About This Book

This book is designed to help you teach yourself how to program with C++. In just 21 days, you'll learn about such fundamentals as the managing I/O, loops and arrays, object-oriented programming, templates, and creating C++ applications—all in well-structured and easy-to-follow lessons. Lessons provide sample listings—complete with sample output and an analysis of the code—to illustrate the topics of the day. Syntax examples are clearly marked for handy reference.

To help you become more proficient, each lesson ends with a set of common questions and answers, exercises, and a quiz. You can check your progress by examining the quiz and exercise answers provided in the book's appendix.

Who Should Read This Book

You don't need any previous experience in programming to learn C++ with this book. This book starts you from the beginning and teaches you both the language and the concepts involved with programming C++. You'll find the numerous examples of syntax and detailed analysis of code an excellent guide as you begin your journey into this rewarding environment. Whether you are just beginning or already have some experience programming, you will find that this book's clear organization makes learning C++ fast and easy.

Conventions

Note: These boxes highlight information that can make your C++ programming more efficient and effective.

Warning: These focus your attention on problems or side effects that can occur in specific situations.

NEW
TERM
These boxes provide clear definitions of essential terms.

DO
DON'T
DO use the "Do/Don't" boxes to find a quick summary of a fundamental principle in a lesson.

DON'T overlook the useful information offered in these boxes.

This book uses various typefaces to help you distinguish C++ code from regular English. Actual C++ code is typeset in a special monospace font. Placeholders—words or characters temporarily used to represent the real words or characters you would type in code—are typeset in *italic monospace*. New or important terms are typeset in *italic*.

In the listings in this book, each real code line is numbered. If you see an unnumbered line in a listing, you'll know that the unnumbered line is really a continuation of the preceding numbered code line (some code lines are too long for the width of the book). In this case, you should type the two lines as one; do not divide them.

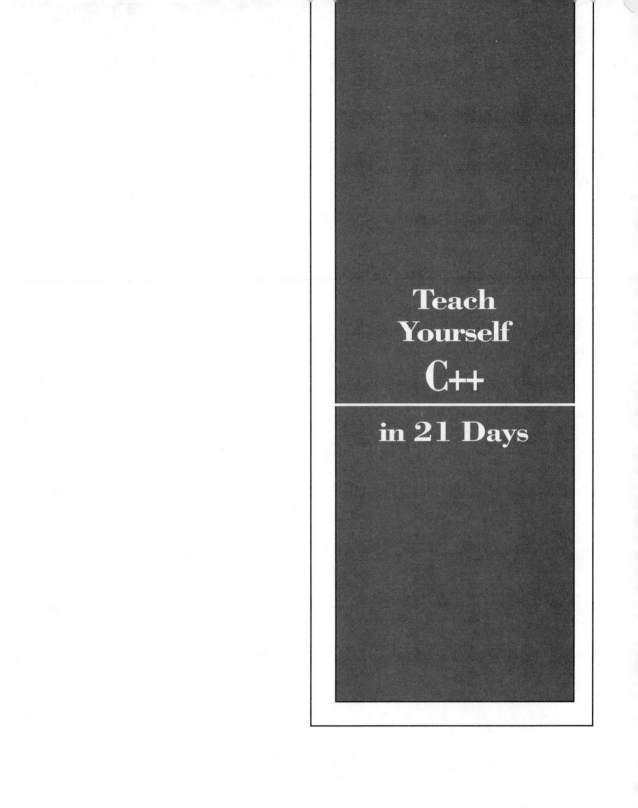

Teach
Yourself
C++
in 21 Days

Teach Yourself
C++
in 21 Days

Jesse Liberty

SAMS
PUBLISHING

201 West 103rd Street, Indianapolis, Indiana 46290

This book is dedicated to the living memory of David Levine.

Copyright © 1994 by Sams Publishing

FIRST EDITION

International Standard Book Number: 0-672-30541-0

Library of Congress Catalog Card Number: 94-66277

97 96 95 94   4   3   2   1

Interpretation of the printing code: the rightmost double-digit number is the year of the book's printing; the rightmost single-digit, the number of the book's printing. For example, a printing code of 94-1 shows that the first printing of the book occurred in 1994.

Composed in AGaramond and MCPdigital by Macmillan Computer Publishing

Printed in the United States of America

Trademarks

Overview

Appendixes

Contents

Acknowledgments

I would like to acknowledge the many people who contributed to this book, both directly and indirectly. First and foremost, Stacey and Robin Liberty, whose support, encouragement and patience made it possible. Also, Mike Kraley, Ed Belove, and Patrick Johnson, who create an intellectual atmosphere at the Interchange Online Network, which makes it a gas to come to work every day, and the many, many developers at Ziff from whom I learned whatever it is I know about C++.

I must particularly acknowledge those who taught me how to program, Skip Gilbrech and David McCune, and those who taught me C++, including Steve Rogers and especially Steven Zagieboylo. Others who contributed directly or indirectly to this book include: Scott Boag, David Bogartz, Gene Broadway, Drew and Al Carlson, Frank Childs, Jim Culbert, Fran Daniels, Thomas Dobbing, James Efstratiou, June Goldstein, Basha Goldstein-Weiss, Michael Griffin, David Heath, Eric Helliwell, Gisele and Ed Herlihy, Mushtaq Khalique, Matt Kingman, Steve Leland, Sangam Pant, Mike Rothman, Michael Smith, Frank Tino, Seth Weiss, Donovan White, Mark Woodbury and Alan Zeitchek. Special thanks go to Wayne Wylupski and Steven Zagieboylo.

Programming is as much a business and creative experience as it is a technical one, and I must therefore acknowledge Tom Hottenstein, Jay Leve, David Rollert, David Shnaider and Robert Spielvogel. I also want to thank the many people at Sams Publishing who worked so hard to create this book, including Christopher Denny, Bradley Jones, and Matthew Usher. If any of what I've written is especially clear, it is thanks to the editors.

Finally, I'd like to thank Mrs. Kalish, who taught my sixth-grade class how to do binary arithmetic in 1965, when neither she nor we knew why.

About the Author

Jesse Liberty

Jesse Liberty has been programming computers professionally for over ten years. He is a Consulting Engineer at the Interchange Online Network, where he was a founding member of the Software Development Team. He is also president of The Liberty Group, Inc., and a former vice president of Citibank's Development Division. Jesse lives with his wife, Stacey, and his daughter, Robin, in the suburbs of Cambridge, Massachusetts. He can be reached via the Internet at `jlibertydi.ziff.com`, or as `jl` on Interchange.

AT A GLANCE

M T W R F S

As you prepare for your first week of learning how to program in C++, you will need a few things: a compiler, an editor, and this book. If you don't have a C++ compiler and an editor, you can still use this book, but you won't get as much out of it as you would if you were to do the exercises.

The best way to learn to program is by writing programs! At the end of each day you will find a workshop containing a quiz and some exercises. Be sure to take the time to answer all the questions, and to evaluate your work as objectively as you can. The later chapters build on the lessons in the earlier chapters, so be sure you fully understand the material before moving on.

1
2
3
4
5
6
7

A Note to C Programmers

The material in the first five days will be familiar to you. Be sure to skim the material and to do the exercises, to make sure you are fully up to speed before going on to Day 6.

Where You Are Going

The first week covers the material you need to get started with programming in general, and with C++ in particular. On Days 1 and 2 you will be introduced to the basic concepts of programming and program flow. On Day 3 you will learn about variables and constants and how to use data in your programs. On Day 4 you will learn how programs branch based on the data provided and the conditions encountered when the program is running. On Day 5 you will learn what functions are and how to use them, and on Day 6 you will learn about classes and objects. Day 7 teaches more about program flow, and by the end of the first week you will be writing real object-oriented programs.

Getting Started

Introduction

Welcome to *Teach Yourself C++ in 21 Days*! Today you will get started on your way to becoming a proficient C++ programmer. You'll learn:

☐ Why C++ is the emerging standard in software development.

☐ The steps to develop a C++ program.

☐ How to enter, compile and link your first working C++ program.

A Brief History of C++

Computer languages have undergone dramatic evolution since the first electronic computers were built to assist in telemetry calculations during World War II. Early on, programmers worked with the most primitive computer instructions, machine language. These instructions were represented by long strings of 1s and 0s. Soon, assemblers were invented to map machine instructions to human readable and manageable mnemonics, such as ADD and MOV.

In time, higher-level languages evolved, such as BASIC and COBOL. These let people work with something approximating words and sentences, such as Let I = 100. These instructions were translated back into machine language by interpreters and compilers. An interpreter translates a program as it reads it, turning the programmer's program instructions, or *code*, directly into actions. Compilers translate the code into an intermediary form. This step is called *compiling*, and produces an object file. The compiler then invokes a linker, which turns the object file into an executable program.

Because interpreters read the code as it is written, and execute the code on the spot, they are easy for the programmer to work with. Compilers introduce the extra steps of compiling and linking the code, which is inconvenient. Compilers produce a program that is very fast each time it is run. However, the time-consuming task of translating the source code into machine language has already been accomplished.

Another advantage of many compiled languages is that you can distribute the executable program to people who don't have the compiler. With an interpretive language, you must have the language to run the program.

For many years, the principal goal of computer programmers was to write short pieces of code that would execute quickly. The program needed to be small, because memory was expensive, and it needed to be fast, because processing power was also expensive. As computers have become smaller, cheaper and faster, and as the cost of memory has fallen, these priorities have changed. Today the cost of a programmer's time far outweighs the cost of most of the computers in use by businesses. Well-written, easy to maintain code is at a premium. Easy to maintain means that as business requirements change, the program can be extended and enhanced without great expense.

The Word "Program"

The word *program* is used in two ways: to describe individual instructions, or *source code*, created by the programmer, and to describe an entire piece of *executable* software. This distinction can cause enormous confusion, so we will try to distinguish between the source code on one hand, and the executable on the other.

NEW☞ TERM A *program* can be defined as either a set of written instructions created by a programmer or as an executable piece of software.

Source code can be turned into an executable program in two ways: interpreters translate the source code into computer instructions, and the computer acts on those instructions immediately. Alternatively, compilers translate source code into a program, which you can run at a later time. While interpreters are easier to work with, most serious programming is done with compilers because compiled code runs much faster. C++ is a compiled language.

Solving Problems

The problems programmers are asked to solve have been changing. Twenty years ago, programs were created to manage large amounts of raw data. The people writing the code and the people using the program were all computer professionals. Today, computers are in use by far more people, and most know very little about how computers and programs work. Computers are tools used by people who are more interested in solving their business problems than struggling with the computer.

Ironically, in order to become easier to use for this new audience, programs have become far more sophisticated. Gone are the days when users typed in cryptic commands at esoteric prompts, only to see a stream of raw data. Today's programs use sophisticated "user-friendly interfaces" involving multiple windows, menus, dialog boxes and all the myriad metaphors with which we've all become familiar. The programs written to support this new approach are far more complex than those written just ten years ago.

As programming requirements have changed, both languages and the techniques used for writing programs have evolved. While the complete history is fascinating, the part that concerns us is the transformation from procedural programming to object-oriented programming.

Procedural, Structured, and Object-Oriented Programming

Until recently, programs were thought of as a series of procedures that acted upon data. A procedure, or *function*, is a set of specific instructions executed one after the other. The data was quite separate from the procedures, and the trick in programming was to keep track of which functions called which other functions, and what data was changed. To make sense of this potentially confusing situation, structured programming was created.

The principle idea behind structured programming is as simple as the idea of divide and conquer. A computer program could be thought of as consisting of a set of tasks. Any task that was too complex to be described simply would be broken down into a set of smaller component tasks, until the tasks were sufficiently small and self contained that they were easily understood.

As an example, computing the average salary of every employee of a company is a rather complex task. You can, however, break it down into these sub-tasks:

1. Find out what each person earns.
2. Count how many people you have.
3. Total all the salaries.
4. Divide the total by the number of people you have.

Totaling the salaries can, itself, be broken down into:

1. Get each employee's record.
2. Access the salary.
3. Add the salary to the running total.
4. Get the next employee's record.

In turn, obtaining each employee's record can be broken down into:

1. Open the file of employees.
2. Go to the correct record.
3. Read the data from disk.

Structured programming remains an enormously successful approach for dealing with complex problems. By the late 1980s, however, some of its deficiencies had became all too clear.

First, the separation of data from the tasks that manipulate the data became harder and harder to comprehend and maintain. It is natural to think of your data (employee records, for example) and what you can do with your data (sort, edit, etc.) as related ideas.

Second, programmers found themselves constantly reinventing new solutions to old problems. This is often called "reinventing the wheel," and is the opposite of reusability. The idea behind reusability is to build components that have known properties, and then to be able to plug them into your program as you need them. This is modeled after the hardware world—when an engineer needs a new transistor she doesn't usually invent one, she goes to the big bin of transistors and finds one that works like she needs, or perhaps modifies it. There was no similar option for a software engineer.

The way we are now using computers—with menus and buttons and windows—fosters a more interactive, "event-driven" approach to computer programming. Event-driven means that an event happens—the user presses a button or chooses from a menu—and the program must respond. Programs are becoming increasingly interactive, and it has became important to design for that kind of functionality.

NEW☞ TERM Old-fashioned programs forced the user to proceed step-by-step through a series of screens. Modern *event-driven* programs present all the choices at once and respond to the user's actions.

Object-oriented programming attempts to respond to these needs, providing techniques for managing enormous complexity, achieving reuse of software components, and coupling data with the tasks that manipulate that data.

The essence of object-oriented programming is to treat data and the procedures that act upon the data as a single "object"—a self-contained entity with an identity and certain characteristics of its own.

C++ and Object-Oriented Programming

C++ fully supports object-oriented programming, including the four pillars of object-oriented development: *encapsulation*, *data hiding*, *inheritance* and *polymorphism*.

Encapsulation and Data Hiding

When an engineer needs to add a resistor to the device she is creating, she doesn't typically build a new one from scratch. She walks over to a bin of resistors, examines the colored bands that indicate the properties, and picks the one she needs. The resistor is a "black box" as far as the engineer is concerned, she doesn't much care how it does its work as long as it conforms to her specifications; she doesn't need to look inside the box to use it in her design.

The property of being a self-contained unit is called *encapsulation*. That the encapsulated unit can be used without regard to how it works is called *data hiding*.

All the properties of the resistor are encapsulated in the resistor object, they are not spread out through the circuitry. It is not necessary to understand how the resistor works in order to use it effectively, its data is hidden inside the resistor's casing.

C++ supports the properties of encapsulation and data hiding through the creation of user-defined types, called *classes*. You'll see how to create classes on Day 6. Once created, a well-defined class acts as a fully encapsulated entity, it is used as a whole unit. The actual inner workings of the class should be hidden; users of a well-defined class do not need to know how the class works, they just need to know how to use it.

Inheritance and Reuse

When the engineers at Acme Motors want to build a new car they have two choices: they can start from scratch, or they can modify an existing model. Perhaps their Star model is nearly perfect, but they'd like to add a turbocharger and a six-speed transmission. The chief engineer would prefer not to start from the ground up, but rather to say, "Let's build another Star, but let's add these additional capabilities. We'll call the new model a Quasar." A Quasar is a kind of Star, but one with new features.

C++ supports the idea of reuse through inheritance. A new type can be declared, which is an extension of an existing type. This new subclass is said to derive from the existing type, and is sometimes called a derived type. The Quasar is derived from the Star and thus inherits all its qualities, but can add to them as needed. Inheritance and its application in C++ is discussed on days 12 and 15.

Polymorphism

The new Quasar might respond differently than a Star does when you press down on the accelerator. The Quasar might engage fuel injection and a turbocharger, while the Star would simply let gasoline into its carburetor. A user, however, does not have to know about these differences, he can just "floor it," and the right thing will happen depending on which car he's driving.

C++ supports this idea, that different objects do "the right thing," through what is called function polymorphism and class polymorphism. *Poly* means many, and *morph* means form. Polymorphism refers to the same name taking many forms, and is discussed on Days 10 and 13.

How C++ Evolved

As object-oriented analysis, design, and programming began to catch on, Bjarne Stroustrup took the most popular language for commercial software development, C, and extended it to provide the features needed to facilitate object-oriented programming. He created C++, and in less than a decade it has gone from being used by only a handful of developers at AT&T to being the programming language of choice for an estimated one million developers worldwide. It is expected that by the end of the decade, C++ will be the predominant language for commercial software development.

While it is true that C++ is a superset of C, and that virtually any legal C program is a legal C++ program, the leap from C to C++ is very significant. C++ benefited from its relationship to C for many years, as C programmers could ease into their use of C++. To really get the full benefit of C++, however, many programmers found they had to unlearn much of what they knew, and learn a whole new way of conceptualizing and solving programming problems.

Should I Learn C First?

The question inevitably arises: since C++ is a superset of C, should you learn C first? Stroustrup and most other C++ programmers agree: not only is it unnecessary to learn C first, it may be advantageous not to do so. This book attempts to meet the needs of people like you, who come to C++ without prior experience of C. In fact, this book assumes no programming experience of any kind.

Preparing to Program

C++, perhaps more than other languages, demands that the programmer design the program before writing it. Trivial problems, such as the ones discussed in the first few chapters of this book, don't require much design. Complex problems, however, such as the ones professional programmers are challenged with every day, do require design, and the more thorough the design, the more likely it is that the program will solve the problems it is designed to solve, on time and on budget. A good design also makes for a program that is relatively bug free and easy to maintain. It has been estimated that fully 90 percent of the cost of software is the combined cost of debugging and maintenance.

To the extent that good design can reduce those costs, it can have a significant impact on the bottom-line cost of the project.

The first question you need to ask when preparing to design any program is, "What is the problem I'm trying to solve?" Every program should have a clear, well-articulated goal, and you'll find that even the simplest programs in this book do so.

The second question every good programmer asks is, "Can this be accomplished without resorting to writing custom software?" Reusing an old program, using pen and paper, or buying software off the shelf are often better solutions to a problem than writing something new. The programmer who can offer these alternatives will never suffer from lack of work; finding less expensive solutions to today's problems will always generate new opportunities later.

Assuming you understand the problem, and it requires writing a new program, you are ready to begin your design.

Your Development Environment

This book makes the assumption that your computer has a mode in which you can write directly to the screen, without worrying about a graphical environment such as the ones in Windows or on the Macintosh.

Your compiler may have its own built-in text editor, or you may be using a commercial text editor or word processor that can produce text files. The important thing is that whatever you write your program in, it must save simple, plain-text files, with no word processing commands embedded in the text. Examples of safe editors include the Windows Notepad, the DOS Edit command, Brief, Epsilon, EMACS, and vi. Many commercial word processors, such as Word Perfect, Word and dozens of others, also offer a method for saving simple text files.

The files you create with your editor are called source files, and for C++ they typically are named with the extension .CPP or .CP or .C. In this book, we'll name all the source code files with the .CPP extension, but check your compiler for what it needs.

Note: Most C++ compilers don't care what extension you give your source code, but if you don't specify otherwise many will use .CPP by default.

DO	**DON'T**

DO use a simple text editor to create your source code, or use the built-in editor that comes with your compiler.

DON'T use a word processor that saves special formatting characters. If you do use a word processor, save the file as ASCII Text.

DO save your files with the .C, .CP or .CPP extension.

DO check your documentation for specifics about your compiler and linker to ensure that you know how to compile and link your programs.

Compiling the Source Code

Although the source code in your file is somewhat cryptic, and anyone who doesn't know C++ will struggle to understand what it is for, it is still in what we call human-readable form. Your source code file is not a program, and it can't be executed, or run, as a program can.

To turn your source code into a program, you use a compiler. How you invoke your compiler, and how you tell it where to find your source code, will vary from compiler to compiler; check your documentation. In Borland's Turbo C++ you pick the RUN menu command or type

```
tc <filename>
```

from the command line, where `<filename>` is the name of your source code file (e.g., `test.cpp`). Other compilers may do things slightly differently.

Note: If you compile the source code from the operating system's command line, you should type the following:

For the Borland C++ compiler:	`bc <filename>`
For the Borland C++ for Windows compiler:	`bcc <filename>`
For the Borland Turbo C++ compiler:	`tc <filename>`
For the Microsoft compilers:	`cl <filename>`

After your source code is compiled, an object file is produced. This file is often named with the extension .OBJ. This is still not an executable program, however. To turn this into an executable program, you must run your linker.

Creating an Executable File with the Linker

C++ programs are typically created by linking together one or more .OBJ files with one or more libraries. A *library* is a collection of linkable files that you created or that were supplied with your compiler or that you purchased separately. All C++ compilers come with a library of useful functions—or procedures—and classes that you can include in your program. A function is a block of code that performs a service, such as adding two numbers or printing to the screen. A class is a collection of data and related functions; we'll be talking about classes a lot, starting on Day 5, "Functions."

The steps to create an executable file are:

1. Create a source code file, with a .CPP extension.

2. Compile the source code into a file with the .OBJ extension.

3. Link your .OBJ file with any needed libraries to produce an executable program.

The Development Cycle

If every program worked the first time you tried it, that would be the complete development cycle: write the program, compile the source code, link the program and run it. Unfortunately, almost every program, no matter how trivial, can and will have errors, or *bugs*, in it. Some bugs will cause the compile to fail, some will cause the link to fail, and some will only show up when you run the program.

Whatever the type of bug you find, you must fix it, and that involves editing your source code, recompiling and relinking, and then rerunning the program. This cycle is represented in Figure 1.1, which diagrams the steps in the development cycle.

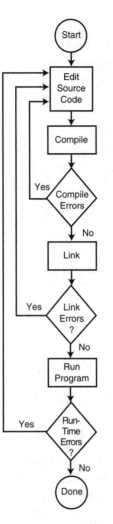

Figure 1.1. *The steps in the development of a C++ program.*

HELLO.CPP—Your First C++ Program

Traditional programming books begin by writing the words Hello World to the screen, or a variation on that statement. This time-honored tradition is carried on here.

Type the first program directly into your editor, exactly as shown. Once you are certain it is correct, save the file, compile it, link it and run it. It will print the words `Hello World` to your screen. Don't worry too much about how it works, this is really just to get you comfortable with the development cycle. Every aspect of this program will be covered over the next couple of days.

> **Warning:** The following listing contains line numbers on the left. These numbers are for reference within the book. They should not be typed in to your editor. For example, in line 1 of Listing 1.1, you should enter:
>
> ```
> #include <iostream.h>
> ```

Listing 1.1. HELLO.CPP, the Hello World program.

```
1: #include <iostream.h>
2:
3: void main()
4: {
5:    cout << "Hello World!\n";
6: }
```

Make certain you enter this exactly as shown. Pay careful attention to the punctuation. The << in line 5 is the redirection symbol, produced on most keyboards by holding the shift key and pressing the comma key. Line 5 ends with a semicolon, don't leave this off!

Also check to make sure you are following your compiler directions properly. Most compilers will link automatically, but check your documentation. If you get errors, look over your code carefully and determine how it is different from the above. If you see an error on line 1, such as `cannot find file iostream.h` check your compiler documentation for directions on setting up your `include path` or `environment variables`. If you receive an error that there is no prototype for main, add the line `void main();` just before line three. You will need to add this line to every program in this book before the beginning of the `main` function. Most compilers don't require this, but a few do.

Your finished program will look like this:

```
1: #include <iostream.h>
2:
4: void main();
5: {
6: cout <<"Hello World!\n";
7: }
```

Try running HELLO.EXE; it should write:

```
Hello World!
```

directly to your screen. If so, congratulations! You've just entered, compiled, and run your first C++ program. It may not look like much, but almost every professional C++ programmer started out with this exact program.

Compile Errors

Compile-time errors can occur for any number of reasons. Usually they are a result of a typo or other inadvertent minor error. Good compilers will not only tell you what you did wrong, they'll point you to the exact place in your code where you made the mistake. The great ones will even suggest a remedy!

You can see this by intentionally putting an error into your program. If HELLO.CPP ran smoothly, edit it now and remove the closing brace on line 6. Your program will now look like listing 1.2.

Listing 1.2. Demonstration of compiler error.

```
1: #include <iostream.h>
2:
3: void main()
4: {
5:     cout << "Hello World!\n";
6:
```

Recompile your program and you should see an error that looks similar to:

```
Hello.cpp, line 5: Compound statement missing terminating } in function main().
```

This error tells you the file and line number of the problem, and what the problem is (although I admit it is somewhat cryptic). Note that the error message points you to line 5. The compiler wasn't sure if you intended to put the closing brace before or after the cout statement on line 5. Sometimes the errors just get you to the general vicinity of the problem. If a compiler could perfectly identify every problem, it would fix the code itself.

Summary

After reading this chapter you should have a good understanding of how C++ evolved and what problems it was designed to solve. You should feel confident that learning C++

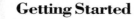

is the right choice for anyone interested in programming in the next decade. C++ provides the tools of object-oriented programming and the performance of a systems level language, which makes C++ the development language of choice.

Today you learned how to enter, compile, link and run your first C++ program, and what the normal development cycle is. You also learned a little of what object-oriented programming is all about. You will return to these topics during the next three weeks.

Q&A

Q What is the difference between a text editor and a word processor?

A A text editor produces files with plain text in them. There are no formatting commands or other special symbols required by a particular word processor. Text files do not have automatic word wrap, bold print, italics and so forth.

Q If my compiler has a built-in editor, must I use it?

A Almost all compilers will compile code produced by any text editor. The advantages of using the built-in text editor, however, might include the ability to quickly move back and forth between the edit and compile steps of the development cycle. Sophisticated compilers include a fully integrated development environment, allowing the programmer to access help files, edit, and compile the code in place, and to resolve compile and link errors without ever leaving the environment.

Q Can I ignore warning messages from my compiler?

A Many books hedge on this one, but I'll stake myself to this position: No! Get into the habit, from day one, of treating warning messages as errors. C++ uses the compiler to warn you when you are doing something you may not intend; heed those warnings and do what is required to make them go away.

Q What is compile-time?

A Compile-time is the time when you run your compiler, as opposed to link-time (when you run the linker) or run-time (when running the program). This is just programmer shorthand to identify the three times when errors usually surface.

Workshop

The Workshop provides quiz questions to help you solidify your understanding of the material covered and exercises to provide you with experience in using what you've learned. Try to answer the quiz and exercise questions before checking the answers in Appendix D, and make sure you understand the answers before continuing to the next chapter.

Quiz

1. What is the difference between an interpreter and a compiler?

2. How do you compile the source code with your compiler?

3. What does the linker do?

4. What are the steps in the development cycle?

Exercises

1. Look at the following program and try to guess what it does without running it.

```
1:  #include <iostream.h>
2:  void main()
3:  {
4:      int x = 5;
5:      int y = 7;
6:      cout "\n";
7:      cout << x + y << "   " << x * y;
8:      cout "\n";
9:  }
```

2. Type in the program from question one, compile and link it. What does it do? Is it what you guessed?

3. Type in the following program and compile it. What error do you receive?

```
1:  include <iostream.h>
2:  void main()
3:  {
4:      cout << "Hello World\n";
5:  }
```

4. Fix the error in the program in question 3 and recompile and link and run it. What does it do?

The Parts of a C++ Program

Introduction

C++ programs consist of objects, functions, variables and other component parts. Most of this book is devoted to explaining these parts in depth, but to get a sense of how a program fits together you must see a complete working program. Today you learn:

☐ The parts of a C++ program.

☐ How the parts work together.

☐ What a function is and what it does.

The Parts of a Simple Program

Even the simple program HELLO.CPP from Day 1 had many interesting parts. This section will review this program in more detail. Listing 2.1 reproduces the original version of HELLO.CPP for your convenience.

Listing 2.1. HELLO.CPP. Demonstrates the parts of a C++ program.

```
1: #include <iostream.h>
2:
3: void main()
4: {
5:     cout << "Hello World!\n";
6: }
```

```
Hello World!
```

On line 1 the file IOSTREAM.H is included into the file. The first character is the # symbol, which is a signal to the preprocessor. Each time you start your compiler, the preprocessor is run. The preprocessor reads through your source code looking for lines that begin with the pound symbol (#), and acts on those lines before the compiler runs.

include is a preprocessor instruction that says, "What follows is a filename, find that file and read it in right here." The angle brackets around the filename tell the preprocessor to "Look in all the usual places for this file." If your compiler is set up correctly, the angle brackets will cause the preprocessor to look for the file IOSTREAM.H in the directory that holds all the .H files for your compiler. The file IOSTREAM.H (Input-Output-STREAM) is used by cout, which assists with writing to the screen. The effect of line 1 is to include the file IOSTREAM.H into this program, as if you had typed it in yourself.

 NEW TERM The preprocessor runs before your compiler, each time the compiler is invoked: it translates any line that begins with a pound symbol (#) into a special command, getting your code file ready for the compiler.

Line 3 begins the actual program with a function named main(). Every C++ program has a main() function. In general, a function is a block of code that performs one or more actions. Usually functions are invoked, or called by other functions, but main() is special. When your program starts, main() is called automatically.

main(), like all functions, must state what kind of value it will return. The return value type for main() in HELLO.CPP is void, which means that this function will not return any value at all. Returning values from functions is discussed in detail on Day 4.

All functions begin with an opening brace ({) and end with a closing brace (}). The braces for the main() function are on lines 4 and 6. Everything between the opening and closing braces is considered a part of the function.

The meat and potatoes of this program are on line 5. The object cout is used to print a message to the screen. We'll cover objects in general on Day 6, and cout and its related object cin in detail on Day 17. These two objects, cout and cin, are used in C++ to print strings and values to the screen. A *string* is just a set of characters.

Here's how cout is used: write the word cout followed by the output redirection operator (<<). Whatever follows the output redirection operator is written to the screen. If you want a string of characters written, be sure to enclose them in double quotes (") as shown on line 5.

NEW TERM A *text string* is a series of printable characters.

The final two characters, \n, tell cout to put a new line after the words Hello World! This special code is explained in detail when cout is discussed on Day 17.

The main() function ends on line 6 with the closing brace.

A Brief Look at *cout*

On Day 16 you will see how to use cout for printing data to the screen. For now, you can use cout without fully understanding how it works. To print a value to the screen, write the word cout, followed by the insertion operator (<<) which you create by typing the less-than character (<) twice. Even though this is two characters, C++ treats it as one.

Follow the insertion character by your data. Listing 2.2 illustrates how this is used. Type in the example exactly as written, except substitute your own name were you see Jesse Liberty (unless your name *is* Jesse Liberty, in which case leave it just the way it is, it's perfect (but I'm still not splitting royalties!).

Listing 2.2. Using cin.

```
1:      // Listing 2.2 using cout
2:
3:      #include <iostream.h>
4:      void main()
5:      {
6:         cout << "Hello there.\n";
7:         cout << "Here is 5: " << 5 << "\n";
8:         cout << "The manipulator endl writes a new line to the screen." << endl;
9:         cout << "Here is a very big number:\t" << 70000 << endl;
10:        cout << "Here is the sum of 8 and 5:\t" << 8+5 << endl;
11:        cout << "Here's a fraction:\t\t" << (float) 5/8 << endl;
12:        cout << "And a very very big number:\t" << (double) 7000 * 7000 << endl;
13:        cout << "Don't forget to replace Jesse Liberty with your name...\n";
14:        cout << "Jesse Liberty is a C++ programmer!\n";
15:     }
```

endl ↑

```
Hello there.
Here is 5: 5
The manipulator endl writes a new line to the screen.
Here is a very big number:      70000
Here is the sum of 8 and 5:     13
Here's a fraction:              0.625
And a very very big number:     4.9e+07
Don't forget to replace Jesse Liberty with your name...
Jesse Liberty is a C++ programmer
```

On line 3 the statement #include <iostream.h> causes the IOSTREAM.H file to be added to your source code. This is *required* if you use cout and its related functions.

On line 6 is the simplest use of cout, printing a string, or series of characters. The symbol \n is a special formatting character, it tells cout to print a new line character to the screen.

On line 7 three values are passed to cout, each separated by the insertion operator. The first value is the string "Here is 5: ". Note the space after the colon, that is part of the string. Next the value 5 is passed to the insertion operator, and next the newline character (always in double quotes or single quotes). This causes the line

```
Here is 5: 5
```

to be printed to the screen. Because there is no new line character after the first string, the next value is printed immediately afterwards. This is called *concatenating* the two values.

On line 8 an informative message is printed, and then the *manipulator* endl is used. The purpose of endl is to write a new line to the screen. (Other uses for endl will be discussed on Day 16).

On line 9 a new formatting character, \t is introduced. This inserts a tab character, and is used on lines 8-12 to line up the output. Line 9 shows that not only integers, but long integers can be printed. Line 10 demonstrates that cout will do simple addition, the value 8+5 is passed to cout but what is printed is 13.

On line 11 the value 5/8 is inserted into cout. The term (float) tells cout that you want this value evaluated as a fraction, and so a fraction is printed. On line 12 the value 7000 * 7000 is given to cout, and the term (double) is used to tell cout that you want this to be printed using *scientific notation*. All of this will be explained tomorrow when data types are discussed on Day 3.

On line 14 you substituted your name, and the output confirmed that you are, indeed a C++ programmer. It must be true, the computer said so!

Comments

When you are writing a program it is always clear and self-evident what you are trying to do. Funny thing, though—a month later, when you return to the program, it can be quite confusing and unclear. I'm not sure how that confusion creeps into your program, but it's always there.

To fight the onset of confusion and to help others to understand your code, you'll want to use comments. Comments are simply text that is ignored by the compiler, but that may inform the reader of what you are doing at any particular point in your program.

Types of Comments

C++ comments come in two flavors. The double-slash (//) comment, which will be referred to as a C++-style comment, tells the compiler to ignore everything that follows this until the end of the line.

The slash-star (/*) comment mark tells the compiler to ignore everything that follows until it finds a star-slash (*/) comment mark. These marks will be referred to as C-style comments. Every /* must be matched with a closing */.

As you might guess, C-style comments are used in the C language as well, but C++-style comments are not part of the official definition of C.

Many C++ programmers use the C++-style comment most of the time, and reserve C-style comments for blocking out large blocks of a program. You can include C++-style comments within a block "commented out" by C++-style comments; everything, including the C++-style comments, is ignored between the comment marks.

Using Comments

As a general rule, the overall program should have comments at the beginning, telling you what the program does. Each function should also have comments explaining what the function does and what values it returns. Finally, any statement in your program that is obscure or less than obvious should be commented as well.

Listing 2.3 demonstrates the use of comments, showing that they do not affect the processing of the program or its output.

Listing 2.3. HELP.CPP demonstrates comments.

```
1: #include <iostream.h>
2:
3: void main()
4: {
5:   /* this is a comment
6:   and it extends until the closing
7:   star-slash comment mark */
8:     cout << "Hello World!\n";
9:     // this comment ends at the end of the line
10:    cout << "That comment ended!";
11:
12:   // double slash comments can be alone on a line
13: /* as can slash-star comments */
14: }
```

```
Hello World!
That comment ended
```

The comments on lines 5 through 7 are completely ignored by the compiler, as are the comments on lines 9, 12, and 13. The comment on line 9 ended with the end of the line, however, while the comments on 5 and 13 required a closing comment mark.

Comments at the Top of Each File

It is a good idea to put a comment block at the top of every file you write. The exact style of this block of comments is a matter of individual taste, but every such header should include at least the following information:

- [ ] The name of the function or program.

- [ ] The name of the file.

- [ ] What the function or program does.

- [ ] A description of how the program works.

- [ ] The author's name.

- [ ] A revision history (notes on each change made).

- [ ] What compilers, linkers, and other tools were used to make this program.

- [ ] Additional notes as needed.

For example, the following block of comments might appear at the top of the Hello World program.

```
/**********************************************************

Program:      Hello World

File:         Hello.cpp

Function:     Main (complete program listing in this file)

Description:  Prints the words "Hello world" to the screen

Author:       Jesse Liberty (jl)

Environment:  Turbo C++ version 4, 486/66 32mb RAM, Windows 3.1
              DOS 6.0.  EasyWin module.

Notes:        This is an introductory, example program.

Revisions:    1.00  10/1/94 (jl) First release
              1.01  10/2/94 (jl) Capitalized "World"

**********************************************************/
```

It is very important that you keep the notes and descriptions up to date. A common problem with headers like this is that they are neglected after their initial creation, and over time they become increasingly misleading. Properly maintained, however, they can be an invaluable guide to the overall program.

The listings in the rest of this book will leave off the headings in an attempt to save room. That does not diminish their importance, however, so they will appear in the programs provided at the end of each week.

A Final Word of Caution About Comments

Comments that state the obvious are less than useful. In fact, they can be counter-productive, because the code may change and the programmer may neglect to update the comment. What is obvious to one person may be obscure to another, however, so judgment is required.

The bottom line is that comments should not say *what* is happening, they should say *why* it is happening.

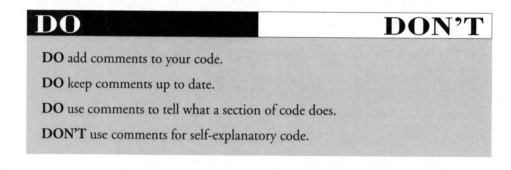

DO   **DON'T**

DO add comments to your code.

DO keep comments up to date.

DO use comments to tell what a section of code does.

DON'T use comments for self-explanatory code.

Functions

While main() is a function, it is an unusual one. Typical functions are called, or invoked, during the course of your program. A program is executed line by line, in the order it appears in your source code, until a function is reached. Then the program branches off to execute the function. When the function finishes, it returns control to the line of code immediately following the call to the function.

A good analogy for this is sharpening your pencil. If you are drawing a picture, and your pencil breaks, you might stop drawing, go sharpen the pencil, and then return to what you were doing. When a program needs a service performed, it can call a function to perform the service and then pick up where it was when the function is finished. Listing 2.4 demonstrates this idea.

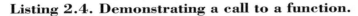

Listing 2.4. Demonstrating a call to a function.

```
1:     #include <iostream.h>
2:
3:     // function Demonstration Function
4:     // prints out a useful message
5:     void DemonstrationFunction()
6:     {
7:         cout << "In Demonstration Function\n";
8:     }
9:
10:    // function main - prints out a message, then
11:    // calls DemonstrationFunction, then prints out
12:    // a second message.
13:    void main()
14:    {
15:        cout << "In main\n" ;
16:        DemonstrationFunction();
17:        cout << "Back in main\n";
18:    }
```

```
In main
In Demonstration Function
Back in main
```

The function DemonstrationFunction() is defined on lines 3–5. When it is called it prints a message to the screen and then returns.

Line 8 is the beginning of the actual program. On line 10, main() prints out a message saying it is in main(). After printing the message, line 11 calls DemonstrationFunction(). This call causes the commands in DemonstrationFunction() to execute. In this case the entire function consists of the code on line 7, which prints another message. When DemonstrationFunction() completes (line 8), it returns back to where it was called from. In this case the program returns to line 17, where main() prints its final line.

Using Functions

Functions either return a value, or they return void, meaning they return nothing. A function that adds two integers might return the sum, and thus would be defined to return an integer value. A function that just prints a message has nothing to return and would be declared to return void.

Functions consist of a header and a body. The header consists, in turn, of the return type, the function name, and the parameters to that function. The parameters to a function allow values to be passed into the function. Thus, if the function were to add two numbers, the numbers would be the parameters to the function. Here's a typical function header

```
int Sum(int a, int b)
```

A parameter is a declaration of what type of value will be passed in; the actual value passed in by the calling function is called the argument. Many programmers use these two terms, "parameters" and "arguments" as synonyms, others are careful about the technical distinction. This book will use the terms interchangeably.

The body of a function consists of an opening brace, zero or more statements, and a closing brace. The statements constitute the work of the function. A function may return a value using a return statement. This statement will also cause the function to exit. If you don't put a return statement into your function, it will automatically return void at the end of the function. The value returned must be of the type declared in the function header.

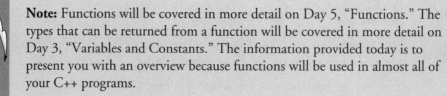

Note: Functions will be covered in more detail on Day 5, "Functions." The types that can be returned from a function will be covered in more detail on Day 3, "Variables and Constants." The information provided today is to present you with an overview because functions will be used in almost all of your C++ programs.

Listing 2.5 demonstrates a function that takes two integer parameters and returns an integer value. Don't worry about the syntax or the specifics of how to work with integer values (for example int x) for now, that will be covered in detail on Day 3.

Listing 2.5. FUNC.CPP demonstrates a simple function.

```
1:    #include <iostream.h>
2:    int Add (int x, int y)
3:    {
4:      cout << "In Add(), received " << x << " and " << y << "\n";
5:      return (x+y);
6:    }
7:
8:    void main()
9:    {
10:        cout << "I'm in main()!\n";
11:        int a, b, c;
12:        cout << "Enter two numbers: ";
13:        cin >> a;
14:        cin >> b;
```

```
15:         cout << "\nCalling Add()\n";
16:         c=Add(a,b);
17:         cout << "\nBack in main().\n";
18:         cout << "c was set to " << c;
19:         cout << "\nExiting...\n\n";
20:     }
```

```
I'm in main()!
Enter two numbers: 3 5
Calling Add()
In Add(), received 3 and 5
Back in main().
c was set to 8
Exiting...
```

The function Add() is defined on line 2. It takes two integer parameters and returns an integer value. The program itself begins on line 10 where it prints a message. The program prompts the user for two numbers (lines 12 to 14). The user types each number, separated by a space and then presses ENTER. Main() passes the two numbers typed in by the user as arguments to the Add() function on line 16.

Processing branches to the Add() function, which starts on line 2. The parameters a and b are printed and then added together. The result is returned on line 5 and the function returns.

In lines 13 and 14, the cin object is used to obtain a number for the variables a and b, and cout is used to write the values to the screen. Variables and other aspects of this program will be explored in depth in the next few days.

Summary

The difficulty in learning a complex subject, such as programming, is that so much of what you learn depends on every thing else there is to learn. This chapter introduced the basic parts of a simple C++ program. It also introduced the development cycle and a number of new important terms.

Q & A

Q What does #include do?

A This is a directive to the preprocessor, which runs when you call your compiler. This specific directive causes the file named after the word include to be read in, as if it were typed in at that location in your source code.

Q What is the difference between // comments and /* style comments.

A The double-slash comments (//) "expire" at the end of the line. Slash-star (/*) comments are in effect until a closing comment (*/). Remember, not even the end of the function terminates a slash-star comment; you must put in the closing comment mark, or you will get a compile time error.

Q What differentiates a good comment from a bad comment?

A A good comment tells the reader why this particular code is doing whatever it is doing, or explains what a section of code is about to do. A bad comment restates what a particular line of code is doing. Lines of code should be written so that they speak for themselves: reading the line of code should tell you what it is doing without needing a comment.

Workshop

The Workshop provides quiz questions to help you solidify your understanding of the material covered and exercises to provide you with experience in using what you've learned. Try to answer the quiz and exercise questions before checking the answers in Appendix D, and make sure you understand the answers before continuing to the next chapter.

Quiz

1. What is the difference between the compiler and the preprocessor?

2. Why is the function main() special?

3. What are the two types of comments, and how do they differ?

4. Can comments be nested?

5. Can comments be longer than one line?

Exercises

1. Write a program that writes I love C++ to the screen.

2. Write the smallest program that can be compiled, linked, and run.

3. **BUG BUSTER:** Enter this program and compile it. Why does it fail? How can you fix it?

```
1: #include <iostream.h>
2: main()
3: {
4:      cout << Is there a bug here?";
5: }
```

4. Fix the bug in question 3 and recompile, link, and run it.

Variables and Constants

Programs need a way to store the data they use. Variables and constants offer various ways to represent and manipulate that data.

Today you will learn:

☐ How to declare and define variables and constants.

☐ How to assign values to variables and manipulate those values.

☐ How to write the value of a variable to the screen.

What Is a Variable?

In C++ a variable is a place to store information. A variable is a location in your computer's memory in which you can store a value and from which you can later retrieve that value.

Your computer's memory can be viewed as a series of cubby holes. Each cubby hole is one of many, many such holes all lined up. Each cubby hole—or memory location—is numbered sequentially. These numbers are known as memory addresses. A variable reserves one or more cubby holes in which you may store a value.

Your variable's name (for example, `myVariable`) is a label on one of these cubby holes so that you can find it easily, without knowing its actual memory address. Figure 3.1 is a schematic representation of this idea. As you can see from the figure, `myVariable` starts at memory address ###. Depending on the size of `myVariable`, it can take up one or more memory addresses.

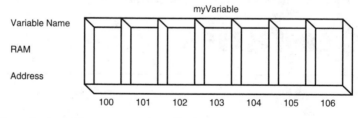

Figure 3.1. *A schematic representation of memory.*

Note: RAM is *random access memory*. When you run your program, it is loaded into RAM from the disk file. All variables are created in RAM as well. When programmers talk of memory, it is usually RAM to which they are referring.

Setting Aside Memory

When you define a variable in C++, you must tell the compiler what *kind* of variable it is: integer, character, and so forth. This information tells the compiler how much room to set aside and what kind of value you want to store in your variable.

Each cubby is one byte large. If the type of variable you create is two bytes in size, it needs two bytes of memory, or two cubbies. The type of the variable (for example, integer) tells the compiler how much memory (how many cubby holes) to set aside for the variable.

Because computers use bits and bytes to represent values, and because memory is measured in bytes, it is important that you understand and are comfortable with these concepts. For a full review of this topic, please read Appendix B, "C++ Keywords."

Size of Integers

On any one computer, each variable type takes up a single unchanging amount of room. That is, an integer might be two bytes on one machine, and four on another, but on either computer it is always the same, day in and day out.

A char variable (used to hold characters) is most often one byte long. A short integer is two bytes on most computers, a long integer is usually four bytes, and an integer (without the keyword short or long) can be two or four bytes. Listing 3.1 should help you determine the exact size of these types on your computer.

NEW TERM A *character* is a single letter, number or symbol that takes up one byte of memory.

Listing 3.1. Determines the size of variable types on your computer.

```
1:   #include <iostream.h>
2:
3:   main()
4:   {
5:     cout << "The size of an int is:\t\t"    << sizeof(int)    << " bytes.\n";
6:     cout << "The size of a short int is:\t" << sizeof(short)  << " bytes.\n";
7:     cout << "The size of a long int is:\t"  << sizeof(long)   << " bytes.\n";
8:     cout << "The size of a char is:\t\t"    << sizeof(char)   << " bytes.\n";
9:     cout << "The size of a float is:\t\t"   << sizeof(float)  << " bytes.\n";
10:    cout << "The size of a double is:\t"    << sizeof(double) << " bytes.\n";
11:
12:  }
```

```
The size of an int is          2 bytes.
The size of a short int is     2 bytes.
The size of a long int is      4 bytes.
The size of a char is          1 bytes.
The size of a float is         4 bytes.
The size of a double is        8 bytes.
```

Note: On your computer, the number of bytes presented might be different!

 Most of Listing 3.1 should be pretty familiar. The one new feature is the use of the `sizeof()` function in lines 5 through 10. `sizeof()` is provided by your compiler, and it tells you the size of the object you pass in as a parameter. For example, on line 5 the keyword `int` is passed into `sizeof()`. Using `sizeof()`, I was able to determine that on my computer, an `int` is equal to a short `int`, which is 2 bytes.

Signed and Unsigned

In addition, all of these types come in two varieties: signed and unsigned. The idea here is that sometimes you need negative numbers, and sometimes you don't. Integers (short and long) without the word "unsigned" are assumed to be signed. Signed integers are either negative or positive. Unsigned integers are always positive.

Because you have the same number of bytes for both signed and unsigned integers, the largest number you can store in an unsigned integer is twice as big as the largest positive number you can store in a signed integer. An unsigned short integer can handle numbers from 0 to 65,535. Half the numbers represented by a signed short are negative, thus a signed short can only represent numbers from –32,767 to 32,768. Again, if this is confusing, be sure to read Appendix A, "Operator Precedence."

Fundamental Variable Types

Several other variable types are built into C++. They can be conveniently divided into integer variables (the type discussed so far), floating-point variables, and character variables.

Floating-point variables have values that can be expressed as fractions—that is, they are "real numbers." Character variables hold a single byte and are used for holding the 256 characters and symbols of the ASCII and extended ASCII character sets.

NEW ☞ The *ASCII character set* is the set of characters standardized for use on com-
TERM puters. ASCII is an acronym for American Standard Code for Information
Interchange. Nearly every computer operating system supports ASCII, though
many support other international character sets as well.

The types of variables used in C++ programs are described in Table 3.1. This table shows
the variable type, how much room this book assumes it takes in memory, and what kinds
of values can be stored in these variables. The values that can be stored are determined
by the size of the variable types, so check your output from Listing 3.1.

Table 3.1. Variable types.

Type	Size	Values
unsigned short int	2 bytes	0 to 65,535
short int	2 bytes	–32,768 to 32,767
unsigned long int	4 bytes	0 to 4,294,967,295
long int	4 bytes	–2,147,483,648 to 2,147,483,647
int	2 bytes	–32,768 to 32,767
unsigned int	2 bytes	0 to 65,535
char	1 byte	256 character values
float	4 bytes	1.2e–38 to 3.4e38
double	8 bytes	2.2e–308 to 1.8e308

Note: The sizes of variables might be different from those shown in Table
3.1, depending on the compiler and the computer you are using. If your
computer had the same output as was presented in Listing 3.1, then Table
3.1 should apply to your compiler. If your output from Listing 3.1 was
different, you should consult your compiler's manual for the values that your
variable types can hold.

Defining a Variable

You create, or define, a variable by stating its type, followed by one or more spaces, followed by the variable name and a semicolon. The variable name can be virtually any combination of letters, but cannot contain spaces. Legal variable names include x, J23qrsnf, and myAge. Good variable names tell you what the variables are for; using good names makes it easier to understand the flow of your program. The following statement defines an integer variable called myAge:

```
int myAge;
```

As a general programming practice, avoid such horrific names as J23qrsnf, and restrict single-letter variable names (such as x or i) to variables that are used only very briefly. Try to use expressive names such as myAge or howMany. Such names are easier to understand three weeks later when you are scratching your head trying to figure out what you meant when you wrote that line of code.

Try this experiment: Guess what these pieces of programs do, based on the first few lines of code:

Example 1

```
main()
{
    unsigned short x;
    unsigned short y;
    ULONG z;
    z = x * y;
}
```

Example 2

```
main ()
{
    unsigned short Width;
    unsigned short Length;
    unsigned short Area;
    Area = Width * Length;
}
```

Clearly, the second program is easier to understand, and the inconvenience of having to type the longer variable names is more than made up for by how much easier it is to maintain the second program.

Case Sensitivity

C++ is case-sensitive. In other words, uppercase and lowercase letters are considered to be different. A variable named age is different from Age, which is different from AGE.

Note: Some compilers allow you to turn case sensitivity off. Don't be tempted to do this; your programs won't work with other compilers, and other C++ programmers will be *very* confused by your code.

There are various conventions for how to name variables, and although it doesn't much matter which method you adopt, it is important to be consistent throughout your program.

Many programmers prefer to use all lowercase letters for their variable names. If the name requires two words (for example, my car), there are two popular conventions: my_car or myCar. The latter form is called camel-notation, because the capitalization looks something like a hump.

Some people find the underscore character (my_car) to be easier to read; others prefer to avoid the underscore because it is more difficult to type. This book uses camel-notation, in which the second and all subsequent words are capitalized: myCar, theQuickBrownFox, and so forth.

Note: Many advanced programmers employ a notation style that is often referred to as *Hungarian notation*. The idea behind Hungarian notation is to prefix every variable with a set of characters that describes its type. Integer variables might begin with a lowercase letter i, or begin longs with a lowercase l. Other notations indicate constants, globals, pointers, and so forth. Most of this is much more important in C programming, because C++ supports the creation of user-defined types (see Day 6) and because C++ is strongly typed.

Keywords

Some words are reserved by C++, and you may not use them as variable names. These are *keywords*, used by the compiler to control your program. Key words include `if`, `while`, `for`, and `main`. Your compiler manual should provide a complete list, but generally, any reasonable name for a variable is almost certainly not a keyword.

DO	DON'T

DO define a variable by writing the type, then the variable name.

DO use meaningful variable names.

DO remember that C++ is case sensitive.

DON'T use C++ keywords as variable names.

DO understand the number of bytes each variable type consumes in memory, and what values can be stored in variables of that type.

DON'T use unsigned variables for negative numbers.

Creating More Than One Variable at a Time

You can create more than one variable of the same type in one statement by writing the type and then the variable names, separated by commas. For example:

```
unsigned int myAge, myWeight;    // two unsigned int variables
long area, width, length;        // three longs
```

As you can see, `myAge` and `myWeight` are each declared as unsigned integer variables. The second line declares three individual long variables named `area`, `width`, and `length`. The type (`long`) is assigned to all the variables, so you cannot mix types in one definition statement.

Assigning Values to Your Variables

You assign a value to a variable by using the *assignment operator* (=). Thus, you would assign 5 to `Width` by writing

```
unsigned short Width;
Width = 5;
```

You can combine these steps and *initialize* Width when you define it by writing

```
unsigned short Width = 5;
```

Initialization looks very much like assignment, and with integer variables, the difference is minor. Later, when constants are covered, you will see that some values *must* be initialized because they cannot be assigned to. The essential difference is that initialization takes place at the moment you create the variable.

Just as you can define more than one variable at a time, you can initialize more than one variable at creation. For example:

```
long width = 5, length = 7;  // create two long variables and initialize them
```

This example initializes the long variable width the value 5 and the long variable length to the value 7. You can even mix definitions and initializations:

```
int myAge = 39, yourAge, hisAge = 40;
```

This example creates three type int variables, and it initializes the first and third.

Listing 3.2 shows a complete program, ready to compile, that computes the area of a rectangle and writes the answer to the screen.

Listing 3.2. Demonstrates the use of variables.

```
1:    // Demonstration of variables
2:    #include <iostream.h>
3:
4:    main()
5:    {
6:       unsigned short int Width = 5, Length; // create two variables,
         ➥initialize first
7:       Length = 10;                        // assign a value to the
         ➥uninitialized variable
8:
9:       // create  an unsigned short and initialize with result of multiplying
         ➥Width by Length
10:      unsigned short int Area  = Width * Length;
11:
12:      cout << "Width:" << Width << "\n";
13:      cout << "Length: "  << Length << endl;
14:      cout << "Area: " << Area;
15:   }
```

```
Width: 5
Length: 10
Area: 50
```

Line 2 includes the required `include` statement for the `iostream`'s library so that `cout` will work. Line 4 begins the program.

On line 6, `Width` is defined as an unsigned short integer, and its value is initialized to 5. Another unsigned short integer, `Length`, is also defined, but it's not initialized. On line 7 the value 10 is assigned to `Length`.

On line 10 an unsigned short integer, `Area`, is defined, and it is initialized with the value obtained by multiplying `Width` times `Length`. On lines 12 through 15 the values of the variables are printed to the screen. Note that the special word `endl` creates a new line.

typedef

It can become tedious, repetitious, and, most important, error-prone to keep writing `unsigned short int`. C++ enables you to create an alias for this phrase by using the keyword `typedef`, which stands for *type definition*.

In effect, you are creating a synonym, and it is important to distinguish this from creating a new type (which you will do on Day 6, "Basic Classes"). `typedef` is used by writing the keyword `typedef` followed by the existing type and then the new name. For example,

```
typedef unsigned short int USHORT
```

creates the new name `USHORT` that you can use anywhere you might have written `unsigned short int`. Listing 3.3 is a replay of Listing 3.2 using the type definition `USHORT` rather than `unsigned short int`.

Listing 3.3. Demonstrates `typedef`.

```
1:   // ****************
2:   // Demonstrates typedef keyword
3:   <#include iostream.h>
4:
5:   typedef USHORT unsigned short integer      // typedef defined
6:
7:   main()
8:   {
9:     USHORT  Width = 5;
10:    USHORT Length;
11:    Length = 10;
```

```
12:    USHORT Area  = Width * Length;
13:    cout << "Width:" << Width << "\n";
14:    cout << "Length: "  << Length << endl;
15:    cout << "Area: " << Area;
16: }
```

```
Width: 5
Length: 10
Area: 50
```

On line 5 USHORT is typedef'd as a synonym for unsigned short int. The program is otherwise identical to Listing 3.2, and the output is the same.

When to Use Short and When to Use Long

One source of confusion for new C++ programmers is when to declare a variable to be type long and when to declare it to be type short. The rule, when understood, is fairly straightforward: If there is any chance that the value you'll want to put into your variable will be too big for its type, use a larger type.

As seen in Table 3.1, unsigned short integers, assuming that they are two bytes, can hold a value only up to 65,535. Signed short integers can hold only half that. Although unsigned long integers can hold an extremely large number—4,294,967,295—that is still quite finite. If you need a larger number, you'll have to go to float or double, and then you lose some precision. Floats and doubles can hold extremely large numbers, but only the first 7 or 19 digits are significant on most computers. That means that the number is rounded off after that many digits.

Wrapping Around in Unsigned Integers

The fact that unsigned long integers have a limit to the values they can hold is only rarely a problem, but what happens if you do run out of room?

When an unsigned integer reaches its maximum value, it *wraps around* and starts over, much as a car odometer might. Listing 3.4 shows what happens if you try to put too large a value into a short integer.

Listing 3.4. Demonstrates putting too large a value in an unsigned integer.

```
1: #include <iostream.h>
2: void main()
3: {
4:     unsigned short int smallNumber;
5:     smallNumber = 65535;
6:     cout << "small number:" << smallNumber << endl;
7:     smallNumber++;
8:     cout << "small number:" << smallNumber << endl;
9:     smallNumber++;
10:    cout << "small number:" << smallNumber << endl;
11: }
```

Output

```
small number: 65535
small number: 0
small number: 1
```

Analysis

On line 4 `smallNumber` is declared to be an `unsigned short int`, which on my computer is a two-byte variable, able to hold a value between 0 and 65,535. On line 5 the maximum value is assigned to `smallNumber`, and it is printed on line 6.

On line 7 `smallNumber` is *incremented*; that is, 1 is added to it. The symbol for incrementing is ++ (as in the name C++—an incremental increase from C). Thus, the value in `smallNumber` would be 65,536. But unsigned small integers can't hold a number larger than 65,535, so the value is *wrapped around* to 0, which is printed on line 8.

On line 9 `smallNumber` is incremented again, and then its new value, 1, is printed.

Wrapping Around a Signed Integer

A signed integer is different from an unsigned integer, in that half of its values are negative. Instead of picturing a traditional car odometer, you might picture one that rotates up for positive numbers and down for negative numbers. One *mile* from zero is either 1 or –1. When you run out of positive numbers, you run right into the largest negative numbers and then count back *down* to zero. Listing 3.5 shows what happens when you add 1 to the maximum positive number in an unsigned short integer.

Listing 3.5. Demonstrates adding too large a number to a signed integer.

```
1:  #include <iostream.h>
2:  void main()
```

```
3:  {
4:      short int smallNumber;
5:      smallNumber = 32767;
6:      cout << "small number:" << smallNumber << endl;
7:      smallNumber++;
8:      cout << "small number:" << smallNumber << endl;
9:      smallNumber++;
10:     cout << "small number:" << smallNumber << endl;
11: }
```

```
small number: 32767
small number: -32768
small number: -32767
```

On line 4 `smallNumber` is declared this time to be a signed short integer (if you don't explicitly say that it is unsigned, it is assumed to be signed). The program proceeds much as the preceding one, but the output is quite different. To fully understand this output, you must be comfortable with how signed numbers are represented as bits in a two-byte integer. For details, check Appendix B.

The bottom line, however, is that just like an unsigned integer, the signed integer *wraps around* from its highest positive value to its highest negative value.

Characters

Character variables (type `char`) are typically 1 byte, enough to hold 256 values (see Appendix A). A `char` can be interpreted as a small number (0–255) or as a member of the ASCII set. ASCII stands for the American Standards Committee for Information Interchange. The ASCII character set and its ISO (International Standards Organization) equivalent are a way to encode all the letters, numerals, and punctuation marks.

> **Note:** Computers do not know about letters, punctuation, or sentences. All they understand are numbers. In fact, all they really know about is whether or not a sufficient amount of electricity is at a particular junction of wires. If so, it is represented internally as a 1; if not, it is represented as a 0. By grouping ones and zeros the computer is able to generate patterns which can be interpreted as numbers, and these in turn can be assigned to letters and punctuation.

In the ASCII code the lowercase letter *a* is assigned the value 32. All the lower- and uppercase letters, all the numerals, and all the punctuation marks are assigned a value between 1 and 128. Another 128 marks and symbols are reserved for use by the computer maker, although the IBM extended character set has become something of a standard.

*char*s and Numbers

When you put a character, for example, `'a'`, into a char variable, what is really there is just a number between 0 and 255. The compiler knows, however, how to translate back and forth between characters (represented by a single quotation mark and then a letter, numeral, or punctuation mark, followed by a closing single quotation mark) and one of the ASCII values.

The value/letter relationship is arbitrary; there is no particular reason that the lowercase *a* is represented by the value 97. But as long as everyone (your keyboard, compiler, and screen) agrees, there is no problem. It is important to realize, however, that there is a big difference between the value 5 and the character `'5'`. The latter is actually valued at 53, much as the letter `'a'` is valued at 97.

Listing 3.6. Printing characters based on numbers.

```
1:    #include <iostreams.h>
2:    void main()
3:    {
4:    for (int i = 32; i<128; i++
5:         cout << (char) i;
6:    }
```

```
!"#$%G'()*+,./0123456789:;<>?@ABCDEFGHIJKLMNOP
➡QRSTUVWXYZ[\]^'abcdefghijklmnopqrstuvwxyz<¦>~
```

This simple program prints the character values for the integers 32 through 128.

Special Printing Characters

The C++ compiler recognizes some special characters for formatting. Table 3.2 shows the most common ones. You put these into your code by typing the backslash (called the escape character), followed by the character. Thus, to put a tab character into your code, you would enter a single quotation mark, the slash, the letter *t*, and then a closing single quotation mark:

```
char tabCharacter = '\t';
```

This example declares a char variable (`tabCharacter`) and initializes it with the character value \t, which is recognized as a tab. The special printing characters are used when printing either to the screen or to a file or other output device.

An *escape character* changes the meaning of the character that follows it. For example, normally the character n means the letter n, but when it is escaped by the escape character (\) it means new line.

Table 3.2. The escape characters.

Character	What it means
\n	new line
\t	tab
\b	backspace
\"	double quote
\'	single quote
\?	question mark
\\	backslash

Constants

Like variables, constants are data storage locations. Unlike variables, and as the name implies, constants don't change. You must initialize a constant when you create it, and you cannot assign a new value later.

Literal Constants

C++ has two types of constants: literal and symbolic.

A literal constant is a value typed directly into your program wherever it is needed. For example:

```
int myAge = 39;
```

`myAge` is a variable, of type `int`; "39" is a literal constant. You can't assign a value to 39, and its value can't be changed.

Symbolic Constants

A symbolic constant is a constant that is represented by a name, just as a variable is. Unlike a variable, however, after a constant is initialized, its value can't be changed.

If your program has one integer variable named `students` and another named `classes`, you could compute how many students you have, given a known number of classes, if you knew there were 15 students per class:

```
students = classes * 15;
```

Note: * indicates multiplication.

In this example `15` is a literal constant. Your code would be easier to read, and easier to maintain, if you substituted a symbolic constant for this value:

```
students = classes * studentsPerClass
```

If you later decided to change the number of students in each class, you could do so where you define the constant `studentsPerClass` without having to make a change everyplace you used that value!

There are two ways to declare a symbolic constant in C++. The old, traditional, and now obsolete way is with a preprocessor directive, `#define`.

Defining Constants with *#define*

To define a constant the traditional way, you would enter this:

```
#define studentsPerClass 15
```

Note that `studentsPerClass` is of no particular type (`int`, `char`, and so on). `#define` does a simple text substitution. Every time the preprocessor sees the word `studentsPerClass`, it puts in the text `15`.

Because the preprocessor runs before the compiler, your compiler never sees your constant; it sees the number `15`.

Defining Constants with *const*

Although `#define` works, there is a new, much better way to define constants in C++:

```
const unsigned short int studentsPerClass = 15;
```

This example also declares a symbolic constant named studentsPerClass, but this time studentsPerClass is typed as an unsigned short int. This method has several advantages in making your code easier to maintain and in preventing bugs. The biggest difference is that this constant has a type, and the compiler can enforce that it is used according to its type.

Note: Constants cannot be changed while the program is running. If you need to change studentsPerClass, for example, you need to change the code and recompile.

DO	DON'T

DON'T use the term int, use short and long to make it clear which size number you intended.

DO watch for numbers overrunning the size of the integer and wrapping around incorrect values.

DO give your variables meaningful names which reflect their use.

DON'T use keywords as variable names.

Enumerated Constants

Enumerated constants enable you to create new types and then to define variables of those types whose values are restricted to a set of possible values. For example, you can declare COLOR to be an enumeration, and you can define that there are five values for COLOR: RED, BLUE, GREEN, WHITE, and BLACK.

The syntax for enumerated constants is to write the keyword enum, followed by the type name, an open brace, each of the legal values separated by a comma, and finally a closing brace and a semicolon. Here's an example:

```
enum COLOR { RED, BLUE, GREEN, WHITE, BLACK };
```

This statement performs two tasks:

1. It makes COLOR the name of an enumeration, that is, a new type.

2. It makes RED a symbolic constant with the value 0, BLUE a symbolic constant with the value 1, GREEN a symbolic constant with the value 2, and so forth.

Every enumerated constant has an integer value. If you don't specify otherwise, the first constant will have the value 0, and the rest will count up from there. Any one of the constants can be initialized with a particular value, however, and those that are not initialized will count upward from the ones before them. Thus, if you write

```
enum Color { RED=100, BLUE, GREEN=500, WHITE, BLACK=700 };
```

then RED will have the value 100; BLUE, the value 101; GREEN, the value 500; WHITE, the value 501; and BLACK, the value 700.

You can define variables of type COLOR, but they can be assigned only one of the enumerated values (in this case, RED, BLUE, GREEN, WHITE, or BLACK, or else 100, 101, 500, 501, or 700). You can assign any color value to your COLOR variable. In fact, you can assign any integer value, even if it is not a legal color, although a good compiler will issue a warning if you do. It is important to realize that enumerator variables actually are of type unsigned int and that the enumerated constants equate to integer variables. It is, however, very convenient to be able to name these values when working with colors, days of the week, or similar sets of values. Listing 3.7 presents a program that uses an enumerated type.

Listing 3.7. Demonstrates enumerated constants.

```
1:  #include <iostream.h>
2:  void main()
3:  {
4:      enum Days { Sunday, Monday, Tuesday, Wednesday, Thursday, Friday,
        ➥Saturday };
5:
6:      Days DayOff;
7:
8:      cout << "What day would you like off (0-6)? ";
9:      cin  >> DayOff;
10:
11:     if (DayOff == Sunday || DayOff == Saturday)
12:         cout << "\nYou're already off on weekends!\n";
13:     else
14:         cout << "\nOkay, I'll put in the vacation day.\n";
15: }
```

```
What day would you like off (0-6)? 1
Okay, I'll put in the vacation day.
```

```
What day would you like off (0-6)? 0
You're already off on weekends!
```

Analysis

On line 4 the enumerated constant DAYS is defined, with seven values counting upward from 0. The user is prompted for a day on line 8. The chosen value, a number between 0 and 6, is compared on line 11 to the enumerated values for Sunday and Saturday, and action is taken accordingly. The if statement will be covered in more detail on Day 4, "Decisions and Program Flow."

You cannot type the word "Sunday" when prompted for a day; the program does not know how to translate the characters in "Sunday" into one of the enumerated values.

> **Note:** For this and all the small programs in this book, I've left out all the code you would normally write to deal with what happens when the user types inappropriate data. For example, this program doesn't check, as it would in a real program, to make sure that the user types a number between 0 and 6. This detail has been left out to keep these programs small and simple, and to focus on the issue at hand.

Summary

This chapter has discussed numeric and character variables and constants, which are used by C++ to store data during the execution of your program. Numeric variables are either integral (char, short, and long int) or they are floating point (float and double). Numeric variables can also be signed or unsigned. Although all the types can be of variant sizes among different computers, the type specifies an exact size on any given computer.

You must declare a variable before it can be used, and then you must store the type of data that you've declared correct for that variable. If you put too large a number into an integral variable, it wraps around and produces an incorrect result.

This chapter also reviewed literal and symbolic constants, as well as enumerated constants, and showed two ways to declare a symbolic constant: using #define and using the keyword const.

Q&A

Q If a short int can run out of room and wrap around, why not always use long integers?

A Both short integers and long integers will run out of room and wrap around, but a long integer will do so with a much larger number. For example, an unsigned short int will wrap around after 65,535, whereas an unsigned long int will not wrap around until 4,294,967,295. However, on most machines, a long integer takes up twice as much memory every time you declare one (4 bytes versus 2 bytes), and a program with 100 such variables will consume an extra 200 bytes of RAM. Frankly, this is less of a problem than it used to be, because most personal computers now come with many thousands (if not millions) of bytes of memory.

Q What happens if I assign a number with a decimal to an integer rather than a float? Consider the following line of code:

```
int aNumber = 5.4;
```

A A good compiler will issue a warning, but the assignment is completely legal. The number you've assigned will be truncated into an integer. Thus, if you assign 5.4 to an integer variable, that variable will have the value 5. Information will be lost, however, and if you then try to assign the value in that integer variable to a float variable, the float variable will have only 5.

Q Why not use literal constants; why go to the bother of using symbolic constants?

A If you use the value in many places throughout your program, a symbolic constant allows all the values to change just by changing the one definition of the constant. Symbolic constants also speak for themselves. It might be hard to understand why a number is being multiplied by 360, but it's much easier to understand what's going on if the number is being multiplied by degreesInACircle.

Q What happens if I assign a negative number to an unsigned variable? Consider the following line of code:

```
unsigned int aPositiveNumber  = -1;
```

A A good compiler will warn, but the assignment is legal. The negative number will be assessed as a bit pattern and assigned to the variable. The value of that variable will then be interpreted as an unsigned number. Thus, –1, whose bit pattern is 11111111 11111111 (0xFF in hex), will be assessed as the unsigned value 65,535. If this information confuses you, reread Appendix A.

Q Can I work with C++ without understanding bit patterns, binary arithmetic, and hexadecimal?

A Yes, but not as effectively as if you do understand these topics. C++ does not do as good a job as some languages at "protecting" you from what the computer is really doing. This is actually a benefit, because it provides you with tremendous power that other languages don't. As with any power tool, however, to get the most out of C++ you must understand how it works. Programmers who try to program in C++ without understanding the fundamentals of the binary system often are confused by their results.

Workshop

The Workshop provides quiz questions to help you solidify your understanding of the material covered, and exercises to provide you with experience in using what you've learned. Try to answer the quiz and exercise questions before checking the answers in Appendix D, and make sure that you understand the answers before continuing to the next chapter.

Quiz

1. What is the difference between an integral variable and a floating-point variable?

2. What are the differences between an unsigned short `int` and a long `int`?

3. What are the advantages of using a symbolic constant rather than a literal?

4. What are the advantages of using the `const` keyword rather than `#define`?

5. What makes for a good or bad variable name?

6. Given this enum, what is the value of `Blue`?

```
enum COLOR { WHITE, BLACK = 100, RED, BLUE, GREEN = 300 };
```

7. Which of the following variable names are good, which are bad, and which are invalid?

   a. `Age`

   b. `!ex`

   c. `R79J`

   d. `TotalIncome`

   e. `__Invalid`

Exercises

1. What would be the correct variable type in which to store the following information?

   a. Your age.

   b. The area of your backyard.

   c. The number of stars in the galaxy.

   d. The average rainfall for the month of January.

2. Create good variable names for this information.

3. Declare a constant for pi as 3.14159.

4. Declare a float variable and initialize it using your pi constant.

4

Expressions and Statements

Introduction

At its heart, a program is a set of commands, executed in sequence. The power in a program comes from its capability to execute one or another set of commands based on whether a particular condition is true or false. Today you will learn:

- [ ] What statements are.

- [ ] What blocks are.

- [ ] What expressions are.

- [ ] How to branch your code based on conditions.

- [ ] What truth is, and how to act on it.

Statements

In C++ a statement controls the sequence of execution, evaluates an expression, or does nothing (the null statement). All C++ statements end with a semicolon, even the null statement, which is just the semicolon and nothing else. One of the most common statements is the following assignment statement:

```
x = a + b;
```

Unlike in algebra, this statement does not mean that x equals a+b. This is read, "Assign the value of the sum of a and b to x," or "Assign to x, a+b." Even though this statement is doing two things, it is one statement and thus has one semicolon. The assignment operator assigns whatever is on the right side to whatever is on the left side.

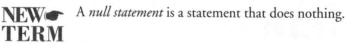 **NEW TERM**   A *null statement* is a statement that does nothing.

Whitespace

Whitespace (tabs, spaces, and newlines) is generally ignored in statements. The assignment statement previously discussed could be written as

```
x=a+b;
```

or as

```
x                    =a
+         b          ;
```

Although this last variation is perfectly legal, it is also perfectly foolish. Whitespace can be used to make your programs more readable and easier to maintain, or it can be used to create horrific and indecipherable code. In this as in all things, C++ provides the power; you supply the judgment.

 NEW TERM Whitespace characters (spaces, tabs, newlines) cannot be seen. If these characters are printed, you see only the white of the paper.

Blocks and Compound Statements

Any place you can put a single statement, you can put a compound statement, also called a block. A block begins with an opening brace ({) and ends with a closing brace (}). Although every statement in the block must end with a semicolon, the block itself does not end with a semicolon. For example:

```
{
    temp = a;
    a = b;
    b = temp;
}
```

This block of code acts as one statement and swaps the values in the variables a and b.

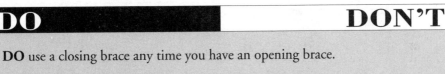

DO	DON'T

DO use a closing brace any time you have an opening brace.

DO end your statements with a semicolon.

DO use whitespace judiciously to make your code clearer.

Expressions

Anything that evaluates to a value is an expression in C++. Expressions are said to *return* a value. Thus, 3+2; returns the value 5 and so is an expression. All expressions are statements.

The myriad pieces of code that qualify as an expression might surprise you. Here are three examples:

```
3.2                    // returns the value 3.2
PI                     // float const that returns the value 3.14
SecondsPerMinute       // int const that returns 60
```

Assuming that `PI` is a const equal to `3.14` and `SecondsPerMinute` is a constant equal to `60`, all three of these statements are expressions.

The complicated expression

```
x = a + b;
```

not only adds a and b and assigns the result to x, but returns the value of that assignment (the value in x) as well. Thus, this statement is also an expression. Because it is an expression, it can be on the right side of an assignment operator:

```
y = x = a + b;
```

This line is evaluated in the following order:

> Add a to b.
> Assign the result of the expression a + b to x.
> Assign the result of the assignment expression x = a + b to y.

If a, b, x, and y are all integers, and if a has the value 2 and b has the value 5, then both x and y will be assigned the value 7.

Listing 4.1. Evaluating complex expressions.

```
1:    #include <iostreams.h>
2:    void main()
3:    {
4:        int a=0, b=0, x=0, y=35;
5:        cout << "a: " << a << " b: " << b;
6:        cout << " x: " << x << " y: " << y << endl;
7:        a = 9;
8:        b = 7;
9:        y = x = a+b;
10:       cout << "a: " << a << " b: " << b;
11:       cout << " x: " << x << "y: " << y << endl;
12:   }
```

```
a: 0 b: 0 x: 0 y: 35
a: 9 b: 7 x: 16 y: 16
```

On line 4, the four variables are declared and initialized. Their values are printed on lines 5 and 6. On line 7, a is assigned the value 9. One line 8, b is assigned the value 7. On line 9, the values of a and b are summed and the result is assigned to x. This expression (x = a+b) evaluates to a value (the sum of a + b), and that value is in turn assigned to y.

Operators

An operator is a symbol that causes the compiler to take an action. Operators act on operands, and in C++ all operands are expressions. In C++ there are several different categories of operators. Two of these categories are:

- ☐ Assignment operators.
- ☐ Mathematical operators.

Assignment Operator

The assignment operator (=) causes the operand on the left side of the assignment operator to have its value changed to the value on the right side of the assignment operator. The expression

```
x = a + b;
```

assigns the value that is the result of adding a and b to the operand x.

An operand that can legally be on the left side of an assignment operator is called an l-value. That which can be on the right side is called (you guessed it) an r-value.

Constants are r-values. They cannot be l-values. Thus, you can write

```
x = 35;          // ok
```

but you can't legally write

```
35 = x;          // error, not an lvalue!
```

NEW TERM An l-value is an operand that can be on the left side of an expression. An r-value is an operand that can be on the right side of an expression. Note that all l-values are r-values, but not all r-values are l-values. An example of an r-value that is not an l-value is a literal. Thus, you can write x = 5;, but you cannot write 5 = x;.

Mathematical Operators

There are five mathematical operators: addition (+), subtraction (-), multiplication (*), division (/), and modulus (%).

Addition and subtraction work as you would expect, although subtraction with unsigned integers can lead to surprising results if the result is a negative number. You saw something much like this yesterday, when variable overflow was described. Listing 4.2

shows what happens when you subtract a large unsigned number from a small unsigned number.

Listing 4.2. Demonstrates subtraction and integer overflow.

```
1: // Listing 4.1 - demonstrates subtraction and
2: // integer overflow
3: #include <iostream.h>
4:
5: void main()
6: {
7:     unsigned int difference;
8:     unsigned int bigNumber = 100;
9:     unsigned int smallNumber = 50;
10:    difference = bigNumber - smallNumber;
11:    cout << "Difference is: " << difference;
12:    difference = smallNumber - bigNumber;
13:    cout << "\nNow difference is: " << difference;
14: }
```

```
Difference is: 50
Now difference is: 65486
```

 The subtraction operator is invoked on line 10, and the result is printed on line 11, much as we might expect. The subtraction operator is called again on line 12, but this time a large unsigned number is subtracted from a small unsigned number. The result would be negative, but because it is evaluated (and printed) as an unsigned number, the result is an overflow as described yesterday. This topic is reviewed in detail in Appendix A.

Integer Division and Modulus

Integer division is somewhat different from everyday division. When you divide 21 by 4, the result is a real number (a number with a fraction). Integers don't have fractions, and so the "remainder" is lopped off. The answer thus is 5. To get the remainder, you take 21 modulus 4 (21 % 4) and the result is 1. The modulus operator tells you the remainder after an integer division.

Finding the modulus can be very useful. For example, you might want to print a statement on every 10th action. Any number whose value is 0 when you modulus 10 with that number is an exact multiple of 10. Thus 1 % 10 is 1, 2 % 10 is 2, and so forth until 10 % 10, whose result is 0. 11 % 10 is back to one, and this pattern continues until the next multiple of 10, which is 20. We'll use this technique when looping is discussed on Day 7.

Warning: Many novice C++ programmers inadvertantly put a semicolon after their `if` statements:

```
if(someValue , 10);
    SomeValue = 10;
```

What was intended here was to test whether `SomeValue` is less than 10, and if so to set it to `10`, making `10` the minimum value for `SomeValue`. Running this code snippet will show that `SomeValue` is *always* set to `10`! Why? The `if` statement terminates with the semicolon (the do-nothing operator).

Remember that indentation has no meaning to the complier. This snippet could more accurately have been written as:

```
if (SomeValue , 10)      // test
    ;                    // do nothing
SomeValue = 10;          // assign
```

Removing the semicolon will make the final line part of the `if` statement, and will make this code do what was intended.

Combining the Assignment and Mathematical Operators

It is not uncommon to want to add a value to a variable, and then to assign the result back into the variable. If you have a variable `myAge` and you want to increase the value by two, you can write

```
int myAge = 5;
int temp;
temp = myAge + 2;   // add 5 + 2 and put it in temp
myAge = temp;              // put it back in myAge
```

This method, however, is terribly convoluted and wasteful. In C++ you can put the same variable on both sides of the assignment operator, and thus the preceding becomes

```
myAge = myAge + 2;
```

which is much better. In algebra this expression would be meaningless, but in C++ it is read as "add two to the value in `myAge` and assign the result to `myAge`."

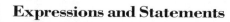

Even simpler to write, but perhaps a bit harder to read is

```
myAge += 2;
```

The self-assigned addition operator (+=) adds the rvalue to the lvalue and then reassigns the result into the lvalue. This operator is pronounced "plus-equals." The statement would be read "myAge plus-equals two." If myAge had the value 4 to start, it would have 6 after this statement.

There are self-assigned subtraction (-=), division (/=), multiplication (*=) and modulus (%=) operators as well.

Increment and Decrement

The most common value to add (or subtract) and then reassign into a variable is 1. In C++ increasing a value by 1 is called incrementing, and decreasing by 1 is called decrementing. There are special operators to perform these actions.

The increment operator (++) increases the value of the variable by 1, and the decrement operator (--) decreases it by 1. Thus, if you have a variable, C, and you want to increment it, you would use this statement:

```
C++;              // Start with C and increment it.
```

This statement is equivalent to the more verbose statement

```
C = C + 1;
```

which you learned is also equivalent to the moderately verbose statement

```
C += 1;
```

Prefix and Postfix

Both the increment operator (++) and the decrement operator(--) come in two varieties: prefix and postfix. The prefix variety is written before the variable name (++myAge); the postfix variety, after (myAge++).

In a simple statement, it doesn't much matter which you use, but in a complex statement, when you are incrementing (or decrementing) a variable and then assigning the result to another variable, it matters very much. The prefix operator is evaluated before the assignment, the postfix is evaluated after. Listing 4.3 shows the use and implications of both types.

Listing 4.3. Demonstrates prefix and postfix operators.

```
 1:  // Listing 4.2 - demonstrates use of
 2:  // prefix and postfix increment and
 3:  // decrement operators
 4:  #include <iostream.h>
 5:  void main()
 6:  {
 7:      int myAge = 39;        // initialize two integers
 8:      int yourAge = 39;
 9:      cout << "I am:\t" << myAge << "\tyears old.\n";
10:      cout << "You are:\t" << yourAge << "\tyears old\n";
11:      myAge++;             // postfix increment
12:      ++yourAge;           // prefix increment
13:      cout << "One year passes...\n";
14:      cout << "I am:\t" << myAge << "\tyears old.\n";
15:      cout << "You are:\t" << yourAge << "\tyears old\n";
16:      cout << "Another year passes\n";
17:      cout << "I am:\t" << myAge++ << "\tyears old.\n";
     ➥//note differences
18:      cout << "You are:\t" << ++yourAge << "\tyears old\n";
     ➥// between these lines
19:      cout << "Let's print it again.\n";
20:      cout << "I am:\t" << myAge << "\tyears old.\n";
21:      cout << "You are:\t" << yourAge << "\tyears old\n";
22:  }
```

Output

```
I am      39 years old
You are   39 years old
One year passes
I am      40 years old
You are   40 years old
Another year passes
I am      41 years old
You are   40 years old
Let's print it again
I am      41 years old
You are   41 years old
```

Analysis

On lines 7 and 8 two integer variables are declared, and each is initialized with the value 39. Their value is printed on lines 9 and 10.

On line 11 myAge is incremented using the postfix increment operator, and on line 12 yourAge is incremented using the prefix increment operator. The results are printed on lines 14 and 15, and they are identical (both 40).

On line 17 myAge is incremented as part of the printing statement, using the postfix increment operator. Because it is postfix, the increment happens *after* the print, and so the value 40 is printed again. In contrast, on line 18 yourAge is incremented using the prefix increment operator. Thus, it is incremented *before* being printed, and the value displays as 41.

Finally, on lines 20 and 21 the values are printed again. Because the increment statement has completed, the value in myAge is now 41, as is the value in yourAge.

Precedence

In the complex statement

```
x = 5 + 3 * 8;
```

which is performed first, the addition or the multiplication? If the addition is performed first, the answer is 8 * 8, or 64. If the multiplication is performed first, the answer is 5 + 24, or 29.

Every operator has a precedence value, and the complete list is shown in Appendix B. Multiplication has higher precedence than addition, and thus the value of the expression is 29.

When two mathematical operators have the same precedence, they are performed in left-to-right order. Thus

```
x = 5 + 3 + 8 * 9 + 6 * 4;
```

is evaluated multiplication first, left to right. Thus, 8*9 = 72, and 6*4 = 24. Now the expression is essentially

```
x = 5 + 3 + 72 + 24;
```

Now the addition, left to right, is 5 + 3 = 8; 8 + 72 = 80; 80 + 24 = 104.

Be careful with this. Some operators, such as assignment, are evaluated in right-to-left order! In any case, what if the precedence order doesn't meet your needs? Consider the expression

```
TotalSeconds = NumMinutesToThink + NumMinutesToType * 60
```

In this expression you do not want to multiply the NumMinutesToType variable by 60 and then add it to NumMinutesToThink. You want to add the two variables to get the total number of minutes, and then you want to multiply that number by 60 to get the total seconds.

In this case you use parentheses to change the precedence order. Items in parentheses are evaluated at a higher precedence than any of the mathematical operators. Thus

```
TotalSeconds = (NumMinutesToThink + NumMinutesToType) * 60
```

will accomplish what you want.

Nesting Parentheses

For complex expressions you might need to nest parentheses one within another. For example, you might need to compute the total seconds and then compute the total number of people who are involved before multiplying seconds times people:

```
Total PersonSeconds = ( ( (NumMinutesToThink + NumMinutesToType) * 60) *
(PeopleInTheOffice + PeopleOnVacation) )
```

This complicated expression is read from the inside out. First, `NumMinutesToThink` is added to `NumMinutesToType`, because these are in the innermost parentheses. Then this sum is multiplied by 60. Next, `PeopleInTheOffice` is added to `PeopleOnVacation`. Finally, the total number of people found is multiplied by the total number of seconds.

This example raises an important related issue. This expression is easy for a computer to understand but very difficult for a human to read, understand, or modify. Here is the same expression rewritten, using some temporary integer variables:

```
TotalMinutes = NumMinutesToThink + NumMinutesToType;
TotalSeconds = TotalMinutes * 60;
TotalPeople = PeopleInTheOffice + PeopleOnVacation;
Total PersonSeconds = TotalPeople * TotalSeconds;
```

This example takes longer to write and uses more temporary variables than the preceding example, but it is far easier to understand. Add a comment at the top to explain what this code does, and change the `60` to a symbolic constant. You then will have code that is easy to understand and maintain.

DO	DON'T

DO remember that expressions have a value.

DO use the prefix operator (`++variable`) to increment or decrement the variable before it is used in the expression.

DO use the postfix operator (`variable++`) to increment or decrement the variable after it is used.

DO use parentheses to change the order of precedence.

DON'T nest too deeply, because the expression becomes hard to understand and maintain.

The Nature of Truth

In C++, 0 (zero) is considered false, and all other values are considered true, although true is usually represented by 1. Thus, if an expression is false, it is equal to zero, and if an expression is equal to zero, it is false. If a statement is true, all you know is that it is nonzero, and any nonzero statement is true.

Relational Operators

The relational operators are used to determine whether two numbers are equal, or if one is greater or less than the other. Every relational statement evaluates to either 1 (true) or 0 (false). The relational operators are presented later in Table 4.1.

If the integer variable myAge has the value 39, and the integer variable yourAge has the value 40, you can determine whether they are equal by using the relational "equals" operator:

```
myAge == yourAge;   // is the value in myAge the same as in yourAge?
```

This expression evaluates to 0, or false, because the variables are not equal. The expression

```
myAge > yourAge;   // is myAge greater than yourAge?
```

evaluates to 1 or true.

Warning: Many novice C++ programmers confuse the assignment operator (=) with the equals operator (==). This can create a nasty bug in your program.

There are six relational operators: equals (==), less than (<), greater than (>), less than or equal to (<=), greater than or equal to (>=), and not equals (!=). Table 4.1 shows each relational operator, its use, and a sample code use.

Table 1.1. The relational operators.

Name	Operator	Sample	Evaluates
Equals	==	100 == 50;	false
		50 == 50;	true

Name	Operator	Sample	Evaluates
Not Equals	!=	100 != 50;	true
		50 != 50;	false
Greater Than	>	100 > 50;	true
		50 > 50;	false
Greater Than or Equals	>=	100 >= 50;	true
		50 >= 50;	true
Less Than	<	100 < 50;	false
		50 < 50;	false
Less Than or Equals	<=	100 <= 50;	false
		50 <= 50;	true

DO / DON'T

DO remember that relational operators return the value 1 (true) or 0 (false).

DON'T confuse the assignment operator (=) with the equals relational operator (==). This is one of the most common C++ programming mistakes—be on guard for it.

The *if* Statement

Normally, your program flows along line by line in the order in which it appears in your source code. The if statement enables you to test for a condition (such as whether two variables are equal) and branch to different parts of your code depending on the result.

The simplest form of an if statement is this:

```
if (expression)
    statement;
```

The expression in the parentheses can be any expression at all, but it usually contains one of the relational expressions. If the expression has the value zero, it is considered false, and the statement is skipped. If it has any nonzero value, it is considered true, and the statement is executed. Consider the following example:

```
if (bigNumber > smallNumber)
    bigNumber = smallNumber;
```

This code compares `bigNumber` and `smallNumber`. If `bigNumber` is larger, the second line sets its value to the value of `smallNumber`.

Because a block of statements surrounded by braces is exactly equivalent to a single statement, the following type of branch can be quite large and powerful:

```
if (expression)
{
    statement1;
    statement2;
    statement3;
}
```

Here's a simple example of this usage:

```
if (bigNumber > smallNumber)
{
    bigNumber = smallNumber;
    cout << "bigNumber: " << bigNumber << "\n";
    cout << "smallNumber: " << smallNumber << "\n";
}
```

This time, if `bigNumber` is larger than `smallNumber`, not only is it set to the value of `smallNumber`, but an informational message is printed. Listing 4.4 shows a fuller example of branching based on relational operators.

Listing 4.4. Demonstrates branching based on relational operators.

```
1:  // Listing 4.3 - demonstrates if statement
2:  // used with relational operators
3:  #include <iostream.h>
4:  main()
5:  {
6:      int RedSoxScore, YankeesScore;
7:      cout << "Enter the score for the Red Sox: ";
8:      cin >> RedSoxScore;
9:
10:     cout << "\nEnter the score for the Yankees: ";
11:     cin >> YankeesScore;
12:
13:     cout << "\n";
14:
15:     if (RedSoxScore > YankeesScore)
16:         cout << "Go Sox!\n";
17:
18:     if (RedSoxScore < YankeesScore)
19:         {
```

```
20:            cout << "Go Yankees!\n";
21:            cout << "Happy days in New York!\n";
22:        }
23:
24:        if (RedSoxScore == YankeesScore)
25:        {
26:            cout << "A tie? Naah, can't be.\n";
27:            cout << "Give me the real score for the Yanks: ";
28:            cin >> YankeesScore;
29:
30:            if (RedSoxScore > YankeesScore)
31:                cout << "Knew it! Go Sox!";
32:
33:            if (YankeesScore > RedSoxScore)
34:                cout << "Knew it! Go Yanks!";
35:
36:            if (YankeesScore == RedSoxScore)
37:                cout << "Wow, it really was a tie!";
38:        }
39:
40:        cout << "\nThanks for telling me.\n";
41:  }
```

Output

```
Enter the score for the Red Sox: 10
Enter the score for the Yankees: 10
A tie? Naah, can't be
Give me the real score for the Yanks: 8
Knew it! Go Sox!
Thanks for telling me.
```

Analysis This program asks for user input of scores for two baseball teams, which are stored in integer variables. The variables are compared in the if statement on lines 15, 18, and 24.

If one score is higher than the other, an informational message is printed. If the scores are equal, the block of code that begins on line 26 and ends on line 38 is entered. The second score is requested again, and then the scores are compared again.

Note that if the initial Yankees score was higher than the Red Sox score, the if statement on line 15 would evaluate as false, and line 16 would not be invoked. The test on line 18 would evaluate as true, and the statements on lines 20 and 21 would be invoked. Then the if statement on line 24 would be tested, and this would be false (if line 18 was true). Thus, the program would skip the entire block, falling through to line 39.

In this example, getting a true result in one if statement does not stop other if statements from being tested.

Indentation Styles

Listing 4.3 shows one style of indenting `if` statements. Nothing is more likely to create a religious war, however, than to ask a group of programmers what is the best style for brace alignment. Although there are dozens of variations, these appear to be the favorite three:

☐ Putting the initial brace after the condition and aligning the closing brace under the `if` to close the statement block.

```
if (expression){
    statements
}
```

☐ Aligning the braces under the `if` and indenting the statements.

```
if (expression)
{
    statements
}
```

☐ Indenting the braces and statements.

```
if (expression)
  {
  statements
  }
```

This book uses the middle alternative, because I find it easier to understand where blocks of statements begin and end if the braces line up with each other and with the condition being tested. Again, it doesn't matter much which style you choose as long as you are consistent with it.

else

Often your program will want to take one branch if your condition is true, another if it is false. In the Listing 4.3, you wanted to print one message ("`Go Sox`") if the first test (`RedSoxScore > Yankees`) evaluated true, and another message ("`Go Yanks!`") if it evaluated false.

The method shown so far, testing first one condition and then the other, works fine but is a bit cumbersome. The keyword `else` can make for far more readable code:

```
if (expression)
```

```
          statement;
else
          statement;
```

Listing 4.5 demonstrates the use of the keyword `else`.

Listing 4.5. Demonstrating the `else` keyword.

```
1:    // Listing 4.4 - demonstrates if statement
2:    // with else clause
3:    #include <iostream.h>
4:    main()
5:    {
6:        int firstNumber, secondNumber;
7:        cout << "Please enter a big number: ";
8:        cin >> firstNumber;
9:        cout << "\nPlease enter a smaller number: ";
10:       cin >> secondNumber;
11:       if (firstNumber > secondNumber)
12:           cout << "\nThanks!\n";
13:       else
14:           cout << "\nOops. The second is bigger!";
15:
16:   }
```

```
Please enter a big number: 10
Please enter a smaller number: 12
Oops. The second is bigger!
```

The `if` statement on line 11 is evaluated. If the condition is true, the statement on line 12 is run; if it is false, the statement on line 14 is run. If the `else` clause on line 13 were removed, the statement on line 14 would run whether or not the `if` statement was true. Remember, the `if` statement ends after line 12. If the `else` was not there, line 14 would just be the next line in the program.

Remember that either or both of these statements could be replaced with a block of code in braces.

The *if* Statement
Form 1

```
if (expression)
    statement;
next statement;
```

If the expression is evaluated as true, the statement is executed and the program continues with the next statement. If the expression is not true, the statement is ignored and the program jumps to the next statement.

71

Remember that the statement can be a single statement ending with a semicolon, or a block enclosed in braces.

Form 2

```
if (expression)
    statement1;
else
    statement2;
next statement;
```

If the expression evaluates true, `statement1` is executed; otherwise, `statement2` is executed. Afterwards, the program continues with the next statement.

Example 1

```
Example
if (SomeValue < 10)
  cout << "SomeValue is less than 10");
else
  cout << "SomeValue is not less than 10!");
cout << "Done." << endl;
```

Advanced *if* Statements

It is worth noting that any statement can be used in an `if` or `else` clause, even another `if` or `else` statement. Thus, you might see complex `if` statements in the following form:

```
if (expression1)
{
    if (expression2)
        statement1;
    else
    {
        if (expression3)
            statement2;
        else
            statement3;
    }
}
else
    statement4;
```

This cumbersome `if` statement says, "If `expression1` is true and `expression2` is true, execute `statement1`. If `expression1` is true but `expression2` is not true, then if `expression3` is true execute `statement2`. If `expression1` is true but `expression2` and `expression3` are false, execute `statement3`. Finally, if `expression1` is not true, execute `statement4`." As you can see, complex `if` statements can be confusing!

Listing 4.6 gives an example of such a complex `if` statement.

Listing 4.6. A complex, nested `if` statement.

```
1:  // Listing 4.5 - a complex nested
2:  // if statement
3:  #include <iostream.h>
4:  void main()
5:  {
6:      // Ask for two numbers
7:      // Assign the numbers to bigNumber and littleNumber
8:      // If bigNumber is bigger than littleNumber,
9:      // see if they are evenly divisible
10:     // If they are, see if they are the same number
11:
12:     int firstNumber, secondNumber;
13:     cout << "Enter two numbers.\nFirst: ";
14:     cin >> firstNumber;
15:     cout << "\nSecond: ";
16:     cin >> secondNumber;
17:     cout << "\n\n";
18:
19:     if (firstNumber >= secondNumber)
20:     {
21:       if ( (firstNumber % secondNumber) == 0) // evenly divisible?
22:       {
23:           if (firstNumber == secondNumber)
24:               cout << "They are the same!\n";
25:           else
26:               cout << "They are evenly divisible!\n";
27:       }
28:       else
29:           cout << "They are not evenly divisible!\n";
30:     }
31:     else
32:       cout << "Hey! The second one is larger!\n";
33: }
```

```
Enter two numbers.
First: 10
Second: 2
They are evenly divisible!
```

Two numbers are prompted for, then compared. The first `if` statement, on line 19, checks to ensure that the first number is greater than or equal to the second. If not, the `else` clause on line 31 is executed.

If the first `if` is true, the block of code beginning on line 20 is executed, and the second `if` statement is tested, on line 21. This checks to see whether the first number modulo the second number yields no remainder. If so, the numbers are either evenly divisible or equal. The if statement on line 23 checks for equality and displays the appropriate message either way.

If the if statement on line 21 fails, the else statement on line 28 is executed.

Use Braces in Nested *if* Statements

Although it is legal to leave out the braces on if statements that are only a single statement, and it is legal to nest if statements, such as

```
if (x > y)              // if x is bigger than y
    if (x < z)          // and if x is smaller than z
        x == y;         // then set x to the value in z
```

when writing large nested statements, this can cause enormous confusion. Remember, whitespace and indentation are a convenience for the programmer; they make no difference to the compiler. It is easy to confuse the logic and inadvertently assign an else statement to the wrong if statement. Listing 4.7 illustrates this problem.

Listing 4.7. Demonstrates why braces help clarify which else statement goes with which if statement.

```
1:   // Listing 4.6 - demonstrates why braces
2:   // are important in nested if statements
3:   #include <iostream.h>
4:   void main()
5:   {
6:     int x;
7:     cout << "Enter a number less than 10 or greater than 100: ";
8:     cin >> x;
9:     cout << "\n";
10:
11:     if (x > 10)
12:       if (x > 100)
13:            cout << "More than 100, Thanks!\n";
14:     else                          // not the else intended!
15:       cout << "Less than 10, Thanks!\n";
16:
17:   }
```

```
Enter a number less than 10 or greater than 100: 20
Less than 10, Thanks!
```

The programmer intended to ask for a number between 10 and 100, check for the correct value, and then print a thank-you note.

If the if statement on line 11 evaluates true, the following statement (line 12) is executed. In this case, line 12 executes when the number entered is greater than 10. Line 12 contains an if statement also. This if statement evaluates true if the number entered is greater than 100. If the number is not greater than 100, the statement on line 13 is executed.

If the number entered is less than or equal to 10, the if on line 10 evaluates to false. Program control goes to the next line following the if, in this case line 16. If you enter a number less than 10, the output is as follows:

```
Enter a number less than 10 or greater than 100: 9
```

The else clause on line 14 was clearly intended to be attached to the if statement on line 11, and thus is indented accordingly. Unfortunately, the else statement is really attached to the if on line 12, and thus this program has a subtle bug.

It is a subtle bug because the compiler will not complain. This is a legal C++ program, but it just doesn't do what was intended. Further, most of the time the programmer tests this program, it will appear to work. As long as a number that is greater than 100 is entered, the program will seem to work just fine.

Listing 4.8 fixes the problem by putting in the necessary braces.

Listing 4.8. Demonstrates the proper use of braces with an if statement.

```
1:    // Listing 4.7 - demonstrates proper use of braces
2:    // in nested if statements
3:    #include <iostream.h>
4:    void main()
5:    {
6:       int x;
7:       cout << "Enter a number less than 10 or greater than 100: ";
8:       cin >> x;
9:       cout << "\n";
10:
11:      if (x > 10)
12:      {
13:         if (x > 100)
14:             cout << "More than 100, Thanks!\n";
15:      }
16:      else                           // not the else intended!
17:         cout << "Less than 10, Thanks!\n";
17:   }
```

```
Enter a number less than 10 or greater than 100: 20
```

The braces on lines 12 and 15 make everything between them into one statement, and now the `else` on line 16 applies to the `if` on line 10 as intended.

The user typed `20`, so the `if` statement on line 11 is true; however, the `if` statement on line 13 is false, so nothing is printed. It would be better if the programmer put another `else` clause after line 14 so that errors would be caught and a message printed.

Note: The programs shown in this book are written to demonstrate the particular issues being discussed. They are kept intentionally simple; there is no attempt to "bulletproof" the code to protect against user error. In professional-quality code, every possible user error is anticipated and handled gracefully.

Logical Operators

Often you want to ask more than one relational question at a time. "Is it true that x is greater than y, and also true that y is greater than z?" A program might need to determine that both of these conditions are true, or that some other condition is true, in order to take an action.

Imagine a sophisticated alarm system that has this logic: "If the door alarm sounds AND it is after six p.m. AND it is NOT a holiday, OR if it is a weekend, then call the police." C++'s three logical operators are used to make this kind of evaluation. These operators are listed in Table 4.2.

Table 4.2. The Logical Operators.

Operator	Symbol	Example
AND	&&	expression1 && expression2
OR	¦¦	expression1 ¦¦ expression2
NOT	!	!expression

Logical *AND*

A logical AND statement evaluates two expressions, and if *both* expressions are true, the logical AND statement is true as well. If it is true that you are hungry, AND it is true that you have money, THEN it is true that you can buy lunch. Thus,

```
if ( (x == 5) && (y == 5) )
```

would evaluate true if both x and y are equal to 5, and it would evaluate false if either one is not equal to 5. Note that both sides must be true for the entire expression to be true.

Note that the logical AND is *two* && symbols. A single & symbol is a different operator, discussed on Day 19.

Logical *OR*

A logical OR statement evaluates two expressions. If *either one* is true, the expression is true. If you have money OR you have a credit card, you can pay the bill. You don't need both money and a credit card; you need only one, although having both would be fine as well. Thus,

```
if ( (x == 5) || (y == 5) )
```

evaluates true if either x or y is equal to 5, or if both are.

Note that the logical OR is *two* || symbols. A single | symbol is a different operator, discussed on Day 19.

Logical *NOT*

A logical NOT statement evaluates true if the expression being tested is false. Again, if the expression being tested is false, the value of the test is true! Thus

```
if ( !(x == 5) )
```

is true only if x is not equal to 5. This is exactly the same as writing

```
if (x != 5)
```

Relational Precedence

Relational operators and logical operators, being C++ expressions, each return a value: 1 (true) or 0 (false). And like all expressions, they have a precedence order (see Appendix

A) that determines which relations are evaluated first. This fact is important when determining the value of the statement

```
if ( x > 5 && y > 5 ¦¦ z > 5)
```

It might be that the programmer wanted this expression to evaluate true if both x and y are greater than 5 or if z is greater than 5. On the other hand, the programmer might have wanted this expression to evaluate true only if x is greater than 5 and if it is also true that either y is greater than 5 or z is greater than 5.

If x is 3, and y and z are both 10, the first interpretation will be true (z is greater than 5, so ignore x and y), but the second will be false (it isn't true that both x and y are greater than 5 nor is it true that z is greater than 5).

Although precedence will determine which relation is evaluated first, parentheses can both change the order and make the statement clearer:

```
if (  (x > 5)  && (y > 5 ¦¦  z > 5) )
```

Using the values from earlier, this statement is false. Because it is not true that x is greater than 5, the left side of the AND statement fails, and thus the entire statement is false. Remember that an AND statement requires that both sides be true—something isn't both "good tasting" AND "good for you" if it isn't good tasting.

> **Note:** It is often a good idea to use extra parentheses to clarify what you want to group. Remember, the goal is to write programs that work *and* that are easy to read and understand.

More About Truth and Falsehood

In C++ zero is false, and any other value is true. Because expressions always have a value, many C++ programmers take advantage of this feature in their if statements. A statement such as

```
if (x)           // if x is true (nonzero)
   x = 0;
```

can be read as "If x has a nonzero value, set it to 0." This is a bit of a cheat; it would be clearer if written

```
if (x != 0)      // if x is nonzero
   x = 0;
```

Both statements are legal, but the latter is clearer. It is good programming practice to reserve the former method for true tests of logic, rather than for testing for nonzero values.

These two statements are also equivalent:

```
if (!x)          // if x is false (zero)
if (x == 0)      // if x is zero
```

The second statement, however, is somewhat easier to understand and is more explicit.

DO	DON'T

DO put parentheses around your logical tests to make them clearer and to make the precedence explicit.

DO use braces in nested `if` statements to make the `else` statements clearer and to avoid bugs.

DON'T use `if(x)` as a synonym for `if(x != 0)`; the latter is clearer.

DON'T use `if(!x)` as a synonym for `if(x == 0)`; the latter is clearer.

Note: It is common to define your own enumerated Boolean (logical) type with `enum Bool {FALSE, TRUE};`. This serves to set `FALSE` to 0 and `TRUE` to 1.

Conditional (Ternary) Operator

The conditional operator (?:) is C++'s only ternary operator; that is, it is the only operator to take three terms.

The conditional operator takes three expressions and returns a value:

```
(expression1) ? (expression2) : (expression3)
```

This line is read as "If *expression1* is true, return the value of *expression2*; otherwise, return the value of *expression3*." Typically, this value would be assigned to a variable.

Listing 4.9 shows an `if` statement rewritten using the conditional operator.

Listing 4.9. Demonstrates the conditional operator.

```
1:   // Listing 4.8 - demonstrates the conditional operator
2:   //
3:   #include <iostream.h>
4:   void main()
5:   {
6:       int x, y, z;
7:       cout << "Enter two numbers.\n";
8:       cout << "First: ";
9:       cin >> x;
10:      cout << "\nSecond: ";
11:      cin >> y;
12:      cout << "\n";
13:
14:      if (x > y)
15:         z = x;
16:      else
17:         z = y;
18:
19:      cout << "z: " << z;
20:      cout << "\n";
21:
22:      z =  (x > y) ? x : y;
23:
24:      cout << "z: " << z;
25:      cout << "\n";
26:  }
```

```
Enter two numbers.
First: 5
Second: 8
z: 8
z: 8
```

Three integer variables are created: x, y, and z. The first two are given values by the user. The if statement on line 14 tests to see which is larger and assigns the larger value to z. This value is printed on line 19.

The conditional operator on line 22 makes the same test and assigns z the larger value. It is read like this: "If x is greater than y, return the value of x; otherwise, return the value of y." The value returned is assigned to z. That value is printed on line 24. As you can see, the conditional statement is a shorter equivalent to the if...else statement.

Summary

This chapter has covered a lot of material. You have learned what C++ statements and expressions are, what C++ operators do, and how C++ if statements work.

You have seen that a block of statements enclosed by a pair of braces can be used anywhere a single statement can be used.

You have learned that every expression evaluates to a value, and that value can be tested in an `if` statement or by using the conditional operator. You've also seen how to evaluate multiple statements using the logical operator, how to compare values using the relational operators, and how to assign values using the assignment operator.

You have explored operator precedence. And you have seen how parentheses can be used to change the precedence and to make precedence explicit and thus easier to manage.

Q&A

Q **Why use unnecessary parentheses when precedence will determine which operators are acted on first?**

A Although it is true that the compiler will know the precedence and that a programmer can look up the precedence order, code that is easy to understand is easier to maintain.

Q **If the relational operators always return 1 or 0, why are other values considered true?**

A The relational operators return 1 or 0, but every expression returns a value, and those values can also be evaluated in an `if` statement. Here's an example:

```
if ( (x = a + b) == 35 )
```

This is a perfectly legal C++ statement. It evaluates to a value even if the sum of a and b is not equal to 35. Also note that x is assigned the value that *is* the sum of a and b in any case.

Q **What effect do tabs, spaces, and new lines have on the program?**

A Tabs, spaces, and new lines (known as whitespace) have no effect on the program, although judicious use of whitespace can make the program easier to read.

Q **Are negative numbers true or false?**

A All nonzero numbers, positive and negative, are true.

Workshop

The Workshop provides quiz questions to help you solidify your understanding of the material covered, and exercises to provide you with experience in using what you've learned. Try to answer the quiz and exercise questions before checking the answers in Appendix D, and make sure that you understand the answers before continuing to the next chapter.

Quiz

1. What is an expression?

2. Is x = 5 + 7 an expression? What is its value?

3. What is the value of 201 / 4?

4. What is the value of 201 % 4?

5. If myAge, a, and b are all int variables, what are their values after:

   ```
   myAge = 39;
   a = myAge++;
   b = ++myAge;
   ```

6. What is the value of 8+2*3?

7. What is the difference between x = 3 and x == 3?

8. Do the following values evaluate to TRUE or FALSE?

   a. 0

   b. 1

   c. -1

   d. x = 0

   e. x == 0   // assume that x has the value of 0

Exercises

1. Write a single if statement that examines two integer variables and changes the larger to the smaller, using only one else clause.

2. Examine the following program. Imagine entering three numbers, and write what output you expect.

```
1:    #include <iostream.h>
2:    void main()
3:    {
4:        int a, b, c;
5:        cout << "Please enter three numbers\n";
6:        cout << "a: ";
7:        cin >> a;
8:        cout << "\nb: ";
9:        cin >> b;
10:       cout << "\nc: ";
11:       cin >> c;
12:
13:       if (c = (a-b))
14:            cout << "a: ";
15:            cout << a;
16:            cout << "minus b: ";
17:            cout << b;
18:            cout << "equals c: ";
19:            cout << c << endl;
20:       else
21:            cout << "a-b does not equal c: " << endl;
22:   }
```

3. Enter the program from Exercise 3; compile, link, and run it. Enter the numbers 20, 10, and 50. Did you get the output you expected? Why not?

4. Examine this program and anticipate the output:

```
1:    #include <iostream.h>
2:    void main()
3:    {
4:        int a = 1, b = 1, c;
5:        if (c = (a-b))
6:            cout << "The value of c is: " << c;
7:    }
```

5. Enter, compile, link, and run the program from Exercise 4. What was the output? Why?

5

Functions

Introduction

Although object-oriented programming has shifted attention from functions and toward objects, functions nonetheless remain a central component of any program. Today you will learn:

- ☐ What a function is and what its parts are.
- ☐ How to declare and define functions.
- ☐ How to pass parameters into functions.
- ☐ How to return a value from a function.

What Is a Function?

A function is, in effect, a subprogram that can act on data and return a value. Every C++ program has at least one function, `main()`. When your program starts, `main()` is called automatically. `main()` might call other functions, some of which might call still others.

Each function has its own name, and when that name is encountered, the execution of the program branches to the body of that function. When the function returns, execution resumes on the next line of the calling function. This flow is illustrated in Figure 5.1.

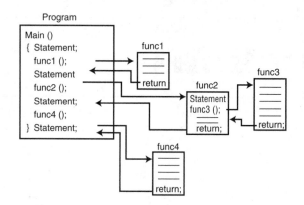

Figure 5.1. *When a program calls a function, execution switches to the function and then resumes at the line after the function call.*

Well-designed functions perform a specific and easily understood task. Complicated tasks should be broken down into multiple functions, and then each can be called in turn.

Functions come in two varieties: user-defined and built-in. Built-in functions are part of your compiler package—they are supplied by the manufacturer for your use.

Declaring and Defining Functions

Using functions in your program requires that you first declare the function and that you then define the function. The declaration tells the compiler the name, return type, and parameters of the function. The definition tells the compiler how the function works. No function can be called from any other function that hasn't first been declared. The declaration of a function is called its prototype.

Declaring the Function

There are three ways to declare a function:

☐ Write your prototype into a file, and then use the #include directive to include it in your program.

☐ Write the prototype into the file in which your function is used.

☐ Define the function before it is called by any other function. When you do this, the definition acts as its own declaration.

Although you can define the function before using it, and thus avoid the necessity of creating a function prototype, this is not good programming practice for three reasons.

First, it is a bad idea to require that functions appear in a file in a particular order. Doing so makes it hard to maintain the program as requirements change.

Second, it is possible that function A() needs to be able to call function B(), but function B() also needs to be able to call function A() under some circumstances. It is not possible to define function A() before you define function B() and also to define function B() before you define function A(), so at least one of them must be declared in any case.

Third, function prototypes are a good and powerful debugging technique. If your prototype declares that your function takes a particular set of parameters, or that it returns a particular type of value, and then your function does not match the prototype, the compiler can flag your error instead of waiting for it to show itself when you run the program.

5

Function Prototypes

Many of the built-in functions you use will have their function prototypes already written in the files you include in your program by using #include. For functions you write yourself, you must include the prototype.

The function prototype is a statement, which means it ends with a semicolon. It consists of the function's return type, name, and parameter list.

The parameter list is a list of all the parameters and their types, separated by commas. Figure 5.2 illustrates the parts of the function prototype.

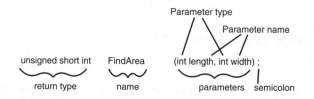

Figure 5.2. *Parts of a function prototype.*

The function prototype and the function definition must agree exactly about the return type, the name, and the parameter list. If they do not agree, you will get a compile-time error. Note, however, that the function prototype does not need to contain the names of the parameters, just their types. A prototype that looks like this is perfectly legal:

```
long Area(int, int);
```

This prototype declares a function named Area() that returns a long and that has two parameters, both integers. Although this is legal, it is not a good idea. Adding parameter names makes your prototype clearer. The same function with named parameters might be:

```
long Area(int length, int width);
```

It is now obvious what this function does and what the parameters are.

Note that all functions have a return type. If none is explicitly stated, the return type defaults to int. Your programs will be easier to understand, however, if you explicitly declare the return type of every function, including main(). Listing 5.1 demonstrates a program that includes a function prototype for the Area() function.

Listing 5.1. Shows a function declaration and the definition and use of that function.

```
1:    // Listing 5.1 - demonstrates the use of function prototypes
2:
3:    typedef unsigned int USHORT;
4:    #include <iostream.h>
5:    USHORT FindArea(USHORT length, USHORT width); //function prototype
6:
7:    void main()
8:    {
9:      USHORT lengthOfYard;
10:     USHORT widthOfYard;
11:     USHORT areaOfYard;
12:
13:     cout << "\nHow wide is your yard? ";
14:     cin >> widthOfYard;
15:     cout << "\nHow long is your yard? ";
16:     cin >> lengthOfYard;
17:
18:     areaOfYard= FindArea(lengthOfYard,widthOfYard);
19:
20:     cout << "\nYour yard is ";
21:     cout << areaOfYard;
22:     cout << " square feet\n\n";
23:   }
24:
25:   USHORT FindArea(USHORT l, USHORT w)
26:   {
27:       return l * w;
28:   }
```

5

 Output

```
How wide is your yard? 100
How long is your yard? 200
Your yard is 20000 square feet
```

 Analysis

The prototype for the FindArea() function is on line 7. Compare the prototype with the definition of the function on line 25. Note that the name, the return type, and the parameter types are the same. If they were different, a compiler error would have been generated. In fact, the only required difference is that the function prototype ends with a semicolon and has no body.

Also note that the parameter names in the prototype are length and width, but the parameter names in the definition are l and w. As discussed, the names in the prototype are not used; they are there as information to the programmer. When they are included, they should match the implementation when possible. This is a matter of good programming style and reduces confusion, but is not required, as you see here.

The arguments are passed in to the function in the order in which they are declared and defined, but there is no matching of the names. Had you passed in widthOfYard, followed

89

by `lengthOfYard`, the `FindArea()` function would have used the value in `widthOfYard` for `length` and `lengthOfYard` for `width`. The body of the function is always enclosed in braces, even when it consists of only one statement, as in this case.

Defining the Function

The definition of a function consists of the function header and its body. The header is exactly like the function prototype, except that the parameters must be named, and there is no terminating semicolon.

The body of the function is a set of statements enclosed in braces. Figure 5.3 shows the header and body of a function.

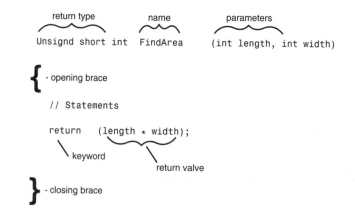

Figure 5.3. *The header and body of a function.*

Syntax

Functions

Function Prototype

```
return_type function_name ( [type [parameterName]]...);
```

Function Definition

```
return_type function_name ( [type parameterName]...)
{
    statements;
}
```

A *function prototype* tells the compiler the return type, name, and parameter list. Functions are not required to have parameters, and if they do, the prototype is not required to list their names, only their types. A prototype always ends with a semi-colon (;).

A *function definition* must agree in return type and parameter list with its prototype. It must provide names for all the parameters, and the body of the function definition must be surrounded by braces. All statements within the body of the function must be terminated with semicolons, but the function itself is not ended with a semicolon; it ends with a closing brace.

If the function returns a value, it should end with a return statement, although return statements can legally appear anywhere in the body of the function.

Every function has a return type. If one is not explicitly designated, the return type will be int. Be sure to give every function an explicit return type. If a function does not return a value, its return type will be void.

Function Prototype Examples

```
long FindArea(long length, long width); // returns long, has two parameters
void PrintMessage(int messageNumber);   // returns void, has one parameter
int GetChoice();                        // returns int, has no parameters
BadFunction();                          // returns int, has no parameters
```

Function Definition Examples

```
long Area(long l, long w)
{
    return l * w;
}

void PrintMessage(int whichMsg)
{
    if (whichMsg == 0)
        cout << "Hello.\n";
    if (whichMsg == 1)
        cout << "Goodbye.\n";
    if (whichMsg > 1)
        cout << "I'm confused.\n";
}
```

Execution of Functions

When you call a function, execution begins with the first statement after the opening brace ({). Branching can be accomplished by using the if statement (and related statements that will be discussed on Day 7). Functions can also call other functions and can even call themselves (see the section "Recursion," later in this chapter).

Local Variables

Not only can you pass in variables to the function, but you also can declare variables within the body of the function. This is done using local variables, so named because they exist only locally within the function itself. When the function returns, the local variables are no longer available.

Local variables are defined like any other variables. The parameters passed in to the function are also considered local variables and can be used exactly as if they had been defined within the body of the function. Listing 5.2 is an example of using parameters and locally defined variables within a function.

Listing 5.2. Demonstrates use of local variables and parameters.

```
1:      #include <iostream.h>
2:
3:      float Convert(float);
4:      void main()
5:      {
6:          float TempFer;
7:          float TempCel;
8:
9:          cout << "Please enter the temperature in Fahrenheit: ";
10:         cin >> TempFer;
11:         TempCel = Convert(TempFer);
12:         cout << "\nHere's the temperature in Celsius: ";
13:         cout << TempCel << endl;
14:     }
15:
16:     float Convert(float TempFer)
17:     {
18:         float TempCel;
19:         TempCel = ((TempFer - 32) * 5) / 9;
20:         return TempCel;
24:     {
```

```
Please enter the temperature in Fahrenheit: 212
Here's the temperature in Celsius: 100

Please enter the temperature in Fahrenheit: 32
Here's the temperature in Celsius: 0

Please enter the temperature in Fahrenheit: 85
Here's the temperature in Celsius: 29.4444
```

On lines 6 and 7, two float variables are declared, one to hold the temperature in Fahrenheit and one to hold the temperature in degrees Celsius. The user is prompted to enter a Fahrenheit temperature on line 9, and that value is passed to the function Convert().

Execution jumps to the first line of the function `Convert()` on line 18, where a local variable, also named `TempCel`, is declared. Note that this local variable is not the same as the variable `TempCel` on line 7. This variable exists only within the function `Convert()`. The value passed as a parameter, `TempFer`, is also just a local copy of the variable passed in by `main()`.

This function could have named the parameter `FerTemp` and the local variable `CelTemp` and the program would work equally well. You can reenter these names and recompile the program to see this work.

The local function variable `Tempcel` is assigned the value that results form subtracting 32 from the parameter `TempFer`, multiplying by 5, and then dividing by 9. This value is then returned as the return value of the function, and on line 11 it is assigned to the variable `TempCel` in the `main()` function. It is printed on line 12.

The program is run three times. The first time, the value 212 is passed in to ensure that the boiling point of water in degrees Fahrenheit (212) generates the correct answer in degrees Celsius (100). The second test is the freezing point of water. The third test is a random number chosen to generate a fractional result.

As an exercise, try reentering the program with other variable names as illustrated here:

```
1:      #include <iostream.h>
2:
3:      float Convert(float):
4:      void main()
5:      {
6:          float TempFer;
7:          float TempCel;
8:
9:          cout << "Please enter the temperature in Fahrenheit: ";
10:         cin >> TempFer;
11:         TempCel = Convert(TempFer);
12:         cout << "\nHere's the temperature in Celsius: ";
13:         cout << TempCel << endl;
14:     }
15:
16:     float Convert(float Fer)
17:     {
18:         float Cel;
19:         Cel = ((Fer - 32 * 5) / 9;
20:         return Cel;
21:     }
```

You should get the same results.

NEW TERM A variable has scope, which determines how long it is available to your program and where it can be accessed. Variables declared within a block are scoped to that block; they can be accessed only within that block and "go to of existence" when that block ends. Global variables have global scope and are available anywhere within your program.

Normally scope is obvious, but there are some tricky exceptions. Currently, variables declared within the header of a for loop (for int i = 0; i<SomeValue; i++) are scoped to the block in which the for loop increated, but there is talk of changing this in the official C++ standard.

None of this matters very much if you are careful not to reuse your variable names within any given function.

Global Variables

Variables defined outside of any function have global scope and thus are available from any function in the program, including main().

Local variables with the same name as global variables do not change the global variables. A local variable with the same name as a global variable *hides* the global variable, however. If a function has a variable with the same name as a global variable, the name refers to the local variable—not the global—when used within the function. Listing 5.3 illustrates these points.

Listing 5.3. Demonstrating global and local variables.

```
1:   #include <iostream.h>
2:   void myFunction();           // prototype
3:
4:   int x = 5, y = 7;            // global variables
5:   void main()
6:   {
7:
8:       cout << "x from main: " << x << "\n";
9:       cout << "y from main: " << y << "\n\n";
10:      myFunction();
11:      cout << "Back from myFunction!\n\n
12:      cout << "x from main: " << x << "\n";
13:      cout << "y from main: " << y << "\n";
14:  }
15:
16:  void myFunction()
17:  {
18:      int y = 10;
19:
20:      cout << "x from myFunction: " << x << "\n";
21:      cout << "y from myFunction: " << y << "\n\n
22:  }
```

Output

```
x from main: 5
y from main: 7

x from myFunction: 5
y from myFunction: 10

Back from myFunction!

x from main: 5
y from main: 7
```

Analysis   This simple program illustrates a few key, and potentially confusing, points about local and global variables. On line 1 two global variables, x and y, are declared. The global variable x is initialized with the value 5, and the global variable y is initialized with the value 7.

On lines 8 and 9 in the function main(), these values are printed to the screen. Note that the function main() defines neither variable; because they are global, they are already available to main().

When myFunction() is called on line 10, program execution passes to line 18, and a local variable, y, is defined and initialized with the value 10. On line 20 myFunction() prints the value of the variable x, and the global variable x is used, just as it was in main(). On line 21, however, when the variable name y is used, the *local* variable y is used, hiding the global variable with the same name.

The function call ends, and control returns to main(), which again prints the values in the global variables. Note that the global variable y was totally unaffected by the value assigned to myFunction()'s local y variable.

5

Global Variables—A Word of Caution

In C++, global variables are legal, but they are almost never used. C++ grew out of C, and in C global variables are a dangerous but necessary tool. They are necessary because there are times when the programmer needs to make data available to many functions and does not want to pass that data as a parameter from function to function.

Globals are dangerous because they are shared data, and one function can change a global variable in a way that is invisible to another function. This can and does create bugs that are very difficult to find.

On Day 14 you'll see a powerful alternative to global variables that C++ offers but that is unavailable in C.

More on Local Variables

Variables declared within the function are said to have "local scope." That means, as discussed, that they are visible and usable only within the function in which they are defined. In fact, in C++ you can define variables anywhere within the function, not just at its top. The scope of the variable is the *block* in which it is defined. Thus, if you define a variable inside a set of braces within the function, that variable is available only within that block. Listing 5.4 illustrates this idea.

Listing 5.4. Demonstrates variables scoped within a block.

```
1:    // Listing 5.4 - demonstrates variables
2:    // scoped within a block
3:
4:    #include <iostream.h>
5:
6:    void myFunc();
7:
8:    void main()
9:    {
10:       int x = 5;
11:       cout << "\nIn main x is: " << x;
12:
13:       myFunc();
14:
15:       cout << "\nBack in main, x is: " << x;
16:    }
17:
18:    void myFunc()
19:    {
20:
21:       int x = 8;
22:       cout << "\nIn myFunc, local x: " << x;
23:
24:       {
25:          cout << "\nIn block in myFunc, x is: " << x;
26:
27:          int x = 9;
28:
29:          cout << "\nVery local x: " << x;
30:       }
31:
32:       cout << "\nOut of block, in myFunc, x: " << x;
33:    }
```

Output

```
In main x is 5
In myFunc, local x: 8
In block in myFunc, x is: 8
Very local x: 9
```

```
Out of block, in myFunc, x: 8
Back in main, x is 5
```

 Analysis This program begins with the initialization of a local variable, x, on line 10, in main(). The printout on line 11 verifies that x was initialized with the value 5.

MyFunc() is called, and a local variable, also named x, is initialized with the value 8 on line 21. Its value is printed on line 22.

A block is started on line 24, and the variable x from the function is printed again on line 25. A new variable also named x, but local to the block, is created on line 27 and initialized with the value 9.

The value of the newest variable x is printed on line 29. The local block ends on line 30, and the variable created on line 27 goes "out of scope" and is no longer visible.

When x is printed on line 32, it is the x that was declared on line 21. This x was unaffected by the x that was defined on line 27; its value is still 8.

On line 33 MyFunc() goes out of scope, and its local variable x becomes unavailable. Execution returns to line 15, and the value of the local variable x, which was created on line 10, is printed. It was unaffected by either of the variables defined in MyFunc().

Needless to say, this program would be far less confusing if these three variables were given unique names!

Function Statements

There is virtually no limit to the number or types of statements that can be in a function body. Although you can't define another function from within a function, you can call a function, and of course main() does just that in nearly every C++ program. Functions can even call themselves, which is discussed soon, in the section on recursion.

Although there is no limit to the size of a function in C++, well-designed functions tend to be small. Many programmers advise keeping your functions short enough to fit on a single screen so that you can see the entire function at one time. This is a rule of thumb, often broken by very good programmers, but a smaller function is easier to understand and maintain.

Each function should carry out a single, easily understood task. If your functions start getting large, look for places where you can divide them into component tasks.

5

Function Arguments

Function arguments do not have to all be of the same type. It is perfectly reasonable to write a function that takes an integer, two longs, and a character as its arguments.

Any valid C++ expression can be a function argument, including constants, mathematical and logical expressions, and other functions that return a value.

Using Functions as Parameters to Functions

Although it is legal to use a function that returns a value as a parameter to another function, it can make for code that is hard to read and hard to debug.

As an example, say you have the functions `double()`, `triple()`, `square()`, and `cube()`, each of which returns a value. You could write

```
Answer = (double(triple(square(cube(myValue)))));
```

This statement takes a variable, `myValue`, and passes it as an argument to the function `cube()`, whose return value is passed as an argument to the function `square()`, whose return value is in turn passed to `triple()`, and that return value is passed to `double()`. The return value of this doubled, tripled, squared, and cubed number is now passed to `Answer`.

It is difficult to be certain what this code does (was the value tripled before or after it was squared?), and if the answer is wrong it will be hard to figure out which function failed.

An alternative is to assign each step to its own intermediate variable:

```
unsigned long myValue = 2;
unsigned long cubed   =   cube(myValue);      // cubed = 8
unsigned long squared = square(cubed);        // squared = 64
unsigned long tripled = triple(squared);      // tripled = 196
unsigned long Answer =  double(tripled);      // Answer = 392
```

Now each intermediate result can be examined, and the order of execution is explicit.

Parameters Are Local Variables

The arguments passed in to the function are local to the function. Changes made to the arguments do not affect the values in the calling function. This is known as *passing by value,* which means a local copy of each argument is made in the function. These local copies are treated just like any other local variables. Listing 5.5 illustrates this point.

Listing 5.5. Demonstrates passing by value.

```
1:    // Listing 5.5 - demonstrates passing by value
2:
3:    #include <iostream.h>
4:
5:    void swap(int x, int y);
6:
7:    void main()
8:    {
9:      int x = 5, y = 10;
10:
11:      cout << "Main. Before swap, x: " << x << " y: " << y << "\n";
12:      swap(x,y);
13:      cout << "Main. After swap, x: " << x << " y: " << y << "\n";
14:    }
15:
16:    void swap (int x, int y)
17:    {
18:      int temp;
19:
20:      cout << "Swap. Before swap, x: " << x << " y: " << y << "\n";
21:
22:      temp = x;
23:      x = y;
24:      y = temp;
25:
26:      cout << "Swap. After swap, x: " << x << " y: " << y << "\n";
27:
28:    }
```

Output

```
Main. Before swap. x: 5 y: 10
Swap. Before swap. x: 5 y: 10
Swap. After swap. x: 10 y: 5
Main. After swap. x: 5 y: 10
```

Analysis This program initializes two variables in main() and then passes them to the swap() function, which appears to swap them. When they are examined again in main(), however, they are unchanged!

The variables are initialized on line 9, and their values are displayed on line 11. swap() is called, and the variables are passed in.

Execution of the program switches to the swap() function, where on line 20 the values are printed again. They are in the same order as they were in main(), as expected. On lines 22 to 24 the values are swapped, and this action is confirmed by the printout on line 26. Indeed, while in the swap() function, the values are swapped.

Execution then returns to line 13, back in main(), where the values are no longer swapped.

As you've figured out, the values passed in to the swap() function are passed by value, meaning that copies of the values are made that are local to swap(). These local variables are swapped in lines 22 to 24, but the variables back in main() are unaffected.

On Days 8 and 10 you'll see alternatives to passing by value that will allow the values in main() to be changed.

Return Values

Functions return a value or return void. Void is a signal to the compiler that no value will be returned.

To return a value from a function, write the keyword return followed by the value you want to return. The value might itself be an expression that returns a value. For example:

```
return 5;
return (x > 5);
return (MyFunction());
```

These are all legal return statements, assuming that the function MyFunction() itself returns a value. The value in the second statement, return (x > 5), will be zero if x is not greater than 5, or it will be 1. What is returned is the value of the expression, 0 (false) or 1 (true), not the value of x.

When the return keyword is encountered, the expression following return is returned as the value of the function. Program execution returns immediately to the calling function, and any statements following the return are not executed.

It is legal to have more than one return statement in a single function. Listing 5.6 illustrates this idea.

Listing 5.6. Demonstrates multiple return statements.

```
1:     // Listing 5.6 - demonstrates multiple return
2:     // statements
3:
4:     #include <iostream.h>
5:
6:     int Doubler(int AmountToDouble);
7:
8:     void main()
9:     {
10:
11:         int result = 0;
12:         int input;
13:
```

```
14:        cout << "Enter a number between 0 and 10,000 to double: ";
15:        cin >> input;
16:
17:        cout << "\nBefore doubler is called... ";
18:        cout << "\ninput: " << input << " doubled: " << result << "\n";
19:
20:        result = Doubler(input);
21:
22:        cout << "\nBack from Doubler...\n";
23:        cout << "\ninput: " << input << "   doubled: " << result << "\n";
24:
25:
26:    }
27:
28:    int Doubler(int original)
29:    {
30:        if (original <= 10000)
31:            return original * 2;
32:        else
33:            return -1;
34:        cout << "You can't get here!\n";
35:    }
```

```
Enter a number between 0 and 10,000 to double: 9000
Before doubler is called...
input: 9000 doubled: 0
Back from doubler...
input: 9000 doubled: 18000

Enter a number between 0 and 10,000 to double: 11000
Before doubler is called...
input: 11000  doubled: 0
Back from doubler...
input: 11000  doubled: -1
```

A number is requested on lines 14 and 15, and printed on line 18, along with the local variable result. The function Doubler() is called on line 20, and the input value is passed as a parameter. The result will be assigned to the local variable result, and the values will be reprinted on lines 22 and 23.

On line 30, in the function Doubler(), the parameter is tested to see whether it is greater than 10,000. If it is not, the function returns twice the original number. If it is greater than 10,000, the function returns -1 as an error value.

The statement on line 34 is never reached, because whether or not the value is greater than 10,000, the function returns before it gets to line 34, on either line 31 or line 33. A good compiler will warn that this statement cannot be executed, and a good programmer will take it out!

Default Parameters

For every parameter you declare in a function prototype and definition, the calling function must pass in a value. The value passed in must be of the declared type. Thus, if you have a function declared as

```
long myFunction(int);
```

the function must in fact take an integer variable. If the function definition differs or if you fail to pass in an integer, you will get a compiler error.

The one exception to this rule is if the function prototype declares a default value for the parameter. A default value is a value to use if none is supplied. The preceding declaration could be rewritten as

```
long myFunction (int x = 50);
```

This prototype says "myFunction() returns a long and takes an integer parameter. If an argument is not supplied, use the default value of 50." Because parameter names are not required in function prototypes, this declaration could have been written as

```
long myFunction (int = 50);
```

The function definition is not changed by declaring a default parameter. The function definition header for this function would be

```
long myFunction (int x)
```

If the calling function did not include a parameter, the compiler would fill x with the default value of 50. The name of the default parameter in the prototype need not be the same as the name in the function header; the default value is assigned by position, not name.

Any or all of the function's parameters can be assigned default values. The one restriction is this: If any of the parameters does not have a default value, no previous parameter may have a default value.

If the function prototype looks like

```
long myFunction (int Param1, int Param2, int Param3);
```

you can assign a default value to Param2 only if you have assigned a default value to Param3. You can assign a default value to Param1 only if you've assigned default values to *both* Param2 and Param3. Listing 5.7 demonstrates the use of default values.

Listing 5.7. Demonstrates default parameter values.

```
1:    // Listing 5.7 - demonstrates use
2:    // of default parameter values
3:
4:    #include <iostream.h>
5:
6:    int AreaCube(int length, int width = 25, int height = 1);
7:
8:    void main()
9:    {
10:       int length = 100;
11:       int width = 50;
12:       int height = 2;
13:       int area;
14:
15:       area = AreaCube(length, width, height);
16:       cout << "First area equals: " << area << "\n";
17:
18:       area = AreaCube(length, width);
19:       cout << "Second time area equals: " << area << "\n";
20:
21:       area = AreaCube(length);
22:       cout << "Third time area equals: " << area << "\n";
23:    }
24:
25:    AreaCube(int length, int width, int height)
26:    {
27:
28:       return (length * width * height);
29:     }
```

5

```
First area equals: 10000
Second time area equals: 5000
Third time area equals: 2500
```

Analysis On line 6 the AreaCube() prototype specifies that the AreaCube() function takes three integer parameters. The last two have default values.

This function computes the area of the cube whose dimensions are passed in. If no width is passed in, a width of 25 is used and a height of 1 is used. If the width but not the height is passed in, a height of 1 is used. It is not possible to pass in the height without passing in a width.

On lines 10–12 the dimensions length, height, and width are initialized, and they are passed to the AreaCube() function on line 15. The values are computed, and the result is printed on line 16.

Execution returns to line 18, where AreaCube() is called again, but with no value for height. The default value is used, and again the dimensions are computed and printed.

Execution returns to line 21, and this time neither the `width` nor the `height` is passed in. Execution branches for a third time to line 27. The default values are used. The area is computed and then printed.

DO	DON'T

DO remember that function parameters act as local variables within the function.

DON'T try to create a default value for a first parameter if there is no default value for the second.

DON'T forget that arguments passed by value can not affect the variables in the calling function.

DON'T forget that changes to a global variable in one function change that variable for all functions.

Overloading Functions

C++ enables you to create more than one function with the same name. This is called function overloading. The functions must differ in their parameter list, with a different type of parameter, a different number of parameters, or both. Here's an example:

```
int myFunction (int, int);
int myFunction (long, long);
int myFunction (long);
```

`myFunction()` is overloaded with three different parameter lists. The first and second versions differ in the types of the parameters, and the third differs in the number of parameters.

The return types can be the same or different on overloaded functions. You should note that two functions with the same name and parameter list but different return types generate a compiler error.

Function overloading is also called function polymorphism. *Poly* means many, and *morph* means form: a polymorphic function is many-formed.

NEW TERM Function polymorphism refers to the ability to "overload" a function with more than one meaning. By changing the number or type of the parameters, you can give two or more functions the same function name, and the right one will be called by matching the parameters used. This allows you to create a function that can average integers, doubles, and other values without having to create individual names for each function, such as `AverageInst()`, `AverageDoubles()`, etc.

Suppose you write a function that doubles whatever input you give it. You would like to be able to pass in an `int`, a `long`, a `float`, or a `double`. Without function overloading, you would have to create four function names:

```
int DoubleInt(int);
long DoubleLong(long);
float DoubleFloat(float);
double DoubleDouble(double);
```

With function overloading, you make this declaration:

```
int Double(int);
long Double(long);
float Double(float);
double Double(double);
```

This is easier to read and easier to use. You don't have to worry about which one to call; you just pass in a variable, and the right function is called automatically. Listing 5.8 illustrates the use of function overloading.

Listing 5.8. Demonstrates function polymorphism.

```
1:     // Listing 5.8 - demonstrates
2:     // function polymorphism
3:
4:     #include <iostream.h>
5:
6:     int Double(int);
7:     long Double(long);
8:     float Double(float);
9:     double Double(double);
10:
11:    void main()
12:    {
13:        int      myInt = 6500;
14:        long     myLong = 65000;
15:        float    myFloat = 6.5;
16:        double   myDouble = 6.5e20;
17:
18:        int      doubledInt;
19:        long     doubledLong;
20:        float    doubledFloat;
21:        double   doubledDouble;
22:
23:        cout << "myInt: " << myInt << "\n";
24:        cout << "myLong: " << myLong << "\n";
25:        cout << "myFloat: " << myFloat << "\n";
```

continues

Listing 5.8. continued

```
26:        cout << "myDouble: " << myDouble << "\n";
27:
28:        doubledInt = Double(myInt);
29:        doubledLong = Double(myLong);
30:        doubledFloat = Double(myFloat);
31:        doubledDouble = Double(myDouble);
32:
33:        cout << "doubledInt: " << doubledInt << "\n";
34:        cout << "doubledLong: " << doubledLong << "\n";
35:        cout << "doubledFloat: " << doubledFloat << "\n";
36:        cout << "doubledDouble: " << doubledDouble << "\n";
37:
38:    }
39:
40:  int Double(int original)
41:  {
42:    cout << "In Double(int)\n";
43:    return 2 * original;
44:  }
45:
46:  long Double(long original)
47:  {
48:    cout << "In Double(long)\n";
49:    return 2 * original;
50:  }
51:
52:  float Double(float original)
53:  {
54:    cout << "In Double(float)\n";
55:    return 2 * original;
56:  }
57:
58:  double Double(double original)
59:  {
60:    cout << "In Double(double)\n";
61:    return 2 * original;
62:  }
```

```
myInt: 6500
myLong: 65000
myFloat: 6.5
myDouble: 6.5e20
In Double(int)
In Double(long)
In Double(float)
In Double(double)
DoubledInt: 13000
DoubledLong:130000
DoubledFloat:13
DoubledDouble: 13e21
```

Analysis The Double() function is overloaded with int, long, float, and double. The prototypes are on lines 6–9, and the definitions are on lines 40–62.

In the body of the main program, eight local variables are declared. On lines 13–16 four of the values are initialized, and on lines 28–31 the other four are assigned the results of passing the first four to the Double() function. Note that when Double() is called, the calling function does not distinguish which one to call; it just passes in an argument, and the correct one is invoked.

The compiler examines the arguments and chooses which of the four Double() functions to call. The output reveals that each of the four was called in turn, as you would expect.

Special Topics

Because functions are so central to programming, a few special topics arise which might be of interest when you confront special problems. Used wisely, inline functions can help you squeak out that last bit of performance. Function recursion is one of those wonderful, esoteric bits of programming which, every once in a while, can cut through a thorny problem otherwise not easily solved.

Inline Functions

When you define a function, normally the compiler creates just one set of instructions in memory. When you call the function, execution of the program jumps to those instructions, and when the function returns, execution jumps back to the next line in the calling function. If you call the function 10 times, your program jumps to the same set of instructions each time. This means there is only one copy of the function, not 10.

There is some performance overhead in jumping in and out of functions. It turns out that some functions are very small, just a line or two of code, and some efficiency can be gained if the program can avoid making these jumps just to execute one or two instructions. When programmers speak of efficiency, they usually mean speed: the program runs faster if the function call can be avoided.

If a function is declared with the keyword inline, the compiler does not create a real function: it copies the code from the inline function directly into the calling function. No jump is made; it is just as if you had written the statements of the function right into the calling function.

Note that inline functions can bring a heavy cost. If the function is called 10 times, the inline code is copied into the calling functions each of those 10 times. The tiny

5

improvement in speed you might achieve is more than swamped by the increase in size of the executable program. Even the speed increase might be illusory. First, today's optimizing compilers do a terrific job on their own, and there is almost never a big gain from declaring a function `inline`. More important, the increased size brings its own performance cost.

What's the rule of thumb? If you have a small function, one or two statements, it is a candidate for `inline`. When in doubt, though, leave it out. Listing 5.9 demonstrates an inline function.

Listing 5.9. Demonstrates an inline function.

```
1:    // Listing 5.9 - demonstrates inline functions
2:
3:    #include <iostream.h>
4:
5:    inline int Double(int);
6:
7:    void main()
8:    {
9:      int target;
10:
11:     cout << "Enter a number to work with: ";
12:     cin >> target;
13:     cout << "\n";
14:
15:     target = Double(target);
16:     cout << "Target: " << target << endl;
17:
18:     target = Double(target);
19:     cout << "Target: " << target << endl;
20:
21:
22:     target = Double(target);
23:     cout << "Target: " << target << endl;
24:   }
25:
26:   int Double(int target)
27:   {
28:     return 2*target;
29:   }
```

```
Enter a number to work with: 20
Target: 40
Target: 80
Target: 160
```

On line 5 `Double()` is declared to be an inline function taking an `int` parameter and returning an `int`. The declaration is just like any other prototype except that the keyword `inline` is prepended just before the return value.

This compiles into code that is the same as if you had written the following:

```
target = 2 * target;
```

everywhere you entered

```
target = Double(target);
```

By the time your program executes, the instructions are already in place, compiled into the .OBJ file. This saves a jump in the execution of the code, at the cost of a larger program.

> **Note:** Inline is a *hint* to the compiler that you would like the function to be inlined. The compiler is free to ignore the hint and make a real function call.

Recursion

A function can call itself. This is called recursion, and recursion can be direct or indirect. It is direct when a function calls itself; it is indirect recursion when a function calls another function that then calls the first function.

Some problems are most easily solved by recursion, usually those in which you act on data and then act in the same way on the result. Both types of recursion, direct and indirect, come in two varieties: those that eventually end and produce an answer, and those that never end and produce a runtime failure. Programmers think that the latter is quite funny (when it happens to someone else).

It is important to note that when a function calls itself, a new copy of that function is run. The local variables in the second version are independent of the local variables in the first, and they cannot affect one another directly, any more than the local variables in main() can affect the local variables in any function it calls, as was illustrated in Listing 5.4.

To illustrate solving a problem using recursion, consider the Fibonacci series:

```
1,1,2,3,5,8,13,21,34...
```

Each number, after the second, is the sum of the two numbers before it. A Fibonacci problem might be to determine what the 12th number in the series is.

One way to solve this problem is to examine the series carefully. The first two numbers are 1. Each subsequent number is the sum of the previous two numbers. Thus, the seventh number is the sum of the sixth and fifth numbers. More generally, the nth number is the sum of $n - 2$ and $n - 1$, as long as $n > 2$.

5

Recursive functions need a stop condition. Something must happen to cause the program to stop recursing, or it will never end. In the Fibonacci series $n < 3$ is a stop condition.

The algorithm to use is this:

1. Ask the user for a position in the series.

2. Call the `fib()` function with that position, passing in the value the user entered.

3. The `fib()` function examines the argument (n). If `n < 3` it returns 1; otherwise, `fib()` calls itself (recursively) passing in `n-2`, calls itself again passing in `n-1`, and returns the sum.

If you call `fib(1)`, it returns 1. If you call `fib(2)`, it returns 1. If you call `fib(3)`, it returns the sum of calling `fib(2)` and `fib(1)`. Because `fib(2)` returns 1 and `fib(1)` returns 1, `fib(3)` will return 2.

If you call `fib(4)`, it returns the sum of calling `fib(3)` and `fib(2)`. We've established that `fib(3)` returns 2 (by calling `fib(2)` and `fib(1)`) and that `fib(2)` returns 1, so `fib(4)` will sum these numbers and return 3, which is the fourth number in the series.

Taking this one more step, if you call `fib(5)`, it will return the sum of `fib(4)` and `fib(3)`. We've established that `fib(4)` returns 3 and `fib(3)` returns 2, so the sum returned will be 5.

This method is not the most efficient way to solve this problem (in `fib(20)` the `fib()` function is called 13,529 times!), but it does work. Be careful: if you feed in too large a number, you'll run out of memory. Every time `fib()` is called, memory is set aside. When it returns, memory is freed. With recursion, memory continues to be set aside before it is freed, and this system can eat memory very quickly. Listing 5.10 implements the `fib()` function:

Warning: When you run Listing 5.10, use a small number (less than 15). Because this uses recursion, it can consume a lot of memory.

Listing 5.10. Demonstrates recursion using the Fibonacci series.

```
1:    // Listing 5.10 - demonstrates recursion
2:    // Fibonacci find.
3:    // Finds the nth Fibonacci number
4:    // Uses this algorithm: Fib(n) = fib(n-1) + fib(n-2)
```

```
5:     // Stop conditions: n = 2 || n = 1
6:
7:     #include <iostream.h>
8:
9:     int fib(int n);
10:
11:    void main()
12:    {
13:
14:      int n, answer;
15:      cout << "Enter number to find: ";
16:      cin >> n;
17:
18:      cout << "\n\n";
19:
20:      answer = fib(n);
21:
22:      cout << answer << " is the " << n << "th Fibonacci number\n";
23:
24:    }
25:
26:    int fib (int n)
27:    {
28:      cout << "Processing fib(" << n << ")... ";
29:
30:      if (n < 3 )
31:      {
32:         cout << "Return 1!\n";
33:         return (1);
34:      }
35:      else
36:      {
37:         cout << "Call fib(" << n-2 << ") and fib(" << n-1 << ").\n";
38:         return( fib(n-2) + fib(n-1));
39:      }
40:    }
```

```
Enter number to find: 5
Processing fib(5)... Call fib(3) and fib(4).     // returns 5
Processing fib(3)... Call fib(1) and fib(2).     // returns 2
Processing fib(1)... Return 1!
Processing fib(2)... Return 1!
Processing fib(4)... Call fib(2) and fib(3)      // returns 3
Processing fib(2)... Return 1!
Processing fib(3)... Call fib(1) and fib(2)
Processing fib(1)... Return 1!
Processing fib(2)... Return 1!
5 is the 5th Fibonacci number.
```

The program asks for a number to find on line 15 and assigns that number to target. It then calls fib() with the target. Execution branches to the fib() function, where, on line 28, it prints its argument.

111

The argument n is tested to see whether it equals 1 or 2 on line 30; if so, fib() returns. Otherwise, it returns the sums of the values returned by calling fib() on n-2 and n-1.

In the example, n is 5 so fib(5) is called from main(). Execution jumps to the fib() function, and n is tested for a value less than 3 on line 30. The test fails, so fib(5) returns the sum of the values returned by fib(3) and fib(4). That is, fib() is called on n-2 (5 - 2 = 3) and n-1 (5 - 1 = 4). fib(4) will return 3 and fib(3) will return 2, so the final answer will be 5.

Because fib(4) passes in an argument that is not less than 3, fib() will be called again, this time with 3 and 2. fib(3) will in turn call fib(2) and fib(1). Finally, the calls to fib(2) and fib(1) will both return 1, because these are the stop conditions.

The output traces these calls and the return values. Compile, link, and run this program, entering first 1, then 2, then 3, building up to 6, and watch the output carefully. Then, just for fun, try the number 20. If you don't run out of memory, it makes quite a show!

Recursion is not used often in C++ programming, but it can be a powerful and elegant tool for certain needs.

Note: Recursion is a very tricky part of advanced programming. It is presented here because it can be very useful to understand the fundamentals of how it works, but don't worry too much if you don't fully understand all the details.

Summary

This chapter introduced functions. A function is, in effect, a subprogram into which you can pass parameters and from which you can return a value. Every C++ program starts in the main() function, and main() in turn can call other functions.

A function is declared with a function prototype, which describes the return value, the function name, and its parameter types. A function can optionally be declared inline. A function prototype can also declare default variables for one or more of the parameters.

The function definition must match the function prototype in return type, name, and parameter list. Function names can be overloaded by changing the number or type of parameters; the compiler finds the right function based on the argument list.

Local function variables, and the arguments passed in to the function, are local to the *block* in which they are declared. Parameters passed by value are copies and cannot affect the value of variables in the calling function.

Q&A

Q Why not make all variables global?

A There was a time when this was exactly how programming was done. As programs became more complex, however, it became very difficult to find bugs in programs because data could be corrupted by any of the functions—global data can be changed anywhere in the program. Years of experience have convinced programmers that data should be kept as local as possible, and access to changing that data should be narrowly defined.

Q When should the keyword `inline` be used in a function prototype?

A If the function is very small, no more than a line or two, and won't be called from many places in your program, it is a candidate for inlining.

Q Why aren't changes to the value of function arguments reflected in the calling function?

A Arguments passed to a function are passed *by value*. That means that the argument in the function is actually a copy of the original value. This concept is explained in depth in the Extra Credit section that follows the Workshop.

Q If arguments are passed by value, what do I do if I need to reflect the changes back in the calling function?

A On Day 8 pointers will be discussed. Use of pointers will solve this problem, as well as provide a way around the limitation of returning only a single value from a function.

Q What happens if I have the following two functions?

```
int Area (int width, int length = 1);
int Area (int size);
```

Will these overload? There are a different number of parameters, but the first one has a default value.

A The declarations will compile, but if you invoke `Area` with one parameter you will receive a compile-time error: `ambiguity between Area(ibt, int) and Area(int)`.

Workshop

The Workshop provides quiz questions to help you solidify your understanding of the material covered, and exercises to provide you with experience in using what you've learned. Try to answer the quiz and exercise questions before checking the answers in Appendix D, and make sure that you understand the answers before continuing to the next chapter.

Quiz

1. What are the differences between the function prototype and the function definition?

2. Do the names of parameters have to agree in the prototype, definition, and call to the function?

3. If a function doesn't return a value, how do you declare the function?

4. If you don't declare a return value, what type of return value is assumed?

5. What is a local variable?

6. What is scope?

7. What is recursion?

8. When should you use global variables?

9. What is function overloading?

10. What is polymorphism?

Exercises

1. Write the prototype for a function named `Perimeter()`, which returns an `unsigned long int` and which takes two parameters, both `unsigned short ints`.

2. Write the definition of the function `Perimeter()` as described in question 1. The two parameters represent the length and width of a rectangle. Have the function return the perimeter (twice the length plus twice the width).

3. **BUG BUSTER:** What is wrong with the function in the following code?

```
#include <iostreams.h>
void myFunc(unsigned short int x);
void main()
{
    unsigned short int x, y;
    y = myFunc(int);
    cout << "x: " << x << " y: " << y << "\n";
}


void myFunc(unsigned short int x)
{
    return (4*x);
}
```

4. **BUG BUSTER:** What is wrong with the function in the following code?

```
#include <iostreams.h>
int myFunc(unsigned short int x);
void main()
{
    unsigned short int x, y;
    y = myFunc(int);
    cout << "x: " << x << " y: " << y << "\n";
}

int myFunc(unsigned short int x)
{
    return (4*x);
}
```

5. Write a function that takes two unsigned short integer arguments and returns the result of dividing the first by the second. Do not do the division if the second number is zero, but do return −1.

6. Write a program that asks the user for two numbers and calls the function you wrote in Exercise 5. Print the answer, or print an error message if you get −1.

7. Write a program that asks for a number and a power. Write a recursive function that takes the number to the power. Thus, if the number is 2 and the power is 4, the function will return 16.

5

Extra Credit
How Functions Work

When you call a function, the code branches to the called function, parameters are passed in, and the body of the function is executed. When the function completes, a value is returned (unless the function returns void), and control returns to the calling function.

How is this task accomplished? How does the code know where to branch to? Where are the variables kept when they are passed in? What happens to variables that are declared in the body of the function? How is the return value passed back out? How does the code know where to resume?

Most introductory books don't try to answer these questions, but without understanding this information, you'll find that programming remains a fuzzy mystery. The explanation requires a brief tangent into a discussion of computer memory.

Levels of Abstraction

One of the principal hurdles for new programmers is grappling with the many layers of intellectual abstraction. Computers, of course, are just electronic machines. They don't know about windows and menus, they don't know about programs or instructions, and they don't even know about 1s and 0s. All that is really going on is that voltage is being measured at various places on an integrated circuit. Even this is an abstraction: electricity itself is just an intellectual concept, representing the behavior of subatomic particles.

Few programmers bother much with any level of detail below the idea of values in RAM. After all, you don't need to understand particle physics to drive a car, make toast, or hit a baseball, and you don't need to understand the electronics of a computer to program one.

You do need to understand how memory is organized, however. Without a reasonably strong mental picture of where your variables are when they are created, and how values are passed among functions, it will all remain an unmanageable mystery.

Partitioning RAM

When you begin your program, your operating system (such as DOS or Microsoft Windows) sets up various areas of memory based on the requirements of your compiler. As a C++ programmer, you'll often be concerned with the global name space, the free store, the registers, the code space, and the stack.

Global variables are in global name space. We'll talk more about global name space and the free store in coming days, but for now we'll focus on the registers, code space, and stack.

Registers are a special area of memory built right into the Central Processing Unit (or CPU). They take care of internal housekeeping. A lot of what goes on in the registers is beyond the scope of this book, but what we are concerned about is the set of registers responsible for pointing, at any given moment, to the next line of code. We'll call these registers, together, the Instruction Pointer. It is the job of the Instruction Pointer to keep track of which line of code is to be executed next.

The code itself is in code space, which is that part of memory set aside to hold the binary form of the instructions you created in your program. Each line of source code is translated into a series of instructions, and each of these instructions is at a particular address in memory. The Instruction Pointer has the address of the next instruction to execute. Figure 5.4 illustrates this idea.

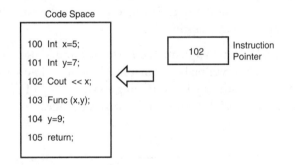

Figure 5.4. *The instruction pointer.*

The stack is a special area of memory allocated for your program to hold the data required by each of the functions in your program. It is called a stack because it is a last-in first-out queue, much like a stack of dishes at a cafeteria, as shown in Figure 5.5.

Last-in first-out means that whatever is added to the stack last will be the first thing taken off. Most queues are like a line at a theater: the first one on line is the first one off. A stack is more like a stack of coins: if you stack 10 pennies on a tabletop and then take some back, the last three you put on will be the first three you take off.

When data is "pushed" onto the stack, the stack grows; as data is "popped" off the stack, the stack shrinks. It isn't possible to pop a dish off of the stack without first popping off all the dishes placed on after that dish.

Figure 5.5. *A stack.*

A stack of dishes is the common analogy. It is fine as far as it goes, but it is wrong in a fundamental way. A more accurate mental picture is of a series of cubbyholes aligned top to bottom. The top of the stack is whatever cubby the *stack pointer* (which is another register) happens to be pointing to.

Each of the cubbies has a sequential address, and one of those addresses is kept in the stack pointer register. Everything below that magic address, known as the top of the stack, is considered to be on the stack. Everything above the top of the stack is considered to be off the stack and invalid. Figure 5.6 illustrates this idea.

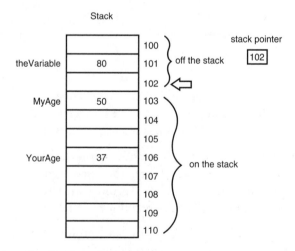

Figure 5.6. *The stack pointer.*

When data is put on the stack, it is placed into a cubby above the stack pointer, and then the stack pointer is moved to the new data. When data is popped off the stack, all that really happens is that the address of the stack pointer is changed by moving it down the stack. Figure 5.7 makes this rule clear.

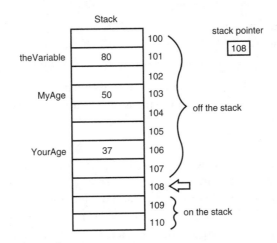

Figure 5.7. *Moving the stack pointer.*

The Stack and Functions

Here's what happens when a program, running on a PC under DOS, branches to a function:

1. The address in the instruction pointer is incremented to the next instruction past the function call. That address is then placed on the stack, and it will be the return address when the function returns.

2. Room is made on the stack for the return type you've declared. On a system with two-byte integers, if the return type is declared to be int, another two bytes are added to the stack, but no value is placed in these bytes.

3. The address of the called function, which is kept in a special area of memory set aside for that purpose, is loaded into the instruction pointer, so the next instruction executed will be in the called function.

4. The current top of the stack is now noted and is held in a special pointer called the Stack Frame. Everything added to the stack from now until the function returns will be considered "local" to the function.

5. All the arguments to the function are placed on the stack.

6. The instruction now in the Instruction Pointer is executed, thus executing the first instruction in the function.

7. Local variables are pushed onto the stack as they are defined.

When the function is ready to return, the return value is placed in the area of the stack reserved at step 2. The stack is then popped all the way up to the stack frame pointer, which effectively throws away all the local variables and the arguments to the function.

The return value is popped off the stack and assigned as the value of the function call itself, and the address stashed away in step 1 is retrieved and put into the Instruction Pointer. The program thus resumes immediately after the function call, with the value of the function retrieved.

Some of the details of this process change from compiler to compiler, or between computers, but the essential ideas are consistent across environments. In general, when you call a function, the return address and the parameters are put on the stack. During the life of the function, local variables are added to the stack. When the function returns, these are all removed by popping the stack.

In coming days we'll look at other places in memory that are used to hold data that must persist beyond the life of the function.

Quiz

1. What are the differences between the function prototype and the function definition?

2. Do the names of parameters have to agree in the prototype, definition, and call to the function?

3. If a function doesn't return a value, how do you declare the function?

4. If you don't declare a return value, what type of return value is assumed?

5. What is a local variable?

6. What is scope?

7. What is recursion?

8. When should you use global variables?

9. What is function overloading?

10. What is polymorphism?

Exercises

1. Write the prototype for a function named `Perimeter`, which returns an unsigned long int and which takes two parameters, both unsigned short ints.

2. Write the definition of the function `Perimeter` as described in question 1. The two parameters represent the length and width of a rectangle, have the function return the perimeter (twice the length plus twice the width).

3. **BUG BUSTER:** What is wrong with the function?

```
#include <iostreams.h>
void myFunc(unsigned short int x);
void main()
{
    unsigned short int x, y;
    y = myFunc(int);
    cout << "x: " << x << " y: " << y << "\n";
}


void myFunc(unsigned short int x)
{
    return (4*x);
}
```

4. **BUG BUSTER:** What is wrong with the function?

```
#include <iostreams.h>
int myFunc(unsigned short int x);
void main()
{
    unsigned short int x, y;
    y = myFunc(int);
    cout << "x: " << x << " y: " << y << "\n";
}


int myFunc(unsigned short int x)
{
    return (4*x);
}
```

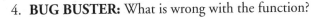

5

5. Write a function which takes two unsigned short int arguments, and returns the result of dividing the first by the second. Do not do the division if the second number is zero, but do return negative 1.

6. Write a program which asks the user for two numbers and calls the function you wrote in Exercise 5. Print the answer, or print an error message if you get −1.

7. Write a program which asks for a number and a power. Write a recursive function which takes the number to the power. Thus if the number is 2 and the power is 4, the function will return 16.

Basic Classes

Classes extend the built-in capabilities of C++ to assist you in representing and solving complex, real-world problems. Today you will learn:

☐ What classes and objects are.

☐ How to define a new class and create objects of that class.

☐ What member functions and member data are.

☐ What constructors are and how to use them.

Creating New Types

You've already learned about a number of variable types, including unsigned integers and characters. The type of a variable tells you quite a bit about it. For example, if you declare `Height` and `Width` to be unsigned integers, you know that each one can hold a number between 0 and 65,535, assuming an integer is two bytes. That is the meaning of saying they are unsigned integers; trying to hold anything else in these variables causes an error. You can't store your name in an unsigned short integer, and you shouldn't try.

Just by declaring these variables to be unsigned short integers, you know that it is possible to add `Height` to `Width` and to assign that number to another number.

The type of these variables tells you:

☐ Their size in memory.

☐ What information they can hold.

☐ What actions can be performed on them.

More generally, a type is a category. Familiar types include car, house, person, fruit, and shape. In C++ the programmer can create any type needed, and each of these new types can have all the functionality and power of the built-in types.

Why Create a New Type?

Programs are usually written to solve real-world problems, such as keeping track of employee records or simulating the workings of a heating system. Although it is possible to solve complex problems by using programs written with only integers and characters, it is far easier to grapple with large, complex problems if you can create representations of the objects that you are talking about. In other words, simulating the workings of a heating system is easier if you can create variables that represent rooms, heat sensors, thermostats and boilers. The closer these variables correspond to reality, the easier it is to write the program.

Classes and Members

You make a new type by declaring a class. A class is just a collection of variables—often of different types—combined with a set of related functions.

One way to think about a car is as a collection of wheels, doors, seats, windows and so forth. Another way is to think about what a car can do: It can move, speed up, slow down, stop, park, and so on. A class enables you encapsulate, or bundle, these various parts and various functions into one collection, which is called an object.

Encapsulating everything you know about a car into one class has a number of advantages for a programmer. Everything is in one place, which makes it easy to refer to, copy, and manipulate the data. Likewise, clients of your class—that is, the parts of the program that use your class—can use your object without worry about what is in it or how it works.

A class can consist of any combination of the variable types and also other class types. The variables in the class are referred to as the member variables or data members. A Car class might have member variables representing the seats, radio type, tires, and so forth.

NEW TERM *Member variables,* also known as *data members,* are the variables in your class. Member variables are part of your class, just like the wheels and engine are part of your car.

The functions in the class typically manipulate the member variables. They are referred to as member functions or methods of the class. Methods of the Car class might include Start() and Brake(). A Cat class might have data members that represent age and weight; its methods might include Sleep(), Meow(), and ChaseMice().

NEW TERM *Member functions,* also known as *methods,* are the functions in your class. Member functions are as much a part of your class as the member variables. They determine what the objects of your class can do.

Declaring a Class

To declare a class, use the class keyword followed by an opening brace, and then list the data members and methods of that class. End the declaration with a closing brace and a semicolon. Here's the declaration of a class called Cat:

```
class Cat
{
```

6

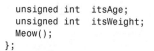
```
    unsigned int   itsAge;
    unsigned int   itsWeight;
    Meow();
};
```

Declaring this class doesn't allocate memory for a Cat. It just tells the compiler what a Cat is, what data it contains (itsAge and itsWeight), and what it can do (Meow()). It also tells the compiler how big a Cat is—that is, how much room the compiler must set aside for each Cat that you create. In this example, if an integer is two bytes, a Cat is only four bytes big: itsAge is two bytes, and itsWeight is another two. Meow() takes up no room, because no storage space is set aside for member functions (methods).

A Word on Naming Conventions

As programmer, you must name all your member variables, member functions, and classes. As you learned on Day 3, these should be easily understood and meaningful names. Cat, Rectangle, and Employee are good class names. Meow(), ChaseMice(), and StopEngine() are good function names, because they tell you what the functions do. Many programmers name the member variables with the prefix its, as in itsAge, itsWeight, and itsSpeed. This helps to distinguish member variables from nonmember variables.

C++ is case-sensitive, and all class names should follow the same pattern. That way you never have to check how to spell your class name—Was it Rectangle, rectangle or RECTANGLE? Some programmers like to prefix every class name with a particular letter—for example, cCat or cPerson—whereas others put the name in all uppercase or all lowercase. The convention that I use is to name all classes with initial-capitalization, as in Cat and Person.

Similarly, many programmers begin all functions with capital letters and all variables with lowercase. Words are usually separated with an underbar—as in Chase_Mice—or by capitalizing each word—for example, ChaseMice or DrawCircle.

The important idea is that you should pick one style and stay with it through each program. Over time, your style will evolve to include not only naming conventions, but also indentation, alignment of braces, and commenting style.

Note: It's common for development companies house standards for many style issues. This ensures that all developers can easily read one another's code.

Defining an Object

You define an object of your new type just as you define an integer variable:

```
unsigned int GrossWeight;        // define an unsigned integer
Cat Frisky;                      // define a Cat
```

This code defines a variable called Gross Weight whose type is an unsigned integer. It also defines Frisky, which is an object whose class (or type) is Cat.

Classes Versus Objects

You never pet the definition of a cat; you pet individual cats. You draw a distinction between the idea of a cat, and the particular cat that right now is shedding all over your living room. In the same way, C++ differentiates between the class Cat, which is the idea of a cat, and each individual Cat object. Thus, Frisky is an object of type Cat in the same way in which GrossWeight is a variable of type unsigned int.

NEW TERM   An *object* is an individual instance of a class.

Accessing Class Members

Once you define an actual Cat object—for example, Frisky—you use the dot operator (.) to access the members of that object. Therefore, to assign 50 to Frisky's Weight member variable, you would write

```
Frisky.Weight = 50;
```

In the same way, to call the Meow() function, you would write

```
Frisky.Meow();
```

When you use a class method, you *call* the method. In this example, you are calling Meow() on Frisky.

Assign to Objects, Not to Classes

In C++ you don't assign values to types, you assign values to variables. For example, you would never write

```
int = 5;                 // wrong
```

The compiler would flag this as an error, because you can't assign five to an integer. Rather, you must define an integer variable and assign 5 to that variable. For example,

```
int  x;              // define x to be an int
x = 5;               // set x's value to 5
```

This is a short hand way of saying, "Assign five to the variable x, which is of type int." In the same way, you wouldn't write

```
cat.age=5;            // wrong
??? I suggest that the "wrong" comment be changed to "cat not defined" or some other
message. The code is not wrong (if Cat has been defined)
```

The compiler would flag this as an error, because you can't assign five to the age part of a Cat. Rather, you must define a Cat object and assign 5 to that object. For example,

```
Cat Frisky;           // just like  int x;
Frisky.age = 5;       // just like  x = 5;
```

If You Don't Declare It, Your Class Won't Have It

Try this experiment: Walk up to a three-year-old and show her a cat. Then say, "This is Frisky. Frisky knows a trick. Frisky, Bark." The child will giggle and say, "No, silly, cats can't bark."

If you wrote

```
Cat  Frisky;          // make a cat named Frisky
Frisky.Bark()         // tell Frisky to bark
```

the compiler would say, No, silly, Cats can't bark. (Your compiler's wording may vary). The compiler knows that Frisky can't bark because the Cat class doesn't have a Bark() function. The compiler wouldn't even let Frisky meow if you didn't define a Meow() function.

DO	DON'T

DO use the key word class to declare a class.

DON'T confuse a declaration with a definition. A declaration says what a class is. A definition sets aside memory for an object.

DON'T confuse a class with an object.

DON'T assign values to a class. Assign values to the data members of an object.

DO use the dot operator (.) to access class members and functions.

Private Versus Public

Other keywords are used in the declaration of a class. Two of the most important are `public` and `private`.

All members of a class—data and methods—are private by default. Private members can be accessed only within methods of the class itself. Public members can be accessed through any object of the class. This distinction is both important and confusing. To make it a bit clearer, consider an example from earlier in this chapter:

```
class Cat
{
    unsigned int  itsAge;
    unsigned int  itsWeight;
    Meow();
};
```

In this declaration, `itsAge`, `itsWeight`, and `Meow()` are all private, because all members of a class are private by default. This means that unless you specify otherwise, they are private.

However, if you write

```
Cat  Boots;
Boots.Age=5;          // error! can't access private data!
```

the compiler flags this as an error. In effect, you've said to the compiler, "I'll access `itsAge`, `itsWeight`, and `Meow()` from only within member functions of the `Cat` class." Yet here you've accessed it from outside a `Cat` method. Just because `Boots` is an object of class `Cat`, that doesn't mean that you can access the parts of `Boots` that are private.

This is a source of endless confusion to new C++ programmers. I can almost hear you yelling, "Hey! I just said Boots is a cat. Why can't Boots access his own age?" The answer is that Boots can, but *you* can't. Boots, in his own methods, can access all his parts— public and private. Even though you've created a `Cat`, that doesn't mean that you can see or change the parts of it that are private.

The way to use `Cat` so that you can access the data members is

```
class Cat
{
public:
    unsigned int  itsAge;
    unsigned int  itsWeight;
    Meow();
};
```

Now `itsAge`, `itsWeight`, and `Meow()` are all public. `Boots.Age=5` compiles without problem.

6

Listing 6.1 shows the declaration of a Cat class with public member variables.

Listing 6.1. Accessing the public members of a simple class.

```
1:   // Demonstrates declaration of a class and
2:   // definition of an object of the class,
3:
4:   #include <iostreams.h>    // for cout
5:
6:   class Cat              // declare the class object
7:   {
8:    public:               // members which follow are public
9:      int itsAge;
10:     int itsWeight;
11:  };
12:
13:
14:  main()
15:  {
16:     Cat Frisky;
17:     Frisky.itsAge = 5;    // assign to the member variable
18:     cout << "Frisky is a cat who is " ;
19:     cout << Frisky.itsAge << " years old.\n";
20:  }
```

```
Frisky is a cat who is 5 years old.
```

Line 6 contains the keyword class. This tells the compiler that what follows is a declaration. The name of the new class comes after the keyword class. In this case, it is Cat.

The body of the declaration begins with the opening brace in line 7 and ends with a closing brace and a semicolon in line 11. Line 8 contains the keyword public, which indicates that everything that follows is public until the keyword private or the end of the class declaration.

Lines 9 and 10 contain the declarations of the class members itsAge and itsWeight.

Line 14 begins the main function of the program. Frisky is defined in line 16 as an instance of a Cat—that is, as a Cat object. Frisky's age is set in line 17 to 5. In lines 18 and 19, the itsAge member variable is used to print out a message about Frisky.

> **Note:** Try commenting out line 8 (`8:    public:`) and try to recompile. You will receive an error on line 17 because `itsAge` will no longer have public access. The default for classes is private access.

Make Member Data Private

As a general rule of design, you should keep the member data of a class private. Therefore, you must create public functions known as accessor methods to set and get the private member variables. These accessor methods are the member functions that other parts of your program call to get and set your private member variables.

NEW☞ TERM A *public accessor method* is a class member function used either to read the value of a private class member variable or to set its value.

Why bother with this extra level of indirect access? After all, it is simpler and easier to use the data, instead of working through accessor functions.

Accessor functions enable you to separate the details of how the data is stored from how it is used. This enables you to change how the data is stored without having to rewrite functions that use the data.

If a function that needs to know a `Cat`'s age accesses `itsAge` directly, that function would need to be rewritten if you, as the author of the `Cat` class, decided to change how that data is stored. By having the function call `GetAge()`, your `Cat` class can easily return the right value no matter how you arrive at the age. The calling function doesn't need to know whether you are storing it as an unsigned integer or a long, or whether you are computing it as needed.

This technique makes your program easier to maintain. It gives your code a longer life because design changes don't make your program obsolete.

Listing 6.2 shows the `Cat` class modified to include private member data and public accessor methods. Note that this is not an executable listing.

Listing 6.2. A class with accessor methods.

```
1:      // Cat class declaration
2:      // Data members are private, public accessor methods
3:      // mediate setting and getting the values of the private data
4:
```

continues

Listing 6.2. continued

```
5:  class Cat
6:  {
7:  public:
8:      // public accessors
9:      unsigned int GetAge();
10:     void SetAge(unsigned int Age);
11:
12:     unsigned int GetWeight();
13:     void SetWeight(unsigned int Weight);
14:
15:      // public member functions
16:     Meow();
17:
18:      // private member data
19: private:
20:     unsigned int  itsAge;
21:     unsigned int  itsWeight;
22:
23: };
```

 This class has five public methods. Lines 9 and 10 contain the accessor methods for itsAge. Lines 12 and 13 contain the accessor methods for itsWeight. These accessor functions set the member variables and return their value.

The public member function Meow() is declared in line 16. Meow() is not an accessor function. It doesn't get or set a member variable; it performs another service for the class, printing the word meow.

The member variables themselves are declared in lines 20 and 21.

To set Frisky's age, you would pass the value to the SetAge() method, as in

```
Cat  Frisky;
Frisky.SetAge(5);    // set Frisky's age using the public accessor
```

Privacy Versus Security

Declaring methods or data private enables the compiler to find programming mistakes before they become bugs. Any programmer worth his consulting fees can find a way around privacy if he wants to. Stroustrup, the inventor of C++ said, "The C++ access control mechanisms provide protection against accident—not against fraud" (ARM, 1990).

The class keyword

```
class class_name
{
// access control keywords here
    // class variables and methods declared here
};
```

You use the `class` keyword to declare new types. A class is a collection of class member data, which are variables of various types, including other classes. The class also contains class functions—or methods—which are functions used to manipulate the data in the class and to perform other services for the class.

You define objects of the new type in much the same way in which you define any variable. State the type (class) and then the variable name (the object). You access the class members and functions by using the dot (.) operator.

You use access control keywords to declare sections of the class as public or private. The default for access control is private. Each keyword changes the access control from that point on to the end of the class or until the next access control keyword. Class declarations end with a closing brace and a semicolon.

Example 1

```
class Cat
{
public:
    unsigned int Age;
    unsigned int Weight;
    void Meow();
};

Cat  frisky;
Frisky.age = 8;
Frisky.Weight = 18;
Frisky.Meow();
```

Example 2

```
class Car
{
public:                         // the next five are public

    void Start();
    void Accelerate();
    void Brake();
    void SetYear(int year);
    int GetYear();

private:                        // the rest is private
```

6

```
      int Year;
      char[255] Model;
};                               // end of class declaration

Car OldFaithful;                 // make an instance of car
int bought;                      // a local variable of type int
OldFaithful.SetYear(84) ;        // assign 84 to the year
bought = OldFaithful.GetYear();  // set bought to 84
OldFaithful.Start();             // call the start method
```

DO	DON'T

DO declare member variables private.

DO use public accessor methods.

DON'T try to use private member variables from outside the class.

DO access private member variables from within class member functions.

Implementing Class Methods

As you've seen, an accessor function provides a public interface to the private member data of the class. Each accessor function, along with any other class methods that you declare, must have an implementation. The implementation is called the function definition.

A member function definition begins with the name of the class, followed by two colons, the name of the function, and its parameters. Listing 6.3 shows the complete declaration of a simple Cat class and the implementation of its accessor function and one general class member function.

Listing 6.3. Implementing the methods of a simple class.

```
1:    // Demonstrates declaration of a class and
2:    // definition of class methods,
3:
4:    #include <iostreams.h>       // for cout
5:
6:    class Cat                    // begin declaration of the class
7:    {
8:      public:                    // begin public section
9:        int GetAge();            // accessor function
10:       void SetAge (int age);   // accessor function
11:       void Meow();             // general function
```

```
12:    private:                    // begin private section
13:      int itsAge;               // member variable
14:  };
15:
16:  // GetAge, Public accessor function
17:  // returns value of itsAge member
18:  int Cat::GetAge()
19:  {
20:      return itsAge;
21:  }
22:
23:  // definition of SetAge, public
24:  // accessor function
25:  // returns sets itsAge member
26:  int Cat::SetAge(age)
27:  {
28:      // set member variable its age to
29:      // value passed in by parameter age
30:      itsAge = age;
31:  }
32:
33:  // definition of Meow method
34:  // returns: void
35:  // parameters: None
36:  // action: Prints "meow" to screen
37:  void Cat::Meow()
38:  {
39:      cout << "Meow.\n";
40:  }
41:
42:  // create a cat, set its age, have it
43:  // meow, tell us its age, then meow again.
44:  void main()
45:  {
46:      Cat Frisky;
47:      Frisky.SetAge(5);
48:      Frisky.Meow();
49:      cout << "Frisky is a cat who is " ;
50:      << Frisky.GetAge() << " years old.\n";
51:      Frisky.Meow();
52:  }
```

```
Meow.
Frisky is a cat who is 5 years old.
Meow.
```

Lines 6 through 14 contain the definintion of the Cat class. Line 8 contains the keyword public, which tells the compiler that what follows is a set of public members. Line 9 has the declaration of the public accessor method GetAge(). GetAge() provides access to the private member variable itsAge, which is declared in line 13. Line 10 has the public accessor function SetAge(). SetAge() takes an integer as an argument and sets itsAge to the value of that argument.

Line 11 has the declaration of the class method Meow(). Meow() is not an accessor function. Here it is a general method that prints the word Meow to the screen.

Line 12 begins the private section, which includes only the declaration in line 13 of the private member variable itsAge. The class declaration ends with a closing brace and semicolon in line 14.

Lines 18 to 21 contain the definition of the member function GetAge(). This method takes no parmeters; it returns an integer. Note that class methods include the class name followed by two colons and the function name (Line 18). This syntax tells the compiler that the GetAge() function that you are defining here is the one that you declared in the Cat class. With the exception of this header line, the GetAge() function is created like any other function.

The GetAge() function takes only one line; it returns the value in itsAge. Note that the main() function cannot access itsAge because itsAge is private to the Cat class. The main() function has access to the public method GetAge(). Because GetAge() is a member function of the Cat class, it has full access to the itsAge variable. This access enables GetAge() to return the value of itsAge to main().

Line 26 contains the definition of the SetAge() member function. It takes an integer parameter and sets the value of itsAge to the value of that parameter in line 30. Because it is a member of the Cat class, SetAge() has direct access to the member variable itsAge.

Line 37 begins the definition, or implementation, of the Meow() method of the Cat class. It is a one-line function that prints the word Meow to the screen followed by a new line. Remember that the \n character prints a new line to the screen.

Line 44 begins the body of the program with the familiar main() function. In this case, it takes no arguments and returns void. In line 46, main() declares a Cat named Frisky. In line 47, the value 5 is assigned to the itsAge member variable by way of the SetAge() accessor method. Note that the method is called by using the class name (Frisky) followed by the member operator (.) and the the method name (SetAge()). In this same way, you can call any of the other methods in a class.

Line 48 calls the Meow() member function, and line 49 prints a message using the GetAge() accessor. Line 51 calls Meow() again.

Constructors and Destructors

There are two ways to define an integer variable. You can define the variable and then assign a value to it later in the program. For example,

```
int Weight;          // define a variable
...                  // other code here
Weight = 7;          // assign it a value
```

Or you can define the integer and immediately initialize it. For example,

```
int Weight = 7;      // define and initialize to 7
```

Initialization combines the definition of the variable with its initial assignment. Nothing stops you from changing that value later. Initialization ensures that your variable is never without a meaningful value.

How do you initialize the member data of a class? Classes have a special member function called a *constructor*. The constructor can take parameters as needed, but it cannot have a return value—not even void. The constructor is a class method with the same name as the class itself.

Whenever you declare a constructor, you'll also want to declare a destructor. Just as constructors create and initialize objects of your class, destructors clean up after your object and free any memory you might have allocated. A destructor always has the name of the class preceded by a tilde (~). Destructors take no arguments and have no return value. Therefore, the Cat declaration includes

```
~Cat();
```

Default Constructors and Destructors

If you don't declare a constructor or a destructor, the compiler makes one for you. The default constructor and destructor take no arguments and do nothing.

What good is a constructor that does nothing? In part, it is a matter of form. All objects must be constructed and destructed, and these do-nothing functions are called at the right time. However, to declare an object without passing in parameters, such as

```
Cat Rags;           // Rags gets no parameters
```

you must have a constructor in the form

```
Cat();
```

When you define an object of a class the constructor is called. If the Cat constructor took two parameters, you might define a Cat object by writing

```
Cat Frisky (5,7);
```

If the constructor took one parameter, you would write

```
Cat Frisky (3);
```

6

In the event that the constructor takes no parameters at all, you leave off the parentheses and write

```
Cat Frisky ;
```

This is an exception to the rule that states all functions require parentheses, even if they take no parameters. This is why you are able to write

```
Cat Frisky;
```

which is a call to the default constructor. It provides no parameters, and it leaves off the parentheses. You don't have to use the compiler-provided default constructor. You are always free to write your own constructor with no parameters. Even constructors with no parameters can have a function body in which they initialize their objects or do other work.

As a matter of form, if you declare a constructor, be sure to declare a destructor, even if your destructor does nothing. Although it is true that the default destructor would work correctly, it doesn't hurt to declare your own. It makes your code clearer.

Listing 6.4 rewrites the Cat class to use a constructor to initialize the Cat object, setting its age to whatever initial age you provide, and it demonstrates where the destructor is called.

Listing 6.4. Using constructors and destructors.

```
1:   // Demonstrates declaration of a constructors and
2:   // destructor for the Cat class
3:
4:   #include <iostreams.h>        // for cout
5:
6:   class Cat                     // begin declaration of the class
7:   {
8:     public:                     // begin public section
9:       Cat(int initialAge);      // constructor
10:      ~Cat();                   // destructor
11:      int GetAge();             // accessor function
12:      void SetAge(int age);     // accessor function
13:      void Meow();
14:    private:                    // begin private section
15:      int itsAge;               // member variable
16:   };
17:
18:   // constructor of Cat,
19:   Cat::Cat(int initialAge);
20:   {
21:       itsAge = initialAge;
22:   }
23:
24:   Cat::~Cat()                   // destructor, takes no action
```

```
25:    {
26:    }
27:
28:    // GetAge, Public accessor function
29:    // returns value of itsAge member
30:    int Cat::GetAge()
31:    {
32:        return itsAge;
33:    }
34:
35:    // Definition of SetAge, public
36:    // accessor function
37:    // returns sets itsAge member
38:    int Cat::SetAge(age)
39:    {
40:        // set member variable its age to
41:        // value passed in by parameter age
42:        itsAge = age;
43:    }
44:
45:    // definition of Meow method
46:    // returns: void
47:    // parameters: None
48:    // action: Prints "meow" to screen
49:    void Cat::Meow()
50:    {
51:        cout << "Meow.\n";
52:    }
53:
54:    // create a cat, set its age, have it
55:    // meow, tell us its age, then meow again.
56:    void main()
57:    {
58:      Cat Frisky(5)
59:      Frisky.Meow();
60:      cout << "Frisky is a cat who is " ;
61:      cout << Frisky.GetAge() << " years old.\n";
62:      Frisky.Meow();
63:      Frisky.SetAge(7);
64:      cout << "Now Frisky is " ;
65:      cout << Frisky.GetAge() << " years old.\n";
66: }
```

```
Meow,
Frisky is a cat who is 5 years old.
Meow.
Now Frisky is 7 years old.
Meow.
```

Listing 6.4 is similar to 6.3, except that line 9 adds a constructor that takes an integer. Line 10 declares the destructor, which takes no parameters. Destructors never take parameters, and neither constructors nor destructors return a value—not even void.

139

Lines 19 to 22 show the implementation of the constructor. It is similar to the implementation of the SetAge() accessor function. There is no return value.

Lines 24 to 26 show the implementation of the destructor ~Cat(). This function does nothing, but you must include the definition of the function if you declare it in the class declaration.

Line 58 contains the definition of a Cat object, Frisky. The value 5 is passed in to Frisky's constructor. There is no need to call SetAge(), because Frisky was created with the value 5 in its member variable itsAge, as shown in line 61. In line 63, Frisky's itsAge variable is reassigned to 7. Line 65 prints the new value.

DO	DON'T

DO use constructors to initialize your objects.

DON'T give constructors or destructors a return value.

DON'T give destructors parameters.

const Member Functions

If you declare a class method const, you are promising that the method won't change the value of any of the members of the class. To declare a class method constant, put the keyword const after the parentheses but before the semicolon. The declaration of the constant member function SomeFunction() takes no arguments and returns void. It looks like this:

```
void SomeFunction() const;
```

Accessor functions are often declared as constant functions by using the const modifier. The Cat class has two accessor functions:

```
void SetAge(int anAge);
int GetAge();
```

SetAge() cannot be const because it changes the member variable itsAge. GetAge(), on the other hand, can and should be const because its doesn't change the class at all. It simply returns the current value of the member variable itsAge. Therefore, the declaration of these functions should be written like this:

```
void SetAge(int anAge);
int GetAge() const;
```

If you declare a function to be const and the implementation of that function changes the object, by changing the value of any of its members. The compiler flags it as an error. For example, if you wrote GetAge() in such a way that it kept count of the number of times that the Cat was asked its age, it would generate a compiler error. This is because you would be changing the Cat object by calling this method.

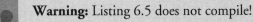

Note: Use const whenever possible. Declare member functions to be const whenever they should not change the object. This lets the compiler help you find errors; it's faster and less expensive than doing it yourself.

It is good programming practice to declare as many methods to be const as possible. Each time you do, you enable the compiler to catch your errors, instead of letting your errors become bugs that will show up when your program is running.

Interface Versus Implementation

As you've learned, clients are the parts of the program that create and use objects of your class. You can think of the interface to your class—the class declaration—as a contract with these clients. The contract tells what data your class has available and how your class will behave.

For example, in the Cat class declaration, you create a contract that every Cat will have a member variable itsAge that can be initialized in its constructor, assigned to by its SetAge() accessor function, and read by its GetAge() accessor. You also promise that every Cat will know how to Meow().

If you make GetAge() a const function—as you should—the contract also promises that GetAge() won't change the Cat on which it is called.

C++ is *strongly typed,* which means that the compiler enforces these contracts by giving you a compiler error when you violate them. Listing 6.5 demonstrates a program that doesn't compile because of violations of these contracts.

Warning: Listing 6.5 does not compile!

Listing 6.5. A demonstration of violations of the interface.

```
1:   // Demonstrates compiler errors
2:
3:
4:   #include <iostreams.h>          // for cout
5:
6:   class Cat
7:   {
8:   public:
9:       Cat(int initialAge);
10:      ~Cat();
11:      int GetAge() const;         // const accessor function
12:      void SetAge (int age);
13:      void Meow();
14:   private:
15:      int itsAge;
16:   };
17:
18:      // constructor of Cat,
19:      Cat::Cat(int initialAge)
20:      {
21:          itsAge = initialAge;
21:          cout << "Cat Constructor\n";
22:      }
23:
24:      Cat::~Cat()                 // destructor, takes no action
25:      {
26:          cout << "Cat Destructor\n";
27:      }
28:   // GetAge, const function
29:   // but we violate const!
30:   int Cat::GetAge() const
31:   {
32:      return (itsAge++);          // violates const!
33:   }
34:
35:   // definition of SetAge, public
36:   // accessor function
37:   // returns sets itsAge member
38:   int Cat::SetAge(age)
39:   {
40:      // set member variable its age to
41:      // value passed in by parameter age
42:      itsAge = age;
43:   }
44:
45:   // definition of Meow method
46:   // returns: void
47:   // parameters: None
48:   // action: Prints "meow" to screen
49:   void Cat::Meow()
50:   {
51:      cout << "Meow.\n";
52:   }
53:
```

```
54:    // demonstrate various violations of the
55:    // interface, and resulting compiler errors
56:    void main()
57:    {
58:        Cat Frisky;                    // doesn't match declaration
59:        Frisky.Meow();
60:        Frisky.Bark();                 // No, silly, cat's can't bark.
61:        Frisky.itsAge = 7;             // itsAge is private
62:    }
```

As it is written, this program doesn't compile. Therefore, there is no output.

This program was fun to write because there are so many errors in it.

Line 11 declares GetAge() to be a const accessor function—as it should be. In the body of GetAge(), however, in line 32, the member variable itsAge is incremented. Because this method is declared to be const, it must not change the value of itsAge. Therefore, it is flagged as an error when the program is compiled.

In line 13, Meow() is not declared const. Although this is not an error, it is bad programming practice. A better design takes into account that this method doesn't change the member variables of Cat. Therefore, Meow() should be const.

Line 58 shows the definition of a Cat object, Frisky. Cats now have a constructor, which takes an integer as a parameter. This means that you must pass a parameter in. Because there is no parameter in line 58, it is flagged as an error.

Line 59 shows a call to a class method, Bark(). Bark() was never declared. Therefore, it is illegal.

Line 61 shows itsAge being assigned the value 7. Because itsAge is a private data member, it is flagged as an error when the program is compiled.

Why Use The Compiler to Catch Errors?

While it would be wonderful to write 100-percent bug-free code, few programmers have been able to do so. However, what many programmers have done is developed a system to help minimize bugs by catching and fixing them early in the process.

Although compiler errors are infuriating and are the bane of a programmer's existence, they are far better than the alternative. A weakly typed language enables you to violate your contracts without a peep from the compiler, but your program will crash at run-time—when, for example, your boss is watching.

Compile-time errors—that is, errors found while you are compiling—are far better than run-time errors—that is, errors found while you are executing the program. This is because compile-time errors can be found much more reliably. It is possible to run a program many times without going down every possible code-path. Thus, a run-time error can hide for quite a while. Compile-time errors are found every time you compile. Thus, they are easier to identify and fix. It is the goal of quality programming to ensure that the code has no run-time bugs. One tried and true technique to accomplish this is to use the compiler to catch your mistakes early in the development process.

Where to Put Class Declarations and Method Definitions

Each function that you declare for your class must have a definition. The definition is also called the function implementation. Like other functions, the definition of a class method has a function header and a function body.

The definition must be in a file that the compiler can find. Most C++ compilers want that file to end with .C, or .CPP. This book uses .CPP, but check your compiler to see what it prefers.

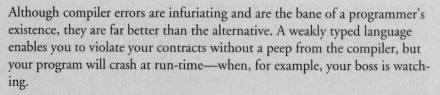

Note: Many compilers assume that files ending with .C are C programs, and that C++ program files end with .CPP. You can use any extension, but .CPP will minimize confusion.

You are free to put the declaration in this file as well, but that is not good programming practice. The convention that most programmers adopt is to put the declaration into what is called a header file, usually with the same name but ending in .H, .HP, or .HPP. This book names the header files with .HPP, but check your compiler to see what it prefers.

For example, you put the declaration of the Cat class into a file named CAT.HPP, and we put the definition of the class methods into a file called CAT.CPP. You then attach the header file to the .CPP file by putting the following code at the top of CAT.CPP:

```
#include Cat.hpp
```

This tells the compiler to read CAT.HPP into the file, just as if you had typed in its contents at this point. Why bother separating them if you're just going to read them back in? Most of the time, clients of your class don't care about the implementation specifics. Reading the header file tells them everything they need to know; they can ignore the implementation files.

> **Note:** The declaration of a class tells the compiler what the class is, what data it holds, and what functions it has. The declaration of the class is called its interface because it tells the user how to interact with the class. The interface is usually stored in an .HPP file, which is referred to as a header file.
>
> The function definition tells the compiler how the function works. The function definition is called the implementation of the class method, and it is kept in a .CPP file. The implementation details of the class are of concern only to the author of the class. Clients of the class—that is, the parts of the program that use the class—don't need to know—and don't care—how the functions are implemented.

6

Inline Implementation

Just as you can ask the compiler to make a regular function inline, you can make class methods inline. The keyword inline appears before the return value. The inline implementation of the GetWeight() function, for example, looks like this:

```
inline int Cat::GetWeight()
{
    return itsWeight;          // return the Weight data member
}
```

You can also put the definition of a function into the declaration of the class, which automatically makes that function inline. For example,

```
class Cat
{
  public:
    int GetWeight() { return itsWeight; }     // inline
    void SetWeight(int aWeight);
};
```

Note the syntax of the `GetWeight()` definition, the body of the inline function begins immediately after the declaration of the class method; there is no semicolon after the parentheses. Like any function, the definition begins with an opening brace and ends with a closing brace. As usual, whitespace doesn't matter; you could have have written the declaration as

```
class Cat
{
public:
    int GetWeight()
        {
            return itsWeight;
        }                          // inline
    void SetWeight(int aWeight);
};
```

Listings 6.6 and 6.7 recreate the `Cat` class, but they put the declaration in CAT.HPP and the implementation of the functions in CAT.CPP. Listing 6.7 also changes the accessor functions and the `Meow()` function to inline.

Listing 6.6. Cat class declaration in CAT.HPP.

```
1:   class Cat
2    {
3:   public:
4:     Cat (int initialAge);
5:     ~Cat();
6:     int GetAge() { return itsAge;}          // inline!
7:     void SetAge (int age) { itsAge + age;}  // inline!
8:     void Meow() { cout << "Meow.;}          // inline!
9:   private:
10:  int itsAge;
11:  };
```

Listing 6.7. Cat implementation in CAT.CPP.

```
1:   // Demonstrates inline functions
2:   // and inclusion of header files
```

```
3:
4:    #include "cat.hpp"  // be sure to include the header files!
5:    #include <iostream.h>
6:
7:    Cat::Cat(int intialAge)    //constructor
8:    {
9:        itsAge = initialAge;
10:   }
11:
12:   Cat::~Cat()                //destructor, takes no action
13:   {
14:   }
15:
16:   // Creat a cat, set its age, have it
17:   // meow, tell us its age, then meow again.
18:   void main()
19:   {
20:       Cat Frisky(5);
21:       Frisky.Meow();
22:       cout << "Frisky is a cat who is " ;
23:       cout << Frisky.GetAge() << " years old.\n";
24:       Frisky.Meow();
25:       Frisky.SetAge(7);
26:       cout << "Now Frisky is " ;
27:       cout << Frisky.GetAge() << " years old.\n";
28:   }
```

Output

```
Meow.
Frisky is a cat who is 5 years old.
Meow.
Now Frisky is 7 years old.
```

Analysis The code presented in Listing 6.6 and Listing 6.7 is similar to Listing 6.4, except that three of the methods are written inline in the declaration file and the declaration has been separated the into CAT.HPP.

GetAge() is declared in line 6, and its inline implementation is provided. Lines 7 and 8 provide more inline functions, but the functionality of these functions is unchanged from the previous "outline" implementations.

Line 4 of listing 6.7 shows "#include cat.hpp", which brings in the listings from CAT.HPP. IOSTREAM.H, which is needed for cout, is included on line 5.

Lines 18 to 28 repeat the main function from listing 6.4. This shows that making these functions inline doesn't change their performance.

Classes with Other Classes as Member Data

It is not uncommon to build up a complex class by declaring simpler classes and including them in the declaration of the more complicated class. For example, you might declare a wheel class, a motor class, a transmission class, and so forth, and then combine them into a car class. This declares a "has a" relationship. A car has a motor; it has wheels; and it has a transmission.

Consider a second example. A rectangle is composed of lines. A line can is defined by two points. A point is defined by an x-coordinate and a y-coordinate. Listing 6.8 shows a complete declaration of a `Rectangle` class, as might appear in RECTANGLE.HPP. Because a rectangle is defined as four lines connecting four points and each point refers to a coordinate on a graph, we first declare a `Point` class, to hold the x,y coordinates of each point. Listing 6.9 shows a complete declaration of both classes.

Listing 6.8. Declaring a complete class.

```
1:   // Begin Rectangle.hp
2:   #include <iostream.h>
3:   class Point      // holds x,y coordinates
4:   {
5:      // no constructor, use default
6:      public:
7:         void SetX(int x) { itsX = x; }
8:         void SetY(int y) { itsY = y; }
9:         int GetX()const { return itsX;}
10:        int GetY()const { return itsY;}
11:     private:
12:        int itsX;
13:        int itsY;
14:  };   // end of Point class declaration
15:
16:
17:  class  Rectangle
18:  {
19:     public:
20:        Rectangle (int top, int left, int bottom, int right);
21:        ~Rectangle () {}
22:
23:        int GetTop() const { return itsTop; }
24:        int GetLeft() const { return itsLeft; }
25:        int GetBottom() const { return itsBottom; }
26:        int GetRight() const { return itsRight; }
27:
28:        Point  GetUpperLeft() const { return itsUpperLeft; }
29:        Point  GetLowerLeft() const { return itsLowerLeft; }
30:        Point  GetUpperRight() const { return itsUpperRight; }
```

```
31:         Point  GetLowerRight() const { return itsLowerRight; }
32:
33:         void SetUpperLeft(Point Location)   {itsUpperLeft = Location;}
34:         void SetLowerLeft(Point Location)   {itsLowerLeft = Location;}
35:         void SetUpperRight(Point Location)  {itsUpperRight = Location;}
36:         void SetLowerRight(Point Location)  {itsLowerRight = Location;}
37:
38:         void SetTop(int top) { itsTop = top; }
39:         void SetLeft (int left) { itsLeft = left; }
40:         void SetBottom (int bottom) { itsBottom = bottom; }
41:         void SetRight (int right) { itsRight = right; }
42:
43:         int GetArea() const;
44:
45:     private:
46:         Point  itsUpperLeft;
47:         Point  itsUpperRight;
48:         Point  itsLowerLeft;
49:         Point  itsLowerRight;
50:         int    itsTop;
51:         int    itsLeft;
52:         int    itsBottom;
53:         int    itsRight;
54: };
55: // end Rectangle.hp
```

Listing 6.9. RECTANGLE.CPP.

```
1:  // Begin Rectangle.cp
2:  Rectangle::Rectangle(int top, int left, int bottom, int right)
3:  {
4:      itsTop = top;
5:      itsLeft = left;
6:      itsBottom = bottom;
7:      itsRight = right;
8:
9:      itsUpperLeft.SetX(left);
10:     itsUpperLeft.SetY(top);
11:
12:     itsUpperRight.SetX(right);
13:     itsUpperRight.SetY(top);
14:
15:     itsLowerLeft.SetX(left);
16:     itsLowerLeft.SetY(bottom);
17:
18:     itsLowerRight.SetX(right);
19:     itsLowerRight.SetY(bottom);
20: }
21:
22:
23: // compute area of the rectangle by finding corners,
24: // establish width and height and then multiply
```

6

continues

149

Listing 6.9. continued

```
25:  int Rectangle::GetArea() const
26:  {
27:        int Width = itsRight-itsLeft;
28:        int Height = itsTop - itsBottom;
29:        return (Width * Height);
30:  }
31:
32:  void main()
33:  {
34:        //initialize a local Rectangle variable
35:        Rectangle MyRectangle (100, 20, 50, 80 );
36:
37:        int Area = MyRectangle.GetArea();
38:
39:        cout << "Area: " << Area << "\n";
40:        cout << "Upper Left X Coordinate: ";
41:        cout << MyRectangle.GetUpperLeft().GetX();
42:  }
```

```
Area: 200
Upper Left X Coordinate: 20
```

Lines 3–14 in Listing 6.8 declare the class Point, which is used to hold a specific x,y coordinate on a graph. As it written, this program doesn't use Points much. However, other drawing methods require Points.

Within the declaration of the class Point, you declare two member variables—itsX and itsY—on lines 12 and 13. These variables hold the values of the coordinates. As the x-coordinate increases, you move to the right on the graph. As the y-coordinate increases, you move upward on the graph. Other graphs use different systems. Some windowing programs, for example, increase the y-coordinate as you move down in the window.

The Point class uses inline accessor functions to get and set the X and Y points declared on lines 7–10. Points use the default constructor and destructor. Therefore, you must set their coordinates explicitly.

Line 17 begins the declaration of a Rectangle class. A Rectangle consists of four points that represent the corners of the Rectangle.

The constructor for the Rectangle (line 20) takes four integers, known as top, left, bottom, and right. The four parameters to the constructor are copied into four member variables (listing 6.9) and then the four Points are established.

In addition to the usual accessor functions, Rectangle has a function GetArea() declared in line 43. Instead of storing the area as a variable, the GetArea() function computes the area on lines 27–29 of listing 6.9. To do this, it computes the width and the height of the rectangle, and then it multiplies these two values.

Getting the x-coordinate of the upper-left corner of the rectangle requires that you access the UpperLeft point and ask that point for its X value. Because GetArea() is a method of Rectangle, it can directly access the private data of Rectangle, including itsUpperLeft. Because itsUpperLeft is a Point and Point's itsX value is private, GetArea() cannot directly access this data. Rather, it must use the public accessor function GetX to obtain that value.

Line 32 of listing 6.9 is the beginning of the body of the actual program. Until line 35, no memory has been allocated, and nothing has really happened. The only thing you've done is to tell the compiler how to make a Point and how to make a Rectangle, in case one is ever needed.

In line 35, you define a Rectangle by passing in values for top, left, bottom, and right.

In line 37, you make a local variable, Area, of type int. This variable holds the area of the Rectangle that you've created. You initialize Area with the value returned by Rectangle's GetArea() function.

A client of Rectangle could create a Rectangle object and get its area without ever looking at the implementation of GetArea().

CAT.HPP is shown in Listing 6.8. Just by looking at the header file, which contains the declaration of the Cat class, the programmer knows that GetArea() returns an int. How GetArea does its magic is not of concern to the user of class Cat. In fact, the author of Cat could change GetArea() without affecting the user of the Cat class.

Structures

A very close cousin to the class keyword is the keyword struct, which is used to declare a structure. In C++ a structure is exactly like a class, except that its members are public by default. You can declare a structure exactly as you declare a class, and you can give it exactly the same data members and functions. In fact, if you follow the good programming practice of always explicitly declaring the private and public sections of your class, there will be no difference whatsoever.

Try re-entering listing 6.8 with these changes:

    In line 3, change class Point to struct Point.
    In line 17, change class Rectangle to struct Rectangle.

Now run the program again and compare the output. There should be no change.

Why Two Keywords Do the Same Thing

You're probably wondering why two keywords do the same thing. This is an accident of history. When C++ was developed, it was built as an extension of the C language. C has structures, although C structures don't have class methods. Bjarne Stroustrup, the creator of C++, built upon `structs`, but he changed the name to `class` to represent the new, expanded functionality.

DO put your class declaration in an .HPP file and your member functions in a .CPP file.

DO use const whenever you can.

DO understand classes before you move on.

Summary

Today you learned how to create new data types called classes. You learned how to define variables of these new types, which are called objects.

A class has data members, which are variables of various types, including other classes. A class also includes member functions—also known as methods. You use these member functions to manipulate the member data and to perform other services.

Class members—both data and functions—can be public or private. Public members are accessible to any part of your program. Private members are accessible only to the member functions of the class.

It is good programming practice to isolate the interface—or declaration—of the class in a header file. You usually do this in a file with an .HPP extension. The implementation of the class methods is written in a file with a .CPP extension.

Class constructors initialize objects. Class destructors destroy objects and are often used to free memory allocated by methods of the class.

Q&A

Q How big is a class object?

A A class object's size in memory is determined by the sum of the sizes of its member variables. Class methods don't take up room as part of the memory set aside for the object.

Some compilers align variables in memory in such a way that two-byte variables actually consume somewhat more than two bytes. Check your compiler manual to be sure, but at this point there is no reason to be concerned with these details.

Q If I declare a class `Cat` with a private member `itsAge` and then define two `Cat` objects, `Frisky` and `Boots`, can `Boots` access `Frisky`'s `itsAge` member variable?

A No. While private data is available to the member functions of a class, different instances of the class caannot access each other's data. In other words, `Frisky`'s member functions can access `Frisky`'s data, but not `Boots`'. In fact, `Frisky` is a completely independent cat from `Boots`, and that is just as it should be.

Q Why shouldn't I make all the member data public?

A Making member data private enables the client of the class to use the data without worrying about how it is stored or computed. For example, if the `Cat` class has a method `GetAge()`, clients of the `Cat` class can ask for the cat's age without knowing or caring if the cat stores its age in a member variable, or computes its age on the fly.

Q If using a `const` function to change the class causes a compiler error, why shouldn't I just leave out the word `const` and be sure to avoid errors?

A If your member function logically shouldn't change the class, using the keyword `const` is a good way to enlist the compiler in helping you find silly mistakes. For example, `GetAge()` might have no reason to change the `Cat` class, but your implementation has this line:

```
if (itsAge = 100)
    cout << "Hey! You're 100 years old\n"
```

Declaring `GetAge()` to be `const` causes this code to be flagged as an error. You meant to check whether `itsAge` is equal to 100, but instead you inadvertently

6

assigned 100 to `itsAge`. Because this assignment changes the class—and you said this method would not change the class—the compiler is able to find the error.

This kind of mistake can be hard to find just by scanning the code—the eye often sees only what it expects to see. More importantly, the program might appear to run correctly, but `itsAge` has now been set to a bogus number. This will cause problems sooner or later.

Q Is there ever a reason to use a structure in a C++ program?

A Many C++ programmers reserve the `struct` keyword for classes that have no functions. This is a throwback to the old C structures, which could not have functions. Frankly, I find it confusing and poor programming practice. Today's method-less structure might need methods tomorrow. Then you'll be forced either to change the type to `class` or to break your rule and end up with a structure with methods.

Workshop

The Workshop provides quiz questions to help you solidify your understanding of the material covered and exercises to provide you with experience in using what you've learned. Try to answer the quiz and exercise questions before checking the answers in Appendix D, and make sure you understand the answers before continuing to the next chapter.

Quiz

1. What is the dot operator, and what is it used for?

2. Which sets aside memory—declaration or definition?

3. Is the declaration of a class its interface or its implementation?

4. What is the difference between public and private data members?

5. Can member functions be private?

6. Can member data be public?

7. If you declare two `Cat` objects, can they have different values in their `itsAge` member data?

8. Do class declarations end with a semicolon? Do class method definitions?

9. What would the header for a `Cat` function, `Meow`, that takes no parameters and returns `void` look like?

10. What function is called to initialize a class?

Exercises

1. Write the code that declares a class called `Employee` with these data members: `age`, `yearsOfService`, and `Salary`.

2. Rewrite the `Employee` class to make the data members private, and provide public accessor methods to get and set each of the data members.

3. Write a program with the `Employee` class that makes two `Employees`; sets their `age`, `YearsOfService`, and `Salary`; and prints their values.

4. Continuing from Exercise 3, provide a method of `Employee` that reports how many thousands of dollars the employee earns, rounded to the nearest 1,000.

5. Change the `Employee` class so that you can initialize `age`, `YearsOfService`, and `Salary` when you create the employee.

6. **BUG BUSTERS:** What is wrong with the following declaration?

```
class Square
{
public:
    int Side;
}
```

7. **BUG BUSTERS:** Why isn't the following class declaration very useful?

```
class Cat
{
    int GetAge()const;
private:
    int itsAge;
};
```

8. **BUG BUSTERS:** What three bugs in this code will the compiler find?

```
class  TV
{
public:
```

```
     void SetStation(int Station);
     int GetStation() const;
private:
     int itsStation;
};

main()
{
    TV myTV;
    myTV.itsStation = 9;
    TV.SetStation(10);
    TV myOtherTv(2);
}
```

More Program
Flow

Introduction

Programs accomplish most of their work by branching and looping. On Day 4 you learned how to branch your program using the `if` statement. Today you learn:

- [ ] What loops are and how they are used.
- [ ] How to build various loops.
- [ ] An alternative to deeply-nested `if`/`else` statements.

Looping

Many programming problems are solved by repeatedly acting on the same data. There are two ways to do this: recursion (discussed yesterday) and iteration. Iteration means doing the same thing again and again. The principal method of iteration is the loop.

The Roots of Looping: *goto*

In the primitive days of early computer science, programs were nasty, brutish, and short. Loops consisted of a label, some statements, and a jump.

In C++, a label is just a name followed by a colon (:). The label is placed to the left of a legal C++ statement, and a jump is accomplished by writing `goto` followed by the label name. Listing 7.1 illustrates this.

Listing 7.1. Looping with the keyword `goto`.

```
1:    // Listing 7.1
2:    // Looping with goto
3:
4:    #include <iostream.h>
5:
6:    void main()
7:    {
8:         int counter = 0;        // initialize counter
9:    loop:   counter ++;             // top of the loop
10:          cout << "counter: " << counter << "\n";
11:          if (counter < 5)        // test the value
12:              goto loop;          // jump to the top
13:
14:          cout << "Complete. Counter: " << counter << ".\n";
15:    }
```

```
counter: 1
counter: 2
counter: 3
counter: 4
counter: 5
Complete. Counter: 5
```

Analysis

On line 8 counter is initialized to zero. The label loop is on line 9 marking the top of the loop. Counter is incremented and its new value is printed. The value of counter is tested on line 11. If it is less than 5 the if statement is true and the goto statement is executed. This causes program execution to jump back to line 9. The program continues looping until counter is equal to 5, at which time it "falls through" the loop and the final output is printed.

Why *goto* Is Shunned

goto has received some rotten press lately, and it's well deserved. goto statements can cause a jump to any location in your source code, backward or forward. The indiscriminate use of goto statements has caused tangled, miserable, impossible-to-read programs known as "spaghetti code." Because of this, computer science teachers have spent the past 20 years drumming one lesson into the heads of their students: "Never, ever, ever use goto! It is evil!"

To avoid the use of goto, more sophisticated, tightly controlled looping commands have been introduced: for, while, and do...while. Using these makes programs that are more easily understood, and goto is generally avoided, but one might argue that the case has been a bit overstated. Like any tool, carefully used and in the right hands, goto can be a useful construct. Kids, don't try this at home.

Syntax

The *goto* Statement

To use the goto statement, you write goto followed by a label name. This causes an unconditioned jump to the label.

Example

```
if (value > 10)
    goto end;

if (value < 10)
    goto end.\

cout << "value is 10!";

end:

cout << "done";
```

>
>
> **Warning:** Use of goto is almost always a sign of bad design. The best advice is to avoid using it. In 10 years of programming, I've only needed it once.

while Loops

A while loop causes your program to repeat a sequence of statements as long as the starting condition remains true. In the example of goto, in listing 7.1, the counter was incremented until it was equal to 5. Listing 7.2 shows the same program rewritten to take advantage of a while loop.

Listing 7.2. while loops.

```
1:    // Listing 7.2
2:    // Looping with while
3:
4:    #include <iostream.h>
5:
6:    void main()
7:    {
8:      int counter = 0;              // initialize the condition
9:
10:     while(counter <= 5)      // test condition still true
11:       {
12:         counter++;                // body of the loop
13:         cout << "counter: " << counter << "\n";
14:       }
15:
16:     cout << "Complete. Counter: " << counter << ".\n";
17:   }
```

```
counter: 0
counter: 1
counter: 2
counter: 3
counter: 4
counter: 5
Complete. Counter: 5
```

Analysis This simple program demonstrates the fundamentals of the while loop. A condition is tested, and if it is true, the body of the while loop is executed. In this case, the condition tested on line 12 is whether counter is less than 5. If the condition is true, the body of the loop is executed—on line 12 the counter is incremented and on line 13 the value is printed. When the conditional statement on line 10 fails (when counter is no longer less than 5) the entire body of the while loop (from lines 11 through 14) is skipped. Program execution falls through to line 15.

The *while* Statement

```
while ( condition )
    statement;
```

Condition is any C++ expression, and *statement* is any valid C++ statement or block of statements. When *condition* evaluates to true (1), the *statement* is executed, and then the *condition* is tested again. This continues until the *condition* tests false, at which time the while loop terminates and execution continues on the first line below the *statement*.

Example

```
// count to 10
int x = 0;
while (x < 10)
    cout << "X: " << x++;
```

More Complicated *while* Statements

The condition tested by a while loop can be as complex as any legal C++ expression. This can include expressions produced using the logical && (and), ¦¦ (or), and ! (not) operators. Listing 7.3 is a somewhat more complicated while statement.

Listing 7.3. Complex while loops.

```
1:     // Listing 7.3
2:     // Complex while statements
3:
4:     #include <iostream.h>
5:
6:     void main()
7:     {
8:        unsigned short small;
9:        unsigned long  large;
10:       const unsigned short MAXSMALL=65535;
11:
12:       cout << "Enter a small number: ";
13:       cin >> small;
14:       cout << "Enter a large number: ";
15:       cin >> large;
16:
17:        cout << "small: " << small << "...";
18:
19:       // for each iteration, test three conditions
```

continues

Listing 7.3. continued

```
20:      while (small < large && large > 0 && small < MAXSMALL)
21:      {
22:        if (small % 5000 == 0)  // write a dot every 5k lines
23:          cout << ".";
24:
25:        small++;
26:
27:        large-=2;
28:      }
29:
30:      cout << "\nSmall: " << small << " Large: " << large << endl;
31:    }
```

```
Enter a small number: 2
Enter a large number: 100000
Small:2......
Small:33335 Large: 33334
```

This program is a game. Enter two numbers, one small and one large. The smaller number will count up by ones, the larger number will count down by twos. The goal of the game is to guess when they'll meet.

On lines 12–15 the numbers are entered. Line 20 sets up a `while` loop, which will continue only as long as three conditions are met:

1. `small` is not bigger than `large`

2. `large` isn't negative

3. `small` doesn't overrun the size of a small integer (`MAXSMALL`).

On line 22 the value in `small` is calculated modulo 5,000. This does not change the value in `small`, however, it only returns the value 0 when `small` is an exact multiple of 5,000. Each time it is, a dot (.) is printed to the screen to show progress. On line 25 `small` is incremented and on line 27 `large` is decremented by 2.

When any of the three conditions in the `while` loop fail, the loop ends and execution of the program continues after the `while` loop's closing brace on line 27.

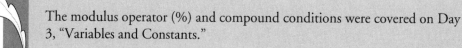

The modulus operator (%) and compound conditions were covered on Day 3, "Variables and Constants."

continue and *break*

At times you'll want to return to the top of a while loop before the entire set of statements in the while loop is executed. The continue statement jumps back to the top of the loop.

At other times, you may want to exit the loop before the exit conditions are met. The break statement immediately exits the while loop, and program execution resumes after the closing brace.

Listing 7.4 demonstrates the use of these statements. This time the game has become more complicated. The user is invited to enter a small number and a large number, a skip number, and a target number. The small number will be incremented by one, and the large number will be decremented by 2. The decrement will be skipped each time the small number is a multiple of the skip. The game ends if small becomes larger than large. If the large number reaches the target exactly, a statement is printed and the game stops.

The user's goal is to put in a target number for the large number that will stop the game.

Listing 7.4. Break and continue.

```
1:     // Listing 7.4
2:     // Demonstrates break and continue
3:
4:     #include <iostream.h>
5:
6:     void main()
7:     {
8:       unsigned short small;
9:       unsigned long  large;
10:      unsigned long  skip;
11:      unsigned long target;
12:      const unsigned short MAXSMALL=65535;
13:
14:      cout << "Enter a small number: ";
15:      cin >> small;
16:      cout << "Enter a large number: ";
17:      cin >> large;
18:      cout << "Enter a skip number: ";
19:      cin >> skip;
20:      cout << "Enter a target number: ";
21:      cin >> target;
22:
23:    cout << "\n";
24:
25:      // set up 3 stop conditions for the loop
26:      while (small < large && large > 0 && small < 65535)
27:      {
28:
```

continues

More Program Flow

Listing 7.4. continued

```
29:                    small++;
30:
31:            if (small % skip == 0)   // skip the decrement?
32:            {
33:              cout << "skipping on " << small << endl;
34:              continue;
35:            }
36:
37:            if (large == target)     // exact match for the target?
38:            {
39:              cout << "Target reached!";
40:              break;
41:            }
42:
43:            large-=2;
44:        }                      // end of while loop
45:
46:        cout << "\nSmall: " << small << " Large: " << large << endl;
47:    }
```

Enter a small number: 2
Enter a large number: 20
Enter a skip number: 4
Enter a target number: 6
skipping on 4
skipping on 8
Small: 10 Large: 8

In this play, the user lost; small became larger than large before the target number of 6 was reached.

On line 26 the while conditions are tested. If small continues to be smaller than large, and large is larger than 0 and small hasn't overrun the maximum value for a small int, the body of the while loop is entered.

On line 31 the small value is taken modulo the skip value. If small is a multiple of skip the continue statement is reached and program execution jumps to the top of the loop at line 26. This effectively skips over the test for the target and the decrement of large.

On line 37 target is tested against the value for large. If they are the same the user has won. A message is printed and the break statement is reached. This causes an immediate break out of the while loop, and program execution resumes on line 45.

Both continue and break should be used with caution. They are the next most dangerous commands after goto, for much the same reason. Programs that suddenly change direction are harder to understand, and liberal use of continue and break can render even a small while loop unreadable.

The *continue* Statement

continue; causes a while or for loop to begin again at the top of the loop.

Example

```
while (condition)
{
    if (condition 2)
        continue;
    //statements;
}
```

The *break* Statement

break; causes the immediate end of a while or for loop. Execution jumps to the closing brace.

Example

```
while (condition)
{
    if (condition2)
        break;
    // statements;
}
```

while (1) Loops

The condition tested in a while loop can be any valid C++ expression. As long as that condition remains true the while loop will continue. You can create a loop that will never end by using the number 1 for the condition to be tested. Since 1 is always true, the loop will never end, unless a break statement is reached. Listing 7.5 demonstrates counting to ten using this construct.

Listing 7.5. while (1) loops.

```
1:    // Listing 7.5
2:    // Demonstrates a while true loop
3:
4:    #include <iostream.h>
5:
6:    void main()
7:    {
8:      int counter = 0;
9:
10:     while (1)
11:     {
12:        counter ++;
13:        if (counter > 10)
14:            break;
15:     }
16:     cout << "Counter: " << counter << "\n";
17:    }
```

counter: 11

On line 10 a while loop is set up with a condition that can never be false. The loop increments the counter variable on line 12 and then on line 13 tests to see if counter has gone past 10. If it hasn't, the while loop iterates. If counter is greater than 10 the break on line 14 ends the while loop, and program execution falls through to line 16, where the results are printed.

This program works, but it isn't pretty. This is a good example of using the wrong tool for the job. The same thing can be accomplished by putting the test of counter's value where it belongs—in the while condition.

Eternal loops such as while(1) can cause your computer to "hang" if the exit condition is never reached. Use these with caution and test them thoroughly.

C++ gives you many different ways to accomplish the same task. The real trick is picking the right tool for the particular job.

SAMS
PUBLISHING

Sams
Learning
Center

DO	DON'T

DON'T use the goto statement.

DO use while loops to iterate while a condition is true.

DO exercise caution when using continue and break statements.

DO make sure your loop will eventually end.

do...while Loops

It is possible that the body of a while loop will never execute. The while statement checks its condition before executing any of its statements, and if the condition evaluates false the entire body of the while loop is skipped. Listing 7.6 illustrates this.

Listing 7.6. Skipping the body of the while Loop

```
1:      // Listing 7.6
2:      // Demonstrates skipping the body of
3:      // the while loop when the condition is false.
4:
5:      #include <iostream.h>
6:
7:      void main()
8:      {
9:          int counter;
10:         cout << "How many hellos?: ";
11:         cin >> counter;
12:         while (counter > 0)
13:         {
14:             cout << "Hello!\n";
15:             counter — ;
16:         }
17:         cout << "Counter is" << counter;
18:      }
```

Output

```
How many hellos?: 2
Hello!
Hello!
Counter is 0
```

7

167

The user is prompted for a starting value on line 10, which is stored in the integer variable `counter`. The value of `counter` is tested on line 12, and decremented in the body of the `while` loop. The first time through `counter` was set to 2, and so the body of the `while` loop ran twice. The second time through, however, the user typed in `0`. The value of `counter` was tested on line 12 and the condition was false; `counter` was not greater than `0`. The entire body of the `while` loop was skipped, and `hello` was never printed.

What if you want to ensure that `hello` is always printed at least once? The `while` loop can't accomplish this, because the `if` condition is tested *before* any printing is done. You can force the issue with an `if` statement just before entering the `while`:

```
if (counter < 1)  // force a minimum value
    counter = 1;
```

but that is what programmers call a "kludge," an ugly and inelegant solution.

do...while

The `do...while` loop executes the body of the loop before its condition is tested, and ensures that the body always executes at least one time. Listing 7.7 demonstrates this program rewritten with a `do...while` loop.

Listing 7.7. Demonstrates `do...while` loop.

```
1:    // Listing 7.7
2:    // Demonstrates do while
3:
4:    #include <iostream.h>
5:
6:    void main()
7:    {
8:        int counter;
9:        cout << "How many hellos? ";
10:       cin >> counter;
11:       do
12:       {
13:           cout << "Hello\n";
14:           counter—;
15:       }  while (counter >0);
16:       cout << "Counter is: " << counter;
17:    }
```

```
Enter starting number: 2
Hello
Hello
Counter is 0
```

The user is prompted for starting a value on line 9, which is stored in the integer variable counter. In the do...while loop the body of the loop is entered *before* the condition is tested, and therefore is guaranteed to be acted on at least once. On line 13 the message is printed, on line 14 the counter is decremented, and on line 15 the condition is tested. If the condition evaluates true, execution jumps to the top of the loop on line 13, otherwise it falls through to line 16.

The continue and break statements work in the do...while loop exactly as they do in the while loop. The only difference between a while loop and a do...while loop is when the *condition* is tested.

Syntax

The *do...while* Statement

```
do
    statement
while (condition);
```

The *statement* is executed, and then the *condition* is evaluated. If the *condition* is true, the loop is repeated, otherwise the loop ends. The *statements* and *conditions* are otherwise identical to the while loop.

Example 1

```
// count to 10
int x = 0;
do
    cout << "X: " << x++;
while (x < 10)
```

Example 2

```
// print lowercase alphabet.
char ch = 'a';
do
{
    cout << ch << ' ';
    ch++;
} while ( ch <= 'z' );
```

DO	**DON'T**

DO use do...while when you want to ensure the loop is executed at least once.

DO use while loops when you want to skip the loop if the condition is false.

DO test all loops to make sure that they do what you expect.

for Loops

When programming while loops, you'll often find yourself setting up a starting condition, testing to see if the condition is true, and incrementing or otherwise changing a variable each time through the loop. Listing 7.8 demonstrates this.

Listing 7.8. While reexamined.

```
1:    // Listing 7.8
2:    // Looping with while
3:
4:    #include <iostream.h>
5:
6:    void main()
7:    {
8:      int counter = 0;
9:
10:     while(counter < 5)
11:     {
12:         counter++;
13:         cout << "Looping!   ";
14:     }
15:
16:     cout << "\nCounter: " << counter << ".\n";
17:   }
```

```
Looping!  Looping!  Looping!  Looping!  Looping!
Counter: 5
```

The condition is set on line 8: counter is initialized to zero. On line 12 counter is tested to see if it is less than 100. Counter is incremented on line 14. On line 15 a simple message is printed, but you can imagine that more important work could be done for each increment of the counter.

A `for` loop combines the three steps of *initialization, test,* and *increment* into one statement. A `for` statement consists of the keyword `for` followed by a pair of parentheses. Within the parentheses are three statements separated by semicolons.

The first statement is the *initialization.* Any legal C++ statement can be put here, but typically this is used to create and initialize a counting variable. Statement 2 is the *test,* and any legal C++ expression can be used here. This serves the same role as the condition in the `while` loop. Statement 3 is the *action.* Typically a value is incremented or decremented, though any legal C++ statement can be put here. Note that statements one and three can be any legal C++ statement, but statement 2 must be an expression—a C++ statement that returns a value. Listing 7.9 demonstrates its use.

Listing 7.9. Demonstrating the `for` loop.

```
1:      // Listing 7.9
2:      // Looping with for
3:
4:      #include <iostream.h>
5:
6:      void main()
7:      {
8:        for (int counter = 0; counter < 5; counter++)
9:          cout << "Looping! ";
10:
11:       cout << "\nCounter: " << counter << ".\n";
12:     }
```

```
Looping!  Looping!  Looping!  Looping!  Looping!
Counter: 5
```

The `for` statement on line 8 combines the initialization of `counter`, the test that `counter` is less than 5, and the increment of `counter` all into one line. The body of the `for` statement is on line 9. Of course, a block could be used here as well.

The *for* Statement

```
for (initialization; test; action )
    statement;
```

The *Initialization* statement is used to initialize the state of a `counter`, or to otherwise prepare for the loop. *test* is any C++ expression and is evaluated each time through the loop. If *test* is true, the *action* in the header is executed (typically the counter is incremented) and then the body of the `for` loop is executed.

Example 1

```
// print hello ten times
for (int i = 0; i<10; i++)
    cout << "Hello! ";
```

Example 2

```
for (int i = 0; i < 10; i++)
{
    cout << "Hello!" << endl;
    cout << "the value of i is: " << i << endl;
}
```

Advanced *for* Loops

For statements are powerful and flexible. The three independent statements (initialization, test, and action) lend themselves to a number of variations.

A `for` loop works in the following sequence:

1. Performs the operations in the initialization.

2. Evaluates the condition.

3. If the condition is true, executes the action statement and the loop.

After each time through the loop repeat steps 2 and 3.

Multiple Initialization and Increments

It is not uncommon to initialize more than one variable, to test a compound logical expression, and to execute more than one statement. The *initialization* and the *action* may be replaced by multiple C++ statements, each separated by a comma. Listing 7.10 demonstrates the initialization and increment of two variables.

Listing 7.10. Demonstrating multiple statements in for loops.

```
1:  //listing 7.10
2:  // demonstrates multiple statements in
3:  // for loops
4:
5:  #include <iostream.h>
6:
7:  void main()
8:  {
```

```
9:        for (int i=0, j=0; i<3; i++, j++)
10:           cout << "i: " << i << " j: " << j << endl;
11:    }
```

```
i: 0  j: 0
i: 1  j: 1
i: 2  j: 2
```

Analysis On line 9 two variables, i and j are each initialized with the value 0. The test (i<3) is evaluated, and since it is true the actions are taken (i and j are incremented). Then the body of the for statement is executed and the values are printed.

Once line 10 completes, the condition is evaluated again, and if it remains true the actions are repeated (i and j are again incremented) and the body of loop is executed again. This continues until the test fails, in which case the action statement is *not* executed, and control falls out of the loop.

Null Statements in *for* Loops

Any or all of the statements in a for loop can be null. To accomplish this, use the semicolon to mark where the statement would have been. To create a for loop which acts exactly like a while loop, leave out the first and third statement. Listing 7.11 illustrates this idea.

Listing 7.11. Null statements in for loops.

```
1:     // Listing 7.11
2:     // For loops with null statements
3:
4:     #include <iostream.h>
5:
6:     void main()
7:     {
8:         int counter = 0;
9:
10:        for( ; counter < 5; )
11:        {
12:            counter++;
13:            cout << "Looping!   ";
14:        }
15:
16:        cout << "\nCounter: " << counter << ".\n";
17:    }
```

7

```
Looping!  Looping!  Looping!  Looping!  Looping!
Counter: 5
```

You may recognize this as exactly like the `while` loop illustrated in listing 7.8! On line 9 the counter variable is initialized. The `for` statement on line 10 does not initialize any values, but it does include a test for `counter < 5`. There is no increment statement, so this loop behaves exactly as if it had been written:

```
while (counter < 5)
```

Once again, C++ gives you a number of ways to accomplish the same thing. No experienced C++ programmer would use a `for` loop in this way, but it does illustrate the flexibility of the `for` statement. In fact, it is possible, using `break` and `continue`, to create a `for` loop with none of the three statements. Listing 7.12 illustrates how.

Listing 7.12. Illustrating empty for loop statement.

```
1:      //Listing 7.12 illustrating
2:      //empty for loop statement
3:
4:      #include <iostream.h>
5:
6:      void main()
7:      {
8:          int counter=0;        // initialization
9:          int max;
10:         cout << "How many hellos?";
11:         cin >> max;
12:         for (;;)               // a for loop that doesn't end
13:         {
14:             if (counter < max)      // test
15:             {
16:               cout << "Hello!\n";
17:               counter++;            // increment
18:             }
19:             else
20:                 break;
21:         }
22:     }
```

```
How many hellos?  3
Hello!
Hello!
Hello!
```

The `for` loop has now been pushed to its absolute limit. Initialization, test, and action have all been taken out of the `for` statement. The initialization is done on line 8, before the `for` loop begins. The test is done in a separate `if` statement on line 14, and if the test succeeds the action, an increment to `counter`, is performed on line 17. If the test fails, breaking out of the loop occurs on line 20.

While this particular program is somewhat absurd, there are times when a `for(;;)` loop or a `while (1)` loop is just what you'll want. You'll see an example of a more reasonable use of such loops when `switch` statements are discussed later today.

Empty *for* Loops

So much can be done in the header of a `for` statement, there are times you won't need the body to do anything at all. In that case, be sure to put a null statement (;) as the body of the loop. The semicolon can be on the same line as the header, but this is easy to overlook. Listing 7.13 illustrates how this is done.

Listing 7.13. Illustrates null statement in `for` loop.

```
1:      //Listing 7.13
2:      //Demonstrates null statement
3:      // as body of for loop
4:
5:      #include <iostream.h>
6:      void main()
7:      {
8:          for (int i = 0; i<5; cout << "i: " << i++ << endl)
9:              ;
10:     }
```

```
i: 0
i: 1
i: 2
i: 3
i: 4
```

The `for` loop on line 8 includes three statements: the initialization statement establishes the counter `i` and initializes it to 0. The condition statement tests for `i<5` and the action statement prints the value in `i` and increments it.

There is nothing left to do in the body of the `for` loop, so the null statement (;) is used. Note that this is not a well-designed `for` loop: the action statement is doing far too much. This would be better rewritten as

```
8:          for (int i = 0; i<5; i++)
9:              cout << "i: " << i << endl;
```

While both do exactly the same thing, this example is easier to understand.

Nested Loops

Loops may be nested, with one loop sitting in the body of another. The inner loop will be executed in full for every execution of the outer loop. Listing 7.14 illustrates writing marks into a matrix using nested `for` loops.

Listing 7.14. Illustrates nested for loops.

```
1:    //Listing 7.14
2:    //Illustrates nested for loops
3:
4:    #include <iostream.h>
5:
6:    void main()
7:    {
8:        int rows, columns;
9:        char theChar;
10:       cout << "How many rows? ";
11:       cin >> rows;
12:       cout << "How many columns? ";
13:       cin >> columns;
14:       cout << "What character? ";
15:       cin >> theChar;
16:       for (int i = 0; i<rows; i++)
17:       {
18:           for (int j = 0; j<columns; j++)
19:               cout << theChar;
20:           cout << "\n";
21:       }
22:   }
```

```
How many rows? 4
How many columns?  12
What character?  x
xxxxxxxxxxxx
xxxxxxxxxxxx
xxxxxxxxxxxx
xxxxxxxxxxxx
```

The user is prompted for the number of rows and columns, and for a character to print. The first for loop, on line 16, initializes a counter (i) to 0 and then the body of the outer for loop is run.

On line 18, the first line of the body of the outer for loop, another for loop is established. A second counter (j) is also initialized to 0, and the body of the inner for loop is executed. On line 19 the chosen character is printed and control returns to the header of the inner for loop. Note that the inner for loop is only one statement (the printing of the character). The condition is tested (j < columns) and if it evaluates true, j is incremented and the next character is printed. This continues until j equals the number of columns.

Once the inner for loop fails its test, in this case after 12 x's are printed, execution falls through to line 20 and a new line is printed. The outer for loop now returns to its header, where *its* condition (i < rows) is tested. If this evaluates true, i is incremented and the body of the loop is executed.

In the second iteration of the outer for loop the inner for loop is started over. Thus j is reinitialized to 0(!) and the entire inner loop is run again.

The important idea here is that by using a nested loop the inner loop is executed for each iteration of the outer loop. Thus the character is printed columns times for each row.

> As an aside, many C++ programmers use the letters i and j as counting variables. This tradition goes all the way back to FORTRAN, in which the letters i, j, k, l, m, and n were the only legal counting variables.
>
> Other programmers prefer to use more descriptive counter variable names, such as Ctr1 and Ctr2. Using i and j in for loop headers should not cause much confusion, however.

Scoping in *for* Loops

You will remember that variables are scoped to the block in which they are created. That is, a local variable is only visible within the block in which it is created. It is important to note that counting variables created in the header of a for loop are scoped to the outer block, not the inner. The implication of this is that if you have two for loops in the same function, you must give them different counter variables or they may interfere with one another.

Summing Up Loops

On Day 5 you learned how to solve the Fibbonacci series problem using recursion. To review, briefly, a Fibbonacci series starts with 1, 1, 2, 3, and all subsequent numbers are the sum of the previous two:

1,1,2,3,5,8,13,21,34...

The Nth Fibbonacci number is the sum of the N-1 and the N-2 Fibbonacci number. The problem solved on Day 5 was finding the value of the Nth Fibbonacci number. This was done with recursion. Listing 7.15 offers a solution using iteration.

Listing 7.15. Solving the Nth Fibonnacci number using iteration.

```
1:    // Listing 7.15
2:    // Demonstrates solving the Nth
3:    // Fibonnacci number using iteration
4:
5:    #include <iostreams.h>
6:
7:    typedef unsigned long int ULONG;
8:
9:    ULONG fib(ULONG position);
10:   void main()
11:   {
12:       ULONG answer, position;
13:       cout << "Which position? ";
14:       cin >> position;
15:       cout << "\n";
16:
17:       answer = fib(position);
18:       cout << answer << " is the ";
19:       cout << position << "th Fibonnacci number.\n";
20:   }
21:
22:   ULONG fib(ULONG n)
23:   {
24:       ULONG minusTwo=1, minusOne=1, answer=2;
25:
26:       if (n < 3)
27:           return 1;
28:
29:       for (n -= 3; n; n—)
30:       {
31:           minusTwo = minusOne;
32:           minusOne = answer;
33:           answer = minusOne + minusTwo;
34:       }
35:
36:       return answer;
37:   }
```

```
Which position? 4
3 is the 4th Fibonnacci number.
Which position? 5
5 is the 5th Fibonnacci number
Which position? 20
6765 is the 20th Fibonnacci number
Which position? 100
3314859971 is the 100th Fibonnacci number
```

Listing 7.15 solves the Fibonnacci series using iteration rather than recursion. This approach is faster, and uses less memory than the recursive solution.

On line 13 the user is asked for the position to check. The function `fib()` is called, which evaluates the position. If it is less than 3 it returns the value 1. Starting with position 3, the function iterates using the following algorithm:

1. Establish the starting position: fill variable `answer` with 2, `minusTwo` with 1 (answer-2) and `minusOne` with 1 (answer-1). Decrement the position by 3, as the first two numbers are handled by the starting position.

2. For every number, count up the Fibonnacci series. This is done by:

    1. Putting the value currently in `minusOne` into `minusTwo`.

    2. Putting the value currently in `answer` into `minusOne`.

    3. Adding `minusOne` and `minusTwo` and putting the sum in `answer`.

    4. Decrementing n.

3. When n reaches 0, return the answer.

This is exactly how you would solve this problem with pencil and paper. If you were asked for the fifth Fibonnacci number, you would write:

```
1, 1, 2,
```

and think, "two more to do." You would then add 2+1 and write 3, and think, "one more to find." Finally you would write 3+2 and the answer would be 5. In effect, you are shifting your attention right one number each time through, and decrementing the number remaining to be found.

Note the condition tested on line 28 (n). This is a C++ idiom, and is exactly equivalent to n != 0. This `for` loop relies on the fact that when n reaches 0 it will evaluate false, because 0 is false in C++. The `for` loop header could have been written:

```
for (n-=3; n>0; n++)
```

which might have been clearer. However, this idiom is so common in C++ there is little sense in fighting it.

Compile, link, and run this program along with the recursive solution offered on Day 5. Try finding position 25 and compare the time it takes each program. Recursion is elegant, but because the function call brings a performance overhead, and because it is called so many times, its performance is noticeably slower than iteration. Microcomputers tend to be optimized for the arithmetic operations, so the iterative solution should be blazingly fast.

switch Statements

On Day 4 you saw how to write `if` and `if/else` statements. These can become quite confusing when nested too deeply, and C++ offers an alternative. Unlike `if`, which evaluates one value, `switch` statements allow you to branch on any of a number of different values. The general form of the `switch` statement is:

```
switch (expression)
{
    case valueOne: statement;
                   break;
    case valueTwo: statement;
                   break;
    ....
    case valueN:   statement;
                   break;
    default:       statement;
}
```

Expression is any legal C++ expression, the *statements* are any legal C++ statements or block of statements. Switch evaluates expression and compares the result to each of the case values. Note, however, that the evaluation is only for equality; relational operators may not be used here, nor can Boolean operations.

If one of the case values matches the expression, execution jumps to those statements and continues to the end of the `switch` block unless a `break` statement is encountered. If nothing matches, execution branches to the optional `default` statement. If there is no default and there is no matching value, execution falls through the `switch` statement and the statement ends.

> **Note:** It is almost always a good idea to have a `default` case in `switch` statements. If you have no other need for the `default`, use it to test for the supposedly impossible case and print out an error message; this can be a tremendous aid in debugging.

It is important to note that if there is no *break* statement at the end of a case statement, execution will fall through to the next case. This is sometimes necessary, but usually is an error. If you decide to let execution fall through, be sure to put a comment indicating that you didn't just forget the break.

Listing 7.16 illustrates use of the `switch` statement.

Listing 7.16. Demonstrating the `switch` statement.

```
1:  //Listing 7.16
2:  // Demonstrates switch statement
3:
4:  #include <iostreams.h>
5:
6:  void main()
7:  {
8:     unsigned short int number;
9:     cout << "Enter a number between 1 and 5: ";
10:    cin >> number;
11:    switch (number)
12:    {
13:       case 0:   cout << "Too small, sorry!";
14:                 break;
15:       case 5:  cout << "Good job!\n";  // fall through
16:       case 4:  cout << "Nice Pick!\n"; // fall through
17:       case 3:  cout << "Excellent!\n"; // fall through
18:       case 2:  cout << "Masterful!\n"; // fall through
19:       case 1:  cout << "Incredible!\n";
20:                break;
21:       default: cout << "Too large!\n";
22:                break;
23:    }
24:    cout << "\n\n";
25: }
```

```
Enter a number between 1 and 5:  3
Excellent!
Masterful!
Incredible!
```

Output

```
Enter a number between 1 and 5: 8
Too large!
```

The user is prompted for a number. That number is given to the `switch` statement. If the number is 0, the case statement on line 13 matches, the message `Too small, sorry!` is printed and the break statement ends the switch. If the value is 5, execution switches to line 15 where a message is printed, and then falls through to line 16, another message is printed, and so forth until hitting the break on line 20.

The net effect of these statements is that for a number between 1 and 5, that many messages are printed. If the value of number is not 0–5 it is assumed to be too large, and the `default` statement is invoked on line 21.

Syntax

The *switch* Statement

```
switch (expression)
{
    case valueOne: statement;
    case valueTwo: statement;
    ....
    case valueN: statement
    default: statement;
}
```

The `switch` statement allows for branching on multiple values of *expression*. The *expression* is evaluated and if it matches any of the `case` values, execution jumps to that line. Execution continues until either the end of the `switch` statement or a `break` statement is encountered.

If *expression* does not match any of the case statements, and if there is a `default` statement, execution switches to the `default` statement, otherwise the `switch` statement ends.

Example 1

```
switch (choice)
{
    choice 0:
            cout << "Zero!" << endl;
            break
    choice 1:
            cout << "One!" << endl;
            break;
    choice 2:
            cout << "Two!" << endl;
    default:
            cout << "Default!" endl;
}
```

Example 2

```
switch (choice)
{
    choice 0:
    choice 1:
    choice 2:
            cout << "Less than 3!";
            break;
    choice 3:
```

```
        cout << "Equals 3!";
        break;
default:
        cout << "greater than 3!";
}
```

Using a *switch* Statement with a Menu

Listing 7.17 returns to the `for(;;)` loop discussed earlier. These loops are also called forever loops, as they will loop forever if a break is not encountered. The forever loop is used to put up a menu, solicit a choice from the user, act on the choice, and then return to the menu. This will continue until the user chooses to exit.

> **Note:** Some programmers like to write
>
> ```
> #define EVER ;;
> for (EVER)
> {
>     // statements...
> }
> ```
>
> Use of `#define` is covered on Day 17, "The Preprocessor."

NEW TERM A *forever loop* is a loop that does not have an exit condition. In order to exit the loop a break statement must be used. Forever loops are also known as eternal loops.

Listing 7.17. Illustrates a forever loop.

```
1:    //Listing 7.17
2:    //Using a forever loop to manage
3:    //user interaction
4:    #include <iostreams.h>
5:
6:    // types & defines
7:    enum BOOL { FALSE, TRUE };
8:    typedef unsigned short int USHORT;
9:
10:   // prototypes
11:   USHORT menu();
12:   void DoTaskOne();
13:   void DoTaskMany(USHORT);
14:
```

continues

Listing 7.17. continued

```
15:    void main()
16:    {
17:
18:        BOOL exit = FALSE;
19:        for (;;)
20:        {
21:            USHORT choice = menu();
22:            switch(choice)
23:            {
24:                case (1):
25:                    DoTaskOne();
26:                    break;
27:                case (2):
28:                    DoTaskMany(2);
29:                    break;
30:                case (3):
31:                    DoTaskMany(3);
32:                    break;
33:                case (4):
34:                    continue;  // redundant!
35:                    break;
36:                case (5):
37:                    exit=TRUE;
38:                    break;
39:                default:
40:                    cout << "Please select again!\n";
41:                    break;
42:            }        // end switch
43:
44:            if (exit)
45:                    break;
46:        }                // end forever
47:    }                    // end main()
48:
49:    USHORT menu()
50:    {
51:        USHORT choice;
52:
53:        cout << " **** Menu ****\n\n";
54:        cout << "(1) Choice one.\n";
55:        cout << "(2) Choice two.\n";
56:        cout << "(3) Choice three.\n";
57:        cout << "(4) Redisplay menu.\n";
58:        cout << "(5) Quit.\n\n";
59:        cout << ": ";
60:        cin >> choice;
61:        return choice;
62:    }
63:
64:    void DoTaskOne()
65:    {
66:        cout << "Task One!\n";
67:    }
```

```
68:
69:    void DoTaskMany(USHORT which)
70:    {
71:        if (which == 2)
72:            cout << "Task Two!\n";
73:        else
74:            cout << "Task Three!\n";
75:    }
```

```
**** Menu ****
(1) Choice one.
(2) Choice two.
(3) Choice three.
(4) Redisplay menu
(5) Quit.
: 1
Task One!
 **** Menu ****
(1) Choice one.
(2) Choice two.
(3) Choice three.
(4) Redisplay menu
(5) Quit.
: 3
Task Three!
 **** Menu ****
(1) Choice one.
(2) Choice two.
(3) Choice three.
(4) Redisplay menu
(5) Quit.
: 5
```

This program brings together a number of concepts from today and previous days. It also shows a common use of the switch statement. On line 7, an enumeration, BOOL is created, with two possible values, FALSE which equals 0 as it should, and TRUE which equals 1. On line 8, typedef is used to create an alias, USHORT, for unsigned short int.

The forever loop begins on 19. The menu() function is called, which prints the menu to the screen and returns the user's selection. The switch statement, which begins on line 22 and ends on line 42, switches on the user's choice.

If the user enters 1, execution jumps to the case 1: statement on line 24. Line 25 switches execution to the DoTaskOne() function, which prints a message and returns. On its return, execution resumes on line 26, where the break ends the switch statement, and execution falls through to line 43. On line 44 the variable exit is evaluated. If it evaluates true, the break on line 45 will be executed and the for(;;) loop will end, but if it evaluates false, execution resumes at the top of the loop on line 19.

Note that the `continue` statement on line 34 is redundant. If it were left out, and the `break` statement were encountered, the `switch` would end, `exit` would evaluate false, the loop would reiterate and the menu would be reprinted. The `continue` does, however, bypass the test of `exit`.

DO	DON'T

DO use `switch` statements to avoid deeply nested `if` statements.

DON'T forget `break` at the end of each case unless you wish to fall through.

DO carefully document all intentional fall-through cases.

DO put a default case in `switch` statements, if only to detect seemingly impossible situations.

Summary

There are a number of different ways of causing a C++ program to loop. `While` loops check a condition, and if it is true, execute the statements in the body of the loop. `Do...while` loops execute the body of the loop and then test the condition. `For` loops initialize a value, then test an expression. If expression is true, the final statement in the `for` header is executed as is the body of the loop. Each subsequent time through the loop the expression is tested again.

The `goto` statement is generally avoided, as it causes an unconditional jump to a seemingly arbitrary location in the code, and thus makes source code difficult to understand and maintain. `Continue` causes `while`, `do...while`, and `for` loops to start over, and `break` causes `while`, `do...while`, `for`, and `switch` statements to end.

Q&A

Q How do you choose between `if/else` and `switch`?

A If there are more than just one or two `else` clauses, and all are testing the same value, consider using a `switch` statement.

Q How do you choose between `while` and `do...while`?

A If the body of the loop should always execute at least once, consider a `do...while` loop, otherwise try to use the `while` loop.

Q How do you choose between `while` and `for`?

A If you are initializing a counting variable, testing that variable and incrementing it each time through the loop, consider the `for` loop. If your variable is already initialized, and is not incremented on each loop, a `while` loop may be the better choice.

Q How do you choose between recursion and iteration?

A Some problems cry out for recursion, but most problems will yield to iteration as well. Put recursion in your back pocket, it may come in handy someday.

Q Is it better to use `while(1)` or `for(;;)`?

A This is no significant difference.

Workshop

The Workshop provides quiz questions to help you solidify your understanding of the material covered, as well as exercises to provide you with experience in using what you've learned. Try to answer the quiz and exercise questions before checking the answers in Appendix D, and make sure you understand the answers before continuing to the next chapter.

Quiz

1. How do I initialize more than one variable in a `for` loop?

2. Why is `goto` avoided?

3. Is it possible to write a `for` loop with a body that is never executed?

4. Is it possible to nest `while` loops within `for` loops?

5. Is it possible to create a loop that never ends? Give an example.

6. What happens if you create a loop that never ends?

Exercises

1. What is the value of x when the `for` loop completes?

   ```
   for (int x = 0; x < 100; x++)
   ```

2. Write a nested `for` loop which prints a 10×10 pattern of 0s.

3. Write a `for` statement to count from 100 to 200 by 2s.

4. Write a `while` loop to count from 100 to 200 by 2s.

5. Write a `do...while` loop to count from 100 to 200 by 2s.

6. **BUG BUSTERS:** What is wrong with this code?

```cpp
int counter = 0
while (counter < 10)
{
    cout << "counter: " << counter;
}
```

7. **BUG BUSTERS:** What is wrong with this code?

```cpp
for (int counter = 0; counter < 10; counter++);
    cout << counter << " ";
```

8. **BUG BUSTERS:** What is wrong with this code?

```cpp
int counter = 100;
while (counter < 10)
{
    cout << "counter now: " << counter;
    counter--;
}
```

9. **BUG BUSTERS:** What is wrong with this code?

```cpp
cout << "Enter a number between 0 and 5: ";
cin >> theNumber;
switch (theNumber)
{
  case 0:
        doZero();
  case 1:                // fall through
  case 2:                // fall through
  case 3:                // fall through
  case 4:                // fall through
  case 5:
        doOneToFive();
        break;
  default:
        doDefault();
        break;
}
```

Week In Review Listing

```
1:      #include <iostream.h>
2:
3:      typedef unsigned short int USHORT;
4:      typedef unsigned long int ULONG;
5:      enum BOOL { FALSE, TRUE};
6:      enum CHOICE { DrawRect = 1, GetArea, GetPerim,
        ➡ChangeDimensions, Quit};
7:
8:      // Rectangle class declaration
9:      class Rectangle
10:     {
11:       public:
12:         // constructors
13:         Rectangle(USHORT width, USHORT height);
14:         ~Rectangle();
15:
16:         // accessors
17:         USHORT GetHeight() const { return
          ➡itsHeight; }
18:         USHORT GetWidth() const { return itsWidth;
          ➡}
19:         ULONG GetArea() const { return itsHeight *
          ➡itsWidth; }
20:         ULONG GetPerim() const { return 2*itsHeight
          ➡+ 2*itsWidth; }
21:         void SetSize(USHORT newWidth, USHORT
          ➡newHeight);
22:
```

```
23:          // Misc. methods
24:          void DrawShape() const;
25:
26:      private:
27:          USHORT itsWidth;
28:          USHORT itsHeight;
29:     };
30:
31:     // Class method implementations
32:     void Rectangle::SetSize(USHORT newWidth, USHORT newHeight)
33:     {
34:         itsWidth = newWidth;
35:         itsHeight = newHeight;
36:     }
37:
38:
39:     Rectangle::Rectangle(USHORT width, USHORT height):
40:         itsWidth(width),        // initializations
41:         itsHeight(height)
42:         {}                      // empty body
43:
44:     Rectangle::~Rectangle() {}
45:
46:     USHORT DoMenu();
47:     void DoDrawRect(Rectangle);
48:     void DoGetArea(Rectangle);
49:     void DoGetPerim(Rectangle);
50:
51:     void main ()
52:     {
53:         // initialize a rectangle to 10,20
54:         Rectangle theRect(30,5);
55:
56:         USHORT choice = DrawRect;
57:         USHORT fQuit = FALSE;
58:
59:         while (!fQuit)
60:         {
61:            choice = DoMenu();
62:            if (choice < DrawRect || choice >  Quit)
63:            {
64:               cout << "\nInvalid Choice, please try again.\n\n";
65:               continue;
66:            }
67:            switch (choice)
68:            {
69:            case  DrawRect:
70:               DoDrawRect(theRect);
71:               break;
72:            case GetArea:
73:               DoGetArea(theRect);
74:               break;
75:            case GetPerim:
76:               DoGetPerim(theRect);
77:               break;
78:            case ChangeDimensions:
79:               USHORT newLength, newWidth;
```

```
80:                cout << "\nNew width: ";
81:                cin >> newWidth;
82:                cout << "New height: ";
83:                cin >> newLength;
84:                theRect.SetSize(newWidth, newLength);
85:                DoDrawRect(theRect);
86:                break;
87:            case Quit:
88:                fQuit = TRUE;
89:                cout << "\nExiting...\n\n";
90:                break;
91:            default:
92:                cout << "Error in choice!\n";
93:                fQuit = TRUE;
94:                break;
95:        }    // end switch
96:    }        // end while
97: }           // end main
98:
99:
100:    USHORT DoMenu()
101:    {
102:       USHORT choice;
103:          cout << "\n\n    *** Menu *** \n";
104:          cout << "(1) Draw Rectangle\n";
105:          cout << "(2) Area\n";
106:          cout << "(3) Perimeter\n";
107:          cout << "(4) Resize\n";
108:          cout << "(5) Quit\n";
109:
110:      cin >> choice;
111:      return choice;
112:    }
113:
114:    void DoDrawRect(Rectangle theRect)
115:    {
116:       USHORT height = theRect.GetHeight();
117:       USHORT width = theRect.GetWidth();
118:
119:       for (USHORT i = 0; i<height; i++)
120:       {
121:          for (USHORT j = 0; j< width; j++)
122:             cout << "*";
123:          cout << "\n";
124:       }
125:    }
126:
127:
128:    void DoGetArea(Rectangle theRect)
129:    {
130:       cout << "Area: " <<  theRect.GetArea() << endl;
131:    }
132:
133:    void DoGetPerim(Rectangle theRect)
134:    {
135:       cout << "Perimeter: " <<  theRect.GetPerim() << endl;
136:    }
```

```
(0)Quit (1)Car (2)Plane: 1
New PartNumber?: 8394
Model Year?: 92
(0)Quit (1)Car (2)Plane: 1
New PartNumber?: 234
Model Year?: 91
(0)Quit (1)Car (2)Plane: 2
New PartNumber?: 7683
Engine Number?: 94
(0)Quit (1)Car (2)Plane: 2
New PartNumber?: 32
Engine Number?: 374693
(0)Quit (1)Car (2)Plane: 2
New PartNumber?: 45
Engine Number?: 374693
(0)Quit (1)Car (2)Plane: 1
New PartNumber?: 324
Model Year?: 92
(0)Quit (1)Car (2)Plane: 0

Part Number: 32
Engine No.: 47013

Part Number: 45
Engine No.: 47013

Part Number: 234
Model Year: 91

Part Number: 234
Model Year: 92

Part Number: 7683
Engine No.: 94

Part Number: 8394
Model Year: 92
```

Analysis This program utilizes most of the skills you learned this week. You should not only be able to enter, compile, link, and run this program, but also understand what it does and how it works, based on the work you did this week.

The first six lines set up the new types and definitions that will be used throughout the program.

Lines 8–29 declare the Rectangle class. There are public accessor methods for obtaining and setting the width and height of the rectangle, as well as for computing the area and perimeter. Lines 31–44 contain the class function definitions that were not declared inline.

The function prototypes, for the non-class member functions, are on lines 46–49 and the program itself begins on line 51. The essence of this program is to generate a rectangle,

then to print out a menu offering five options: Draw the rectangle, determine its area, determine its perimeter, resize the rectangle, or quit.

A flag is set on line 57, and when that flag is not set to TRUE the menu loop continues. The flag is only set to TRUE if the user picks "Quit" from the menu.

Each of the other choices, with the exception of ChangeDimensions, calls out to a function. This makes the switch statement cleaner. ChangeDimensions *cannot* call out to a function because it must change the dimensions of the rectangle. If the rectangle were passed (by value) to a function such as DoChangeDimensions(), the dimensions would be changed on the local copy of the rectangle in DoChangeDimensions(), and not on the rectangle in main(). On Days 8 and 10 you'll learn how to overcome this restriction, but for now the change is made in the main() function.

Note how the use of an enumeration makes the switch statement much cleaner and easier to understand. Had the switch depended on the numeric choices (1–5) of the user, you would have to constantly refer back to the description of the menu to see which pick was which.

On line 62 the user's choice is checked to make sure it is in range. If not, an error message is printed and the menu is reprinted. Note that the switch statement includes an "impossible" default condition. This is an aid in debugging. If the program is working that statement can never be reached.

Week In Review

Congratulations! You've completed the first week! Now you can create and understand sophisticated C++ programs. Of course, there's much more to do, and next week starts with one of the most difficult concepts in C++: *pointers*. Don't give up now, you're about to delve deep into the meaning and use of object-oriented programming, virtual functions, and many of the advanced features of this powerful language.

Take a break, bask in the glory of your accomplishment, then turn the page to start Week 2.

You have finished the first week of learning how to program in C++. By now you should feel comfortable entering programs, using your compiler, and thinking about objects, classes, and program flow.

Where You Are Going

Week 2 begins with pointers. Pointers are traditionally a difficult subject for new C++ programmers, but you will find them explained fully and clearly, and they should not be a stumbling block. Day 9 teaches references, which are a close cousin to pointers. On Day 10 you will see how to overload functions, and on Day 11 you will learn how to work with arrays and collections. Day 12 introduces inheritance, a fundamental concept in object-oriented programming. Day 13 extends the lessons of Day 12 to discuss polymorphism, and Day 14 ends the week with a discussion of static functions and friends.

8

Pointers

One of the most powerful tools available to a C++ programmer is the ability to manipulate computer memory directly by using pointers. Today you will learn:

☐ What pointers are.

☐ How to declare and use pointers.

☐ What the free store is and how to manipulate memory.

Pointers present two special challenges when learning C++: They can be somewhat confusing, and it isn't immediately obvious why they are needed. This chapter explains how pointers work, step by step. You will understand the need for pointers, however, only as the book progresses.

What Is a Pointer?

NEW☞ TERM A *pointer* is a variable that holds a memory address.

To understand pointers, you must know a little about computer memory. Computer memory is divided into sequentially numbered memory locations. Each variable is located at a unique location in memory, known as its address. (This is discussed in the "Extra Credit" section following Day 5.) Figure 8.1 shows a schematic representation of the storage of an unsigned long integer variable the Age.

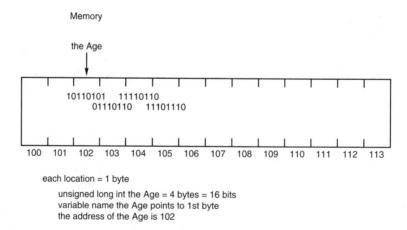

Memory

the Age

10110101 11110110
01110110 11101110

100 101 102 103 104 105 106 107 108 109 110 111 112 113

each location = 1 byte

unsigned long int the Age = 4 bytes = 16 bits
variable name the Age points to 1st byte
the address of the Age is 102

Figure 8.1. *A schematic representation of* the Age.

Different computers number this memory using different, complex schemes. Usually programmers don't need to know the particular address of any given variable, because the compiler handles the details. If you want this information, though, you can use the address of operator (&), which is illustrated in Listing 8.1.

Listing 8.1. Demonstrating address of variables.

```
1:    // Listing 8.1 Demonstrates address of operator
2:    // and addresses of local variables
3:
4:    #include <iostream.h>
5:
6:    void main()
7:    {
8:        unsigned short shortVar=5;
9:        unsigned long  longVar=65535;
10:       long sVar = -65535;
11:
12:       cout << "shortVar:\t" << shortVar << " Address of shortVar:\t" <<  &shortVar
          ➥<< "\n";
13:
14:       cout << "longVar:\t"  << longVar  << " Address of longVar:\t"  <<  &longVar
          ➥<< "\n";
15:
16:       cout << "sVar:\t"     << sVar     << " Address of sVar:\t"     <<  &sVar
          ➥<< "\n";
17:
18:   }
```

```
shortVar: 5       Address of shortVar: 0x8fc9:fff4
longVar:  65535   Address of longVar:  0x8fc9:fff2
sVar:     -65535  Address of sVar:     0x8fc9:ffee
```

(Your printout may look different.)

Three variables are declared and initialized: a short in line 8, an unsigned long in line 9, and a long in line 10. Their values and addresses are printed in lines 12-16, by using the address of operator (&).

The value of shortVar is 5—as expected—and its address is 0x8fc9:fff4 when run on my 80386-based computer. This complicated address is computer-specific, and may change slightly each time the program is run. Your results will be different. What doesn't change, however, is that the difference in the first two addresses is two bytes if your computer uses two-byte short integers. The difference between the second and third is four bytes if your computer uses four-byte long integers. Figure 8.2 illustrates how the variables in this program would be stored in memory.

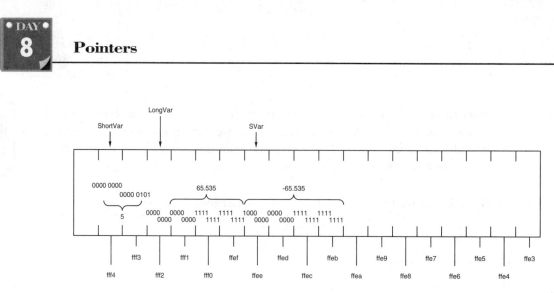

Figure 8.2. *Illustration of variable storage.*

There is no reason why you need to know the actual numeric value of the address of each variable. What you care about is that each one has an address and that the right amount of memory is set aside. You tell the compiler how much memory to allow for your variables by declaring the variable type; the compiler automatically assigns an address for it. For example, a `long` integer is typically four bytes, meaning that the variable has an address to four bytes of memory.

Storing the Address in a Pointer

Every variable has an address. Even without knowing the specific address of a given variable, you can store that address in a pointer.

For example, suppose that `howOld` is an integer. To declare a pointer called `pAge` to hold its address, you would write

```
int *pAge = 0;
```

This declares `pAge` to be a `pointer to int`. That is, `pAge` is declared to hold the address of an `int`.

Note that `pAge` is a variable like any of the variables. When you declare an integer variable (type `int`), it is set up to hold an integer. When you declare a pointer variable like `pAge`, it is set up to hold an address. `pAge` is just a different type of variable.

In this example, `pAge` is initialized to zero. A pointer whose value is zero is called a null pointer. All pointers, when they are created, should be initialized to something. If you don't know what you want to assign to the pointer, assign 0. A pointer that is not initialized is called a *wild pointer*. Wild pointers are very dangerous.

> **Note:** Practice safe computing: Initialize your pointers!

If you do initialize the pointer to zero, you must specifically assign the address of howOld to pAge. Here's an example that shows how to do that:

```
unsigned short int howOld = 50;      // make a variable
unsigned short int * pAge = 0;       // make a pointer
pAge = &howOld;                      // put howOld's address in pAge
```

The first line creates a variable—howOld, whose type is unsigned short int—and initializes it with the value 50. The second line declares pAge to be a pointer to type unsigned short int and initializes it to zero. You know that pAge is a pointer because of the asterisk (*) after the variable type and before the variable name.

The third and final line assigns the address of howOld to the pointer pAge. You can tell that the address of howOld is being assigned because of the address of operator (&). If the address of operator had not been used, the value of howOld would have been assigned. That might—or might not—have been a valid address.

At this point, pAge has as its value the address of howOld. HowOld, in turn, has the value 50. You could have accomplished this with one fewer step, as in

```
unsigned short int howOld = 50;          // make a variable
unsigned short int * pAge = &howOld;     // make pointer to howOld
```

pAge is a pointer that now contains the address of the howOld variable. Using pAge, you can actually determine the value of howOld, which in this case is 50. Accessing howOld by using the pointer pAge is called *indirection* because you are indirectly accessing howOld by means of pAge. Later today you will see how to use indirection to access a variable's value.

NEW TERM *Indirection* means accessing the value at the address held by a pointer. The pointer provides an indirect way to get the value held at that address.

Pointer Names

Pointers can have any name that is legal for other variables. This book follows the convention of naming all pointers with an initial p, as in pAge or pNumber.

The Indirection Operator

The indirection operator (*) is also called the dereference operator. When a pointer is dereferenced, the value at the address stored by the pointer is retrieved.

Normal variables provide direct access to their own values. If you create a new variable of type `unsigned short int` called `yourAge`, and you want to assign the value in `howOld` to that new variable, you would write

```
unsigned short int yourAge;
yourAge = howOld;
```

A pointer provides indirect access to the value of the variable whose address it stores. To assign the value in `howOld` to the new variable `yourAge` by way of the pointer `pAge`, you would write

```
unsigned short int yourAge;
yourAge = *pAge;
```

The indirection operator (*) in front of the variable `pAge` means "the value stored at." This assignment says, "Take the value stored at the address in `pAge` and assign it to `yourAge`."

> **Note:** The indirection operator (*) is used in two distinct ways with pointers: declaration and dereference. When a pointer is declared, the star indicates that it is a pointer, not a normal variable. For example,
>
> ```
> unsigned short * pAge = 0;     // make a pointer to an unsigned short
> ```
>
> When the pointer is dereferenced, the indirection operator indicates that the value at the memory location stored in the pointer is to be accessed, rather than the address itself.
>
> ```
> *pAge = 5;                 // assign 5 to the value at pAge
> ```
>
> Also note that this same character (*) is used as the multiplication operator. The compiler knows which operator to call based on context.

Pointers, Addresses, and Variables

It is important to distinguish between a pointer, the address that the pointer holds, and the value at the address held by the pointer. This is the source of much of the confusion about pointers.

Consider the following code fragment:

```
int theVariable = 5;
int * pPointer = &theVariable ;
```

theVariable is declared to be an integer variable initialized with the value 5. pPointer is declared to be a pointer to an integer; it is initialized with the address of theVariable. pPointer is the pointer. The address that pPointer holds is the address of theVariable. The value at the address that pPointer holds is 5. Figure 8.3 shows a schematic representation of theVariable and pPointer.

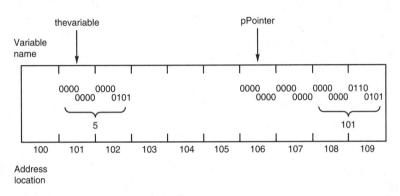

Figure 8.3. *A schematic representation of memory.*

Manipulating Data by Using Pointers

Once a pointer is assigned the address of a variable, you can use that pointer to access the data in that variable. Listing 8.2 demonstrates how the address of a local variable is assigned to a pointer and how the pointer manipulates the values in that variable.

Listing 8.2. Manipulating data by using pointers.

```
1:     // Listing 8.2 Using pointers
2:
3:     #include <iostream.h>
4:
5:     typedef unsigned short int USHORT;
6:     void main()
7:     {
8:        USHORT myAge;           // a variable
9:        USHORT * pAge = 0;      // a pointer
10:       myAge = 5;
11:       cout << "myAge: " << myAge << "\n";
12:
13:       pAge = &myAge;          // assign address of myAge to pAge
14:
15:       cout << " *pAge: " << *pAge << "\n\n";
16:
```

Listing 8.2. continued

```
17:        cout << "*pAge = 7\n";
18:
19:        *pAge = 7;           // sets myAge to 7
20:
21:        cout << "*pAge: " << *pAge << "\n";
22:        cout << "myAge: " << myAge << "\n\n";
23:
24:
25:        cout << "myAge = 9\n";
26:
27:        myAge = 9;
28:
29:        cout << "myAge: " << myAge << "\n";
30:        cout << "*pAge: " << *pAge << "\n";
31:
32:    }
```

```
myAge: 5
*pAge: 5

*pAge = 7
*pAge: 7
myAge: 7

myAge =9
myAge: 9
*pAge: 9
```

Analysis This program declares two variables: an unsigned short myAge and a pointer to pAge, a pointer to the unsigned short myAge. myAge is assigned the value 5 in line 10; this is verified by the printout in line 11.

In line 13, pAge is assigned the address of myAge. In line 15, pAge is dereferenced and printed, showing that the value at the address that pAge stores is the 5 stored in myAge. In line 17, the value 7 is assigned to the variable at the address stored in pAge. This sets myAge to 7, and the printouts in lines 21–22 confirm this.

In line 27, the value 9 is assigned to the variable myAge. This value is obtained directly in line 29 and indirectly—by dereferencing pAge—in line 30.

Examining the Address

Pointers enable you to manipulate addresses without ever knowing their real value. After today, you'll take it on faith that when you assign the address of a variable to a pointer, it really has the address of that variable as its value. But just this once, why not check to make sure? Listing 8.3 illustrates this idea.

Listing 8.3. Finding out what is stored in pointers.

```
1:      // Listing 8.3 What is stored in a pointer.
2:
3:      #include <iostream.h>
4:
5:      typedef unsigned short int USHORT;
6:      void main()
7:      {
8:         unsigned short int myAge = 5, yourAge = 10;
9:         unsigned short int * pAge = &myAge;   // a pointer
10:
11:        cout << "myAge:\t" << myAge <<  "\tyourAge:\t" << yourAge << "\n";
12:        cout << "&myAge:\t" << &myAge <<  "\t&yourAge:\t" << &yourAge <<"\n";
13:
14:        cout << "pAge:\t" << pAge << "\n";
15:        cout << "*pAge:\t" << *pAge << "\n";
16:
17:        pAge = &yourAge;         // reassign the pointer
18:
19:        cout << "myAge:\t" << myAge <<  "\tyourAge:\t" << yourAge << "\n";
20:        cout << "&myAge:\t" << &myAge <<  "\t&yourAge:\t" << &yourAge <<"\n";
21:
22:        cout << "pAge:\t" << pAge << "\n";
23:        cout << "*pAge:\t" << *pAge << "\n";
24:
25:        cout << "&pAge:\t" << &pAge << "\n";
26:     }
```

```
myAge:      5              yourAge:  10
&myAge:     0xfb3fff4      &yourAge: 0xfb3fff2
pAge:       0xfd1:fff4
*pAge:      5
myAge:      5              yourAge:  10
&myAge:     0xfb3fff4      &yourAge: 0xfb3fff2
pAge:       0xfd1:fff2
*pAge:      10
&pAge:      0xfd1:fff0
```

(Your output may look different.)

In line 8, myAge and yourAge are declared to be variables of type unsigned short integer. In line 9, pAge is declared to be a pointer to an unsigned short integer, and it is initialized with the address of the variable myAge.

Lines 11 and 12 print the values and the addresses of myAge and yourAge. Line 14 prints the contents of pAge, which is the address of myAge. Line 15 prints the result of dereferencing pAge, which prints the value at pAge—the value in myAge, or 5.

This is the essence of pointers. Line 14 shows that pAge stores the address of myAge, and line 15 shows how to get the value stored in myAge by dereferencing the pointer pAge. Make sure that you understand this fully, before you go on. Study the code and look at the output.

In line 17, pAge is reassigned to point to the address of yourAge. The values and addresses are printed again. The output shows that pAge now has the address of the variable yourAge and that dereferencing obtains the value in yourAge.

Line 25 prints the address of pAge itself. Like any variable, it too has an address, and that address can be stored in a pointer. (Assigning the address of a pointer to another pointer will be discussed shortly.)

DO	DON'T

DO use the indirection operator (*) to access the data stored at the address in a pointer.

DO initialize all pointers either to a valid address or to null (0).

DO remember the difference between the address in a pointer and the value at that address.

Syntax

Pointers

To declare a pointer, write the type of the variable or object whose address will be stored in the pointer, followed by the pointer operator (*) and the name of the pointer. For example,

```
unsigned short int * pPointer = 0;
```

To assign or initialize a pointer, prepend the name of the variable whose address is being assigned with the address of operator (&). For example,

```
unsigned short int theVariable = 5;
unsigned short int * pPointer = & theVariable;
```

To dereference a pointer, prepend the pointer name with the dereference operator (*). For example,

```
unsigned short int theValue = *pPointer
```

Why Would You Use Pointers?

So far you've seen step-by-step details of a variable's address to a pointer. In practice, though, you would never do this. After all, why bother with a pointer when you already have a variable with access to that value? The only reason for this kind of pointer manipulation of an automatic variable is to demonstrate how pointers work. Now that you are comfortable with the syntax of pointers, you can put them to good use. Pointers are used, most often, for three tasks:

☐ Managing data on the free store.

☐ Accessing class member data and functions.

☐ Passing variables by reference to functions.

This rest of this chapter focuses on managing data on the free store and accessing class member data and functions. Tomorrow you will learn about passing variables by reference.

The Stack and the Free Store

In the "Extra Credit" section following the discussion of functions in Day 5, five areas of memory are mentioned:

> Global name space
> The free store
> Registers
> Code space
> The stack

Local variables are on the stack, along with function parameters. Code is in code space, of course, and global variables are in global name space. The registers are used for internal housekeeping functions, such as keeping track of the top of the stack and the instruction pointer. Just about all remaining memory is given over to the free store, which is sometimes referred to as the heap.

The problem with local variables is that they don't persist: When the function returns, the local variables are thrown away. Global variables solve that problem at the cost of unrestricted access throughout the program—which leads to the creation of code that is difficult to understand and maintain. Putting data in the free store solves both of these problems.

You can think of the free store as a massive section of memory in which thousands of sequentially numbered cubbyholes lie waiting for your data. You can't label these cubbyholes, though, as you can with the stack. You must ask for the address of the cubbyhole's hole that you reserve and then stash that address away in a pointer.

One way to think about this is with an analogy: A friend gives you the 800 number for Acme Mail Order. You go home and program your telephone with that number, and then you throw away the piece of paper with the number on it. If you push the button, a telephone rings somewhere, and Acme Mail Order answers. You don't remember the number, and you don't know where the other telephone is located, but the button gives you access to Acme Mail Order. Acme Mail Order is your data on the free store. You don't know where it is, but you know how to get to it. You access it by using its address—in this case, the telephone number. You don't have to know that number; you just have to put it into a pointer—the button. The pointer gives you access to your data without bothering you with the details.

The stack is cleaned automatically when a function returns. All the local variables go out of scope, and they are removed from the stack. The free store is not cleaned until your program ends, and it is your responsibility to free any memory that you've reserved when you are done with it.

The advantage to the free store is that the memory you reserve remains available until you explicitly free it. If you reserve memory on the free store while in a function, the memory is still available when the function returns.

The advantage of accessing memory in this way, rather than using global variables, is that only functions with access to the pointer have access to the data. This provides a tightly controlled interface to that data, and it eliminates the problem of one function changing that data in unexpected and unanticipated ways.

For this to work, you must be able to create a pointer to an area on the free store and to pass that pointer among functions. The following sections describe how to do this.

new

You allocate memory on the free store in C++ by using the new keyword. new is followed by the type of the object that you want to allocate so that the compiler knows how much memory is required. Therefore, new unsigned short int allocates two bytes in the free store, and new long allocates four.

The return value from new is a memory address. It must be assigned to a pointer. To create an unsigned short on the free store, you might write

```
unsigned short int * pPointer;
pPointer = new unsigned short int;
```

You can, of course, initialize the pointer at its creation with

```
unsigned short int * pPointer = new unsigned short int;
```

In either case, pPointer now points to an unsigned short int on the free store. You can use this like any other pointer to a variable and assign a value into that area of memory by writing

```
*pPointer = 72;
```

This means, "Put 72 at the value in pPointer," or "Assign the value 72 to the area on the free store to which pPointer points."

If new cannot create memory on the free store—memory is, after all, a limited resource—it returns the null pointer. You *must* check your pointer for null each time you request new memory.

 Warning: Each time you allocate memory using the new keyword, you must check to make sure the pointer is not null.

delete

When you are finished with your area of memory, you must call delete on the pointer. delete returns the memory to the free store. Remember that the pointer itself—as opposed to the memory to which it points—is a local variable. When the function in which it is declared returns, that pointer goes out of scope and is lost. The memory allocated with the new is not freed automatically, however. That memory becomes unavailable—a situation called a *memory leak*. It's called a memory leak because that memory can't be recovered until the program ends. It is as though the memory has leaked out of your computer.

To restore the memory to the free store, you use the keyword delete. For example,

```
delete pPointer;
```

When you delete the pointer, what you are really doing is freeing up the memory whose address is stored in the pointer. You are saying, "Return to the free store the memory that this pointer points to." The pointer is still a pointer, and it can be reassigned. Listing 8.4 demonstrates allocating a variable on the heap, using that variable, and deleting it.

 Warning: When you call delete on a pointer, the memory it points to is freed. Calling delete on that pointer again will crash your program! When

you delete a pointer, set it to zero (null). Calling `delete` on a null pointer is guaranteed to be safe. For example:

```
Animal *pDag = new Animal;
delete pDog; //frees the memory
  pDog = 0; //sets pointer to null
  //...
delete pDog; //harmless
```

Listing 8.4. Allocating, using, and deleting pointers.

```
1:      // Listing 8.4
2:      // Allocating and deleting a pointer
3:
4:      #include <iostream.h>
5:      void main()
6:      {
7:         int localVariable = 5;
8:         int * pLocal= &localVariable;
9:         int * pHeap = new int;
10:        if (pHeap == NULL)
11:         {
12:             cout << "Error! No memory for pHeap!!";
13:             return;
14:         }
15:        *pHeap = 7;
16:        cout << "localVariable: " << localVariable << "\n";
17:        cout << "*pLocal: " << *pLocal << "\n";
18:        cout << "*pHeap: " << *pHeap << "\n";
19:        delete pHeap;
20:        pHeap = new int;
21:        if (pHeap == NULL)
22:        {
23:             cout << "Error! No memory for pHeap!!";
24:             return;
25:        }
26:        *pHeap = 9;
27:        cout << "*pHeap: " << *pHeap << "\n";
28:        delete pHeap;
29:      }
```

```
localVariable: 5
*pLocal: 5
*pHeap: 7
*pHeap: 9
```

Line 7 declares and initializes a local variable. Line 8 declares and initializes a pointer with the address of the local variable. Line 9 declares another pointer but initializes it with the result obtained from calling `new int`. This allocates space on the free store for an `int`. Line 10 verifies that memory was allocated and the pointer is valid (not null). If no memory can be allocated, the pointer is null and an error message is printed.

To keep things simple, this error checking often won't be reproduced in future programs, but you *must* include some sort of error checking in your own programs.

Line 15 assigns the value 7 to the newly allocated memory. Line 16 prints the value of the local variable, and line 18 prints the value pointed to by `pLocal`. As expected, these are the same. Line 19 prints the value pointed to by `pHeap`. It shows that the value assigned in line 15 is, in fact, accessible.

In line 19, the memory allocated in line 9 is returned to the free store by a call to `delete`. This frees the memory and disassociates the pointer from that memory. `pHeap` is now free to point to other memory. It is reassigned in lines 20 and 26, and line 27 prints the result. Line 28 restores that memory to the free store.

Although line 28 is redundant—the end of the program would have returned that memory—it is a good idea to free this memory explicitly. If the program changes or is extended, it will be beneficial that this step was already taken care of.

Memory Leaks

Another way you might inadvertently create a memory leak is by reassigning your pointer before deleting the memory to which it points. Consider this code fragment:

```
1:    unsigned short int * pPointer = new unsigned short int;
2:    *pPointer = 72;
3:    pPointer = new unsigned short int;
4:    *pPointer = 84;
```

Line 1 creates `pPointer` and assigns it the address of an area on the free store. Line 2 stores the value 72 in that area of memory. Line 3 reassigns `pPointer` to another area of memory. Line 4 places the value 84 in that area. The original area—in which the value 72 is now held—is unavailable because the pointer to that area of memory has been reassigned. There is no way to access that original area of memory, nor is there any way to free it before the program ends.

The code should have been written like this:

```
1: unsigned short int * pPointer = new unsigned short int;
2: *pPointer = 72;
3: delete pPointer;
```

```
4: pPointer = new unsigned short int;
5: *pPointer = 84;
```

Now the memory originally pointed to by `pPointer` is deleted—and thus freed—in line 4.

> **Note:** For every time in your program that you call `new`, there should be a call to `delete`. It is important to keep track of which pointer owns an area of memory and to ensure that the memory is returned to the free store when you are done with it.

Creating Objects on the Free Store

Just as you can create a pointer to an integer, you can create a pointer to any object. If you have declared an object of type `Cat`, you can declare a pointer to that class and instantiate a `Cat` object on the free store, just as you can make one on the stack. The syntax is the same as for integers:

```
Cat *pCat = new Cat;
```

This calls the default constructor—the constructor that takes no parameters. The constructor is called whenever an object is created—on the stack or on the free store.

Deleting Objects

When you call `delete` on a pointer to an object on the free store, that object's destructor is called before the memory is released. This gives your class a chance to clean up, just as it does for objects destroyed on the stack. Listing 8.5 illustrates creating and deleting objects on the free store.

Listing 8.5. Creating and deleting objects on the free store.

```
1:    // Listing 8.5
2:    // Creating objects on the free store
3:
4:    #include <iostream.h>
5:
6:    class SimpleCat
7:    {
8:    public:
9:          SimpleCat();
10           ~SimpleCat();
```

```
11      private:
12              int itsAge;
13      };
14
15      SimpleCat::SimpleCat()
16      {
17              cout << "Constructor called.\n";
18              itsAge = 1;
19      }
20
21      SimpleCat::~SimpleCat()
22      {
23              cout << "Destructor called.\n";
24      }
25
26      void main()
27      {
28              cout << "SimpleCat Frisky...\n";
29              SimpleCat Frisky;
30              cout << "SimpleCat *pRags = new SimpleCat...\n";
31              SimpleCat * pRags = new SimpleCat;
32              cout << "delete pRags...\n";
33              delete pRags;
34              cout << "Exiting, watch Frisky go...\n";
35      }
```

```
SimpleCat Frisky...
Constructor called.
SimpleCat * pRags = new SimpleCat..
Constructor called.
delete pRags...
Destructor called.
Exiting, watch Frisky go...
Destructor called.
```

Lines 6–13 declare the stripped-down class SimpleCat. Line 9 declares SimpleCat's constructor, and lines 15–19 contain its definition. Line 10 declares SimpleCat's destructor, and lines 21–24 contain its definition.

In line 29, Frisky is created on the stack, which causes the constructor to be called. In line 31, the SimpleCat pointed to by pRags is created on the heap; the constructor is called again. In line 33, delete is called on pRags, and the destructor is called. When the function ends, Frisky goes out of scope, and the destructor is called.

Accessing Data Members

You accessed data members and functions by using the dot (.) operator for Cat objects created locally. To access the Cat object on the free store, you must dereference the pointer and call the dot operator on the object pointed to by the pointer. Therefore, to access the GetAge member function, you would write

```
(*pRags).GetAge();
```

Parentheses are used to assure that pRags is dereferenced before GetAge() is accessed.

Because this is cumbersome, C++ provides a shorthand operator for indirect access: the points-to operator (->), which is created by typing the dash (-) immediately followed by the greater-than symbol (>). C++ treats this as a single symbol. Listing 8.6 demonstrates accessing member variables and functions of objects created on the free store.

Listing 8.6. Accessing member data of objects on the free store.

```
1:      // Listing 8.6
2:      // Accessing data members of objects on the heap
3:
4:      #include <iostream.h>
5:
6:      class SimpleCat
7:      {
8:      public:
9:          SimpleCat() {itsAge = 2; }
10:          ~SimpleCat() {}
11:          int GetAge() const { return itsAge; }
12:          void SetAge(int age) { itsAge = age; }
13:      private:
14:          int itsAge;
15:      };
16:
17:      void main()
18:      {
19:          SimpleCat * Frisky = new SimpleCat;
20:          cout << "Frisky is " << Frisky->GetAge() << " years old\n";
21:          Frisky->SetAge(5);
22:          cout << "Frisky is " << Frisky->GetAge() << " years old\n";
23:          delete Frisky;
24:      }
```

```
Frisky is 2 years old
Frisky is 5 years old
```

In line 19, a SimpleCat object is instantiated on the free store. The default constructor sets its age to 2, and the GetAge() method is called in line 20. Because this is a pointer, the indirection operator (->) is used to access the member data and functions. In line 21, the SetAge() method is called, and GetAge() is accessed again in line 22.

Member Data on the Free Store

One or more of the data members of a class can be a pointer to an object on the free store. The memory can be allocated in the class constructor or in one of its methods, and it can be deleted in its destructor, as Listing 8.7 illustrates.

Listing 8.7. Pointers as member data.

```
1:   // Listing 8.7
2:   // Pointers as data members
3:
4:      #include <iostream.h>
5:
6:      class SimpleCat
7:      {
8:      public:
9:             SimpleCat();
10:            ~SimpleCat();
11:            int GetAge() const { return *itsAge; }
12:            void SetAge(int age) { *itsAge = age; }
13:
14:            int GetWeight() const { return *itsWeight; }
15:            void setAge(int weight) { *itsWeight = weight; }
16:
17:     private:
18:            int * itsAge;
19:            int * itsWeight;
20:         };
21:
22:      SimpleCat::SimpleCat()
23:      {
24:            itsAge = new int(2);
25:            itsWeight = new int(5);
26:      }
27:
28:      SimpleCat::~SimpleCat()
29:      {
30:         delete itsAge;
31:         delete itsWeight;
32:      }
33:
34:      void main()
35:      {
36:            SimpleCat *Frisky = new SimpleCat;
37:            cout << "Frisky is " << Frisky->GetAge() << " years old\n";
38:            Frisky->SetAge(5);
39:            cout << "Frisky is " << Frisky->GetAge() << " years old\n";
40:            delete Frisky;
41:      }
```

Frisky is 2 years old
Frisky is 5 years old

The class SimpleCat is declared to have two member variables—both of which are pointers to integers—on lines 14 and 15. The constructor (lines 22–26) initializes the pointers to memory on the free store and to the default values.

The destructor (lines 28–32) cleans up the allocated memory. Because this is the destructor, there is no point in assigning these pointers to null, as they will no longer be accessible. This is one of the safe places to break the rule that deleted pointers should be assigned to null, although following the rule doesn't hurt.

The calling function—in this case, main()—is unaware that itsAge and itsWeight are pointers to memory on the free store. main() continues to call GetAge() and SetAge(), and the details of the memory management are hidden in the implementation of the class—as they should be.

When Frisky is deleted in line 40, its destructor is called. The destructor deletes each of its member pointers. If these, in turn, point to objects of other user-defined classes, their destructors are called as well.

The *this* Pointer

Every class member function has a hidden parameter: the this pointer. this points to the individual object. Therefore, in each call to GetAge() or SetAge(), the this pointer for the object is included as a hidden parameter.

It is possible to use the this pointer explicitly, as Listing 8.8 illustrates.

Listing 8.8. Using the this pointer.

```
1:      // Listing 8.8
2:      // Using the this pointer
3:
4:      #include <iostream.h>
5:
6:      class Rectangle
7:      {
8:      public:
9:          Rectangle();
10:         ~Rectangle();
11:         void SetLength(int length) { this->itsLength = length; }
12:         int GetLength() const { return this->itsLength; }
13:
14:         void SetWidth(int width) { itsWidth = width; }
15:         int GetWidth() const { return itsWidth; }
```

```
16:
17:        private:
18:              int itsLength;
19:              int itsWidth;
20:        };
21:
22:        Rectangle::Rectangle():
23:        itsWidth(5),
24:        itsLength(10)
25:        {}
26:
27:        Rectangle::~Rectangle()
28:        {}
29:
30:        void main()
31:        {
32:              Rectangle theRect;
33:              cout << "theRect is " << theRect.GetLength() << " feet long.\n";
34:              cout << "theRect is " << theRect.GetWidth() << " feet wide.\n";
35:              theRect.SetLength(20);
36:              theRect.SetWidth(10);
37:              cout << "theRect is " << theRect.GetLength()<< " feet long.\n";
38:              cout << "theRect is " << theRect.GetWidth()<< " feet wide.\n";
39:        }
```

```
theRect is 10 feet long
theRect is 5 feet long
theRect is 20 feet long
theRect is 10 feet long
```

The SetLength() and GetLength() accessor functions explicitly use the this pointer to access the member variables of the Rectangle object. The SetWidth and GetWidth accessors do not. There is no difference in their behavior, although the syntax is easier to understand.

If that were all there was to the this pointer, there would be little point in bothering you with it. The this pointer, however, is a pointer; it stores the memory address of an object. As such, it can be a powerful tool.

You'll see a practical use for the this pointer on Day 10, when operator overloading is discussed. For now, your goal is to know about the this pointer and to understand what it is: a pointer to the object itself.

You don't have to worry about creating or deleting the this pointer. The compiler takes care of that.

Stray or Dangling Pointers

One source of bugs that are nasty and difficult to find is stray pointers. A stray pointer is created when you call delete on a pointer—thereby freeing the memory that it points to—and later try to use that pointer again without reassigning it.

It is as though the Acme Mail Order company moved away, and you still pressed the programmed button on your phone. It is possible that nothing terrible happens—a telephone rings in a deserted warehouse. Perhaps the telephone number has been reassigned to a munitions factory, and your call detonates an explosive and blows up your whole city!

In short, be careful not to use a pointer after you have called delete on it. The pointer still points to the old area of memory, but the compiler is free to put other data there; using the pointer can cause your program to crash. Worse, your program might proceed merrily on its way and crash several minutes later. This is called a time bomb, and it is no fun. To be safe, after you delete a pointer, set it to null (0). This disarms the pointer.

Note: Stray pointers are often called wild pointers or dangling pointers.

Listing 8.9 illustrates creating a stray pointer.

Listing 8.9. Creating a stray pointer.

```
1:     // Listing 8.9
2:     // Demonstrates a stray pointer
3:     typedef unsigned short int USHORT;
4:     #include <iostream.h>
5:
6:     void main()
7:     {
8:        USHORT * pInt = new USHORT;
9:        *pInt = 10;
10:       cout << "*pInt: " << *pInt << endl;
11:       delete pInt;
12:       pInt = 0;
13:       long * pLong = new long;
14:       *pLong = 90000;
15:       cout << "*pLong: " << *pLong << endl;
16:
17:       *pInt = 20;      // uh oh, this was deleted!
18:
19:       cout << "*pInt: " << *pInt  << endl;
20:       cout << "*pLong: " << *pLong  << endl;
21:       delete pLong;
22:     }
```

```
*pInt:   10
*pLong:  90000
*pInt:   20
*pLong:  65556
```

(Your output may look different.)

Line 8 declares pInt to be a pointer to USHORT, and pInt is pointed to newly allocated memory. Line 9 puts the value 10 in that memory, and line 10 prints its value. After the value is printed, delete is called on the pointer. pInt is now a stray, or dangling, pointer.

Line 13 declares a new pointer, pLong, which is pointed at the memory allocated by new. Line 14 assigns the value 90000 to pLong, and line 15 prints its value.

Line 17 assigns the value 20 to the memory that pInt points to, but pInt no longer points anywhere that is valid. The memory that pInt points to was freed by the call to delete, so assigning a value to that memory is certain disaster.

Line 19 prints the value at pInt. Sure enough, it is 20. Line 20, prints 20, the value at pLong; it has suddenly been changed to 65556. Two questions arise:

1. How could pLong's value change, given that pLong wasn't touched?

2. Where did the 20 go when pInt was used in line 17?

As you might guess, these are related questions. When a value was placed at pInt in line 17, the compiler happily placed the value 20 at the memory location that pInt previously pointed to. However, because that memory was freed in line 11, the compiler was free to reassign it. When pLong was created in line 14, it was given pInt's old memory location. (On some computers this may not happen, depending on where in memory these values are stored.) When the value 20 was assigned to the location that pInt previously pointed to, it wrote over the value pointed to by pLong. This is called "stomping on a pointer." It is often the unfortunate outcome of using a stray pointer.

This is a particularly nasty bug, because the value that changed wasn't associated with the stray pointer. The change to the value at pLong was a side effect of the misuse of pInt. In a large program, this would be very difficult to track down.

Just for fun, here are the details of how 65,556 got into that memory address:

1. pInt was pointed at a particular memory location, and the value 10 was assigned.

2. delete was called on pInt, which told the compiler that it could put something else at that location. Then pLong was assigned the same memory location.

3. The value `90000` was assigned to `*pLong`. The particular computer used in this example stored the four-byte value of 90,000—00 01 5F 90—in byte-swapped order. Therefore, it was stored as 5F 90 00 01.

4. `pInt` was assigned the value `20`—or 00 14 in hexadecimal notation. Because `pInt` still pointed to the same address, the first two bytes of `pLong` were over-written, leaving 00 14 00 01.

5. The value at `pLong` was printed, reversing the bytes back to their correct order of 00 01 00 14, which was translated into the DOS value of `65556`.

DO   **DON'T**

DO use `new` to create objects on the free store.

DO use `delete` to destroy objects on the free store and to return their memory.

DON'T forget to balance all new statements with a `delete` statement.

DON'T forget to assign `NULL` (0) to all pointers that you call `delete` on.

DO check the value returned by `new`.

const Pointers

You can use the keyword `const` for pointers before the type, after the type, or in both places. For example, all of the following are legal declarations:

```
const int * pOne;
int * const pTwo;
const int * const pThree;
```

`pOne` is a pointer to a constant integer. The value that is pointed to can't be changed.

`pTwo` is a constant pointer to an integer. The integer can be changed, but `pTwo` can't point to anything else.

`pThree` is a constant pointer to a constant integer. The value that is pointed to can't be changed, and `pThree` can't be changed to point to anything else.

The trick to keeping this straight is to look to the right of the keyword `const` to find out what is being declared constant. If the type is to the right of the keyword, it is the value that is constant. If the variable is to the right of the keyword `const`, it is the pointer variable itself that is constant.

```
const int * p1;   // the int pointed to is constant
int * const p2;   // p2 is constant, it can't point to anything else
```

const Pointers and *const* Member Functions

On Day 6, "Basic Classes," you learned that you can apply the keyword const to a member function. When a function is declared const, the compiler flags as an error any attempt to change data in the object from within that function.

If you declare a pointer to a const object, the only methods that you can call with that pointer are const methods. Listing 8.10 illustrates this.

Listing 8.10. Using pointers to const objects.

```
1:     // Listing 8.10
2:     // Using pointers with const methods
3:
4:     #include <iostream.h>
5:
6:     class Rectangle
7:     {
8:     public:
9:         Rectangle();
10:        ~Rectangle();
11:        void SetLength(int length) { itsLength = length; }
12:        int GetLength() const { return itsLength; }
13:
14:        void SetWidth(int width) { itsWidth = width; }
15:        int GetWidth() const { return itsWidth; }
16:
17:    private:
18:        int itsLength;
19:        int itsWidth;
20:    };
21:
22:     Rectangle::Rectangle():
23:     itsWidth(5),
24:     itsLength(10)
25:     {}
26:
27:     Rectangle::~Rectangle()
28:     {}
29:
30:     void main()
31:     {
32:         Rectangle* pRect =  new Rectangle;
33:         const Rectangle * pConstRect = new Rectangle;
34:         Rectangle * const pConstPtr = new Rectangle;
```

continues

Listing 8.10. continued

```
35:
36:            cout << "pRect width: " << pRect->GetWidth() << " feet\n";
37:            cout << "pConstRect width: " << pConstRect->GetWidth() << " feet\n";
38:            cout << "pConstPtr width: " << pConstPtr->GetWidth() << " feet\n";
39:
40:            pRect->SetWidth(10);
41:            // pConstRect->SetWidth(10);
42:            pConstPtr->SetWidth(10);
43:
44:            cout << "pRect width: " << pRect->GetWidth() << " feet\n";
45:            cout << "pConstRect width: " << pConstRect->GetWidth() << " feet\n";
46:            cout << "pConstPtr width: " << pConstPtr->GetWidth() << " feet\n";
47:    }
```

```
pRect width:       5 feet
pConstRect width:  5 feet
pConstPtr width:   5 feet
pRect width:       10 feet
pConstRect width:  5 feet
pConstPtr width:   10 feet
```

Lines 6–20 declare Rectangle. Line 12 declares the GetWidth() member method const. Line 32 declares a pointer to Rectangle. Line 33 declares pConstRect, which is a pointer to a constant Rectangle. Line 34 declares pConstPtr, which is a constant pointer to Rectangle.

Lines 36–38 print their values.

In line 40, pRect is used to set the width of the rectangle to 10. In line 41, pConstRect would be used, but it was declared to point to a constant rectangle. Therefore, it cannot legally call a non-const member function; it is commented out. In line 38, pConstPtr calls SetAge(). pConstPtr is declared to be a constant pointer to a rectangle. In other words, the pointer is constant and cannot point to anything else, but the rectangle is not constant.

const this Pointers

When you declare an object to be const, you are in effect declaring that the this pointer is a pointer to a const object. A const this pointer can be used only with const member functions.

Constant objects and constant pointers will be discussed again tomorrow, when references to constant objects are discussed.

DO	DON'T

DO protect objects passed by reference with `const` if they should not be changed.

DO pass by reference when the object can be changed.

DO pass by value when small objects should not be changed.

Summary

Pointers provide a powerful way to access data by indirection. Every variable has an address, which can be obtained using the `address of` operator (`&`). The address can be stored in a pointer.

Pointers are declared by writing the type of object that they point to, followed by the indirection operator (`*`) and the name of the pointer. Pointers should be initialized to point to an object or to `NULL` (0).

You access the value at the address stored in a pointer by using the indirection operator (`*`). You can declare `const` pointers—which can't be reassigned to point to other objects—and pointers to `const` objects—which can't be used to change the objects to which they point.

To create new objects on the free store, you use the `new` keyword and assign the address that is returned to a pointer. You free that memory by calling the `delete` keyword on the pointer. `delete` frees the memory, but it doesn't destroy the pointer. Therefore, you must reassign the pointer after its memory has been freed.

Q&A

Q Why are pointers so important?

A Today you saw how pointers are used to hold the address of objects on the free store and how they are used to pass arguments by reference. In addition, on Day 13 you'll see how pointers are used in class polymorphism.

Q Why should I bother to declare anything on the free store?

A Objects on the free store persist after the return of a function. Additionally, the ability to store objects on the free store enables you to decide at run-time how many objects you need, instead of having to declare this in advance. This is explored in greater depth tomorrow.

Q Why should I declare an object const if it limits what I can do with it?

A As a programmer, you want to enlist the compiler in helping you find bugs. One serious bug that is difficult to find is a function that changes an object in ways that aren't obvious to the calling function. Declaring an object const prevents such changes.

Workshop

The Workshop provides quiz questions to help you solidify your understanding of the material covered and exercises to provide you with experience in using what you've learned. Try to answer the quiz and exercise questions before checking the answers in Appendix D, and make sure you understand the answers before continuing to the next chapter.

Quiz

1. What operator is used to determine the address of a variable?

2. What operator is used to find the value stored at an address held in a pointer?

3. What is a pointer?

4. What is the difference between the address stored in a pointer and the value at that address?

5. What is the difference between the indirection operator and the `address of` operator?

6. What is the difference between const int * ptrOne and int * const ptrTwo?

Exercises

1. What do these declarations do?

    a. `int * pOne;`

    b. `int vTwo;`

    c. `int * pThree = &vTwo;`

2. If you have an unsigned short variable named yourAge, how would you declare a pointer to manipulate yourAge?

3. Assign the value 50 to the variable yourAge by using the pointer that you declared in Exercise 2.

4. Write a small program that declares an integer and a pointer to integer. Assign the address of the integer to the pointer. Use the pointer to set a value in the integer variable.

5. **BUG BUSTERS:** What is wrong with this code?

```
#include <iostream.h>
void main()
{
    int *pInt;
    *pInt = 9;
    cout << "The value at pInt: " << *pInt;
}
```

6. **BUG BUSTERS:** What is wrong with this code?

```
void main()
{
    int SomeVariable = 5;
    cout << "SomeVariable: " << SomeVariable << "\n";
    int *pVar = & SomeVariable;
    pVar = 9;
    cout << "SomeVariable: " << *pVar << "\n";
}
```

References

Introduction

Yesterday you learned how to use pointers to manipulate objects on the free store and how to refer to those objects indirectly. References, the topic of today's chapter, give you almost all the power of pointers but with a much easier syntax. Today you learn the following:

☐ What references are.

☐ How references differ from pointers.

☐ How to create references and use them.

☐ What the limitations of references are.

☐ How to pass values and objects into and out of functions by reference.

What Is a Reference?

A reference is an alias; when you create a reference, you initialize it with the name of another object, the target. From that moment on, the reference acts as an alternative name for the target, and anything you do to the reference is really done to the target.

You create a reference by writing the type of the target object, followed by the reference operator (&), followed by the name of the reference. References can use any legal variable name, but for this book we'll prefix all reference names with "r." Thus, if you have an integer variable named someInt, you can make a reference to that variable by writing the following:

```
int &rSomeRef = someInt;
```

This is read as "rSomeRef is a reference to integer that is initialized to refer to someInt." Listing 9.1 shows how references are created and used.

> **Note:** Note that the reference operator (&) is the same symbol as the one used for the address of the operator. These are *not* the same operators, however, though clearly they are related.

Listing 9.1. Creating and using references.

```
1:      //Listing 9.1
2:      // Demonstrating the use of References
3:
4:      #include <iostream.h>
5:
6:      void main()
7:      {
8:          int  intOne;
9:          int &rSomeRef = intOne;
10:
11:         intOne = 5;
12:         cout << "intOne: " << intOne << endl;
13:         cout << "rSomeRef: " << rSomeRef << endl;
14:
15:         rSomeRef = 7;
16:         cout << "intOne: " << intOne << endl;
17:         cout << "rSomeRef: " << rSomeRef << endl;
18:     }
```

```
intOne: 5
rSomeRef: 5
intOne: 7
rSomeRef: 7
```

On line 8, a local int variable, intOne, is declared. On line 9, a reference to an int, rSomeRef, is declared and initialized to refer to intOne. If you declare a reference but don't initialize it, you will get a compile-time error. References *must* be initialized.

On line 11, intOne is assigned the value 5. On lines 12 and 13, the values in intOne and rSomeRef are printed, and are of course the same.

On line 15, 7 is assigned to rSomeRef. Since this is a reference it is an alias for intOne, and thus the 7 is really assigned to intOne, as is shown by the printouts on lines 16 and 17.

Using the Address of Operator & on References

If you ask a reference for its address, it returns the address of its target. That is the nature of references. They are aliases for the target. Listing 9.2 demonstrates this.

229

Listing 9.2. Taking the address of a reference.

```
1:      //Listing 9.2
2:      // Demonstrating the use of References
3:
4:      #include <iostream.h>
5:
6:      void main()
7:      {
8:          int  intOne;
9:          int &rSomeRef = intOne;
10:
11:         intOne = 5;
12:         cout << "intOne: " << intOne << endl;
13:         cout << "rSomeRef: " << rSomeRef << endl;
14:
15:         cout << "&intOne: "  << &intOne << endl;
16:         cout << "&rSomeRef: " << &rSomeRef << endl;
17:
18:     }
```

```
intOne: 5
rSomeRef: 5
&intOne:   0x3500
&rSomeRef: 0x3500
```

Once again rSomeRef is initialized as a reference to intOne. This time the addresses of the two variables are printed, and they are identical. C++ gives you no way to access the address of the reference itself because it is not meaningful, as it would be if you were using a pointer or other variable. References are initialized when created, and always act as a synonym for their target, even when the *address of* operator is applied.

For example, if you have a class called President, you might declare an instance of that class as follows:

```
President  William_Jefferson_Clinton;
```

You might then declare a reference to President and initialize it with this object:

```
President &Bill_Clinton = William_Jefferson_Clinton;
```

There is only one President; both identifiers refer to the same object of the same class. Any action you take on Bill_Clinton will be taken on William_Jefferson_Clinton as well.

Be careful to distinguish between the & symbol on line 9 of Listing 9.2, which declares a reference to int named rSomeRef, and the & symbols on lines 15 and 16, which return the addresses of the integer variable intOne and the reference rSomeRef.

Normally, when you use a reference, you do not use the *address of* operator. You simply use the reference as you would use the target variable. This is shown on line 13.

Even experienced C++ programmers, who know the rule that references cannot be reassigned and are always aliases for their target, can be confused by what happens when you try to reassign a reference. What appears to be a reassignment turns out to be the assignment of a new value to the target. Listing 9.3 illustrates this fact.

Listing 9.3. Assigning to a reference.

```
1:      //Listing 9.3
2:      //Reassigning a reference
3:
4:      #include <iostream.h>
5:
6:      void main()
7:      {
8:          int  intOne;
9:          int &rSomeRef = intOne;
10:
11:          intOne = 5;
12:          cout << "intOne:\t" << intOne << endl;
13:          cout << "rSomeRef:\t" << rSomeRef << endl;
14:          cout << "&intOne:\t"  << &intOne << endl;
15:          cout << "&rSomeRef:\t" << &rSomeRef << endl;
16:
17:          int intTwo = 8;
18:          rSomeRef = intTwo;  // not what you think!
19:          cout << "\nintOne:\t" << intOne << endl;
20:          cout << "intTwo:\t" << intTwo << endl;
21:          cout << "rSomeRef:\t" << rSomeRef << endl;
22:          cout << "&intOne:\t"  << &intOne << endl;
23:          cout << "&intTwo:\t"  << &intTwo << endl;
24:          cout << "&rSomeRef:\t" << &rSomeRef << endl;
25:      }
```

```
intOne:                 5
rSomeRef:       5
&intOne:                0x213e
&rSomeRef:      0x213e

intOne:                 8
intTwo:                 8
rSomeRef:       8
&intOne:                0x213e
&intTwo:                0x2130
&rSomeRef:      0x213e
```

Once again, an integer variable and a reference to an integer are declared, on lines 8 and 9. The integer is assigned the value 5 on line 11, and the values and their addresses are printed on lines 12–15.

231

On line 17 a new variable, `intTwo`, is created and initialized with the value 8. On line 18 the programmer tries to reassign `rSomeRef` to now be an alias to the variable `intTwo`, but that is not what happens. What actually happens is that `rSomeRef` continues to act as an alias for `intOne`, so this assignment is exactly equivalent to the following:

```
intOne = intTwo;
```

Sure enough, when the values of `intOne` and `rSomeRef` are printed (lines 19–21) they are the same as `intTwo`. In fact, when the addresses are printed on lines 22–24, you see that `rSomeRef` continues to refer to `intOne` and not `intTwo`.

DO	DON'T
DO use references to create an alias to an object.	
DO initialize all references.	
DON'T try to reassign a reference.	
DON'T confuse the address of operator with the reference operator.	

What Can Be Referenced?

Any object can be referenced, including user-defined objects. Note that you create a reference to an object, not to a class. You do not write this:

```
int & rIntRef = int;     // wrong
```

You must initialize `rIntRef` to a particular integer, such as this:

```
int howBig = 200;
int & rIntRef = howBig;
```

In the same way, you don't initialize a reference to a `CAT`:

```
CAT & rCatRef = CAT;     // wrong
```

You must initialize `rCatRef` to a particular `CAT` object:

```
CAT frisky;
CAT & rCatRef = frisky;
```

References to objects are used just like the object itself. Member data and methods are accessed using the normal class member access operator (.), and just as with the built-in types, the reference acts as an alias to the object. Listing 9.4 illustrates this.

Listing 9.4. References to objects.

```
1:    // Listing 9.4
2:    // References to class objects
3:
4:    #include <iostream.h>
5:
6:    class SimpleCat
7:    {
8:       public:
9:          SimpleCat (int age, int weight);
10:         ~SimpleCat() {}
11:         int GetAge() { return itsAge; }
12:         int GetWeight() { return itsWeight; }
13:      private:
14:         int itsAge;
15:         int itsWeight;
16:   };
17:
18:   SimpleCat::SimpleCat(int age, int weight):
19:   itsAge(age), itsWeight(weight) {}
20:
21:   void main()
22:   {
23:         SimpleCat Frisky(5,8);
24:         SimpleCat & rCat = Frisky;
25:
26:         cout << "Frisky is: ";
27:         cout << Frisky.GetAge() << " years old. \n";
28:         cout << "And Frisky weighs: ";
29:         cout << rCat.GetWeight() << " pounds. \n";
30:   }
```

```
Frisky is 5 years old.

And Frisky weighs 8 pounds.
```

On line 23, Frisky is declared to be a SimpleCat object. On line 24, a SimpleCat reference, rCat, is declared and initialized to refer to Frisky. On lines 26 and 27, the SimpleCat accessor methods are accessed by using first the SimpleCat object and then the SimpleCat reference. Note that the access is identical. Again, the reference is an alias for the actual object.

References

Declare a reference by writing the type, followed by the reference operator (&), followed by the reference name. References must be initialized at the time of creation.

Example 1

```
int hisAge;
int &rAge = hisAge;
```

Example 2

```
CAT boots;
CAT &rCatRef = boots;
```

Null Pointers and Null References

When pointers are not initialized, or when they are deleted, they ought to be assigned to null (0). This is not true for references. In fact, a reference cannot be null, and a program with a reference to a null object is considered an invalid program. When a program is invalid, just about anything can happen. It can appear to work, or it can erase all the files on your disk. Both are possible outcomes of an invalid program.

Most compilers will support a null object without much complaint, crashing only if you try to use the object in some way. Taking advantage of this, however, is still not a good idea. When you move your program to another machine or compiler, mysterious bugs may develop if you have null objects.

Passing Function Arguments by Reference

On Day 5, you learned that functions have two limitations: arguments are passed by value, and the return statement can return only one value.

Passing values to a function by reference can overcome both of these limitations. In C++, passing by reference is accomplished in two ways: using pointers and using references. The syntax is different, but the net effect is the same: rather than a copy being created within the scope of the function, the actual original object is passed into the function.

> **Note:** If you read the extra credit section after Day 5, you learned that functions are passed their parameters on the stack. When a function is passed a value by reference (either using pointers or references), the address of the object is put on the stack, not the entire object.
>
> In fact, on some computers the address is actually held in a register and nothing is put on the stack. In either case, the compiler now knows how to get to the original object, and changes are made there and not in a copy.

Passing an object by reference allows the function to change the object being referred to.

Recall that Listing 5.5 demonstrated that a call to the swap() function did not affect the values in the calling function. Listing 5.5 is reproduced here for your convenience.

Listing 9.5 (5.5). Demonstrating pass by value.

```
1:      //Listing 5.5 Demonstrates passing by value
2:
3:      #include <iostream.h>
4:
5:      void swap(int x, int y);
6:
7:      void main()
8:      {
9:        int x = 5, y = 10;
10:
11:         cout << "Main. Before swap, x: " << x << " y: " << y << "\n";
12:         swap(x,y);
13:         cout << "Main. After swap, x: " << x << " y: " << y << "\n";
14:      }
15:
16:       void swap (int x, int y)
17:       {
18:         int temp;
19:
20:         cout << "Swap. Before swap, x: " << x << " y: " << y << "\n";
21:
22:         temp = x;
23:         x = y;
24:         y = temp;
25:
26:         cout << "Swap. After swap, x: " << x << " y: " << y << "\n";
27:
28:        }
```

```
Main. Before swap. x: 5 y: 10
Swap. Before swap. x: 5 y: 10
Swap. After swap. x: 10 y: 5
Main. After swap. x: 5 y: 10
```

This program initializes two variables in main() and then passes them to the swap() function, which appears to swap them. But when they are examined again in main(), they are unchanged!

The problem here is that x and y are being passed to swap() by value. That is, local copies were made in the function. What you want is to pass x and y by reference.

There are two ways to solve this problem in C++: you can make the parameters of swap() pointers to the original values, or you can pass in references to the original values.

Making *swap()* Work with Pointers

When you pass in a pointer, you pass in the address of the object, and thus the function can manipulate the value at that address. To make swap() change the actual values using pointers, the function, swap(), should be declared to accept two int pointers. Then, by dereferencing the pointers, the values of x and y will, in fact, be swapped. Listing 9.6 demonstrates this idea.

Listing 9.6. Passing by reference using pointers.

```
1:     //Listing 9.6 Demonstrates passing by reference
2:
3:     #include <iostream.h>
4:
5:     void swap(int *x, int *y);
6:
7:     void main()
8:     {
9:       int x = 5, y = 10;
10:
11:       cout << "Main. Before swap, x: " << x << " y: " << y << "\n";
12:       swap(&x,&y);
13:       cout << "Main. After swap, x: " << x << " y: " << y << "\n";
14:     }
15:
16:     void swap (int *px, int *py)
17:     {
18:       int temp;
19:
20:       cout << "Swap. Before swap, *px: " << *px << " *py: " << *py << "\n";
21:
22:       temp = *px;
23:       *px = *py;
24:       *py = temp;
25:
26:       cout << "Swap. After swap, *px: " << *px << " *py: " << *py << "\n";
27:
28:     }
```

```
Main. Before swap. x: 5 y: 10
Swap. Before swap. *px: 5 *py: 10
Swap. After swap. *px: 10 *py: 5
Main. After swap. x: 10 y: 5
```

Success! On line 5, the prototype of swap() is changed to indicate that its two parameters will be pointers to int rather than int variables. When swap() is called on line 12, the addresses of x and y are passed as the arguments.

On line 18, a local variable, temp, is declared in the swap() function. Temp need not be a pointer; it will just hold the value of *px (that is, the value of x in the calling function) for the life of the function. After the function returns, temp will no longer be needed.

On line 22, `temp` is assigned the value at `px`. On line 23, the value at `px` is assigned to the value at `py`. On line 24, the value stashed in `temp` (that is, the original value at `px`) is put into `py`.

The net effect of this is that the values in the calling function, whose address was passed to `swap()`, are in fact swapped.

Implementing *swap()* with References

The preceding program works, but the syntax of the `swap()` function is cumbersome in two ways. First, the repeated need to dereference the pointers within the swap function makes it error-prone and hard to read. Second, the need to pass the address of the variables in the calling function makes the inner workings of `swap()` overly apparent to its users.

It is a goal of C++ to prevent the user of a function from worrying about how it works. Passing by pointers puts the burden on the calling function rather than on the called function, where it belongs. Listing 9.7 rewrites the `swap()` function, using references.

Listing 9.7. Swap rewritten with references.

```
1:      //Listing 9.7 Demonstrates passing by reference
2:      // using references!
3:
4:      #include <iostream.h>
5:
6:      void swap(int &x, int &y);
7:
8:      void main()
9:      {
10:         int x = 5, y = 10;
11:
12:         cout << "Main. Before swap, x: " << x << " y: " << y << "\n";
13:         swap(x,y);
14:         cout << "Main. After swap, x: " << x << " y: " << y << "\n";
15:      }
16:
17:      void swap (int &rx, int &ry)
18:      {
19:        int temp;
20:
21:         cout << "Swap. Before swap, rx: " << rx << " ry: " << ry << "\n";
22:
23:         temp = rx;
24:         rx = ry;
25:         ry = temp;
26:
27:         cout << "Swap. After swap, rx: " << rx << " ry: " << ry << "\n";
28:
29:          }
```

```
Main. Before swap, x:5 y: 10
Swap. Before swap, x:5 y:10
Swap. After swap, x:10 y:5
Main. After swap, x:10, y:5
```

Just as in the example with pointers, two variables are declared on line 10 and their values are printed on line 12. On line 13 the function swap() is called, but note that x and y are passed, *not* their addresses. The calling function simply passes the variables.

When swap() is called, program execution jumps to line 17, where the variables are identified as references. Their values are printed on line 21, but note that no special operators are required. These are aliases for the original values, and can be used as such.

On lines 23–25 the values are swapped, and then they're printed on line 27. Program execution jumps back to the calling function, and on line 14 the values are printed in main(). Because the parameters to swap() are declared to be references, the values from main() are passed by reference, and thus are changed in main() as well.

References provide the convenience and ease of use of normal variables, with the power and pass-by-reference ability of pointers!

Understanding Function Headers and Prototypes

Listing 9.6 shows swap() using pointers, and Listing 9.7 shows it using references. Using the function that takes references is easier, and the code is easier to read, but how does the calling function know if the values are passed by reference or by value? As a client (or user) of swap(), the programmer must ensure that swap() will in fact change the parameters.

This is another use for the function prototype. By examining the parameters declared in the prototype, which is typically in a header file along with all the other prototypes, the programmer knows that the values passed into swap() are passed by reference, and thus will be swapped properly.

If swap() had been a member function of a class, the class declaration, also available in a header file, would have supplied this information.

In C++, clients of classes and functions rely on the header file to tell all that is needed; it acts as the interface to the class or function. The actual implementation is hidden from the client. This allows the programmer to focus on the problem at hand and to use the class or function without concern for how it works.

9

When Colonel Roebling built the Brooklyn Bridge, he worried in detail about how the concrete was poured and how the wire for the bridge was manufactured. He was intimately involved in the mechanical and chemical processes required to create his materials. Today, however, engineers make more efficient use of their time by using well-understood building materials, without regard to how their manufacturer produced them.

It is the goal of C++ to allow programmers to rely on well-understood classes and functions without regard to their internal workings. These "component parts" can be assembled to produce a program, much the same way wires, pipes, clamps, and other parts are assembled to produce buildings and bridges.

In much the same way that an engineer examines the spec sheet for a pipe to determine its load-bearing capacity, volume, fitting size, and so forth, a C++ programmer reads the interface of a function or class to determine what services it provides, what parameters it takes, and what values it returns.

Returning Multiple Values

As discussed, functions can only return one value. What if you need to get two values back from a function? One way to solve this problem is to pass two objects into the function, by reference. The function can then fill the objects with the correct values. Since passing by reference allows a function to change the original objects, this effectively lets the function return two pieces of information. This approach bypasses the return value of the function, which can then be reserved for reporting errors.

Once again, this can be done with references or pointers. Listing 9.8 demonstrates a function that returns three values, two as pointer parameters and one as the return value of the function.

Listing 9.8. Returning values with pointers.

```
1:     //Listing 9.8
2:     // Returning multiple values from a function
3:
4:     #include <iostream.h>
5:
6:     typedef unsigned short USHORT;
7:
8:     short Factor(USHORT, USHORT*, USHORT*);
9:
10:    void main()
11:    {
12:       USHORT number, squared, cubed;
```

continues

Listing 9.8. continued

```
13:        short error;
14:
15:        cout << "Enter a number (0 - 20): ";
16:        cin >> number;
17:
18:        error = Factor(number, &squared, &cubed);
19:
20:        if (!error)
21:        {
22:            cout << "number: " << number << "\n";
23:            cout << "square: " << squared << "\n";
24:            cout << "cubed: "  << cubed   << "\n";
25:        }
26:        else
27:        cout << "Error encountered!!\n";
28:    }
29:
30:    short Factor(USHORT n, USHORT *pSquared, USHORT *pCubed)
31:    {
32:    short return Value = 0
33:        if (n > 20)
34:            return Value = 1;
35:        else
36:        {
37:            *pSquared = n*n;
38:            *pCubed = n*n*n;
39:            return Value = 0;
41:            return
42:            return Value:
```

```
Enter a number (0-20): 3
number: 3
square: 9
cubed: 27
```

On line 12, number, squared, and cubed are defined as USHORTs. number is assigned a value based on user input. This number and the addresses of squared and cubed are passed to the function Factor().

Factor() examines the first parameter, which is passed by value. If it is greater than 20 (the maximum value this function can handle), it sets return Value to a simple error value. Note that the return value from Function() is reserved for either this error value or the value 0, indicating all went well, and note that the function returns this value on line 41.

The actual values needed, the square and cube of number, are returned not by using the return mechanism, but rather by changing the pointers that were passed into the function.

On lines 37 and 38, the pointers are assigned their return values. On line 39, return Value is assigned a success value. On line 41, return Value is returned.

One improvement to this program might be to declare the following:

```
enum ERROR_VALUE { SUCCESS, FAILURE};
```

Then, rather than returning 0 or 1, the program could return SUCCESS or FAILURE.

Returning Values by Reference

Although Listing 9.8 works, it can be made easier to read and maintain by using references rather than pointers. Listing 9.9 shows the same program rewritten to use references and to incorporate the ERROR enumeration.

Listing 9.9. Listing 9.8 rewritten using references.

```
1:      //Listing 9.8
2:      // Returning multiple values from a function
3:      // using references
4:
5:      #include <iostream.h>
6:
7:      typedef unsigned short USHORT;
8:      enum ERR_CODE { SUCCESS, ERROR };
9:
10:     ERR_CODE Factor(USHORT, USHORT&, USHORT&);
11:
12:     void main()
13:     {
14:         USHORT number, squared, cubed;
15:         ERR_CODE result;
16:
17:         cout << "Enter a number (0 - 20): ";
18:         cin >> number;
19:
20:         result = Factor(number, squared, cubed);
21:
22:         if (result == SUCCESS)
23:         {
24:             cout << "number: " << number << "\n";
25:             cout << "square: " << squared << "\n";
26:             cout << "cubed: "  << cubed   << "\n";
27:         }
28:         else
29:         cout << "Error encountered!!\n";
30:     }
31:
32:     ERR_CODE Factor(USHORT n, USHORT &rSquared, USHORT &rCubed)
33:     {
34:         if (n > 20)
```

continues

Listing 9.9. continued

```
35:                return ERROR;    // simple error code
36:            else
37:            {
38:                rSquared = n*n;
39:                rCubed = n*n*n;
40:                return SUCCESS;
41:            }
42:      }
```

```
Enter a number

(0-20): 3
number: 3
square: 9
cubed: 27
```

Listing 9.8 is identical to 9.8, with two exceptions. The `ERR_CODE` enumeration makes the error reporting a bit more explicit on lines 35 and 40, as well as the error handling on line 22.

The larger change, however, is that `Factor()` is now declared to take references to `squared` and `cubed` rather than to pointers. This makes the manipulation of these parameters far simpler and easier to understand.

Passing by Reference for Efficiency

Each time you pass an object into a function by value, a copy of the object is made. Each time you return an object from a function by value, another copy is made.

In the extra credit section at the end of Day 5, you learned that these objects are copied onto the stack. Doing so takes time and memory. For small objects, such as the built-in integer values, this is a trivial cost.

However, with larger, user-created objects the cost is greater. The size of a user-created object on the stack is the sum of each of its member variables. These, in turn, can each be user-created objects, and passing such a massive structure by copying it onto the stack can be very expensive in performance and memory consumption.

There is another cost as well. With the classes you create, each of these temporary copies is created when the compiler calls a special constructor: the copy constructor. Tomorrow you will learn how copy constructors work and how you can make your own, but for now it is enough to know that the copy constructor is called each time a temporary copy of the object is put on the stack.

When the temporary object is destroyed, which happens when the function returns, the object's destructor is called. If an object is returned by the function by value, a copy of that object must be made and destroyed as well.

With large objects, these constructor and destructor calls can be expensive in speed and use of memory. To illustrate this idea, Listing 9.9 creates a stripped-down user-created object: SimpleCat. A real object would be larger and more expensive, but this is sufficient to show how often the copy constructor and destructor are called.

Listing 9.10 creates the SimpleCat object and then calls two functions. The first function receives the Cat by value and then returns it by value. The second one receives a pointer to the object, rather than the object itself, and returns a pointer to the object.

Listing 9.10. Passing objects by reference.

```
1:    //Listing 9.10
2:    // Passing pointers to objects
3:
4:    #include <iostream.h>
5:
6:    class SimpleCat
7:    {
8:    public:
9:            SimpleCat ();                   // constructor
10:           SimpleCat(SimpleCat&);     // copy constructor
11:           ~SimpleCat();                   // destructor
12:    };
13:
14:   SimpleCat::SimpleCat()
15:   {
16:           cout << "Simple Cat Constructor...\n";
17:   }
18:
19:   SimpleCat::SimpleCat(SimpleCat&)
20:   {
21:           cout << "Simple Cat Copy Constructor...\n";
22:   }
23:
24:   SimpleCat::~SimpleCat()
25:   {
26:           cout << "Simple Cat Destructor...\n";
27:   }
28:
29:   SimpleCat FunctionOne (SimpleCat theCat);
30:   SimpleCat* FunctionTwo (SimpleCat *theCat);
31:
32:   void main()
33:   {
34:           cout << "Making a cat...\n";
35:           SimpleCat Frisky;
36:           cout << "Calling FunctionOne...\n";
37:           FunctionOne(Frisky);
```

continues

Listing 9.10. continued

```
38:          cout << "Calling FunctionTwo...\n";
39:          FunctionTwo(&Frisky);
40:    }
41:
42:    // FunctionOne, passes by value
43:    SimpleCat FunctionOne(SimpleCat theCat)
44:    {
45:             cout << "Function One. Returning...\n";
46:             return theCat;
47:    }
48:
49:    // functionTwo, passes by reference
50:    SimpleCat* FunctionTwo (SimpleCat   *theCat)
51:    {
52:             cout << "Function Two. Returning...\n";
53:             return theCat;
54:    }
```

```
1:   Making a cat...
2:   Simple Cat Constructor...
3:   Calling FunctionOne...
4:   Simple Cat Copy Constructor...
5:   Function One. Returning...
6:   Simple Cat Copy Constructor...
7:   Simple Cat Destructor...
8:   Simple Cat Destructor...
9:   Calling FunctionTwo...
10:  Function Two. Returning...
11:  Simple Cat Destructor...
```

Note: Line numbers will not print. They were added to aid in the analysis.

A very simplified `SimpleCat` class is declared on lines 6–12. The constructor, copy constructor, and destructor all print an informative message so that you can tell when they've been called.

On line 34, `main()` prints out a message, and that is seen on output line 1. On line 35, a `SimpleCat` object is instantiated. This causes the constructor to be called, and the output from the constructor is seen on output line 2.

On line 36, `main()` reports that it is calling `FunctionOne`, which creates output line 3. Because `FunctionOne()` is called passing the `SimpleCat` object by value, a copy of the `SimpleCat` object is made on the stack as an object local to the called function. This causes the copy constructor to be called, which creates output line 4.

Program execution jumps to line 45 in the called function, which prints an informative message, output line 5. The function then returns, and returns the SimpleCat object by value. This creates yet another copy of the object, calling the copy constructor and producing line 6.

The return value from FunctionOne() is not assigned to any object, and so the temporary created for the return is thrown away, calling the destructor, which produces output line 7. Since FunctionOne() has ended, its local copy goes out of scope and is destroyed, calling the destructor and producing line 8.

Program execution returns to main(), and FunctionTwo() is called, but the parameter is passed by reference. No copy is produced, so there's no output. FunctionTwo() prints the message that appears as output line 10 and then returns the SimpleCat object, again by reference, and so again produces no calls to the constructor or destructor.

Finally, the program ends and Frisky goes out of scope, causing one final call to the destructor and printing output line 11.

The net effect of this is that the call to FunctionOne(), because it passed the cat by value, produced two calls to the copy constructor and two to the destructor, while the call to FunctionTwo() produced none.

Passing a *const* Pointer

Although passing a pointer to FunctionTwo() is more efficient, it is dangerous. FunctionTwo() is not allowed to change the SimpleCat object it is passed, yet it is given the address of the SimpleCat. This seriously exposes the object to change and defeats the protection offered in passing by value.

Passing by value is like giving a museum a photograph of your masterpiece instead of the real thing. If vandals mark it up, there is no harm done to the original. Passing by reference is like sending your home address to the museum and inviting guests to come over and look at the real thing.

The solution is to pass a const pointer to SimpleCat. Doing so prevents calling any non-const method on SimpleCat, and thus protects the object from change. Listing 9.11 demonstrates this idea.

Listing 9.11. Passing const pointers.

```
1:  //Listing 9.11
2:      // Passing pointers to objects
3:
4:      #include <iostream.h>
```

Listing 9.11. continued

```
5:
6:         class SimpleCat
7:         {
8:         public:
9:                 SimpleCat();
10:                SimpleCat(SimpleCat&);
11:                ~SimpleCat();
12:
13:                int GetAge() const { return itsAge; }
14:                void SetAge(int age) { itsAge = age; }
15:
16:        private:
17:                int itsAge;
18:          };
19:
20:          SimpleCat::SimpleCat()
21:          {
22:                  cout << "Simple Cat Constructor...\n";
23:                  itsAge = 1;
24:          }
25:
26:          SimpleCat::SimpleCat(SimpleCat&)
27:          {
28:                  cout << "Simple Cat Copy Constructor...\n";
29:          }
30:
31:          SimpleCat::~SimpleCat()
32:          {
33:                  cout << "Simple Cat Destructor...\n";
34:          }
35:
36:          const    SimpleCat * const FunctionTwo (const SimpleCat * const
           ➥theCat);
37:
38:          void main()
39:          {
40:                  cout << "Making a cat...\n";
41:                  SimpleCat Frisky;
42:                  cout << "Frisky is " << Frisky.GetAge() << " years
                   ➥old\n";
43:                  int age = 5;
44:                  Frisky.SetAge(age);
45:                  cout << "Frisky is " << Frisky.GetAge() << " years
                   ➥old\n";
46:                  cout << "Calling FunctionTwo...\n";
47:                  FunctionTwo(&Frisky);
48:                  cout << "Frisky is " << Frisky.GetAge() << " years
                   ➥old\n";
49:          }
50:
51:          // functionTwo, passes a const pointer
52:          const SimpleCat * const FunctionTwo (const SimpleCat * const theCat)
53:          {
54:                          cout << "Function Two. Returning...\n";
55:                          cout << "Frisky is now " << theCat->GetAge();
```

```
56:                              cout << " years old \n";
57:                              // theCat->SetAge(8);    const!
58:                              return theCat;
59:             }
```

```
Making a cat...
Simple Cat constructor...
Frisky is 1 years old
Frisky is 5 years old
Calling FunctionTwo
FunctionTwo. Returning...
Frisky is now 5 years old
Frisky is 5 years old
Simple Cat Destructor...
```

SimpleCat has added two accessor functions, GetAge() on line 13, which is a const function, and SetAge() on line 14, which is not. It has also added the member variable itsAge on line 17.

The constructor, copy constructor, and destructor are still defined to print their messages. The copy constructor is never called, however, because the object is passed by reference and so no copies are made. On line 41 an object is created, and its default age is printed on line 42.

On line 43, itsAge is set using the accessor SetAge, and the result is printed on line 45. FunctionOne is not used in this program, but FunctionTwo() is called. FunctionTwo() has changed slightly; the parameter and return value are now declared, on line 36, to take a constant pointer to a constant object and to return a constant pointer to a constant object.

Because the parameter and return value are still passed by reference, no copies are made and the copy constructor is not called. The pointer in FunctionTwo(), however, is now constant, and thus cannot call the non-const method, SetAge(). If the call to SetAge() on line 57 was not commented out, the program would not compile.

Note that the object created in main() is not constant, and Frisky *can* call SetAge(). The address of this non-constant object is passed to FunctionTwo(), but because FunctionTwo()'s declaration declares the pointer to be a pointer to a constant object, the object is treated as if it were constant!

References as an Alternative

Listing 9.11 solves the problem of making extra copies, and thus saves the calls to the copy constructor and destructor. It uses constant pointers to constant objects, and thereby solves the problem of the function changing the object. It is still somewhat cumbersome, however, because the objects passed to the function are pointers.

Since you know the object will never be null, it would be easier to work with in the function if a reference were passed in, rather than a pointer. Listing 9.12 illustrates this.

Listing 9.12. Passing references to objects.

```
1:  //Listing 9.12
2:  // Passing references to objects
3:
4:    #include <iostream.h>
5:
6:    class SimpleCat
7:    {
8:  public:
9:          SimpleCat();
10:         SimpleCat(SimpleCat&);
11:         ~SimpleCat();
12:
13:         int GetAge() const { return itsAge; }
14:         void SetAge(int age) { itsAge = age; }
15:
16:  private:
17:         int itsAge;
18:      };
19:
20:    SimpleCat::SimpleCat()
21:    {
22:          cout << "Simple Cat Constructor...\n";
23:          itsAge = 1;
24:    }
25:
26:    SimpleCat::SimpleCat(SimpleCat&)
27:    {
28:          cout << "Simple Cat Copy Constructor...\n";
29:    }
30:
31:    SimpleCat::~SimpleCat()
32:    {
33:          cout << "Simple Cat Destructor...\n";
34:    }
35:
36:    const     SimpleCat & FunctionTwo (const SimpleCat & theCat);
37:
38:    void main()
39:    {
40:          cout << "Making a cat...\n";
41:          SimpleCat Frisky;
42:          cout << "Frisky is " << Frisky.GetAge() << " years old\n";
43:          int age = 5;
44:          Frisky.SetAge(age);
45:          cout << "Frisky is " << Frisky.GetAge() << " years old\n";
46:          cout << "Calling FunctionTwo...\n";
47:          FunctionTwo(Frisky);
48:          cout << "Frisky is " << Frisky.GetAge() << " years old\n";
49:    }
50:
```

```
51:     // functionTwo, passes a ref to a const object
52:     const SimpleCat & FunctionTwo (const SimpleCat & theCat)
53:     {
54:                 cout << "Function Two. Returning...\n";
55:                 cout << "Frisky is now " << theCat.GetAge();
56:                 cout << " years old \n";
57:                 // theCat.SetAge(8);   const!
58:                 return theCat;
59:     }
```

9

Output

```
Making a cat...
Simple Cat constructor...
Frisky is 1 years old
Frisky is 5 years old
Calling FunctionTwo
FunctionTwo. Returning...
Frisky is now 5 years old
Frisky is 5 years old
Simple Cat Destructor...
```

Analysis

The output is identical to that produced by Listing 9.11. The only significant change is that FunctionTwo() now takes and returns a reference to a constant object. Once again, working with references is somewhat simpler than working with pointers, and the same savings and efficiency, as well as the safety provided by using const, is achieved.

> **Note:** Const References
>
> C++ programmers do not usually differentiate between "constant reference to a SimpleCat object" and "reference to a constant SimpleCat object." References themselves can never be reassigned to refer to another object, and so are always constant. If the keyword const is applied to a reference, it is to make the object referred to constant.

When to Use References and When to Use Pointers

C++ programmers strongly prefer references to pointers. References are cleaner and easier to use, and they do a better job of hiding information, as we saw in the previous example.

References cannot be reassigned, however. If you need to point first to one object and then another, you must use a pointer. References cannot be null, so if there is any chance

that the object in question may be null, you must not use a reference. You must use a pointer.

An example of the latter concern is the operator new. If new cannot allocate memory on the free store, it returns a null pointer. Since a reference can't be null, you must not initialize a reference to this memory until you've checked that it is not null. The following example shows how to handle this:

```
int *pInt = new int;
if (pInt != NULL)
    int &rInt = *pInt;
```

In this example a pointer to int, pInt, is declared and initialized with the memory returned by the operator new. The address in pInt is tested, and if it is not null, pInt is dereferenced. The result of dereferencing an int variable is an int object, and rInt is initialized to refer to that object. Thus, rInt becomes an alias to the int returned by the operator new.

DO	DON'T
DO pass parameters by reference whenever possible.	
DO return by reference whenever possible.	
DON'T use pointers if references will work.	
DO use const to protect references and pointers whenever possible.	
DON'T return a reference to a local object.	

Mixing References and Pointers

It is perfectly legal to declare both pointers and references in the same function parameter list, along with objects passed by value. Here's an example:

```
CAT * SomeFunction (Person &theOwner, House *theHouse, int age);
```

This declaration says that SomeFunction takes three parameters. The first is a reference to a Person object, the second is a pointer to a house object, and the third is an integer. It returns a pointer to a CAT object.

> **Note:** The question of where to put the reference (&) or indirection (*) operator when declaring these variables is a great controversy. You may legally write any of the following:
>
> ```
> 1:  CAT&  rFrisky;
> 2:  CAT & rFrisky;
> 3:  CAT  &rFrisky;
> ```
>
> White space is completely ignored, so anywhere you see a space here you may put as many spaces, tabs, and new lines as you like.
>
> Setting aside freedom of expression issues, which is best? Here are the arguments for all three:
>
> The argument for case 1 is that rFrisky is a variable whose name is rFrisky and whose type can be thought of as "reference to CAT object." Thus, this argument goes, the & should be with the type.
>
> The counterargument is that the type is CAT. The & is part of the "declarator," which includes the variable name and the ampersand. More important, having the & near the CAT can lead to the following bug:
>
> ```
> CAT&  rFrisky, rBoots;
> ```
>
> Casual examination of this line would lead you to think that both rFrisky and rBoots are references to CAT objects, but you'd be wrong. This really says that rFrisky is a reference to a CAT, and rBoots (despite its name) is not a reference but a plain old CAT variable. This should be rewritten as follows:
>
> ```
> CAT   &rFrisky, rBoots;
> ```
>
> The answer to this objection is that declarations of references and variables should never be combined like this. Here's the right answer:
>
> ```
> CAT& rFrisky;
> CAT  boots;
> ```
>
> Finally, many programmers opt out of the argument and go with the middle position, that of putting the & in the middle of the two, as illustrated in case 2 above.
>
> Of course, everything said so far about the reference operator (&) applies equally well to the indirection operator (*). The important thing is to

9

recognize that reasonable people differ in their perceptions of the one true way. Choose a style that works for you, and be consistent within any one program; clarity is, and remains, the goal.

This book will adopt two conventions when declaring references and pointers:

1. Put the ampersand and asterisk in the middle, with a space on either side.

2. Never declare references, pointers, and variables all on the same line.

Don't Return a Reference to an Object that isn't in Scope!

Once C++ programmers learn to pass by reference, they have a tendency to go hog-wild. It is possible, however, to overdo it. Remember that a reference is always an alias to some other object. If you pass a reference into or out of a function, be sure to ask yourself, "What is the object I'm aliasing, and will it still exist every time it's used?"

Listing 9.13 illustrates the danger of returning a reference to an object that no longer exists.

Listing 9.13. Returning a reference to a non-existent object.

```
1:     // Listing 9.13
2:     // Returning a reference to an object
3:     // which no longer exists
4:
5:     #include <iostream.h>
6:
7:     class SimpleCat
8:     {
9:     public:
10:            SimpleCat (int age, int weight);
11:            ~SimpleCat() {}
12:            int GetAge() { return itsAge; }
13:            int GetWeight() { return itsWeight; }
14:     private:
15:            int itsAge;
16:            int itsWeight;
17:     };
18:
19:     SimpleCat::SimpleCat(int age, int weight):
20:     itsAge(age), itsWeight(weight) {}
```

```
21:
22:      SimpleCat &TheFunction();
23:
24:      void main()
25:      {
26:          SimpleCat &rCat = TheFunction();
27:          int age = rCat.GetAge();
28:          cout << "rCat is " << age << " years old!\n";
29:      }
30:
31:      SimpleCat &TheFunction()
32:      {
33:          SimpleCat Frisky(5,9);
34:          return Frisky;
35:      }
```

Compile error: Attempting to return a reference to a local object!

Warning: This program won't compile!

On lines 7–17, SimpleCat is declared. On line 26, a reference to a SimpleCat is initialized with the results of calling TheFunction(), which is declared on line 22 to return a reference to a SimpleCat.

The body of TheFunction() declares a local object of type SimpleCat and initializes its age and weight. It then returns that local object by reference. Some compilers are smart enough to catch this error and won't let you run the program. Others will let you run the program, with unpredictable results.

When TheFunction() returns, the local object, Frisky, will be destroyed (painlessly, I assure you). The reference returned by this function will be an alias to a non-existent object, and this is a bad thing.

Returning a Reference to an Object on the Heap

You might be tempted to solve the problem in Listing 9.13 by having TheFunction() create Frisky on the heap. That way, when you return from TheFunction(), Frisky will still exist.

The problem with this approach is: What do you do with the memory allocated for Frisky when you are done with it? Listing 9.14 illustrates this problem.

Listing 9.14. Memory leaks.

```
1:      // Listing 9.14
2:      // Resolving memory leaks
3:      #include <iostream.h>
4:
5:      class SimpleCat
6:      {
7:      public:
8:              SimpleCat (int age, int weight);
9:              ~SimpleCat() {}
10:             int GetAge() { return itsAge; }
11:             int GetWeight() { return itsWeight; }
12:
13      private:
14:             int itsAge;
15:             int itsWeight;
16:         };
17:
18:      SimpleCat::SimpleCat(int age, int weight):
19:      itsAge(age), itsWeight(weight) {}
20:
21:      SimpleCat & TheFunction();
22:
23:      void main()
24:      {
25:          SimpleCat & rCat = TheFunction();
26:          int age = rCat.GetAge();
27:          cout << "rCat is " << age << " years old!\n";
28:          cout << "&rCat: " << &rCat << endl;
29:          // How do you get rid of that memory?
30:          SimpleCat * pCat = &rCat;
31:          delete pCat;
32:          // Uh oh, rCat now refers to ??
33:      }
34:
35:      SimpleCat &TheFunction()
36:      {
37:          SimpleCat * pFrisky = new SimpleCat(5,9);
38:          cout << "pFrisky: " << pFrisky << endl;
39:          return *pFrisky;
40:      }
```

Output

```
pFrisky:  0x2bf4
rCat is 5 years old
&rCat:    0x2bf4
```

Warning: This compiles, links, and appears to work. But it is a time bomb waiting to go off.

The function TheFunction() has been changed so that it no longer returns a reference to a local variable. Memory is allocated on the free store and assigned to a pointer on line 37. The address that pointer holds is printed, and then the pointer is dereferenced and the SimpleCat object is returned by reference.

On line 25, the return of TheFunction() is assigned to a reference to a SimpleCat, and that object is used to obtain the cat's age, which is printed on line 27.

To prove that the reference declared in main() is referring to the object put on the free store in TheFunction(), the *address of* operator is applied to rCat. Sure enough, it displays the address of the object it refers to and this matches the address of the object on the free store.

So far, so good. But how will that memory be freed? You can't call delete on the reference. One clever solution is to create another pointer and initialize it with the address obtained from rCat. This does delete the memory, and plugs the memory leak. One small problem, though: What is rCat referring to after line 31? As stated earlier, a reference must always alias an actual object; if it references a null object (as this does now), the program is invalid.

Note: It cannot be overemphasized that a program with a reference to a null object may compile, but it is invalid and its performance is unpredictable.

There are actually three solutions to this problem. The first is to declare a SimpleCat object on line 25, and to return that cat from TheFunction by value. The second is to go ahead and declare the SimpleCat on the free store in TheFunction(), but have TheFunction() return a pointer to that memory. Then the calling function can delete the pointer when it is done.

The third workable solution, and the right one, is to declare the object in the calling function and then to pass it to TheFunction() by reference.

Pointer, Pointer, Who Has the Pointer?

When your program allocates memory on the free store, a pointer is returned. It is imperative that you keep a pointer to that memory, because once the pointer is lost, the memory cannot be deleted and becomes a memory leak.

As you pass this block of memory between functions, someone will "own" the pointer. Typically the value in the block will be passed using references, and the function that created the memory is the one that deletes it. But this is a general rule, not an ironclad one.

It is dangerous for one function to create memory and another to free it, however. Ambiguity about who owns the pointer can lead to one of two problems: forgetting to delete a pointer or deleting it twice. Either one can cause serious problems in your program. It is safer to build your functions so that they delete the memory they create.

If you are writing a function that needs to create memory and then pass it back to the calling function, consider changing your interface. Have the calling function allocate the memory and then pass it into your function by reference. This moves all memory management out of your program and back to the function that is prepared to delete it.

DO	DON'T
DO pass parameters by value when you must.	
DO return by value when you must.	
DON'T pass by reference if the item referred to may go out of scope.	
DON'T use references to null objects.	

Summary

Today you learned what references are and how they compare to pointers. You saw that references must be initialized to refer to an existing object, and cannot be reassigned to refer to anything else. Any action taken on a reference is in fact taken on the reference's target object. Proof of this is that taking the address of a reference returns the address of the target.

You saw that passing objects by reference can be more efficient than passing by value. Passing by reference also allows the called function to change the value in the arguments back in the calling function.

You saw that arguments to functions and values returned from functions can be passed by reference, and that this can be implemented with pointers or with references.

You saw how to use const pointers and const references to safely pass values between functions while achieving the efficiency of passing by reference.

Q&A

Q Why have references if pointers can do everything references can?

A References are easier to use and understand. The indirection is hidden, and there is no need to repeatedly dereference the variable.

Q Why have pointers if references are easier?

A References cannot be null, and they cannot be reassigned. Pointers offer greater flexibility, but are slightly more difficult to use.

Q Why would you ever return by value from a function?

A If the object being returned is local, you must return by value or you will be returning a reference to a non-existent object.

Q Given the danger in returning by reference, why not always return by value?

A There is far greater efficiency in returning by reference. Memory is saved and the program runs faster.

Workshop

The Workshop contains quiz questions to help solidify your understanding of the material covered and exercises to provide you with experience in using what you've learned. Try to answer the quiz and exercise questions before checking the answers in Appendix D, and make sure you understand the answers before going to the next chapter.

Quiz

1. What is the difference between a reference and a pointer?

2. When must you use a pointer rather than a reference?

3. What does new return if there is insufficient memory to make your new object?

4. What is a constant reference?

5. What is the difference between passing *by* reference and passing *a* reference?

Exercises

1. Write a program that declares an int, a reference to an int, and a pointer to an int. Use the pointer and the reference to manipulate the value in the int.

2. Write a program that declares a constant pointer to a constant integer. Initialize the pointer to an integer variable, varOne. Assign 6 to varOne. Use the pointer to assign 7 to varOne. Create a second integer variable, varTwo. Reassign the pointer to varTwo.

3. Compile the program in Exercise 2. What produces errors? What produces warnings?

4. Write a program that produces a stray pointer.

5. Fix the program from Exercise 4.

6. Write a program that produces a memory leak.

7. Fix the program from Exercise 6.

8. **BUG BUSTERS:** What is wrong with this program?

```
1:      #include <iostreams.h>
2:
3:      class CAT
4:      {
5:        public:
6:            CAT(int age) { itsAge = age; }
7:            ~CAT(){}
8:            int GetAge() const { return itsAge;}
9:        private:
10:           int itsAge;
```

```
11:    };
12:
13:    CAT & MakeCat(int age);
14:    void main()
15:    {
16:       int age = 7;
17:       CAT Boots = MakeCat(age);
18:       cout << "Boots is " << Boots.GetAge() << " years old\n";
19:    }
20:
21:    CAT & MakeCat(int age)
22:    {
23:       CAT * pCat = new CAT(age);
24:       return *pCat;
25:    }
```

9. Fix the program from Exercise 8.

Advanced Functions

Introduction

On Day 5, you learned the fundamentals of working with functions. Now that you know how pointers and references work, there is more you can do with functions. Today you learn the following:

☐ How to overload member functions.

☐ How to overload operators.

☐ How to write functions to support classes with dynamically allocated variables.

Overloaded Member Functions

On Day 5, you learned how to implement function polymorphism, or function overloading, by writing two or more functions with the same name but with different parameters. Class member functions can be overloaded as well, in much the same way.

The Rectangle class, demonstrated in Listing 10.1, has two DrawShape() functions. One, which takes no parameters, draws the Rectangle based on the class's current values. The other takes two values, a width and a length, and draws the Rectangle based on those values, ignoring the current class values.

Listing 10.1. Illustrates overloading member functions.

```
1:      //Listing 10.1 Overloading class member functions
2:      #include <iostream.h>
3:
4:      typedef unsigned short int USHORT;
5:      enum BOOL { FALSE, TRUE};
6:
7:      // Rectangle class declaration
8:      class Rectangle
9:      {
10:     public:
11:         // constructors
12:         Rectangle(USHORT width, USHORT height);
13:         ~Rectangle(){}
14:
15:         // overloaded class function DrawShape
16:         void DrawShape() const;
17:         void DrawShape(USHORT aWidth, USHORT aHeight) const;
18:
19:     private:
20:         USHORT itsWidth;
21:         USHORT itsHeight;
22:     };
```

```
23:
24:    //Constructor implementation
25:    Rectangle::Rectangle(USHORT width, USHORT height)
26:    {
27:       itsWidth = width;
28:       itsHeight = height;
29:    }
30:
31:
32:    // Overloaded DrawShape - takes no values
33:    // Draws based on current class member values
34:    void Rectangle::DrawShape() const
35:    {
36:        DrawShape(itsHeight, itsWidth);
37:    }
38:
39:
40:    // overloaded DrawShape - takes two values
41:    // draws shape based on the parameters
42:    void Rectangle::DrawShape(USHORT height, USHORT width) const
43:    {
44:       for (USHORT i = 0; i<height; i++)
45:       {
46:          for (USHORT j = 0; j< width; j++)
47:          {
48:             cout << "*";
49:          }
50:          cout << "\n";
51:       }
52:    }
53:
54:    // Driver program to demonstrate overloaded functions
55:    void main ()
56:    {
57:       // initialize a rectangle to 10,20
58:       Rectangle theRect(30,5);
59:       cout << "DrawShape(): \n";
60:       DrawShape();
61:       cout << "\nDrawShape(40,2): \n";
62:       DrawShape(40,2);
63:    }
```

```
DrawShape():
******************************
******************************
******************************
******************************
******************************

DrawShape(40,2):
************************************************************
************************************************************
```

263

Listing 10.1 represents a stripped-down version of the Week in Review project from Week 1. The test for illegal values has been taken out to save room, as have some of the accessor functions. The main program has been stripped down to a simple driver program, rather than a menu.

The important code, however, is on lines 16 and 17, where DrawShape() is overloaded. The implementation for these overloaded class methods is on lines 32–52. Note that the version of DrawShape() that takes no parameters simply calls the version that takes two parameters, passing in the current member variables. Try very hard to avoid duplicating code in two functions. Otherwise, keeping them in synch when changes are made to one or the other will be difficult and error-prone.

The driver program, on lines 55–63, creates a rectangle object and then calls DrawShape(), first passing in no parameters, and then passing in two unsigned short integers.

The compiler decides which method to call based on the number and type of parameters entered. One can imagine a third overloaded function named DrawShape() that takes one dimension and an enumeration for whether it is the width or height, at the user's choice.

Using Default Values

Just as non-class functions can have one or more default values, so can each member function of a class. The same rules apply for declaring the default values, as illustrated in Listing 10.2.

Listing 10.2. Using default values.

```
1:      //Listing 10.2 Default values in member functions
2:      #include <iostream.h>
3:
4:      typedef unsigned short int USHORT;
5:      enum BOOL { FALSE, TRUE};
6:
7:      // Rectangle class declaration
8:      class Rectangle
9:      {
10:     public:
11:         // constructors
12:         Rectangle(USHORT width, USHORT height);
13:         ~Rectangle(){}
14:         void DrawShape(USHORT aWidth, USHORT aHeight, BOOL UseCurrentVals =
            ➡FALSE) const;
15:
16:     private:
17:         USHORT itsWidth;
18:         USHORT itsHeight;
```

```
19:    };
20:
21:    //Constructor implementation
22:    Rectangle::Rectangle(USHORT width, USHORT height):
23:    itsWidth(width),        // initializations
24:    itsHeight(height)
25:    {}                      // empty body
26:
27:
28:    // default values used for third parameter
29:    void Rectangle::DrawShape(
30:        USHORT width,
31:        USHORT height,
32:        BOOL UseCurrentValue
33:        ) const
34:    {
35:        int printWidth;
36:        int printHeight;
37:
38:        if (UseCurrentValue == TRUE)
39:        {
40:            printWidth = itsWidth;        // use current class values
41:            printHeight = itsHeight;
42:        }
43:        else
44:        {
45:            printWidth = width;           // use parameter values
46:            printHeight = height;
47:        }
48:
49:
50:        for (int i = 0; i<printHeight; i++)
51:        {
52:            for (int j = 0; j< printWidth; j++)
53:            {
54:                cout << "*";
55:            }
56:            cout << "\n";
57:        }
58:    }
59:
60:    // Driver program to demonstrate overloaded functions
61:    void main ()
62:    {
63:        // initialize a rectangle to 10,20
64:        Rectangle theRect(30,5);
65:        cout << "DrawShape(0,0,TRUE)...\n";
66:        theRect.DrawShape(0,0,TRUE);
67:        cout <<"DrawShape(40,2)...\n";
68:        theRect.DrawShape(40,2);
69:    }
```

Output

```
DrawShape(0,0,TRUE)...
*****************************
*****************************
```

```
*******************************
*******************************
*******************************

DrawShape(40,2)...
***************************************************************
***************************************************************
```

Analysis Listing 10.2 replaces the overloaded `DrawShape()` function with a single function with default parameters. The function is declared on line 14 to take three parameters. The first two, `aWidth` and `aHeight`, are `USHORT`s, and the third, `UseCurrentValue`, is a `BOOL` (true or false) that defaults to `FALSE`.

>
>
> **Note:** Boolean values are those that evaluate to true or false. C++ considers 0 to be false and all other values to be true.

The implementation for this somewhat awkward function begins on line 28. The third parameter, `UseCurrentValue`, is evaluated. If it is `TRUE`, the member variables `itsWidth` and `itsHeight` are used to set the local variables `printWidth` and `printHeight`, respectively.

If `UseCurrentValue` is `FALSE`, either because it has defaulted `FALSE` or was set by the user, the first two parameters are used for setting `printWidth` and `printHeight`.

Note that if `UseCurrentValue` is `TRUE`, the values of the other two parameters are completely ignored.

Choosing Between Default Values and Overloaded Functions

Listing 10.1 and 10.2 accomplish the same thing, but the overloaded functions in 10.1 are simpler to understand and more natural to use. Also, if a third variation is needed—perhaps the user wants to supply either the width *or* the height, but not both—it is easy to extend the overloaded functions. The default value, however, will quickly become unusably complex as new variations are added.

How do you decide whether to use function overloading or default values? Here's a rule of thumb:

Look to function overloading when

☐ There is no reasonable default value.

☐ You need different algorithms.

☐ You need to support variant types in your parameter list.

The Default Constructor

As discussed on Day 6, if you do not explicitly declare a constructor for your class, a default constructor is created that takes no parameters and does nothing. You are free to make your own default constructor, however, that takes no arguments but that "sets up" your object as required.

The constructor provided for you is called the "default" constructor, but by convention so is any constructor that takes no parameters. This can be a bit confusing, but it is usually clear from context which is meant.

Take note that if you make any constructors at all, the default constructor is not made by the compiler. So if you want a constructor that takes no parameters, and you've created any other constructors, you must make the default constructor yourself!

Overloading Constructors

The point of a constructor is to establish the object; for example, the point of a Rectangle constructor is to make a rectangle. Before the constructor runs, there is no rectangle, just an area of memory. After the constructor finishes, there is a complete, ready-to-use rectangle object.

Constructors, like all member functions, can be overloaded. The ability to overload constructors is very powerful and very flexible.

For example, you might have a rectangle object that has two constructors: The first takes a length and a width, and makes a rectangle of that size. The second takes no values, and makes a default-sized rectangle. Listing 10.3 illustrates this idea.

Listing 10.3. Overloading the constructor.

```
1:      // Listing 10.3
2:       // Overloading constructors
3:
```

continues

Listing 10.3. continued

```
4:      #include <iostreams.h>
5:
6:      class Rectangle
7:      {
8:      public:
9:            Rectangle();
10:           Rectangle(int width, int length);
11:           ~Rectangle() {}
12:           int GetWidth() const { return itsWidth; }
13:           int GetLength() const { return itsLength; }
14:     private:
15:           int itsWidth;
16:           int itsLength;
17:      };
18:
19:      Rectangle::Rectangle()
20:      {
21:           itsWidth = 5;
22:           itsLength = 10;
23:      }
24:
25:      Rectangle::Rectangle (int width, int length)
26:      {
27:           itsWidth = width;
28:           itsLength = length;
29:      }
30:
31:      void main()
32:      {
33:           Rectangle Rect1;
34:           cout << "Rect1 width: " << Rect1.GetWidth() << endl;
35:           cout << "Rect1 length: " << Rect1.GetLength() << endl;
36:
37:           int aWidth, aLength;
38:           cout << "Enter a width: ";
39:           cin >> aWidth;
40:           cout << "\nEnter a length: ";
41:           cin >> aLength;
42:
43:           Rectangle Rect2(aWidth, aLength);
44:           cout << "\nRect2 width: " << Rect2.GetWidth() << endl;
45:           cout << "Rect2 length: " << Rect2.GetLength() << endl;
46:      }
```

```
Rect1 width: 5
Rect1 length: 10
Enter a width: 20
Enter a length: 50
Rect2 width: 20
Rect2 length: 50
```

Analysis The Rectangle class is declared on lines 6–17. Two constructors are declared: the "default constructor" on line 9, and a constructor taking two integer variables.

On line 33, a rectangle is created using the default constructor, and its values are printed on lines 34–35. On lines 37–41, the user is prompted for a width and length, and the constructor taking two parameters is called on line 43. Finally, the width and height for this rectangle are printed on lines 44–45.

The compiler chooses the right constructor just as it does any overloaded function: based on the number and type of the parameters.

Initializing Objects

Up until now, you've been setting the member variables of objects in the body of the constructor. Constructors, however, are invoked in two stages: the initialization stage and the body.

Most variables can be set in either stage, either by initializing in the initialization stage or by assigning in the body of the constructor. It is cleaner, and often more efficient, to initialize member variables at the initialization stage. The following example shows how to initialize member variables:

```
CAT():          // constructor name and parameters
    itsAge(5),    // initialization list
    itsWeight(8)
{ }                // body of constructor
```

After the closing parentheses on the constructor's parameter list, write a colon. Then write the name of the member variable and a pair of parentheses. Inside the parentheses, write the expression to be used to initialize that member variable. If there is more than one initialization, separate each one with a comma. Listing 10.4 shows the definition of the constructors from Listing 10.3, with initialization of the member variables rather than assignment.

Listing 10.4. A code snippet showing initialization of member variables.

```
1:    Rectangle::Rectangle():
2:        itsWidth(5),
3:        itsLength(10)
4:    {
5:    }
6:
```

continues

269

Listing 10.4. continued

```
7:   Rectangle::Rectangle (int width, int length)
8:       itsWidth(width),
9:       itsLength(length)
10:  {
11:  }
```

There are some variables that must be initialized and cannot be assigned to: references and constants. It is common to have other assignments or action statements in the body of the constructor; however, it is best to use initialization as much as possible.

The Copy Constructor

In addition to providing a default constructor and destructor, the compiler provides a default copy constructor. The copy constructor is called every time a copy of an object is made.

When you pass an object by value, either into a function or as a function's return value, a temporary copy of that object is made. If the object is a user-defined object, the class's copy constructor is called, as you saw yesterday in Listing 9.6.

All copy constructors take one parameter, a reference to an object of the same class. It is a good idea to make it a constant reference, because the constructor will not have to alter the object passed in. For example:

```
CAT(const CAT & theCat);
```

Here the CAT constructor takes a constant reference to an existing CAT object. The goal of the copy constructor is to make a copy of theCAT.

The default copy constructor simply copies each member variable from the object passed as a parameter to the member variables of the new object. This is called a member-wise (or shallow) copy, and although this is fine for most member variables, it breaks pretty quickly for member variables that are pointers to objects on the free store.

NEW TERM A shallow or member-wise copy copies the exact values of one object's member valuables into another object. Pointers in both objects end up pointing to the same memory. A deep copy copies the values allocated on the heap to newly allocated memory.

If the CAT class includes a member variable, itsAge, that points to an integer on the free store, the default copy constructor will copy the passed-in CAT's itsAge member variable to the new CAT's itsAge member variable. The two objects will now point to the same memory, as illustrated in Figure 10.1.

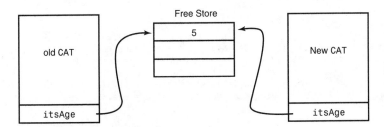

Figure 10.1. *Using the default copy constructor.*

This will lead to a disaster when either CAT goes out of scope. As mentioned on Day 8, the job of the destructor is to clean up this memory. If the original CAT's destructor frees this memory and the new CAT is still pointing to the memory, a stray pointer has been created, and the program is in mortal danger. Figure 10.2 illustrates this problem.

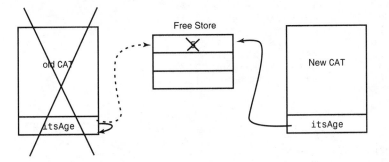

Figure 10.2. *Creating a stray pointer.*

The solution to this is to create your own copy constructor and to allocate the memory as required. Once the memory is allocated, the old values can be copied into the new memory. This is called a deep copy. Listing 10.5 illustrates how to do this.

Listing 10.5. Copy constructors.

```
1:    // Listing 10.5
2:    // Copy constructors
3:
4:    #include <iostreams.h>
```

continues

Listing 10.5. continued

```
5:
6:    class CAT
7:    {
8:        public:
9:            CAT();                          // default constructor
10:           CAT (const CAT &);    // copy constructor
11:           ~CAT();                         // destructor
12:           int GetAge() const { return *itsAge; }
13:           int GetWeight() const { return *itsWeight; }
14:           void SetAge(int age) { *itsAge = age; }
15:
16:       private:
17:           int *itsAge;
18:           int *itsWeight;
19:    };
20:
21:    CAT::CAT()
22:    {
23:        itsAge = new int;
24:        itsWeight = new int;
25:        *itsAge = 5;
26:        *itsWeight = 9;
27:    }
28:
29:    CAT::CAT(const CAT & rhs)
30:    {
31:        itsAge = new int;
32:        itsWeight = new int;
33:        *itsAge = rhs.GetAge();
34:        *itsWeight = rhs.GetWeight();
35:    }
36:
37:    CAT::~CAT()
38:    {
39:        delete itsAge;
40:        itsAge = 0;
41:        delete itsWeight;
42:        itsWeight = 0;
43:    }
44:
45:    void main()
46:    {
47:        CAT frisky;
48:        cout << "frisky's age: " << frisky.GetAge() << endl;
49:        cout << "Setting frisky to 6...\n";
50:        frisky.SetAge(6);
51:        cout << "Creating boots from frisky\n";
52:        CAT boots(frisky);
53:        cout << "frisky's age: " <<      frisky.GetAge() << endl;
54:        cout << "boots' age: " << boots.GetAge() << endl;
55:        cout << "setting frisky to 7...\n";
56:        frisky.SetAge(7);
57:        cout << "frisky's age: " <<      frisky.GetAge() << endl;
58:        cout << "boot's age: " << boots.GetAge() << endl;
59:    }
```

```
frisky's age: 5
Setting frisky to 6
Creating boots from frisky
frisky's age: 6
boots' age:  6
Setting frisky to 7
frisky's age: 7
boots' age: 6
```

On lines 6–19, the CAT class is declared. Note that on line 9 a default constructor is declared, and on line 10 a copy constructor is declared.

On lines 17 and 18, two member variables are declared, each as a pointer to an integer. Typically there'd be little reason for a class to store int member variables as pointers, but this was done to illustrate how to manage member variables on the free store.

The default constructor, on lines 21–27, allocates room on the free store for two int variables, and then assigns values to them.

The copy constructor begins on line 29. Note that the parameter is rhs. It is common to refer to the parameter to a copy constructor as rhs, which stands for *right-hand side*. When you look at the assignments in lines 33 and 34, you'll see that the object passed in as a parameter is on the right-hand side of the equals sign. Here's how it works.

On lines 31 and 32, memory is allocated on the free store. Then, on lines 33 and 34, the value at the new memory location is assigned the values from the existing CAT.

The parameter rhs is a CAT that is passed into the copy constructor as a constant reference. The member function rhs.GetAge() returns the value stored in the memory pointed to by rhs's member variable itsAge. As a CAT object, rhs has all the member variables of any other CAT.

When the copy constructor is called to create a new CAT, an existing CAT is passed in as a parameter. The new CAT can refer to its own member variables directly; however, it must access rhs's member variables using the public accessor methods.

Figure 10.3 diagrams what is happening here. The values pointed to by the existing CAT are copied to the memory allocated for the new CAT.

On line 47, a CAT is created, called frisky. frisky's age is printed, and then his age is set to 6 on line 50. On line 52 a new CAT is created, boots, using the copy constructor, and passing in frisky. Had frisky been passed as a parameter to a function, this same call to the copy constructor would have been made by the compiler.

On lines 53 and 54, the ages of both CATs are printed. Sure enough, boots has frisky's age, 6, not the default age of 5. On line 56, frisky's age is set to 7, and then the ages are printed again. This time `frisky`'s age is 7 but `boots`' age is still 6, demonstrating that they are stored in separate areas of memory.

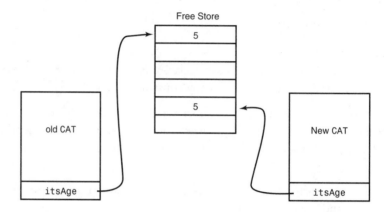

Figure 10.3. *Deep copy illustrated.*

When the `CAT`s fall out of scope, their destructors are automatically invoked. The implementation of the `CAT` destructor is shown on lines 37–43. `delete` is called on both pointers, `itsAge` and `itsWeight`, returning the allocated memory to the free store. Also, for safety, the pointers are reassigned to `NULL`.

Operator Overloading

C++ has a number of built-in types, including `int`, `real`, `char`, and so forth. Each of these has a number of built-in operators, such as addition (+) and multiplication (*). C++ enables you to add these operators to your own classes as well.

In order to explore operator overloading fully, Listing 10.6 creates a new class, `Counter`. A `Counter` object will be used in counting (surprise!) in loops and other applications where a number must be incremented, decremented, or otherwise tracked.

Listing 10.6. The `Counter` class.

```
1:      // Listing 10.5
2:      // The Counter class
3:
4:      typedef unsigned short  USHORT;
5:      #include <iostreams.h>
6:
7:      class Counter
```

```
8:      {
9:          public:
10:             Counter();
11:             ~Counter(){}
12:             USHORT GetItsVal()const { return itsVal; }
13:             void SetItsVal(USHORT x) {itsVal = x; }
14:
15:          private:
16:             USHORT itsVal;
17:
18:      };
19:
20:      Counter::Counter():
21:      itsVal(0)
22:      {};
23:
24:      void main()
25:      {
26:          Counter i;
27:          cout << "The value of i is " << i.GetItsVal() << endl;
28:      }
```

```
The value of i is 0.
```

As it stands, this is a pretty useless class. It is defined on lines 7–18. Its only member variable is a USHORT. The default constructor, which is declared on line 10 and whose implementation is on line 20, initializes the one member variable, itsVal, to zero.

Unlike an honest, red-blooded USHORT, the counter object cannot be incremented, decremented, added, assigned, or otherwise manipulated. In exchange for this, it makes printing its value far more difficult!

Writing an Increment Function

Operator overloading restores much of the functionality that has been stripped out of this class. For example, there are two ways to add the ability to increment a Counter object. The first is to write an increment method, as shown in Listing 10.7

Listing 10.7. Adding an increment operator.

```
1:      // Listing 10.7
2:      // The Counter class
3:
4:      typedef unsigned short  USHORT;
5:      #include <iostreams.h>
```

continues

Listing 10.7. continued

```
6:
7:     class Counter
8:     {
9:        public:
10:           Counter();
11:           ~Counter(){}
12:           USHORT GetItsVal()const { return itsVal; }
13:           void SetItsVal(USHORT x) {itsVal = x; }
14:           void Increment() { ++itsVal; }
15:
16:        private:
17:           USHORT itsVal;
18:
19:     };
20:
21:     Counter::Counter():
22:     itsVal(0)
23:     {};
24:
25:     void main()
26:     {
27:        Counter i;
28:        cout << "The value of i is " << i.GetItsVal() << endl;
29:        i.Increment();
30:        cout << "The value of i is " << i.GetItsVal() << endl;
31:     }
```

```
The value of i is 0
The value of i is 1
```

Listing 10.7 adds an `Increment` function, defined on line 14. Although this works, it is cumbersome to use. The program cries out for the ability to add a ++ operator, and of course this can be done.

Overloading the *prefix* Operator

Prefix operators can be overloaded by declaring functions with the form:

```
returnType Operator op (parameters)
```

Here, *op* is the operator to overload. Thus the ++ operator can be overloaded with the following syntax:

```
void operator++ ()
```

Listing 10.8 demonstrates this alternative.

Listing 10.8. Overloading operator++.

```
1:    // Listing 10.8
2:    // The Counter class
3:
4:    typedef unsigned short  USHORT;
5:    #include <iostreams.h>
6:
7:    class Counter
8:    {
9:       public:
10:          Counter();
11:          ~Counter(){}
12:          USHORT GetItsVal()const { return itsVal; }
13:          void SetItsVal(USHORT x) {itsVal = x; }
14:          void Increment() { ++itsVal; }
15:          void operator++ () { ++itsVal; }
16:
17:       private:
18:          USHORT itsVal;
19:
20:    };
21:
22:    Counter::Counter():
23:    itsVal(0)
24:    {};
25:
26:    void main()
27:    {
28:       Counter i;
29:       cout << "The value of i is " << i.GetItsVal() << endl;
30:       i.Increment();
31:       cout << "The value of i is " << i.GetItsVal() << endl;
32:       ++i;
33:       cout << "The value of i is " << i.GetItsVal() << endl;
34:    }
```

```
The value of i is 0
The value of i is 1
The value of i is 2
```

On line 15 operator++ is overloaded, and it's used on line 32. This is far closer to the syntax one would expect with the Counter object. At this point, you might consider putting in the extra abilities for which counter was created in the first place: such as detecting when the counter overruns its maximum size.

There is a significant defect in the way the Increment operator was written, however. If you want to put the counter on the right side of an assignment, it will fail. For example:

```
counter a = ++i;
```

This code intends to create a new counter, a, and then assign to it the value in i after i is incremented. The built-in copy constructor will handle the assignment, but the current Increment operator does not return a Counter object. It returns void. You can't assign a void object to a Counter object. (You can't make something from nothing!)

Returning Types in Overloaded Operator Functions

Clearly, what you want is to return a Counter object so that it can be assigned to another Counter object. Which object should be returned? One approach would be to create a temporary object and return that. Listing 10.9 illustrates this approach.

Listing 10.9. Returning a temporary object.

```
1:      // Listing 10.9
2:      // operator++ returns a temporary object
3:
4:      typedef unsigned short  USHORT;
5:      #include <iostreams.h>
6:
7:      class Counter
8:      {
9:        public:
10:           Counter();
11:           ~Counter(){}
12:           USHORT GetItsVal()const { return itsVal; }
13:           void SetItsVal(USHORT x) {itsVal = x; }
14:           void Increment() { ++itsVal; }
15:           Counter operator++ ();
16:
17:        private:
18:           USHORT itsVal;
19:
20:      };
21:
22:      Counter::Counter():
23:      itsVal(0)
24:      {};
25:
26:      Counter Counter::operator++()
27:      {
28:          ++itsVal;
29:          Counter temp;
30:          temp.SetItsVal(itsVal);
31:          return temp;
32:      }
33:
34:      void main()
35:      {
36:          Counter i;
```

```
37:        cout << "The value of i is " << i.GetItsVal() << endl;
38:        i.Increment();
39:        cout << "The value of i is " << i.GetItsVal() << endl;
40:        ++i;
41:        cout << "The value of i is " << i.GetItsVal() << endl;
42:        Counter a = ++i;
43:        cout << "The value of a: " << a.GetItsVal();
44:        cout << " and i: " << i.GetItsVal() << endl;
45:    }
```

```
The value of i is 0
The value of i is 1
The value of i is 2
The value of a: 3 and i: 3
```

In this version, `operator++` has been declared on line 15 to return a `Counter` object. On line 28 a temporary variable, `temp`, is created and its value is set to match that in the current object. That temporary variable is returned and immediately assigned to a on line 42.

Returning Nameless Temporaries

There is really no need to name the temporary object created on line 29. If `Counter` had a constructor that took a value, you could simply return the result of that constructor as the return value of the `Increment` operator. Listing 10.10 illustrates this idea.

Listing 10.10. Returning a nameless temporary object.

```
1:    // Listing 10.10
2:    // operator++ returns a nameless temporary object
3:
4:    typedef unsigned short   USHORT;
5:    #include <iostreams.h>
6:
7:    class Counter
8:    {
9:        public:
10:           Counter();
11:           Counter(USHORT val);
12:           ~Counter(){}
13:           USHORT GetItsVal()const { return itsVal; }
14:           void SetItsVal(USHORT x) {itsVal = x; }
15:           void Increment() { ++itsVal; }
16:           Counter operator++ ();
17:
18:        private:
19:           USHORT itsVal;
20:
```

continues

Listing 10.10. continued

```
21:    };
22:
23:    Counter::Counter():
24:    itsVal(0)
25:    {}
26:
27:    Counter::Counter(USHORT val):
28:    itsVal(val)
29:    {}
30:
31:    Counter Counter::operator++()
32:    {
33:        ++itsVal;
34:        return Counter (itsVal);
35:    }
36:
37:    void main()
38:    {
39:        Counter i;
40:        cout << "The value of i is " << i.GetItsVal() << endl;
41:        i.Increment();
42:        cout << "The value of i is " << i.GetItsVal() << endl;
43:        ++i;
44:        cout << "The value of i is " << i.GetItsVal() << endl;
45:        Counter a = ++i;
46:        cout << "The value of a: " << a.GetItsVal();
47:        cout << " and i: " << i.GetItsVal() << endl;
48:    }
```

```
The value of i is 0
The value of i is 1
The value of i is 2
The value of a: 3 and i: 3
```

On line 11, a new constructor is declared that takes a USHORT. The implementation is on lines 27–29. It initializes itsVal with the passed-in value.

The implementation of operator++ is now simplified. On line 33, itsVal is incremented. Then on line 34, a temporary Counter object is created, initialized to the value in itsVal, and then returned as the result of the operator++.

This is more elegant, but begs the question, "Why create a temporary object at all?" Remember that each temporary object must be constructed and later destroyed, each one potentially an expensive operation. And the object i already exists and already has the right value, so why not return *it*?

Using the *this* Pointer

The this pointer, as discussed yesterday, was passed to the operator++ member function as to all member functions. The this pointer points to i, and if it's dereferenced it will return the object i, which already has the right value in its member variable itsVal. Listing 10.9 illustrates returning the dereferenced this pointer and avoiding the creation of an unneeded temporary object.

Listing 10.11. Returning the this pointer.

```
1:      // Listing 10.11
2:      // Returning the dereferenced this pointer
3:
4:      typedef unsigned short   USHORT;
5:      #include <iostreams.h>
6:
7:      class Counter
8:      {
9:         public:
10:           Counter();
11:           ~Counter(){}
12:           USHORT GetItsVal()const { return itsVal; }
13:           void SetItsVal(USHORT x) {itsVal = x; }
14:           void Increment() { ++itsVal; }
15:           const Counter& operator++ ();
16:
17:         private:
18:           USHORT itsVal;
19:
20:      };
21:
22:      Counter::Counter():
23:      itsVal(0)
24:      {};
25:
26:      const Counter& Counter::Operator++()
27:      {
28:          ++itsVal;
29:          return *this;
30:      }
31:
32:      void main()
33:      {
34:          Counter i;
35:          cout << "The value of i is " << i.GetItsVal() << endl;
36:          i.Increment();
37:          cout << "The value of i is " << i.GetItsVal() << endl;
38:          ++i;
39:          cout << "The value of i is " << i.GetItsVal() << endl;
40:          Counter a = ++i;
41:          cout << "The value of a: " << a.GetItsVal();
42:          cout << " and i: " << i.GetItsVal() << endl;
43:      }
```

10

The value of i is 0
The value of i is 1
The value of i is 2
The value of a: 3 and i: 3

The implementation of operator++, on lines 26–30, has been changed to dereference the `this` pointer and to return the current object. This provides a `Counter` object to be assigned to a. As discussed above, if the `Counter` object allocated memory, it would be important to override the copy constructor. In this case, the default copy constructor works fine.

Note that the value returned is a `Counter` reference, thereby avoiding the creation of an extra temporary object. It is a `const` reference because the value should not be changed by the function using this `Counter`.

Overloading the *postfix* Operator

So far you've overloaded the prefix operator. What if you want to overload the postfix `Increment` operator? Here the compiler has a problem: How is it to differentiate between prefix and postfix? By convention, an integer variable is supplied as a parameter to the operator declaration. The parameter's value is ignored; it is just a signal that this is the postfix operator. Listing 10.12 demonstrates the use of both the prefix and the postfix operators.

Listing 10.12. Prefix and postfix operators.

```
1:     // Listing 10.12
2:     // Returning the dereferenced this pointer
3:
4:     typedef unsigned short  USHORT;
5:     #include <iostreams.h>
6:
7:     class Counter
8:     {
9:     public:
10:        Counter();
11:        ~Counter(){}
12:        USHORT GetItsVal()const { return itsVal; }
13:        void SetItsVal(USHORT x) {itsVal = x; }
14:        const Counter& operator++ ();       // prefix
15:        const Counter& operator++ (int); // postfix
16:
17:     private:
18:        USHORT itsVal;
19:
20:     };
21:
22:     Counter::Counter():
```

```
23:     itsVal(0)
24:     {}
25:
26:     const Counter& Counter::operator++()
27:     {
28:         ++itsVal;
29:         return *this;
30:     }
31:
32:     const Counter& Counter::operator++(int x)
33:     {
34:         itsVal++;
35:         return *this;
36:     }
37:
38:     void main()
39:     {
40:         Counter i;
41:         cout << "The value of i is " << i.GetItsVal() << endl;
42:         i++;
43:         cout << "The value of i is " << i.GetItsVal() << endl;
44:         ++i;
45:         cout << "The value of i is " << i.GetItsVal() << endl;
46:         Counter a = ++i;
47:         cout << "The value of a: " << a.GetItsVal();
48:         cout << " and i: " << i.GetItsVal() << endl;
49:         a = i++;
50:         cout << "The value of a: " << a.GetItsVal();
51:         cout << " and i: " << i.GetItsVal() << endl;
52:     }
```

```
The value of i is 0
The value of i is 1
The value of i is 2
The value of a: 3 and i: 3
The value of a: 4 and i: 4
```

The postfix operator is declared on line 15 and implemented on lines 32–36. Note that the call to the prefix operator on line 14 does not include the flag integer (x), but is used with its normal syntax. The postfix operator uses a flag value (x) to signal that it is the postfix and not the prefix. The flag value (x) is never used, however.

Operator Overloading Unary Operators

Declare an overloaded operator as you would a function. Use the keyword operator followed by the operator to overload. Unary operator functions do not take parameters, with the exception of the postfix increment and decrement, which take an integer as a flag.

Example 1

```
const Counter& Counter::operator++ ();
```

Example 2

```
Counter Counter::operator—(int);
```

DO	DON'T

DO use a parameter to operator++ if you want the postfix operator.

DO return a const reference to the object from operator++.

DON'T create temporary object as return values from operator++.

Operator+

The Increment operator is a unary operator. It operates on one object only. The addition operator (+) is a binary operator, where two objects are involved. How do you implement overloading the + operator for Count?

The goal is to be able to declare two Counter variables and then add them, as in this example:

```
Counter varOne, varTwo, varThree;
VarThree = VarOne + VarTwo;
```

Once again, you could start by writing a function, Add(), which would take a Counter as its argument, add the values, and then return a Counter with the result. Listing 10.13 illustrates this approach.

Listing 10.13. The Add() function.

```
1:     // Listing 10.13
2:     // Add function
3:
4:     typedef unsigned short   USHORT;
5:     #include <iostreams.h>
6:
7:     class Counter
8:     {
9:     public:
10:        Counter();
11:        Counter(USHORT initialValue);
12:        ~Counter(){}
```

```
13:        USHORT GetItsVal()const { return itsVal; }
14:        void SetItsVal(USHORT x) {itsVal = x; }
15:        Counter Add(const Counter &);
16:
17:    private:
18:        USHORT itsVal;
19:
20:    };
21:
22:    Counter::Counter(USHORT initialValue):
23:    itsVal(initialValue)
24:    {}
25:
26:    Counter::Counter():
27:    itsVal(0)
28:    {}
29:
30:    Counter Counter::Add(const Counter & rhs)
31:    {
32:        return Counter(itsVal+ rhs.GetItsVal());
33:    }
34:
35:    void main()
36:    {
37:        Counter varOne(2), varTwo(4), varThree;
38:        varThree = varOne.Add(varTwo);
39:        cout << "varOne: " << varOne.GetItsVal()<< endl;
40:        cout << "varTwo: " << varTwo.GetItsVal() << endl;
41:        cout << "varThree: " << varThree.GetItsVal() << endl;
42:
43:    }
```

Output

```
varOne: 2
varTwo: 4
varThree: 6
```

Analysis

The Add() function is declared on line 15. It takes a constant Counter reference, which is the number to add to the current object. It returns a Counter object, which is the result to be assigned to the left side of the assignment statement, as shown on line 38. That is, VarOne is the object, varTwo is the parameter to the Add() function, and the result is assigned to VarThree.

In order to create varThree without having to initialize a value for it, a default constructor is required. The default constructor initializes itsVal to zero, as shown on lines 26–28. Since varOne and varTwo need to be initialized to a non-zero value, another constructor was created, as shown on lines 22–24. Another solution to this problem is to provide the default value 0 to the constructor declared on line 11.

Overloading *operator+*

The Add() function itself is shown on lines 30–33. It works, but its use is unnatural.
Overloading the operator + would make for a more natural use of the Counter class.
Listing 10.14 illustrates this.

Listing 10.14. operator+.

```
1:      // Listing 10.12
2:      //Overload operator plus (+)
3:
4:      typedef unsigned short  USHORT;
5:      #include <iostreams.h>
6:
7:      class Counter
8:      {
9:      public:
10:         Counter();
11:         Counter(USHORT initialValue);
12:         ~Counter(){}
13:         USHORT GetItsVal()const { return itsVal; }
14:         void SetItsVal(USHORT x) {itsVal = x; }
15:         Counter operator+ (const Counter &);
16:     private:
17:         USHORT itsVal;
18:     };
19:
20:     Counter::Counter(USHORT initialValue):
21:     itsVal(initialValue)
22:     {}
23:
24:     Counter::Counter():
25:     itsVal(0)
26:     {}
27:
28:     Counter Counter::operator+ (const Counter & rhs)
29:     {
30:         return Counter(itsVal + rhs.GetItsVal());
31:     }
32:
33:     void main()
34:     {
35:         Counter varOne(2), varTwo(4), varThree;
36:         varThree = varOne + varTwo;
37:         cout << "varOne: " << varOne.GetItsVal()<< endl;
38:         cout << "varTwo: " << varTwo.GetItsVal() << endl;
39:         cout << "varThree: " << varThree.GetItsVal() << endl;
40:
41:     }
```

```
varOne: 2
varTwo: 4
varThree: 6
```

Analysis operator+ is declared on line 15 and defined on lines 28–31. Compare these with the declaration and definition of the Add() function in the previous listing; they are nearly identical. The syntax of their use, however, is quite different. It is more natural to say this:

```
varThree = varOne + varTwo;
```

than it is to say this:

```
varThree = varOne.Add(varTwo);
```

Not a big change, but enough to make the program easier to use and understand.

> **Note:** The techniques used for overloading operator++ can be applied to the other unary operators, such as operator—.

Syntax

Operator Overloading: Binary Operators

Binary operators are created like unary operators, except that they do take a parameter. The parameter is a constant reference to an object of the same type.

Example 1

```
Counter Counter::operator+ (const Counter & rhs);
```

Example 2

```
Counter Counter::operator-(const Counter & rhs);
```

Issues in Operator Overloading

Overloaded operators can be member functions, as described in this chapter, or can be non-member functions. The latter will be described on Day 14 when we discuss friend functions.

The only operators that must be class members are the assignment (=), subscript([ ]), function call (( )) and indirection (->) operators.

operator[] will be discussed tomorrow, when arrays are covered. Overloading operator-> will be discussed on Day 14, when smart pointers are discussed.

Limitations on Operator Overloading

Operators on built-in types (such as int) cannot be overloaded. The precedence order cannot be changed, and the *arity* of the operator, that is, whether it is unary or binary, cannot be changed. You cannot make up new operators, so you cannot declare ** to be the "power of" operator.

What to Overload

Operator overloading is one of the aspects of C++ most overused and abused by new programmers. It is tempting to create new and interesting uses for some of the more obscure operators, but these invariably lead to code that is confusing and difficult to read.

Of course, making the + operator *subtract* and the * operator *add* can be fun, but no professional programmer would do that. The greater danger lies in the well-intentioned but idiosyncratic use of an operator—using + to mean *concatenate a series of letters*, or / to mean *split a string*. There is good reason to consider these uses, but there is even better reason to proceed with caution. Remember, the goal of overloading operators is to increase usability and understanding.

DO	DON'T
DO use operator overloading when it will clarify the program.	
DON'T create counter-intuitive operators.	
DO return an object of the class from overloaded operators.	

operator=

The fourth and final function that is supplied by the compiler, if you don't specify one, is operator equals (operator=()). This operator is called whenever you assign to an object. For example:

```
CAT catOne(5,7);
CAT catTwo(3,4);
// ... other code here
catTwo = catOne;
```

Here catOne is created and initialized with itsAge equal to 5 and itsWeight equal to 7. catTwo is then created and assigned the values 3 and 4.

After a while, `catTwo` is assigned the values in `catOne`. Two issues are raised here: What happens if `itsAge` is a pointer, and what happens to the original values in `catTwo`?

Handling member variables that store their values on the free store was discussed earlier during the examination of the copy constructor. The same issues arise here, as illustrated in Figures 10.1 and 10.2.

C++ programmers differentiate between a *shallow* or *member-wise* copy on the one hand, and a "deep copy" on the other. A shallow copy just copies the members, and both objects end up pointing to the same area on the free store. A deep copy allocates the necessary memory. This is illustrated in Figure 10.3.

There is an added wrinkle with the assignment operator, however. The object `catTwo` already exists, and already has memory allocated. That memory must be deleted if there is to be no memory leak. But what happens if you assign `catTwo` to itself?

```
catTwo = catTwo;
```

No one is likely to do this on purpose, but the program must be able to handle it. More important, it is possible for this to happen by accident when references and dereferenced pointers hide the fact that the assignment is to itself.

If you did not handle this problem carefully, `catTwo` would delete its memory allocation. Then, when it was ready to copy in the memory from the right-hand side of the assignment, it would have a very big problem: the memory would be gone.

To protect against this, your assignment operator must check to see if the right-hand side of the assignment operator is the object itself. It does this by examining the `this` pointer. Listing 10.15 shows a class with an assignment operator.

Listing 10.15. An assignment operator.

```
1:      // Listing 10.15
2:      // Copy constructors
3:
4:      #include <iostreams.h>
5:
6:      class CAT
7:      {
8:          public:
9:              CAT();                          // default constructor
10:     // copy constructor and destructor elided!
11:             int GetAge() const { return *itsAge; }
12:             int GetWeight() const { return *itsWeight; }
13:             void SetAge(int age) { *itsAge = age; }
14:             CAT operator=(const CAT &);
15:
```

continues

Listing 10.15. continued

```
16:            private:
17:                int *itsAge;
18:                int *itsWeight;
19:        };
20:
21:        CAT::CAT()
22:        {
23:            itsAge = new int;
24:            itsWeight = new int;
25:            *itsAge = 5;
26:            *itsWeight = 9;
27:        }
28:
29:
30:        CAT CAT::operator=(const CAT & rhs)
31:        {
32:          if (this == &rhs)
33:            return *this;
34:            itsAge = new int;
35:            itsWeight = new int;
36:            *itsAge = rhs.GetAge();
37:            *itsWeight = rhs.GetWeight();
38:        }
39:
40:
41:        void main()
42:        {
43:            CAT frisky;
44:            cout << "frisky's age: " << frisky.GetAge() << endl;
45:            cout << "Setting frisky to 6...\n";
46:            frisky.SetAge(6);
47:            CAT whiskers;
48:            cout << "whiskers' age: " << whiskers.GetAge() << endl;
49:            cout << "copying frisky to whiskers...\n";
50:            whiskers = frisky;
51:            cout << "whiskers' age: " << whiskers.GetAge() << endl;
52:        }
```

```
frisky's age: 5
Setting frisky to 6;
whisker's age: 5
copying frisky to whiskers...
whisker's age: 6
```

Listing 10.15 brings back the CAT class, and leaves out the copy constructor and destructor to save room. On line 14 the assignment operator is declared, and on lines 30–38 it is defined.

On line 32, the current object (the CAT being assigned to) is tested to see if it is the same as the CAT being assigned. This is done by checking if the address of rhs is the same as the address stored in the this pointer.

This works fine for single inheritance, but if you are using multiple inheritance, as discussed on Day 13, this test will fail. An alternative test is to dereference the this pointer and see if the two objects are the same:

```
if (*this == rhs)
```

Of course, the equality operator (==) can be overloaded as well, allowing you to determine for yourself what it means for your objects to be equal.

Conversion Operators

What happens when you try to assign a variable of a built-in type, such as int or unsigned short, to an object of a user-defined class? Listing 10.16 brings back the Counter class, and attempts to assign a variable of type USHORT to a Counter object.

Warning: Listing 10.16 will not compile!

Listing 10.16. Attempting to assign a counter to a USHORT.

```
1:     // Listing 10.16
2:     // This code won't compile!
3:
4:     typedef unsigned short  USHORT;
5:     #include <iostreams.h>
6:
7:     class Counter
8:     {
9:        public:
10:          Counter();
11:          ~Counter(){}
12:          USHORT GetItsVal()const { return itsVal; }
13:          void SetItsVal(USHORT x) {itsVal = x; }
14:        private:
15:          USHORT itsVal;
16:
17:     };
18:
19:     Counter::Counter():
20:     itsVal(0)
21:     {}
22:
23:     void main()
24:     {
```

continues

Listing 10.16. continued

```
25:       USHORT theShort = 5;
26:       Counter theCtr = theShort;
27:       cout << "theCtr: " << theCtr.GetItsVal() << endl;
28:    }
```

Compiler error! Unable to convert USHORT to Counter

The Counter class declared on lines 7–17 has only a default constructor. It declares no particular method for turning a USHORT into a Counter object, and so line 26 causes a compile error. The compiler cannot figure out, unless you tell it, that given a USHORT it should assign that value to the member variable itsVal.

Listing 10.17 corrects this by creating a conversion operator: a constructor that takes a USHORT and produces a Counter object.

Listing 10.17. Converting USHORT to Counter.

```
1:       // Listing 10.17
2:       // Constructor as conversion operator
3:
4:       typedef unsigned short   USHORT;
5:       #include <iostreams.h>
6:
7:       class Counter
8:       {
9:          public:
10:             Counter();
11:             Counter(USHORT val);
12:             ~Counter(){}
13:             USHORT GetItsVal()const { return itsVal; }
14:             void SetItsVal(USHORT x) {itsVal = x; }
15:          private:
16:             USHORT itsVal;
17:
18:       };
19:
20:       Counter::Counter():
21:       itsVal(0)
22:       {}
23:
24:    Counter::Counter(USHORT val):
25:    itsVal(val)
26:    {}
27:
28:
```

```
29:    void main()
30:    {
31:        USHORT theShort = 5;
32:        Counter theCtr = theShort;
33:        cout << "theCtr: " << theCtr.GetItsVal() << endl;
34:    }
```

theCtr: 5

The important change is on line 11, where the constructor is overloaded to take a USHORT, and on lines 20–22, where the constructor is implemented. The effect of this constructor is to create a Counter out of a USHORT.

Given this, the compiler is able to call the constructor that takes a USHORT as its argument. What happens, however, if you try to reverse the assignment with the following?

```
1:   Counter theCtr(5);
2:   USHORT theShort = theCtr;
3:   cout << "theShort : " << theShort  << endl;
```

Once again, this will generate a compile error. Although the compiler now knows how to create a Counter out of a USHORT, it does not know how to reverse the process.

Operator *unsigned short()*

To solve this and similar problems, C++ provides conversion operators that can be added to your class. This allows your class to specify how to do implicit conversions to built-in types. Listing 10.18 illustrates this. One note, however: conversion operators do *not* specify a return value, even though they do, in effect, return a converted value.

Listing 10.18. Converting from Counter to unsigned short().

```
1:   // Listing 10.18
2:   // conversion operator
3:
4:   typedef unsigned short   USHORT;
5:   #include <iostreams.h>
6:
7:   class Counter
8:   {
9:     public:
10:        Counter();
11:        Counter(USHORT val);
12:        ~Counter(){}
```

continues

293

Listing 10.18. continued

```
13:        USHORT GetItsVal()const { return itsVal; }
14:        void SetItsVal(USHORT x) {itsVal = x; }
15:        operator unsigned short();
16:    private:
17:        USHORT itsVal;
18:
19:    };
20:
21:    Counter::Counter():
22:    itsVal(0)
23:    {}
24:
25:  Counter::Counter(USHORT val):
26:  itsVal(val)
27:  {}
28:
29:  Counter::operator unsigned short ()
30:  {
31:      return ( USHORT (itsVal) );
32:  }
33:
34:  void main()
35:  {
36:      Counter ctr(5);
37:      USHORT theShort = ctr;
38:      cout << "theShort: " << theShort << endl;
39:  }
```

```
theShort: 5
```

On line 15 the conversion operator is declared. Note that it has no return value. The implementation of this function is on lines 29–32. Line 31 returns the value of itsVal converted to a USHORT.

Now the compiler knows how to turn USHORTS into Counter objects and vice versa, and they can be assigned to one another freely.

Summary

Today you learned how to overload member functions of your classes. You also learned how to supply default values to functions, and how to decide when to use default values and when to overload.

Overloading class constructors allows you to create flexible classes that can be created from other objects. Initialization of objects happens at the initialization stage of construction, and is more efficient than assigning values in the body of the constructor.

The copy constructor and operator= are supplied by the compiler if you don't create your own, but they do a member-wise copy of the class. In classes in which member data includes pointers to the free store, these methods must be overridden so that you allocate memory for the target object.

Almost all C++ operators can be overloaded, though you want to be cautious not to create operators whose use is counterintuitive. You cannot change the arity of operators, nor can you invent new operators.

The this pointer refers to the current object, and is an invisible parameter to all member functions. The dereferenced this pointer is often returned by overloaded operators.

Conversion operators allow you to create classes that can be used in expressions that expect a different type of object. They are exceptions to the rule that all functions return an explicit value; like constructors and destructors, they have no return type.

Q&A

Q Why would you ever use default values when you can overload a function?

A It is easier to maintain one function than two, and often easier to understand a function with default parameters than to study the bodies of two functions. Furthermore, updating one of the functions and neglecting to update the second is a common source of bugs.

Q Given the problems with overloaded functions, why not always use default values instead?

A Overloaded functions supply capabilities not available with default variables, such as varying the list of parameters by type rather than just by number.

Q When writing a class constructor, how do you decide what to put in the initialization and what to put in the body of the constructor?

A A simple rule of thumb is to do as much as possible in the initialization phase; that is, initialize all member variables there. Some things, like computations and print statements, must be in the body of the constructor.

Q Can an overloaded function have a default parameter?

A Yes. There is no reason not to combine these powerful features. One or more of the overloaded functions can have their own default values, following the normal rules for default variables in any function.

Q Why are some member functions defined within the class declaration and others are not?

A Defining the implementation of a member function within the declaration makes it inline. Generally, this is done only if the function is extremely simple. Note that you can also make a member function inline by using the keyword `inline`, even if the function is declared outside the class declaration.

Workshop

The Workshop provides quiz questions to help solidify your understanding of the material covered and exercises to provide you with experience in using what you've learned. Try to answer the quiz and exercise questions before checking the answers in Appendix D, and make sure you understand the answers before going to the next chapter.

Quiz

1. When you overload member functions, in what ways must they differ?
2. What is the difference between a declaration and a definition?
3. When is the copy constructor called?
4. When is the destructor called?
5. How does the copy constructor differ from the assignment operator (=)?
6. What is the `this` pointer?
7. How do you differentiate between overloading the prefix increment and the postfix?
8. Can you overload the operator+ for short integers?
9. Is it legal in C++ to overload `operator++` so that it decrements a value in your class?
10. What return value must conversion operators have in their declaration?

Exercises

1. Write a `SimpleCircle` class declaration (only) with one member variable: `itsRadius`. Include a default constructor, a destructor, and accessor methods for radius.

2. Using the class you created in Exercise 1, write the implementation of the default constructor, initializing `itsRadius` with the value 5.

3. Using the same class, add a second constructor that takes a value as its parameter and assigns that value to `itsRadius`.

4. Create a prefix and postfix `Increment` operator for your `SimpleCircle` class that increments `itsRadius`.

5. Change `SimpleCircle` to store `itsRadius` on the free store, and fix the existing methods.

6. Provide a copy constructor for `SimpleCircle`.

7. Provide an `operator=` for `SimpleCircle`.

8. Write a program that creates two `SimpleCircle` objects. Use the default constructor on one and instantiate the other with the value 9. Call `Increment` on each and then print their values. Finally, assign the second to the first and print its values.

9. **BUG BUSTERS:** What is wrong with this implementation of the assignment operator?

```
SQUARE SQUARE ::operator=(const SQUARE & rhs)
{
    itsSide = new int;
    *itsSide = rhs.GetSide();
    return *this;
}
```

10. **BUG BUSTERS:** What is wrong with this implementation of `operator+`?

```
VeryShort  VeryShort::operator+ (const VeryShort& rhs)
{
   itsVal += rhs.GetItsVal();
   return *this;
}
```

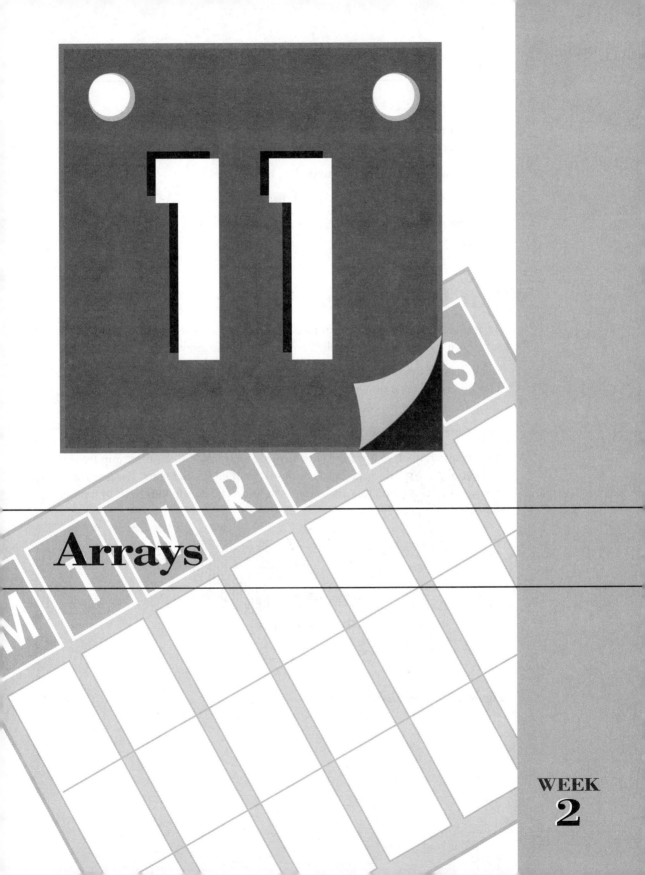

11

Arrays

In previous chapters, you declared a single int, char, or other object. You often want to declare a collection of objects, such as 20 ints or a litter of CATs. Today, you learn:

☐ What arrays are and how to declare them.

☐ What strings are and how to use character arrays to make them.

☐ The relationship between arrays and pointers.

☐ How to use pointer arithmetic with arrays.

What Is an Array?

An array is a collection of data storage locations, each of which holds the same type of data. Each storage location is called an element of the array.

You declare an array by writing the type, followed by the array name and the subscript. The subscript is the number of elements in the array, surrounded by square brackets. For example,

```
long LongArray[25];
```

declares an array of 25 long integers, named LongArray. When the compiler sees this declaration, it sets aside enough memory to hold all 25 elements. Because each long integer requires 4 bytes, this declaration sets aside 100 contiguous bytes of memory, as illustrated in Figure 11.1.

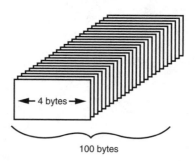

◄— 4 bytes —►

100 bytes

Figure 11.1. *Declaring an array.*

Array Elements

You access each of the array elements by referring to an offset from the array name. Array elements are counted from zero. Therefore, the first array element is arrayName[0]. In the LongArray example, LongArray[0] is the first array element, LongArray[1] the second, and so forth.

This can be somewhat confusing. The array SomeArray[3] has three elements. They are SomeArray[0], SomeArray[1], and SomeArray[2]. More generally, SomeArray[n] has n elements that are numbered SomeArray[0] through SomeArray[n-1].

Therefore, LongArray[25] is numbered from LongArray[0] through LongArray[24]. Listing 11.1 shows how to declare an array of five integers and fill each with a value.

Listing 11.1. Using an integer array.

```
1:      //Listing 11.1 - Arrays
2:      #include <iostream.h>
3:
4:      void main()
5:      {
6:          int myArray[5];
7:          for (int i=0; i<5; i++)   // 0-4
8:          {
9:              cout << "Value for myArray[" << i << "]: ";
10:             cin >> myArray[i];
11:         }
12:         for (i = 0; i<5; i++)
13:             cout << i << ": " << myArray[i] << "\n";
14:     }
```

```
Value for myArray[0]:   3
Value for myArray[1]:   6
Value for myArray[2]:   9
Value for myArray[3]:   12
Value for myArray[4]:   15

0: 3
1: 6
2: 9
3: 12
4: 15
```

Line 6 declares an array called myArray, which holds five integer variables. Line 7 establishes a loop that counts from 0 through 4, which is the proper set of offsets for a five-element array. The user is prompted for a value, and that value is saved at the correct offset into the array.

The first value is saved at `myArray[0]`, the second at `myArray[1]`, and so forth. The second `for` loop prints each value to the screen.

> **Note:** Arrays count from 0, not from 1. This is the cause of many bugs in programs written by C++ novices. Whenever you use an array, remember that an array with 10 elements counts from `ArrayName[0]` to `ArrayName[9]`. There is no `ArrayName[10]`.

Writing Past the End of an Array

When you write a value to an element in an array, the compiler computes where to store the value based on the size of each element and the subscript. Suppose that you ask to write over the value at `LongArray[5]`, which is the sixth element. The compiler multiplies the offset—5—by the size of each element—in this case, 4. It then moves that many bytes—20—from the beginning of the array and writes the new value at that location.

If you ask to write at `LongArray[50]`, the compiler ignores the fact that there is no such element. It computes how far past the first element it should look—200 bytes—and then writes over whatever is at that location. This can be virtually any data, and writing your new value there might have unpredictable results. If you're lucky, your program will crash immediately. If you're unlucky, you'll get strange results much later in your program, and you'll have a difficult time figuring out what went wrong.

The compiler is like a blind man pacing off the distance from a house. He starts out at the first house, `MainStreet[0]`. When you ask him to go to the sixth house on Main Street, he says to himself, "I must go five more houses. Each house is four big paces. I must go an additional 20 steps." If you ask him to go to `MainStreet[100]`, and Main Street is only 25 houses long, he will pace off 400 steps. Long before he gets there, he will, no doubt, step in front of a moving bus. So be careful where you send him.

Listing 11.2 shows what happens when you write past the end of an array.

> **Caution:** Do not run this program—it may crash your system!

Listing 11.2. Writing past the end of an array.

```
1:      //Listing 11.2
2:      // Demonstrates what happens when you write past the end
3:      // of an array
4:
5:      #include <iostream.h>
6:      void main()
7:      {
8:          // sentinels
9:          long sentinelOne[3];
10:         long sentinelTwo[3];
11:         long TargetArray[25]; // array to fill
12:
13:         for (int i=0; i<3; i++)
14:             sentinelOne[i] = sentinelTwo[i] = 0;
15:
16:         for (i=0; i<25; i++)
17:             TargetArray[i] = 0;
18:
19:         cout << "Test 1: \n";   // test current values (should be 0)
20:         cout << "TargetArray[0]: " << TargetArray[0] << "\n";
21:         cout << "TargetArray[24]: " << TargetArray[24] << "\n\n";
22:
23:         for (i = 0; i<3; i++)
24:         {
25:             cout << "sentinelOne[" << i << "]: " << sentinelOne[i] << "\n";
26:             cout << "sentinelTwo[" << i << "]: " << sentinelTwo[i]<< "\n";
27:         }
28:
29:         cout << "\nAssigning...";
30:         for (i = 0; i<=25; i++)
31:             TargetArray[i] = 20;
32:
33:         cout << "\nTest 2: \n";
34:         cout << "TargetArray[0]: " << TargetArray[0] << "\n";
35:         cout << "TargetArray[24]: " << TargetArray[24] << "\n";
36:         cout << "TargetArray[25]: " << TargetArray[25] << "\n\n";
37:         for (i = 0; i<3; i++)
38:         {
39:             cout << "sentinelOne[" << i << "]: " << sentinelOne[i]<< "\n";
40:             cout << "sentinelTwo[" << i << "]: " << sentinelTwo[i]<< "\n";
41:         }
42:
43:     }
```

11

```
Test 1:
TargetArray[0]: 0
TargetArray[24]: 0

SentinelOne[0]: 0
SentinelTwo[0]: 0
SentinelOne[1]: 0
SentinelTwo[1]: 0
SentinelOne[2]: 0
SentinelTwo[2]: 0

Assigning...
Test 2:
TargetArray[0]:   20
TargetArray[24]:  20
TargetArray[25]:  20

SentinelOne[0]: 0
SentinelTwo[0]: 20
SentinelOne[1]: 0
SentinelTwo[1]: 0
SentinelOne[2]: 0
SentinelTwo[2]: 0
```

Lines 9 and 10 declare two arrays of three integers that act as sentinels around `TargetArray`. These sentinel arrays are initialized with the value `0`. If memory is written to beyond the end of `TargetArray`, the sentinels are likely to be changed. Some compilers count down in memory; others count up. For this reason, the sentinels are placed on both sides of `TargetArray`.

Lines 19–27 confirm the sentinel values in Test 1. In line 31 `TargetArray`'s members are all initialized to the value `20`, but the counter counts to `TargetArray` offset 25, which doesn't exist in `TargetArray`.

Lines 34–36 print `TargetArray`'s values in Test 2. Note that `TargetArray[25]` is perfectly happy to print the value `20`. However, when `SentinelOne` and `SentinelTwo` are printed, `SentinelTwo[0]` reveals that its value has changed. This is because the memory that is 25 elements after `TargetArray[0]` is the same memory that is at `SentinelTwo[0]`. When the nonexistent `TargetArray[0]` was accessed, what was actually accessed was `SentinelTwo[0]`.

This nasty bug can be very hard to find, because `SentinelTwo[0]`'s value was changed in a part of the code that was not writing to `SentinelTwo` at all.

This code uses "magic numbers," such as 3 for the size of the sentinel arrays and 25 for the size of `TargetArray`. It is safer to use constants, so that when one changes, they all reflect the change.

Fence Post Errors

It is so common to write to one past the end of an array that this bug has its own name. It is called a fence post error. This refers to the problem in counting how many fence posts you need for a 10-foot fence if you need one post for every foot. Most people answer 10, but of course you need 11. Figure 11.2 makes this clear.

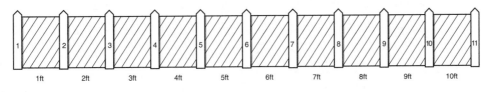

Figure 11.2. *Fence post errors.*

This sort of "off by one" counting can be the bane of any programmer's life. Over time, however, you'll get used to the idea that a 25-element array counts only to element 24, and that everything counts from 0. (Programmers are often confused why office buildings don't have a floor zero. Indeed, some have been known to push the 4 elevator button when they want to get to the fifth floor.)

> **Note:** Some programmers refer to `ArrayName[0]` as the zeroth element. Getting into this habit is a big mistake. If `ArrayName[0]` is the zeroth element, what is `ArrayName[1]`? The oneth? If so, when you see `ArrayName[24]`, will you realize that it is not the 24th element, but rather the 25th? It is far better to say that `ArrayName[0]` is at offset zero and is the first element.

Initializing Arrays

You can initialize a simple array of built-in types, such as integers and characters, when you first declare the array. After the array name, you put an equal sign (=) and a list of comma-separated values enclosed in braces. For example,

```
int IntegerArray[5] = { 10, 20, 30, 40, 50 };
```

declares `IntegerArray` to be an array of five integers. It assigns `IntegerArray[0]` the value 10, `IntegerArray[1]` the value 20, and so forth.

If you omit the size of the array, an array just big enough to hold the initialization is created. Therefore, if you write

```
int IntegerArray[] = { 10, 20, 30, 40, 50 };
```

you will create exactly the same array as you did in the previous example.

If you need to know the size of the array, you can ask the compiler to compute it for you. For example,

```
const USHORT IntegerArrayLength = sizeof(IntegerArray)/sizeof(IntegerArray[0]);
```

sets the constant `USHORT` variable `IntegerArrayLength` to the result obtained from dividing the size of the entire array by the size of each individual entry in the array. That quotient is the number of members in the array.

You cannot initialize more elements than you've declared for the array. Therefore,

```
int IntegerArray[5] = { 10, 20, 30, 40, 50, 60};
```

generates a compiler error because you've declared a five-member array and initialized six values. It is legal, however, to write

```
int IntegerArray[5] = { 10, 20};
```

Although uninitialized array members have no guaranteed value, they do have a value. The array still points to memory, so you will get whatever happens to be in memory at the time. It is always safer to initialize array members at the time you declare the array than to take the chance of getting random data back when you use the array.

DO	DON'T
DO let the compiler set the size of initialized arrays.	
DON'T write past the end of the array.	
DO give arrays meaningful names, as you would with any variable.	
DO remember that the first member of the array is at offset 0.	

Declaring Arrays

Arrays can have any legal variable name, but they cannot have the same name as another variable or array within their scope. Therefore, you cannot have an array named myCats[5] and a variable named myCats at the same time.

You can dimension the array size with a const or with an enumeration. Listing 11.3 illustrates this.

Listing 11.3. Using consts and enums in arrays.

```
1:     // Listing 11.3
2:     // Dimensioning arrays with consts and enumerations
3:
4:     #include <iostream.h>
5:     void main()
6:     {
7:         enum WeekDays { Sun, Mon, Tue, Wed, Thu, Fri, Sat, DaysInWeek };
8:
9:         int ArrayWeek[DaysInWeek] = { 10, 20, 30, 40, 50, 60, 70 };
10:
11:        cout << "The value at Tuesday is: " << ArrayWeek[Tue];
12:    }
```

The value at Tuesday is: 30

Line 7 creates an enumeration called WeekDays. It has eight members. Sunday is equal to 0, and DaysInWeek is equal to 7.

Line 11 uses the enumerated constant Tue as an offset into the array. Because Tue evaluates to 2, the third element of the array, DaysInWeek[2], is returned and printed in line 12.

Arrays

To declare an array, write the type of object stored, followed by the name of the array and a subscript with the number of objects to be held in the array.

Example 1

```
int MyIntegerArray[90];
```

Example 2

```
long * ArrayOfPointersToLongs[100];
```

To access members of the array, use the subscript operator.

Example 1

```
int theNinethInteger = MyIntegerArray[8];
```

Example 2

```
long * pLong = ArrayOfPointersToLongs[8]
```

Arrays count from zero. An array of *n* items is numbered from 0 to *n*–1.

Arrays of Objects

Any object, whether built-in or user-defined, can be stored in an array. When you declare the array, you tell the compiler the type of object to store and the number of objects for which to allocate room. The compiler knows how much room is needed for each object based on the class declaration. The class must have a default constructor that takes no arguments so that the objects can be created when the array is defined.

Accessing member data in an array of objects is a two-step process. You identify the member of the array by using the index operator ([ ]), and then you add the member operator (.) to access the particular member variable. Listing 11.4 demonstrates how you would create an array of five CATs.

Listing 11.4. Creating an array of objects.

```
1:      // Listing 11.4 - An array of objects
2:
3:      #include <iostreams.h>
4:
5:      class CAT
6:      {
7:         public:
8:            CAT() { itsAge = 1; itsWeight=5; }        // default constructor
9:            ~CAT() {}                                 // destructor
10:           int GetAge() const { return itsAge; }
11:           int GetWeight() const { return itsWeight; }
12:           void SetAge(int age) { itsAge = age; }
13:
14:        private:
15:           int itsAge;
16:           int itsWeight;
17:     };
```

```
18:
19:     void main()
20:     {
21:         CAT Litter[5];
22:         int i;
23:         for (i = 0; i < 5; i++)
24:             Litter[i].SetAge(2*i +1);
25:
26:         for (i = 0; i < 5; i++)
27:             cout << "Cat #" << i+1<< ": " << Litter[i].GetAge() << endl;
28:     }
```

```
cat #1:  1
cat #2:  3
cat #3:  5
cat #4:  7
cat #5:  9
```

Lines 5–17 declare the CAT class. The CAT class must have a default constructor so that CAT objects can be created in an array. Remember that if you create any other constructor, the compiler-supplied default constructor is not created; you must create your own.

The first for loop (lines 23 and 24) sets the age of each of the five CATs in the array. The second for loop (lines 26 and 27) accesses each member of the array and calls GetAge().

Each individual CAT's GetAge() method is called by accessing the member in the array, Litter[i], followed by the dot operator (.), and the member function.

Multidimensional Arrays

It is possible to have arrays of more than one dimension. Each dimension is represented as a subscript in the array. Therefore, a two-dimensional array has two subscripts; a three-dimensional array has three subscripts; and so on. Arrays can have any number of dimensions, although it is likely that most of the arrays you create will be of one or two dimensions.

A good example of a two-dimensional array is a chess board. One dimension represents the eight rows; the other dimension represents the eight columns. Figure 11.3 illustrates this idea.

Suppose that you have a class named SQUARE. The declaration of an array named Board that represents it would be

```
SQUARE Board[8][8];
```

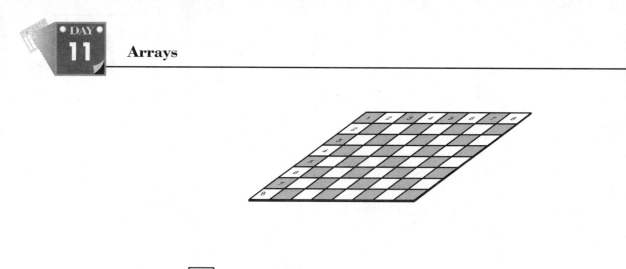

Figure 11.3. *A chess board and a two-dimensional array.*

You could also represent the same data with a one-dimension, 64-square array. For example,

```
SQUARE Board[64]
```

This doesn't correspond as closely to the real-world object as the two-dimension. When the game begins, the king is located in the fourth position in the first row. Counting from zero, that position corresponds to

```
Board[0][3];
```

assuming that the first subscript corresponds to row, and the second to column. The layout of positions for the entire board is illustrated in Figure 11.3.

Initializing Multidimensional Arrays

You can initialize multidimensional arrays. You assign the list of values to array elements in order, with the last array subscript changing while each of the former hold steady. Therefore, if you have an array

```
int theArray[5][3]
```

the first three elements go into theArray[0]; the next three into theArray[1]; and so forth.

You initialize this array by writing

```
int theArray[5][3] = { 1,2,3,4,5,6,7,8,9,10,11,12,13,14,15 }
```

For the sake of clarity, you could group the initializations with braces. For example,

```
int theArray[5][3] = {  {1,2,3},
                        {4,5,6},
                        {7,8.9},
                        {10,11,12},
                        {13,14,15} };
```

The compiler ignores the inner braces, which make it easier to understand how the numbers are distributed.

Each value must be separated by a comma, without regard to the braces. The entire initialization set must be within braces, and it must end with a semicolon.

Listing 11.5 creates a two-dimensional array. The first dimension is the set of numbers from 0 to 5. The second dimension consists of the double of each value in the first dimension.

Listing 11.5. Creating a multidimensional array.

```
1:      #include <iostreams.h>
2:      void main()
3:      {
4:          int SomeArray[5][2] = { {0,0}, {1,2}, {2,4}, {3,6}, {4,8}};
5:          for (int i = 0; i<5; i++)
6:             for (int j=0; j<2; j++)
7:             {
8:                cout << "SomeArray[" << i << "][" << j << "]: ";
9:                cout << SomeArray[i][j]<< endl;
10:            }
11:
12:     }
```

```
SomeArray[0][0]: 0
SomeArray[0][1]: 0
SomeArray[1][0]: 1
SomeArray[1][1]: 2
SomeArray[2][0]: 2
SomeArray[2][1]: 4
SomeArray[3][0]: 3
SomeArray[3][1]: 6
SomeArray[4][0]: 4
SomeArray[4][1]: 8
```

Line 4 declares SomeArray to be a two-dimensional array. The first dimension consists of five integers; the second dimension consists of two integers. This creates a 5×2 grid, as Figure 11.4 shows.

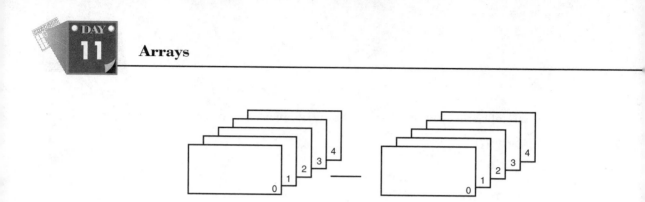

Some Array [5] [2]

Figure 11.4. *A 5×2 array.*

The values are initialized in pairs, although they could be computed as well. Lines 5 and 6 create a nested `for` loop. The outer `for` loop ticks through each member of the first dimension. For every member in that dimension, the inner `for` loop ticks through each member of the second dimension. This is consistent with the printout. `SomeArray[0][0]` is followed by `SomeArray[0][1]`. The first dimension is incremented only after the second dimension is incremented by 1. Then the second dimension starts over.

A Word About Memory

When you declare an array, you tell the compiler exactly how many objects you expect to store in it. The compiler sets aside memory for all the objects, even if you never use it. This isn't a problem with arrays for which you have a good idea of how many objects you'll need. For example, a chess board has 64 squares, and CATs have between 1 and 10 kittens. When you have no idea of how many objects you'll need, however, you must use more advanced data structures.

This book looks at arrays of pointers, arrays built on the free store, and various other collections. Other more advanced data structures that solve large data storage problems are beyond the scope of this book. Two of the great things about programming are that there are always more things to learn and that there are always more books from which to learn.

Arrays of Pointers

The arrays discussed so far store all their members on the stack. Usually stack memory is severely limited, whereas free store memory is far larger. It is possible to declare each object on the free store and then to store only a pointer to the object in the array. This dramatically reduces the amount of stack memory used. Listing 11.6 rewrites the array from Listing 11.4, but it stores all the objects on the free store. As an indication of the greater memory that this enables, the array is expanded from 5 to 500, and the name is changed from `Litter` to `Family`.

Listing 11.6. Storing an array on the free store.

```
1:      // Listing 11.6 - An array of pointers to objects
2:
3:      #include <iostreams.h>
4:
5:      class CAT
6:      {
7:         public:
8:            CAT() { itsAge = 1; itsWeight=5; }        // default constructor
9:            ~CAT() {}                                 // destructor
10:            int GetAge() const { return itsAge; }
11:            int GetWeight() const { return itsWeight; }
12:            void SetAge(int age) { itsAge = age; }
13:
14:         private:
15:            int itsAge;
16:            int itsWeight;
17:      };
18:
19:      void main()
20:      {
21:         CAT * Family[500];
22:         int i;
23:         CAT * pCat;
24:         for (i = 0; i < 500; i++)
25:         {
26:            pCat = new CAT;
27:            pCat->SetAge(2*i +1);
28:            Family[i] = pCat;
29:         }
30:
31:         for (i = 0; i < 500; i++)
32:            cout << "Cat #" << i+1 << ": " << Family[i]->GetAge() << endl;
33:      }
```

Output

```
Cat #1: 1
Cat #2: 3
Cat #3: 5
...
Cat #499: 997
Cat #500: 999
```

Analysis

The CAT object declared in lines 5–17 is identical with the CAT object declared in Listing 11.4. This time, however, the array declared in line 21 is named Family, and it is declared to hold 500 pointers to CAT objects.

In the initial loop (lines 24–29), 500 new CAT objects are created on the free store, and each one has its age set to twice the index plus one. Therefore, the first CAT is set to 1, the second CAT to 3, the third CAT to 5, and so on. Finally, the pointer is added to the array.

Because the array has been declared to hold pointers, the pointer—rather than the dereferenced value in the pointer—is added to the array.

The second loop (lines 31 and 32) prints each of the values. The pointer is accessed by using the index, `Family[i]`. That address is then used to access the `GetAge()` method.

In this example, the array `Family` and all its pointers are stored on the stack, but the 500 `CAT`s that are created are stored on the free store.

Declaring Arrays on the Free Store

It is possible to put the entire array on the free store, also known as the heap. You do this by calling new and using the subscript operator. The result is a pointer to an area on the free store that holds the array. For example,

```
CAT *Family = new CAT[500];
```

declares `Family` to be a pointer to the first in an array of 500 `CAT`s. In other words, `Family` points to—or has the address of—`Family[0]`.

The advantage of using `Family` in this way is that you can use pointer arithmetic to access each member of `Family`. For example, you can write

```
CAT *Family = new CAT[500];
CAT *pCat = Family;             //pCat points to Family[0]
pCat->SetAge(10);               // set Family[0] to 10
pCat++;                         // advance to Family[1]
pCat->SetAge(20);               // set Family[1] to 20
```

This declares a new array of 500 `CAT`s and a pointer to point to the start of the array. Using that pointer, the first `CAT`'s `SetAge()` function is incremented to point to the next `CAT`, and the second `Cat`'s `SetAge()` method is then called.

A Pointer to an Array Versus an Array of Pointers

Examine these three declarations:

```
1:  Cat   FamilyOne[500]
2:  CAT * FamilyTwo[500];
3:  CAT * FamilyThree = new CAT[500];
```

`FamilyOne` is an array of 500 `CAT`s. `FamilyTwo` is an array of 500 pointers to `CAT`s. `FamilyThree` is a pointer to an array of 500 `CAT`s.

The differences among these three code lines dramatically affect how these arrays operate. What is perhaps even more surprising is that `FamilyThree` is a variant of `FamilyOne` but is very different from `FamilyTwo`.

This raises the thorny issue of how pointers relate to arrays. In the third case, FamilyThree is a pointer to an array. That is, the address in FamilyThree is the address of the first item in that array. This is exactly the case for FamilyOne.

Pointers and Array Names

In C++ an array name is a constant pointer to the first element of the array. Therefore, in the declaration

```
CAT Family[50];
```

Family is a pointer to &Family[0], which is the address of the first element of the array Family.

It is legal to use array names as constant pointers, and vice versa. Therefore, Family + 4 is a legitimate way of accessing the data at Family[4].

The compiler does all the arithmetic when you add to, increment, and decrement pointers. The address accessed when you write Family + 4 isn't 4 bytes past the address of Family—it is four objects. If each object is 4 bytes long, Family + 4 is 16 bytes. If each object is a CAT that has four long member variables of 4 bytes each and two short member variables of 2 bytes each, each CAT is 20 bytes, and Family + 4 is 80 bytes past the start of the array.

Listing 11.7 illustrates declaring and using an array on the free store.

Listing 11.7. Creating an array by using new.

```
1:      // Listing 11.7 - An array on the free store
2:
3:      #include <iostreams.h>
4:
5:      class CAT
6:      {
7:        public:
8:          CAT() { itsAge = 1; itsWeight=5; }      // default constructor
9:          ~CAT();                                 // destructor
10:         int GetAge() const { return itsAge; }
11:         int GetWeight() const { return itsWeight; }
12:         void SetAge(int age) { itsAge = age; }
13:
14:       private:
15:          int itsAge;
16:          int itsWeight;
17:      };
18:
```

continues

315

Listing 11.7. continued

```
19:     CAT :: ~CAT()
20:     {
21:        // cout << "Destructor called!\n";
22:     }
23:
24:     void main()
25:     {
26:        CAT * Family = new CAT[500];
27:        int i;
28:        CAT * pCat;
29:        for (i = 0; i < 500; i++)
30:        {
31:           pCat = new CAT;
32:           pCat->SetAge(2*i +1);
33:           Family[i] = *pCat;
34:        }
35:
36:        for (i = 0; i < 500; i++)
37:           cout << "Cat #" << i+1 << ": " << Family[i].GetAge() << endl;
38:
39:        delete [] Family;
40:
41:     }
```

```
Cat #1: 1
Cat #2: 3
Cat #3: 5
...
Cat #499: 997
Cat #500: 999
```

Line 26 declares the array Family, which holds 500 CAT objects. The entire array is created on the free store with the call to new CAT[500].

Each CAT object added to the array also is created on the free store (line 31). Note, however, that the pointer isn't added to the array this time; the object itself is. This array isn't an array of pointers to CATs. It is an array of CATs.

Deleting Arrays on the Free Store

Family is a pointer, a pointer to the array on the free store. When, on line 33, the pointer pCat is dereferenced, the CAT object itself is stored in the array (why not? the array is on the free store). But pCat is used again in the next iteration of the loop. Isn't there a danger that there will now be no pointer to that CAT object, and a memory leak has been created?

This would be a big problem, except that deleting Family returns all the memory set aside for the array. The compiler is smart enough to destroy each object in the array and to return its memory to the free store.

To see this, change the size of the array from 500 to 10 in lines 26, 29, and 36. Then uncomment the cout statement in line 21. When line 39 is reached and the array is destroyed, each CAT object destructor is called.

When you create an item on the heap by using new, you always delete that item and free its memory with delete. Similarly, when you create an array by using new <class>[size], you delete that array and free all its memory with delete[]. The brackets signal the compiler that this array is being deleted.

If you leave the brackets off only the first object in the array will be deleted. You can prove this to yourself by removing the brackets on line 39. If you edited line 21 so that the destructor prints, you should now see only one CAT object destroyed. Congratulations! You just created a memory leak.

11

DO	DON'T

DO remember that an array of *n* items is numbered from zero through *n*−1.

DON'T write or read past the end of an array.

DON'T confuse an array of pointers with a pointer to an array.

DO use array indexing with pointers that point to arrays.

char Arrays

A string is a series of characters. The only strings you've seen until now have been unnamed string constants used in cout statements, such as

```
cout << "hello world.\n";
```

In C++ a string is an array of chars ending with a null character. You can declare and initialize a string just as you would any other array. For example,

```
char Greeting[] = { 'H', 'e', 'l', 'l', 'o', ' ', 'W','o','r','l','d', '\0' };
```

The last character, '\0', is the null character, which many C++ functions recognize as the terminator for a string. Although this character-by-character approach works, it is difficult to type and admits too many opportunities for error. C++ enables you to use a shorthand form of the previous line of code. It is

```
char Greeting[] = "Hello World";
```

You should note two things about this syntax:

☐ Instead of single quoted characters separated by commas and surrounded by braces, you have a double-quoted string, no commas, and no braces.

☐ You don't need to add the null character because the compiler adds it for you.

The string Hello World is 12 bytes. Hello is 5 bytes, the space 1, World 5, and the null character 1.

You can also create uninitialized character arrays. As with all arrays, it is important to ensure that you don't put more into the buffer than there is room for.

Listing 11.8 demonstrates the use of an uninitialized buffer.

Listing 11.8. Filling an array.

```
1:      //listing 11.8 char array buffers
2:
3:      #include <iostream.h>
4:
5:      void main()
6:      {
7:         char buffer[80];
8:         cout << "Enter the string: ";
9:         cin >> buffer;
10:        cout << "Here's buffer:  " << buffer << endl;
11:     }
```

```
Enter the string: Hello World
Here's the buffer: Hello
```

On line 7 a buffer is declared to hold 80 characters. This is large enough to hold a 79 character string and a terminating null character.

On line 8 the user is prompted to enter a string, which is entered into buffer on line 9. It is the syntax of cin to write a terminating null to buffer after it writes the string.

There are two problems with the program in Listing 11.8. First, if the user enters more than 79 characters, cin writes past the end of the buffer. Second, if the user enters a space, cin thinks that it is the end of the string, and it stops writing to the buffer.

To solve these problems, you must call a special method on cin: get(). Cin.get() takes three parameters:

> The buffer to fill
> The maximum number of characters to get
> The delimiter that terminates input

The default delimiter is newline. Listing 11.9 illustrates its use.

Listing 11.9. Filling an array.

```
1:      //listing 11.9 using cin.get()
2:
3:      #include <iostream.h>
4:
5:      void main()
6:      {
7:         char buffer[80];
8:         cout << "Enter the string: ";
9:         cin.get(buffer, 79);        // get up to 79 or newline
10:        cout << "Here's buffer:  " << buffer << endl;
11:     }
```

Output

```
Enter the string: Hello World
Here's the buffer: Hello World
```

Analysis

Line 9 calls the method get() of cin. The buffer declared in line 7 is passed in as the first argument. The second argument is the maximum number of characters to get. In this case, it must be 79 to allow for the terminating null. There is no need to provide a terminating character because the default value of newline is sufficient.

Cin and all its variations are covered on Day 17, "The Preprocessor," when streams are discussed in depth.

strcpy() and *strncpy()*

C++ inherits from C a library of functions for dealing with strings. Among the many functions provided are two for copying one string into another: strcpy() and strncpy(). strcpy() copies the entire contents of one string into a designated buffer. Listing 11.10 demonstrates its use.

Listing 11.10. Using `strcpy()`.

```
1:      #include <iostreams.h>
2:      #include <string.h>
3:      void main()
4:      {
5:          char String1[] = "No man is an island";
6:          char String2[80];
7:
8:          strcpy(String2,String1);
9:
10:         cout << "String1: " << String1 << endl;
11:         cout << "String2: " << String2 << endl;
12:     }
```

```
String1: No man is an island
String2: No man is an island
```

The header file STRING.H is included in line 2. This file contains the prototype of the `strcpy()` function. `strcpy()` takes two character arrays—a destination followed by a source. If the source were larger than the destination, `strcpy()` would overwrite past the end of the buffer.

To protect against this, the standard library also includes `strncpy()`. This variation takes a maximum number of characters to copy. `strncpy()` copies up to the first null character or the maximum number of characters specified into the destination buffer.

Listing 11.11 illustrates the use of `strncpy()`.

Listing 11.11. Using `strncpy()`.

```
1:      #include <iostreams.h>
2:      #include <string.h>
3:      void main()
4:      {
5:          const int MaxLength = 80;
6:          char String1[] = "No man is an island";
7:          char String2[MaxLength+1];
8:
9:
10:         strncpy(String2,String1,MaxLength);
11:
12:         cout << "String1: " << String1 << endl;
13:         cout << "String2: " << String2 << endl;
14:     }
```

```
String1: No man is an island
String2: No man is an island
```

In line 10, the call to strcpy() has been changed to a call to strncpy(), which takes a third parameter: the maximum number of characters to copy. The buffer String2 is declared to take MaxLength+1 characters. The extra character is for the null, which both strcpy() and strncpy() automatically add to the end of the string.

String Classes

Most C++ compilers come with a class library that includes a large set of classes for data manipulation. A standard component of a class library is a String class.

C++ inherited the null-terminated string and the library of functions that includes strcpy() from C, but these functions aren't integrated into an object-oriented framework. A String class provides an encapsulated set of data and functions for manipulating that data, as well as accessor functions so that the data itself is hidden from the clients of the String class.

If your compiler doesn't already provide a String class—and perhaps even if it does— you might want to write your own. The remainder of this chapter discusses the design and partial implementation of String classes.

At a minimum, a String class should overcome the basic limitations of character arrays. Like all arrays, character arrays are static. You define how large they are. They always take up that much room in memory even if you don't need it all. Writing past the end of the array is disastrous.

A good String class allocates only as much memory as it needs, and always enough to hold whatever it is given. If it can't allocate enough memory, it should fail gracefully.

Listing 11.12 provides a first approximation of a String class.

Listing 11.12. Using a String class.

```
1:      //Listing 11.12
2:
3:      #include <iostreams.h>
4:      #include <string.h>
5:
6:      // Rudimentary string class
7:      class String
8:      {
9:         public:
10:            // constructors
11:            String();
12:            String(const char *const);
```

continues

Listing 11.12. continued

```
13:          String(const String &);
14:          ~String();
15:
16:          // overloaded operators
17:          char & operator[](unsigned short offset);
18:          char operator[](unsigned short offset) const;
19:          String operator+(const String&);
20:          void operator+=(const String&);
21:          String & operator= (const String &);
22:
23:          // General accessors
24:          unsigned short GetLen()const { return itsLen; }
25:          const char * GetString() const { return itsString; }
26:
27:       private:
28:          String (unsigned short);          // private constructor
29:          char * itsString;
30:          unsigned short itsLen;
31:       };
32:
33:       // default constructor creates string of 0 bytes
34:       String::String()
35:       {
36:          itsString = new char[1];
37:          itsString[0] = '\0';
38:          itsLen=0;
39:       }
40:
41:       // private (helper) constructor, used only by
42:       // class methods for creating a new string of
43:       // required size. Null filled.
44:       String::String(unsigned short len)
45:       {
46:          itsString = new char[len+1];
47:          for (unsigned short i = 0; i<=len; i++)
48:             itsString[1] = '\0';
49:          itsLen=len;
50:       }
51:
52:       // Converts a character array to a String
53:       String::String(const char * const cString)
54:       {
55:          itsLen = strlen(cString);
56:          itsString = new char[itsLen+1];
57:          for (unsigned short i = 0; i<itsLen; i++)
58:             itsString[i] = cString[i];
59:          itsString[itsLen]='\0';
60:       }
61:
62:       // copy constructor
63:       String::String (const String & rhs)
64:       {
65:          itsLen=rhs.GetLen();
66:          itsString = new char[itsLen+1];
```

```
67:        for (unsigned short i = 0; i<itsLen;i++)
68:            itsString[i] = rhs[i];
69:        itsString[itsLen] = '\0';
70:    }
71:
72:    // destructor, frees allocated memory
73:    String::~String ()
74:    {
75:        delete [] itsString;
76:        itsLen = 0;
77:    }
78:
79:    // operator equals, frees existing memory
80:    // then copies string and size
81:    String& String::operator=(const String & rhs)
82:    {
83:        if (this == &rhs)
84:            return *this;
85:        delete [] itsString;
86:        itsLen=rhs.GetLen();
87:        itsString = new char[itsLen+1];
88:        for (unsigned short i = 0; i<itsLen;i++)
89:            itsString[i] = rhs[i];
90:        itsString[itsLen] = '\0';
91:        return *this;
92:    }
93:
94:    //nonconstant offset operator, returns
95:    // reference to character so it can be
96:    // changed!
97:    char & String::operator[](unsigned short offset)
98:    {
99:        if (offset > itsLen)
100:           return itsString[itsLen-1];
101:       else
102:           return itsString[offset];
103:   }
104:
105:   // constant offset operator for use
106:   // on const objects (see copy constructor!)
107:   char String::operator[](unsigned short offset) const
108:   {
109:       if (offset > itsLen)
110:           return itsString[itsLen-1];
111:       else
112:           return itsString[offset];
113:   }
114:
115:   // creates a new string by adding current
116:   // string to rhs
117:   String String::operator+(const String& rhs)
118:   {
119:       unsigned short  totalLen = itsLen + rhs.GetLen();
120:       String temp(totalLen);
121:       for (unsigned short i = 0; i<itsLen; i++)
```

continues

Listing 11.12. continued

```
122:          temp[i] = itsString[i];
123:       for (unsigned short j = 0; j<rhs.GetLen(); j++, i++)
124:          temp[i] = rhs[j];
125:       temp[totalLen]='\0';
126:       return temp;
127:    }
128:
129:    // changes current string, returns nothing
130:    void String::operator+=(const String& rhs)
131:    {
132:       unsigned short rhsLen = rhs.GetLen();
133:       unsigned short totalLen = itsLen + rhsLen;
134:       String  temp(totalLen);
135:       for (unsigned short i = 0; i<itsLen; i++)
136:          temp[i] = itsString[i];
137:       for (unsigned short j = 0; j<rhs.GetLen(); j++, i++)
138:          temp[i] = rhs[i-itsLen];
139:       temp[totalLen]='\0';
140:       *this = temp;
141:    }
142:
143:    void main()
144:    {
145:       String s1("initial test");
146:       cout << "S1:\t" << s1.GetString() << endl;
147:
148:       char * temp = "Hello World";
149:       s1 = temp;
150:       cout << "S1:\t" << s1.GetString() << endl;
151:
152:       char tempTwo[20];
153:       strcpy(tempTwo,"; nice to be here!");
154:       s1 += tempTwo;
155:       cout << "tempTwo:\t" << tempTwo << endl;
156:       cout << "S1:\t" << s1.GetString() << endl;
157:
158:       cout << "S1[4]:\t" << s1[4] << endl;
159:       s1[4]='x';
160:       cout << "S1:\t" << s1.GetString() << endl;
161:
162:       cout << "S1[999]:\t" << s1[999] << endl;
163:
164:       String s2(" Another string");
165:       String s3;
166:       s3 = s1+s2;
167:       cout << "S3:\t" << s3.GetString() << endl;
168:
169:       String s4;
170:       s4 = "Why does this work?";
171:       cout << "S4:\t" << s4.GetString() << endl;
172:    }
```

```
S1:        initial test
S1:        Hello world
TempTwo;   ;nice to be here!
S1:        Hello world; nice to be here!
S1[4]:     o
S1:        Hellx World; nice to be here!
S1[999]    !
S3:        Hellx World; nice to be here! Another string
S4:        Why does this work?
```

Analysis Lines 7-31 are the declaration of a simple String class. Lines 11–13 contain three constructors: the default constructor, the copy constructor, and a constructor that takes an existing null-terminated (C-style) string.

This String class overloads the offset operator ([ ]), operator plus (t), and operator plus-equals (t=). The offset operator is overloaded twice: once as a constant function returning a char and again as a nonconstant function returning a reference to a char.

The nonconstant version is used in statements such as

```
SomeString[4]='\x';
```

as seen in line 158. This enables direct access to each of the characters in the string. A reference to the character is returned so that the calling function can manipulate it.

The constant version is used when a constant String object is being accessed, such as in the implementation of the copy constructor, (line 63). Note that rhs[i] is accessed, yet rhs is declared as a const String &. It isn't legal to access this object by using a nonconstant member function. Therefore, the reference operator must be overloaded with a constant accessor.

If the object being returned were large, you might want to declare the return value to be a constant reference. However, because a char is only one byte, there would be no point in doing that.

The default constructor is implemented in lines 33–39. It creates a string whose length is 0. It is the convention of this String class to report its length not counting the terminating null. This default string contains only a terminating null.

The copy constructor is implemented in lines 63–72. It sets the new string's length to that of the existing string—plus 1 for the terminating null. It copies each character from the existing string to the new string, and it null-terminates the new string.

Lines 52–60 implement the constructor that takes an existing C-style string. This constructor is similar to the copy constructor. The length of the existing string is established by a call to the standard String library function strlen().

11

On line 28 another constructor, String(int), is declared to be a *private* member function. It is the intent of the designer of this class that no client class ever create a String of arbitrary length. This constructor exists only to help in the internal creation of Strings as required, for example, by operator+=, on line 136. This will be discussed in depth when operator+= is described, below.

The String(unsigned short) constructor fills every member of its array with NULL. Therefore, the for loop checks for i<=len rather than i<len.

The destructor, implemented in lines 73–77, deletes the character string maintained by the class. Be sure to include the brackets in the call to the delete operator, so that every member of the array is deleted, instead of only the first.

The assignment operator first checks whether the right-hand side of the assignment is the same as the left-hand side. If it isn't, the current string is deleted, and the new string is created and copied into place. A reference is returned to facilitate assignments like

```
String1 = String2 = String3;
```

The offset operator is overloaded twice. Rudimentary bounds checking is performed both times. If the user attempts to access a character at a location beyond the end of the array, the last character—that is, len-1—is returned.

Lines 117–129 implement operator plus as a concatenation operator. It is convenient to be able to write

```
String3 = String1 + String2;
```

and have String3 be the concatenation of the other two strings. To accomplish this, the operator plus function computes the combined length of the two strings and creates a temporary string temp. This invokes the private constructor, which takes an integer, and creates a string filled with nulls. The nulls are then replaced by the contents of the two strings. The left-hand side string (*this) is copied first, followed by the right-hand side string (rhs).

The first for loop counts through the string on the left-hand side and adds each character to the new string. The second for loop counts through the right-hand side. Note that i continues to count the place for the new string, even as j counts into the rhs string.

Operator plus returns the temp string by value, which is assigned to the string on the left-hand side of the assignment (string1). Operator += operates on the existing string—that is, the left-hand side of the statement string1 += string2. It works just like operator plus, except that the temp value is assigned to the current string (*this = temp) in line 140.

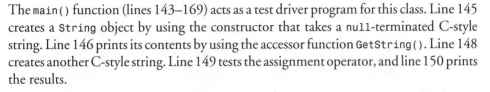

The main() function (lines 143–169) acts as a test driver program for this class. Line 145 creates a String object by using the constructor that takes a null-terminated C-style string. Line 146 prints its contents by using the accessor function GetString(). Line 148 creates another C-style string. Line 149 tests the assignment operator, and line 150 prints the results.

Line 152 creates a third C-style string, tempTwo. Line 153 invokes strcpy to fill the buffer with the characters ; nice to be here! Line 154 invokes operator += and concatenates tmpTwo onto the existing string s1. Line 156 prints the results.

In line 158, the fifth character in s1 is accessed and printed. It is assigned a new value in line 159. This invokes the nonconstant offset operator ([ ]). Line 160 prints the result, which shows that the actual value has, in fact, been changed.

Line 162 attempts to access a character beyond the end of the array. The last character of the array is returned, as designed.

Lines 164–165 create two more String objects, and line 166 the operator plus. Line 167 prints the results.

Line 169 creates a new String object, s4. Line 170 invokes the assignment operator. Line 174 prints the results. You might be thinking, "The assignment operator is defined to take a constant String reference in line 21, but here the program passes in a C-style string. Why is this legal?"

The answer is that the compiler expects a String, but it is given a character array. Therefore, it checks whether it can create a String from what it is given. In line 12, you declared a constructor that creates Strings from character arrays. The compiler creates a temporary String from the character array and passes it to the assignment operator. This is known as implicit casting, or promotion. If you had not declared—and provided the implementation for—the constructor that takes a character array, this assignment would have generated a compiler error.

Linked Lists and Other Structures

Arrays are much like Tupperware. They are great containers, but they are of a fixed size. If you pick a container that is too large, you waste space in your storage area. If you pick one that is too small, its contents spill all over and you have a big mess.

One way to solve this problem is with a linked list. A linked list is a data structure that consists of small containers that are designed to fit and that are linked together as needed. The idea is to write a class that holds one object of your data—such as one CAT or one

`Rectangle`—and that can point at the next container. You create one container for each object that you need to store, and you chain them together as needed.

The containers are called nodes. The first node in the list is called the head, and the last node in the list is called the tail.

Lists come in three fundamental forms. From simplest to most complex, they are

Singly linked
Doubly linked
Trees

In a singly linked list, each node points to the next one, but not backward. To find a particular node, you start at the top and go from node to node, as in a treasure hunt ("The next node is under the sofa"). A doubly linked list enables you move backward and forward in the chain. A tree is a complex structure built from nodes, each of which can point in two or three directions. Figure 11.5 shows these three fundamental structures.

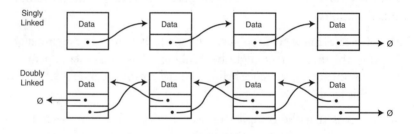

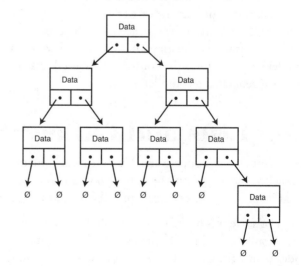

Figure 11.5. *Linked lists.*

Computer scientists have created even more complex and clever data structures, nearly all of which rely on interconnecting nodes. Listing 11.13 shows how to create and use a simple linked list.

Listing 11.13. Implementing a linked list.

```
1:    // Listing 11.13
2:    // Linked list simple implementation
3:
4:    #include <iostreams.h>
5:
6:    // object to add to list
7:    class CAT
8:    {
9:    public:
10:       CAT() { itsAge = 1;}
11:       CAT(int age):itsAge(age){}
12:       ~CAT(){};
13:       int GetAge() const { return itsAge; }
14:    private:
15:       int itsAge;
16:    };
17:
18:    // manages list, orders by cat's age!
19:    class Node
20:    {
21:    public:
22:       Node (CAT*);
23:       ~Node();
24:       void SetNext(Node * node) { itsNext = node; }
25:       Node * GetNext() const { return itsNext; }
26:       CAT * GetCat() const { return itsCat; }
27:       void Insert(Node *);
28:       void Display();
29:    private:
30:       CAT *itsCat;
31:       Node * itsNext;
32:    };
33:
34:
35:    Node::Node(CAT* pCat):
36:    itsCat(pCat),
37:    itsNext(0)
38:    {}
39:
40:    Node::~Node()
41:    {
42:       cout << "Deleting node...\n";
43:       delete itsCat;
44:       itsCat = 0;
45:       delete itsNext;
46:       itsNext = 0;
47:    }
```

continues

Listing 11.13. continued

```
48:
49:       // ************************************
50:       // Insert
51:       // Orders cats based on their ages
52:       // Algorithim: If you are last in line, add the cat
53:       // Otherwise, if the new cat is older than you
54:       // and also younger than next in line, insert it after
55:       // this one. Otherwise call insert on the next in line
56:       // ************************************
57:       void Node::Insert(Node* newNode)
58:       {
59:          if (!itsNext)
60:             itsNext = newNode;
61:          else
62:          {
63:             int NextCatsAge = itsNext->GetCat()->GetAge();
64:             int NewAge =  newNode->GetCat()->GetAge();
65:             int ThisNodeAge = itsCat->GetAge();
66:
67:             if (  NewAge > ThisNodeAge && NewAge < NextCatsAge  )
68:             {
69:                newNode->SetNext(itsNext);
70:                itsNext = newNode;
71:             }
72:             else
73:                itsNext->Insert(newNode);
74:          }
75:       }
76:
77:       void Node::Display()
78:       {
79:          if (itsCat->GetAge() > 0)
80:             cout << "My cat is " << itsCat->GetAge() << " years old\n";
81:          if (itsNext)
82:             itsNext->Display();
83:       }
84:
85:       void main()
86:       {
87:
88:          Node *pNode = 0;
89:          CAT * pCat = new CAT(0);
90:          int age;
91:
92:          Node *pHead = new Node(pCat);
93:
94:          while (1)
95:          {
96:             cout << "New Cat's age? (0 to quit): ";
97:             cin >>  age;
98:             if (!age)
99:                break;
100:            pCat = new CAT(age);
```

```
101:                pNode = new Node(pCat);
102:                pHead->Insert(pNode);
103:            }
104:        pHead->Display();
105:        delete pHead;
106:        cout << "Exiting...\n\n";
107:    }
```

Output

```
New Cat's age? (0 to quit): 1
New Cat's age? (0 to quit): 9
New Cat's age? (0 to quit): 3
New Cat's age? (0 to quit): 7
New Cat's age? (0 to quit): 2
New Cat's age? (0 to quit): 5
New Cat's age? (0 to quit): 0
My cat is 1 years old
My cat is 2 years old
My cat is 3 years old
My cat is 5 years old
My cat is 7 years old
My cat is 9 years old
Deleting node...
Deleting node...
Deleting node...
Deleting node...
Deleting node...
Deleting node...
Deleting node...
Exiting...
```

Analysis

Lines 7–16 declare a simplified CAT class. It has two constructors, a default constructor that initializes the member variable itsAge to 1, and a constructor that takes an integer and initializes itsAge to that value.

Lines 18–32 declare the class Node. Node is designed specifically to hold a CAT object in a list. Normally, you would hide Node inside a CatList class. It is exposed here to illustrate how linked lists work.

It is possible to make a more generic Node that would hold any kind of object in a list. You'll learn about doing that on Day 14, "Special Classes and Functions," when templates are discussed.

Node's constructor takes a pointer to a CAT object. The copy constructor and assignment operator have been left out to save space. In a real-world application, they would be included.

Three accessor functions are defined. SetNext() sets the member variable itsNext to point to the Node object supplied as its parameter. GetNext() and GetCat() return the appropriate member variables. GetNext() and GetCat() are declared const because they don't change the Node object.

Insert() is the most powerful member function in the class. Insert() maintains the linked list and adds Nodes to the list based on the age of the CAT that they point to.

The program begins at line 85. The pointer pNode is created and initialized to 0. A dummy CAT object is created, and its age is initialized to 0, to ensure that the pointer to the head of the list (pHead) is always first.

Beginning on line 94, the user is prompted for an age. If the user presses 0, this is taken as a signal that no more CAT objects are to be created. For all other values, a CAT object is created on line 100, and the member variable itsAge is set to the supplied value. The CAT objects are created on the free store. For each CAT created a Node object is created on line 101.

After the CAT and Node objects are created, the first Node in the list is told to insert the newly created node, on line 102.

Note that the program doesn't know—or care—how Node is inserted or how the list is maintained. That is entirely up to the Node object itself.

The call to Insert() causes program execution to jump to line 57. Insert() is always called on pHead first.

The test in line 59 fails the first time a new Node is added. Therefore, pHead is pointed at the first new Node. In the output, this is the node with a CAT whose itsAge value was set to 1.

When the second CAT object's itsAge variable is set to 9, pHead is called again. This time, its member variable itsNext isn't null, and the else statement in lines 61 to 74 is invoked.

Three local variables—NextCatsAge, NewAge, and ThisNodeAge—are filled with the values of

   The current Node's age—the age of pHead's CAT is 0
   The age of the CAT held by the new Node—in this case, 9
   The age of the CAT object held by the next node in line—in this case, 1

The test in line 67 could have been written as

```
if (  newNode->GetCat()->GetAge() > itsCat->GetAge() && \\
                  newNode->GetCat()->GetAge()< itsNext->GetCat()->GetAge())
```

which would have eliminated the three temporary variables while creating code that is more confusing and harder to read. Some C++ programmers see this as macho—until they have a bug and can't figure out which one of the values is wrong.

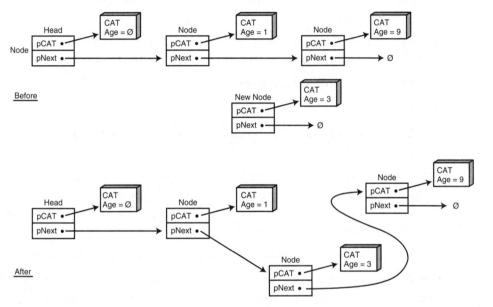

If the new CAT's age is greater than the current CAT's age and less than the next CAT's age, the proper place to insert the new CAT's age is immediately after the current Node. In this case, the if statement is true. The new Node is set to point to what the current Node points to, and the current Node is set to point to the new Node. Figure 11.6 illustrates this.

Figure 11.6. *Inserting a* Node.

If the test fails, this isn't the proper place to insert the node, and Insert() is called on the next Node in the list. Note that the current call to Insert() doesn't return until after the recursive call to Insert() returns. Therefore, these calls pile up on the stack. If the list gets too long, it will blow the stack and crash the program. There are other ways to do this that aren't so stack-intensive, but they are beyond the scope of this book.

Once the user is finished adding CAT objects, display is called on the first Node, pHead. The CAT object's age is displayed if the current Node points to a CAT (pHead does not). Then, if the current Node points to another Node, display() is called on that Node.

Finally, delete is called on pHead. Because the destructor deletes the pointer to the next Node, delete is called on that Node as well. It walks the entire list, eliminating each Node and freeing the memory of itsCat. Note that the last Node has its member variable itsNext set to zero, and delete is called on that pointer as well. It is always safe to call delete on zero, for it has no effect.

Array Classes

Writing your own `Array` class has many advantages over using the built-in arrays. For starters, you can prevent array overruns. You might also consider making your array class dynamically sized: at creation it might have only one member, growing as needed during the course of the program.

You might want to sort or otherwise order the members of the array. There are a number of powerful `Array` variants you might consider, among the most popular are:

- [ ] **Ordered collection:** Each member is in sorted order.

- [ ] **Set:** No member appears more than once.

- [ ] **Dictionary:** This uses matched pairs in which one value acts as a key to retrieve the other value.

- [ ] **Sparse array:** Indices are permitted for a large set, but only those values actually added to the array consume memory. Thus, you can ask for `SparseArray[5]` or `SparseArray[200]`, but it is possible that memory is allocated only for a small number of entries.

- [ ] **Bag:** An unordered collection that is added to and retrieved in random order.

By overloading the index operator (`[ ]`), you can turn a linked list into an ordered collection. By excluding duplicates, you can turn a collection into a set. If each object in the list has a pair of matched values, you can use a linked list to build a dictionary or a sparse array.

Summary

Today you learned how to create arrays in C++. An array is a fixed-size collection of objects that are all of the same type.

Arrays don't do bounds checking. Therefore it is legal—even if disastrous—to read or write past the end of an array. Arrays count from 0. A common mistake is to write to offset *n* of an array of *n* members.

Arrays can be single dimensional or multidimensional. In either case, the members of the array can be initialized, as long as the array contains either built-in types, such as `int`, or objects of a class that has a default constructor.

Arrays and their contents can be on the free store or on the stack. If you delete an array on the free store, remember to use the brackets in the call to `delete`.

Array names are constant pointers to the first elements of the array. Pointers and arrays use pointer arithmetic to find the next element of an array.

You can create linked lists to manage collections whose size you won't know at compile time. From linked lists, you can create any number of more complex data structures.

Strings are arrays of characters, or chars. C++ provides special features for managing char arrays, including the ability to initialize them with quoted strings.

Q&A

Q What happens if I write to element 25 in a 24-member array?

A You will write to other memory, with potentially disastrous effects on your program.

Q What is in an uninitialized array element?

A Whatever happens to be in memory at a given time. The results of using this member without assigning a value are unpredictable.

Q Can I combine arrays?

A Yes. With simple arrays you can use pointers to combine them into a new, larger array. With strings you can use some of the built-in functions, such as strcat, to combine strings.

Q Why should I create a linked list if an array will work?

A An array must have a fixed size, whereas a linked list can be sized dynamically at runtime.

Q Why would I ever use built-in arrays if I can make a better array class?

A Built-in arrays are quick and easy to use.

Q Must a string class use a char * to hold the contents of the string?

A No. It can use any memory storage the designer thinks is best.

Workshop

The Workshop provides quiz questions to help you solidify your understanding of the material covered and exercises to provide you with experience in using what you've learned. Try to answer the quiz and exercise questions before checking the answers in

Appendix D, and make sure you understand the answers before continuing to the next chapter.

Quiz

1. What are the first and last elements in `SomeArray[25]`?

2. How do you declare a multidimensional array?

3. Initialize the members of the array in question 2.

4. How many elements are in the array `SomeArray[10][5][20]`?

5. What is the maximum number of elements that you can add to a linked list?

6. Can you use subscript notation on a linked list?

7. What is the last character in the string "Brad is a nice guy?"?

Exercises

1. Declare a two-dimensional array that represents a tic-tac-toe game board.

2. Write the code that initializes all the elements in the array you created in Exercise 1 to the value 0.

3. Write the declaration for a `Node` class that holds unsigned `short` integers.

4. **BUG BUSTERS:** What is wrong with this code fragment?

```
unsigned short SomeArray[5][4];
for (int i = 0; i<4; i++)
    for (int j = 0; j<5; j++)
        SomeArray[i][j] = i+j;
```

5. **BUG BUSTERS:** What is wrong with this code fragment?

```
unsigned short SomeArray[5][4];
for (int i = 0; i<=5; i++)
    for (int j = 0; j<=4; j++)
        SomeArray[i][j] = 0;
```

12

Inheritance

Introduction

It is a fundamental aspect of human intelligence to seek out, recognize, and create relationships among concepts. We build hierarchies, matrices, networks, and other interrelationships to explain and understand the ways in which things interact. C++ attempts to capture this in inheritance hierarchies. Today you will learn:

☐ What inheritance is.

☐ How to derive one class from another.

☐ What protected access is and how to use it.

☐ What virtual functions are.

What Is Inheritance?

What is a dog? When you look at your pet, what do you see? A biologist sees a network of interacting organs, a physicist sees atoms and forces at work, and a taxonomist sees a representative of the species *canine domesticus*.

It is that last assessment that interests us at the moment. A dog is a kind of canine, a canine is a kind of mammal, and so forth. Taxonomists divide the world of living things into Kingdom, Phyla, Class, Order, Family, Genus, and Species.

This hierarchy establishes an *is-a* relationship. A dog *is a* kind of canine. We see this relationship everywhere: a Toyota *is a* kind of car, which *is a* kind of vehicle. A sundae *is a* kind of dessert, which *is a* kind of food.

What do we mean when we say something *is a* kind of something else? We mean that it is a specialization of that thing. That is, a car is a special kind of vehicle.

Inheritance and Derivation

The concept *dog inherits*, that is, it automatically gets, all the features of a mammal. Because it is a mammal, we know that it moves and that it breathes air—all mammals move and breathe air by definition. The concept of a dog adds the idea of barking, wagging its tail, and so forth to that definition. We can further divide dogs into hunting dogs and terriers, and we can divide terriers into Yorkshire Terriers, Dandie Dinmont Terriers, and so forth.

A Yorkshire Terrier is a kind of terrier, therefore it is a kind of dog, therefore a kind of mammal, therefore a kind of animal, and therefore a kind of living thing. This hierarchy is represented in Figure 12.1.

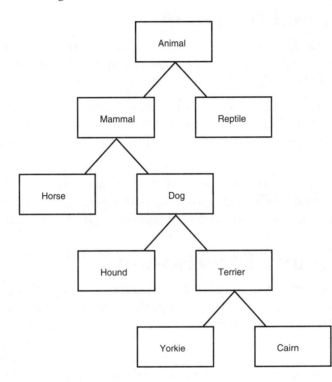

Figure 12.1. *Hierarchy of Animals.*

C++ attempts to represent these relationships by enabling you to define classes that *derive* from one another. Derivation is a way of expressing the *is a* relationship. You derive a new class, Dog, from the class Mammal. You don't have to state explicitly that dogs move, because they *inherit* that from Mammal.

NEW TERM A class which adds new functionality to an existing class is said to *derive* from that original class. The original class is said to be the new class's *base class*.

If the Dog class derives from the Mammal class, then Mammal is a base class of Dog. Derived classes are *supersets* of their base classes. Just as dog adds certain features to the idea of a mammal, the Dog class will add certain methods or data to the Mammal class.

Typically, a base class will have more than one derived class. Just as dogs, cats, and horses are all types of mammals, their classes would all derive from the `Mammal` class.

The Animal Kingdom

To facilitate the discussion of derivation and inheritance, this chapter will focus on the relationships among a number of classes representing animals. You can imagine that you have been asked to design a children's game—a simulation of a farm.

In time you will develop a whole set of farm animals, including horses, cows, dogs, cats, sheep, and so forth. You will create methods for these classes so that they can act in the ways the child might expect, but for now you'll stub-out each method with a simple `print` statement.

Stubbing-out a function means you'll write only enough to show that the function was called, leaving the details for later when you have more time. Please feel free to extend the minimal code provided in this chapter to enable the animals to act more realistically.

The Syntax of Derivation

When you declare a class, you can indicate what class it derives from by writing a colon after the class name, the type of derivation (public or otherwise), and the class from which it derives. The following is an example.

```
class Dog : public Mammal
```

The type of derivation will be discussed later in this chapter. For now, always use `public`. The class from which you derive must have been declared earlier, or you will get a compiler error. Listing 12.1 illustrates how to declare a `Dog` class that is derived from a `Mammal` class.

Listing 12.1. Simple inheritance.

```
1:     //Listing 12.1 Simple inheritance
2:
3:     #include <iostreams.h>
4:     enum BREED { YORKIE, CAIRN, DANDIE, SHETLAND, DOBERMAN, LAB };
5:
6:     class Mammal
7:     {
8:     public:
9:         // constructors
10:        Mammal();
11:        ~Mammal();
12:
```

```
13:         //accessors
14:         int GetAge()const;
15:         void SetAge(int);
16:         int GetWeight() const;
17:         void SetWeight();
18:
19:         //Other methods
20:         void Speak();
21:         void Sleep();
22:
23:
24:     protected:
25:         int itsAge;
26:         int itsWeight;
27:     };
28:
29:     class Dog : public Mammal
30:     {
31:     public:
32:
33:         // Constructors
34:         Dog();
35:         ~Dog();
36:
37:         // Accessors
38:         BREED GetBreed() const;
39:         void SetBreed(BREED);
40:
41:         // Other methods
42:         // WagTail();
43:         // BegForFood();
44:
45:     protected:
46:         BREED itsBreed;
47:     }
```

Analysis This program has no output because it is only a set of class declarations without their implementations. Nonetheless, there is much to see here.

On lines 6–27 the Mammal class is declared. Note that in this example, Mammal does not derive from any other class. In the real world mammals do derive—that is, mammals are kinds of animals. In a C++ program you can represent only a fraction of the information you have about any given object. Reality is far too complex to capture all of it, so every C++ hierarchy is an arbitrary representation of the data available. The trick of a good design is to represent the areas that you care about in a way that maps back to reality reasonably faithfully.

The hierarchy has to begin somewhere; this program begins with Mammal. Because of this decision, some member variables that might properly belong in a higher base class are now represented here. For example, certainly all animals have an age and weight, so if `Mammal` derived from `Animal` we might expect to inherit those attributes. As it is, the attributes appear in the `Mammal` class.

To keep the program reasonably simple and manageable, only six methods have been put in the `Mammal` class—four accessor methods, `Speak()`, and `Sleep()`.

The `Dog` class inherits from `Mammal`, as indicated on line 29. Every `Dog` object will have three member variables: `itsAge`, `itsWeight`, and `itsBreed`. Note that the class declaration for `Dog` does not include the member variables `itsAge` and `itsWeight`. `Dog` objects inherit these variables from the `Mammal` class, along with all of `Mammal`'s methods *except* the copy operator and the constructors and destructor.

Private Versus Protected

You may have noticed that a new access keyword, `protected`, has been introduced on lines 24 and 45 of Listing 12.1. Previously, class data had been declared `private`. However, `private` members are not available to derived classes. You could make `itsAge` and `itsWeight` public, but that is not desirable. You don't want other classes accessing these data members directly.

What you want is a designation that says, "make these visible to this class and to classes that derive from this class." That designation is `protected`. Protected data members and functions are fully visible to derived classes, but are otherwise private.

There are, in total, three access specifiers: *public*, *protected*, and *private*. If a function has an object of your class, it can access all the public member data and functions. The member functions, in turn, can access all private data members and functions of their own class, and all protected data members and functions of any class from which they derive.

Thus, the function `Dog::WagTail()` can access the private data `itsBreed` and can access the protected data in the `Mammal` class.

Even if other classes are layered between `Mammal` and `Dog` (for example, `DomesticAnimals`) the `Dog` class will still be able to access the protected members of `Mammal`, assuming that these other classes all use public inheritance. Private inheritance is discussed on Day 15, "Advanced Inheritance."

Listing 12.2 demonstrates how to create objects of type `Dog` and access the data and functions of that type.

Listing 12.2. Using a derived object.

```
1:    //Listing 12.2 Using a derived object
2:
3:    #include <iostreams.h>
4:    enum BREED { YORKIE, CAIRN, DANDIE, SHETLAND, DOBERMAN, LAB };
5:
6:    class Mammal
7:    {
8:    public:
9:        // constructors
10:       Mammal():itsAge(2), itsWeight(5){}
11:       ~Mammal(){}
12:
13:       //accessors
14:       int GetAge()const { return itsAge; }
15:       void SetAge(int age) { itsAge = age; }
16:       int GetWeight() const { return itsWeight; }
17:       void SetWeight(int weight) { itsWeight = weight; }
18:
19:       //Other methods
20:       void Speak()const { cout << "Mammal sound!\n"; }
21:       void Sleep()const { cout << "shhh. I'm sleeping.\n"; }
22:
23:
24:    protected:
25:        int itsAge;
26:        int itsWeight;
27:    };
28:
29:    class Dog : public Mammal
30:    {
31:    public:
32:
33:        // Constructors
34:        Dog():itsBreed(YORKIE){}
35:        ~Dog(){}
36:
37:        // Accessors
38:        BREED GetBreed() const { return itsBreed; }
39:        void SetBreed(BREED breed) { itsBreed = breed; }
40:
41:        // Other methods
42:        void WagTail() { cout << "Tail wagging...\n"; }
43:        void BegForFood() { cout << "Begging for food...\n"; }
44:
45:    private:
46:        BREED itsBreed;
47:    };
48:
49:    void main()
50:    {
51:        Dog fido;
52:        fido.Speak();
53:        fido.WagTail();
54:        cout << "Fido is " << fido.GetAge() << " years old\n";
55:    }
```

12

```
Mammal sound!
Tail wagging...
Fido is 2 years old.
```

On lines 6–27 the Mammal class is declared (all of its functions are inline to save space here). On lines 29–47 the Dog class is declared, as a derived class of Mammal. Thus, by these declarations, all Dogs have an age, a weight, and a breed.

On line 51 a Dog is declared, Fido. Fido inherits all the attributes of a Mammal, as well as all the attributes of a Dog. Thus Fido knows how to WagTail(), but also knows how to Speak() and Sleep().

Constructors and Destructors

Dog objects *are* Mammal objects. This is the essence of the *is a* relationship. When Fido is created, his base constructor is called first, creating a Mammal. Then the Dog constructor is called, completing the construction of the Dog object. Because we gave Fido no parameters, the default constructor was called in each case. Fido doesn't exist until he is completely constructed, which means that both his Mammal part and his Dog part must be constructed. Thus, both constructors must be called.

When Fido is destroyed, first the Dog destructor will be called, and then the destructor for the Mammal part of Fido. Each destructor is given an opportunity to clean up after its own part of Fido. Remember to clean up after your Dog! Listing 12.3 demonstrates this.

Listing 12.3. Constructors and destructors called.

```
1:     //Listing 12.3 Constructors and destructors called.
2:
3:     #include <iostreams.h>
4:     enum BREED { YORKIE, CAIRN, DANDIE, SHETLAND, DOBERMAN, LAB };
5:
6:     class Mammal
7:     {
8:     public:
9:         // constructors
10:        Mammal();
11:        ~Mammal();
12:
13:        //accessors
14:        int GetAge() const { return itsAge; }
15:        void SetAge(int age) { itsAge = age; }
16:        int GetWeight() const { return itsWeight; }
17:        void SetWeight(int weight) { itsWeight = weight; }
18:
19:        //Other methods
20:        void Speak() const { cout << "Mammal sound!\n"; }
21:        void Sleep() const { cout << "shhh. I'm sleeping.\n"; }
```

```
22:
23:
24:    protected:
25:        int itsAge;
26:        int itsWeight;
27:    };
28:
29:    class Dog : public Mammal
30:    {
31:    public:
32:
33:        // Constructors
34:        Dog();
35:        ~Dog();
36:
37:        // Accessors
38:        BREED GetBreed() const { return itsBreed; }
39:        void SetBreed(BREED breed) { itsBreed = breed; }
40:
41:        // Other methods
42:        void WagTail() { cout << "tail wagging...\n"; }
43:        void BegForFood() { cout << "begging for food...\n"; }
44:
45:    private:
46:        BREED itsBreed;
47:    };
48:
49:    Mammal::Mammal():
50:    itsAge(1),
51:    itsWeight(5)
52:    {
53:        cout << "Mammal constructor...\n";
54:    }
55:
56:    Mammal::~Mammal()
57:    {
58:        cout << "Mammal destructor...\n";
59:    }
60:
61:    Dog::Dog():
62:    itsBreed(YORKIE)
63:    {
64:        cout << "Dog constructor...\n";
65:    }
66:
67:    Dog::~Dog()
68:    {
69:        cout << "Dog destructor...\n";
70:    }
71:    void main()
72:    {
73:        Dog fido;
74:        fido.Speak();
75:        fido.WagTail();
76:        cout << "Fido is " << fido.GetAge() << " years old\n";
77:    }
```

12

```
Mammal constructor...
Dog constructor...
Mammal sound!
Tail wagging...
Fido is 1 years old.
Dog destructor...
Mammal destructor...
```

Listing 12.3 is just like Listing 12.2, except that the constructors and destructors now print to the screen when called. Mammal's constructor is called, then Dog's. At that point the Dog fully exists, and its methods can be called. When fido goes out of scope Dog's destructor is called, followed by a call to Mammal's destructor.

Passing Arguments to Base Constructors

It is possible that you'll want to overload the constructor of Mammal to take a specific age, and that you'll want to overload the Dog constructor to take a breed. How do you get the age and weight parameters passed up to the right constructor in Mammal? What if Dogs want to initialize weight but Mammals don't?

Base class initialization can be performed during class initialization by writing the base class name, followed by the parameters expected by the base class. Listing 12.4 demonstrates this.

Listing 12.4. Overloading constructors in derived classes.

```
1:    //Listing 12.4 Overloading constructors in derived classes
2:
3:    #include <iostreams.h>
4:    enum BREED { YORKIE, CAIRN, DANDIE, SHETLAND, DOBERMAN, LAB };
5:
6:    class Mammal
7:    {
8:    public:
9:       // constructors
10:      Mammal();
11:      Mammal(int age);
12:      ~Mammal();
13:
14:      //accessors
15:      int GetAge() const { return itsAge; }
16:      void SetAge(int age) { itsAge = age; }
17:      int GetWeight() const { return itsWeight; }
18:      void SetWeight(int weight) { itsWeight = weight; }
19:
20:      //Other methods
21:      void Speak() const { cout << "Mammal sound!\n"; }
22:      void Sleep() const { cout << "shhh. I'm sleeping.\n"; }
23:
24:
```

```
25:    protected:
26:        int itsAge;
27:        int itsWeight;
28:    };
29:
30:    class Dog : public Mammal
31:    {
32:    public:
33:
34:        // Constructors
35:        Dog();
36:        Dog(int age);
37:        Dog(int age, int weight);
38:        Dog(int age, BREED breed);
39:        Dog(int age, int weight, BREED breed);
40:        ~Dog();
41:
42:        // Accessors
43:        BREED GetBreed() const { return itsBreed; }
44:        void SetBreed(BREED breed) { itsBreed = breed; }
45:
46:        // Other methods
47:        void WagTail() { cout << "tail wagging...\n"; }
48:        void BegForFood() { cout << "begging for food...\n"; }
49:
50:    private:
51:        BREED itsBreed;
52:    };
53:
54:    Mammal::Mammal():
55:    itsAge(1),
56:    itsWeight(5)
57:    {
58:        cout << "Mammal constructor...\n";
59:    }
60:
61:    Mammal::Mammal(int age):
62:    itsAge(age),
63:    itsWeight(5)
64:    {
65:        cout << "Mammal(int) constructor...\n";
66:    }
67:
68:    Mammal::~Mammal()
69:    {
70:        cout << "Mammal destructor...\n";
71:    }
72:
73:    Dog::Dog():
74:    Mammal(),
75:    itsBreed(YORKIE)
76:    {
77:        cout << "Dog constructor...\n";
78:    }
79:
80:    Dog::Dog(int age):
```

12

continues

Listing 12.4. continued

```
81:    Mammal(age),
82:    itsBreed(YORKIE)
83:    {
84:        cout << "Dog(int) constructor...\n";
85:    }
86:
87:    Dog::Dog(int age, int weight):
88:    Mammal(age),
89:    itsBreed(YORKIE)
90:    {
91:        itsWeight = weight;
92:        cout << "Dog(int, int) constructor...\n";
93:    }
94:
95:    Dog::Dog(int age, int weight, BREED breed):
96:    Mammal(age),
97:    itsBreed(breed)
98:    {
99:        itsWeight = weight;
100:       cout << "Dog(int, int, BREED) constructor...\n";
101:   }
102:
103:   Dog::Dog(int age, BREED breed):
104:   Mammal(age),
105:   itsBreed(breed)
106:   {
107:       cout << "Dog(int, BREED) constructor...\n";
108:   }
109:
110:   Dog::~Dog()
111:   {
112:       cout << "Dog destructor...\n";
113:   }
114:   void main()
115:   {
116:       Dog fido;
117:       Dog rover(5);
118:       Dog buster(6,8);
119:       Dog yorkie (3,YORKIE);
120:       Dog dobbie (4,20,DOBERMAN);
121:       fido.Speak();
122:       rover.WagTail();
123:       cout << "Yorkie is " << yorkie.GetAge() << " years old\n";
124:       cout << "Dobbie weighs " << dobbie.GetWeight() << " pounds\n";
125:   }
```

Note: The output has been numbered so that each line can be referred to in this analysis.

Output

```
1:  Mammal constructor...
2:  Dog constructor...
3:  Mammal(int) constructor...
4:  Dog(int) constructor...
5:  Mammal(int) constructor...
6:  Dog(int, int) constructor...
7:  Mammal(int) constructor...
8:  Dog(int, BREED) constructor....
9:  Mammal(int) constructor...
10: Dog(int, int, BREED) constructor...
11: Mammal sound!
12: Tail wagging...
13: Yorkie is 3 years old.
14: Dobie weighs 20 pounds.
15: Mammal destructor...
16: Dog destructor...
17: Mammal destructor...
18: Dog destructor...
19: Mammal destructor...
20: Dog destructor...
21: Mammal destructor...
22: Dog destructor...
23: Mammal destructor...
```

Analysis

In Listing 12.4, Mammal's constructor has been overloaded on line 11 to take an integer, the Mammal's age. The implementation on lines 61–66 initializes itsAge with the value passed into the constructor, and itsWeight with the value 5.

Dog has overloaded five constructors, on lines 35–39. The first is the default constructor. The second takes the age, which is the same parameter that the Mammal constructor takes. The third constructor takes both the age and the weight, the fourth takes the age and breed, and the fifth takes the age, weight, and breed.

Note that on line 74 Dog's default constructor calls Mammal's default constructor. Although it is not strictly necessary to do this, it serves as documentation that you *intended* to call the base constructor, which takes no parameters. The base constructor would be called in any case, but actually doing so makes your intentions explicit.

The implementation for the Dog constructor, which takes an integer, is on lines 80–85. In its initialization phase (lines 81–82) Dog initializes its base class, passing in the parameter, and then it initializes its breed.

Another Dog constructor is on lines 87–93. This one takes two parameters. Once again it initializes its base class by calling the appropriate constructor, but this time it also assigns weight to its base class's variable itsWeight. Note that you *cannot* assign to the base class variable in the initialization phase. Because Mammal does not have a constructor that takes this parameter, you must do this within the body of the Dog's constructor.

Walk through the remaining constructors to make sure you are comfortable with how they work. Note what is initialized and what must wait for the body of the constructor.

The output has been numbered so that each line can be referred to in this analysis. The first two lines of output represent the instantiation of Fido, using the default constructor.

In the output, lines 3 and 4 represent the creation of rover. Lines 5 and 6 represent buster. Note that the Mammal constructor that was called is the constructor that takes one integer, but the Dog constructor is the constructor that takes two integers.

After all the objects are created they are used and then go out of scope. As each object is destroyed, first the Dog destructor and then the Mammal destructor is called; five of each in total.

Overriding Functions

A Dog object has access to all the member functions in class Mammal, as well as to any member functions, such as WagTail(), that the declaration of the Dog class might add. It can also *override* a base class function. Overriding a function means changing the implementation of a base class function in a derived class. When you make an object of the derived class, the correct function is called.

NEW TERM When a derived class creates a function with the same return type and signature as a member function in the base class, but with a mew implementation, it is said to be *overriding* that method.

When you override a function, it must agree in return type and in signature with the function in the base class. The signature is the function prototype other than the return type: that is, the name, the parameter list, and the keyword const if used.

NEW TERM The *signature* of a function is its name, as well as the number and type of its parameters. The signature does *not* include the return type.

Listing 12.5 illustrates what happens if the Dog class overrides the speak() method in Mammal. To save room, the accessor functions have been left out of these classes.

Listing 12.5. Overriding a base class method in a derived class.

```
1:    //Listing 12.5 Overriding a base class method in a derived class
2:
3:    #include <iostreams.h>
4:    enum BREED { YORKIE, CAIRN, DANDIE, SHETLAND, DOBERMAN, LAB };
5:
6:    class Mammal
7:    {
8:    public:
9:       // constructors
10:      Mammal() { cout << "Mammal constructor...\n"; }
```

```
11:        ~Mammal() { cout << "Mammal destructor...\n"; }
12:
13:        //Other methods
14:        void Speak()const { cout << "Mammal sound!\n"; }
15:        void Sleep()const { cout << "shhh. I'm sleeping.\n"; }
16:
17:
18:     protected:
19:        int itsAge;
20:        int itsWeight;
21:     };
22:
23:     class Dog : public Mammal
24:     {
25:     public:
26:
27:        // Constructors
28:        Dog(){ cout << "Dog constructor...\n"; }
29:        ~Dog(){ cout << "Dog destructor...\n"; }
30:
31:        // Other methods
32:        void WagTail() { cout << "tail wagging...\n"; }
33:        void BegForFood() { cout << "begging for food...\n"; }
34:        void Speak()const { cout << "Woof!\n"; }
35:
36:     private:
37:        BREED itsBreed;
38:     };
39:
40:     void main()
41:     {
42:        Mammal bigAnimal;
43:        Dog fido;
44:        bigAnimal.Speak();
45:        fido.Speak();
46:     }
```

```
1:  Mammal constructor...
2:  Dog constructor...
3:  Mammal constructor...
4:  Mammal sound!
5:  Woof!
14: Dog destructor...
15: Mammal destructor...
15: Mammal destructor...
```

On line 34 the Dog class overrides the Speak() method, causing Dog objects to say Woof! when the Speak() method is called. On line 42 a Mammal object, bigAnimal, is created, causing the first line of output when the Mammal constructor is called. On line 43 a Dog object, fido, is created, causing the next two lines of output, where the Mammal constructor and then the Dog constructor are called.

On line 44 the `Mammal` object calls its `Speak()` method, then on line 45 the `Dog` object calls *its* `Speak()` method. The output reflects that the correct methods were called. Finally, the two objects go out of scope and the destructors are called.

Overloading Versus Overriding

These terms are similar and they do similar things. When you *overload* a method you create more than one method with the same name, but with a different signature. When you *override* a method, you create a method in a derived class with the same name as a method in the base class *and the same signature*.

Hiding the Base Class Method

In the previous listing the `Dog` class's method `Speak()` hides the base class's method. This is just what is wanted, but it can have unexpected results. If `Mammal` has a method, `Move()`, which is overloaded, and `Dog` overrides that method, the `Dog` method will hide all of the `Mammal` methods with that name.

If `Mammal` overloads `Move()` as three methods—one that takes no parameters, one that takes an integer, and one that takes an integer and a direction—and `Dog` overrides just the `Move()` method, which takes no parameters, it will not be easy to access the other two methods using a `Dog` object. Listing 12.6 illustrates this problem.

Listing 12.6. Hiding methods.

```
1:      //Listing 12.6 Hiding methods
2:
3:      #include <iostreams.h>
4:
5:      class Mammal
6:      {
7:      public:
8:         void Move() const { cout << "Mammal move one step\n"; }
9:         void Move(int distance) const { cout << "Mammal move " << distance <<"
           steps.\n"; }
10:     protected:
11:        int itsAge;
12:        int itsWeight;
13:     };
14:
15:     class Dog : public Mammal
16:     {
17:     public:
18:        void Move() const { cout << "Dog move 5 steps.\n"; }
19:     };      // You may receive a warning that you are hiding a function!
20:
```

```
21:     void main()
22:     {
23:         Mammal bigAnimal;
24:         Dog fido;
25:         bigAnimal.Move();
26:         bigAnimal.Move(2);
27:         fido.Move();
28:         // fido.Move(10);
29:     }
```

Output

```
Mammal move one step
Mammal move 2 steps
Dog move 5 steps
```

Analysis

All of the extra methods and data have been removed from these classes. On lines 8 and 9 the `Mammal` class declares the overloaded `Move()` methods. On line 18, `Dog` overrides the version of `Move()` with no parameters. These are invoked on lines 25–27, and the output reflects this as executed.

Line 28, however, is commented out, as it causes a compile-time error. While the `Dog` class *could* have called the `Move(int)` method if it had not overridden the version of `Move()` without parameters, now that it has done so it must override both if it wishes to use both. This is reminiscent of the rule that if you supply any constructor, the compiler will no longer supply a default constructor.

It is a common mistake to hide a base class method when you intend to override it, by forgetting to include the keyword `const`. `const` is part of the signature, and leaving it off changes the signature and thus hides the method rather than overriding it.

Overriding Versus Hiding

In the next section virtual methods are described. Overriding a virtual method supports polymorphism—hiding it undermines polymorphism. You'll see more on this very soon.

Calling the Base Method

If you have overridden the base method, it is still possible to call it by fully qualifying the name of the method. You do this by writing the base name, followed by two colons and then the method name. For example: `Mammal::Move()`.

It would have been possible to rewrite line 28 in Listing 12.6 so that it would compile, by writing

```
28:     fido.Mammal::Move(10);
```

This calls the `Mammal` method explicitly. Listing 12.7 fully illustrates this idea.

Listing 12.7. Calling base method from overridden method.

```
1:      //Listing 12.7 Calling base method from overridden method.
2:
3:      #include <iostreams.h>
4:
5:      class Mammal
6:      {
7:      public:
8:          void Move() const { cout << "Mammal move one step\n"; }
9:          void Move(int distance) const { cout << "Mammal move " << distance << "
            steps.\n"; }
10:     protected:
11:         int itsAge;
12:         int itsWeight;
13:     };
14:
15:     class Dog : public Mammal
16:     {
17:     public:
18:         void Move()const;
19:
20:     };
21:
22:     void Dog::Move() const
23:     {
24:         cout << "In dog move...\n";
25:         Mammal::Move(3);
26:     }
27:
28:     void main()
29:     {
30:         Mammal bigAnimal;
31:         Dog fido;
32:         bigAnimal.Move(2);
33:         fido.Mammal::Move(6);
34:     }
```

```
Mammal move 2 steps
Mammal move 6 steps
```

Analysis On line 30 a `Mammal`, `bigAnimal` is created, and on line 31 a `Dog`, `Fido` is created. The method call on line 32 invokes the `Move()` method of `Mammal`, which takes an `int`.

The programmer wanted to invoke `Move(int)` on the `Dog` object, but had a problem. `Dog` overrides the `Move()` method, but does not overload it and does not provide a version that takes an `int`. This is solved by the explicit call to the base class `Move(int)` method on line 33.

DO	**DON'T**

DO extend the functionality of tested classes by deriving.

DO change the behavior of certain functions in the derived class by overriding the base class methods.

DON'T hide a base class function by changing the function signature.

Virtual Methods

This chapter has emphasized the fact that a `Dog` object *is a* `Mammal` object. So far that has meant only that the `Dog` object has inherited the attributes (data) and capabilities (methods) of its base class. In C++ the *is a* relationship runs deeper than that, however.

C++ extends its polymorphism to allow pointers to base classes to be assigned to derived class objects. Thus, you can write

```
Mammal* pMammal = new Dog;
```

This creates a new `Dog` object on the heap and returns a pointer to that object, which it assigns to a pointer to `Mammal`. This is fine, because a Dog *is a* Mammal.

> **Note:** This is the essence of polymorphism. You could, for example, create many different types of windows, including dialog boxes, scrollable windows, and list boxes, and give them each a virtual `draw()` method. By creating a pointer to window and assigning dialog boxes and other derived types to that pointer you can call `draw()` without regard to the actual runtime type of the object pointed to. The correct `draw()` function will be called.

12

You can then use this pointer to invoke any method on `Mammal`. What you would like is for those methods that are overridden in `Dog()` to call the correct function. Virtual functions let you do that. Listing 12.8 illustrates how this works, and what happens with non-virtual methods.

Listing 12.8. Using virtual methods.

```
1:     //Listing 12.8 Using virtual methods
2:
3:     #include <iostreams.h>
4:
5:     class Mammal
6:     {
7:     public:
8:         Mammal():itsAge(1) { cout << "Mammal constructor...\n"; }
9:         ~Mammal() { cout << "Mammal destructor...\n"; }
10:        void Move() const { cout << "Mammal move one step\n"; }
11:        virtual void Speak() const { cout << "Mammal speak!\n"; }
12:    protected:
13:        int itsAge;
14:
15:    };
16:
17:    class Dog : public Mammal
18:    {
19:    public:
20:        Dog() { cout << "Dog Constructor...\n"; }
21:        ~Dog() { cout << "Dog destructor...\n"; }
22:        void WagTail() { cout << "Wagging Tail...\n"; }
23:        void Speak()const { cout << "Woof!\n"; }
24:        void Move()const { cout << "Dog moves 5 steps...\n"; }
25:    };
26:
27:    void main()
28:    {
29:
30:        Mammal *pDog = new Dog;
31:        pDog->Move();
32:        pDog->Speak();
33:
34:    }
```

```
Mammal constructor...
Dog Constructor...
Mammal move one step
Woof!
```

On line 11 `Mammal` is provided a virtual method—`speak()`. The designer of this class thereby signals that she expects this class to eventually be another class's base type. The derived class will probably want to override this function.

On line 30 a pointer to Mammal is created, pDog, but it is assigned the address of a new Dog object. Because a Dog is a Mammal, this is a legal assignment. The pointer is then used to call the Move() function. Because the compiler knows pDog only to be a Mammal it looks to the Mammal object to find the Move() method.

On line 32 the pointer then calls the Speak() method. Because Speak() is virtual, the Speak() method overridden in Dog is invoked.

This is almost magical, as far as the calling function knew it had a Mammal pointer, but here a method on Dog was called. In fact, if you had an array of pointers to Mammal, each of which pointed to a subclass of Mammal, you could call each in turn and the correct function would be called. Listing 12.9 illustrates this idea.

Listing 12.9. Multiple virtual functions called in turn.

```
1:      //Listing 12.9 Multiple virtual functions called in turn
2:
3:      #include <iostreams.h>
4:
5:    class Mammal
6:    {
7:    public:
8:       Mammal():itsAge(1) {  }
9:       ~Mammal() { }
10:      virtual void Speak() const { cout << "Mammal speak!\n"; }
11:    protected:
12:       int itsAge;
13:    };
14:
15:    class Dog : public Mammal
16:    {
17:    public:
18:       void Speak()const { cout << "Woof!\n"; }
19:    };
20:
21:
22:    class Cat : public Mammal
23:    {
24:    public:
25:       void Speak()const { cout << "Meow!\n"; }
26:    };
27:
28:
29:    class Horse : public Mammal
30:    {
31:    public:
32:       void Speak()const { cout << "Winnie!\n"; }
33:    };
34:
35:    class Pig : public Mammal
36:    {
37:    public:
```

continues

Listing 12.9. continued

```
38:      void Speak()const { cout << "Oink!\n"; }
39:   };
40:
41:   void main()
42:   {
43:      Mammal* theArray[5];
44:      Mammal* ptr;
45:      int choice;
46:      for (int i = 0; i<5; i++)
47:      {
48:         cout << "(1)dog (2)cat (3)horse (4)pig: ";
49:         cin >> choice;
50:         switch (choice)
51:         {
52:            case 1: ptr = new Dog;
53:            break;
54:            case 2: ptr = new Cat;
55:            break;
56:            case 3: ptr = new Horse;
57:            break;
58:            case 4: ptr = new Pig;
59:            break;
60:            default: ptr = new Mammal;
61:            break;
62:         }
63:         theArray[i] = ptr;
64:      }
65:      for (i=0;i<5;i++)
66:         theArray[i]->Speak();
67:   }
```

```
(1)dog (2)cat (3)horse (4)pig: 1
(1)dog (2)cat (3)horse (4)pig: 2
(1)dog (2)cat (3)horse (4)pig: 3
(1)dog (2)cat (3)horse (4)pig: 4
(1)dog (2)cat (3)horse (4)pig: 5
Woof!
Meow!
Winnie!
Oink!
Mammal Speak!
```

This stripped-down program, which provides only the barest functionality to each class, illustrates virtual functions in their purest form. Four classes are declared, Dog, Cat, Horse, and Pig, all derived from Mammal.

On line 10, Mammal's Speak() function is declared to be virtual. On lines 18, 25, 32, and 38, the four derived classes override the implementation of Speak().

The user is prompted to pick which objects to create, and the pointers are added to the array on lines 46 through 63.

Note: Note that at compile time it is impossible to know which objects will be created, and thus which `Speak()` methods will be invoked. The pointer `ptr` is bound to its object at run-time. This is called *dynamic binding*, or *run-time binding*, as opposed to *static binding*, or *compile-time binding*.

How Virtual Functions Work

When a derived object, such as a `Dog` object, is created, first the constructor for the base class is called and then the constructor for the derived class is called. Figure 12.2 shows what the `Dog` object looks like after it is created. Note that the `Mammal` part of the object is contiguous in memory with the `Dog` part.

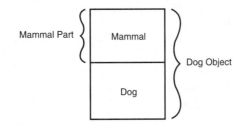

Figure 12.2. *The* `Dog` *object after it is created.*

When a virtual function is created in an object, the object must keep track of that function. Many compilers build a *virtual function table*, called a v-table. One of these is kept for each type, and each object of that type keeps a virtual table pointer (called a `vptr` or v-pointer), which points to that table.

While implementations vary, all compilers must accomplish the same thing, so you won't be too wrong with this description.

Each object's `vptr` points to the v-table which, in turn, has a pointer to each of the virtual functions. (Note, pointers to functions will be discussed in depth on Day 14, "Special Classes and Functions.") When the `Mammal` part of the `Dog` is created, the `vptr` is initialized to point to the correct part of the v-table, as shown in Figure 12.3.

12

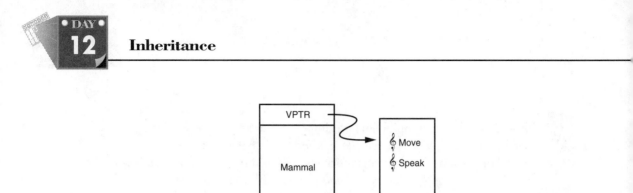

Figure 12.3. *The v-table of a* `Mammal`.

When the `Dog` constructor is called, and the `Dog` part of this object is added, the `vptr` is adjusted to point to the virtual function overrides (if any) in the `Dog` object, as illustrated in Figure 12.4.

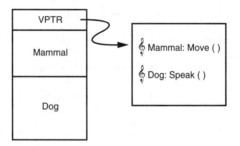

Figure 12.4. *The v-table of a* `Dog`.

When a pointer to a `Mammal` is used, the `vptr` continues to point to the correct function, depending on the "real" type of the object. Thus, when `Speak()` is invoked, the correct function is invoked.

You Can't Get There from Here

If the `Dog` object had a method, `WagTail()`, which is not in the `Mammal`, you could not use the pointer to `Mammal` to access that method (unless you cast it to be a pointer to `Dog`). Because `WagTail()` is not a virtual function, and because it is not in a `Mammal` object, you can't get there without either a `Dog` object or a `Dog` pointer.

Although you can transform the `Mammal` pointer into a `Dog` pointer, there are usually far better and safer ways to call the `WagTail()` method. C++ frowns on explicit casts because

they are error-prone. This subject will be addressed in-depth when multiple-inheritance is covered tomorrow, and again when templates are covered on Day 20, "Exceptions and Error Handling."

Slicing

Note that the virtual function magic only operates on pointers and references. Passing an object by value will not enable the virtual functions to be invoked. Listing 12.10 illustrates this problem.

Listing 12.10. Data slicing when passing by value.

```
1:      //Listing 12.10 Data slicing with passing by value
2:
3:      #include <iostreams.h>
4:
5:      enum BOOL { FALSE, TRUE };
6:      class Mammal
7:      {
8:      public:
9:          Mammal():itsAge(1) {  }
10:         ~Mammal() { }
11:         virtual void Speak() const { cout << "Mammal speak!\n"; }
12:     protected:
13:         int itsAge;
14:     };
15:
16:     class Dog : public Mammal
17:     {
18:     public:
19:         void Speak()const { cout << "Woof!\n"; }
20:     };
21:
22:     class Cat : public Mammal
23:     {
24:     public:
25:         void Speak()const { cout << "Meow!\n"; }
26:     };
27:
28:     void ValueFunction (Mammal);
29:     void PtrFunction    (Mammal*);
30:     void RefFunction (Mammal&);
31:     void main()
32:     {
33:         Mammal* ptr=0;
34:         int choice;
35:         while (1)
36:         {
37:             BOOL fQuit = FALSE;
38:             cout << "(1)dog (2)cat (0)Quit: ";
39:             cin >> choice;
```

continues

Listing 12.10. continued

```
40:          switch (choice)
41:          {
42:             case 0: fQuit = TRUE;
43:             break;
44:             case 1: ptr = new Dog;
45:             break;
46:             case 2: ptr = new Cat;
47:             break;
48:             default: ptr = new Mammal;
49:             break;
50:          }
51:           if (fQuit)
52:              break;
53:           PtrFunction(ptr);
54:           RefFunction(*ptr);
55:           ValueFunction(*ptr);
56:      }
57:  }
58:
59:  void ValueFunction (Mammal MammalValue)
60:  {
61:      MammalValue.Speak();
62:  }
63:
64:  void PtrFunction (Mammal * pMammal)
65:  {
66:      pMammal->Speak();
67:  }
68:
69:  void RefFunction (Mammal & rMammal)
70:  {
71:      rMammal.Speak();
72:  }
```

```
(1)dog (2)cat (0)Quit: 1
Woof
Woof
Mammal Speak!
(1)dog (2)cat (0)Quit: 2
Meow!
Meow!
Mammal Speak!
(1)dog (2)cat (0)Quit: 0
```

On lines 6–27 stripped-down versions of the Mammal, Dog, and Cat classes are declared. Three functions are declared—PtrFunction(), RefFunction(), and ValueFunction(). They take a pointer to a Mammal, a Mammal reference, and a Mammal object, respectively. All three functions then do the same thing—they call the Speak() method.

The user is prompted to choose a `Dog` or `Cat`, and based on the choice he makes, a pointer to the correct type is created on lines 44–49.

In the first line of the output, the user chooses `Dog`. The `Dog` object is created on the free store on line 44. The `Dog` is then passed as a pointer, as a reference, and by value to the three functions.

The pointer and references all invoke the virtual functions, and the `Dog->Speak()` member function is invoked. This is shown on the first two lines of output after the user's choice.

The dereferenced pointer, however, is passed by value. The function expects a `Mammal` object, and so the compiler slices down the `Dog` object to just the `Mammal` part. At that point, the `Mammal Speak()` method is called, as reflected in the third line of output after the user's choice.

This experiment is then repeated for the `Cat` object, with similar results.

Virtual Destructors

It is legal and common to pass a pointer to a derived object when a pointer to a base object is expected. What happens when that pointer to a derived subject is deleted? If the destructor is virtual, as it should be, the right thing happens—the derived class's destructor is called. Because the derived class's destructor will automatically invoke the base class's destructor, the entire object will be properly destroyed.

The rule of thumb is this: If any of the functions in your class are virtual, the destructor should be as well.

12

Virtual Copy Constructors

As previously stated, no constructor can be virtual. Nonetheless, there are times when your program desperately needs to be able to pass in a pointer to a base object, and have a copy of the correct derived object that is created. A common solution to this problem is to create a *clone* method in the base class, and to make that be virtual. The clone method creates a new object copy of the current class, and returns that object.

Because each derived class overrides the clone method, a copy of the derived class is created. Listing 12.11 illustrates how this is used.

Listing 12.11. Virtual copy constructor.

```
1:    //Listing 12. Virtual copy constructor
2:
3:    #include <iostreams.h>
4:
5:    class Mammal
6:    {
7:    public:
8:        Mammal():itsAge(1) { cout << "Mammal constructor...\n"; }
9:        ~Mammal() { cout << "Mammal destructor...\n"; }
10:       Mammal (const Mammal & rhs);
11:       virtual void Speak() const { cout << "Mammal speak!\n"; }
12:       virtual Mammal* Clone() { return new Mammal(*this); } // virtual
          ➥constructor
13:       int GetAge()const { return itsAge; }
14:   protected:
15:       int itsAge;
16:   };
17:
18:   Mammal::Mammal (const Mammal & rhs):itsAge(rhs.GetAge())
19:   {
20:       cout << "Mammal Copy Constructor...\n";
21:   }
22:
23:   class Dog : public Mammal
24:   {
25:   public:
26:       Dog() { cout << "Dog constructor...\n"; }
27:       ~Dog() { cout << "Dog destructor...\n"; }
28:       Dog (const Dog & rhs);
29:       void Speak()const { cout << "Woof!\n"; }
30:       virtual Mammal* Clone() { return new Dog(*this); }
31:   };
32:
33:   Dog::Dog(const Dog & rhs):
34:   Mammal(rhs)
35:   {
36:       cout << "Dog copy constructor...\n";
37:   }
38:
39:   class Cat : public Mammal
40:   {
41:   public:
42:       Cat() { cout << "Cat constructor...\n"; }
43:       ~Cat() { cout << "Cat destructor...\n"; }
44:       Cat (const Cat &);
45:       void Speak()const { cout << "Meow!\n"; }
46:       virtual Mammal* Clone() { return new Cat(*this); }
47:   };
48:
49:   Cat::Cat(const Cat & rhs):
50:   Mammal(rhs)
51:   {
52:       cout << "Cat copy constructor...\n";
53:   }
```

```
54:
55:    enum ANIMALS { MAMMAL, DOG, CAT};
56:    const int NumAnimalTypes = 3;
57:    void main()
58:    {
59:        Mammal *theArray[NumAnimalTypes];
60:        Mammal* ptr;
61:        int choice;
62:        for (int i = 0; i<NumAnimalTypes; i++)
63:        {
64:            cout << "(1)dog (2)cat (3)Mammal: ";
65:            cin >> choice;
66:            switch (choice)
67:            {
68:                case DOG: ptr = new Dog;
69:                break;
70:                case CAT: ptr = new Cat;
71:                break;
72:                default: ptr = new Mammal;
73:                break;
74:            }
75:            theArray[i] = ptr;
76:        }
77:        Mammal *OtherArray[NumAnimalTypes];
78:        for (i=0;i<NumAnimalTypes;i++)
79:        {
80:            theArray[i]->Speak();
81:            OtherArray[i] = theArray[i]->Clone();
82:        }
83:        for (i=0;i<NumAnimalTypes;i++)
84:            OtherArray[i]->Speak();
85:    }
```

Output

```
1:  (1)dog (2)cat (3)Mammal: 1
2:  Mammal constructor...
3:  Dog Constructor...
4:  (1)dog (2)cat (3)Mammal: 2
5:  Mammal constructor...
6:  Cat constructor...
7:  (1)dog (2)cat (3)Mammal: 3
8:  Mammal constructor...
9:  Woof!
10: Mammal constructor...
11: Dog copy constructor...
12: Meow!
13: Mammal constructor...
14: Cat copy constructor...
15: Mammal speak!
16: Mammal constructor...
17: Woof!
18: Meow!
19: Mammal speak!
```

12

Analysis Listing 12.11 is very similar to the previous two listings, except that a new virtual method has been added to the Mammal class: clone(). This method returns a pointer to a new Mammal object by calling the copy constructor, passing in itself (*this) as a const reference.

Dog and Cat both override the clone() method, initializing their data and passing in copies of themselves to their own copy constructors. Because clone() is virtual, this will effectively create a virtual copy constructor, as shown on line 81.

The user is prompted to choose dogs, cats, or mammals, and these are created on lines 62–74. A pointer to each choice is stored in an array on line 75.

As the program iterates over the array, each object has its Speak() and its Clone() method called, in turn, on lines 80 and 81. The result of the Clone() call is a pointer to a copy of the object, which is then stored in a second array on line 81.

On line 1 of the output, the user is prompted and responds with 1, choosing to create a dog. The Mammal and Dog constructors are invoked. This is repeated for Cat and for Mammal on lines 4–8 of the constructor.

Line 9 of the constructor represents the call to Speak on the first object, the Dog. The virtual Speak() method is called, and the correct version of Speak() is invoked. The Clone() function is then called, and as this is also virtual, Dog's Clone method is invoked, causing the Mammal constructor and the Dog copy constructor to be called. Note that as part of the call to the Dog copy constructor, the Mammal constructor, but not the Mammal copy constructor, is called. This is why the Dog copy constructor must initialize the itsAge variable.

The same is repeated for Cat on lines 12–14, and then for Mammal on lines 15 and 16. Finally, the new array is iterated, and each of the new objects has Speak() invoked.

The Cost of Virtual Methods

Because objects with virtual methods must maintain a v-table, there is some overhead in having virtual methods. If you have a very small class, from which you do not expect to derive other classes, there may be no reason to have any virtual methods at all.

Once you declare *any* methods virtual, you've paid most of the price of the v-table (although each entry does add a small memory overhead). At that point, you'll want the destructor to be virtual, and the assumption will be that all other methods probably will be virtual as well. Take a long hard look at any non-virtual methods, and be certain you understand why they are *not* virtual.

DO	DON'T

DO use virtual methods when you expect to derive from a class.

DO use a virtual destructor if any methods are virtual.

DON'T mark the constructor as virtual.

Summary

Today you learned how derived classes inherit from base classes. This chapter discussed public inheritance and virtual functions. Classes inherit all the public and protected data and functions from their base classes.

Protected access is public to derived classes and private to all other objects. Even derived classes cannot access private data or functions in their base classes.

Constructors can be initialized before the body of the constructor. It is at this time that base constructors are invoked and parameters can be passed to the base class.

Functions in the base class can be overridden in the derived class. If the base class functions are virtual, and if the object is accessed by pointer or reference, the derived class's functions will be invoked based on the runtime type of the object pointed to.

Methods in the base class can be invoked by explicitly naming the function with the prefix of the base class name and two colons. For example, if `Dog` inherits from `Mammal`, `Mammal`'s `walk()` method can be called with `Mammal::Walk()`.

In classes with virtual methods, the destructor should almost always be made virtual. A virtual destructor ensures that the derived part of the object will be freed when `delete` is called on the pointer. Constructors cannot be virtual. Virtual copy constructors can be effectively created by making a virtual member function that calls the copy constructor.

12

Q&A

Q Are inherited members and functions passed along to subsequent genera-
tions? If Dog derives from Mammal and Mammal derives from Animal does Dog
inherit Animal's functions and data?

A Yes. As derivation continues, derived classes inherit the sum of all the functions
and data in all their base classes.

Q If, in the example above, Mammal overrides a function in Animal, which does
Dog get, the original or the overridden function?

A If Dog inherits from Mammal, it gets the function in the state Mammal has it: the
overridden function.

Q Can a derived class make a public base function private?

A Yes, and it remains private for all subsequent derivation.

Q Why not make all class functions virtual?

A There is overhead with the first virtual function in the creation of a v-table.
After that, the overhead is trivial. Many C++ programmers feel that if one
function is virtual all others should be. Other programmers disagree, feeling
that there should always be a reason for what you do.

Q If a function, SomeFunc() is virtual in a base class and is also overloaded, so
as to take either an integer or two integers, and the derived class overrides
the form taking one integer, what is called when a pointer to a derived
object calls the two integer form?

A The overriding of the one int form hides the entire base class function, and
thus you will get a compile error complaining that that function requires only
one int.

Workshop

The Workshop provides quiz questions to help you solidify your understanding of the
material that was covered, and exercises to provide you with experience in using what
you've learned. Try to answer the quiz and exercise questions before checking the answers
in Appendix D, and make sure you understand the answers before continuing to the next
chapter.

Quiz

1. What is a v-table?

2. What is a virtual destructor?

3. How do you show the declaration of a virtual constructor?

4. How can you create a virtual copy constructor?

5. How do you invoke a base member function from a derived class in which you've overridden that function?

6. How do you invoke a base member function from a derived class in which you have *not* overridden that function?

7. If a base class declares a function to be virtual, and a derived class does not use the term virtual when overriding that class, is it still virtual when inherited by a third-generation class?

8. What is the `protected` keyword used for?

Exercises

1. Show the declaration of a virtual function that takes an integer parameter and returns `void`.

2. Show the declaration of a class `Square`, which derives from `Rectangle`, which in turn derives from `Shape`.

3. If, in Exercise 2, `Shape` takes no parameters, `Rectangle` takes two (length and width), but `Square` takes only one (length), show the constructor initialization for `Square`.

4. Write a virtual copy constructor for the class `Square` (above).

5. **BUG BUSTERS:** What is wrong with this code snippet?

```
void SomeFunction (Shape);
Shape * pRect = new Rectangle;
SomeFunction(*pRect);
```

6. **BUG BUSTERS:** What is wrong with this code snippet?

```
class Shape()
{
public:
    Shape();
    virtual ~Shape();
    virtual Shape(const Shape&);
};
```

13

Polymorphism

Introduction

Yesterday, you learned how to write virtual functions in derived classes. This is the fundamental building block of polymorphism: the capability to bind specific, derived class objects to base class pointers at runtime. Today, you learn:

☐ What multiple inheritance is and how to use it.

☐ What virtual inheritance is.

☐ What abstract data types are.

☐ What pure virtual functions are.

Problems with Single Inheritance

Suppose you've been working with your animal classes for a while and you've divided the class hierarchy into `Birds` and `Mammals`. The `Bird` class includes the member function `Fly()`. The `Mammal` class has been divided into a number of types of `Mammals`, including `Horse`. The `Horse` class includes the member functions `Whinny()` and `Gallop()`.

Suddenly, you realize you need a `Pegasus` object: a cross between a `Horse` and a `Bird`. A `Pegasus` can `Fly()`, and it can `Whinny()` and it can `Gallop()`. With single inheritance, you're in quite a jam.

You can make `Pegasus` a `Bird`, but then it won't be able to `Whinny()` or `Gallop()`. You can make it a `Horse`, but then it won't be able to `Fly()`.

Your first solution is to copy the `Fly()` method into the `Pegasus` class and derive `Pegasus` from `Horse`. This works fine, at the cost of having the `Fly()` method in two places (`Bird` and `Pegasus`). If you change one, you must remember to change the other. Of course, a developer who comes along months or years later to maintain your code must also know to fix both places.

Soon, however, you have a new problem. You wish to create a list of `Horse` objects and a list of `Bird` objects. You'd like to be able to add your `Pegasus` objects to either list, but if a `Pegasus` is a horse, you can't add it to a list of birds.

You have a couple of potential solutions. You can rename the `Horse` method `Gallop()` to `Move()`, and then override `Move()` in your `Pegasus` object to do the work of `Fly()`. You would then override `Move()` in your other horses to do the work of `Gallop()`. Perhaps `Pegasus` could be clever enough to gallop short distances and fly longer distances.

```
Pegasus::Move(long distance)
{
    if (distance > veryFar)
        fly(distance);
    else
        gallop(distance);
}
```

This is a bit limiting. Perhaps one day Pegasus will want to fly a short distance or gallop a long distance. Your next solution might be to move Fly() up into Horse, as illustrated in Listing 13.1. The problem is that most horses can't fly, so you have to make this method do nothing unless it is a Pegasus.

Listing 13.1. If horses could fly...

```
1:      // Listing 13.1. If horses could fly...
2:      // Percolating Fly() up into Horse
3:
4:      #include <iostreams.h>
5:
6:      class Horse
7:      {
8:      public:
9:          void Gallop(){ cout << "Galloping...\n"; }
10:         virtual void Fly() { cout << "Horses can't fly.\n" ; }
11:     private:
12:         int itsAge;
13:     };
14:
15:     class Pegasus : public Horse
16:     {
17:     public:
18:         virtual void Fly() { cout << "I can fly! I can fly! I can fly!\n"; }
19:     };
20:
21:     const int NumberHorses = 5;
22:     void main()
23:     {
24:         Horse* Ranch[NumberHorses];
25:         Horse* pHorse;
26:         int choice;
27:         for (int i=0; i<NumberHorses; i++)
28:         {
29:             cout << "(1)Horse (2)Pegasus: ";
30:             cin >> choice;
31:             if (choice == 2)
32:                 pHorse = new Pegasus;
33:             else
34:                 pHorse = new Horse;
35:             Ranch[i] = pHorse;
36:         }
37:         cout << "\n";
38:         for (i=0; i<NumberHorses; i++)
```

13

continues

Listing 13.1. continued

```
39:        {
40:           Ranch[i]->Fly();
41:           delete Ranch[i];
42:        }
43:    }
```

```
(1)Horse (2)Pegasus: 1
(1)Horse (2)Pegasus: 2
(1)Horse (2)Pegasus: 1
(1)Horse (2)Pegasus: 2
(1)Horse (2)Pegasus: 1

Horses can't fly.
I can fly! I can fly! I can fly!
Horses can't fly.
I can fly! I can fly! I can fly!
Horses can't fly.
```

This program certainly works, though at the expense of the Horse class having a Fly() method. On line 10, the method Fly() is provided to Horse. In a real world class, you might have it issue an error, or fail quietly. On line 18, the Pegasus class overrides the Fly() method to "do the right thing," represented here by printing a happy message.

The array of Horse pointers on line 24 is used to demonstrate that the correct Fly() method is called based on the runtime binding of the Horse or Pegasus object.

Percolating Upward

Putting the required function higher in the class hierarchy is a common solution to this problem, and results in many functions "percolating up" into the base class. The base class is then in grave danger of becoming a global namespace for all the functions that might be used by any of the derived classes. This can seriously undermine the class typing of C++, and can create a large and cumbersome base class.

In general, you want to percolate shared functionality up the hierarchy, without migrating the interface of each class. This means that if two classes that share a common base class (for example, Horse and Bird both share Animal) have a function in common (both birds and horses eat, for example), you'll want to move that functionality up into the base class and create a virtual function.

What you'll want to avoid, however, is percolating an interface (like Fly up where it doesn't belong), just so you can call that function only on some derived classes.

Casting Down

An alternative to this approach, still within single inheritance, is to keep the Fly() method within Pegasus, and only call it if the pointer is actually pointing to a Pegasus object. To make this work, you'll need to be able to ask your pointer what type it is really pointing to. This is known as Run Time Type Identification (RTTI). Using RTTI has only recently become an official part of C++.

If your compiler does not support RTTI, you can mimic it by putting a method that returns an enumerated type in each of the classes. You can then test that type at run-time and call Fly() if it returns Pegasus.

> **Note:** Beware of adding RTTI to your classes. Use of it may be an indication of poor design. Consider using virtual functions, templates, or multiple inheritance instead.

In order to call Fly() however, you must cast the pointer, telling it that the object it is pointing to is a Pegasus object, not a Horse. This is called *casting down*, because you are casting the Horse object *down* to a more derived type. Casting down is often a sign of poor design, as is illustrated by Listing 13.2.

Listing 13.2. Run time type identification.

```
1:      // Listing 13.2 Run time type identification.
2:      // Using rtti
3:
4:      #include <iostreams.h>
5:      enum TYPE { HORSE, PEGASUS };
6:
7:      class Horse
8:      {
9:      public:
10:         void Gallop(){ cout << "Galloping...\n"; }
11:         virtual TYPE GetType() { return HORSE; }
12:     private:
13:         int itsAge;
14:     };
15:
16:     class Pegasus : public Horse
17:     {
18:     public:
19:         TYPE GetType() { return PEGASUS; }
20:         virtual void Fly() { cout << "I can fly! I can fly! I can fly!\n"; }
21:     };
```

continues

Listing 13.2. continued

```
22:
23:    const int NumberHorses = 5;
24:    void main()
25:    {
26:       Horse* Ranch[NumberHorses];
27:       Horse* pHorse;
28:       int choice;
29:       for (int i=0; i<NumberHorses; i++)
30:       {
31:          cout << "(1)Horse (2)Pegasus: ";
32:          cin >> choice;
33:          if (choice == 2)
34:             pHorse = new Pegasus;
35:          else
36:             pHorse = new Horse;
37:          Ranch[i] = pHorse;
38:       }
39:       cout << "\n";
40:       for (i=0; i<NumberHorses; i++)
41:       {
42:          if (Ranch[i]->GetType() == PEGASUS)
43:             ((Pegasus *)(Ranch[i]))->Fly();
44:
45:          delete Ranch[i];
46:       }
47:    }
```

```
(1)Horse (2)Pegasus: 1
(1)Horse (2)Pegasus: 2
(1)Horse (2)Pegasus: 1
(1)Horse (2)Pegasus: 2
(1)Horse (2)Pegasus: 1

I can fly! I can fly! I can fly!
I can fly! I can fly! I can fly!
```

This solution also works. Fly() is kept out of Horse, and is not called on Horse objects. When it is called on Pegasus objects, however, they must be explicitly cast; Horse objects don't have the method Fly(), so the pointer must be told it is pointing to a Pegasus object before being used.

The need for you to cast the Pegasus object is a warning that something may be wrong with your design. Here, the program must test each object at runtime, as shown on line 42. In this case, a simple if statement is used to differentiate the two types, but if there were dozens of types a very large and hard-to-maintain switch statement would have been required.

This program effectively undermines the virtual function polymorphism, because it depends on casting the object to its real runtime type.

Adding to Two Lists

The other problem with these solutions is that you've declared Pegasus to be a type of Horse, so you cannot add a Pegasus object to a list of Birds. You've paid the price of either moving Fly() up into Horse, or casting down the pointer, and yet you still don't have the full functionality you need.

One final single inheritance solution presents itself. You can push Fly(), Whinny(), and Gallop() all up into a common base class of both Bird and Horse: Animal. Now, instead of having a list of Birds and a list of Horses, you can have one unified list of Animals. This works, but percolates more functionality up into the base classes.

Alternatively, you can leave the methods where they are, but cast down Horses and Birds and Pegasus objects, but that is even worse!

DO   DON'T

DO move functionality up the inheritance hierarchy.

DON'T move interface up the inheritance hierarchy.

DO avoid switching on the runtime type of the object—use virtual methods, templates, and multiple inheritance.

DON'T cast pointers to base objects down to derived objects.

Multiple Inheritance

It is possible to derive a new class from more than one base class. This is called *Multiple Inheritance*. To derive from more than the base class, you separate each base class by commas in the class designation. Listing 13.3 illustrates how to declare Pegasus so that it derives from both Horses and Birds. The program then adds Pegasus objects to both types of lists.

Listing 13.3. Multiple inheritance.

```
1:    // Listing 13.3. Multiple inheritance.
2:    // Multiple Inheritance
3:
4:    #include <iostreams.h>
5:
```

continues

377

Listing 13.3. continued

```
6:    class Horse
7:    {
8:    public:
9:        Horse() { cout << "Horse constructor... "; }
10:       virtual ~Horse() { cout << "Horse destructor... "; }
11:       virtual void Whinny() const { cout << "Whinny!... "; }
12:    private:
13:       int itsAge;
14:    };
15:
16:    class Bird
17:    {
18:    public:
19:        Bird() { cout << "Bird constructor... "; }
20:       virtual ~Bird() { cout << "Bird destructor... "; }
21:       virtual void Chirp() const { cout << "Chirp... ";  }
22:       virtual void Fly() const { cout << "I can fly! I can fly! I can fly! "; }
23:    private:
24:       int itsWeight;
25:    };
26:
27:    class Pegasus : public Horse, public Bird
28:    {
29:    public:
30:       void Chirp() const { Whinny(); }
31:       Pegasus() { cout << "Pegasus constructor... "; }
32:       ~Pegasus() { cout << "Pegasus destructor...  "; }
33:    };
34:
35:    const int MagicNumber = 2;
36:    void main()
37:    {
38:       Horse* Ranch[MagicNumber];
39:       Bird* Aviary[MagicNumber];
40:       Horse * pHorse;
41:       Bird * pBird;
42:       int choice;
43:       for (int i=0; i<MagicNumber; i++)
44:       {
45:          cout << "\n(1)Horse (2)Pegasus: ";
46:          cin >> choice;
47:          if (choice == 2)
48:             pHorse = new Pegasus;
49:          else
50:             pHorse = new Horse;
51:          Ranch[i] = pHorse;
52:       }
53:       for (i=0; i<MagicNumber; i++)
54:       {
55:          cout << "\n(1)Bird (2)Pegasus: ";
56:          cin >> choice;
57:          if (choice == 2)
58:             pBird = new Pegasus;
59:          else
```

```
60:             pBird = new Bird;
61:          Aviary[i] = pBird;
62:       }
63:
64:       cout << "\n";
65:       for (i=0; i<MagicNumber; i++)
66:       {
67:          cout << "\nRanch[" << i << "]: " ;
68:          Ranch[i]->Whinny();
69:          delete Ranch[i];
70:       }
71:
72:       for (i=0; i<MagicNumber; i++)
73:       {
74:          cout << "\nAviary[" << i << "]: " ;
75:          Aviary[i]->Chirp();
76:          Aviary[i]->Fly();
77:          delete Aviary[i];
78:       }
79:    }
```

Output

```
(1)Horse (2)Pegasus: 1
Horse constructor...
(1)Horse (2)Pegasus: 2
Horse constructor... Bird constructor... Pegasus constructor
(1)Bird (2)Pegasus: 1
Bird constructor...
(1)Bird (2)Pegasus: 2
Horse constructor... Bird constructor... Pegasus constructor

Ranch[0]: Whinny!... Horse destructor...
Ranch[1]: Whinny!... Pegasus destructor.. Bird destructor... Horse destructor...
Aviary[0]: Chirp... I can fly! I can fly! I can fly! Bird destructor...
Aviary[1]: Whinny!... I can fly! I can fly! I can fly! Pegasus destructor.. Bird
destructor... Horse destructor...
```

Analysis

On lines 6–14, a Horse class is declared. The constructor and destructor print out a message, and the Whinny() method prints the word Whinny!

On lines 16–25, a Bird class is declared. In addition to its constructor and destructor, this class has two methods: Chirp() and Fly(), both of which print identifying messages. In a real program these might, for example, activate the speaker or generate animated images.

Finally, on lines 27–33, the class Pegasus is declared. It derives both from Horse and from Bird. The Pegasus class overrides the Chirp() method to call the Whinny() method, which it inherits from Horse.

Two lists are created, a Ranch with pointers to Horse on line 38, and an Aviary with pointers to Bird on line 39. On lines 43–52, Horse and Pegasus objects are added to the Ranch. On lines 53–62, Bird and Pegasus objects are added to the Aviary.

13

Invocations of the virtual methods on both the `Bird` pointers and the `Horse` pointers do the right things for `Pegasus` objects. For example, on line 75 the members of the `Aviary` array are used to call `Chirp()` on the objects to which they point. The `Bird` class declares this to be a virtual method, so the right function is called for each object.

Note that each time a `Pegasus` object is created, the output reflects that both the `Bird` part and the `Horse` part of the `Pegasus` object is also created. When a `Pegasus` object is destroyed, the `Bird` and `Horse` parts are destroyed as well, thanks to the destructors being made virtual.

Declaring Multiple Inheritance

Declare an object to inherit from more than one class by listing the base classes following the colon after the class name. Separate the base classes by commas.

Example 1:

```
class Pegasus : public Horse, public Bird
```

Example 2:

```
class Schnoodle : public Schnauzer, public Poodle
```

The Parts of a Multiply Inherited Object

When the `Pegasus` object is created in memory, both of the base classes form part of the `Pegasus` object, as illustrated in Figure 13.1

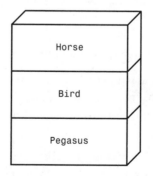

Figure 13.1. *Multiply inherited objects.*

A number of issues arise with objects with multiple base classes. For example, what happens if two base classes that happen to have the same name have virtual functions or data? How are multiple base class constructors initialized? What happens if multiple base classes both derive from the same class? The next sections will answer these questions, and explore how multiple inheritance can be put to work.

Constructors in Multiply Inherited Objects

If Pegasus derives from both Horse and Bird, and each of the base classes has constructors that take parameters, the Pegasus class initializes these constructors in turn. Listing 13.4 illustrates how this is done.

Listing 13.4. Calling multiple constructors.

```
1:  // Listing 13.4
2:  // Calling multiple constructors
3:  #include <iostreams.h>
4:  typedef int HANDS;
5:  enum COLOR { Red, Green, Blue, Yellow, White, Black, Brown } ;
6:  enum BOOL { FALSE, TRUE };
7:
8:  class Horse
9:  {
10: public:
11:     Horse(COLOR color, HANDS height);
12:     virtual ~Horse() { cout << "Horse destructor...\n"; }
13:     virtual void Whinny()const { cout << "Whinny!... "; }
14:     virtual HANDS GetHeight() const { return itsHeight; }
15:     virtual COLOR GetColor() const { return itsColor; }
16: private:
17:     HANDS itsHeight;
18:     COLOR itsColor;
19: };
20:
21: Horse::Horse(COLOR color, HANDS height):
22:     itsColor(color),itsHeight(height)
23: {
24:     cout << "Horse constructor...\n";
25: }
26:
27: class Bird
28: {
29: public:
30:     Bird(COLOR color, BOOL migrates);
31:     virtual ~Bird() {cout << "Bird destructor...\n";  }
32:     virtual void Chirp()const { cout << "Chirp... ";  }
33:     virtual void Fly()const { cout << "I can fly! I can fly! I can fly! "; }
34:     virtual COLOR GetColor()const { return itsColor; }
35:     virtual BOOL GetMigration() const { return itsMigration; }
36:
37: private:
38:     COLOR itsColor;
```

continues

Listing 13.4. continued

```
39:        BOOL itsMigration;
40:    };
41:
42:    Bird::Bird(COLOR color, BOOL migrates):
43:        itsColor(color), itsMigration(migrates)
44:    {
45:        cout << "Bird constructor...\n";
46:    }
47:
48:    class Pegasus : public Horse, public Bird
49:    {
50:    public:
51:        void Chirp()const { Whinny(); }
52:        Pegasus(COLOR, HANDS, BOOL,long);
53:        ~Pegasus() {cout << "Pegasus destructor...\n";}
54:        virtual long GetNumberBelievers() const { return  itsNumberBelievers; }
55:
56:    private:
57:        long itsNumberBelievers;
58:    };
59:
60:    Pegasus::Pegasus(COLOR aColor, HANDS height, BOOL migrates, long NumBelieve):
61:    Horse(aColor, height),
62:    Bird(aColor, migrates),
63:    itsNumberBelievers(NumBelieve)
64:    {
65:        cout << "Pegasus constructor...\n";
66:    }
67:
68:    void main()
69:    {
70:        Pegasus *pPeg = new Pegasus(Red, 5, TRUE, 10);
71:        pPeg->Fly();
72:        pPeg->Whinny();
73:        cout << "\nYour Pegasus is " << pPeg->GetHeight();
74:        cout << " hands tall and ";
75:        if (pPeg->GetMigration())
76:           cout << "it does migrate.";
77:        else
78:           cout << "it does not migrate.";
79:        cout << "\nA total of " << pPeg->GetNumberBelievers();
80:        cout << " people believe it exists.\n";
81:        delete pPeg;
82:    }
```

```
Horse constructor...
Bird constructor...
Pegasus constructor...
I can fly! I can fly! I can fly! Whinny
Your Pegasus is 5 hands tall and it does migrate.
A total of 10 people believe it exists.
Pegasus destructor...
Bird destructor...
Horse destructor...
```

On lines 8–19, the Horse class is declared. The constructor takes two parameters, both using enumerations declared on lines 5 and 6. The implementation of the constructor on lines 21–25 simply initializes the member variables and prints a message.

On lines 27–40, the Bird class is declared, and the implementation of its constructor is on lines 42–46. Again, the Bird class takes two parameters. Interestingly, the Horse constructor takes color (so that you can detect horses of different colors), and the Bird constructor takes the color of the feathers (so those of one feather can stick together). This leads to a problem when you want to ask the Pegasus for its color, which you'll see in the next example.

The Pegasus class itself is declared on lines 48–58, and its constructor is on lines 60–66. The initialization of the Pegasus object includes three statements. First, the Horse constructor is initialized with color and height. Then the Bird constructor is initialized with color and the Boolean. Finally, the Pegasus member variable itsNumberBelievers is initialized. Once all that is accomplished, the body of the Pegasus constructor is called.

In the main() function, a Pegasus pointer is created and used to access the member functions of the base objects. On line 79, the Pegasus accessor GetNumberBelievers() is called, though the data member itsNumberBelievers could have been called directly.

Ambiguity Resolution

In Listing 13.4, both the Horse class and the Bird class have a method GetColor(). You may need to ask the Pegasus object to return its color, but you have a problem: the Pegasus class inherits from both Bird and Horse. They both have a color, and their methods for getting that color have the same names and signature. This creates an ambiguity for the compiler, which you must resolve.

If you simply write

```
COLOR currentColor = pPeg->GetColor();
```

you will get a compiler error:

```
Member is ambiguous: 'Horse::GetColor' and 'Bird::GetColor'
```

You can resolve the ambiguity with an explicit call to the function you wish to invoke:

```
COLOR currentColor = pPeg->Horse::GetColor();
```

Anytime you need to resolve which class a member function or member data inherits from, you can fully qualify the call by prepending the class name to the base class data or function.

13

Note that if `Pegasus` were to override this function, then the problem would be moved, as it should be, into the `Pegasus` member function:

```
virtual COLOR GetColor()const { return Horse::itsColor; }
```

This hides the problem from clients of the `Pegasus` class, and encapsulates within `Pegasus` the knowledge of which base class it wishes to inherit its color from. A client is still free to force the issue by writing:

```
COLOR currentColor = pPeg->Bird::GetColor();
```

Inheriting from Shared Base Class

What happens if both `Bird` and `Horse` inherit from a common base class, such as `Animal`? Figure 13.2 illustrates what this looks like.

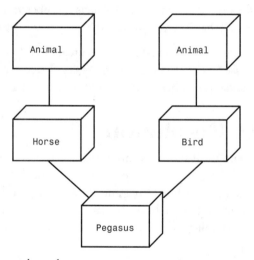

Figure 13.2. *Common base classes.*

As you can see in Figure 13.2, two base class objects exist. When a function or data member is called in the shared base class, another ambiguity exists. For example, if `Animal` declares `itsAge` as a member variable and `GetAge()` as a member function, and you call `pPeg->GetAge()`, did you mean to call the `GetAge()` function you inherit from `Animal` by way of `Horse`, or by way of `Bird`? You must resolve this ambiguity as well, as illustrated in Listing 13.5.

Listing 13.5. Common base classes.

```
1:    // Listing 13.5
2:    // Common base classes
3:    #include <iostreams.h>
4:
5:    typedef int HANDS;
6:    enum COLOR { Red, Green, Blue, Yellow, White, Black, Brown } ;
7:    enum BOOL { FALSE, TRUE };
8:
9:    class Animal        // common base to both horse and bird
10:   {
11:   public:
12:       Animal(int);
13:       virtual ~Animal() { cout << "Animal destructor...\n"; }
14:       virtual int GetAge() const { return itsAge; }
15:       virtual void SetAge(int age) { itsAge = age; }
16:   private:
17:       int itsAge;
18:   };
19:
20:   Animal::Animal(int age):
21:   itsAge(age)
22:   {
23:       cout << "Animal constructor...\n";
24:   }
25:
26:   class Horse : public Animal
27:   {
28:   public:
29:       Horse(COLOR color, HANDS height, int age);
30:       virtual ~Horse() { cout << "Horse destructor...\n"; }
31:       virtual void Whinny()const { cout << "Whinny!... "; }
32:       virtual HANDS GetHeight() const { return itsHeight; }
33:       virtual COLOR GetColor() const { return itsColor; }
34:   protected:
35:       HANDS itsHeight;
36:       COLOR itsColor;
37:   };
38:
39:   Horse::Horse(COLOR color, HANDS height, int age):
40:       Animal(age),
41:       itsColor(color),itsHeight(height)
42:   {
43:       cout << "Horse constructor...\n";
44:   }
45:
46:   class Bird : public Animal
47:   {
48:   public:
49:       Bird(COLOR color, BOOL migrates, int age);
50:       virtual ~Bird() {cout << "Bird destructor...\n";  }
51:       virtual void Chirp()const { cout << "Chirp... ";  }
52:       virtual void Fly()const { cout << "I can fly! I can fly! I can fly! "; }
53:       virtual COLOR GetColor()const { return itsColor; }
```

continues

Listing 13.5. continued

```
54:         virtual BOOL GetMigration() const { return itsMigration; }
55:
56:     protected:
57:         COLOR itsColor;
58:         BOOL itsMigration;
59:     };
60:
61:     Bird::Bird(COLOR color, BOOL migrates, int age):
62:         Animal(age),
63:         itsColor(color), itsMigration(migrates)
64:     {
65:         cout << "Bird constructor...\n";
66:     }
67:
68:     class Pegasus : public Horse, public Bird
69:     {
70:     public:
71:         void Chirp()const { Whinny(); }
72:         Pegasus(COLOR, HANDS, BOOL, long, int);
73:         ~Pegasus() {cout << "Pegasus destructor...\n";}
74:         virtual long GetNumberBelievers() const { return  itsNumberBelievers; }
75:         virtual COLOR GetColor()const { return Horse::itsColor; }
76:         virtual int GetAge() const { return Horse::GetAge(); }
77:
78:     private:
79:         long itsNumberBelievers;
80:     };
81:
82:     Pegasus::Pegasus(
83:         COLOR aColor,
84:         HANDS height,
85:         BOOL migrates,
86:         long NumBelieve,
87:         int age):
88:     Horse(aColor, height,age),
89:     Bird(aColor, migrates,age),
90:     itsNumberBelievers(NumBelieve)
91:     {
92:         cout << "Pegasus constructor...\n";
93:     }
94:
95:     void main()
96:     {
97:         Pegasus *pPeg = new Pegasus(Red, 5, TRUE, 10, 2);
98:         int age = pPeg->GetAge();
99:         cout << "This pegasus is " << age << " years old.\n";
100:        delete pPeg;
101:    }
```

```
1:  Animal constructor...
2:  Horse constructor...
3:  Animal constructor...
4:  Bird constructor...
```

```
5:  Pegasus constructor...
6:  This pegasus is 2 years old.
7:  Pegasus destructor...
8:  Bird destructor...
9:  Animal destructor...
10: Horse destructor...
11: Animal destructor...
```

Analysis There are a number of interesting features to this listing. The `Animal` class is declared on lines 9–18. `Animal` adds one member variable, `itsAge` and an accessor, `SetAge()`.

On line 26, the `Horse` class is declared to derive from `Animal`. The `Horse` constructor now has a third parameter, `age`, which it passes to its base class, `Animal`. Note that the `Horse` class does *not* override `GetAge()`, it simply inherits it.

On line 46, the `Bird` class is declared to derive from `Animal`. Its constructor also takes an age and uses it to initialize its base class, `Animal`. It also inherits `GetAge()` without overriding it.

`Pegasus` inherits from both `Bird` and from `Animal`, and so has two `Animal` classes in its inheritance chain. If you were to call `GetAge()` on a `Pegasus` object, you would have to disambiguate, or fully qualify, the method you want if `Pegasus` did not override the method.

This is solved on line 76 when the `Pegasus` object overrides `GetAge()` to do nothing more than to *chain up*—that is, to call the same method in a base class.

Chaining up is done for two reasons: either to disambiguate which base class to call, as in this case, or to do some work and then let the function in the base class do some more work. At times, you may want to do work and then chain up, or chain up and then do the work when the base class function returns.

The `Pegasus` constructor takes five parameters: the creature's color, its height (in HANDS), whether or not it migrates, how many believe in it, and its age. The constructor initializes the `Horse` part of the `Pegasus` with the color, height, and age on line 88. It initializes the `Bird` part with color, whether it migrates, and age on line 89. Finally, it initializes `itsNumberBelievers` on line 90.

The call to the `Horse` constructor on line 88 invokes the implementation shown on line 39. The `Horse` constructor uses the age parameter to initialize the `Animal` part of the `Horse` part of the `Pegasus`. It then goes on to initialize the two member variables of `Horse`— `itsColor` and `itsAge`.

The call to the `Bird` constructor on line 89 invokes the implementation shown on line 46. Here too, the age parameter is used to initialize the `Animal` part of the `Bird`.

13

Note that the `color` parameter to the `Pegasus` is used to initialize member variables in each of `Bird` and `Horse`. Note also that the age is used to initialize `itsAge` in the `Horse`'s base `Animal` and in the `Bird`'s base `Animal`.

Virtual Inheritance

In Listing 13.5, the `Pegasus` class went to some lengths to disambiguate which of its `Animal` base classes it meant to invoke. Most of the time, the decision as to which one to use is arbitrary—after all, the `Horse` and the `Bird` have exactly the same base class.

It is possible to tell C++ that you do not want two copies of the shared base class, as shown in Figure 13.2, but rather to have a single shared base class, as shown in Figure 13.3.

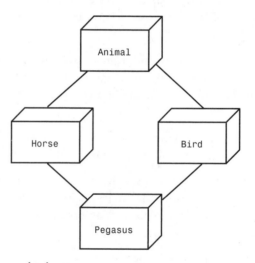

Figure 13.3. *A diamond inheritance.*

You accomplish this by making `Animal` a virtual base class of both `Horse` and `Bird`. The `Animal` class does not change at all. The `Horse` and `Bird` classes change only in their use of the term virtual in their declarations. `Pegasus`, however, changes substantially.

Normally, a class's constructor initializes only its own variables and its base class. Virtually inherited base classes are an exception, however. They are initialized by their *most derived* class. Thus, `Animal` is initialized not by `Horse` and `Bird`, but by `Pegasus`. `Horse` and `Bird` have to initialize `Animal` in their constructors, but these initializations will be ignored when a `Pegasus` object is created.

Listing 13.6 rewrites Listing 13.5 to take advantage of virtual derivation.

Listing 13.6. Illustrates use of virtual inheritance.

```
1:      // Listing 13.5
2:      // Virtual inheritance
3:      #include <iostreams.h>
4:
5:      typedef int HANDS;
6:      enum COLOR { Red, Green, Blue, Yellow, White, Black, Brown } ;
7:      enum BOOL { FALSE, TRUE };
8:
9:      class Animal          // common base to both horse and bird
10:     {
11:     public:
12:         Animal(int);
13:         virtual ~Animal() { cout << "Animal destructor...\n"; }
14:         virtual int GetAge() const { return itsAge; }
15:         virtual void SetAge(int age) { itsAge = age; }
16:     private:
17:         int itsAge;
18:     };
19:
20:     Animal::Animal(int age):
21:     itsAge(age)
22:     {
23:         cout << "Animal constructor...\n";
24:     }
25:
26:     class Horse : virtual public Animal
27:     {
28:     public:
29:         Horse(COLOR color, HANDS height, int age);
30:         virtual ~Horse() { cout << "Horse destructor...\n"; }
31:         virtual void Whinny()const { cout << "Whinny!... "; }
32:         virtual HANDS GetHeight() const { return itsHeight; }
33:         virtual COLOR GetColor() const { return itsColor; }
34:     protected:
35:         HANDS itsHeight;
36:         COLOR itsColor;
37:     };
38:
39:     Horse::Horse(COLOR color, HANDS height, int age):
40:         Animal(age),
41:         itsColor(color),itsHeight(height)
42:     {
43:         cout << "Horse constructor...\n";
44:     }
45:
46:     class Bird : virtual public Animal
47:     {
48:     public:
49:         Bird(COLOR color, BOOL migrates, int age);
50:         virtual ~Bird() {cout << "Bird destructor...\n";  }
51:         virtual void Chirp()const { cout << "Chirp... ";  }
52:         virtual void Fly()const { cout << "I can fly! I can fly! I can fly! "; }
53:         virtual COLOR GetColor()const { return itsColor; }
54:         virtual BOOL GetMigration() const { return itsMigration; }
```

continues

Listing 13.6. continued

```
55:
56:    protected:
57:       COLOR itsColor;
58:       BOOL itsMigration;
59:    };
60:
61:    Bird::Bird(COLOR color, BOOL migrates, int age):
62:       Animal(age),
63:       itsColor(color), itsMigration(migrates)
64:    {
65:       cout << "Bird constructor...\n";
66:    }
67:
68:    class Pegasus : public Horse, public Bird
69:    {
70:    public:
71:       void Chirp()const { Whinny(); }
72:       Pegasus(COLOR, HANDS, BOOL, long, int);
73:       ~Pegasus() {cout << "Pegasus destructor...\n";}
74:       virtual long GetNumberBelievers() const { return  itsNumberBelievers; }
75:       virtual COLOR GetColor()const { return Horse::itsColor; }
76:
77:    private:
78:       long itsNumberBelievers;
79:    };
80:
81:    Pegasus::Pegasus(
82:       COLOR aColor,
83:       HANDS height,
84:       BOOL migrates,
85:       long NumBelieve,
86:       int age):
87:    Horse(aColor, height,age),
88:    Bird(aColor, migrates,age),
89:    Animal(age*2),
90:    itsNumberBelievers(NumBelieve)
91:    {
92:       cout << "Pegasus constructor...\n";
93:    }
94:
95:    void main()
96:    {
97:       Pegasus *pPeg = new Pegasus(Red, 5, TRUE, 10, 2);
98:       int age = pPeg->GetAge();
99:       cout << "This pegasus is " << age << " years old.\n";
100:      delete pPeg;
101:   }
```

```
Animal constructor...
Horse constructor...
Bird constructor...
Pegasus constructor...
This pegasus is 4 years old
```

```
Pegasus destructor...
Bird destructor...
Horse destructor...
Animal destructor...
```

 On line 26, Horse declares that it inherits *virtually* from Animal, and on line 46, Bird makes the same declaration. Note that the constructors for both Bird and Animal still initialize the Animal object.

Pegasus inherits from both Bird and Animal, and as the most derived object of Animal, it also initializes Animal. It is Pegasus' initialization which is called, however, and the calls to Animal's constructor in Bird and Horse are ignored. You can see this because the value 2 is passed in, and Horse and Bird pass it along to Animal, but Pegasus doubles it. The result, 4, is reflected in the printout on line 99 and as shown in the output.

Pegasus no longer has to disambiguate the call to GetAge(), and so is free to simply inherit this function from Animal. Note that Pegasus must still disambiguate the call to GetColor(), as this function is in both of its base classes and not in Animal.

Declaring Classes for Virtual Inheritance

To ensure that derived classes have only one instance of common base classes, declare the intermediate classes to inherit virtually from the base class.

Example 1:

```
class Horse : virtual public Animal
class Bird : virtual public Animal
class Pegasus : public Horse, public Bird
```

Example 2:

```
class Schnauzer : virtual public Dog
class Poodle : virtual public Dog
class Schnoodle : public Schnauzer, public Poodle
```

Problems with Multiple Inheritance

Although multiple inheritance offers a number of advantages over single inheritance, there are many C++ programmers who are reluctant to use it. The problems they cite are that many compilers don't support it yet, that it makes debugging harder, and that nearly everything that can be done with multiple inheritance can be done without it.

These are valid concerns, and you will want to be on your guard against installing needless complexity into your programs. Some debuggers have a hard time with multiple inheritance, and some designs are needlessly made complex by using multiple inheritance when it is not needed.

DO	**DON'T**

DO use multiple inheritance when a new class needs functions and features from more than one base class.

DO use virtual inheritance when the most derived classes must have only one instance of the shared base class.

DO initialize the shared base class from the most derived class when using virtual base classes.

DON'T use multiple inheritance when single inheritance will do.

Mixins and Capabilities Classes

One way to strike a middle ground between multiple inheritance and single inheritance is to use what are called *Mixins*. Thus, you might have your Horse class derive from Animal and from Displayable. Displayable would just add a few methods for displaying any object on-screen.

 NEW TERM A Mixin, or capability class, is a class that adds functionality without adding much or any data.

Capability classes are mixed into a derived class like any other class might be, by declaring the derived class to inherit publicly from them. The only difference between a Capability class and any other class is that the Capability class has little or no data. This is an arbitrary distinction, of course, and is just a shorthand way of noting that at times all you want to do is mix in some additional capabilities without complicating the derived class.

This will, for some debuggers, make it easier to work with Mixins than with more complex multiply-inherited objects. There is also less likelihood of ambiguity in accessing the data in the other principal base class.

For example, if Horse derives from Animal and from Displayable, Displayable would have no data. Animal would be just as it always was, so all the data in Horse would derive from Animal, but the functions in Horse would derive from both.

The term Mixin comes from an ice-cream store in Sommerville, Massachusetts, where candies and cakes were mixed into the basic ice-cream flavors. This seemed like a good metaphor to some of the object-oriented programmers who used to take a summer break there, especially while working with the object-oriented programming language SCOOPS.

Abstract Data Types

Often, you will create a hierarchy of classes together. For example, you might create a Shape class, and derive from that Rectangle and Circle. From Rectangle, you might derive Square, as a special case of Rectangle.

Each of the derived classes will override the Draw() method, the GetArea() method, and so forth. Listing 13.7 illustrates a bare-bones implementation of the Shape class and its derived Circle and Rectangle classes.

Listing 13.7. Shape classes.

```
1:    //Listing 13.7. Shape classes.
2:
3:    #include <iostreams.h>
4:
5:    enum BOOL { FALSE, TRUE };
6:
7:    class Shape
8:    {
9:    public:
10:       Shape(){}
11:       ~Shape(){}
12:       virtual long GetArea() { return -1; } // error
13:       virtual long GetPerim() { return -1; }
14:       virtual void Draw() {}
15:    private:
16:    };
17:
18:    class Circle : public Shape
19:    {
20:    public:
21:         Circle(int radius):itsRadius(radius){}
22:         ~Circle(){}
23:         long GetArea() { return 3 * itsRadius * itsRadius; }
24:         long GetPerim() { return 9 * itsRadius; }
25:         void Draw();
26:    private:
27:       int itsRadius;
28:       int itsCircumference;
29:    };
30:
31:    void Circle::Draw()
32:    {
33:       cout << "Circle drawing routine here!\n";
34:    }
```

continues

Listing 13.7. continued

```
35:
36:
37:    class Rectangle : public Shape
38:    {
39:    public:
40:          Rectangle(int len, int width):
41:              itsLength(len), itsWidth(width){}
42:          ~Rectangle(){}
43:          virtual long GetArea() { return itsLength * itsWidth; }
44:          virtual long GetPerim() {return 2*itsLength + 2*itsWidth; }
45:          virtual int GetLength() { return itsLength; }
46:          virtual int GetWidth() { return itsWidth; }
47:          virtual void Draw();
48:    private:
49:       int itsWidth;
50:       int itsLength;
51:    };
52:
53:    void Rectangle::Draw()
54:    {
55:       for (int i = 0; i<itsLength; i++)
56:       {
57:          for (int j = 0; j<itsWidth; j++)
58:             cout << "x ";
59:
60:          cout << "\n";
61:       }
62:    }
63:
64:    class Square : public Rectangle
65:    {
66:    public:
67:          Square(int len);
68:          Square(int len, int width);
69:          ~Square(){}
70:          long GetPerim() {return 4 * GetLength();}
71:    };
72:
73:    Square::Square(int len):
74:       Rectangle(len,len)
75:    {}
76:
77:    Square::Square(int len, int width):
78:       Rectangle(len,width)
79:
80:    {
81:       if (GetLength() != GetWidth())
82:          cout << "Error, not a square... a Rectangle??\n";
83:    }
84:
85:    void main()
86:    {
87:       int choice;
88:       BOOL fQuit = FALSE;
```

```
89:        Shape * sp;
90:
91:        while (1)
92:        {
93:           cout << "(1)Circle (2)Rectangle (3)Square (0)Quit: ";
94:           cin >> choice;
95:
96:           switch (choice)
97:           {
98:              case 1: sp = new Circle(5);
99:              break;
100:             case 2: sp = new Rectangle(4,6);
101:             break;
102:             case 3: sp = new Square(5);
103:             break;
104:             default: fQuit = TRUE;
105:             break;
106:          }
107:          if (fQuit)
108:             break;
109:
110:          sp->Draw();
111:          cout << "\n";
112:       }
113:    }
```

```
(1)Circle (2)Rectangle (3)Square (0)Quit: 2
x x x x x x
x x x x x x
x x x x x x
x x x x x x
(1)Circle (2)Rectangle (3)Square (0)Quit:3
x x x x x
x x x x x
x x x x x
x x x x x
x x x x x
(1)Circle (2)Rectangle (3)Square (0)Quit:0
```

On lines 7–16, the Shape class is declared. The GetArea() and GetPerim() methods
return an error value, and Draw() takes no action. After all, what does it mean to draw
a Shape? Only types of shapes (circles, rectangle, and so on) can be drawn, Shapes
as an abstraction cannot be drawn.

Circle derives from Shape and overrides the three virtual methods. Note that there is no
reason to add the word *virtual*, as that is part of their inheritance. But there is no harm
in doing so either, as shown in the Rectangle class on lines 43, 44, and 47. It is a good
idea to include the term *virtual* as a reminder, a form of documentation.

Square derives from Rectangle, and it too overrides the GetPerim() method, inheriting
the rest of the methods defined in Rectangle.

13

It is troubling, though, that a client might try to instantiate a Shape object, and it might be desirable to make that impossible. The Shape class exists only to provide an interface for the classes derived from it; as such it is an *abstract data type*, or ADT.

NEW TERM An abstract data type represents a concept (like shape) rather than an object (like circle). In C++, an ADT is always the base class to other classes, and it is not valid to make an instance of an ADT.

Pure Virtual Functions

C++ supports the creation of abstract data types with pure virtual functions. A virtual function is made pure by initializing it with zero, as in:

```
virtual void Draw() = 0;
```

Any class with one or more pure virtual functions is an ADT, and it is illegal to instantiate an object of a class that is an ADT. Trying to do so will cause a compile-time error. Putting a pure virtual function in your class signals two things to clients of your class:

1. Don't make an object of this class derive from it and

2. Make sure you override the pure virtual function.

Any class that derives from an ADT inherits the pure virtual function as pure, and so must override every pure virtual function if it wants to instantiate objects. Thus, if Rectangle inherits from Shape, and Shape has three pure virtual functions, Rectangle must override all three or it too will be an ADT. Listing 13.8 rewrites the Shape class to be an abstract data type. To save space, the rest of Listing 13.7 is not reproduced here. Replace the declaration of Shape in Listing 13.7, lines 7–16, with the declaration of Shape in Listing 13.8 and run the program again.

Listing 13.8. Abstract data types.

```
1:  class Shape
2:  {
3:  public:
4:        Shape(){}
5:        ~Shape(){}
6:        virtual long GetArea() = 0; // error
7:        virtual long GetPerim()= 0;
8:        virtual void Draw() = 0;
9:  private:
10: };
```

```
(1)Circle (2)Rectangle (3)Square (0)Quit:2
x x x x x x
x x x x x x
x x x x x x
x x x x x x
(1)Circle (2)Rectangle (3)Square (0)Quit:3
x x x x x
x x x x x
x x x x x
x x x x x
x x x x x
(1)Circle (2)Rectangle (3)Square (0)Quit:0
```

Analysis

As you can see, the workings of the program are totally unaffected. The only difference is that it would now be impossible to make an object of class Shape.

Syntax

Abstract Data Types

Declare a class to be an abstract data type by including one or more pure virtual functions in the class declaration. Declare a pure virtual function by writing = 0 after the function declaration.

Example:

```
class Shape
{
    virtual void Draw = 0;    // pure virtual
};
```

Implementing Pure Virtual Functions

Typically, the pure virtual functions in an abstract base class are never implemented. Because no objects of that type are ever created, there is no reason to provide implementations, and the ADT works purely as the definition of an interface to objects which derive from it.

It is possible, however, to provide an implementation to a pure virtual function. The function can then be called by objects *derived* from the ADT, perhaps to provide common functionality to all the overridden functions. Listing 13.9 reproduces Listing 13.7, this time with Shape as an ADT and with an implementation for the pure virtual function Draw(). The Circle class overrides Draw(), as it must, but it then *chains up* to the base class function for additional functionality.

In this example, the additional functionality is simply an additional message printed, but one can imagine that the base class provides a shared drawing mechanism, perhaps setting up a window that all derived classes will use.

Listing 13.9. Implementing pure virtual functions.

```
1:      //Implementing pure virtual functions
2:
3:      #include <iostreams.h>
4:
5:      enum BOOL { FALSE, TRUE };
6:
7:      class Shape
8:      {
9:      public:
10:        Shape(){}
11:        ~Shape(){}
12:        virtual long GetArea() = 0; // error
13:        virtual long GetPerim()= 0;
14:        virtual void Draw() = 0;
15:      private:
16:      };
17:
18:       void Shape::Draw()
19:      {
20:        cout << "Abstract drawing mechanism!\n";
21:      }
22:
23:      class Circle : public Shape
24:      {
25:      public:
26:          Circle(int radius):itsRadius(radius){}
27:          ~Circle(){}
28:          long GetArea() { return 3 * itsRadius * itsRadius; }
29:          long GetPerim() { return 9 * itsRadius; }
30:          void Draw();
31:      private:
32:        int itsRadius;
33:        int itsCircumference;
34:      };
35:
36:      void Circle::Draw()
37:      {
38:        cout << "Circle drawing routine here!\n";
39:        Shape::Draw();
40:      }
41:
42:
43:      class Rectangle : public Shape
44:      {
45:      public:
46:          Rectangle(int len, int width):
47:              itsLength(len), itsWidth(width){}
48:          ~Rectangle(){}
49:          long GetArea() { return itsLength * itsWidth; }
50:          long GetPerim() {return 2*itsLength + 2*itsWidth; }
51:          virtual int GetLength() { return itsLength; }
52:          virtual int GetWidth() { return itsWidth; }
53:          void Draw();
54:      private:
```

```
55:        int itsWidth;
56:        int itsLength;
57:    };
58:
59:    void Rectangle::Draw()
60:    {
61:        for (int i = 0; i<itsLength; i++)
62:        {
63:            for (int j = 0; j<itsWidth; j++)
64:                cout << "x ";
65:
66:            cout << "\n";
67:        }
68:        Shape::Draw();
69:    }
70:
71:
72:    class Square : public Rectangle
73:    {
74:    public:
75:        Square(int len);
76:        Square(int len, int width);
77:        ~Square(){}
78:        long GetPerim() {return 4 * GetLength();}
79:    };
80:
81:    Square::Square(int len):
82:        Rectangle(len,len)
83:    {}
84:
85:    Square::Square(int len, int width):
86:        Rectangle(len,width)
87:
88:    {
89:        if (GetLength() != GetWidth())
90:            cout << "Error, not a square... a Rectangle??\n";
91:    }
92:
93:    void main()
94:    {
95:        int choice;
96:        BOOL fQuit = FALSE;
97:        Shape * sp;
98:
99:        while (1)
100:       {
101:           cout << "(1)Circle (2)Rectangle (3)Square (0)Quit: ";
102:           cin >> choice;
103:
104:           switch (choice)
105:           {
106:               case 1: sp = new Circle(5);
107:               break;
108:               case 2: sp = new Rectangle(4,6);
109:               break;
110:               case 3: sp = new Square (5);
```

continues

Listing 13.9. continued

```
111:             break;
112:             default: fQuit = TRUE;
113:             break;
114:         }
115:         if (fQuit)
116:             break;
117:
118:         sp->Draw();
119:         cout << "\n";
120:     }
121: }
```

```
(1)Circle (2)Rectangle (3)Square (0)Quit: 2
x x x x x x
x x x x x x
x x x x x x
x x x x x x
Abstract drawing mechanism!
(1)Circle (2)Rectangle (3)Square (0)Quit:3
x x x x x
x x x x x
x x x x x
x x x x x
x x x x x
Abstract drawing mechanism!
(1)Circle (2)Rectangle (3)Square (0)Quit:0
```

On lines 7–16, the abstract data type Shape is declared, with all three of its accessor methods declared to be pure virtual. Note that this is not necessary. If any one were declared pure virtual, the class would have been an ADT.

The GetAre() and GetPerim() methods are not implemented, but GetDraw() is. Circle and Rectangle both override GetDraw(), and both chain up to the base method, taking advantage of shared functionality in the base class.

Complex Hierarchies of Abstraction

At times, you will derive ADTs from other ADTs. It may be that you will want to make some of the derived pure virtual functions non-pure, and leave others pure.

If you create the Animal class, you may make Eat(), Sleep(), Move(), and Reproduce() all be pure virtual functions. Perhaps from Animal you derive Mammal and Fish.

On examination, you decide that every Mammal will reproduce in the same way, and so you make Mammal::Reproduce() be non-pure, but you leave Eat(), Sleep(), and Move() as pure virtual functions.

From Mammal you derive Dog, and Dog must override and implement the three remaining pure virtual functions so that you can make objects of type Dog.

What you've said, as class designer, is that no Animals or Mammals can be instantiated, but that all Mammals may inherit the provided Reproduce() method without overriding it.

Listing 13.10 illustrates this technique with a bare-bones implementation of these classes.

Listing 13.10. Deriving ADTs from other ADTs.

```
1:      // Listing 13.10
2:      // Deriving ADTs from other ADTs
3:      #include <iostreams.h>
4:
5:      enum COLOR { Red, Green, Blue, Yellow, White, Black, Brown } ;
6:      enum BOOL { FALSE, TRUE };
7:
8:      class Animal         // common base to both horse and bird
9:      {
10:     public:
11:         Animal(int);
12:         virtual ~Animal() { cout << "Animal destructor...\n"; }
13:         virtual int GetAge() const { return itsAge; }
14:         virtual void SetAge(int age) { itsAge = age; }
15:         virtual void Sleep() const = 0;
16:         virtual void Eat() const = 0;
17:         virtual void Reproduce() const = 0;
18:         virtual void Move() const = 0;
19:         virtual void Speak() const = 0;
20:     private:
21:         int itsAge;
22:     };
23:
24:     Animal::Animal(int age):
25:     itsAge(age)
26:     {
27:         cout << "Animal constructor...\n";
28:     }
29:
30:     class Mammal : public Animal
31:     {
32:     public:
33:         Mammal(int age):Animal(age){ cout << "Mammal constructor...\n";}
34:         ~Mammal() { cout << "Mammal destructor...\n";}
35:         virtual void Reproduce() const { cout << "Mammal reproduction
depicted...\n"; }
36:     };
37:
38:     class Fish : public Animal
39:     {
40:     public:
41:         Fish(int age):Animal(age){ cout << "Fish constructor...\n";}
```

continues

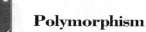

Listing 13.10. continued

```
42:        virtual ~Fish() {cout << "Fish destructor...\n";  }
43:        virtual void Sleep() const { cout << "fish snoring...\n"; }
44:        virtual void Eat() const { cout << "fish feeding...\n"; }
45:        virtual void Reproduce() const { cout << "fish laying eggs...\n"; }
46:        virtual void Move() const { cout << "fish swimming...\n";    }
47:        virtual void Speak() const { }
48:
49:    };
50:
51:    class Horse : public Mammal
52:    {
53:    public:
54:        Horse(int age, COLOR color ):
55:            Mammal(age), itsColor(color) { cout << "Horse constructor...\n"; }
56:        virtual ~Horse() { cout << "Horse destructor...\n"; }
57:        virtual void Speak()const { cout << "Whinny!... \n"; }
58:        virtual COLOR GetItsColor() const { return itsColor; }
59:        virtual void Sleep() const { cout << "Horse snoring...\n"; }
60:        virtual void Eat() const { cout << "Horse feeding...\n"; }
61:        virtual void Move() const { cout << "Horse running...\n";}
62:
63:    protected:
64:        COLOR itsColor;
65:    };
66:
67:    class Dog : public Mammal
68:    {
69:    public:
70:        Dog(int age, COLOR color ):
71:            Mammal(age), itsColor(color) { cout << "Dog constructor...\n"; }
72:        virtual ~Dog() { cout << "Dog destructor...\n"; }
73:        virtual void Speak()const { cout << "Whoof!... \n"; }
74:        virtual void Sleep() const { cout << "Dog snoring...\n"; }
75:        virtual void Eat() const { cout << "Dog eating...\n"; }
76:        virtual void Move() const  { cout << "Dog running...\n"; }
77:        virtual void Reproduce() const { cout << "Dogs reproducing...\n"; }
78:
79:    protected:
80:        COLOR itsColor;
81:    };
82:
83:    void main()
84:    {
85:        Animal *pAnimal=0;
86:        int choice;
87:        BOOL fQuit = FALSE;
88:
89:        while (1)
90:        {
91:            cout << "(1)Dog (2)Horse (3)Bird (0)Quit: ";
92:            cin >> choice;
93:
94:            switch (choice)
95:            {
```

```
96:             case 1: pAnimal = new Dog(5,Brown);
97:             break;
98:             case 2: pAnimal = new Horse(4,Black);
99:             break;
100:            case 3: pAnimal = new Fish (5);
101:            break;
102:            default: fQuit = TRUE;
103:            break;
104:        }
105:        if (fQuit)
106:            break;
107:
108:        pAnimal->Speak();
109:        pAnimal->Eat();
110:        pAnimal->Reproduce();
111:        pAnimal->Move();
112:        pAnimal->Sleep();
113:        delete pAnimal;
114:        cout << "\n";
115:    }
116:
117:
118:
119:  }
```

Output

```
(1)Dog (2)Horse (3)Bird (0)Quit: 1
Animal constructor...
Mammal constructor...
Dog constructor...
Whoof!...
Dog eating...
Dog reproducing....
Dog running...
Dog snoring...
Dog destructor...
Mammal destructor...
Animal destructor...
(1)Dog (2)Horse (3)Bird (0)Quit: 0
```

13

Analysis

On lines 8–22, the abstract data type Animal is declared. Animal has non-pure virtual accessors for itsAge, which are shared by all Animal objects. It has five pure virtual functions, Sleep(), Eat(), Reproduce(), Move(), and Speak().

Animal is derived from Mammal, and is declared on lines 30–36 and adds no data. It overrides Reproduce() however, providing a common form of reproduction for all mammals. Fish *must* override Reproduce(), because Fish derives directly from Animal and cannot take advantage of Mammalian reproduction (and a good thing, too!).

Mammal classes no longer have to override the Reproduce() function, but they are free to do so if they choose, as Dog does on line 77. Fish, Horse, and Dog all override the remaining pure virtual functions, so that objects of their type can be instantiated.

In the body of the program, an Animal pointer is used to point to the various derived objects in turn. The virtual methods are invoked, and based on the runtime binding of the pointer, the correct method is called in the derived class.

It would be a compile-time error to try to instantiate an Animal or a Mammal, as both are abstract data types.

Which Types Are Abstract?

In one program the class Animal is abstract, in another it is not. What determines whether to make a class abstract or not?

The answer to this question is decided not by any real-world intrinsic factor, but by what makes sense in your program. If you are writing a program that depicts a farm or a zoo, you may want Animal to be an abstract data type, but Dog to be a class from which you can instantiate objects.

On the other hand, if you are making an animated kennel, you may want to keep Dog as an abstract data type, and only instantiate types of dogs: retrievers, terriers, and so forth. The level of abstraction is a function of how finely you need to distinguish your types.

DO	DON'T

DO use abstract data types to provide common functionality for a number of related classes.

DO override all pure virtual functions.

DO make pure virtual any function that must be overridden.

DON'T try to instantiate an object of an abstract data type.

Q&A

Q What does percolating functionality upwards mean?

A This refers to the idea of moving shared functionality upwards into a common base class. If more than one class shares a function, it is desirable to find a common base class in which that function can be stored.

Q Is percolating upwards always a good thing?

A Yes, if you are percolating *shared* functionality upwards, no if all you are moving is *interface*. That is, if all the derived classes can't use the method, it is a mistake to move it up into a common base class. If you do, you'll have to switch on the runtime type of the object before deciding if you can invoke the function.

Q Why is switching on the runtime type of an object bad?

A With large programs, the switch statements become big and hard to maintain. The point of virtual functions is to let the virtual table, rather than the programmer, determine the runtime type of the object.

Q Why is casting bad?

A Casting isn't bad if it is done in a way that is type-safe. If a function is called that *knows* that the object *must* be of a particular type, casting to that type is fine. Casting can be used to undermine the strong type checking in C++, and that is what you want to avoid. If you are switching on the runtime type of the object and then casting a pointer, that may be a warning sign that something is wrong with your design.

Q Why not make all functions virtual?

A Virtual functions are supported by a virtual function table, which incurs runtime overhead, both in the size of the program and in the performance of the program. If you have very small classes which you don't expect to subclass, you may not want to make any of the functions virtual.

Q When should the destructor be made virtual?

A Anytime you think the class will be subclassed, and a pointer to the base class will be used to access an object of the subclass. As a general rule of thumb, if you've made *any* functions in your class virtual, be sure to make the destructor virtual as well.

Q Why bother making an abstract data type—why not just make it non-abstract and avoid creating any objects of that type?

A The purpose of many of the conventions in C++ is to enlist the compiler in finding bugs, so as to avoid runtime bugs in code that you give your customers. Making a class abstract, that is, giving it pure virtual functions, causes the compiler to flag any objects created of that abstract type as errors.

Workshop

The Workshop provides quiz questions to help you solidify your understanding of the material covered, and exercises to provide you with experience in using what you've learned. Try to answer the quiz and exercise questions before checking the answers in Appendix D, and make sure you understand the answers before continuing to the next chapter.

Quiz

1. What is a down cast?

2. What is the `v-ptr`?

3. If a round-rectangle has straight edges and rounded corners, and your `RoundRect` class inherits both from `Rectangle` and from `Circle`, and they in turn both inherit from `Shape`, how many `Shapes` are created when you create a `RoundRect`?

4. If `Horse` and `Bird` inherit from `Animal` using public virtual inheritance, do their constructors initialize the `Animal` constructor? If `Pegasus` inherits from both `Horse` and `Bird`, how does it initialize `Animal`'s constructor?

5. Declare a class, `vehicle` and make it an abstract data type.

6. If a base class is an ADT, and it has three pure virtual functions, how many of these *must* be overridden in its derived classes?

Exercises

1. Show the declaration for a class `JetPlane`, which inherits from `Rocket` and `Airplane`.

2. Show the declaration for `747`, which inherits from the `JetPlane` class described in Exercise 1.

3. Write a program that derives `Car` and `Bus` from the class `Vehicle`. Make `Vehicle` be an ADT with two pure virtual functions. Make `Car` and `Bus` not be ADTs.

4. Modify the program in Exercise 1 so that `Car` is an ADT, and derive `SportsCar`, `Wagon`, and `Coupe` from `Car`. In the `Car` class, provide an implementation for one of the pure virtual functions in `Vehicle` and make it non-pure.

14

Special Classes and Functions

C++ offers a number of ways to limit the scope and impact of variables and pointers. So far you've seen how to create global variables, local function variables, pointers to variables, and class member variables. Today you learn:

☐ What static member variables and static member functions are.

☐ How to use static member variables and static member functions.

☐ How to create and manipulate pointers to functions and pointers to member functions.

☐ How to work with arrays of pointers to functions.

Static Member Data

Until now, you have probably thought of the data in each object as unique to that object and not shared among objects in a class. For example, if you have five Cat objects, each has its own age, weight, and other data. The age of one does not affect the age of another.

There are times, however, when you'll want to keep track of a pool of data. For example, you might want to know how many objects for a specific class have been created in your program, and how many are still in existence. Static member variables are shared among all instances of a class. They are a compromise between global data, which is available to all parts of your program, and member data, which is usually available only to each object.

You can think of a static member as belonging to the class rather than to the object. Normal member data is one per object, but static members are one per class. Listing 14.1 declares a Cat object with a static data member, HowManyCats. This variable keeps track of how many Cat objects have been created. This is done by incrementing the static variable, HowManyCats, with each construction and decrementing it with each destruction.

Listing 14.1. Static member data.

```
1:      //Listing 14.1 static data members
2:
3:      #include <iostreams.h>
4:
5:      class Cat
6:      {
7:      public:
8:          Cat(int age):itsAge(age){HowManyCats++; }
9:          virtual ~Cat() { HowManyCats—; }
10:         virtual int GetAge() { return itsAge; }
```

```
11:        virtual void SetAge(int age) { itsAge = age; }
12:        static int HowManyCats;
13:
14:    private:
15:        int itsAge;
16:
17:    };
18:
19:    int Cat::HowManyCats = 0;
20:
21:    void main()
22:    {
23:        const int MaxCats = 5;
24:        Cat *CatHouse[MaxCats];
25:        for (int i = 0; i<MaxCats; i++)
26:            CatHouse[i] = new Cat(i);
27:
28:        for (i = 0; i<MaxCats; i++)
29:        {
30:            cout << "There are ";
31:            cout << Cat::HowManyCats;
32:            cout << " cats left!\n";
33:            cout << "Deleting the one which is ";
34:            cout << CatHouse[i]->GetAge();
35:            cout << " years old\n";
36:            delete CatHouse[i];
37:            CatHouse[i] = 0;
38:        }
39:    }
```

```
There are 5 cats left!
Deleting the one which is 2 years old
There are 4 cats left!
Deleting the one which is 3 years old
There are 3 cats left!
Deleting the one which is 4 years old
There are 2 cats left!
Deleting the one which is 5 years old
There are 1 cats left!
Deleting the one which is 6 years old
```

On lines 5 to 17 the simplified class Cat is declared. On line 12, HowManyCats is declared to be a static member variable of type int.

The declaration of HowManyCats does not define an integer; no storage space is set aside. Unlike the non-static member variables, no storage space is set aside by instantiating a Cat object, because the HowManyCats member variable is not *in* the object. Thus, on line 19 the variable is defined and initialized.

It is a common mistake to forget to define the static member variables of classes. Don't let this happen to you! Of course, if it does, the linker will catch it with a pithy error message such as the following:

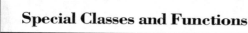

```
undefined symbol Cat::HowManyCats
```

You don't need to do this for itsAge because it is a non-static member variable and is defined each time you make a Cat object, which you do here on line 26.

The constructor for Cat increments the static member variable on line 8. The destructor decrements it on line 9. Thus, at any moment, HowManyCats has an accurate measure of how many Cat objects were created but not yet destroyed.

The driver program on lines 21–39 instantiates five Cats and puts them in an array. This calls five Cat constructors, and thus HowManyCats is incremented five times from its initial value of 0.

The program then loops through each of the five positions in the array and prints out the value of HowManyCats before deleting the current Cat pointer. The printout reflects that the starting value is five (after all, five are constructed), and that each time the loop is run, one fewer Cat remains.

Note that HowManyCats is public and is accessed directly by main(). There is no reason to expose this member variable in this way. It is preferable to make it private along with the other member variables and provide a public accessor method, as long as you will always access the data through an instance of Cat. On the other hand, if you'd like to access this data directly without necessarily having a Cat object available, you have two options: keep it public, as shown in Listing 14.2, or provide a static member function, as discussed later in this chapter.

Listing 14.2. Accessing static members without an object.

```
1:      //Listing 14.2 static data members
2:
3:      #include <iostreams.h>
4:
5:      class Cat
6:      {
7:      public:
8:          Cat(int age):itsAge(age){HowManyCats++; }
9:          virtual ~Cat() { HowManyCats—; }
10:         virtual int GetAge() { return itsAge; }
11:         virtual void SetAge(int age) { itsAge = age; }
12:         static int HowManyCats;
13:
14:     private:
15:         int itsAge;
16:
17:     };
18:
```

```
19:     int Cat::HowManyCats = 0;
20:
21:     void TelepathicFunction();
22:
23:     void main()
24:     {
25:        const int MaxCats = 5;
26:        Cat *CatHouse[MaxCats];
27:        for (int i = 0; i<MaxCats; i++)
28:        {
29:           CatHouse[i] = new Cat(i);
30:           TelepathicFunction();
31:        }
32:
33:        for ( i = 0; i<MaxCats; i++)
34:        {
35:           delete CatHouse[i];
36:           TelepathicFunction();
37:        }
38:     }
39:
40:     void TelepathicFunction()
41:     {
42:        cout << "There are " << Cat::HowManyCats << " cats alive!\n";
43:     }
```

```
There are 1 cats alive
There are 2 cats alive
There are 3 cats alive
There are 4 cats alive
There are 5 cats alive
There are 4 cats alive
There are 3 cats alive
There are 2 cats alive
There are 1 cats alive
There are 0 cats alive
```

Analysis Listing 14.2 is much like Listing 14.1 except for the addition of a new function, TelepathicFunction(). This function does not create a Cat object, nor does it take a Cat object as a parameter, yet it can access the HowManyCats member variable. Again, it is worth reemphasizing that this member variable is *not* in any particular object; it is in the class as a whole, and, if public, can be accessed by any function in the program.

The alternative to making this member variable public is to make it private. If you do, you can access it through a member function, but then you must have an object of that class available. Listing 14.3 shows this approach. The alternative, static member functions, is discussed immediately after the analysis of Listing 14.3.

14

Listing 14.3. Accessing static members using non-static member functions.

```
1:     //Listing 14.3 private static data members
2:
3:     #include <iostreams.h>
4:
5:     class Cat
6:     {
7:     public:
8:         Cat(int age):itsAge(age){HowManyCats++; }
9:         virtual ~Cat() { HowManyCats—; }
10:        virtual int GetAge() { return itsAge; }
11:        virtual void SetAge(int age) { itsAge = age; }
12:        virtual int GetHowMany() { return HowManyCats; }
13:
14:
15:    private:
16:        int itsAge;
17:        static int HowManyCats;
18:    };
19:
20:    int Cat::HowManyCats = 0;
21:
22:    void main()
23:    {
24:        const int MaxCats = 5;
25:        Cat *CatHouse[MaxCats];
26:        for (int i = 0; i<MaxCats; i++)
27:            CatHouse[i] = new Cat(i);
28:
29:        for (i = 0; i<MaxCats; i++)
30:        {
31:            cout << "There are ";
32:            cout << CatHouse[i]->GetHowMany();
33:            cout << " cats left!\n";
34:            cout << "Deleting the one which is ";
35:            cout << CatHouse[i]->GetAge()+2;
36:            cout << " years old\n";
37:            delete CatHouse[i];
38:            CatHouse[i] = 0;
39:        }
40:    }
```

```
There are 5 cats left!
Deleting the one which is 2 years old
There are 4 cats left!
Deleting the one which is 3 years old
There are 3 cats left!
Deleting the one which is 4 years old
There are 2 cats left!
Deleting the one which is 5 years old
There are 1 cats left!
Deleting the one which is 6 years old
```

Analysis On line 17, the static member variable `HowManyCats` is declared to have private access. Now you cannot access this variable from non-member functions, such as `TelepathicFunction` from the previous listing.

Even though `HowManyCats` is static, it is still within the scope of the class. Any class function, such as `GetHowMany()`, can access it, just as member functions can access any member data. However, for a function to call `GetHowMany()`, it must have an object on which to call the function.

DO	DON'T

DO use static member variables to share data among all instances of a class.

DO make static member variables protected or private if you wish to restrict access to them.

DON'T use static member variables to store data for one object. Static member data is shared among all objects of its class.

Static Member Functions

Static member functions are like static member variables: they exist not in an object but in the scope of the class. Thus, they can be called without having an object of that class, as illustrated in Listing 14.4.

Listing 14.4. Static member functions.

```
1:      //Listing 14.1 static data members
2:
3:      #include <iostreams.h>
4:
5:      class Cat
6:      {
7:      public:
8:          Cat(int age):itsAge(age){HowManyCats++; }
9:          virtual ~Cat() { HowManyCats—; }
10:         virtual int GetAge() { return itsAge; }
11:         virtual void SetAge(int age) { itsAge = age; }
12:         static int GetHowMany() { return HowManyCats; }
13:     private:
14:         int itsAge;
15:         static int HowManyCats;
```

continues

413

Listing 14.4. continued

```
16:     };
17:
18:     int Cat::HowManyCats = 0;
19:
20:     void TelepathicFunction();
21:
22:     void main()
23:     {
24:         const int MaxCats = 5;
25:         Cat *CatHouse[MaxCats];
26:         for (int i = 0; i<MaxCats; i++)
27:         {
28:             CatHouse[i] = new Cat(i);
29:             TelepathicFunction();
30:         }
31:
32:         for ( i = 0; i<MaxCats; i++)
33:         {
34:             delete CatHouse[i];
35:             TelepathicFunction();
36:         }
37:     }
38:
39:     void TelepathicFunction()
40:     {
41:         cout << "There are " << Cat::GetHowMany() << " cats alive!\n";
42:     }
```

```
There are 1 cats alive
There are 2 cats alive
There are 3 cats alive
There are 4 cats alive
There are 5 cats alive
There are 4 cats alive
There are 3 cats alive
There are 2 cats alive
There are 1 cats alive
There are 0 cats alive
```

The static member variable HowManyCats is declared to have private access on line 15 of the Cat declaration. The public accessor function, GetHowMany(), is declared to be both public and static on line 12.

Since GetHowMany() is public, it can be accessed by any function, and since it is static there is no need to have an object of type Cat on which to call it. Thus, on line 41, the function TelepathicFunction() is able to access the public static accessor, even though it has no access to a Cat object. Of course, you could have called GetHowMany() on the Cat objects available in main(), just as with any other accessor functions.

> **Note:** Static member functions do not have a *this* pointer. Thus they cannot be declared const. Also, since member data variables are accessed in member functions using the *this* pointer, static member functions cannot access any non-static member variables!

Static Member Functions

You can access static member functions by calling them on an object of the class just as you do any other member function, or you can call them without an object by fully qualifying the class and object name.

Example

```
class Cat
{
public:
    static int GetHowMany() { return HowManyCats; }
private:
    static int HowManyCats;
};
    int Cat::HowManyCats = 0;
void main()
{
    int howMany;
    CAT theCat;                          // define a cat
    howMany = theCat.GetHowMany();       // access through an object
    howMany = Cat::GetHowMany();         // access without an object
}
```

Pointers to Functions

Just as an array name is a constant pointer to the first element of the array, a function name is a constant pointer to the function. It is possible to declare a pointer variable that points to a function, and to invoke the function by using that pointer. This can be very useful; it allows you to create programs that decide which functions to invoke based on user input.

The only tricky part about function pointers is understanding the type of the object being pointed to. A pointer to int points to an integer variable, and a pointer to a function must point to a function of the appropriate return type and signature.

In the declaration

```
long (* funcPtr) (int);
```

14

`funcPtr` is declared to be a pointer (not the `*` in front of the name) that points to a function that takes an integer parameter and returns a `long`. The parentheses around `* funcPtr` are necessary because the parentheses around `int` bind more tightly, that is they have higher precedence than the indirection operator (`*`). Without the first parentheses this would declare a function that takes an integer and returns a pointer to a `long`. (Remember that spaces are meaningless here.)

Examine these two declarations:

```
long * Function (int);
long (* funcPtr) (int);
```

The first, `Function ()`, is a function taking an integer and returning a pointer to a variable of type `long`. The second, `funcPtr`, is a pointer to a function taking an integer and returning a variable of type `long`.

The declaration of a function pointer will always include the return type and the parentheses indicating the type of the parameters, if any. Listing 14.5 illustrates the declaration and use of function pointers.

Listing 14.5. Pointers to functions.

```
1:     // Listing 14.5 Using function pointers
2:
3:     #include <iostreams.h>
4:
5:     void Square (int&,int&);
6:     void Cube (int&, int&);
7:     void Swap (int&, int &);
8:     void GetVals(int&, int&);
9:     void PrintVals(int, int);
10:    enum BOOL { FALSE, TRUE };
11:
12:    void main()
13:    {
14:        void (* pFunc) (int &, int &);
15:        BOOL fQuit = FALSE;
16:
17:        int valOne=1, valTwo=2;
18:        int choice;
19:        while (fQuit == FALSE)
20:        {
21:            cout << "(0)Quit (1)Change Values (2)Square (3)Cube (4)Swap: ";
22:            cin >> choice;
23:            switch (choice)
24:            {
25:                case 1: pFunc = GetVals; break;
26:                case 2: pFunc = Square; break;
27:                case 3: pFunc = Cube; break;
28:                case 4: pFunc = Swap; break;
29:                default : fQuit = TRUE; break;
```

```
30:            }
31:
32:            if (fQuit)
33:                break;
34:
35:            PrintVals(valOne, valTwo);
36:            pFunc(valOne, valTwo);
37:            PrintVals(valOne, valTwo);
38:        }
39:    }
40:
41:    void PrintVals(int x, int y)
42:    {
43:        cout << "x: " << x << " y: " << y << endl;
44:    }
45:
46:    void Square (int & rX, int & rY)
47:    {
48:        rX *= rX;
49:        rY *= rY;
50:    }
51:
52:    void Cube (int & rX, int & rY)
53:    {
54:        int tmp;
55:
56:        tmp = rX;
57:        rX *= rX;
58:        rX = rX * tmp;
59:
60:        tmp = rY;
61:        rY *= rY;
62:        rY = rY * tmp;
63:    }
64:
65:    void Swap(int & rX, int & rY)
66:    {
67:        int temp;
68:        temp = rX;
69:        rX = rY;
70:        rY = temp;
71:    }
72:
73:    void GetVals (int & rValOne, int & rValTwo)
74:    {
75:        cout << "New value for ValOne: ";
76:        cin >> rValOne;
77:        cout << "New value for ValTwo: ";
78:        cin >> rValTwo;
79:    }
```

```
(0)Quit (1)Change Values (2)Square (3)Cube (4)Swap: 1
x: 1 y:2
New value for ValOne: 2
New value for ValTwo: 3
```

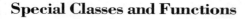
```
(0)Quit (1)Change Values (2)Square (3)Cube (4)Swap: 3
x: 2 y:3
x: 8 y: 27
(0)Quit (1)Change Values (2)Square (3)Cube (4)Swap: 2
x: 8 y: 27
x:64 y:729
(0)Quit (1)Change Values (2)Square (3)Cube (4)Swap: 4
x:64 y:729
x:729 y:64
(0)Quit (1)Change Values (2)Square (3)Cube (4)Swap: 0
```

On lines 5–8 four functions are declared, each with the same return type and signature, returning void and taking two references to integers.

On line 14, pFunc is declared to be a pointer to a function that returns void and takes two integer reference parameters. Any of the previous functions can be pointed to by pFunc. The user is repeatedly offered the choice of which functions to invoke, and pFunc is assigned accordingly. On lines 35–36, the current value of the two integers is printed, the currently assigned function is invoked, and then the values are printed again.

Pointer to Function

A pointer to function is invoked exactly like the functions it points to, except that the function pointer name is used instead of the function name.

Assign a pointer to function to a specific function by assigning to the function name without the parentheses. The function name is a constant pointer to the function itself. Use the pointer to function just as you would the function name. The pointer to function must agree in return value and signature with the function to which you assign it.

Example

```
long (*pFuncOne) (int, int);
long SomeFunction (int, int);
pFuncOne = SomeFunction;
pFuncOne(5,7);
```

Why Use Function Pointers?

You certainly could write the program in Listing 14.5 without function pointers, but the use of these pointers makes the intent and use of the program explicit: pick a function from a list, and then invoke it.

Listing 14.6 uses the function prototypes and definitions from Listing 14.5, but the body of the program does not use a function pointer. Examine the differences between these two listings.

Note: To compile this program, place lines 41–79 from Listing 14.5 immediately after line 55.

Listing 14.6. Rewriting 14.5 without the pointer to function.

```
1:    // Listing 14.6 Without function pointers
2:
3:    #include <iostreams.h>
4:
5:    void Square (int&,int&);
6:    void Cube (int&, int&);
7:    void Swap (int&, int &);
8:    void GetVals(int&, int&);
9:    void PrintVals(int, int);
10:   enum BOOL { FALSE, TRUE };
11:
12:   void main()
13:   {
14:      BOOL fQuit = FALSE;
15:      int valOne=1, valTwo=2;
16:      int choice;
17:      while (fQuit == FALSE)
18:      {
19:         cout << "(0)Quit (1)Change Values (2)Square (3)Cube (4)Swap: ";
20:         cin >> choice;
21:         switch (choice)
22:         {
23:            case 1:
24:               PrintVals(valOne, valTwo);
25:               GetVals(valOne, valTwo);
26:               PrintVals(valOne, valTwo);
27:               break;
28:
29:            case 2:
30:               PrintVals(valOne, valTwo);
31:               Square(valOne,valTwo);
32:               PrintVals(valOne, valTwo);
33:               break;
34:
35:            case 3:
36:               PrintVals(valOne, valTwo);
37:               Cube(valOne, valTwo);
38:               PrintVals(valOne, valTwo);
39:               break;
40:
41:            case 4:
42:               PrintVals(valOne, valTwo);
43:               Swap(valOne, valTwo);
44:               PrintVals(valOne, valTwo);
45:               break;
```

continues

14

Listing 14.6. continued

```
46:
47:                    default :
48:                    fQuit = TRUE;
49:                    break;
50:            }
51:
52:        if (fQuit)
53:            break;
54:        }
55:    }
```

```
(0)Quit (1)Change Values (2)Square (3)Cube (4)Swap: 1
x: 1 y:2
New value for ValOne: 2
New value for ValTwo: 3
(0)Quit (1)Change Values (2)Square (3)Cube (4)Swap: 3
x: 2 y:3
x: 8 y: 27
(0)Quit (1)Change Values (2)Square (3)Cube (4)Swap: 2
x: 8 y: 27
x:64 y:729
(0)Quit (1)Change Values (2)Square (3)Cube (4)Swap: 4
x:64 y:729
x:729 y:64
(0)Quit (1)Change Values (2)Square (3)Cube (4)Swap: 0
```

The implementation of the functions has been left out because it is identical to that provided in Listing 14.5. As you can see, the output is unchanged, but the body of the program has expanded from 27 lines to 38. The calls to PrintVals() must be repeated for each case.

It was tempting to put PrintVals() at the top of the while loop and again at the bottom, rather than in each case statement. This would have called PrintVals() even for the exit case, however, and that was not part of the specification.

Setting aside the increased size of the code and the repeated calls to do the same thing, the overall clarity is somewhat diminished. This is an artificial case, however, created to show how pointers to functions work. In real-world conditions the advantages are even clearer: pointers to functions can eliminate duplicate code, clarify your program, and allow you to make tables of functions to call based on runtime conditions.

Shorthand Invocation

The pointer to function does not need to be dereferenced, though you are free to do so. Therefore, if pFunc is a pointer to a function taking an integer and returning a variable of type long, and you assign pFunc to a matching function, you can invoke that function with either

```
pFunc(x);
```

or

```
(*pFunc)(x);
```

The two forms are identical. The former is just a shorthand version of the latter.

Arrays of Pointers to Functions

Just as you can declare an array of pointers to integers, you can declare an array of pointers to functions returning a specific value type and with a specific signature. Listing 14.7 again rewrites Listing 14.5, this time using an array to invoke all the choices at once.

Note: To compile this program, place lines 41–79 of Listing 14.5 immediately after line 38.

Listing 14.7. Demonstrates use of an array of pointers to functions.

```
1:      // Listing 14.7 demonstrates use of an array of pointers to functions
2:
3:      #include <iostreams.h>
4:
5:      void Square (int&,int&);
6:      void Cube (int&, int&);
7:      void Swap (int&, int &);
8:      void GetVals(int&, int&);
9:      void PrintVals(int, int);
10:     enum BOOL { FALSE, TRUE };
11:
12:     void main()
13:     {
14:        int valOne=1, valTwo=2;
15:        int choice;
16:        const MaxArray = 5;
17:        void (*pFuncArray[MaxArray])(int&, int&);
18:
```

continues

Listing 14.7. continued

```
19:        for (int i=0;i<MaxArray;i++)
20:        {
21:            cout << "(1)Change Values (2)Square (3)Cube (4)Swap: ";
22:            cin >> choice;
23:            switch (choice)
24:            {
25:                case 1:pFuncArray[i] = GetVals; break;
26:                case 2:pFuncArray[i] = Square; break;
27:                case 3:pFuncArray[i] = Cube; break;
28:                case 4:pFuncArray[i] = Swap; break;
29:                default:pFuncArray[i] = 0;
30:            }
31:        }
32:
33:        for (i=0;i<MaxArray; i++)
34:        {
35:            pFuncArray[i](valOne,valTwo);
36:            PrintVals(valOne,valTwo);
37:        }
38:    }
```

Output

```
(1)Change Values (2)Square (3)Cube (4)Swap: 1
(1)Change Values (2)Square (3)Cube (4)Swap: 1
(1)Change Values (2)Square (3)Cube (4)Swap: 1
(1)Change Values (2)Square (3)Cube (4)Swap: 1
(1)Change Values (2)Square (3)Cube (4)Swap: 1
New Value for ValOne: 2
New Value for ValTwo: 3
x: 2 y: 3
x: 4 y: 9
x: 64 y: 729
x: 729 y: 64
x: 7153 y:4896
```

Analysis
Once again the implementation of the functions has been left out to save space, but it is the same as in Listing 14.5. On line 17, the array pFuncArray is declared to be an array of 5 pointers to functions that return void and that take two integer references.

On lines 19–31, the user is asked to pick the functions to invoke, and each member of the array is assigned the address of the appropriate function. On lines 33–37, each function is invoked in turn. The result is printed after each invocation.

Passing Pointers to Functions to Other Functions

The pointers to functions (and arrays of pointers to functions, for that matter) can be passed to other functions, which may take action and then call the right function using the pointer.

For example, you might improve Listing 14.5 by passing the chosen function pointer to another function (outside of main()), which prints the values, invokes the function, and then prints the values again. Listing 14.8 illustrates this variation.

Note: To compile this program, place lines 46–79 of Listing 14.5 immediately after line 44.

Listing 14.8. Passing pointers to functions as function arguments.

```
1:      // Listing 14.8 Without function pointers
2:
3:      #include <iostreams.h>
4:
5:      void Square (int&,int&);
6:      void Cube (int&, int&);
7:      void Swap (int&, int &);
8:      void GetVals(int&, int&);
9:      void PrintVals(void (*)(int&, int&),int&, int&);
10:     enum BOOL { FALSE, TRUE };
11:
12:     void main()
13:     {
14:        int valOne=1, valTwo=2;
15:        int choice;
16:        BOOL fQuit = FALSE;
17:
18:        void (*pFunc)(int&, int&);
19:
20:        while (fQuit == FALSE)
21:        {
22:           cout << "(0)Quit (1)Change Values (2)Square (3)Cube (4)Swap: ";
23:           cin >> choice;
24:           switch (choice)
25:           {
26:              case 1:pFunc = GetVals; break;
```

continues

423

Listing 14.8. continued

```
27:              case 2:pFunc = Square; break;
28:              case 3:pFunc = Cube; break;
29:              case 4:pFunc = Swap; break;
30:              default:fQuit = TRUE; break;
31:          }
32:          if (fQuit == TRUE)
33:              break;
34:          PrintVals ( pFunc, valOne, valTwo);
35:      }
36:
37:  }
38:
39:  void PrintVals( void (*pFunc)(int&, int&),int& x, int& y)
40:  {
41:      cout << "x: " << x << " y: " << y << endl;
42:      pFunc(x,y);
43:      cout << "x: " << x << " y: " << y << endl;
44:  }
```

Output

```
(0)Quit (1)Change Values (2)Square (3)Cube (4)Swap: 1
x: 1 y:2
New value for ValOne: 2
New value for ValTwo: 3
x: 2 y:3
(0)Quit (1)Change Values (2)Square (3)Cube (4)Swap: 3
x: 2 y:3
x: 8 y: 27
(0)Quit (1)Change Values (2)Square (3)Cube (4)Swap: 2
x: 8 y: 27
x:64 y:729
(0)Quit (1)Change Values (2)Square (3)Cube (4)Swap: 4
x:64 y:729
x:729 y:64
(0)Quit (1)Change Values (2)Square (3)Cube (4)Swap: 0
```

Analysis

On line 18, pFunc is declared to be a pointer to a function returning void and taking two parameters, both integer references. On line 9, PrintVals is declared to be a function taking three parameters. The first is a pointer to a function that returns void but takes two integer reference parameters, and the second and third arguments to PrintVals are integer references. The user is again prompted for which functions to call, and then on line 34 PrintVals is called.

Go find a C++ programmer and ask him what this declaration means:

```
void PrintVals(void (*)(int&, int&),int&, int&);
```

This is the kind of declaration that you use infrequently and probably look up in the book each time you need it, but it will save your program on those rare occasions when it is exactly the required construct.

Using *typedef* with Pointers to Functions

The construct void (*)(int&, int&) is cumbersome, at best. You can use typedef to simplify this, by declaring a type VPF as a pointer to a function returning void and taking two integer references. Listing 14.9 rewrites Listing 14.8 using this typedef statement.

Listing 14.9. Using typedef to make pointers to functions more readable.

```
1:     // Listing 14.9. using typedef to make pointers to functions more ➥readable
2:
3:     #include <iostreams.h>
4:
5:     void Square (int&,int&);
6:     void Cube (int&, int&);
7:     void Swap (int&, int &);
8:     void GetVals(int&, int&);
9:     typedef  void (*VPF) (int&, int&) ;
10:    void PrintVals(VPF,int&, int&);
11:    enum BOOL { FALSE, TRUE };
12:
13:    void main()
14:    {
15:       int valOne=1, valTwo=2;
16:       int choice;
17:       BOOL fQuit = FALSE;
18:
19:       VPF pFunc;
20:
21:       while (fQuit == FALSE)
22:       {
23:          cout << "(0)Quit (1)Change Values (2)Square (3)Cube (4)Swap: ";
24:          cin >> choice;
25:          switch (choice)
26:          {
27:             case 1:pFunc = GetVals; break;
28:             case 2:pFunc = Square; break;
29:             case 3:pFunc = Cube; break;
30:             case 4:pFunc = Swap; break;
31:             default:fQuit = TRUE; break;
32:          }
33:          if (fQuit == TRUE)
34:             break;
35:          PrintVals ( pFunc, valOne, valTwo);
36:       }
37:
38:    }
39:
40:    void PrintVals( VPF pFunc,int& x, int& y)
41:    {
42:       cout << "x: " << x << " y: " << y << endl;
43:       pFunc(x,y);
44:       cout << "x: " << x << " y: " << y << endl;
45:    }
```

14

```
(0)Quit (1)Change Values (2)Square (3)Cube (4)Swap: 1
x: 1 y:2
New value for ValOne: 2
New value for ValTwo: 3
x: 2 y:3
(0)Quit (1)Change Values (2)Square (3)Cube (4)Swap: 3
x: 2 y:3
x: 8 y: 27
(0)Quit (1)Change Values (2)Square (3)Cube (4)Swap: 2
x: 8 y: 27
x:64 y:729
(0)Quit (1)Change Values (2)Square (3)Cube (4)Swap: 4
x:64 y:729
x:729 y:64
(0)Quit (1)Change Values (2)Square (3)Cube (4)Swap: 0
```

On line 9, typedef is used to declare VPF to be of the type "function that returns void and takes two parameters, both integer references."

On line 10, the function PrintVals() is declared to take three parameters, a VPF and two integer references. On line 19, pFunc is now declared to be of type VPF.

Once the type VPF is defined, all subsequent uses, to declare pFunc and PrintVals(), are much cleaner. As you can see, the output is identical.

Pointers to Member Functions

Up until this point, all of the function pointers you've created have been for general, non-class functions. It is also possible to create pointers to functions that are members of classes.

To create a pointer to member function, use the same syntax as with a pointer to function, but include the class name and the scoping operator (::). Thus, if pFunc points to a member function of the class Shape, which takes two integers and returns void, the declaration for pFunc is the following:

```
void (Shape::*pFunc) (int, int);
```

Pointers to member functions are used in exactly the same way as pointers to functions, except that they require an object of the correct class on which to invoke them. Listing 14.10 illustrates the use of pointers to member functions.

Listing 14.10. Pointers to member functions.

```
1:    //Listing 14.10 Pointers to member functions Using virtual methods
2:
3:    #include <iostreams.h>
4:
```

```
5:      enum BOOL {FALSE, TRUE};
6:      class Mammal
7:      {
8:      public:
9:         Mammal():itsAge(1) {   }
10:        ~Mammal() { }
11:        virtual void Speak() const = 0;
12:        virtual void Move() const = 0;
13:     protected:
14:        int itsAge;
15:     };
16:
17:     class Dog : public Mammal
18:     {
19:     public:
20:        void Speak()const { cout << "Woof!\n"; }
21:        void Move() const { cout << "Walking to heel...\n"; }
22:     };
23:
24:
25:     class Cat : public Mammal
26:     {
27:     public:
28:        void Speak()const { cout << "Meow!\n"; }
29:        void Move() const { cout << "slinking...\n"; }
30:     };
31:
32:
33:     class Horse : public Mammal
34:     {
35:     public:
36:        void Speak()const { cout << "Winnie!\n"; }
37:        void Move() const { cout << "Galloping...\n"; }
38:     };
39:
40:
41:     void main()
42:     {
43:        void (Mammal::*pFunc)() const =0;
44:        Mammal* ptr =0;
45:        int Animal;
46:        int Method;
47:        BOOL fQuit = FALSE;
48:
49:        while (fQuit == FALSE)
50:        {
51:           cout << "(0)Quit (1)dog (2)cat (3)horse: ";
52:           cin >> Animal;
53:           switch (Animal)
54:           {
55:              case 1: ptr = new Dog; break;
56:              case 2: ptr = new Cat; break;
57:              case 3: ptr = new Horse; break;
58:              default: fQuit = TRUE; break;
59:           }
```

14

continues

Listing 14.10. continued

```
60:        if (fQuit)
61:            break;
62:
63:        cout << "(1)Speak  (2)Move: ";
64:        cin >> Method;
65:        switch (Method)
66:        {
67:            case 1: pFunc = Mammal::Speak; break;
68:            default: pFunc = Mammal::Move; break;
69:        }
70:
71:        (ptr->*pFunc)();
72:        delete ptr;
73:    }
74: }
```

```
(0)Quit (1)Dog (2)Cat (3)Horse: 1
(1)Speak (2)Move: 1
Woof!
(0)Quit (1)Dog (2)Cat (3)Horse: 2
(1)Speak (2)Move: 1
Meow!
(0)Quit (1)Dog (2)Cat (3)Horse: 3
(1)Speak (2)Move: 2
Galloping
(0)Quit (1)Dog (2)Cat (3)Horse: 0
```

On lines 6–15, the abstract data type `Mammal` is declared, with two pure virtual methods, `Speak()` and `Move()`. `Mammal` is subclassed into `Dog`, `Cat`, and `Horse`, each of which overrides `Speak()` and `Move()`.

The driver program in `main()` asks the user to choose which type of animal to create, and then a new subclass of `Animal` is created on the free store and assigned to `ptr` on lines 55–57.

The user is then prompted for which method to invoke, and that method is assigned to the pointer `pFunc`. On line 71, the method chosen is invoked by the object created, by using the pointer `ptr` to access the object and `pFunc` to access the function.

Finally, on line 72, `delete` is called on the pointer `ptr` to return the memory set aside for the object to the free store. Note that there is no reason to call `delete` on `pFunc` because this is a pointer to code, not to an object on the free store. In fact, attempting to do so will generate a compile-time error.

Arrays of Pointers to Member Functions

As with pointers to functions, pointers to member functions can be stored in an array. The array can be initialized with the addresses of various member functions, and these can be invoked by offsets into the array. Listing 14.11 illustrates this technique.

Listing 14.11. Array of pointers to member functions.

```
1:      //Listing 14.11 Array of pointers to member functions
2:
3:      #include <iostreams.h>
4:
5:      enum BOOL {FALSE, TRUE};
6:
7:      class Dog
8:      {
9:      public:
10:         void Speak()const { cout << "Woof!\n"; }
11:         void Move() const { cout << "Walking to heel...\n"; }
12:         void Eat() const { cout << "Gobbling food...\n"; }
13:         void Growl() const { cout << "Grrrrr\n"; }
14:         void Whimper() const { cout << "Whining noises...\n"; }
15:         void RollOver() const { cout << "Rolling over...\n"; }
16:         void PlayDead() const { cout << "Is this the end of Little Caeser?\n"; }
17:      };
18:
19:      typedef void (Dog::*PDF)()const ;
20:      void main()
21:      {
22:         const int MaxFuncs = 7;
23:         PDF DogFunctions[MaxFuncs] =
24:            { Dog::Speak,
25:              Dog::Move,
26:              Dog::Eat,
27:              Dog::Growl,
28:              Dog::Whimper,
29:              Dog::RollOver,
30:              Dog::PlayDead };
31:
32:         Dog* pDog =0;
33:         int Method;
34:         BOOL fQuit = FALSE;
35:
36:         while (!fQuit)
37:         {
38:            cout <<    "(0)Quit (1)Speak (2)Move (3)Eat (4)Growl";
39:            cout << " (5)Whimper (6)Roll Over (7)Play Dead: ";
40:            cin >> Method;
41:            if (Method == 0)
42:            {
43:               fQuit = TRUE;
```

continues

14

Listing 14.11. continued

```
44:            break;
45:        }
46:        else
47:        {
48:            pDog = new Dog;
49:            (pDog->*DogFunctions[Method-1])();
50:            delete pDog;
51:        }
52:    }
53: }
```

```
(0)Quit (1)Speak (2)Move (3)Eat (4)Growl (5)Whimper (6)Roll Over (7)Play Dead: 1
Woof!
(0)Quit (1)Speak (2)Move (3)Eat (4)Growl (5)Whimper (6)Roll Over (7)Play Dead: 4
Grrr...
(0)Quit (1)Speak (2)Move (3)Eat (4)Growl (5)Whimper (6)Roll Over (7)Play Dead: 7
Is this the end of Little Caeser?
(0)Quit (1)Speak (2)Move (3)Eat (4)Growl (5)Whimper (6)Roll Over (7)Play Dead: 0
```

On lines 7–17, the class Dog is created, with 7 member functions all sharing the same return type and signature. On line 19, a typedef declares PDF to be a pointer to a member function of Dog that takes no parameters and returns no values, and that is const: the signature of the 7 member functions of Dog.

On lines 23–30, the array DogFunctions is declared to hold 7 such member functions, and it is initialized with the addresses of these functions.

On lines 38 and 39, the user is prompted to pick a method. Unless they pick Quit, a new Dog is created on the heap, and then the correct method is invoked on the array on line 49. Here's another good line to show to the hotshot C++ programmers in your company; ask them what this does:

```
(pDog->*DogFunctions[Method-1])();
```

Once again, this is a bit esoteric, but when you need a table built from member functions, it can make your program far easier to read and understand.

DO	DON'T
DO invoke pointers to member functions on a specific object of a class.	
DO use typedef to make pointer to member function declarations easier to read.	
DON'T use pointer to member functions when there are simpler solutions.	

Summary

Today you learned how to create static member variables in your class. Each class, rather than each object, has one instance of the static member variable. It is possible to access this member variable without an object of the class type by fully qualifying the name, assuming you've declared the static member to have public access.

Static member variables can be used as counters across instances of the class. Because they are not part of the object, the declaration of static member variables does not allocate memory, and static member variables must be defined and initialized outside the declaration of the class.

Static member functions are part of the class in the same way that static member variables are. They can be accessed without a particular object of the class, and can be used to access static member data. Static member functions cannot be used to access non-static member data because they do not have a *this* pointer.

Because static member functions do not have a *this* pointer, they also cannot be made const. const in a member function indicates that the *this* pointer is const.

You also learned how to declare and use pointers to functions and pointers to member functions. You saw how to create arrays of these pointers and how to pass them to functions.

Pointers to functions and pointers to member functions can be used to create tables of functions that can be selected from at runtime. This can add flexibility to your program not easily achieved without these pointers.

Q&A

Q **Why use static data when you can use global data?**

A Static data is scoped to the class, and thus is available only through an object of the class, through an explicit and full call using the class name if they are public, or by using a static member function. Static data is typed to the class type, however, and the restricted access and strong typing makes static data safer than global data.

Q **Why use static member functions when you can use global functions?**

A Static member functions are scoped to the class, and can be called only by using an object of the class or an explicit full specification (such as `ClassName::FunctionName()`).

Q **Is it common to use many pointers to functions and pointers to member functions?**

A No, these have their special uses but are not common constructs. Many complex and powerful programs have neither.

Workshop

The Workshop contains quiz questions to help solidify your understanding of the material covered and exercises to provide you with experience in using what you've learned. Try to answer the quiz and exercise questions before checking the answers in Appendix D, and make sure you understand the answers before going to the next chapter.

Quiz

1. Can static member variables be private?

2. Show the declaration for a static member variable.

3. Show the declaration for a static function pointer.

4. Show the declaration for a pointer to function returning long and taking an integer parameter.

5. Modify the pointer in Question 4 so it's a pointer to member function of class Car.

6. Show the declaration for an array of 10 pointers as defined in Question 5.

Exercises

1. Write a short program declaring a class with one member variable and one static member variable. Have the constructor initialize the member variable and increment the static member variable. Have the destructor decrement the member variable.

2. Using the program from Exercise 1, write a short driver program that makes three objects and then displays their member variables and the static member variable. Then destroy each object and show the effect on the static member variable.

3. Modify the program from Exercise 2 to use a static member function to access the static member variable. Make the static member variable private.

4. Write a pointer to member function to access the non-static member data in the program in Exercise 3, and use that pointer to print the value of that data.

5. Add two more member variables to the class from the previous questions. Add accessor functions that get the value of these values, and give all the member functions the same return values and signatures. Use the pointer to member function to access these functions.

14

2

WEEK

IN REVIEW

8

9

10

11

12

13

14

The Week in Review program for Week 2 brings together many of the skills you've acquired over the past fortnight and produces a powerful program.

This demonstration of linked lists utilizes virtual functions, pure virtual functions, function overriding, polymorphism, public inheritance, function overloading, forever loops, pointers, references, and more.

The goal of this program is to create a linked list. The nodes on the list are designed to hold parts, as might be used in a factory. While this is not the final form of this program, it does make a good demonstration of a fairly advanced data structure. The code list is 300 lines. Try to analyze the code on your own before reading the analysis that follows the output.

```
1:    // ****************************************************
2:    //
3:    // Title:       Week 2 in review
4:    //
5:    // File:        Week2
6:    //
7:    // Description:  Provide a linked list demonstration program
8:    //
9:    // Classes:      PART - holds part numbers and potentially other
10:   //                      information about parts
11:   //
12:   //               PartNode - acts as a node in a PartsList
13:   //
14:   //               PartsList - provides the mechanisms for a linked list of parts
15:   //
16:   // Author:       Jesse Liberty (jl)
17:   //
18:   // Developed:    486/66 32mb RAM  MVC 1.5
19:   //
20:   // Target:       Platform independent
21:   //
22:   // Rev History:  9/94 - First release (jl)
23:   //
24:   // ****************************************************
25:
26:   #include <iostreams.h>
27:
28:   typedef unsigned long ULONG;
29:   typedef unsigned short USHORT;
30:
31:
32:   // *************** Part ************
33:
34:   // Abstract base class of parts
35:   class Part
36:   {
37:   public:
38:      Part():itsPartNumber(1) {}
39:      Part(ULONG PartNumber):itsPartNumber(PartNumber){}
40:      virtual ~Part(){};
41:      ULONG GetPartNumber() const { return itsPartNumber; }
42:      virtual void Display() const =0;  // must be overridden
43:   private:
44:      ULONG itsPartNumber;
45:   };
46:
47:   // implementation of pure virtual function so that
48:   // derived classes can chain up
49:   void Part::Display() const
50:   {
51:       cout << "\nPart Number: " << itsPartNumber << endl;
52:   }
53:
54:   // *************** Car Part ************
55:
56:   class CarPart : public Part
```

```
57:     {
58:     public:
59:         CarPart():itsModelYear(94){}
60:         CarPart(USHORT year, ULONG partNumber);
61:         virtual void Display() const { Part::Display(); cout << "Model Year: " <<
        ➡itsModelYear << endl;   }
62:     private:
63:         USHORT itsModelYear;
64:     };
65:
66:     CarPart::CarPart(USHORT year, ULONG partNumber):
67:         itsModelYear(year),
68:         Part(partNumber)
69:     {}
70:
71:
72:     // *************** AirPlane Part ************
73:
74:     class AirPlanePart : public Part
75:     {
76:     public:
77:         AirPlanePart():itsEngineNumber(1){};
78:         AirPlanePart(USHORT EngineNumber, ULONG PartNumber);
79:         virtual void Display() const{ Part::Display(); cout << "Engine No.: " <<
        ➡itsEngineNumber << endl;   }
80:     private:
81:         USHORT itsEngineNumber;
82:     };
83:
84:     AirPlanePart::AirPlanePart(USHORT EngineNumber, ULONG PartNumber):
85:         itsEngineNumber(EngineNumber),
86:         Part(PartNumber)
87:     {}
88:
89:     // *************** Part Node ************
90:     class PartNode
91:     {
92:     public:
93:         PartNode (Part*);
94:         ~PartNode();
95:         void SetNext(PartNode * node) { itsNext = node; }
96:         PartNode * GetNext() const;
97:         Part * GetPart() const;
98:     private:
99:         Part *itsPart;
100:        PartNode * itsNext;
101:    };
102:
103:    // PartNode Implementations...
104:
105:    PartNode::PartNode(Part* pPart):
106:    itsPart(pPart),
107:    itsNext(0)
108:    {}
109:
110:    PartNode::~PartNode()
```

```
111:    {
112:       delete itsPart;
113:       itsPart = 0;
114:       delete itsNext;
115:       itsNext = 0;
116:    }
117:
118:    // Returns NULL if no next PartNode
119:    PartNode * PartNode::GetNext() const
120:    {
121:          return itsNext;
122:    }
123:
124:    Part * PartNode::GetPart() const
125:    {
126:       if (itsPart)
127:          return itsPart;
128:       else
129:          return NULL; //error
130:    }
131:
132:    // *************** Part List ***********
133:    class PartsList
134:    {
135:    public:
136:       PartsList();
137:       ~PartsList();
138:       // needs copy constructor and operator equals!
139:       Part*     Find(ULONG & position, ULONG PartNumber)  const;
140:       ULONG     GetCount() const { return itsCount; }
141:       Part*     GetFirst() const;
142:       static    PartsList& GetGlobalPartsList() { return  GlobalPartsList; }
143:       void      Insert(Part *);
144:       void      Iterate(void (Part::*f)()const) const;
145:       Part*     operator[](ULONG) const;
146:    private:
147:       PartNode * pHead;
148:       ULONG itsCount;
149:       static PartsList GlobalPartsList;
150:    };
151:
152:    PartsList PartsList::GlobalPartsList;
153:
154:    // Implementations for Lists...
155:
156:    PartsList::PartsList():
157:       pHead(0),
158:       itsCount(0)
159:       {}
160:
161:    PartsList::~PartsList()
162:    {
163:       delete pHead;
164:    }
165:
166:    Part*   PartsList::GetFirst() const
```

```
167:    {
168:        if (pHead)
169:            return pHead->GetPart();
170:        else
171:            return NULL;  // error catch here
172:    }
173:
174:    Part *  PartsList::operator[](ULONG offSet) const
175:    {
176:        PartNode* pNode = pHead;
177:
178:        if (!pHead)
179:            return NULL; // error catch here
180:
181:        if (offSet > itsCount)
182:            return NULL; // error
183:
184:        for (ULONG i=0;i<offSet; i++)
185:            pNode = pNode->GetNext();
186:
187:      return    pNode->GetPart();
188:    }
189:
190:    Part*   PartsList::Find(ULONG & position, ULONG PartNumber)   const
191:    {
192:        PartNode * pNode = 0;
193:        for (pNode = pHead, position = 0;
194:              pNode!=NULL;
195:              pNode = pNode->GetNext(), position++)
196:        {
197:            if (pNode->GetPart()->GetPartNumber() == PartNumber)
198:              break;
199:        }
200:        if (pNode == NULL)
201:            return NULL;
202:        else
203:            return pNode->GetPart();
204:    }
205:
206:    void PartsList::Iterate(void (Part::*func)()const) const
207:    {
208:        if (!pHead)
209:            return;
210:        PartNode* pNode = pHead;
211:        do
212:            (pNode->GetPart()->*func)();
213:        while (pNode = pNode->GetNext());
214:    }
215:
216:    void PartsList::Insert(Part* pPart)
217:    {
218:        PartNode * pNode = new PartNode(pPart);
219:        PartNode * pCurrent = pHead;
220:        PartNode * pNext = 0;
221:
222:        ULONG New =  pPart->GetPartNumber();
```

```
223:        ULONG Next = 0;
224:        itsCount++;
225:
226:        if (!pHead)
227:        {
228:            pHead = pNode;
229:            return;
230:        }
231:
232:        // if this one is smaller than head
233:        // this one is the new head
234:        if (pHead->GetPart()->GetPartNumber() > New)
235:        {
236:            pNode->SetNext(pHead);
237:            pHead = pNode;
238:            return;
239:        }
240:
241:        for (;;)
242:        {
243:            // if there is no next, append this new one
244:            if (!pCurrent->GetNext())
245:            {
246:                pCurrent->SetNext(pNode);
247:                return;
248:            }
249:
250:            // if this goes after this one and before the next
251:            // then insert it here, otherwise get the next
252:            pNext = pCurrent->GetNext();
253:            Next = pNext->GetPart()->GetPartNumber();
254:            if (Next > New)
255:            {
256:                pCurrent->SetNext(pNode);
257:                pNode->SetNext(pNext);
258:                return;
259:            }
260:            pCurrent = pNext;
261:        }
262:    }
263:
264:    void main()
265:    {
266:        PartsList pl = PartsList::GetGlobalPartsList();
267:        Part * pPart = 0;
268:        ULONG PartNumber;
269:        USHORT value;
270:        ULONG choice;
271:
272:        while (1)
273:        {
274:            cout << "(0)Quit (1)Car (2)Plane: ";
275:            cin >> choice;
276:
277:            if (!choice)
278:                break;
```

```
279:
280:        cout << "New PartNumber?: ";
281:        cin >>  PartNumber;
282:
283:        if (choice == 1)
284:        {
285:            cout << "Model Year?: ";
286:            cin >> value;
287:            pPart = new CarPart(value,PartNumber);
288:        }
289:        else
290:        {
291:            cout << "Engine Number?: ";
292:            cin >> value;
293:            pPart = new AirPlanePart(value,PartNumber);
294:        }
295:
296:        pl.Insert(pPart);
297:    }
298:    void (Part::*pFunc)()const = Part::Display;
299:    pl.Iterate(pFunc);
300:  }
```

Output

```
(0)Quit (1)Car (2)Plane: 1
New PartNumber?: 2837
Model Year? 90

(0)Quit (1)Car (2)Plane: 2
New PartNumber?: 378
Engine Number?: 4938

(0)Quit (1)Car (2)Plane: 1
New PartNumber?: 4499
Model Year? 94

(0)Quit (1)Car (2)Plane: 1
New PartNumber?: 3000
Model Year? 93

(0)Quit (1)Car (2)Plane: 0

Part Number: 378
Engine No. 4938

Part Number: 2837
Model Year: 90

Part Number: 3000
Model Year: 93

Part Number 4499
Model Year: 94
```

The Week 2 in Review provides a linked list implementation for Part objects. A linked list is a dynamic data structure, that is it is like an array but it is sized to fit as objects are added and deleted.

This particular linked list is designed to hold objects of class Part, where Part is an abstract data type serving as a base class to any objects with a part number. In this example, Part has been subclassed into CarPart and AirplanePart.

Class Part is declared on lines 34–43, and consists of a part number and some accessors. Presumably this class could be fleshed out to hold other important information about the parts such as what components they are used in, how many are in stock, and so forth. Part is an abstract data type, enforced by the pure virtual function Display().

Note that Display() does have an implementation, on lines 50–52. It is the designers intention that derived classes will be forced to create their own Display() method, but may chain up to this method as well.

Two simple derived classes, CarPart and AirPlanePart are provided on lines 56–69 and 74–87, respectively. Each provides an overridden Display() method, which does in fact chain up to the base class Display() method.

The class PartNode serves as the interface between the Part class and the PartList class. It contains a pointer to a part and a pointer to the next node in the list. Its only methods are to get and set the next node in the list and to return the Part to which it points.

The intelligence of the list is, appropriately, in the class PartsList, whose declaration is on lines 133–150. The PartsList keeps a pointer to the first element in the list (pHead) and uses that to access all other methods by *walking the list*. Walking the list means asking each node in the list for the next node, until you reach a node whose next pointer is NULL.

This is only a partial implementation, a fully developed list would provide either greater access to its first and last nodes, or would provide an iterator object, which allowed clients to easily walk the list.

The PartsList nonetheless provides a number of interesting methods, which are listed in alphabetical order. This is often a good idea, as it makes finding the functions easier.

Find() takes a PartNumber and a ULONG. If the part corresponding to the PartNumber is found, it returns a pointer to the Part and fills the ULONG with the position of that part in the list. If the PartNumber is not found, it returns NULL and the position is meaningless.

`GetCount()` returns the number of elements in the list. `PartsList` keeps this number as a member variable, `itsCount`, though it could of course compute this number by walking the list.

`GetFirst()` returns a pointer to the first `Part` in the list, or returns `NULL` if the list is empty.

`GetGlobalPartsList()` returns a *reference* to the static member variable `GlobalPartsList`. This is a static instance of this class; every program with a `PartsList` also has one `GlobalPartsList`, though of course it is free to make other `PartsLists` as well. A full implementation of this idea would modify the constructor of `Part` to ensure that every part is created on the `GlobalPartsList`.

`Insert` takes a pointer to a `Part`, creates a `PartNode` for it and adds it to the list, ordered by `PartNumber`.

`Iterate` takes a pointer to a member function of `Part`, which takes no parameters, returns `void` and is `const`. It calls that function for every `Part` object in the list. In the example program this is called on `Display()`, which is a virtual function, so the appropriate `Display()` method will be called based on the run-time type of the `Part` object called.

`Operator[]` allows direct access to the `Part` at the offset provided. Rudimentary bounds checking is provided, if the list is `NULL` or if the offset requested is greater than the size of the list, NULL is returned as an error condition.

Note that in a real program these comments on the functions would be written into the class declaration.

The driver program is on lines 264–300. A pointer to `PartsList` is declared on line 266 and initialized with the `GlobalPartsList`. Note that the `GlobalPartsList` itself is initialized on line 152. This is necessary as the declaration of a static member variable does not define it; definition must be done outside the declaration of the class.

On lines 272–294 the user is repeatedly prompted to choose whether to enter a car part or an airplane part. Depending on the choice the right value is requested and the appropriate part is created. Once created the part is inserted into the list on line 296.

The implementation for the `Insert()` method of `PartsList` is on lines 216–262. When the first part number is entered, `2837`, a `CarPart` with that part number and the model year `90` is created and passed in to `LinkedList::Insert()`.

On line 218 a new `PartNode` is created with that part, and the variable `New` is initialized with the part number. The `PartsList`'s `itsCount` member variable is incremented on line 224.

On line 226 the test that pHead is NULL will evaluate true. Since this is the first node, it *is* true that the PartsList's pHead pointer has zero. Thus on line 228 pHead is set to point to the new node and this function returns.

The user is prompted to enter a second part, and this time an AirPlane part with part number 378 and engine number 4938 is entered. Once again PartsList::Insert() is called, and once again pNode is initialized with the *new* node. The static member variable itsCount is incremented to 2, and pHead is tested. Since pHead was assigned last time, it is no longer null and the test fails.

On line 234 the part number held by pHead, 2837, is compared against the current part number, 378. Since the new one is smaller than the one held by pHead, the new one must become the new head pointer, and the test on line 234 is true.

On line 236 the new node is set to point to the node currently pointed to by pHead. Note that this does not point the new node to pHead itself, but rather to the node that pHead was pointing to! On line 237 pHead is set to point to the new node.

The third time through the loop, the user enters the part number 4499 for a Car with model year 94. The counter is incremented and the number this time is *not* less than the number pointed to by pHead, so the for loop which begins on line 241 is entered.

The value pointed to by pHead is 378. The value pointed to by the second node is 2837. The current value is 4499. The pointer pCurrent points to the same node as pHead and so it does have a next value, it points to the second node, and so the test on line 244 fails.

The pointer pCurrent is set to point to the next node and the loop repeats. This time the test on line 145 succeeds, there is no next item, so the current node is told to point to the new node on line 246 and the insert is finished.

The fourth time through the part number 3000 is entered. This proceeds just like the previous, but this time when the current node is pointing to 2837 and the next node has 4499, the test on line 254 returns TRUE and the new node is inserted into position.

When the user finally presses 0 the test on line 277 evaluates true and the while(1) loop breaks. On line 298 the member function Display() is assigned to the pointer to member function pFunc. In a real program this would be assigned dynamically, based on the user's choice of method.

The pointer to member function is passed to the PartsList Iterate() method. On line 208 the Iterate() method ensures that the list is not empty. Then on lines 211–213 each Part on the list is called using the pointer to member function. This calls the appropriate Display() method for the Part, as shown in the output.

3

You have finished the second week of learning C++. By now you should feel comfortable with some of the more advanced aspects of object-oriented programming, including encapsulation and polymorphism.

Where You Are Going

The last week begins with a discussion of advanced inheritance. On Day 16 you will learn about streams in depth, and on Day 17 you will learn advanced tricks of the preprocessor. Day 18 is a departure: rather than focusing on the syntax of the language you take a day out to learn about object-oriented analysis and design. On Day 19 templates are introduced, and on Day 20 exceptions are explained. Day 21, the last day of this book, covers some miscellaneous subjects not covered elsewhere, and then there is a discussion of the next steps to take in becoming a C++ guru.

15

Advanced Inheritance

So far you have worked with single and multiple inheritance to create *is-a* relationships. Today you will learn:

☐ What containment is and how to model it.

☐ What delegation is and how to model it.

☐ How to implement one class in terms of another.

☐ How to use private inheritance.

Containment

As you have seen in previous examples, it is possible for the member data of a class to include objects of another class. C++ programmers say that the outer class *contains* the inner class. Thus, an Employee class might contain string objects (for the name of the employee) as well as integers (for the employee's salary) and so forth.

Listing 15.1 describes an incomplete but still useful String class. This listing does not produce any output. Instead it will be used with later listings.

Listing 15.1. The String class.

```
1:      #include <iostreams.h>
2:      #include <string.h>
3:
4:      class String
5:      {
6:        public:
7:            // constructors
8:            String();
9:             String(const char *const);
10:            String(const String &);
11:            ~String();
12:
13:            // overloaded operators
14:            char & operator[](int offset);
15:            char operator[](int offset) const;
16:            String operator+(const String&);
17:            void operator+=(const String&);
18:            String & operator= (const String &);
19:
20:            // General accessors
21:            int GetLen()const { return itsLen; }
22:            const char * GetString() const { return itsString; }
23:            // static int ConstructorCount;
24:
25:        private:
26:            String (int);           // private constructor
27:            char * itsString;
```

```
28:        unsigned short itsLen;
29:
30:    };
31:
32:    // default constructor creates string of 0 bytes
33:    String::String()
34:    {
35:        itsString = new char[1];
36:        itsString[0] = '\0';
37:        itsLen=0;
38:        // cout << "\tDefault string constructor\n";
39:        // ConstructorCount++;
40:    }
41:
42:    // private (helper) constructor, used only by
43:    // class methods for creating a new string of
44:    // required size.  Null filled.
45:    String::String(int len)
46:    {
47:        itsString = new char[len+1];
48:        for (int i = 0; i<=len; i++)
49:            itsString[1] = '\0';
50:        itsLen=len;
51:        // cout << "\tString(int) constructor\n";
52:        // ConstructorCount++;
53:    }
54:
55:    // Converts a character array to a String
56:    String::String(const char * const cString)
57:    {
58:        itsLen = strlen(cString);
59:        itsString = new char[itsLen+1];
60:        for (int i = 0; i<itsLen; i++)
61:            itsString[i] = cString[i];
62:        itsString[itsLen]='\0';
63:        // cout << "\tString(char*) constructor\n";
64:        // ConstructorCount++;
65:    }
66:
67:    // copy constructor
68:    String::String (const String & rhs)
69:    {
70:        itsLen=rhs.GetLen();
71:        itsString = new char[itsLen+1];
72:        for (int i = 0; i<itsLen;i++)
73:            itsString[i] = rhs[i];
74:        itsString[itsLen] = '\0';
75:        // cout << "\tString(String&) constructor\n";
76:        // ConstructorCount++;
77:    }
78:
79:    // destructor, frees allocated memory
80:    String::~String ()
81:    {
```

continues

Listing 15.1. continued

```
82:        delete [] itsString;
83:        itsLen = 0;
84:        // cout << "\tString destructor\n";
85:    }
86:
87:    // operator equals, frees existing memory
88:    // then copies string and size
89:    String& String::operator=(const String & rhs)
90:    {
91:        if (this == &rhs)
92:            return *this;
93:        delete [] itsString;
94:        itsLen=rhs.GetLen();
95:        itsString = new char[itsLen+1];
96:        for (int i = 0; i<itsLen;i++)
97:            itsString[i] = rhs[i];
98:        itsString[itsLen] = '\0';
99:        return *this;
100:       // cout << "\tString operator=\n";
101:   }
102:
103:   //non constant offset operator, returns
104:   // reference to character so it can be
105:   // changed!
106:   char & String::operator[](int offset)
107:   {
108:       if (offset > itsLen)
109:           return itsString[itsLen-1];
110:       else
111:           return itsString[offset];
112:   }
113:
114:   // constant offset operator for use
115:   // on const objects (see copy constructor!)
116:   char String::operator[](int offset) const
117:   {
118:       if (offset > itsLen)
119:           return itsString[itsLen-1];
120:       else
121:           return itsString[offset];
122:   }
123:
124:   // creates a new string by adding current
125:   // string to rhs
126:   String String::operator+(const String& rhs)
127:   {
128:       int  totalLen = itsLen + rhs.GetLen();
129:       String temp(totalLen);
130:       for (int i = 0; i<itsLen; i++)
131:           temp[i] = itsString[i];
132:       for (int j = 0; j<rhs.GetLen(); j++, i++)
133:           temp[i] = rhs[j];
134:       temp[totalLen]='\0';
```

```
135:        return temp;
136:    }
137:
138:    // changes current string, returns nothing
139:    void String::operator+=(const String& rhs)
140:    {
141:        unsigned short rhsLen = rhs.GetLen();
142:        unsigned short totalLen = itsLen + rhsLen;
143:        String  temp(totalLen);
144:        for (int i = 0; i<itsLen; i++)
145:            temp[i] = itsString[i];
146:        for (int j = 0; j<rhs.GetLen(); j++, i++)
147:            temp[i] = rhs[i-itsLen];
148:        temp[totalLen]='\0';
149:        *this = temp;
150:    }
151:
152:    // int String::ConstructorCount = 0;
```

Output None.

Analysis Listing 15.1 provides a `String` class much like the one used in Listing 11.14. The significant difference here is that the constructors and a few other functions have print statements to show their use, which are currently commented out. These will be used in later examples.

On line 23 the static member variable `ConstructorCount` is declared, and on line 152 it is initialized. This variable is incremented in each string constructor. All of this is currently commented out; it will be used in a later listing.

Listing 15.2 describes an `Employee` class that contains three string objects. Note that a number of statements are commented out; they will be used in later listings.

Listing 15.2. The `Employee` class and driver program.

```
1:    class Employee
2:    {
3:
4:    public:
5:        Employee();
6:        Employee(char *, char *, char *, long);
7:        ~Employee();
8:        Employee(const Employee&);
9:        Employee & operator= (const Employee &);
10:
11:        const String & GetFirstName() const { return itsFirstName; }
```

continues

Listing 15.2. continued

```
12:        const String & GetLastName() const { return itsLastName; }
13:        const String & GetAddress() const { return itsAddress; }
14:        long GetSalary() const { return itsSalary; }
15:
16:        void SetFirstName(const String & fName) { itsFirstName = fName; }
17:        void SetLastName(const String & lName) { itsLastName = lName; }
18:        void SetAddress(const String & address) { itsAddress = address; }
19:        void SetSalary(long salary) { itsSalary = salary; }
20:    private:
21:        String    itsFirstName;
22:        String    itsLastName;
23:        String    itsAddress;
24:        long      itsSalary;
25:    };
26:
27:    Employee::Employee():
28:        itsFirstName(""),
29:        itsLastName(""),
30:        itsAddress(""),
31:        itsSalary(0)
32:    {}
33:
34:    Employee::Employee(char * firstName, char * lastName,
35:        char * address, long salary):
36:        itsFirstName(firstName),
37:        itsLastName(lastName),
38:        itsAddress(address),
39:        itsSalary(salary)
40:    {}
41:
42:    Employee::Employee(const Employee & rhs):
43:        itsFirstName(rhs.GetFirstName()),
44:        itsLastName(rhs.GetLastName()),
45:        itsAddress(rhs.GetAddress()),
46:        itsSalary(rhs.GetSalary())
47:    {}
48:
49:    Employee::~Employee() {}
50:
51:    Employee & Employee::operator= (const Employee & rhs)
52:    {
53:        if (this == &rhs)
54:            return *this;
55:
56:        itsFirstName = rhs.GetFirstName();
57:        itsLastName = rhs.GetLastName();
58:        itsAddress = rhs.GetAddress();
59:        itsSalary = rhs.GetSalary();
60:
61:        return *this;
62:    }
63:
64:    void main()
65:    {
```

```
66:        Employee Edie("Jane","Doe","1461 Shore Parkway", 20000);
67:        Edie.SetSalary(50000);
68:        String LastName("Levine");
69:        Edie.SetLastName(LastName);
70:        Edie.SetFirstName("Edythe");
71:
72:        cout << "Name: ";
73:        cout << Edie.GetFirstName().GetString();
74:        cout << " " << EmployeeOne.GetLastName().GetString();
75:        cout << ".\nAddress: ";
76:        cout << Edie.GetAddress().GetString();
77:        cout << ".\nSalary: " ;
78:        cout << Edie.GetSalary();
79:    }
```

Note: Put the code from Listing 15.1 into a file called STRING.HPP. Then any time you need the String class you can include Listing 15.1 by using #include. For example, at the top of Listing 15.2 add the line #include String.hpp. This will add the String class to your program.

```
Name; Edythe Levine
Address: 1461 Shore Parkway
Salary: 50000
```

Listing 15.2 shows the Employee class, which contains three string objects: itsFirstName, itsLastName, and itsAddress.

On line 66 an employee object is created, and four values are passed in to initialize the employee object. On line 67 the Employee access function SetSalary() is called, with the constant value 50000. Note that in a real program this would either be a dynamic value (set at runtime) or a constant.

On line 68, a string is created and initialized using a C++ string constant. This string object is then used as an argument to SetLastName() on line 69.

On line 70, the Employee function SetFirstName() is called with yet another string constant. However, if you are paying close attention you will notice that Employee does not have a function SetFirstName() that takes a character string as its argument; SetFirstName() requires a constant string reference.

The compiler resolves this because it knows how to make a string from a constant character string. It knows this because you told it how to do so on line 9 of listing 15.1.

Accessing Members of the Contained Class

Employee objects do not have special access to the member variables of String. If the employee object Edie tried to access the member variable itsLen of its own itsFirstName member variable, it would get a compile-time error. This is not much of a burden, however. The accessor functions provide an interface for the String class, and the Employee class need not worry about the implementation details, any more than it worries about how the integer variable, itsSalary, stores its information.

Filtering Access to Contained Members

Note that the String class provides the operator+. The designer of the Employee class has blocked access to the operator+ being called on employee objects by declaring that all the string accessors, such as GetFirstName(), return a constant reference. Because operator+ is not (and can't be) a const function (it changes the object it is called on), attempting to write the following will cause a compile-time error:

```
String buffer = Edie.GetFirstName() + Edie.GetLastName();
```

GetFirstName() returns a constant String, and you can't call operator+ on a constant object.

To fix this, overload GetFirstName() to be non-const:

```
const String & GetFirstName() const { return itsFirstName; }
String & GetFirstName()  { return itsFirstName; }
```

Note that the return value is no longer const and that the member function itself is no longer const. Changing the return value is not sufficient to overload the function name; you must change the constancy of the function itself.

Cost of Containment

It is important to note that the user of an Employee class pays the price of each of those string objects each time one is constructed or a copy of the Employee is made.

Uncommenting the cout statements in Listing 15.1, lines 38, 51, 63, 75, 84, and 100, reveals how often these are called. Listing 15.3 rewrites the driver program to add print statements indicating where in the program objects are being created:

Note: To compile this listing:

1. Uncomment lines 38, 51, 63, 75, 84, and 100 in Listing 15.1.

2. Edit Listing 15.2. Remove lines 64–79 and substitute Listing 15.3.

3. Add #include string.hpp as previously noted.

Listing 15.3. Contained class constructors.

```
1:     void main()
2:     {
3:         cout << "Creating Edie...\n";
4:         Employee Edie("Jane","Doe","1461 Shore Parkway", 20000);
5:         Edie.SetSalary(20000);
6:         cout << "Calling SetFirstName with char *...\n";
7:         Edie.SetFirstName("Edythe");
8:         cout << "Creating temporary string LastName...\n";
9:         String LastName("Levine");
10:        Edie.SetLastName(LastName);
11:
12:        cout << "Name: ";
13:        cout << Edie.GetFirstName().GetString();
14:        cout << " " << Edie.GetLastName().GetString();
15:        cout << ".\nAddress: ";
16:        cout << Edie.GetAddress().GetString();
17:        cout << ".\nSalary: " ;
18:        cout << Edie.GetSalary();
19:        cout << endl;
20:     }
```

Output

```
1:     Creating Edie...
2:             String(char*) constructor
3:             String(char*) constructor
4:             String(char*) constructor
5:     Calling SetFirstName with char *...
6:             String(char*) constructor
7:             String destructor
8:     Creating temporary string LstName...
9:             String(char*) constructor
10:    Name: Edythe Levine
11:    Address: 1461 Shore Parkway
12:    Salary: 20000
13:            String destructor
14:            String destructor
15:            String destructor
16:            String destructor
```

Listing 15.3 uses the same class declarations as Listings 15.1 and 15.2. However, the cout statements have been uncommented. The output from Listing 15.3 has been numbered to make analysis easier.

On line 3 of Listing 15.3 the statement Creating Edie... is printed, as reflected on line 1 of the output. On line 4 an Employee object, Edie, is created with four parameters. The output reflects the constructor for String being called three times, as expected.

Line 6 prints an information statement, and then on line 7 is the statement Edie.SetFirstName("Edythe"). This statement causes a temporary string to be created from the character string "Edythe", as reflected on lines 6 and 7 of the output. Note that the temporary is destroyed immediately after it is used in the assignment statement.

On line 9 a string object is created in the body of the program. Here the programmer is doing explicitly what the compiler did implicitly on the previous statement. This time you see the constructor on line 9 of the output, but no destructor. This object will not be destroyed until it goes out of scope at the end of the function.

On lines 13–16, the strings in the employee object are destroyed as the employee object falls out of scope, and the string LastName, created on line 9, is destroyed as well when it falls out of scope.

Copying by Value

Listing 15.3 illustrates how the creation of one employee object caused five string constructor calls. Listing 15.4 again rewrites the driver program. This time the print statements are not used, but the string static member variable ConstructorCount is uncommented and used.

Examination of Listing 15.1 shows that ConstructorCount is incremented each time a string constructor is called. The driver program in 15.4 calls the print functions, passing in the Employee object, first by reference and then by value. ConstructorCount keeps track of how many string objects are created when the employee is passed as a parameter.

Note: To compile this listing:

1. Uncomment lines 38, 51, 63, 75, 84, and 100 in Listing 15.1.

2. Edit Listing 15.2. Remove lines 64–79 and substitute Listing 15.4.

3. Add #include string.hpp as previously noted.

Listing 15.4. Passing by value.

```
1:    void PrintFunc(Employee);
2:    void rPrintFunc(const Employee&);
3:
4:    void main()
5:    {
6:        Employee Edie("Jane","Doe","1461 Shore Parkway", 20000);
7:        Edie.SetSalary(20000);
8:        Edie.SetFirstName("Edythe");
9:        String LastName("Levine");
10:       Edie.SetLastName(LastName);
11:
12:       cout << "Constructor count: " << String::ConstructorCount << endl;
13:       rPrintFunc(Edie);
14:       cout << "Constructor count: " << String::ConstructorCount << endl;
15:       PrintFunc(Edie);
16:       cout << "Constructor count: " << String::ConstructorCount << endl;
17:    }
18:    void PrintFunc (Employee Edie)
19:    {
20:
21:        cout << "Name: ";
22:        cout << Edie.GetFirstName().GetString();
23:        cout << " " << Edie.GetLastName().GetString();
24:        cout << ".\nAddress: ";
25:        cout << Edie.GetAddress().GetString();
26:        cout << ".\nSalary: " ;
27:        cout << Edie.GetSalary();
28:        cout << endl;
29:
30:    }
31:
32:    void rPrintFunc (const Employee& Edie)
33:    {
34:        cout << "Name: ";
35:        cout << Edie.GetFirstName().GetString();
36:        cout << " " << Edie.GetLastName().GetString();
37:        cout << ".\nAddress: ";
38:        cout << Edie.GetAddress().GetString();
39:        cout << ".\nSalary: " ;
40:        cout << Edie.GetSalary();
41:        cout << endl;
42:    }
```

```
Constructor count: 5
Name: Edythe Levine
Address: 1461 Shore Parkway
Salary: 20000
Constructor count: 5
Name: Edythe Levine
Address: 1461 Shore Parkway
Salary: 20000
Constructor count: 8
```

The output shows that five string objects were created as part of creating one employee object. When the employee object is passed to rPrintFunc() by reference, no additional employee objects are created, and so no additional string objects are created. (They too are passed by reference.)

When, on line 15, the employee object is passed to PrintFunc() by value, a copy of the employee is created and three more string objects are created (by calls to the copy constructor).

Implemented in Terms of Versus Delegation

At times one class wants to draw on some of the attributes of another class. For example, let's say you need to create a PartsCatalog class. The specification you've been given defines a PartsCatalog as a collection of parts; each part has a unique part number. The PartsCatalog does not allow duplicate entries, and does allow access by part number.

The listing for the Week in Review for Week 2 provides a linked list class. This linked list is well-tested and understood, and you'd like to build on that technology when making your PartsCatalog, rather than inventing it from scratch.

You could create a new PartsCatalog class and have it contain a linked list. The PartsCatalog could delegate management of the linked list to its contained linked list object.

An alternative would be to make the PartsCatalog derive from Linked List and thereby inherit the properties of a linked list. Remembering, however, that public inheritance provides an *is-a* relationship, you should question whether a PartsCatalog really *is a* type of linked list.

One way to answer the question of whether PartsCatalog is a linked list is to assume that LinkedList is the base and PartsCatalog is the derived class, and then to ask these other questions:

1. Is there anything in the base class that should not be in the derived? For example, does the linked list base class have functions that are inappropriate for the PartsCatalog class? If so, you probably don't want public inheritance.

2. Might the class you are creating have more than one of the base? For example, might a PartsCatalog need two linked lists in each object? If it might, you almost certainly want to use containment.

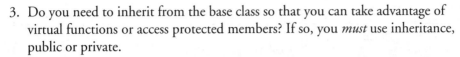

3. Do you need to inherit from the base class so that you can take advantage of virtual functions or access protected members? If so, you *must* use inheritance, public or private.

Based on the answers to these questions, you must chose between public inheritance (the *is a* relationship) and either private inheritance or containment.

 □ **Contained**—An object declared as a member of another class contained by that class.

□ **Delegation**—Using the attributes of a contained class to accomplish functions not otherwise available to the containing class.

□ **Implemented in terms of**—Building one class on the capabilities of another without using public inheritance.

Delegation

Why not derive PartsCatalog from LinkedList? The PartsCatalog isn't a linked list because linked lists are ordered collections and each member of the collection can repeat. The PartsCatalog has unique entries that are not ordered. The fifth member of the PartsCatalog is *not* part number 5.

Certainly it would have been possible to inherit publicly from PartsList and then override Insert() and the offset operators ([]) to do the right thing, but then you would have changed the essence of the PartsList class. Instead you'll build a PartsCatalog that has no offset operator, does not allow duplicates, and defines the operator+ to combine two sets.

The first way to accomplish this is with containment. The PartsCatalog will delegate list management to a contained LinkedList. Listing 15.5 illustrates this approach.

Listing 15.5. Delegating to a contained linked list.

```
1:     #include <iostreams.h>
2:
3:     typedef unsigned long ULONG;
4:     typedef unsigned short USHORT;
5:
6:
7:     // *************** Part ************
8:
9:     // Abstract base class of parts
10:    class Part
11:    {
```

continues

Listing 15.5. continued

```
12:     public:
13:         Part():itsPartNumber(1) {}
14:         Part(ULONG PartNumber):itsPartNumber(PartNumber){}
15:         virtual ~Part(){};
16:         ULONG GetPartNumber() const { return itsPartNumber; }
17:         virtual void Display() const =0;   // must be overridden
18:     private:
19:         ULONG itsPartNumber;
20:     };
21:
22:     // implementation of pure virtual function so that
23:     // derived classes can chain up
24:     void Part::Display() const
25:     {
26:         cout << "\nPart Number: " << itsPartNumber << endl;
27:     }
28:
29:     // *************** Car Part ************
30:
31:     class CarPart : public Part
32:     {
33:     public:
34:         CarPart():itsModelYear(94){}
35:         CarPart(USHORT year, ULONG partNumber);
36:         virtual void Display() const { Part::Display(); cout << "Model Year:  <<
            ➥itsModelYear << endl;  }
37:     private:
38:         USHORT itsModelYear;
39:     };
40:
41:     CarPart::CarPart(USHORT year, ULONG partNumber):
42:         itsModelYear(year),
43:         Part(partNumber)
44:     {}
45:
46:
47:     // *************** AirPlane Part ************
48:
49:     class AirPlanePart : public Part
50:     {
51:     public:
52:         AirPlanePart():itsEngineNumber(1){};
53:         AirPlanePart(USHORT EngineNumber, ULONG PartNumber);
54:         virtual void Display() const{ Part::Display(); cout << "Engine No.: " <<
            ➥itsEngineNumber << endl;  }
55:     private:
56:         USHORT itsEngineNumber;
57:     };
58:
59:     AirPlanePart::AirPlanePart(USHORT EngineNumber, ULONG PartNumber):
60:         itsEngineNumber(EngineNumber),
61:         Part(PartNumber)
62:     {}
63:
```

```
64:     // *************** Part Node ************
65:     class PartNode
66:     {
67:     public:
68:        PartNode (Part*);
69:        ~PartNode();
70:        void SetNext(PartNode * node) { itsNext = node; }
71:        PartNode * GetNext() const;
72:        Part * GetPart() const;
73:     private:
74:        Part *itsPart;
75:        PartNode * itsNext;
76:     };
77:
78:
79:     // *************** Part List ************
80:     class PartsList
81:     {
82:     public:
83:        PartsList();
84:        ~PartsList();
85:        // needs copy constructor and operator equals!
86:        void      Iterate(void (Part::*f)()const) const;
87:        Part*     Find(ULONG & position, ULONG PartNumber)  const;
88:        Part*     GetFirst() const;
89:        void      Insert(Part *);
90:        Part*     operator[](ULONG) const;
91:        ULONG     GetCount() const { return itsCount; }
92:        static    PartsList& GetGlobalPartsList() { return  GlobalPartsList; }
93:     private:
94:        PartNode * pHead;
95:        ULONG itsCount;
96:        static PartsList GlobalPartsList;
97:     };
98:
99:     PartsList PartsList::GlobalPartsList;
100:
101:    class PartsCatalog
102:    {
103:    public:
104:       void Insert(Part *);
105:       ULONG Exists(ULONG PartNumber);
106:       Part * Get(int PartNumber);
107:       operator+(const PartsCatalog &);
108:       void ShowAll() { thePartsList.Iterate(Part::Display); }
109:    private:
110:       PartsList thePartsList;
111:    };
112:
113:    void PartsCatalog::Insert(Part * newPart)
114:    {
115:       ULONG partNumber =  newPart->GetPartNumber();
116:       ULONG offset;
117:
118:       if (!thePartsList.Find(offset, partNumber))
```

continues

461

Listing 15.5. continued

```
119:
120:            thePartsList.Insert(newPart);
121:      else
122:      {
123:          cout << partNumber << " was the ";
124:          switch (offset)
125:          {
126:             case 0:  cout << "first "; break;
127:             case 1:  cout << "second "; break;
128:             case 2:  cout << "third "; break;
129:             default: cout << offset+1 << "th ";
130:          }
131:          cout << "entry. Rejected!\n";
132:      }
133:  }
134:
135:  ULONG PartsCatalog::Exists(ULONG PartNumber)
136:  {
137:     ULONG offset;
138:     thePartsList.Find(offset,PartNumber);
139:         return offset;
140:  }
141:
142:  Part * PartsCatalog::Get(int PartNumber)
143:  {
144:     ULONG offset;
145:     Part * thePart = thePartsList.Find(offset, PartNumber);
146:     return thePart;
147:  }
148:
149:  void main()
150:  {
151:     PartsCatalog pc;
152:     Part * pPart = 0;
153:     ULONG PartNumber;
154:     USHORT value;
155:     ULONG choice;
156:
157:     while (1)
158:     {
159:        cout << "(0)Quit (1)Car (2)Plane: ";
160:        cin >> choice;
161:
162:        if (!choice)
163:           break;
164:
165:        cout << "New PartNumber?: ";
166:        cin >>  PartNumber;
167:
168:        if (choice == 1)
169:        {
170:           cout << "Model Year?: ";
171:           cin >> value;
172:           pPart = new CarPart(value,PartNumber);
```

```
173:        }
174:        else
175:        {
176:            cout << "Engine Number?: ";
177:            cin >> value;
178:            pPart = new AirPlanePart(value,PartNumber);
179:        }
180:        pc.Insert(pPart);
181:    }
182:    pc.ShowAll();
183: }
```

```
(0)Quit (1)Car (2)Plane:  1
New Part Number?: 1234
Model Year?: 94
(0)Quit (1)Car (2)Plane:  1
New Part Number?: 4434
Model Year?: 93
(0)Quit (1)Car (2)Plane:  1
New Part Number?: 1234
Model Year?: 94
1234 was the first entry. Rejected!
(0)Quit (1)Car (2)Plane:  1
New Part Number?: 2345
Model Year?: 93
(0)Quit (1)Car (2)Plane:  0

Part Number: 1234
Model Year: 94

Part Number: 2345
Model Year: 93

Part Number: 4434
Model Year: 93
```

Listing 15.7 reproduces the interface to the Part, PartNode, and PartList classes from Week 2 in Review, but to save room it does not reproduce the implementation of their methods.

A new class, PartsCatalog, is declared on lines 101–111. PartsCatalog has a PartsList as its data member, to which it delegates list management. Another way to say this is that the PartsCatalog is implemented in terms of this PartsList.

Note that clients of the PartsCatalog do not have access to the PartsList directly. The interface is through the PartsCatalog, and as such the behavior of the PartsList is dramatically changed. For example, the PartsCatalog::Insert() method does not allow duplicate entries into the PartsList.

The implementation of PartsCatalog::Insert() starts on line 113. The Part that is passed in as a parameter is asked for the value of its itsPartNumber member variable. This value is fed to the `PartsList`'s `Find()` method, and if no match is found the number is inserted; otherwise an informative error message is printed.

Note that `PartsCatalog` does the actual insert by calling `Insert()` on its member variable, `pl`, which is a `PartsList`. The mechanics of the actual insertion, the maintenance of the linked list, as well as searching and retrieving from the linked list, is maintained in the contained `PartsList` member of `PartsCatalog`. There is no reason for `PartsCatalog` to reproduce this code; it can take full advantage of the well-defined interface.

This is the essence of reusability within C++: `PartsCatalog` can reuse the `PartsList` code, and the designer of `PartsCatalog` is free to ignore the implementation details of `PartsList`. The interface to `PartsList` (that is, the class declaration) provides all the information needed by the designer of the `PartsCatalog` class.

Private Inheritance

If `PartsCatalog` needed access to the protected members of `LinkedList` (in this case there are none), or needed to override any of the `LinkedList` methods, then `PartsCatalog` would be forced to inherit from `PartsList`.

Since a `PartsCatalog` is not a `PartsList` object, and since you don't want to expose the entire set of functionality of `PartsList` to clients of `PartsCatalog`, you need to use private inheritance.

The first thing to know about private inheritance is that all of the base member variables and functions are treated as if they were declared to be private, regardless of their actual access level in the base. Thus, to any function that is not a member function of `PartsCatalog`, every function inherited from `PartsList` is inaccessible. This is critical: private inheritance does not involve inheriting interface, just implementation.

To clients of the `PartsCatalog` class, the `PartsList` class is invisible. None of its interface is available: you can't call any of its methods. You can call `PartsCatalog` methods, however, and they can access all of `LinkedLists`, because they are derived from `LinkedLists`.

The important thing here is that the `PartsCatalog` isn't a `PartsList`, as would have been implied by public inheritance. It is implemented in terms of a `PartsList`, just as would have been the case with containment. The private inheritance is just a convenience.

Listing 15.6 demonstrates the use of private inheritance by rewriting the `PartsCatalog` class as privately derived from `PartsList`.

Note: To compile this program, copy lines 1–100 from Listing 15.5 to the top of this listing.

Listing 15.6. Private inheritance.

```
1:   //listing 15.6 demonstrates private inheritance
2:
3:   //rewrites PartsCatalog from listing 15.7
4:
5:   //see attached notes on compiling
6:
7:      class PartsCatalog : private PartsList
8:      {
9:      public:
10:        void Insert(Part *);
11:        ULONG Exists(ULONG PartNumber);
12:        Part * Get(int PartNumber);
13:        operator+(const PartsCatalog &);
14:        void ShowAll() { Iterate(Part::Display); }
15:      private:
16:      };
17:
18:      void PartsCatalog::Insert(Part * newPart)
19:      {
20:        ULONG partNumber =  newPart->GetPartNumber();
21:        ULONG offset;
22:
23:        if (!Find(offset, partNumber))
24:           PartsList::Insert(newPart);
25:        else
26:        {
27:           cout << partNumber << " was the ";
28:           switch (offset)
29:           {
30:              case 0:  cout << "first "; break;
31:              case 1:  cout << "second "; break;
32:              case 2:  cout << "third "; break;
33:              default: cout << offset+1 << "th ";
34:           }
35:           cout << "entry. Rejected!\n";
36:        }
37:      }
38:
39:      ULONG PartsCatalog::Exists(ULONG PartNumber)
40:      {
41:        ULONG offset;
42:        Find(offset,PartNumber);
43:        return offset;
44:      }
45:
```

continues

Listing 15.6. continued

```
46:    Part * PartsCatalog::Get(int PartNumber)
47:    {
48:       ULONG offset;
49:       return (Find(offset, PartNumber));
50:
51:    }
52:
53:    void main()
54:    {
55:       PartsCatalog pc;
56:       Part * pPart = 0;
57:       ULONG PartNumber;
58:       USHORT value;
59:       ULONG choice;
60:
61:       while (1)
62:       {
63:          cout << "(0)Quit (1)Car (2)Plane: ";
64:          cin >> choice;
65:
66:          if (!choice)
67:             break;
68:
69:          cout << "New PartNumber?: ";
70:          cin >>  PartNumber;
71:
72:          if (choice == 1)
73:          {
74:             cout << "Model Year?: ";
75:             cin >> value;
76:             pPart = new CarPart(value,PartNumber);
77:          }
78:          else
79:          {
80:             cout << "Engine Number?: ";
81:             cin >> value;
82:             pPart = new AirPlanePart(value,PartNumber);
83:          }
84:          pc.Insert(pPart);
85:       }
86:       pc.ShowAll();
87:    }
```

```
(0)Quit (1)Car (2)Plane:  1
New Part Number?: 1234
Model Year?: 94
(0)Quit (1)Car (2)Plane:  1
New Part Number?: 4434
Model Year?: 93
(0)Quit (1)Car (2)Plane:  1
New Part Number?: 1234
Model Year?: 94
```

```
1234 was the first entry. Rejected!
(0)Quit (1)Car (2)Plane: 1
New Part Number?: 2345
Model Year?: 93
(0)Quit (1)Car (2)Plane:  0

Part Number: 1234
Model Year: 94

Part Number: 2345
Model Year: 93

Part Number: 4434
Model Year: 93
```

Analysis Listing 15.6 shows only the changed interface to `PartsCatalog` and the rewritten driver program. The interfaces to the other classes are unchanged from Listing 15.5.

On line 7 of Listing 15.6, `PartsCatalog` is declared to derive privately from `PartsList`. The interface to `PartsCatalog` doesn't change from Listing 15.5, though of course it no longer needs an object of type `PartsList` as member data.

The `PartsCatalog` `ShowAll()` function calls `PartsList` `Iterate()` with the appropriate pointer to member function of class `Part`. `ShowAll()` acts as a public interface to `Iterate()`, providing the correct information but preventing client classes from calling `Iterate()` directly. Although `PartsList` might allow other functions to be passed to `Iterate()`, `PartsCatalog` does not.

The `Insert()` function has changed as well. Note, on line 23, that `Find()` is now called directly, because it is inherited from the base class. The call on line 24 to `Insert()` must be fully qualified, of course, or it would endlessly recurse into itself.

In short, when methods of `PartsCatalog` want to call `PartsList` methods, they may do so directly. The only exception is when `PartsCatalog` has overridden the method and the `PartsList` version is needed, in which case the function name must be qualified fully.

Private inheritance allows the `PartsCatalog` to inherit what it can use, but still provide mediated access to `Insert` and other methods to which client classes should not have direct access.

DO	DON'T

DO inherit publicly when the derived object *is a* kind of the base class.

DO use containment when you want to delegate functionality to another class, but you don't need access to its protected members.

> **DO** use private inheritance when you need to implement one class in terms of another, and you need access to the base class's protected members.
>
> **DON'T** use private inheritance when you need to use more than one of the base class. You must use containment. For example, if PartsCatalog needed two PartsLists, you could not have used private inheritance.
>
> **DON'T** use public inheritance when members of the base class should not be available to clients of the derived class.

Friend Classes

Sometimes you will create classes together, as a set. For example, PartNode and PartsList were tightly coupled, and it would have been convenient if PartsList could have read PartNode's Part pointer, itsPart, directly.

You wouldn't want to make itsPart public, or even protected, because this is an implementation detail of PartNode and you want to keep it private. You do want to expose it to PartsList, however.

If you want to expose your private member data or functions to another class, you must declare that class to be a *friend*. This extends the interface of your class to include the friend class.

Once PartsNode declares PartsList to be a friend, all of PartsNode's member data and functions are public as far as PartsList is concerned.

It is important to note that friendship cannot be transferred. Just because you are my friend and Joe is your friend doesn't mean Joe is *my* friend. Friendship is not inherited either. Again, just because you are my friend and I'm willing to share my secrets with you doesn't mean I'm willing to share my secrets with your children.

Finally, friendship is not commutative. Assigning Class One to be a friend of Class Two does not make Class Two a friend of Class One. Just because you are willing to tell me your secrets doesn't mean I am willing to tell you mine.

Listing 15.7 illustrates friendship by rewriting the example from Listing 15.6, making PartsList a friend of PartNode. Note that this does not make PartNode a friend of PartsList.

> **Note:** To compile this program insert lines 7–63 from Listing 15.6 between lines 5 and 6.

Listing 15.7. Friend class illustrated.

```
1:      #include <iostreams.h>
2:
3:      typedef unsigned long ULONG;
4:      typedef unsigned short USHORT;
5:
6:
7:      class PartsList;
8:
9:      // *************** Part Node ************
10:     class PartNode
11:     {
12:     public:
13:         friend class PartsList;
14:         PartNode (Part*);
15:         ~PartNode();
16:         void SetNext(PartNode * node) { itsNext = node; }
17:         PartNode * GetNext() const;
18:         Part * GetPart() const;
19:     private:
20:         Part *itsPart;
21:         PartNode * itsNext;
22:     };
23:
24:     // *************** Part List ************
25:     class PartsList
26:     {
27:     public:
28:         PartsList();
29:         ~PartsList();
30:         // needs copy constructor and operator equals!
31:         void     Iterate(void (Part::*f)()const) const;
32:         Part*     Find(ULONG & position, ULONG PartNumber)  const;
33:         Part*    GetFirst() const;
34:         void      Insert(Part *);
35:         Part*    operator[](ULONG) const;
36:         ULONG    GetCount() const { return itsCount; }
37:         static    PartsList& GetGlobalPartsList() { return  GlobalPartsList;}
38:     private:
39:         PartNode * pHead;
40:         ULONG itsCount;
41:         static PartsList GlobalPartsList;
42:     };
43:
44:     PartsList PartsList::GlobalPartsList;
```

continues

Listing 15.7. continued

```
45:
46:    // Implementations for Lists...
47:
48:    PartsList::PartsList():
49:       pHead(0),
50:       itsCount(0)
51:       {}
52:
53:    PartsList::~PartsList()
54:    {
55:       delete pHead;
56:    }
57:
58:    Part*   PartsList::GetFirst() const
59:    {
60:       if (pHead)
61:          return pHead->itsPart;
62:       else
63:          return NULL;  // error catch here
64:    }
65:
66:    Part *  PartsList::operator[](ULONG offSet) const
67:    {
68:       PartNode* pNode = pHead;
69:
70:       if (!pHead)
71:          return NULL; // error catch here
72:
73:       if (offSet > itsCount)
74:          return NULL; // error
75:
76:       for (ULONG i=0;i<offSet; i++)
77:          pNode = pNode->itsNext;
78:
79:       return   pNode->itsPart;
80:    }
81:
82:    Part*   PartsList::Find(ULONG & position, ULONG PartNumber)  const
83:    {
84:       PartNode * pNode = 0;
85:       for (pNode = pHead, position = 0;
86:             pNode!=NULL;
87:             pNode = pNode->itsNext, position++)
88:       {
89:          if (pNode->itsPart->GetPartNumber() == PartNumber)
90:             break;
91:       }
92:       if (pNode == NULL)
93:          return NULL;
94:       else
95:          return pNode->itsPart;
96:    }
97:
98:    void PartsList::Iterate(void (Part::*func)()const) const
```

```
99:     {
100:        if (!pHead)
101:            return;
102:        PartNode* pNode = pHead;
103:        do
104:            (pNode->itsPart->*func)();
105:        while (pNode = pNode->itsNext);
106:     }
107:
108:    void PartsList::Insert(Part* pPart)
109:    {
110:        PartNode * pNode = new PartNode(pPart);
111:        PartNode * pCurrent = pHead;
112:        PartNode * pNext = 0;
113:
114:        ULONG New =  pPart->GetPartNumber();
115:        ULONG Next = 0;
116:        itsCount++;
117:
118:        if (!pHead)
119:        {
120:            pHead = pNode;
121:            return;
122:        }
123:
124:        // if this one is smaller than head
125:        // this one is the new head
126:        if (pHead->itsPart->GetPartNumber() > New)
127:        {
128:            pNode->itsNext = pHead;
129:            pHead = pNode;
130:            return;
131:        }
132:
133:        for (;;)
134:        {
135:            // if there is no next, append this new one
136:            if (!pCurrent->itsNext)
137:            {
138:                pCurrent->itsNext = pNode;
139:                return;
140:            }
141:
142:            // if this goes after this one and before the next
143:            // then insert it here, otherwise get the next
144:            pNext = pCurrent->itsNext;
145:            Next = pNext->itsPart->GetPartNumber();
146:            if (Next > New)
147:            {
148:                pCurrent->itsNext = pNode;
149:                pNode->itsNext = pNext;
150:                return;
151:            }
152:            pCurrent = pNext;
153:        }
```

continues

471

Listing 15.7. continued

```
154:    }
155:
156:    class PartsCatalog : private PartsList
157:    {
158:    public:
159:        void Insert(Part *);
160:        ULONG Exists(ULONG PartNumber);
161:        Part * Get(int PartNumber);
162:        operator+(const PartsCatalog &);
163:        void ShowAll() { Iterate(Part::Display); }
164:    private:
165:    };
166:
167:    void PartsCatalog::Insert(Part * newPart)
168:    {
169:        ULONG partNumber = newPart->GetPartNumber();
170:        ULONG offset;
171:
172:        if (!Find(offset, partNumber))
173:            PartsList::Insert(newPart);
174:        else
175:        {
176:            cout << partNumber << " was the ";
177:            switch (offset)
178:            {
179:                case 0:  cout << "first "; break;
180:                case 1:  cout << "second "; break;
181:                case 2:  cout << "third "; break;
182:                default: cout << offset+1 << "th ";
183:            }
184:            cout << "entry. Rejected!\n";
185:        }
186:    }
187:
188:    ULONG PartsCatalog::Exists(ULONG PartNumber)
189:    {
190:        ULONG offset;
191:        Find(offset,PartNumber);
192:        return offset;
193:    }
194:
195:    Part * PartsCatalog::Get(int PartNumber)
196:    {
197:        ULONG offset;
198:        return (Find(offset, PartNumber));
199:
200:    }
201:
202:    void main()
203:    {
204:        PartsCatalog pc;
205:        Part * pPart = 0;
206:        ULONG PartNumber;
207:        USHORT value;
```

```
208:        ULONG choice;
209:
210:        while (1)
211:        {
212:            cout << "(0)Quit (1)Car (2)Plane: ";
213:            cin >> choice;
214:
215:            if (!choice)
216:                break;
217:
218:            cout << "New PartNumber?: ";
219:            cin >>  PartNumber;
220:
221:            if (choice == 1)
222:            {
223:                cout << "Model Year?: ";
224:                cin >> value;
225:                pPart = new CarPart(value,PartNumber);
226:            }
227:            else
228:            {
229:                cout << "Engine Number?: ";
230:                cin >> value;
231:                pPart = new AirPlanePart(value,PartNumber);
232:            }
233:            pc.Insert(pPart);
234:        }
235:        pc.ShowAll();
236:    }
```

```
(0)Quit (1)Car (2)Plane:   1
New Part Number?: 1234
Model Year?: 94
(0)Quit (1)Car (2)Plane:   1
New Part Number?: 4434
Model Year?: 93
(0)Quit (1)Car (2)Plane:   1
New Part Number?: 1234
Model Year?: 94
1234 was the first entry. Rejected!
(0)Quit (1)Car (2)Plane:   1
New Part Number?: 2345
Model Year?: 93
(0)Quit (1)Car (2)Plane:   0

Part Number: 1234
Model Year: 94

Part Number: 2345
Model Year: 93

Part Number: 4434
Model Year: 93
```

Analysis Listing 15.7 shows only the changed interface to Listing 15.8; that is, the changes to PartNode and PartsList.

On line 13, the class PartsList is declared to be a friend to the PartNode class. Because PartsList has not yet been declared, the compiler would complain that this type is not known. On line 7, the PartsList name is declared to the compiler without a full declaration of the class. This is known as a forward declaration and is how you say to the compiler, "I'm about to use the name PartsList; that is a class name and I'll declare it in just a moment, I promise."

This listing places the friend declaration in the public section, but this is not required; it can be put anywhere in the class declaration without changing the meaning of the statement. Because of this statement, all the private member data and functions are available to any member function of class PartsList.

On line 61, the implementation of the member function GetFirst() reflects this change. Rather than returning pHead->GetPart, this function can now return the otherwise private member data by writing pHead->itsPart. Similarly, the Insert() function can now write pNode->itsNext = pHead, rather than writing pNode->SetNext(pHead).

Admittedly these are trivial changes, and there is not a good enough reason to make PartsList a friend of PartNode, but they do serve to illustrate how the keyword friend works.

Declarations of friend classes should be used with extreme caution. If two classes are inextricably entwined, and one must frequently access data in the other, there may be good reason to use this declaration. But use it sparingly; it is often just as easy to use the public accessor methods, and doing so allows you to change one class without having to recompile the other.

> **Note:** You will often hear novice C++ programmers complain that friend declarations "undermine" the encapsulation so important to object-oriented programming. This is, frankly, errant nonsense. The friend declaration makes the declared friend part of the class interface, and is no more an undermining of encapsulation than is public derivation.

Syntax

Friend Class

Declare one class to be a friend of another by putting the word `friend` into the class granting the access rights. That is, I can declare you to be my friend, but you can't declare yourself to be my friend.

Example:

```
class PartNode{
public:
    friend class PartList;  // declares PartList to be a friend of PartNode
};
```

Friend Functions

At times you will want to grant this level of access not to an entire class, but only to one or two functions of that class. You can do this by declaring the member functions of the other class to be friends, rather than declaring the entire class to be a friend. In fact, you can declare any function, whether or not it is a member function of another class, to be a friend function.

Friend Functions and Operator Overloading

Listing 15.1 provided a `String` class that overrode the `operator+`. It also provided a constructor that took a constant character pointer, so that string objects could be created from C-style strings. This allowed you to create a string and add to it with a C-style string.

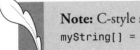

> **Note:** C-style strings are null-terminated character arrays, such as `char myString[] = "Hello World."`

What you could not do, however, was to create a C-style string (a character string) and add to it using a string object, as shown in this example:

```
char cString[] = {"Hello"};
String sString(" World");
String sStringTwo = cString + sString;  //error!
```

C-style strings don't have an overloaded operator+. As discussed on Day 10, when you say cString + sString; what you are really calling is cString.operator+(sString). Since you can't call operator+() on a C-style string, this causes a compile-time error.

You can solve this problem by declaring a friend function in String, which overloads operator+ but takes two string objects. The C-style string will be converted to a string object by the appropriate constructor, and then operator+ will be called using the two string objects.

Listing 15.8. Friendly operator+.

```
1:     //Listing 15.8 - friendly operators
2:
3:     #include <iostreams.h>
4:     #include <string.h>
5:
6:     // Rudimentary string class
7:     class String
8:     {
9:        public:
10:           // constructors
11:           String();
12:           String(const char *const);
13:           String(const String &);
14:           ~String();
15:
16:           // overloaded operators
17:           char & operator[](int offset);
18:           char operator[](int offset) const;
19:           String operator+(const String&);
20:           friend String operator+(const String&, const String&);
21:           void operator+=(const String&);
22:           String & operator= (const String &);
23:
24:           // General accessors
25:           int GetLen()const { return itsLen; }
26:           const char * GetString() const { return itsString; }
27:
28:        private:
29:           String (int);        // private constructor
30:           char * itsString;
31:           unsigned short itsLen;
32:     };
33:
34:     // creates a new string by adding current
35:     // string to rhs
36:     String String::operator+(const String& rhs)
37:     {
38:        int  totalLen = itsLen + rhs.GetLen();
39:        String temp(totalLen);
40:        for (int i = 0; i<itsLen; i++)
41:           temp[i] = itsString[i];
42:        for (int j = 0; j<rhs.GetLen(); j++, i++)
```

```
43:             temp[i] = rhs[j];
44:         temp[totalLen]='\0';
45:         return temp;
46:     }
47:
48:     // creates a new string by adding
49:     // one string to another
50:     String operator+(const String& lhs, const String& rhs)
51:     {
52:         int  totalLen = lhs.GetLen() + rhs.GetLen();
53:         String temp(totalLen);
54:         for (int i = 0; i<lhs.GetLen(); i++)
55:             temp[i] = lhs[i];
56:         for (int j = 0; j<rhs.GetLen(); j++, i++)
57:             temp[i] = rhs[j];
58:         temp[totalLen]='\0';
59:         return temp;
60:     }
61:
62:     void main()
63:     {
64:         String s1("String One ");
65:         String s2("String Two ");
66:         char *c1 = { "C-String One " } ;
67:         String s3;
68:         String s4;
69:         String s5;
70:
71:         cout << "s1: " << s1.GetString() << endl;
72:         cout << "s2: " << s2.GetString() << endl;
73:         cout << "c1: " << c1 << endl;
74:         s3 = s1 + s2;
75:         cout << "s3: " << s3.GetString() << endl;
76:         s4 = s1 + c1;
77:         cout << "s4: " << s4.GetString() << endl;
78:         s5 = c1 + s1;
79:         cout << "s5: " << s5.GetString() << endl;
80:     }
```

Output

```
s1: String One
s2: String Two
c1: C-String One
s3: String One String Two
s4: String One C-String One
s5: C-String One String Two
```

Analysis The implementation of all of the string methods except operator+ are unchanged
from Listing 15.1, and so are left out of this listing. On line 20, a new operator+
is overloaded to take two constant string references and to return a string, and this
function is declared to be a friend.

Note that this operator+ is not a member function of this or any other class. It is declared within the declaration of the String class only so that it can be made a friend, but because it is declared no other function prototype is needed.

The implementation of this operator+ is on lines 50–60. Note that it is similar to the earlier operator+, except that it takes two strings and accesses them both through their public accessor methods.

The driver program demonstrates the use of this function on line 78, where operator+ is now called on a C-style string!

Syntax

Friend Functions

Declare a function to be a friend by using the keyword friend and then the full specification of the function. Declaring a function to be a friend does not give the friend function access to your this pointer, but it does provide full access to all private and protected member data and functions.

Example

```
class PartNode
{
    friend void PartsList::Insert(Part *);  // make another class's member function a
    ➥friend
    friend int SomeFunction();               // make a global function a friend };
```

Overloading the Insertion Operator

You are finally ready to give your String class the ability to use cout like any other type. Until now, when you've wanted to print a string, you've been forced to write the following:

```
cout << theString.GetString();
```

What you would like to do is write this:

```
cout << theString;
```

To accomplish this, you must override operator<<(). On Day 18, you will see all the ins and outs (cins and couts?) of working with iostreams; for now Listing 15.9 illustrates how operator<< can be overloaded using a friend function.

Listing 15.9. Overloading operator<<().

```
1:      #include <iostreams.h>
2:      #include <string.h>
3:
4:      class String
5:      {
6:        public:
7:          // constructors
8:          String();
9:           String(const char *const);
10:           String(const String &);
11:          ~String();
12:
13:          // overloaded operators
14:          char & operator[](int offset);
15:          char operator[](int offset) const;
16:          String operator+(const String&);
17:          void operator+=(const String&);
18:          String & operator= (const String &);
19:          friend ostream& operator<<( ostream& theStream,String& theString);
20:          // General accessors
21:          int GetLen()const { return itsLen; }
22:          const char * GetString() const { return itsString; }
23:          // static int ConstructorCount;
24:
25:        private:
26:          String (int);            // private constructor
27:          char * itsString;
28:          unsigned short itsLen;
29:
30:      };
31:
32:      ostream& operator<<( ostream& theStream,String& theString)
33:      {
34:          theStream << theString.GetString();
35:          return theStream;
36:      }
37:      void main()
38:      {
39:          String theString("Hello world.");
40:          cout << theString;
41:      }
```

```
Hello world.
```

To save space, the implementation of all of String's methods is left out, as they are unchanged from the previous examples.

On line 19, `operator<<` is declared to be a friend function that takes an `ostream` reference and a `String` reference and returns an `ostream` reference. Note that this is not a member function of `String`. It returns a reference to an `ostream` so that you can concatenate calls to `operator<<`, such as this:

```
cout << "myAge: " << itsAge << " years.";
```

The implementation of this friend function is on lines 32–35. All this really does is hide the implementation details of feeding the string to the `ostream`, and that is just as it should be. You'll see more about overloading this operator and `operator>>` on Day 18.

Summary

Today you saw how to delegate functionality to a contained object. You also saw how to implement one class in terms of another by using either containment or private inheritance. Containment is restricted in that the new class does not have access to the protected members of the contained class, and it cannot override the member functions of the contained object. Containment is simpler to use than private inheritance, and should be used when possible.

You also saw how to declare both friend functions and friend classes. Using a friend function, you saw how to overload the extraction operator, to allow your new classes to use `cout` just as the built-in classes do.

Remember that public inheritance expresses *is-a*, containment expresses *has-a* and private inheritance expresses *implemented in terms of*. The relationship *delegates to* can be expressed using either containment or private inheritance, though containment is more common.

Q&A

Q Why is it so important to distinguish between *is-a*, *has-a*, and *implemented in terms of*?

A The point of C++ is to implement well designed, object-oriented programs. Keeping these relationships straight helps to ensure that your design corresponds to the reality of what you are modeling. Furthermore, a well understood design will more likely be reflected in well designed code.

15

Q Why is containment preferred over private inheritance?

A The challenge in modern programming is to cope with complexity. The more you can use objects as black boxes, the fewer details you have to worry about and the more complexity you can manage. Contained classes hide their details; private inheritance exposes the implementation details.

Q Why not make all classes friends of all the classes they use?

A Making one class a friend of another exposes the implementation details and reduces encapsulation. The ideal is to keep as many of the details of each class hidden from all other classes as possible.

Q If a function is overloaded, do you need to declare each form of the function to be a friend?

A Yes, if you overload a function and declare it to be a friend of another class, you must declare friend for each form that you wish to grant this access to.

Workshop

The Workshop contains quiz questions to help solidify your understanding of the material covered and exercises to provide you with experience in using what you've learned. Try to answer the quiz and exercise questions before checking the answers in Appendix D, and make sure you understand the answers before going to the next chapter.

Quiz

1. How do you establish an *is-a* relationship?

2. How do you establish a *has-a* relationship?

3. What is the difference between containment and delegation?

4. What is the difference between delegation and implemented in terms of?

5. What is a friend function?

6. What is a friend class?

7. If Dog is a friend of Boy, is Boy a friend of Dog?

8. If Dog is a friend of Boy, and Terrier derives from Dog, is Terrier a friend of Boy?

9. If Dog is a friend of Boy and Boy is a friend of House, is Dog a friend of House?

10. Where must the declaration of a friend function appear?

Exercises

1. Show the declaration of a class, Animal, that contains a datamember that is a string object.

2. Show the declaration of a class BoundedArray that *is* an array.

3. Show the declaration of a class, Set, that is declared in terms of an array.

4. Modify Listing 15.11 to provide the String class with an extraction operator (>>).

5. **BUG BUSTER:** What is wrong with this program?

```
1:      #include <iostream.h>
2:
3:      class Animal;
4:
5:      void setValue(Animal& , int);
6:
7:
8:      class Animal
9:      {
10:     public:
11:         int GetWeight()const { return itsWeight; }
12:         int GetAge() const { return itsAge; }
13:     private:
14:         int itsWeight;
15:         int itsAge;
16:     };
17:
18:     void setValue(Animal& theAnimal, int theWeight)
19:     {
20:         friend class Animal;
21:         theAnimal.itsWeight = theWeight;
22:     }
23:
24:     void main()
```

```
25:     {
26:         Animal peppy;
27:         setValue(peppy,5);
28:     }
```

6. Fix the listing in Exercise 5 so it compiles.

7. **BUG BUSTERS:** What is wrong with this code?

```
1:      #include <iostream.h>
2:
3:      class Animal;
4:
5:      void setValue(Animal& , int);
6:      void setValue(Animal& ,int,int);
7:
8:      class Animal
9:      {
10:     friend void setValue(Animal& ,int);
11:     private:
12:         int itsWeight;
13:         int itsAge;
14:     };
15:
16:     void setValue(Animal& theAnimal, int theWeight)
17:     {
18:         theAnimal.itsWeight = theWeight;
19:     }
20:
21:
22:     void setValue(Animal& theAnimal, int theWeight, int ➥theAge)
23:     {
24:         theAnimal.itsWeight = theWeight;
25:         theAnimal.itsAge = theAge;
26:     }
27:
28:     void main()
29:     {
30:         Animal peppy;
31:         setValue(peppy,5);
```

```
32:        setValue(peppy,7,9);
33:    }
```

8. Fix Exercise 7 so it compiles.

16

Streams

WEEK
3

Until now, you've been using `cout` to write to the screen and `cin` to read from the keyboard without a full understanding of how they work. Today, you learn:

☐ What streams are and how they are used.

☐ How to manage input and output using streams.

☐ How to write to and read from files using streams.

Overview of Streams

C++ does not, as part of the language, define how data is written to the screen or to a file, nor how data is read into a program. These are clearly essential parts of working with C++, however, and the standard C++ library now includes the `iostream` library, which facilitates input and output (I/O).

The advantage of having the input and output kept apart from the language and handled in libraries is that it is easier to make the language "platform-independent." That is, you can write C++ programs on a PC and then recompile them and run them on a Sun Workstation. The compiler manufacturer just supplies the right library, and everything works. At least that's the theory.

> **Note:** A library is a collection of .OBJ files which can be linked to your program to provide additional functionality. This is the most basic form of code reuse, and has been around since ancient programmers chiseled 1s and 0s into the walls of caves.

Encapsulation

The `iostream` classes view the flow of data from your program to the screen as being a stream of data, one byte following another. If the destination of the stream is a file or the screen, the source is usually some part of your program. If the stream is reversed, the data can come from the keyboard or a disk file and be "poured" into your data variables.

One principal goal of streams is to encapsulate the problems of getting the data to and from the disk or the screen. Once a stream is created, your program works with the stream and the stream sweats the details. Figure 16.1 illustrates this fundamental idea.

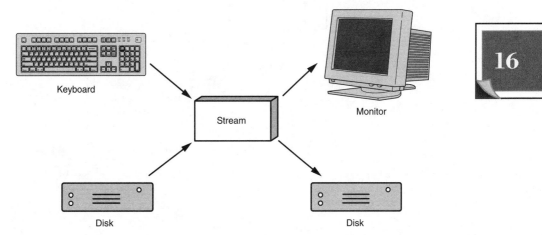

Figure 16.1. *Encapsulation through streams.*

Buffering

Writing to the disk (and to a lesser extent the screen) is very "expensive." It takes a long time (relatively speaking) to write data to the disk or to read data from the disk, and execution of the program is generally blocked by disk writes and reads. To solve this problem, streams provide "buffering." Data is written into the stream, but it is not written back out to the disk immediately. Instead, the stream's buffer fills and fills and when it is full it writes to the disk all at once.

Picture water trickling into the top of a tank, and the tank filling and filling, but no water running out the bottom. Figure 16.2 illustrates this idea.

When the water (data) reaches the top, the valve opens and all the water flows out in a rush. Figure 16.3 illustrates this.

Once the buffer is empty, the bottom valve closes, the top valve opens, and more water flows into the buffer tank. Figure 16.4 illustrates this.

Every once in a while you need to get the water out of the tank even before it is full. This is called "flushing the buffer." Figure 16.5 illustrates this idea.

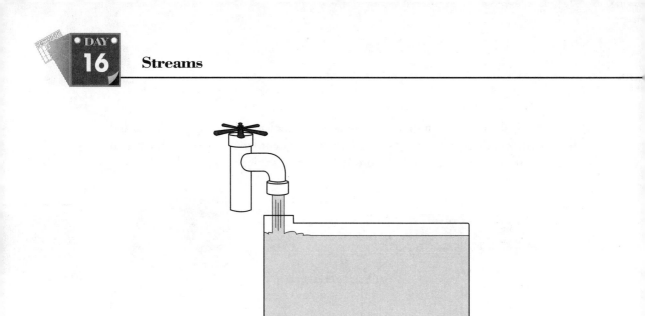

Figure 16.2. *Filling the buffer.*

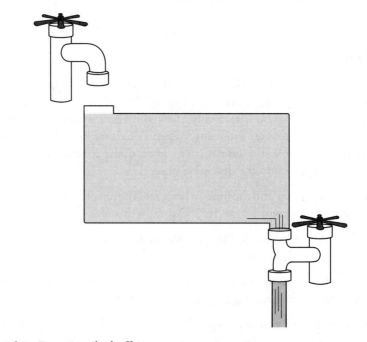

Figure 16.3. *Emptying the buffer.*

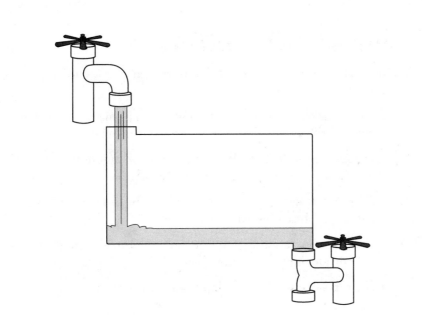

Figure 16.4. *Refilling the buffer.*

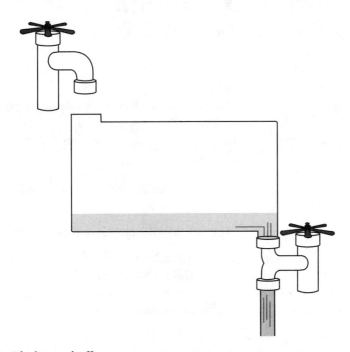

Figure 16.5. *Flushing a buffer.*

Streams and Buffers

As you might expect, C++ takes an object-oriented view toward implementing streams and buffers.

☐ The streambuf class manages the buffer and its member functions provide the ability to fill, empty, flush, and otherwise manipulate the buffer.

☐ The ios class is the base class to the input and output stream classes. The ios class *has* a streambuf object as a member variable.

☐ The istream and ostream classes derive from the ios class and specialize input and output stream behavior, respectively.

☐ The iostream class is derived from both the istream and the ostream classes and provides input and output methods for writing to the screen.

☐ The fstream classes provide input and output from files.

Standard I/O Objects

When a C++ program that includes the iostream classes starts, four objects are created and initialized:

> **Note:** The iostream class library is added automatically to your program by the compiler. All you need to do to use these functions is to put the appropriate include statement at the top of your program listing.

☐ cin (pronounced "see-in") handles input from the standard input, the keyboard.

☐ cout (pronounced "see-out") handles output to the standard output, the screen.

☐ cerr (pronounced "see-err") handles unbuffered output to the standard error device, the screen. Because this is unbuffered, everything sent to cerr is written to the standard error device immediately, without waiting for the buffer to fill or for a flush command to be received.

☐ clog (pronounced "see-log") handles buffered error messages that are output to the standard error device, the screen. It is common for this to be "redirected" to a log file, as described in the following section.

Redirection

Each of the standard devices, input, output, and error, can be *redirected* to other devices. Standard error is often redirected to a file, and standard input and output can be *piped* to files using operating system commands.

NEW **TERM** *Redirecting* refers to sending output (or input) to a place different than the default. The redirection operators for DOS and UNIX are (<) redirect input and (>) redirect output.

> *Piping* refers to using the output of one program as the input of another.

DOS provides rudimentary redirection commands such as *redirect output* (>) and *redirect input* (<). UNIX provides more advanced redirection capabilities, but the general idea is the same: take the output intended for the screen and write it to a file, or pipe it into another program. Alternatively, the input for a program can be extracted from a file rather than from the keyboard.

Redirection is more a function of the operating system than of the `iostream` libraries. C++ just provides access to the four standard devices; it is up to the user to redirect the devices to whatever alternatives are needed.

Input Using *cin*

The global object `cin` is responsible for input and is made available to your program when you include `iostream.h`. In previous examples, you used the overloaded extraction operator (>>) to put data into your program's variables. How does this work? The syntax, as you may remember, is the following:

```
int someVariable;
cout << "Enter a number: ";
cin >> someVariable;
```

The global object `cout` is discussed later today; for now, focus on the third line, `cin >> someVariable;`. What can you guess about `cin`?

Clearly it must be a global object, because you didn't define it in your own code. You know from previous operator experience that `cin` has overloaded the extraction operator (>>) and that the effect is to write whatever data `cin` has in its buffer into your local variable, `someVariable`.

What may not be immediately obvious is that `cin` has overloaded the extraction operator for a great variety of parameters, among them `int&`, `short&`, `long&`, `double&`, `float&`, `char&`, `char*`, and so forth. When you write `cin >> someVariable;`, the type of someVariable is assessed. In the example above, someVariable is an integer, so the following function is called:

```
istream & operator>> (int &)
```

Note that because the parameter is passed by reference, the extraction operator is able to act on the original variable. Listing 16.1 illustrates the use of cin.

Listing 16.1. cin handles different data types.

```
1:      //Listing 16.2 — character strings and cin
2:
3:      #include <iostream.h>
4:
5:      void main()
6:      {
7:          int myInt;
8:          long myLong;
9:          double myDouble;
10:         float myFloat;
11:         unsigned int myUnsigned;
12:
13:         cout << "int: ";
14:         cin >> myInt;
15:         cout << "Long: ";
16:         cin >> myLong;
17:         cout << "Double: ";
18:         cin >> myDouble;
19:         cout << "Float: ";
20:         cin >> myFloat;
21:         cout << "Unsigned: ";
22:         cin >> myUnsigned;
23:
24:         cout << "\n\nInt:\t" << myInt << endl;
25:         cout << "Long:\t" << myLong << endl;
26:         cout << "Double:\t" << myDouble << endl;
27:         cout << "Float:\t" << myFloat << endl;
28:         cout << "Unsigned:\t" << myUnsigned << endl;
29:     }
```

```
int: 2
Long: 70000
Double: 987654321
Float: 3.33
Unsigned: 25

Int:        2
Long:       70000
Double:     9.87654e+08
Float:      3.33
Unsigned:   25
```

On lines 7–11, variables of various types are declared. On lines 13–22, the user is prompted to enter values for these variables, and the results are printed (using cout) on lines 24–28.

The output reflects that the variables were put into the right "kinds" of variables, and the program works as you might expect.

Strings

cin can also handle character pointer (char*) arguments; thus, you can create a character buffer and use cin to fill it. For example, you can write this:

```
char YourName[50]
cout << "Enter your name: ";
cin >> YourName;
```

If you enter Jesse, the variable YourName will be filled with the characters 'J', 'e', 's', 's', 'e', '\0'. The last character is a NULL; cin automatically ends the string with a NULL, and you must have enough room in the buffer to allow for the entire string plus the NULL. The NULL signals "end of string" to the standard library functions discussed on Day 21.

String Problems

After all this success with cin, you might be surprised when you try to enter a full name into a string. cin believes that white space is a separator. When it sees a space or a new line it assumes the input for the parameter is complete, and in the case of strings it adds a NULL right then and there. Listing 16.2 illustrates this problem.

Listing 16.2. Trying to write more than one word to cin.

```
1:     //Listing 16.2 — character strings and cin
2:
3:     #include <iostream.h>
4:
5:     void main()
6:     {
7:         char YourName[50];
8:         cout << "Your first name: ";
9:         cin >> YourName;
10:        cout << "Here it is: " << YourName << endl;
11:        cout << "Your entire name: ";
12:        cin >> YourName;
13:        cout << "Here it is: " << YourName << endl;
14:    }
```

```
Your first name: Jesse
Here it is: Jesse
Your entire name: Jesse Liberty
Here it is: Jesse
```

On line 7, a character array is created to hold the user's input. On line 8, the user is prompted to enter one name, and that name is stored properly as shown in the output.

On line 11, the user is again prompted, this time for a full name. cin reads the input, and when it sees the space between the names, it puts a NULL after the first word and terminates input. This is not exactly what was intended.

To understand why this works this way, examine Listing 16.3, which shows input for a number of fields.

Listing 16.3. Multiple input.

```
1:      //Listing 16.2 - character strings and cin
2:
3:      #include <iostream.h>
4:
5:      void main()
6:      {
7:          int myInt;
8:          long myLong;
9:          double myDouble;
10:         float myFloat;
11:         unsigned int myUnsigned;
12:         char myWord[50];
13:
14:         cout << "int: ";
15:         cin >> myInt;
16:         cout << "Long: ";
17:         cin >> myLong;
18:         cout << "Double: ";
19:         cin >> myDouble;
20:         cout << "Float: ";
21:         cin >> myFloat;
22:         cout << "Word: ";
23:         cin >> myWord;
24:         cout << "Unsigned: ";
25:         cin >> myUnsigned;
26:
27:         cout << "\n\nInt:\t" << myInt << endl;
28:         cout << "Long:\t" << myLong << endl;
29:         cout << "Double:\t" << myDouble << endl;
30:         cout << "Float:\t" << myFloat << endl;
31:         cout << "Word: \t" << myWord << endl;
32:         cout << "Unsigned:\t" << myUnsigned << endl;
33:
34:         cout << "\n\nInt, Long, Double, Float, Word, Unsigned: ";
35:         cin >> myInt >> myLong >> myDouble >> myFloat >> myWord >> myUnsigned;
```

```
36:
37:        cout << "\n\nInt:\t" << myInt << endl;
38:        cout << "Long:\t" << myLong << endl;
39:        cout << "Double:\t" << myDouble << endl;
40:        cout << "Float:\t" << myFloat << endl;
41:        cout << "Word: \t" << myWord << endl;
42:        cout << "Unsigned:\t" << myUnsigned << endl;
43:
44:
45:    }
```

```
Int: 2
Long: 30303
Double: 393939397834
Float: 3.33
Word: Hello
Unsigned: 85

Int:      2
Long:     30303
Double    3.93939e+11
Float:    3.33
Word:     Hello
Unsigned: 85

Int, Long, Double, Float, Word, Unsigned: 3 304938 393847473 6.66 bye -2

Int:      3
Long:     304938
Double    3.93847e+08
Float:    6.66
Word:     bye
Unsigned: 65534
```

Once again, a number of variables are created, this time including a char array. The user is prompted for input and the output is faithfully printed.

On line 34, the user is prompted for all the input at once, and then each "word" of input is assigned to the appropriate variable. It is in order to facilitate this kind of multiple assignment that cin must consider each word in the input to be the full input for each variable. If cin was to consider the entire input to be part of one variable's input, this kind of concatenated input would be impossible.

Note that on line 35 the last object requested was an unsigned integer, but the user entered -2. Because cin believes it is writing to an unsigned integer, the bit pattern of -2 was evaluated as an unsigned integer, and when written out by cout the value 65534 was displayed. The unsigned value 65534 has the exact bit pattern of the signed value -2.

Later in this chapter you will see how to enter an entire string into a buffer, including multiple words. For now, the question arises, "How does the extraction operator manage this trick of concatenation?"

operator>> Returns a Reference to an *istream* Object

The return value of cin is a reference to an istream object. Because cin itself is an istream object, the return value of one extraction operation can be the input to the next extraction.

```
int VarOne, varTwo, varThree;
cout << "Enter three numbers: "
cin >> VarOne >> varTwo >> varThree;
```

When you write cin >> VarOne >> varTwo >> varThree;, the first extraction is evaluated (cin >> VarOne). The return value from this is another istream object, and that object's extraction operator gets the variable varTwo. It is as if you had written this:

```
((cin >> varOne) >> varTwo) >> varThree;
```

You'll see this technique repeated later when cout is discussed.

Other Member Functions of *cin*

In addition to overloading operator>>, cin has a number of other member functions. These are used when finer control over the input is required.

Single Character Input

operator>> taking a character reference can be used to get a single character from the standard input. The member function get() can also be used to obtain a single character, and can do so in two ways. get() can be used with no parameters, in which case the return value is used, or it can be used with a reference to a character.

Using *get()* with No Parameters

The first form of get() is without parameters. This returns the value of the character found, and will return EOF (end of file) if the end of the file is reached. get() with no parameters is not often used. It is not possible to concatenate this use of get() for multiple input, because the return value is not an iostream object. Thus, the following won't work:

```
cin.get() >>myVarOne >> myVarTwo; //   illegal
```

The return value of (cin.get() >> myVarOne) is an integer, not an iostream object.

A common use of get() with no parameters is illustrated in Listing 16.4.

Listing 16.4. Using get() with no parameters.

```
1:     // Listing
2:     #include <iostream.h>
3:
4:     void main()
5:     {
6:        char ch;
7:        while ( (ch = cin.get()) != EOF)
8:        {
9:           cout << "ch: " << ch << endl;
10:       }
11:       cout << "\nDone!\n";
12:    }
```

Note: To exit this program you must send end of file from the keyboard. On DOS computers use Ctrl+Z, on UNIX units use Ctrl+D.

```
Hello
ch: H
ch: e
ch: l
ch: l
ch: o
ch:

World
ch: W
ch: o
ch: r
ch: l
ch: d
ch:

(ctrl-z)
Done!
```

On line 6, a local character variable is declared. The while loop assigns the input received from cin.get() to ch, and if it is not EOF the string is printed out. This output is buffered until an end of line is read, however. Once EOF is encountered (by pressing Ctrl+Z on a DOS machine, or Ctrl+D on a UNIX machine), the loop exits.

Note that not every implementation of istream supports this version of get().

Using *get()* with a Character Reference Parameter

When a character is passed as input to get(), that character is filled with the next character in the input stream. The return value is an iostream object, and so this form of get() can be concatenated, as illustrated in Listing 16.5.

Listing 16.5 Using get() with parameters.

```
1:      // Listing
2:      #include <iostream.h>
3:
4:      void main()
5:      {
6:         char a, b, c;
7:
8:         cout << "Enter three letters: ";
9:
10:        cin.get(a).get(b).get(c);
11:
12:        cout << "a: " << a << "\nb: " << b << "\nc: " << c << endl;
13:     }
```

```
Enter three letters: one
a: o
b: n
c: e
```

On line 6, three character variables are created. On line 10, cin.get() is called three times, concatenated. First cin.get(a) is called. This puts the first letter into a and returns cin so that when it is done, cin.get(b) is called, putting the next letter into b. The end result of this is that cin.get(c) is called and the third letter is put in c.

Because cin.get(a) evaluates to cin, you could have written this:

cin.get(a) >> b;

In this form, cin.get(a) evaluates to cin, so the second phrase is cin >> b;.

DO	DON'T

DO use the extraction operator (>>) when you need to skip over whitespace.

DO use get() with a character parameter when you need to examine every character, including whitespace.

DON'T use get() with no parameters at all; it is more or less obsolete.

Getting Strings from Standard Input

The extraction operator (>>) can be used to fill a character array, as can the member functions get() and getline().

The final form of get() takes three parameters. The first parameter is a pointer to a character array, the second parameter is the maximum number of characters to read plus one, and the third parameter is the termination character.

If you enter 20 as the second parameter, get() will read 19 characters and then will null terminate the string, which it will store in the first parameter. The third parameter, the termination character, defaults to newline ('\n'). If a termination character is reached before the maximum number of characters is read, a NULL is written *and the termination character is left in the buffer.*

Listing 16.6 illustrates the use of this form of get().

Listing 16.6. Using get() with a character array.

```
1:     // Listing
2:     #include <iostream.h>
3:
4:     void main()
5:     {
6:         char stringOne[256];
7:         char stringTwo[256];
8:
9:         cout << "Enter string one: ";
10:        cin.get(stringOne,256);
11:        cout << "stringOne: " << stringOne << endl;
12:
13:        cout << "Enter string two: ";
14:        cin >> stringTwo;
15:        cout << "StringTwo: " << stringTwo << endl;
16:    }
```

```
Enter string one: Now is the time
String One: Now is the time
Enter string two: For all good
String Two: For
```

On lines 6 and 7, two character arrays are created. On line 9 the user is prompted to enter a string, and cin.get() is called on line 10. The first parameter is the buffer to fill, and the second is one more than the maximum number for get() to accept (the extra position being given to NULL ('\0')). The defaulted third parameter is a newline.

The user enters "Now is the time". Because the user ends the phrase with a newline, that phrase is put into stringOne, followed by a terminating NULL.

The user is prompted for another string on line 13, and this time the extraction operator is used. Because the extraction operator takes everything up to the first white space, the string For, with a terminating NULL, is stored in the second string, which of course is not what was intended.

Another way to solve this problem is to use getline(), as illustrated in Listing 16.7.

Listing 16.7. Using getline().

```
1:    // Listing
2:    #include <iostream.h>
3:
4:    void main()
5:    {
6:        char stringOne[256];
7:        char stringTwo[256];
8:        char stringThree[256];
9:
10:       cout << "Enter string one: ";
11:       cin.getline(stringOne,256);
12:       cout << "stringOne: " << stringOne << endl;
13:
14:       cout << "Enter string two: ";
15:       cin >> stringTwo;
16:       cout << "stringTwo: " << stringTwo << endl;
17:
18:       cout << "Enter string three: ";
19:       cin.getline(stringThree,256);
20:       cout << "stringThree: " << stringThree << endl;
21:   }
```

```
Enter string one: one two three
stringOne: one two three
Enter string two: four five six
String two: four
Enter string three: stringThree: five six
```

This example warrants careful examination; there are some potential surprises. On lines 6-8, three character arrays are declared.

On line 10 the user is prompted to enter a string, and that string is read by getline(). Like get(), getline() takes a buffer and a maximum number of characters. Unlike get(), however, the terminating new line is read and thrown away. With get() the terminating new line is not thrown away. It is left in the input buffer.

On line 14 the user is prompted again, and this time the extraction operator is used. The user enters four five six and the first word; four is put in string two. The string Enter string three is then displayed, and getline() is called again. Because five six is still in the input buffer, it is immediately read up to the new line; getline() terminates and the string in stringThree is printed on line 20.

The user has no chance to enter string three, because the second getline() call is fulfilled by the string remaining in the input buffer after the call to the extraction operator on line 15.

The extraction operator (>>) reads up to the first white space and puts the word into the character array.

The member function get() is overloaded. In one version, it takes no parameters and returns the value of the character it receives. In the second version, it takes a single character reference and returns the istream object by reference.

In the third and final version, get() takes a character array, a number of characters to get, and a termination character (which defaults to newline). This version of get() reads characters into the array until it gets to one fewer than its maximum number of characters or it encounters the termination character, whichever comes first. If get() encounters the termination character, it leaves that character in the input buffer and stops reading characters.

The member function getline() also takes three parameters: the buffer to fill, one more than the maximum number of characters to get, and the termination character. It functions exactly like get() does with these parameters, except getline() throws away the terminating character.

Using *cin.ignore()*

At times you want to ignore the remaining characters on a line until you hit either end of line (EOL) or end of file (EOF). The member function ignore() serves this purpose. ignore() takes two parameters, the maximum number of characters to ignore and the termination character. If you write ignore(80, '\n'), up to 80 characters will be thrown away until a newline character is found. The newline is then thrown away and the ignore() statement ends. Listing 16.8 illustrates the use of ignore().

Listing 16.8. Using `ignore()`.

```
1:     // Listing
2:     #include <iostream.h>
3:
4:     void main()
5:     {
6:         char stringOne[255];
7:         char stringTwo[255];
8:
9:         cout << "Enter string one:";
10:        cin.get(stringOne,255);
11:        cout << "String one" << stringOne << endl;
12:
13:        cout << "Enter string two: ";
14:        cin.getline(stringTwo,255);
15:        cout << "String two: " << stringTwo << endl;
16:
17:        cout << "\n\nNow try again...\n";
18:
19:        cout << "Enter string one: ";
20:        cin.get(stringOne,255);
21:        cout << "String one: " << stringOne << endl;
22:
23:        cin.ignore(255,'\n');
24:
25:        cout << "Enter string two: ";
26:        cin.getline(stringTwo,255);
27:        cout << "String Two: " << stringTwo << endl;
28:    }
```

```
Enter string one: once upon a time
String one: once upon a time
Enter string two: String two:

Now try again...
Enter string one: once upon a time
String one: once upon a time
Enter string two: there was a
String two: there was a
```

On lines 6 and 7 two character arrays are created. On line 9 the user is prompted for input and types Once upon a time, followed by Enter. On line 10, `get()` is used to read this string. `get()` fills `stringOne` and terminates on the newline, but leaves the newline character in the input buffer.

On line 13 the user is prompted again, but the `getline()` on line 14 reads the newline that is already in the buffer and terminates immediately, before the user can enter any input.

On line 19 the user is prompted again and puts in the same first line of input. This time, however, on line 23, ignore() is used to "eat" the newline character. Thus, when the getline() call on line 26 is reached, the input buffer is empty, and the user can input the next line of the story.

peek() and putback()

16

The input object cin has two additional methods that can come in rather handy: peek(), which looks at but does not extract the next character, and putback(), which inserts a character into the input stream. Listing 16.9 illustrates how these might be used.

Listing 16.9. Using peek() and putback().

```
1:     // Listing
2:     #include <iostream.h>
3:
4:     void main()
5:     {
6:         char ch;
7:         cout << "enter a phrase: ";
8:         while ( cin.get(ch) )
9:         {
10:            if (ch == '!')
11:                cin.putback('$');
12:            else
13:                cout << ch;
14:            while (cin.peek() == '#')
15:                cin.ignore(1,'#');
16:         }
17:     }
```

```
enter a phrase: Now!is#the!time#for!fun#!
Now$isthe$timefor$fun$
```

On line 6 a character variable, ch, is declared, and on line 7 the user is prompted to enter a phrase. The purpose of this program is to turn any exclamation marks (!) into dollar signs ($) and to remove any pound symbols (#).

The program loops as long as it is getting characters other than the end of file (remember that cin.get() returns 0 for end of file). If the current character is a dollar sign, it is thrown away and the $ symbol is put back into the input buffer; it will be read the next time through. If the current item is not an exclamation mark, it is printed. The next character is "peeked" at, and when pound symbols are found, they are removed.

This is not the most efficient way to do either of these things (and it won't find a pound symbol if it is the first character), but it does illustrate how these methods work. They are relatively obscure, so don't spend a lot of time worrying about when you might really use them. Put them into your bag of tricks; they'll come in handy sooner or later.

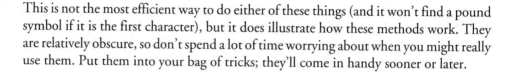

Tip: peek() and putback() are typically used for parsing strings and other data, such as when writing a compiler.

Output with *cout*

You have used cout to write strings, integers, and other numeric data to the screen with the overloaded insertion operator (<<). It is also possible to format the data, aligning columns and writing the numeric data in decimal and hexadecimal. This section will show you how.

Flushing the Output

You've already seen that using endl will flush the output buffer. Endl calls cout's member function flush(), which writes all of the data it is buffering. You can call the flush() method directly, either by calling the flush() member method or by writing the following:

```
cout << flush
```

This can be convenient when you need to ensure that the output buffer is emptied and the contents written to the screen.

Related Functions

Just as the extraction operator can be supplemented with get() and getline(), the insertion operator can be supplemented with put() and write().

The function put() is used to write a single character to the output device. Because put() returns an ostream reference, and because cout is an ostream object, you can concatenate put() just as you do the insertion operator. Listing 16.10 illustrates this idea.

Listing 16.10. Using put().

```
1:      // Listing
2:      #include <iostream.h>
3:
4:      void main()
5:      {
6:          cout.put('H').put('e').put('l').put('l').put('o').put('\n');
7:      }
```

```
Hello
```

Line 6 is evaluated like this: cout.put('H') writes the letter H to the screen and returns the cout object. This leaves the following:

```
cout.put('e').put('l').put('l').put('o').put('\n');
```

The letter e is written, leaving cout.put('l')... This process repeats, each letter being written and the cout object returned until the final character ('\n') is written and the function returns.

The function write() works just like the insertion operator (<<), except that it takes a parameter that tells the function the maximum number of characters to write. Listing 16.11 illustrates its use.

Listing 16.11. Using write().

```
1:      // Listing
2:      #include <iostream.h>
3:      #include <string.h>
4:
5:      void main()
6:      {
7:          char One[] = "One if by land";
8:
9:
10:
11:         int fullLength = strlen(One);
12:         int tooShort = fullLength -4;
13:         int tooLong = fullLength + 6;
14:
15:         cout.write(One,fullLength) << "\n";
16:         cout.write(One,tooShort) << "\n";
17:         cout.write(One,tooLong) << "\n";
18:     }
```

Output

```
One if by land
One if by
One if by land i?!
```

Note: The last line of output may look different on your computer.

Analysis

On lines 7-9, three phrases are created. On line 11 the integer fullLength is set to the length of the second phrase and tooShort is set to that length minus four, while tooLong is set to fullLength plus six.

On line 15, phrase two is printed using write(). The length is set to the actual length of the phrase, and the correct phrase is printed.

On line 16 the phrase is printed again, but is four characters shorter than the full phrase, and that is reflected in the output.

On line 17 the phrase is printed again, but this time write() is instructed to write an extra six characters. Once the phrase is written, the next six bytes of contiguous memory are written. The first extra byte is the null character at the end of phrase two; this is followed by the first five characters of phrase one.

Manipulators, Flags, and Formatting Instructions

The output stream maintains a number of state flags, determining which base (decimal or hexadecimal) to use, how wide to make the fields, and what character to use to fill in fields. A state flag is just a byte whose individual bits are each assigned a special meaning. Manipulating bits in this way is discussed on Day 21. Each of ostream's flags can be set using member functions and manipulators.

Using *cout.width()*

The default width of your output will be just enough space to print the number, character, or string in the output buffer. You can change this by using width(). Because width() is a member function, it must be invoked with a cout object. It only changes the width of the very next output field and then immediately reverts to the default. Listing 16.12 illustrates its use.

Listing 16.12. Adjusting the width of output.

```
1:      // Listing
2:      #include <iostream.h>
3:
4:      void main()
5:      {
6:         cout << "Start >";
7:         cout.width(25);
8:         cout << 123 << "< End\n";
9:
10:        cout << "Start >";
11:        cout.width(25);
12:        cout << 123<< "< Next >";
13:        cout << 456 << "< End\n";
14:
15:        cout << "Start >";
16:        cout.width(4);
17:        cout << 123456 << "< End\n";
18:
19:
20:     }
```

16

```
Start >                    123< End
Start >                    123< Next >456< End
Start >123456< End
```

The first output, on lines 6-8, prints the number 123 within a field whose width is set to 25 on line 7. This is reflected in the first line of output.

The second line of output first prints the value 123 in the same field whose width is set to 25, and then prints the value 456. Note that 456 is printed in a field whose width is reset to just large enough; as stated, the effect of width() lasts only as long as the very next output.

The final output reflects that setting a width that is smaller than the output is exactly like setting a width that is just large enough.

Setting the Fill Characters

Normally cout fills the empty field created by a call to width() with spaces, as shown above. At times you may want to fill the area with other characters, such as asterisks. To do this, you call fill() and pass in as a parameter the character you want used as a fill character. Listing 16.13 illustrates this.

Listing 16.13. Using `fill()`.

```
1:      // listing 16.3 fill()
2:
3:      #include <iostream.h>
4:
5:      void main()
6:      {
7:         cout << "Start >";
8:         cout.width(25);
9:         cout << 123 << "< End\n";
10:
11:
12:          cout << "Start >";
13:         cout.width(25);
14:         cout.fill('*');
15:         cout << 123 << "< End\n";
16:
17:      }
```

```
Start >                      123< End
Start >*******************123< End
```

Lines 7-9 repeat the functionality from the previous example. Lines 12-15 repeat this again, but this time, on line 14, the fill character is set to asterisks, as reflected in the output.

Set Flags

The `iostream` objects keep track of their state by using flags. You can set these flags by calling `setf()` and passing in one or another of the predefined enumerated constants.

NEW☞
TERM Objects are said to have *state* when some or all of their data represents a *condition* which can change during the course of the program.

For example, you can set whether or not to show trailing zeros (so that 20.00 does not become truncated to 20). To turn trailing zeros on, call `setf(ios::showpoint)`.

The enumerated constants are scoped to the `iostream` class (`ios`) and thus are called with the full qualification `ios::`*flagname*, such as `ios::showpoint`.

You can turn the plus sign (+) on before positive numbers by using `ios::showpos`. You can change the alignment of the output by using `ios::left`, `ios::right`, or `ios::internal`.

Finally, you can set the base of the numbers for display by using `ios::dec` (decimal), `ios::oct` (octal—base eight), or `ios::hex` (hexadecimal—base sixteen). These flags can also be concatenated into the insertion operator. Listing 16.14 illustrates these settings.

As a bonus, Listing 16.14 also introduces the setw manipulator, which sets the width but can also be concatenated with the insertion operator.

Listing 16.14. Using setf.

```
1:     // Listing
2:     #include <iostream.h>
3:     #include <iomanip.h>
4:
5:     void main()
6:     {
7:        const int number = 185;
8:        cout << "The number is " << number << endl;
9:
10:       cout << "The number is " << hex <<  number << endl;
11:
12:       cout.setf(ios::showbase);
13:       cout << "The number is " << hex <<  number << endl;
14:
15:       cout << "The number is " ;
16:       cout.width(10);
17:       cout << hex << number << endl;
18:
19:       cout << "The number is " ;
20:       cout.width(10);
21:       cout.setf(ios::left);
22:       cout << hex << number << endl;
23:
24:       cout << "The number is " ;
25:       cout.width(10);
26:       cout.setf(ios::internal);
27:       cout << hex << number << endl;
28:
29:       cout << "The number is:" << setw(10) << hex << number << endl;
30:
31:    }
```

```
The number is 185
The number is b9
The number is 0xb9
The number is        0xb9
The number is 0xb9
The number is 0x        b9
The number is 0x        b9
```

On line 7 the constant int number is initialized to the value 185. This is displayed on line 8.

The value is displayed again on line 10, but this time the manipulator hex is concatenated, causing the value to be displayed in hexadecimal as b9. (b=11; 11*16=176+9=185).

On line 12 the flag showbase is set. This causes the prefix 0x to be added to all hexadecimal numbers, as reflected in the output.

On line 16 the width is set to 10, and the value is pushed to the extreme right. On line 20 the width is again set to 10, but this time the alignment is set to the left, and the number is again printed flush left.

On line 25 once again the width is set to 10, but this time the alignment is internal. Thus the 0x is printed flush left, but the value, b9, is printed flush right.

Finally, on line 29, the concatenation operator setw() is used to set the width to 10, and the value is printed again.

Streams Versus the *printf()* Function

Most C++ implementations also provide the standard C I/O libraries, including the printf() statement. Although printf() is in some ways easier to use than cout, it is far less desirable.

printf() does not provide type safety, so it is easy to inadvertently tell it to display an integer as if it was a character and vice versa. printf() also does not support classes, and so it is not possible to teach it how to print your class data; you must feed each class member to printf() one by one.

On the other hand, printf() does make formatting much easier, because you can put the formatting characters directly into the printf() statement. Because printf() has its uses and many programmers still make extensive use of it, this section will briefly review its use.

To use printf(), be sure to include the STDIO.H header file. In its simplest form, printf() takes a formatting string as its first parameter and then a series of values as its remaining parameters.

The formatting string is a quoted string of text and conversion specifiers. All conversion specifiers must begin with the percent symbol (%). The common conversion specifiers are presented in Table 16.1.

Table 16.1. The common conversion specifiers.

Specifier	Used For
%s	strings

Specifier	Used For
%d	integers
%l	long integer
%ld	long integers
%f	float

Each of the conversion specifiers can also provide a width statement and a precision statement, expressed as a float, where the digits to the left of the decimal are used for the total width and the digits to the right of the decimal provide the precision for floats. Thus, %5d is the specifier for a five-digit-wide integer, and %15.5f is the specifier for a 15-digit-wide float, of which the final five digits are dedicated to the decimal portion. Listing 16.15 illustrates various uses of printf().

Listing 16.15. Printing with printf().

```
1:      #include <stdio.h>
2:      void main()
3:      {
4:          printf("%s","hello world\n");
5:
6:          char *phrase = "Hello again!\n";
7:          printf("%s",phrase);
8:
9:          int x = 5;
10:         printf("%d\n",x);
11:
12:         char *phraseTwo = "Here's some values: ";
13:         char *phraseThree = " and also these: ";
14:         int y = 7, z = 35;
15:         long longVar = 98456;
16:         float floatVar =  8.8;
17:
18:         printf("%s %d %d %s %ld %f\n",phraseTwo,y,z,phraseThree,longVar,floatVar);
19:
20:         char *phraseFour = "Formatted: ";
21:         printf("%s %5d %10d  %10.5f\n",phraseFour,y,z,floatVar);
22:     }
```

```
hello world
Hello again!
5
Here's some values: 7 35 and also these: 98456 8.800000
Formatted:         7            35       8.800000
```

The first `printf()` statement, on line 4, uses the standard form: the term `printf`, followed by a quoted string with a conversion specifier (in this case `%s`), followed by a value to insert into the conversion specifier.

The `%s` indicates that this is a string, and the value for the string is, in this case, the quoted string `"hello world."`

The second `printf()` statement is just like the first, but this time a `char` pointer is used, rather than quoting the string right in place in the `printf()` statement.

The third `printf()`, on line 10, uses the integer conversion specifier, and for its value the integer variable `x`. The fourth `printf()` statement, on line 18, is more complex. Here six values are concatenated. Each conversion specifier is supplied, and then the values are provided, separated by commas.

Finally, on line 21, format specifications are used to specify width and precision. As you can see, all of this is somewhat easier than using manipulators.

As stated previously, however, the limitation here is that there is no type checking and `printf()` cannot be declared a friend or member function of a class. So if you want to print the various member data of a class, you must feed each accessor method to the `printf()` statement explicitly.

File Input and Output

Streams provide a uniform way of dealing with data coming from the keyboard or the hard disk and going out to the screen or hard disk. In either case, you can use the insertion and extraction operators or the other related functions and manipulators. To open and close files, you create `ifstream` and `ofstream` objects as described in the next few sections.

ofstream

The particular objects used to read from or write to files are called `ofstream` objects. These are derived from the `iostream` objects you've been using so far.

To get started with writing to a file, you must first create an `ofstream` object and then associate that object with a particular file on your disk. To use `ofstream` objects, you must be sure to include `fstream.h` in your program.

16

Note: Because `fstream.h` includes `iostream.h`, there is no need for you to include `iostream` explicitly.

Condition States

The `iostream` objects maintain flags that report on the state of your input and output. You can check each of these flags using the boolean functions, `eof()`, `bad()`, `fail()`, and `good()`. The function `eof()` returns true if the `iostream` object has encountered EOF, end of file. The function `bad()` returns true if you attempt an invalid operation. The function `fail()` returns true anytime `bad()` is true or an operation fails. Finally, the function `good()` returns true anytime all three of the other functions are false.

Opening Files for Input and Output

To open the file `myfile.cpp` with an `ofstream` object, declare an instance of an `ofstream` object and pass in the filename as a parameter:

```
ofstream fout("myfile.cpp");
```

Opening this file for input works exactly the same way, except it uses an `ifstream` object:

```
ifstream fin("myfile.cpp");
```

Note that `fout` and `fin` are names you assign; here `fout` has been used to reflect its similarity to `cout`, and `fin` has been used to reflect its similarity to `cin`.

One important file stream function that you will need right away is `close()`. Every file stream object you create opens a file for either reading or writing (or both). It is important to `close()` the file after you finish reading or writing; this ensures that the file won't be corrupted and that the data you've written is flushed to the disk.

Once the stream objects are associated with files, they can be used like any other stream objects. Listing 16.16 illustrates this.

Listing 16.16. Opening files for read and write.

```
1:      #include <fstream.h>
2:      void main()
3:      {
```

continues

Listing 16.16. continued

```
4:        char fileName[80];
5:        char buffer[255];    // for user input
6:        cout << "File name: ";
7:        cin >> fileName;
8:
9:        ofstream fout(fileName);  // open for writing
10:       fout << "This line written directly to the file...\n";
11:       cout << "Enter text for the file: ";
12:       cin.ignore(1,'\n');  // eat the new line after the file name
13:       cin.getline(buffer,255);  // get the user's input
14:       fout << buffer << "\n";  // and write it to the file
15:       fout.close();            // close the file, ready for reopen
16:
17:       ifstream fin(fileName);    // reopen for reading
18:       cout << "Here's the contents of the file:\n";
19:       char ch;
20:       while (fin.get(ch))
21:           cout << ch;
22:
23:       cout << "\n***End of file contents.***\n";
24:
25:       fin.close();             // always pays to be tidy
26:   }
```

```
File name: test1
Enter text for the file: This text is written to the file!
Here's the contents of the file:
This line written directly to the file...
This text is written to the file!

***End of file contents.***
```

On line 4 a buffer is set aside for the filename, and on line 5 another buffer is set aside for user input. The user is prompted to enter a filename on line 6, and this response is written to the `fileName` buffer. On line 9 an `ofstream` object is created, `fout`, which is associated with the new filename. This opens the file; if the file already exists, its contents are thrown away.

On line 10 a string of text is written directly to the file. On line 11 the user is prompted for input. The newline character left over from the user's input of the filename is eaten on line 12, and the user's input is stored into `buffer` on line 13. That input is written to the file along with a newline character on line 14, and then the file is closed on line 15.

On line 17 the file is reopened, this time in input mode, and the contents are read, one character at a time, on lines 20 and 21.

Changing the Default Behavior of *ofstream* on Open

The default behavior upon opening a file is to create the file if it doesn't yet exist and to truncate the file (that is, delete all its contents) if it does exist. If you don't want this default behavior, you can explicitly provide a second argument to the constructor of your ofstream object.

Valid arguments include:

☐ ios::app—Appends to the end of existing files rather than truncating them.

☐ ios::ate—Places you at the end of the file, but you can write data anywhere in the file.

☐ ios::trunc—The default. Causes existing files to be truncated.

☐ ios::nocreate—If the file does not exist, the open fails.

☐ ios::noreplace—If the file does already exist, the open fails.

Note that app is short for append; ate is short for at end, and trunc is short for truncate. Listing 16.17 illustrates using append by reopening the file from Listing 16.16 and appending to it.

Listing 16.17. Appending to the end of a file.

```
1:     #include <fstream.h>
2:     int main()   // returns 1 on error
3:     {
4:         char fileName[80];
5:         char buffer[255];
6:         cout << "Please re-enter the file name: ";
7:         cin >> fileName;
8:
9:         ifstream fin(fileName);
10:        if (fin)                // already exists?
11:        {
12:            cout << "Current file contents:\n";
13:            char ch;
14:            while (fin.get(ch))
15:                cout << ch;
16:            cout << "\n***End of file contents.***\n";
17:        }
18:        fin.close();
19:
20:        cout << "\nOpening " << fileName << " in append mode...\n";
21:
```

continues

Listing 16.17. continued

```
22:        ofstream fout(fileName,ios::app);
23:        if (!fout)
24:        {
25:           cout << "Unable to open " << fileName << " for appending.\n";
26:           return(1);
27:        }
28:
29:        cout << "\nEnter text for the file: ";
30:        cin.ignore(1,'\n');
31:        cin.getline(buffer,255);
32:        fout << buffer << "\n";
33:        fout.close();
34:
35:        fin.open(fileName);   // reassign existing fin object!
36:        if (!fin)
37:        {
38:           cout << "Unable to open " << fileName << " for reading.\n";
39:           return(1);
40:        }
41:        cout << "\nHere's the contents of the file:\n";
42:        char ch;
43:        while (fin.get(ch))
44:           cout << ch;
45:        cout << "\n***End of file contents.***\n";
46:        fin.close();
47:        return 0;
48:    }
```

```
Please re-enter the file name: test1
Current file contents:
This line written directly to the file...
This text is written to the file!

***End of file contents.***

Opening test1 in append mode...

Enter text for the file: More text for the file!

Here's the contents of the file:
This line written directly to the file...
This text is written to the file!
More text for the file!

***End of file contents.***
```

The user is again prompted to enter the filename. This time an input file stream object is created on line 9. That open is tested on line 10, and if the file already exists its contents are printed on lines 12 to 16. Note that `if(fin)` is synonymous with `if (fin.good())`.

The input file is then closed, and the same file is reopened, this time in append mode, on line 22. After this open (and every open), the file is tested to ensure that the file was opened properly. Note that if(!fout) is the same as testing if (fout.fail()). The user is then prompted to enter text, and the file is closed again on line 33.

Finally, as in Listing 16.16, the file is reopened in read mode; however, this time fin does not need to be redeclared. It is just reassigned to the same filename. Again the open is tested, on line 36, and if all is well the contents of the file are printed to the screen and the file is closed for the final time.

DO	**DON'T**

DO test each open of a file to ensure that it opened successfully.

DO reuse existing ifstream and ofstream objects.

DO close all fstream objects when you are done using them.

DON'T try to close or reassign cin or cout.

Binary Versus Text Files

Some operating systems, such as DOS, distinguish between text files and binary files. Text files store everything as text (as you might have guessed), so large numbers such as 54,325 are stored as a string of numerals ('5', '4', ',', '3', '2', '5'). This can be inefficient, but has the advantage that the text can be read using simple programs such as the DOS program, type.

To help the file system distinguish between text and binary files, C++ provides the ios::binary flag. On many systems this flag is ignored, because all data is stored in binary format. On some rather prudish systems, the ios::binary flag is illegal and won't compile!

Binary files can store not only integers and strings, but entire data structures. You can write all the data at one time by using the write() method of fstream.

If you use write(), you can recover the data using read(). Each of these functions expects a pointer to character, however, so you must cast the address of your class to be a pointer to character.

The second argument to these functions is the number of characters to write, which you can determine using sizeof(). Note that what is being written is just the data, not the methods. What is recovered is just data. Listing 16.18 illustrates writing the contents of a class to a file.

Listing 16.18. Writing a class to a file.

```
1:     #include <fstream.h>
2:
3:     class Animal
4:     {
5:     public:
6:         Animal(int weight, long days):itsWeight(weight),itsNumberDaysAlive(days){}
7:         ~Animal(){}
8:
9:         int GetWeight()const { return itsWeight; }
10:        void SetWeight(int weight) { itsWeight = weight; }
11:
12:        long GetDaysAlive()const { return  itsNumberDaysAlive; }
13:        void SetDaysAlive(long days) { itsNumberDaysAlive = days; }
14:
15:    private:
16:        int itsWeight;
17:        long itsNumberDaysAlive;
18:    };
19:
20:    int main()    // returns 1 on error
21:    {
22:        char fileName[80];
23:        char buffer[255];
24:
25:        cout << "Please enter the file name: ";
26:        cin >> fileName;
27:        ofstream fout(fileName,ios::binary);
28:        if (!fout)
29:        {
30:            cout << "Unable to open " << fileName << " for writing.\n";
31:            return(1);
32:        }
33:
34:        Animal Bear(50,100);
35:        fout.write((char*) &Bear,sizeof Bear);
36:
37:        fout.close();
38:
39:        ifstream fin(fileName,ios::binary);
40:        if (!fin)
41:        {
42:            cout << "Unable to open " << fileName << " for reading.\n";
43:            return(1);
44:        }
45:
46:        Animal BearTwo(1,1);
47:
```

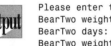

```
48:        cout << "BearTwo weight: " << BearTwo.GetWeight() << endl;
49:        cout << "BearTwo days: " << BearTwo.GetDaysAlive() << endl;
50:
51:        fin.read((char*) &BearTwo, sizeof BearTwo);
52:
53:        cout << "BearTwo weight: " << BearTwo.GetWeight() << endl;
54:        cout << "BearTwo days: " << BearTwo.GetDaysAlive() << endl;
55:        fin.close();
56:        return 0;
57:    }
```

Output

```
Please enter the file name: Animals
BearTwo weight: 1
BearTwo days: 1
BearTwo weight: 50
BearTwo days: 100
```

On lines 3-18 a stripped-down Animal class is declared. On lines 22-32 a file is created and opened for output in binary mode. An animal whose weight is 50 and who is 100 days old is created on line 34, and its data is written to the file on line 35.

The file is closed on line 37 and reopened for reading in binary mode on line 39. A second animal is created on line 46 whose weight is 1 and who is only one day old. The data from the file is read into the new animal object on line 51, wiping out the existing data and replacing it with the data from the file.

Command-Line Processing

Many operating systems, such as DOS and UNIX, enable the user to pass parameters to your program when the program starts. These are called command-line options, and are typically separated by spaces on the command line. For example:

```
SomeProgram Param1 Param2 Param3
```

These parameters are not passed to main() directly. Instead, every program's main() function is passed two parameters. The first is an integer count of the number of arguments on the command line. The program name itself is counted, so every program has at least one parameter. The example command line shown previously has four. (The name SomeProgram plus the three parameters makes a total of four command-line arguments.)

The second parameter passed to main() is an array of pointers to character strings. Because an array name is a constant pointer to the first element of the array, you can declare this argument to be a pointer to a pointer to char, a pointer to an array of char, or an array of arrays of char.

Typically, the first argument is called `argc` (argument count), but you may call it anything you like. The second argument is often called `argv` (argument vector), but again this is just a convention.

It is common to test `argc` to ensure you've received the expected number of arguments, and to use `argv` to access the strings themselves. Note that `argv[0]` is the name of the program, and `argv[1]` is the first parameter to the program, represented as a string. If your program takes two numbers as arguments, you will need to translate these numbers to strings. On Day 19 you will see how to use the standard library conversions. Listing 16.19 illustrates how to use the command-line arguments.

Listing 16.19. Using command-line arguments.

```
1:    #include <iostream.h>
2:    void main(int argc, char **argv)
3:    {
4:       cout << "Received " << argc << " arguments...\n";
5:       for (int i=0; i<argc; i++)
6:          cout << "argument " << i << ": " << argv[i] << endl;
7:    }
```

```
TestProgram  Teach Yourself C++ In 21 Days
Received 7 arguments
argumnet 0: TestProgram.exe
argument 1: Teach
argument 2: Yourself
argument 3: C++
argument 4: In
argument 5: 21
argument 6: Days
```

The function `main()` declares two arguments: `argc` is an integer that contains the count of command-line arguments, and `argv` is a pointer to the array of strings. Each string in the array pointed to by `argv` is a command-line argument. Note that `argv` could just as easily have been declared as `char *argv[]` or `char argv[][]`. It is a matter of programming style how you declare `argv`; even though this program declared it as a pointer to a pointer, array offsets were still used to access the individual strings.

On line 4, `argc` is used to print the number of command-line arguments: 7 in all, counting the program name itself.

On lines 5 and 6, each of the command-line arguments is printed, passing the null-terminated strings to `cout` by indexing into the array of strings.

A more common use of command-line arguments is illustrated by modifying Listing 16.18 to take the filename as a command-line argument. This listing does not include the class declaration, which is unchanged.

Listing 16.20. Using command-line arguments.

```
1:      #include <iostream.h>
2:      int main(int argc, char *argv[])    // returns 1 on error
3:      {
4:          if (argc != 2)
5:          {
6:              cout << "Usage: " << argv[0] << " <filename>" << endl;
7:              return(1);
8:          }
9:
10:         ofstream fout(argv[1],ios::binary);
11:         if (!fout)
12:         {
13:             cout << "Unable to open " << argv[1] << " for writing.\n";
14:             return(1);
15:         }
16:
17:         Animal Bear(50,100);
18:         fout.write((char*) &Bear,sizeof Bear);
19:
20:         fout.close();
21:
22:         ifstream fin(argv[1],ios::binary);
23:         if (!fin)
24:         {
25:             cout << "Unable to open " << argv[1] << " for reading.\n";
26:             return(1);
27:         }
28:
29:         Animal BearTwo(1,1);
30:
31:         cout << "BearTwo weight: " << BearTwo.GetWeight() << endl;
32:         cout << "BearTwo days: " << BearTwo.GetDaysAlive() << endl;
33:
34:         fin.read((char*) &BearTwo, sizeof BearTwo);
35:
36:         cout << "BearTwo weight: " << BearTwo.GetWeight() << endl;
37:         cout << "BearTwo days: " << BearTwo.GetDaysAlive() << endl;
38:         fin.close();
39:         return 0;
40:     }
```

```
BearTwo weight: 1
BearTwo days: 1
BearTwo weight: 50
BearTwo days: 100
```

The declaration of the Animal class is the same as in Listing 16.16, and so is left out of this example. This time, however, rather than prompting the user for the filename, command-line arguments are used. On line 2, main() is declared to take two parameters: the count of the command-line arguments and a pointer to the array of command-line argument strings.

On lines 4-8, the program ensures that the expected number of arguments (exactly 2) is received. If the user fails to supply a single filename, an error message is printed:

```
Usage TestProgram <filename>
```

Then the program exits. Note that by using `argv[0]` rather than hard-coding a program name, you can compile this program to have any name and this usage statement will work automatically.

On line 10, the program attempts to open the supplied filename for binary output. There is no reason to copy the filename into a local temporary buffer. It can be used directly by accessing `argv[1]`.

This technique is repeated on line 22 when the same file is reopened for input, and is used in the error condition statements when the files cannot be opened, on lines 13 and 25.

Summary

Today streams were introduced, and the global objects `cout` and `cin` were described. The goal of the `istream` and `ostream` objects is to encapsulate the work of writing to device drivers, and buffering input and output.

There are four standard stream objects created in every program: `cout`, `cin`, `cerr`, and `clog`. Each of these can be "redirected" by many operating systems.

The `istream` object `cin` is used for input, and its most common use is with the overloaded extraction operator (`>>`). The `ostream` object `cout` is used for output, and its most common use is with the overloaded insertion operator (`<<`).

Each of these objects has a number of other member functions, such as `get()` and `put()`. Because the common forms of each of these methods returns a reference to a stream object, it is easy to concatenate each of these operators and functions.

The state of the stream objects can be changed by using manipulators. These can set the formatting and display characteristics and various other attributes of the stream objects.

File I/O can be accomplished by using the `fstream` classes, which derive from the stream classes. In addition to supporting the normal insertion and extraction operators, these objects also support `read()` and `write()` for storing and retrieving large binary objects.

Q&A

Q How do you know when to use the insertion and extraction operators and when to use the other member functions of the `stream` classes?

A In general, it is easier to use the insertion and extraction operators, and they are preferred when their behavior is what is needed. In those unusual circumstances when these operators don't do the job (such as reading in a string of words), the other functions can be used.

Q What is the difference between `cerr` and `clog`?

A `cerr` is not buffered. Everything written to `cerr` is immediately written out. This is fine for errors to be written to the screen, but may have too high a performance cost for writing logs to disk. `clog` buffers its output, and thus can be more efficient.

Q Why were streams created if `printf()` works well?

A `printf()` does not support the strong type system of C++, and it does not support user-defined classes.

Q When would you ever use `putback()`?

A When one read operation is used to determine whether or not a character is valid, but a different read operation (perhaps by a different object) needs the character to be in the buffer. This is most often used when parsing a file; for example, the C++ compiler might use `putback()`.

Q When would you use `ignore()`?

A A common use of this is after using `get()`. Because `get()` leaves the terminating character in the buffer, it is not uncommon to immediately follow a call to `get()` with a call to `ignore(1,'\n');`. Once again, this is often used in parsing.

Q My friends use `printf()` in their C++ programs. Can I?

A Sure. You'll gain some convenience, but you'll pay by sacrificing type safety.

Workshop

The Workshop contains quiz questions to help solidify your understanding of the material covered and exercises to provide you with experience in using what you've learned. Try to answer the quiz and exercise questions before checking the answers in Appendix D, and make sure you understand the answers before going to the next chapter.

Quiz

1. What is the insertion operator, and what does it do?

2. What is the extraction operator, and what does it do?

3. What are the three forms of `cin.get()`, and what are their differences?

4. What is the difference between `cin.read()` and `cin.getline()`?

5. What is the default width for ouputting a long integer using the insertion operator?

6. What is the return value of the insertion operator?

7. What parameter does the constructor to an `ofstream` object take?

8. What does the `ios::ate` argument do?

Exercises

1. Write a program that writes to the four standard iostream objects: `cin`, `cout`, `cerr`, and `clog`.

2. Write a program that prompts the user to enter her full name and then displays it on the screen.

3. Rewrite Listing 16.9 to do the same thing, but without using `putback()` or `ignore()`.

4. Write a program that takes a filename as a parameter and opens the file for reading. Read every character of the file and display only the letters and punctuation to the screen. (Ignore all nonprinting characters.) Then close the file and exit.

5. Write a program that displays its command-line arguments in reverse order and that does not display the program name.

17

The Preprocessor

Most of what you write in your source code files is C++. These are interpreted by the compiler and turned into your program. Before the compiler runs, however, the preprocessor runs; and this provides an opportunity for *conditional compilation*. Today you will learn:

☐ What conditional compilation is and how to manage it.

☐ How to write macros using the preprocessor.

☐ How to use the preprocessor in finding bugs.

The Preprocessor and the Compiler

Every time you run your compiler, your preprocessor runs first. The preprocessor looks for preprocessor instructions, each of which begins with a pound symbol (#). The effect of each of these instructions is a change to the text of the source code. The result is a new source code file, a temporary file which you normally don't see, but which you can instruct the compiler to save so that you can examine it if you wish.

The compiler does not read your original source code file, it reads the output of the preprocessor, and compiles *that* file. You've seen the effect of this already with the #include directive. This instructs the preprocessor to find the file whose name follows the #include directive, and to write it into the intermediate file at that location. It is as if you had typed that entire file right into your source code, and by the time the compiler sees the source code the included file is there.

Seeing the Intermediate Form

Just about every compiler has a "switch" which you can set either in the integrated development environment (IDE) or at the command line, which instructs the compiler to save the intermediate file. Check your compiler manual for the right switches to set for your compiler if you'd like to examine this file.

Using *#define*

The #define command defines a string substitution. If you write

```
#define BIG 512
```

you have instructed the precompiler to substitute the string 512 wherever it sees the string BIG. This is not a string in the C++ sense. The characters 512 are substituted in your source code wherever the token BIG is seen. A token is a string of characters that can be used wherever a string or constant or other set of letters might be used. Thus if you write

```
#define BIG 512
int myArray[BIG];
```

The intermediate file produced by the precompiler will look like this:

```
int myArray[512];
```

Note that the #define statement is gone. Precompiler statements are all removed from the intermediate file, they do not appear in the final source code *at all*.

Using *#define* for Constants

One way to use #define is as a substitute for constants. This is almost never a good idea, however, as #define merely makes a string substitution, and does *no* type checking. As explained in the section on constants, there are tremendous advantages to using the const keyword rather than #define.

Using *#define* for Tests

A second way to use #define, however, is simply to declare that a particular character string *is* defined. Thus you could write:

```
#define BIG
```

Later, you can test whether or not BIG has been defined, and take action accordingly. The precompiler commands to test whether a string has been defined are #ifdef and #ifndef. Both of these must be followed by the command #endif before the block ends (before the next closing brace).

#ifdef evaluates *true* if the string it tests *has* been defined already. Thus, you can write

```
#ifdef DEBUG
    cout << "Debug defined";
#endif
```

When the precompiler reads the #ifdef it checks a table it has built to see if you've defined DEBUG. If so, the #ifdef evaluates true, and everything to the next #else or #endif is written into the intermediate file for compiling. If it evaluates false, nothing between #ifdef DEBUG and #endif will be written into the intermediate file, it will be as if it were never in the source code in the first place.

Note that #ifndef is the logical reverse of #ifdef. #ifndef evaluates true if the string has *not* been defined up to that point in the file.

The *#else* Precompiler Command

As you might imagine, the term #else can be inserted between either #ifdef or #ifndef and the closing #endif. Listing 17.1 illustrates how these terms are used.

Listing 17.1. Using #define.

```
1:    #define DemoVersion
2:    #define DOS_VERSION 5
3:    #include <iostreams.h>
4:
5:
6:    void main()
7:    {
8:
9:    cout << "Checking on the definitions of DemoVersion, DOS_VERSION
      ➥and WINDOWS_VERSION...\n";
10:
11:   #ifdef DemoVersion
12:       cout << "DemoVersion defined.\n";
13:   #else
14:       cout << "DemoVersion not defined.\n";
15:   #endif
16:
17:   #ifndef DOS_VERSION
18:       cout << "DOS_VERSION not defined!\n";
19:   #else
20:       cout << "DOS_VERSION defined as: " << DOS_VERSION << endl;
21:   #endif
22:
23:   #ifdef WINDOWS_VERSION
24:       cout << "WINDOWS_VERSION defined!\n";
25:   #else
26:       cout << "WINDOWS_VERSION was not defined.\n";
27:   #endif
28:
29:     cout << "Done.\n";
30:   }
```

```
Checking on the definitions of DemoVersion, DOS_VERSION and WINDOWS_VERSION...
DemoVersion defined
DOS_VERSION defined as: 5
WINDOWS_VERSION was not defined.
Done.
```

On lines 1 and 2 DemoVersion and DOS_VERSION are defined, with DOS_VERSION defined with the string 5. On line 11 the definition of DemoVersion is tested, and since DemoVersion is defined, albeit with no value, the test is true and the string on line 12 is printed.

On line 17 is the test that DOS_VERSION is *not* defined. Since DOS_VERSION *is* defined, this test fails and execution jumps to line 20. Here the string 5 is substituted for the word DOS_VERSION, and this is seen by the compiler as

```
cout << "DOS_VERSION defined as: " << 5 << endl;
```

Note that the first word DOS_VERSION is *not* substituted because it is in a quoted string. The second DOS_VERSION is substituted, however, and thus the compiler sees 5 as if you had typed 5 there.

Finally, on line 23 the program tests for WINDOWS_VERSION. Since you did not define WINDOWS_VERSION the test fails and the message on line 24 is printed.

Inclusion and Inclusion Guards

You will create projects with many different files. You will probably organize your directories so that each class has its own header file (.HPP) with the class declaration, and its own implementation file (.CPP) with the source code for the class methods.

Your main() function will be in its own .CPP file, and all the .CPP files will be compiled into .OBJ files, which will then be linked together into a single program by the linker.

Because your programs will use methods from many classes, many header files will be included in each file. Also, header files often need to include one another. For example, the header file for a derived class's declaration *must* include the header file for its base class.

Imagine that the Animal class is declared in the file ANIMAL.HPP. The Dog class, which derives from Animal must, in DOG.HPP include the file ANIMAL.HPP, or it will not be able to derive from Animal. The Cat header also includes ANIMAL.HPP for the same reason. If you create a method that uses both a Cat and a Dog, you will be in danger of including ANIMAL.HPP twice.

This will generate a compile-time error, as it is not legal to declare a class (Animal) twice, even though the declarations are identical. You can solve this problem with "inclusion guards." At the top of your ANIMAL header file you will write these lines:

```
#ifndef ANIMAL_HPP
#define ANIMAL_HPP
...                    // the whole file goes here
#endif
```

This says, if you haven't defined the term ANIMAL_HPP, go ahead and define it now. Between the #define statement and the closing #endif are the *entire* contents of the file.

The first time your program includes this file it reads the first line and the test evaluates *true*; that is, you have not yet defined ANIMAL_HPP. Thus, it goes ahead and defines it and then includes the entire file.

The second time your program includes the ANIMAL.HPP file, it reads the first line and the test evaluates *false*; ANIMALL_HPP *has* been defined. It therefore skips to the next #else (there isn't one) or the next #endif (at the end of the file). Thus, it skips the entire contents of the file and the class is not declared twice.

The actual name of the defined symbol (ANIMAL_HPP) is not important, though it is customary to use the filename in all uppercase with the dot (.) changed to an underscore. This is purely convention, however.

 Note: It never hurts to use inclusion guards. Often they will save you hours of debugging time.

Defining on the Command Line

Almost all C++ compilers will let you #define values either from the command line or from the integrated development environment (and usually both). Thus you can leave out lines 1 and 2 from Listing 11.1, and define DemoVersion and BetaTestVersion from the command line for some compilations, and not for others.

It is common to put in special debugging code surrounded by #ifdef DEBUG and #endif. This allows all of the debugging code to be easily removed from the source code when you compile the final version: just don't define the term DEBUG.

Undefining

If you have a name defined and you'd like to turn it off from within your code, you can use #undef. This works as the antidote to #define. Listing 17.2 provides an illustration of its use.

Listing 17.2. Using #undef.

```
1:     #define DemoVersion
2:     #define DOS_VERSION 5
3:     #include <iostreams.h>
4:
5:
6:     void main()
7:     {
8:
9:     cout << "Checking on the definitions of DemoVersion, DOS_VERSION and
       ➥WINDOWS_VERSION...\n";
10:
11:    #ifdef DemoVersion
12:        cout << "DemoVersion defined.\n";
13:    #else
14:        cout << "DemoVersion not defined.\n";
15:    #endif
16:
17:    #ifndef DOS_VERSION
18:        cout << "DOS_VERSION not defined!\n";
19:    #else
20:        cout << "DOS_VERSION defined as: " << DOS_VERSION << endl;
21:    #endif
22:
23:    #ifdef WINDOWS_VERSION
24:        cout << "WINDOWS_VERSION defined!\n";
25:    #else
26:        cout << "WINDOWS_VERSION was not defined.\n";
27:    #endif
28:
29:    #undef DOS_VERSION
30:
31:     #ifdef DemoVersion
32:        cout << "DemoVersion defined.\n";
33:    #else
34:        cout << "DemoVersion not defined.\n";
35:    #endif
36:
37:    #ifndef DOS_VERSION
38:        cout << "DOS_VERSION not defined!\n";
39:    #else
40:        cout << "DOS_VERSION defined as: " << DOS_VERSION << endl;
41:    #endif
42:
43:    #ifdef WINDOWS_VERSION
44:        cout << "WINDOWS_VERSION defined!\n";
45:    #else
46:        cout << "WINDOWS_VERSION was not defined.\n";
47:    #endif
48:
49:     cout << "Done.\n";
50:    }
```

```
Checking on the definitions of DemoVersion, DOS_VERSION and WINDOWS_VERSION...
DemoVersion defined
DOS_VERSION defined as: 5
WINDOWS_VERSION was not defined.
DemoVersion defined
DOS_VERSION not defined!
WINDOWS_VERSION was not defined.
Done.
```

Listing 17.2 is the same as Listing 17.1 until line 29 when #undef DOS_VERSION is called. This removes the definition of the term DOS_VERSION without changing the other defined terms (in this case, DemoVersion.) The rest of the listing just repeats the printouts. The test for DemoVersion and WINDOWS_VERSION act as they did the first time, but the test for DOS_VERSION now evaluates TRUE. In this second case DOS_VERSION does *not* exist as a defined term.

Conditional Compilation

By combining #define or command line definitions with #ifdef, #else, and #ifndef you can write one program, which compiles different code depending on what is already #define'd. This can be used to create one set of source code to compile on two different platforms, such as DOS and Windows.

Another common use of this technique is to conditionally compile in some code based on whether or not debug has been defined, as you'll see in a few moments.

DO	DON'T

DO use conditional compilation when you need to create more than one version of your code at the same time.

DON'T let your conditions get too complex to manage.

DO use #undef as often as possible to avoid leaving stray definitions in your code.

DO use inclusion guards!

Macro Functions

The #define directive can also be used to create *macro functions*. A macro function is a symbol created using #define, which takes an argument, much like a function does. The preprocessor will substitute the substitution string for whatever argument it is given. For example, you can define the macro TWICE as:

```
#define TWICE(x) ( (x) * 2 )
```

and then in your code you write

```
TWICE(4)
```

The entire string TWICE(4) will be removed and the value 8 will be substituted! When the precompiler sees the 4, it will substitute ((4) * 2) which will then evaluate to 4 * 2 or 8.

A macro can have more than one parameter, and each parameter can be used repeatedly in the replacement text. Two common macros are MAX and MIN

```
#define MAX(x,y) ( (x) > (y) ? (x) : (y) )
#define MIN(x,y) ( (x) < (y) ? (x) : (y) )
```

Note that in a macro function definition, the opening parenthesis for the parameter list must *immediately* follow the macro name, with no spaces. The preprocessor is not as forgiving of white space as is the compiler.

If you were to write

```
#define MAX (x,y) ( (x) > (y) ? (x) : (y) )
```

and then to try to use MAX like this

```
int x = 5, y = 7, z;
z = MAX(x,y);
```

the intermediate code would be:

```
int x = 5, y = 7, z;
z = (x,y) ( (x) > (y) ? (x) : (y) ) (x,y)
```

A simple text substitution would be done, rather than invoking the macro function. Thus the token MAX would have substituted for it (x,y) ((x) > (y) ? (x) : (y)) and then that would be followed by the (x,y) which followed Max.

By removing the space between MAX and (x,y), however, the intermediate code becomes:

```
int x = 5, y = 7, z;
z =7;
```

Why All the Parentheses?

You may be wondering why there are so many parentheses in many of the macros presented so far. The preprocessor does not demand that parentheses be placed around

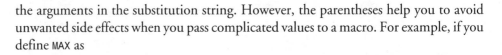

the arguments in the substitution string. However, the parentheses help you to avoid unwanted side effects when you pass complicated values to a macro. For example, if you define MAX as

```
#define MAX (x,y) x > y ? x : y
```

and pass in the values 5 and 7, the macro works as intended. But if you pass in a more complicated expression, you'll get unintended results, as shown in Listing 17.3.

Listing 17.3. Using parentheses in macros.

```
1:      // Listing 17.3 Macro Expansion
2:      #include <iostreams.h>
3:
4:      #define CUBE(a) ( (a) * (a) * (a) )
5:      #define THREE(a) a * a * a
6:
7:      void main()
8:      {
9:          long x = 5;
10:         long y = CUBE(x);
11:         long z = THREE(x);
12:
13:         cout << "y: " << y << endl;
14:         cout << "z: " << z << endl;
15:
16:         long a = 5, b = 7;
17:         y = CUBE(a+b);
18:         z = THREE(a+b);
19:
20:         cout << "y: " << y << endl;
21:         cout << "z: " << z << endl;
22:     }
```

```
y: 125
z: 125
y: 1728
z: 82
```

On line 4 the macro CUBE is defined, with the argument x put into parentheses each time it is used. On line 5 the macro THREE is defined, without the parentheses.

In the first use of these macros, the value 5 is given as the parameter, and both macros work fine. CUBE(5) expands to ((5) * (5) * (5)) which evaluates to 125, and THREE(5) expands to 5 * 5 * 5 which also evaluates to 125.

In the second use, on lines 16-18, the parameter is 5 + 7. In this case CUBE(5+7) evaluates to

```
( (5+7) * (5+7) * (5+7) )
```

which evaluates to

```
( (12) * (12) * (12) )
```

which in turn evaluates to 1,728. THREE(5+7), however, evaluates to

```
5 + 7 * 5 + 7 * 5 + 7
```

Because multiplication has a higher precedence than addition, this becomes

```
5 + (7 * 5) + (7 * 5) + 7
```

which evaluates to

```
5 + (35) + (35) + 7
```

which finally evaluates to 82.

Macros Versus Functions and Templates

Macros suffer from four problems in C++. The first is that they can be confusing if they get large, as all macros must be defined on one line. You can extend that line by using the backslash character (\), but large macros quickly become difficult to manage.

The second problem is that macros are expanded in line each time they are used. This means that if a macro is used a dozen times, the substitution will appear 12 times in your program, rather than once as a function call will. On the other hand, they are usually quicker than a function call because the overhead of a function call is avoided.

The fact that they are expanded inline leads to the third problem, which is that the macro does not appear in the intermediate source code used by the compiler, and thus is unavailable in most debuggers. This makes debugging macros tricky.

The final problem, however, is the biggest: macros are not type-safe. While it is convenient that absolutely any argument may be used with a macro, this completely undermines the strong typing of C++ and so is anathema to C++ programmers. Templates overcome this problem, as you'll see on Day 19.

Inline Functions

It is often possible to declare an inline function, rather than a macro. For example, Listing 17.4 creates a CUBE function, which accomplishes the same thing as the CUBE macro in Listing 17.3, but does so in a type-safe way.

Listing 17.4. Using inline rather than a macro.

```
1:      #include <iostream.h>
2:
3:      inline unsigned long Square(unsigned long a) { return a * a; }
4:      inline unsigned long Cube(unsigned long a) { return a * a * a; }
5:      void main()
6:      {
7:          unsigned long x=1 ;
8:
9:          for (;;)
10:         {
11:             cout << "Enter a number (0 to quit): ";
12:             cin >> x;
13:             if (x == 0)
14:                 break;
15:             cout << "You entered: " << x;
16:             cout << ".  Square(" << x << "): "  << Square(x) << ". Cube("
              ↪<< x << "): " << Cube(x) << "." << endl;
17:         }
18:     }
```

```
Enter a number (0 to quit): 1
You entered: 1. Square(1): 1. Cube(1): 1.
Enter a number (0 to quit): 2
You entered: 2. Square(1): 4. Cube(1): 8.
Enter a number (0 to quit): 3
You entered: 3. Square(1): 9. Cube(1): 27
Enter a number (0 to quit): 4
You entered: 4. Square(1): 16. Cube(1): 64
Enter a number (0 to quit): 5
You entered: 5. Square(1): 25. Cube(1): 125.
Enter a number (0 to quit): 6
You entered: 6. Square(1): 36. Cube(1): 216.
Enter a number (0 to quit): 0
```

On lines 3 and 4, two inline functions are declared, Square() and Cube(). Each is declared to be inline, so like a macro function these will be expanded in place for each call, and there will be no function call overhead.

As a reminder, expanded inline means that the content of the function will be placed into the code wherever the function call is made (for example, on line 16). Because the function call is never made, there is no overhead of putting the return address and the parameters on the stack. If this sounds unfamiliar, please reread the section on function calls on Day 5.

On line 16 the function Square is called as is the function Cube. Again, because these are inline functions, it is exactly as if this line had been written:

```
16:         cout << ".  Square(" << x << "): "  << x * x << ". Cube(" << x << "): "
<< x * x * x <<
 "." << endl;
```

String Manipulation

The preprocessor provides two special operators for manipulating strings in macros. The stringizing operator (#) substitutes a quoted string for whatever follows the stringizing operator. The concatenation operator bonds two strings together into one.

Stringizing

The stringizing operator(#) puts quotes around any characters following the operator, up to the next white space. Thus, if you write:

```
#define WRITESTRING(x) cout << #x
```

and then call

```
WRITESTRING(This is a string);
```

the precompiler will turn it into:

```
cout << "This is a string";
```

Note that the string `This is a string` is put into quotes, as required by `cout`.

Concatenation

The concatenation operator allows you to bond together more than one term into a new word. The new word is actually a *token* which can be used as a class name, a variable name, an offset into an array, or anywhere else a series of letters might appear.

Assume for a moment that you have five functions, named `fOnePrint`, `fTwoPrint`, `fThreePrint`, `fFourPrint` and `fFivePrint`. You can then declare:

```
#define fPRINT(x) f ## x ## Print
```

and then use it with `fPRINT(Two)` to generate `fTwoPrint` and with `fPRINT(Three)` to generate `fThreePrint`.

At the conclusion of Week 2 a `PartsList` class was developed. This list could only handle objects of type `List`. Let's say that this list works well, and you'd like to be able to make lists of animals, cars, computers, etc.

One approach would be to create `AnimalList`, `CarList`, `ComputerList`, and so forth, cutting and pasting the code in place. This will quickly become a nightmare, as every change to one list must be written to all the others.

An alternative is to use macros and the concatenation operator. For example you could define:

```
#define Listof(Type)  class Type##List \
{ \
public: \
    Type##List(){} \
private:          \
    int itsLength; \
};
```

This example is overly sparse, but the idea would be to put in all the necessary methods and data. When you were ready to create an `AnimalList` you would write

```
Listof(Animal)
```

and this would be turned into the declaration of the `AnimalList` class. There are some problems with this approach, all of which are discussed in detail on Day 19, when templates are discussed.

Predefined Macros

Many compilers predefine a number of useful macros, including `__DATE__`, `__TIME__`, `__LINE__`, and `__FILE__`. Each of these names is surrounded by two underscore characters to reduce the likelihood that the names will conflict with names you've used in your program.

When the precompiler sees one of these macros it makes the appropriate substitutes. For `__DATE__`, the *current* Date is substituted. For `__TIME__`, the current time is substituted. `__LINE__` and `__FILE__` are replaced with the source code line number and filename respectively. You should note that this substitution is made when the source is precompiled, not when the program is run. If you asked the program to print `__DATE__`, you will not get the current date, instead you will get the date the program was compiled. These defined macros are *very* useful in debugging.

assert()

Many compilers offer an `assert()` macro. The `assert()` macro returns true if its parameter evaluates true and takes some kind of action if it evaluates false. Many compilers will abort the program on an `assert()` that fails, others will thrown an exception (see Day 20).

One powerful feature of the `assert()` macro is that the preprocessor collapses it into no code at all if DEBUG is not defined. It is a great help during development, but when the final product ships there is no performance penalty nor increase in the size of the executable version of the program.

Rather than depending on the compiler provided assert(), you are free to write your own assert() macro. Listing 17.5 provides a simple assert() macro and shows its use.

Listing 17.5. A simple assert() macro.

```
1:      // Listing 17.5 ASSERTS
2:      #define DEBUG
3:      #include <iostreams.h>
4:
5:      #ifndef DEBUG
6:          #define ASSERT(x)
7:      #else
8:          #define ASSERT(x) \
9:                  if (! (x)) \
10:                 { \
11:                     cout << "ERROR!! Assert " << #x << " failed\n"; \
12:                     cout << " on line " << __LINE__ << "\n"; \
13:                     cout << " in file " << __FILE__ << "\n";   \
14:                 }
15:     #endif
16:
17:
18:     void main()
19:     {
20:         int x = 5;
21:         cout << "First assert: \n";
22:         ASSERT(x==5);
23:         cout << "\nSecond assert: \n";
24:         ASSERT(x != 5);
25:         cout << "\nDone.\n";
26:     }
```

17

```
First assert:

Second assert:
ERROR!! Assert x!=5 failed
 on line 24
 in file test1804.cpp
```

On line 2 the term DEBUG is defined. Typically this would be done from the command line (or the IDE) at compile time, so that you can turn this on and off at will. On lines 8-15 the assert() macro is defined. Typically this would be done in a header file, and that header (ASSERT.HPP) would be included in all of your implementation files.

On line 5 the term DEBUG is tested. If it is *not* defined, assert() is defined to create no code at all. If DEBUG is defined, then the functionality defined on lines 8-14 is applied.

The assert() itself is one long statement, split across 7 source code lines, as far as the precompiler is concerned. On line 9 the value passed in as a parameter is tested; if it evaluates false, the statements on lines 11-13 are invoked, printing an error message. If the value passed in evaluates TRUE, no action is taken.

Debugging with *assert()*

When writing your program you will often *know* deep down in your soul that something is true: a function has a certain value, a pointer is valid, and so forth. It is the nature of bugs that what you know to be true might not be under some conditions. For example, you *know* that a pointer is valid, yet the program crashes. assert() can help you find this type of bug, but only if you make it a regular practice to use assert()s liberally in your code. *Every time* you assign or are passed a pointer as a parameter or function return value, be sure to assert that the pointer is valid. Any time your code depends on a particular value being in a variable, assert() that that is true.

There is no penalty for frequent use of assert()s; they are removed from the code when you undefine debugging. They also provide good internal documentation, reminding the reader of what you believe is true at any given moment in the flow of the code.

assert() Versus Exceptions

On Day 20 you will learn how to work with exceptions to handle error conditions. It is important to note that assert()s are *not* intended to handle run-time error conditions such as bad data, out of memory conditions, unable to open file, and so forth. assert()s are created to catch *programming* errors only. That is, if an assert() "fires," you know you have a bug in your code.

This is critical, because when you ship your code to your customers the assert()s will be removed. You can not depend on an assert() to handle a runtime problem, because the assert() won't be there.

It is a common mistake to use assert() to test the return value from a memory assignment:

```
Animal *pCat = new Cat;
Assert(pCat);   // bad use of assert
pCat->SomeFunction();
```

This is a classic programming error; every time the programmer runs the program there is enough memory and the assert() never fires. After all, the programmer is running with lots of extra RAM to speed up the compiler, debugger, and so forth. The programmer then ships the executable and the poor user, who has less memory, reaches this part of the program and the call to new fails and returns null. The assert(), however, is no longer in the code and there is nothing to indicate that the pointer points to null. As soon as the statement pCat->SomeFunction() is reached, the program crashes.

Getting NULL back from a memory assignment is *not* a programming error, though it is an exceptional situation. Your program *must* be able to recover from this condition, if only by throwing an exception. Remember: The entire assert() statement is *gone* when debug is undefined. Exceptions are covered in detail on Day 20.

Side Effects

It is not uncommon to find that a bug appears only after the assert()s are removed. This is almost always due to the program unintentionally depending on side effects of things done in assert()s and other debug-only code. For example, if you write

```
ASSERT (x = 5)
```

when you mean to test whether x == 5, you will create a particularly nasty bug.

Let's say that just prior to this assert() you called a function that set x equal to zero. With this assert() you *think* you are testing whether x is equal to 5; in fact, you are set-ting x equal to five. The test returns true, because x = 5 not only sets x to five, but returns the value 5, and since 5 is non-zero it evaluates as TRUE.

Once you pass the assert() statement x really is equal to five (you just set it!). Your program runs just fine, and you're ready to ship it, so you turn debugging off. Now the assert() disappears and you are no longer setting x to five. Since x was set to zero just before this, it remains at zero and your program breaks.

In frustration, you turn debugging back on, but hey! Presto! The bug is gone. Once again, this is rather funny to watch, but not to live through, so be very careful about side effects in debugging code. If you see a bug that only appears when debugging is turned off, take a look at your debugging code with an eye out for nasty side effects.

Class Invariants

Most classes have some conditions that should always be true whenever you are finished with a class member function. These class *invariants* are the *sine qua non* of your class. For example, it may be true that your CIRCLE object should never have a radius of zero, or that your ANIMAL should always have an age greater than zero and less than 100.

It can be very helpful to declare an Invariants() method that returns true only if each of these conditions is still true. You can then Assert(Invariants()) at the start and completion of every class method. The exception would be that your Invariants() would not expect to return true before your constructor runs or after your destructor ends. Listing 17.6 demonstrates the use of the Invariants() method in a trivial class.

Listing 17.6. Using Invariants().

```
1:     #define DEBUG
2:     #define SHOW_INVARIANTS
3:     #include <iostreams.h>
4:     #include <string.h>
5:
6:     #ifndef DEBUG
7:     #define ASSERT(x)
8:     #else
9:     #define ASSERT(x) \
10:            if (! (x)) \
11:            { \
12:                cout << "ERROR!! Assert " << #x << " failed\n"; \
13:                cout << " on line " << __LINE__ << "\n"; \
14:                cout << " in file " << __FILE__ << "\n"; \
15:            }
16:     #endif
17:
18:     enum BOOL { FALSE, TRUE } ;
19:
20:     class String
21:     {
22:        public:
23:            // constructors
24:            String();
25:            String(const char *const);
26:            String(const String &);
27:            ~String();
28:
29:            char & operator[](int offset);
30:            char operator[](int offset) const;
31:
32:            String & operator= (const String &);
33:            int GetLen()const { return itsLen; }
34:            const char * GetString() const { return itsString; }
35:            BOOL Invariants();
36:
37:        private:
38:            String (int);          // private constructor
39:            char * itsString;
40:            unsigned short itsLen;
41:     };
42:
43:     // default constructor creates string of 0 bytes
44:     String::String()
45:     {
```

```
46:        itsString = new char[1];
47:        itsString[0] = '\0';
48:        itsLen=0;
49:        ASSERT(Invariants());
50:    }
51:
52:    // private (helper) constructor, used only by
53:    // class methods for creating a new string of
54:    // required size.  Null filled.
55:    String::String(int len)
56:    {
57:        itsString = new char[len+1];
58:        for (int i = 0; i<=len; i++)
59:            itsString[1] = '\0';
60:        itsLen=len;
61:        ASSERT(Invariants());
62:    }
63:
64:    // Converts a character array to a String
65:    String::String(const char * const cString)
66:    {
67:        itsLen = strlen(cString);
68:        itsString = new char[itsLen+1];
69:        for (int i = 0; i<itsLen; i++)
70:            itsString[i] = cString[i];
71:        itsString[itsLen]='\0';
72:        ASSERT(Invariants());
73:    }
74:
75:    // copy constructor
76:    String::String (const String & rhs)
77:    {
78:        itsLen=rhs.GetLen();
79:        itsString = new char[itsLen+1];
80:        for (int i = 0; i<itsLen;i++)
81:            itsString[i] = rhs[i];
82:        itsString[itsLen] = '\0';
83:        ASSERT(Invariants());
84:    }
85:
86:    // destructor, frees allocated memory
87:    String::~String ()
88:    {
89:        ASSERT(Invariants());
90:        delete [] itsString;
91:        itsLen = 0;
92:    }
93:
94:    // operator equals, frees existing memory
95:    // then copies string and size
96:    String& String::operator=(const String & rhs)
97:    {
98:        ASSERT(Invariants());
99:        if (this == &rhs)
100:           return *this;
```

continues

Listing 17.6. continued

```
101:        delete [] itsString;
102:        itsLen=rhs.GetLen();
103:        itsString = new char[itsLen+1];
104:        for (int i = 0; i<itsLen;i++)
105:            itsString[i] = rhs[i];
106:        itsString[itsLen] = '\0';
107:        ASSERT(Invariants());
108:        return *this;
109:    }
110:
111:    //non constant offset operator, returns
112:    // reference to character so it can be
113:    // changed!
114:    char & String::operator[](int offset)
115:    {
116:        ASSERT(Invariants());
117:        if (offset > itsLen)
118:            return itsString[itsLen-1];
119:        else
120:            return itsString[offset];
121:        ASSERT(Invariants());
122:    }
123:
124:    // constant offset operator for use
125:    // on const objects (see copy constructor!)
126:    char String::operator[](int offset) const
127:    {
128:        ASSERT(Invariants());
129:        if (offset > itsLen)
130:            return itsString[itsLen-1];
131:        else
132:            return itsString[offset];
133:        ASSERT(Invariants());
134:    }
135:
136:
137:    BOOL String::Invariants()
138:    {
139: #ifdef SHOW_INVARIANTS
140:        cout << " String OK ";
141: #endif
142:        return ( (itsLen && itsString) ¦¦ (!itsLen && !itsString) );
143:    }
144:
145:    class Animal
146:    {
147:    public:
148:        Animal():itsAge(1),itsName("John Q. Animal"){ASSERT(Invariants());}
149:        Animal(int, const String&);
150:        ~Animal(){}
151:        int GetAge() { ASSERT(Invariants()); return itsAge;}
152:        void SetAge(int Age) { ASSERT(Invariants()); itsAge = Age;
            ➡ASSERT(Invariants()); }
153:        String& GetName() { ASSERT(Invariants()); return itsName;  }
```

```
154:        void SetName(const String& name)
155:              { ASSERT(Invariants()); itsName = name; ASSERT(Invariants());}
156:        BOOL Invariants();
157:    private:
158:        int itsAge;
159:        String itsName;
160:    };
161:
162:    Animal::Animal(int age, const String& name):
163:    itsAge(age),
164:    itsName(name)
165:    {
166:        ASSERT(Invariants());
167:    }
168:
169:    BOOL Animal::Invariants()
170:    {
171:    #ifdef SHOW_INVARIANTS
172:        cout << " Animal OK ";
173:    #endif
174:        return (itsAge > 0 && itsName.GetLen());
175:    }
176:
177:    void main()
178:    {
179:        Animal sparky(5,"Sparky");
180:        cout << "\n" << sparky.GetName().GetString() << " is ";
181:        cout << sparky.GetAge() << " years old.";
182:        sparky.SetAge(8);
183:        cout << "\n" << sparky.GetName().GetString() << " is ";
184:        cout << sparky.GetAge() << " years old.";
185:    }
```

Output

```
String OK  String OK  String OK  String OK  String OK  String OK String OK
➥String OK
Animal OK  Animal OK
Sparky is  Animal OK  5 years old. Animal OK  Animal OK  Animal OK
Sparky is Animal OK 8 years old. String OK  String OK
```

Analysis

On lines 6-16 the assert() macro is defined. If DEBUG is defined this will write out an error message when the assert() macro evaluates false.

On line 35 the String class member function Invariants() is declared; it is defined on lines 137-143. The constructor is declared on lines 44-50, and on line 49, after the object is fully constructed, Invariants() is called to confirm proper construction.

This pattern is repeated for the other constructors, and the destructor calls Invariants() only *before* it sets out to destroy the object. The remaining class functions call Invariants() both before taking any action and then again before returning. This both affirms and validates a fundamental principal of C++: member functions other than constructors and destructors should work on valid objects and should leave them in a valid state.

On line 155 class `Animal` declares its own `Invariants()` method, implemented on lines 169-175. Note on lines 151, 152, 153, and 155 that inline functions can call the `Ivariants()` method.

Printing Interim Values

In addition to asserting that something is true using the `assert()` macro, you may want to print the current value of pointers, variables, and strings. This can be very helpful in checking your assumptions about the progress of your program, and in locating off-by-one bugs in loops. Listing 17.7 illustrates this idea.

Listing 17.7. Printing values in `DEBUG` mode.

```
1:     // Listing 17.7
2:     #include <iostreams.h>
3:     #define DEBUG
4:
5:     #ifndef DEBUG
6:     #define PRINT(x)
7:     #else
8:     #define PRINT(x) \
9:        cout << #x << ":\t" << x << endl;
10:    #endif
11:
12:    enum BOOL { FALSE, TRUE } ;
13:
14:    void main()
15:    {
16:       int x = 5;
17:       long y = 738981;
18:       PRINT(x);
19:       for (int i = 0; i < x; i++)
20:       {
21:          PRINT(i);
22:       }
23:
24:       PRINT (y);
25:       PRINT("Hi.");
26:       int *px = &x;
27:       PRINT(px);
28:       PRINT (*px);
29:    }
```

```
x:        5
i:        0
i:        1
i:        2
i:        3
i:        4
```

```
y:              73898
"Hi.":          Hi
px:             0x2100
*px:            5
```

The macro on lines 5 to 10 provides printing of the current value of the supplied parameter. Note that the first thing fed to cout is the *stringized* version of the parameter, that is if you pass in x cout receives "x".

Next cout receives the quoted string ":\t" which prints a colon and then a tab. Third, cout receives the value of the parameter (x) and then finally, endl, which writes a new line and flushes the buffer.

Debugging Levels

In large, complex projects, you may want more control than simply turning DEBUG on and off. You can define *debug levels*, and test for these levels when deciding which macros to use and which to strip out.

To define a level, simply follow the #define DEBUG statement with a number. While you can have any number of levels, a common system is to have four levels: HIGH, MEDIUM, LOW, and NONE. Listing 17.8 illustrates how this might be done, using the String and Animal classes from Listing 16.6. The definitions of the class methods other than Invariants() have been left out to save space, as they are unchanged from Listing 16.6.

Note: To compile this code, copy lines 43-136 of Listing 17.6 between lines 64 and 65 of this listing.

Listing 17.8. Levels of debugging.

```
1:      enum LEVEL { NONE, LOW, MEDIUM, HIGH };
2:      enum BOOL { FALSE, TRUE } ;
3:
4:      #define DEBUGLEVEL MEDIUM
5:
6:      #include <iostreams.h>
7:      #include <string.h>
8:
9:      #if DEBUGLEVEL < LOW  // must be medium or high
10:     #define ASSERT(x)
11:     #else
12:     #define ASSERT(x) \
```

continues

Listing 17.8. continued

```
13:                    if (! (x)) \
14:                    { \
15:                       cout << "ERROR!! Assert " << #x << " failed\n"; \
16:                       cout << " on line " << __LINE__ << "\n"; \
17:                       cout << " in file " << __FILE__ << "\n"; \
18:                    }
19:    #endif
20:
21:    #if DEBUGLEVEL < MEDIUM
22:    #define EVAL(x)
23:    #else
24:    #define EVAL(x) \
25:       cout << #x << ":\t" << x << endl;
26:    #endif
27:
28:    #if DEBUGLEVEL < HIGH
29:    #define PRINT(x)
30:    #else
31:    #define PRINT(x) \
32:       cout << x << endl;
33:    #endif
34:
35:
36:    class String
37:    {
38:       public:
39:          // constructors
40:          String();
41:          String(const char *const);
42:          String(const String &);
43:          ~String();
44:
45:          char & operator[](int offset);
46:          char operator[](int offset) const;
47:
48:          String & operator= (const String &);
49:          int GetLen()const { return itsLen; }
50:          const char * GetString() const { return itsString; }
51:          BOOL Invariants() const;
52:
53:       private:
54:          String (int);          // private constructor
55:          char * itsString;
56:          unsigned short itsLen;
57:    };
58:
59:    BOOL String::Invariants() const
60:    {
61:       PRINT("(String Invariants Checked)");
62:       return ( (BOOL) (itsLen && itsString) || (!itsLen && !itsString) );
63:    }
64:
65:    class Animal
66:    {
```

```
67:      public:
68:          Animal():itsAge(1),itsName("John Q. Animal"){ASSERT(Invariants());}
69:          Animal(int, const String&);
70:          ~Animal(){}
71:          int GetAge() {  ASSERT(Invariants()); return itsAge;}
72:          void SetAge(int Age) { ASSERT(Invariants()); itsAge = Age;
             ➡ASSERT(Invariants()); }
73:          String& GetName() { ASSERT(Invariants()); return itsName;  }
74:          void SetName(const String& name)
75:                { ASSERT(Invariants()); itsName = name; ASSERT(Invariants());}
76:          BOOL Invariants();
77:      private:
78:          int itsAge;
79:          String itsName;
80:      };
81:
82:      BOOL Animal::Invariants()
83:      {
84:          PRINT("(Animal Invariants Checked)");
85:          return (itsAge > 0 && itsName.GetLen());
86:      }
87:
88:      void main()
89:      {
90:          const int AGE = 5;
91:          EVAL(AGE);
92:          Animal sparky(AGE,"Sparky");
93:          cout << "\n" << sparky.GetName().GetString() << " is ";
94:          cout << sparky.GetAge() << " years old.";
95:          sparky.SetAge(8);
96:          cout << "\n" << sparky.GetName().GetString() << " is ";
97:          cout << sparky.GetAge() << " years old.";
98:      }
```

```
DEBUGLEVEL = HIGH
AGE:     5
(String Invariants Checked)
(String Invariants Checked)
(String Invariants Checked)
(String Invariants Checked)
(String Invariants Checked)
(String Invariants Checked)
(String Invariants Checked)
(String Invariants Checked)
(String Invariants Checked)
(String Invariants Checked)

Sparky is (Animal Invariants Checked)
5 Years old. (Animal Invariants Checked)
(Animal Invariants Checked)
(Animal Invariants Checked)

Sparky is (Animal Invariants Checked)
8 years old. (String Invariants Checked)
(String Invariants Checked)
```

```
// run again with DEBUG = MEDIUM

AGE:     5
Sparky is 5 years old.
Sparky is 8 years old.
```

On lines 9 to 19 the assert() macro is defined to be stripped if DEBUGLEVEL is less than LOW (that is DEBUGLEVEL is NONE). If any debugging is enabled the assert() macro will work. On line 21, EVAL is declared to be stripped if DEBUG is less than MEDIUM; if DEBUGLEVEL is NONE or LOW then EVAL is stripped.

Finally, on lines 28-33 the PRINT macro is declared to be stripped if DEBUGLEVEL is less than HIGH. PRINT is used only when DEBUGLEVEL is high, and you can eliminate this macro by setting DEBUGLEVEL to MEDIUM, and still maintain your use of EVAL and of assert().

PRINT is used within the Invariants() methods to print an informative message. EVAL is used on line 91 to evaluate the current value of the constant integer AGE.

DO	DON'T

DO use capitals for your macro names. This is a pervasive convention, and other programmers will be confused if you don't.

DON'T allow your macros to have side effects. Don't increment variables, or assign values from within a macro.

DO surround all arguments with parentheses in macro functions.

Summary

Today you learned more details about working with the preprocessor. Each time you run the compiler the preprocessor runs first and translates your preprocessor directives such as #define and #ifdef.

The preprocessor does text substitution, though with the use of macros these can be somewhat complex. By using #ifdef, #else, and #ifndef you can accomplish conditional compilation, compiling in some statements under one set of conditions and another set of statements under other conditions. This can assist in writing programs for more than one platform, and is often used to conditionally include debugging information.

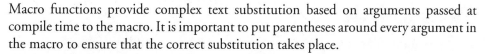

Macro functions provide complex text substitution based on arguments passed at compile time to the macro. It is important to put parentheses around every argument in the macro to ensure that the correct substitution takes place.

Macro functions, and the preprocessor in general, are less important in C++ than they were in C. C++ provides a number of language features, such as const variables and templates, which offer superior alternatives to use of the preprocessor.

Q&A

Q If C++ offers better alternatives than the preprocessor, why is this option still available?

A First, C++ is backwards compatible with C, and all significant parts of C must be supported in C++. Second, there are some uses of the preprocessor which are still used frequently in C++, such as inclusion guards.

Q Why use macro functions when you can use a regular function?

A Macro functions are expanded in line, and are used as a substitute for repeatedly typing the same commands with minor variations. Again, though, templates offer a better alternative.

Q How do you know when to use a macro verses an inline function?

A Often it doesn't matter much, use whichever is simpler. However, macros offer character substitution, stringizing, and concatenation. None of these are available with functions.

Q What is the alternative to using the preprocessor to print interim values during debugging?

A The best alternative is to use watch statements within a debugger. For information on watch statements consult your compiler or debugger documentation.

Q How do you decide when to use an assert() and when to throw an exception?

A If the situation you're testing can be true without your having committed a programming error, use an exception. If the only reason for this situation to ever be true is a bug in your program, use an assert().

Workshop

The Workshop provides quiz questions to help you solidify your understanding of the material covered and exercises to provide you with experience in using what you've learned. Try to answer the quiz and exercise questions before checking the answers in Appendix D, and make sure you understand the answers before continuing to the next chapter.

Quiz

1. What is an inclusion guard?

2. How do you instruct your compiler to print the contents of the intermediate file showing the effects of the preprocessor?

3. What is the difference between `#define debug 0` and `#undef debug`?

4. Name four predefined Macros.

5. Why can't you call `invariants()` as the first line of your constructor?

Exercises

1. Write the inclusion guard statements for the header file STRING.H.

2. Write an `assert()` macro that prints an error message and the file and line number if debug level is 2, just a message (without file and line number) if the level is 1, and does nothing if the level is 0.

3. Write a macro `DPrint` that tests if debug is defined and if it is prints the value passed in as a parameter.

4. Write a function that prints an error message. The function should print the line number and filename where the error occurred. Note that the line number and filename are passed in to this function.

5. How would you call the preceding error function?

6. Write an `assert()` macro that uses the error function from number 4, and write a driver program that calls this `assert()` macro.

Object-Oriented
Analysis and Design

It is easy to become focused on the syntax of C++ and to lose sight of how and why you use these techniques to build programs. Today you will learn:

☐ How to analyze problems from an object-oriented perspective.

☐ How to design your program from an object-oriented perspective.

☐ How to design for reusability and extensibility.

The Development Cycle

Many volumes have been written about the development cycle. Some propose a "waterfall" method, in which designers determine what the program should do; architects determine how the program will be built, what classes will be used, and so forth; and then programmers implement the design and architecture. By the time the design and architecture is given to the programmer, it is complete; all the programmer need do is implement the required functionality.

Even if the waterfall method worked, it would probably be a poor method for writing good programs. As the programmer proceeds, there is a necessary and natural feedback between what has been written so far and what remains to be done. While it is true that good C++ programs are designed in great detail before a line of code is written, it is not true that that design remains unchanged throughout the cycle.

The amount of design that must be finished "up front," before programming begins, is a function of the size of the program. A highly complex effort, involving dozens of programmers working for many months, will require a more fully articulated architecture than a quick and dirty utility written in one day by a single programmer.

This chapter will focus on the design of large, complex programs which will be expanded and enhanced over many years. Many programmers enjoy working at the bleeding edge of technology; they tend to write programs whose complexity pushes at the limits of their tools and understanding. In many ways, C++ was designed to extend the complexity that a programmer or team of programmers could manage.

This chapter will examine a number of design problems from an object-oriented perspective. The goal will be to review the analysis process, and then to understand how you apply the syntax of C++ to implement these design objectives.

Simulating an Alarm System

A simulation is a computer model of a part of a real-world system. There are many reasons to build a simulation, but a good design must start with an understanding of what questions you hope the simulation will answer.

As a starting point, examine this problem: you have been asked to simulate the alarm system for a house. The house is a center hall colonial with four bedrooms, a finished basement, and an under-the-house garage.

The downstairs has the following windows: three in the kitchen, four in the dining room, one in the half-bathroom, two each in the living room and the family room, and two small windows next to the door. All four bedrooms are upstairs, each of which has two windows except for the master bedroom which has four. There are two baths, each with one window. Finally, there are four half-windows in the basement, and one window in the garage.

Normal access to the house is through the front door. Additionally, the kitchen has a sliding glass door and the garage has two doors for the cars, and one door for easy access to the basement. There is also a cellar door in the backyard.

All the windows and doors are alarmed, and there are panic buttons on each phone and next to the bed. The grounds are alarmed as well, though these are carefully calibrated so that they are not set off by small animals or birds.

There is a central alarm system in the basement, which sounds a warning chirp when the alarm has been tripped. If the alarm is not disabled within a setable amount of time, the police are called. If a panic button is pushed, the police are called immediately.

The alarm is also wired into the fire and smoke detectors and the sprinkler system, and the alarm system itself is fault tolerant, has its own internal backup power supply and is encased in a fireproof box.

Preliminary Design

You begin by asking, "What questions might this simulation answer?" For example, you might be able to use the simulation to answer the questions, "How long might a sensor be broken before anyone notices?" or "Is there a way to defeat the window alarms without the police being notified?"

Once you understand the purpose of the simulation you will know what parts of the real system the program must model. Once *that* is well understood, it becomes much easier to design the program itself.

What Are the Objects?

One way to approach this problem is to set aside issues relating to the user interface and to focus only on the components of the "problem space." A first approximation of an object-oriented design might be to list the objects that you need to simulate, and then to examine what these objects "know" and "do."

 The *problem space* is the set of problems and issues your program is trying to solve. The *solution space* is the set of possible solutions to the problems.

For example, clearly you have sensors of various types, a central alarm system, buttons, wires, and telephones. Further thought convinces you that you must also simulate rooms, perhaps floors, and possibly groups of people such as owners, and police.

The sensors can be divided into motion detectors, trip wires, sound detectors, smoke detectors, and so forth. All of these are types of sensors, though there is no such thing as a sensor per se. This is a good indication that *sensor* is an abstract data type (ADT).

As an ADT, the class sensor would provide the complete interface for all types of sensors, and each derived type would provide the implementation. Clients of the various sensors would use them without regard to which type of sensor they are, and they would each "do the right thing" based on their real type.

To create a good ADT, you need to have a complete understanding of what sensors do (rather than how they work). For example, are sensors passive devices or are they active? Do they wait for some element to heat up, a wire to break, a piece of caulk to melt or do they probe their environment? Perhaps some sensors have only a binary state (alarm state or okay) but others have a more analog state (what is the current temperature?). The interface to the abstract data type should be sufficiently complete to handle all the anticipated needs of the myriad derived classes.

Other Objects

The design continues in this way, teasing out the various other classes that will be required to meet the specification. For example, if a log is to be kept, probably a timer will be needed; should the timer poll each sensor or should each sensor file its own report periodically?

The user is going to need to be able to set up, disarm and program the system, and so a terminal of some sort will be required, and you may want a separate object in your simulation for the alarm program itself.

What Are the Classes?

As you solve these problems, you will begin to design your classes. For example, you already have an indication that HeatSensor will derive from Sensor. If the sensor is to make periodic reports, it may also derive via multiple inheritance from Timer, or it may have a timer as a member variable.

The heat sensor will probably have member functions such as CurrentTemp() and SetTempLimit() and will probably inherit functions such as SoundAlarm() from its base class, Sensor.

A frequent issue in object-oriented design is that of encapsulation. You could imagine a design in which the alarm system has a setting for MaxTemp. The alarm system asks the heat sensor what the current temperature is and compares it to the maximum temperature, and sounds the alarm if it is too hot. One could argue that this violates the principle of encapsulation. Perhaps it would be better if the alarm system didn't know or care what the details are of temperature analysis: arguably that should be in the HeatSensor.

Whether or not you agree with that argument, it is the kind of decision you want to focus on during the analysis of the problem. To continue this analysis, one could argue that only the sensor and the log object should know any details of how sensor activity is logged; the alarm object shouldn't know or care.

Good encapsulation is marked by each class having a coherent and complete set of *responsibilities*, and no other class having the same responsibilities. If the sensor is responsible for noting the current temperature, no other class should have that responsibility.

On the other hand, other classes might help deliver the necessary functionality. For example, while it might be the responsibility of the sensor class to note and log the current temperature, it might implement that responsibility by delegating to a log object the job of actually recording the data.

Maintaining a firm division of responsibilities makes your program easier to extend and maintain. When you decide to change the alarm system for an enhanced module, its interface to the log and to the sensors will be narrow and well defined. Changes to the alarm system should not affect the sensor classes, and vice versa.

18

Should the `HeatSensor` have a `ReportAlarm()` function? All sensors will need the ability to report an alarm. This is a good indication that `ReportAlarm()` should be a virtual method of `Sensor`, and that `Sensor` may be an abstract base class. It is possible that `HeatSensor` will chain up to `Sensor`'s more general `ReportAlarm()` method, the overridden function would just fill in the details it is uniquely qualified to supply.

How Are Alarms Reported?

When your sensors report an alarm condition, they will want to provide a lot of information to the object that phones the police and to the log. It may well be that you'll want to create a `Condition` Class, whose constructor takes a number of measurements. Depending on the complexity of the measurements, these too might be objects, or they might be simple scalar values such as integers.

It is possible that condition objects are passed to the central alarm object; or that condition objects are subclassed into alarm objects, which themselves know how to take emergency action. Perhaps there is no central object; instead there might be sensors, which know how to create condition objects. Some condition objects would know how to log themselves, others might know how to contact the police.

A well-designed "event driven" system need not have a central coordinator. One can imagine the sensors all independently receiving and sending message objects to one another, setting parameters, taking readings, monitoring the house. When a fault is detected, an alarm object is created, which logs the problem (by sending a message to the log object?) and takes the appropriate action.

Event Loops

To simulate such an event-driven system, your program needs to create an event loop. An event loop is typically an infinite loop such as `while(1)`, which gets messages from the operating system (mouse clicks, keyboard presses, etc.) and dispatches them one by one, returning to the loop until an exit condition is satisfied. Listing 18.1 shows a rudimentary event loop.

Listing 18.1. A simple event loop.

```
1:     // Listing 16.1
2:
3:     #include <iostreams.h>
4:
5:     class Condition
6:     {
```

```
7:      public:
8:         Condition() { }
9:         virtual ~Condition() {}
10:        virtual void Log() = 0;
11:     };
12:
13:     class Normal : public Condition
14:     {
15:     public:
16:        Normal() { Log(); }
17:        virtual ~Normal() {}
18:        virtual void Log() { cout << "Logging normal conditions...\n"; }
19:     };
20:
21:     class Error : public Condition
22:     {
23:     public:
24:        Error() {Log();}
25:        virtual ~Error() {}
26:        virtual void Log() { cout << "Logging error!\n"; }
27:     };
28:
29:     class Alarm : public Condition
30:     {
31:     public:
32:        Alarm ();
33:        virtual   ~Alarm() {}
34:        virtual void Warn() { cout << "Warning!\n"; }
35:        virtual void Log() { cout << "General Alarm log\n"; }
36:        virtual void Call() = 0;
37:
38:     };
39:
40:     Alarm::Alarm()
41:     {
42:         Log();
43:        Warn();
44:     }
45:     class FireAlarm : public Alarm
46:     {
47:     public:
48:        FireAlarm(){Log();};
49:        virtual ~FireAlarm() {}
50:        virtual void Call() { cout<< "Calling Fire Dept.!\n"; }
51:        virtual void Log() { cout << "Logging fire call.\n"; }
52:     };
53:
54:     void main()
55:     {
56:        int input;
57:        int okay = 1;
58:        Condition * pCondition;
59:        while (okay)
60:        {
61:            cout << "(0)Quit (1)Normal (2)Fire: ";
```

continues

Listing 18.1. continued

```
62:            cin >> input;
63:            okay = input;
64:            switch (input)
65:            {
66:                case 0: break;
67:                case 1:
68:                    pCondition = new Normal;
69:                    delete pCondition;
70:                    break;
71:                case 2:
72:                    pCondition = new FireAlarm;
73:                    delete pCondition;
74:                    break;
75:                default:
76:                    pCondition = new Error;
77:                    delete pCondition;
78:                    okay = 0;
79:                    break;
80:            }
81:        }
82:    }
```

```
(0)Quit (1)Normal (2)Fire: 1
Logging normal conditions...
(0)Quit (1)Normal (2)Fire: 2
General Alarm log
Warning!
Logging fire call.
(0)Quit (1)Normal (2)Fire
```

The simple loop created on lines 59–80 allows the user to enter input simulating a normal report from a sensor and a report of a fire. Note that the effect of this report is to spawn a condition object, whose constructor calls various member functions.

Calling virtual member functions from a constructor can cause confusing results if you are not mindful of the order of construction of objects. For example, when the FireAlarm object is created on line 72 the order of construction is Condition, Alarm, FireAlarm. The Alarm constructor calls Log, but it is Alarm's Log() which is invoked, not FireAlarm's despite Log() being declared virtual. This is because at the time Alarm's constructor runs, there is no fire alarm object. Later, when FireAlarm itself is constructed, its constructor calls Log() again, and this time FireAlarm::Log() is called.

PostMaster

Here's another problem on which to practice your object-oriented analysis: you have been hired by Acme Software Inc. to start a new software project and to hire a team of C++ programmers to implement your program. Jim Grandiose, vice-president of New Product Development, is your new boss. He wants you to design and build PostMaster, a utility to read electronic mail from various unrelated e-mail providers. The potential customer is a business person who uses more than one e-mail product, for example Interchange, CompuServe, Prodigy, America OnLine, Delphi, Internet Mail, Lotus Notes, AppleMail, CC:Mail, and so forth.

The customer will be able to "teach" PostMaster how to dial up or otherwise connect to each of the e-mail providers and PostMaster will get the mail and then present it in a uniform manner, allowing the customer to organize the mail, reply, forward letters among services, and so forth.

PostMasterProfessional, to be developed as version 2 of PostMaster is already antici-pated. It will add an Administrative Assistant mode, which will allow the user to designate another person to read some or all of the mail, to handle routine correspondence, and so forth. There is also speculation in the marketing department that an artificial intelligence component might add the ability for PostMaster to pre-sort and prioritize the mail based on subject and content keywords and associations.

Other enhancements have been talked about, including the ability to handle not only mail but discussion groups such as Interchange discussions, CompuServe Forums, Internet Newsgroups, and so forth. It is obvious that Acme has great hopes for PostMaster, and you are under severe time constraints to bring it to market, though you seem to have a nearly unlimited budget.

Measure Twice, Cut Once

You set up your office and order your equipment, and then your first order of business is to get a good specification for the product. After examining the market, you decide to recommend that development be focused on a single platform, and you set out to decide among DOS, UNIX, the Macintosh, and Windows, Windows NT, and OS/2.

You have many painful meetings with Jim Grandiose, and it becomes clear that there is no right choice, and so you decide to separate the front end, that is the user interface or

18

UI, from the backend, the communications and database part. To get things going quickly, you decide to write for DOS first, followed by Win32, the Mac, then UNIX and OS/2.

This simple decision has enormous ramifications for your project. It quickly becomes obvious that you will need a class library or a series of libraries to handle memory management, the various user interfaces and perhaps also the communications and database components.

Mr. Grandiose believes strongly that projects live or die by having one person with a clear vision, so he asks that you do the initial architectural analysis and design before hiring any programmers. You set out to analyze the problem.

Divide and Conquer

It quickly becomes obvious that you really have more than one problem to solve. You divide the project into these significant sub-projects:

1. Communications: the ability for the software to dial into the e-mail provider via modem, or to connect over a network.

2. Database: the ability to store data and to retrieve it from disk.

3. E-mail: the ability to read various e-mail formats and to write new messages to each system.

4. Editing: providing state-of-the-art editors for the creation and manipulation of messages.

5. Platform issues: the various UI issues presented by each platform (DOS, Macintosh, etc.).

6. Extensibility: planning for growth and enhancements.

7. Organization and scheduling: managing the various developers and their code interdependencies. Each group must devise and publish schedules, and then be able to plan accordingly. Senior management and marketing need to know when the product will be ready.

You decide to hire a manager to handle item seven, organization, and scheduling. You then hire senior developers to help you analyze and design, and then to manage the implementation of the remaining areas. These senior developers will create the following teams:

1. Communications: responsible for both dial-up and network communications. They deal with packets, streams and bits, rather than with e-mail messages per se.

2. Message Format: responsible for converting messages from each e-mail provider to a canonical form (PostMaster standard), and back. It is also their job to write these messages to disk and to get them back off the disk as needed.

3. Message editors: this group is responsible for the entire UI of the product, on each platform. It is their job to ensure that the interface between the back end and the front end of the product is sufficiently narrow that extending the product to other platforms does not require duplication of code.

Message Format

You decide to focus on the message format first, setting aside the issues relating to communications and user interface. These will follow once you understand more fully what it is you are dealing with. There is little sense in worrying about how to present the information to the user until you understand what information you are dealing with.

An examination of the various e-mail formats reveals that they have many things in common, despite their various differences. Each e-mail message has a point of origination, a destination, and a creation date. Nearly all such messages have a title or subject line, and a body which may consist of simple text, rich text (text with formatting), graphics, and perhaps even sound or other fancy additions. Most such e-mail services also support attachments, so that users can send programs and other files.

You confirm your early decision that you will read each mail message out of its original format and into PostMaster Format. This way you will only have to store one record format, and writing to and reading from the disk will be simplified. You also decide to separate the "header" information (sender, recipient, date, title, etc.) from the body of the message. Often the user will want to scan the headers without necessarily reading the contents of all the messages. You anticipate that a time may come when users will want to download only the headers from the message provider, without getting the text at all, but for now you intend that version one of PostMaster will always get the full message, though it may not display them to the user.

Initial Class Design

This analysis of the messages leads you to design the `Message` class. In anticipation of extending the program to non-e-mail messages, you derive `EmailMessage` from the abstract base `Message`. From `EmailMessage` you derive `PostMasterMessage`, `InterchangeMessage`, `CISMessage`, `ProdigyMessage`, and so forth.

Messages are a natural choice for objects in a program handling mail messages, but finding all the right objects in a complex system is the single greatest challenge of object-oriented programming. In some cases, such as with messages, the primary objects seem to "fall out" of your understanding of the problem. More often, however, you have to think long and hard about what you are trying to accomplish to find the right objects.

Don't despair. Most designs are not perfect the first time. A good starting point is to describe the problem out loud. Make a list of all the nouns and verbs you use when describing the project. The nouns are good candidates for objects. The verbs might be the methods of those objects (or they may be objects in their own right). This is not a foolproof method, but it is a good technique to use when getting started on your design.

That was the easy part. Now the question arises, "Should the message header be a separate class from the body?" If so, do you need parallel hierarchies, `CompuServeBody` and `CompuServeHeader`, as well as `ProdigyBody` and `ProdigyHeader`?

Parallel hierarchies are often a warning sign of a bad design. It is a common error in object-oriented design to have a set of objects in one hierarchy, and a matching set of "managers" of those objects in another. The burden of keeping these heartaches up to date and in synch with each other soon becomes overwhelming: a classic maintenance nightmare.

There are no hard and fast rules, of course, and at times such parallel heartaches are the most efficient way to solve a particular problem. Nonetheless, if you see your design moving in this direction you should rethink the problem; there may be a more elegant solution available.

When the messages arrive from the e-mail provider they will not necessarily be separated into header and body; many will be one large stream of data, which your program will have to disentangle. Perhaps your hierarchy should reflect that idea directly.

Further reflection on the tasks at hand leads you to try to list the properties of these messages, with an eye towards introducing capabilities and data storage at the right level of abstraction. Listing properties of your objects is a good way to find the data members, as well as to "shake out" other objects you might need.

Mail messages will need to be stored, as will the user's preferences, phone numbers, and so forth. Storage clearly needs to be high up in the hierarchy. Should the mail messages *necessarily* share a base class with the preferences?

Rooted Hierarchies Versus Non-Rooted

There are two overall approaches to inheritance hierarchies: you can have all, or nearly all of your classes descend from a common root class, or you can have more than one inheritance hierarchy. An advantage of a common root class is that you often can avoid multiple-inheritance; a disadvantage is that many times *implementation* will percolate up into the base class.

NEW ☞ A set of classes is *rooted* if all share a common ancestor.
TERM *Non-rooted* hierarchies do not all share a common base class.

18

Because you know that your product will be developed on many platforms, and because multiple inheritance is complex, and not necessarily well supported by all compilers on all platforms, your first decision is to use a rooted hierarchy and single inheritance. You decide to identify those places where multiple inheritance might be used in the future, and to design so that breaking apart the hierarchy and adding multiple inheritance at a later time need not be traumatic to your entire design.

You decide to prefix the name of all of your internal classes with the letter p, so that you can easily and quickly tell which classes are yours and which are from other libraries. On Day 21 you'll learn about *name spaces*, which can reinforce this idea, but for now the initial will do nicely.

Your root class will be pObject; virtually every class you create will descend from this object. pObject itself will be kept fairly simple; only that data which absolutely every item shares will appear in this class.

If you want a rooted hierarchy, you'll want to give the root class a fairly generic name (like pObject) and few capabilities. The point of a root object is to be able to create collections of all its descendents and refer to them as instances of pObject. The trade off is that rooted hierarchies often percolate interface up into the root class.

The next likely candidates for top of the hierarchy status are pStored and pWired. pStored objects are saved to disk at various times (for example when the program is not in use) and pWired objects are sent over the modem or network. Since nearly all of your objects will need to be stored to disk, it makes sense to push this functionality up high in the hierarchy. Since all the objects that are sent over the modem must be stored, but not all stored objects must be sent over the wire, it makes sense to derive pWired from pStored.

Each derived class acquires all the knowledge (data) and functionality (methods) of its base class, and each should add one discreet additional ability. Thus pWired may add various methods, but all are in service of adding the ability to be transferred over the modem.

It is possible that all wired objects are stored, or that all stored objects are wired, or that neither of these statements is true. If only some wired objects are stored, and only some stored objects are wired, you will be forced either to use multiple inheritance or to "hack around" the problem. A potential "hack" for such a situation would be to inherit, for example, Wired from Stored, and then for those objects that are sent via modem but are never stored, to make the stored methods do nothing or return an error.

In fact you realize that some stored objects clearly are *not* wired, for example: user preferences. All wired objects, however, *are* stored, and so your inheritance hierarchy so far is as reflected in Figure 18.1.

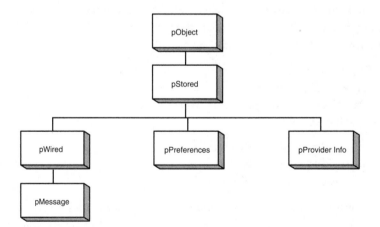

Figure 18.1. *Initial inheritance hierarchy.*

Designing the Interfaces

It is important, at this stage of designing your product, to avoid being concerned with implementation. You want to focus all of your energies on designing a clean interface among the classes, and then delineating what data and methods each class will need.

It is often a good idea to have a solid understanding of the base classes before trying to design the more derived classes, so you decide to focus on pObject, pStored and pWired.

The root class, pObject, will only have those data and methods that are common to everything on your system. Perhaps every object should have a unique identification number? You could create pID (PostMaster ID) and make that a member of pObject; but first you must ask yourself, "Does any object that is not stored and not wired need such a number?" That begs the question, "Are there any objects that are not stored but that are part of this hierarchy?"

If there are no such objects, you may want to consider collapsing pObject and pStored into one class; after all if all objects are stored, what is the point of the differentiation? Thinking this through you realize that there may be some objects, such as address objects, which it would be beneficial to derive from pObject, but that will never be stored on their own; if they are stored it will be as part of some other object.

That says that for now having a separate pObject class would be useful. One can imagine that there will be an address book that would be a collection of pAddress objects, and while no pAddress will ever be stored on its own, there would be utility in having each one have its own unique identification number. You tentatively assign pID to pObject, and this means that pObject, at a minimum will look like this:

```
class pOjbect
{
public:
    pObject();
    ~pObject();
    pID GetID()const;
    void SetID();
private:
    pID  itsID;
}
```

There are a number of things to note about this class declaration. First, this class is not declared to derive from any other; this is your root class. Second, there is no attempt to show implementation, even for methods such as GetID(), which are likely to have inline implementation when you are done.

Third, `const` methods are already identified; this is part of the interface not the implementation. Finally, a new data type is implied: `pID`. Defining `pID` as a type, rather than using, for example, `unsigned long`, puts greater flexibility into your design.

If it turns out that you don't need an `unsigned long`, or that an `unsigned long` is not sufficiently large, you can modify `pID`. That modification will affect every place `pID` is used, and you won't have to track down and edit every file with a `pID` in it.

For now, you will use `typedef` to declare `pID` to be `ULONG`, which in turn you will declare to be `unsigned long`. This raises the question: where do these declarations go?

When programming a large project, an overall design of the files is needed. A standard approach, one which you will follow for this project, is that each class appears in its own header file, and the implementation for the class methods appears in an associated .CPP file. Thus, you will have a file called OBJECT.HPP and another called OBJECT.CPP. You anticipate having other files such as MSG.HPP and MSG.CPP with the declaration of `pMessage` and the implementation of its methods, respectively.

Buy it or write it? One question that you will confront throughout the design phase of your program is which routines might you buy and which must your write yourself. It is entirely possible that you can take advantage of existing commercial libraries to solve some or all of your communications issues. Licensing fees and other non-technical concerns must also be resolved.

It is often advantageous to purchase such a library, and to focus your energies on your specific program, rather than to "reinvent the wheel," about secondary technical issues. You might even want to consider purchasing libraries that were not necessarily intended for use with C++, if they can provide fundamental functionality you'd otherwise have to engineer yourself. This can be instrumental in helping you hit your deadlines.

Building a Prototype

For a project as large as PostMaster, it is unlikely that your initial design will be complete and perfect. It would be easy to become overwhelmed by the sheer scale of the problem, and trying to create all the classes and to complete their interface before writing a line of working code is a recipe for disaster.

There are a number of good reasons to try out your design on a prototype; a quick and dirty working example of your core ideas. There are a number of different types of prototypes, however, each meeting different needs.

An *interface design prototype* provides the chance to test the look and feel of your product with potential users.

A *functionality prototype* might be designed that does not have the final user interface, but which allows users to try out various features, such as forwarding messages or attaching files without worrying about the final interface.

Finally, an *architecture prototype* might be designed to give you a chance to develop a smaller version of the program and to assess how easily your design decisions will "scale up," as the program is fleshed out.

It is imperative to keep your prototyping goals clear. Are you examining the user interface, experimenting with functionality, or building a scale model of your final product? A good architecture prototype makes a poor user Interface prototype, and vice versa.

It is also important to keep an eye on over-engineering the prototype, or becoming so concerned with the investment you've made in the prototype that you are reluctant to tear the code down and redesign as you progress.

The 80/80 Rule

A good design rule of thumb at this stage is to design for those things that 80 percent of the people want to do 80 percent of the time, and to set aside your concerns about the remaining 20 percent. The "boundary conditions" will need to be addressed sooner or later, but the core of your design should focus on the 80/80.

In the face of this you might decide to start by designing the principal classes, setting aside the need for the secondary classes. Further, when you identify multiple classes that will have similar designs, with only minor refinements, you might choose to pick one representative class and focus on that, leaving until later the design and implementation of its close cousins.

> **Note:** There is another rule, the 80/20 rule, which states that "the first 20 percent of your program will take 80 percent of your time to code, the remaining 80 percent of your program will take the other 80 percent of your time!"

Designing the *PostMasterMessage* Class

In keeping with these considerations, you decide to focus on the `PostMasterMessage`. This is the class that is most under your direct control.

As part of its interface, `PostMasterMessage` will need to talk with other types of messages, of course. You hope to be able to work closely with the other message providers, and to get their message format specifications, but for now you can make some smart guesses just by observing what is sent to your computer as you use their services.

In any case, you know that every `PostMasterMessage` will have a sender, a recipient, a date and a subject, as well as the body of the message, and perhaps attached files. This tells you that you'll need accessor methods for each of these attributes, as well as methods to report on the size of the attached files, the size of the messages, and so forth.

Some of the services to which you will connect will use rich text, that is text with formatting instructions to set the font, character size and attributes such as bold and italic. Other services do not support these attributes, and those which do may or may not use their own proprietary scheme for managing rich text. Your class will need conversion methods for turning rich text into plain ASCII, and perhaps for turning other formats into PostMaster formats.

Application Program Interface

An Application Program Interface (API) is a set of documentation and routines for using a service. Many of the mail providers will give you an API so that PostMaster mail will be able to take advantage of their more advanced features, such as rich text and embedding files. PostMaster will also want to publish its own API, so that other providers can plan for working with PostMaster in the future.

Your `PostMasterMessage` class will want to have a well-designed public interface, and the conversion functions will be a principal component of PostMaster's API. Listing 18.2 illustrates what `PostMasterMessage`'s interface looks like so far.

Listing 18.2. `PostMasterMessage`'s interface.

```
1:    class PostMasterMessage : public MailMessage
2:    {
3:    public:
4:      PostMasterMessage();
5:      PostMasterMessage(
```

```
6:          pAddress Sender,
7:          pAddress Recipient,
8:          pString Subject,
9:          pDate creationDate);
10:
11:      // other constructors here
12:      // remember to include copy constructor
13:      // as well as constructor from storage
14:      // and constructor from wire format
15:      // Also include constructors from other formats
16:      ~PostMasterMessage();
17:      pAddress& GetSender() const;
18:      void SetSender(pAddress&);
19:      // other member accessors
20:
21:      // operator methods here, including operator equals
22:      // and conversion routines to turn PostMaster messages
23:      // into messages of other formats.
24:
25:  private:
26:       pAddress itsSender;
27:       pAddress itsRecipient;
28:       pString  itsSubject;
29:       pDate itsCreationDate;
30:       pDate itsLastModDate;
31:       pDate itsReceiptDate;
32:       pDate itsFirstReadDate;
33:       pDate itsLastReadDate;
34:   };
```

18

 None

 Class `PostMasterMessage` is declared to derive from `MailMessage`. A number of constructors will be provided, facilitating the creation of `PostMasterMessages` from other types of mail messages.

A number of accessor methods are anticipated for reading and setting the various member data, as well as operators for turning all or part of this message into other message formats. You anticipate storing these messages to disk, and reading them from the wire, so accessor methods are noted for those purposes as well.

Programming in Large Groups

Even this preliminary architecture is enough to indicate how the various development groups ought to proceed. The communications group can go ahead and start work on the communications back end, negotiating a narrow interface with the Message format group.

The Message Format group will probably lay out the general interface to the Message classes, as was begun above, and then will turn its attention to the question of how to write data to the disk and read it back. Once this disk interface is well understood, they will be in a good position to negotiate the interface to the communications layer.

The message editors will be tempted to create editors with an intimate knowledge of the internals of the message class, but this would be a bad design mistake. They too must negotiate a very narrow interface to the message class; message editor objects should know very little about the internal structure of messages.

Ongoing Design Considerations

As the project continues, you will repeatedly confront this basic design issue: in which class should you put a given set of functionality (or information)? Should the message class have this function, or should the address class? Should the editor store this information, or should the message store it itself?

Your classes should operate on a "need to know" basis, much like secret agents. They shouldn't share any more knowledge than is absolutely necessary.

Design Decisions

As you progress with your program you will face hundreds of design issues. They will range from the more global questions, "What do we want this to do?" to the more specific, "How do we make this work?"

While the details of your implementation won't be finalized until you ship the code, and some of the interfaces will continue to shift and change as you work, you must ensure that your design is well understood early in the process. It is imperative that you know what you are trying to build before you write the code. The single most frequent cause of software dying on the vine must be that there was not sufficient agreement, early enough in the process, about what was being built.

Decisions, Decisions

To get a feel for what the design process is like, examine this question, "What will be on the menu?" For PostMaster, the first choice is probably "new mail message," and this immediately raises another design issue: when the user presses New Message what happens? Does an editor get created, which in turn creates a mail message, or does a new mail message get created, which then creates the editor?

The command you are working with is "new mail message" so creating a new mail message seems like the obvious thing to do. But what happens if the user hits CANCEL after starting to write the message? Perhaps it would be cleaner to first create the editor and have *it* create (and own) the new message.

The problem with this approach is that the editor will need to act differently if it is creating a message than if it is editing the message, whereas if the message is created first and then handed to the editor, only one set of code need exist: everything is an edit of an existing message.

If a message is created first, who creates it? Is it created by the menu command code? If so, does the menu also tell the message to edit itself, or is this part of the constructor method of the message?

It makes sense for the constructor to do this at first glance, after all, every time you create a message you'll probably want to edit it. Nonetheless, this is not a good design idea. First, it is very possible that the premise is wrong: you may well create "canned" messages (e.g., error messages mailed to the system operator) which are *not* put into an editor. Second, and more important, a constructor's job is to create an object: it should do no more and no less than that. Once a mail message is created, the constructor's job is done; adding a call to the edit method just confuses the role of the constructor and makes the mail message vulnerable to failures in the editor.

What is worse, the edit method will call another class: the editor; causing *its* constructor to be called. Yet the editor is not a base class of the message, nor is it contained within the message; it would be unfortunate if the construction of the message depended on successful construction of the editor.

Finally, you won't want to call the editor at all if the message can't be successfully created; yet successful creation would, in this scenario, depend on calling the editor! Clearly you want to fully return from message's constructor before calling `Message::Edit()`.

DO	DON'T

DO look for objects that arise naturally out of your design.

DO redesign as your understanding of the problem space improves.

DON'T share more information among the classes than is absolutely necessary.

DO look for opportunities to take advantage of C++'s polymorphism.

Working with Driver Programs

One approach to surfacing design issues is to create a "driver program," early in the process. For example, the driver program for Post Master might offer a very simple menu, which will create `PostMasterMessage` objects, manipulate them and otherwise exercise some of the design.

 NEW TERM A *driver program* is a function that exists only to demonstrate or test other functions.

Listing 18.3 illustrates a somewhat more robust definition of the `PostMasterMessage` class and a simple driver program.

Listing 18.3. A driver program for `PostMasterMessage`.

```
1:      #include <iostreams.h>
2:      #include <string.h>
3:
4:      typedef unsigned long pDate;
5:      enum SERVICE { PostMaster, Interchange, CompuServe, Prodigy, AOL, Internet };
6:
7:      class String
8:      {
9:        public:
10:          // constructors
11:          String();
12:           String(const char *const);
13:           String(const String &);
14:          ~String();
15:
16:          // overloaded operators
17:          char & operator[](int offset);
18:          char operator[](int offset) const;
19:          String operator+(const String&);
20:          void operator+=(const String&);
21:          String & operator= (const String &);
22:          friend ostream& operator<<( ostream& theStream,String& theString);
23:          // General accessors
24:          int GetLen()const { return itsLen; }
25:          const char * GetString() const { return itsString; }
26:          // static int ConstructorCount;
27:
28:        private:
29:          String (int);           // private constructor
30:          char * itsString;
31:          unsigned short itsLen;
32:
33:      };
34:
35:      // default constructor creates string of 0 bytes
```

```
36:    String::String()
37:    {
38:        itsString = new char[1];
39:        itsString[0] = '\0';
40:        itsLen=0;
41:        // cout << "\tDefault string constructor\n";
42:        // ConstructorCount++;
43:    }
44:
45:    // private (helper) constructor, used only by
46:    // class methods for creating a new string of
47:    // required size.  Null filled.
48:    String::String(int len)
49:    {
50:        itsString = new char[len+1];
51:        for (int i = 0; i<=len; i++)
52:            itsString[1] = '\0';
53:        itsLen=len;
54:        // cout << "\tString(int) constructor\n";
55:        // ConstructorCount++;
56:    }
57:
58:    // Converts a character array to a String
59:    String::String(const char * const cString)
60:    {
61:        itsLen = strlen(cString);
62:        itsString = new char[itsLen+1];
63:        for (int i = 0; i<itsLen; i++)
64:            itsString[i] = cString[i];
65:        itsString[itsLen]='\0';
66:        // cout << "\tString(char*) constructor\n";
67:        // ConstructorCount++;
68:    }
69:
70:    // copy constructor
71:    String::String (const String & rhs)
72:    {
73:        itsLen=rhs.GetLen();
74:        itsString = new char[itsLen+1];
75:        for (int i = 0; i<itsLen;i++)
76:            itsString[i] = rhs[i];
77:        itsString[itsLen] = '\0';
78:        // cout << "\tString(String&) constructor\n";
79:        // ConstructorCount++;
80:    }
81:
82:    // destructor, frees allocated memory
83:    String::~String ()
84:    {
85:        delete [] itsString;
86:        itsLen = 0;
87:        // cout << "\tString destructor\n";
88:    }
89:
90:    // operator equals, frees existing memory
```

continues

Listing 18.3. continued

```
91:     // then copies string and size
92:     String& String::operator=(const String & rhs)
93:     {
94:        if (this == &rhs)
95:           return *this;
96:        delete [] itsString;
97:        itsLen=rhs.GetLen();
98:        itsString = new char[itsLen+1];
99:        for (int i = 0; i<itsLen;i++)
100:          itsString[i] = rhs[i];
101:       itsString[itsLen] = '\0';
102:       return *this;
103:       // cout << "\tString operator=\n";
104:    }
105:
106:    //non constant offset operator, returns
107:    // reference to character so it can be
108:    // changed!
109:    char & String::operator[](int offset)
110:    {
111:       if (offset > itsLen)
112:          return itsString[itsLen-1];
113:       else
114:          return itsString[offset];
115:    }
116:
117:    // constant offset operator for use
118:    // on const objects (see copy constructor!)
119:    char String::operator[](int offset) const
120:    {
121:       if (offset > itsLen)
122:          return itsString[itsLen-1];
123:       else
124:          return itsString[offset];
125:    }
126:
127:    // creates a new string by adding current
128:    // string to rhs
129:    String String::operator+(const String& rhs)
130:    {
131:       int  totalLen = itsLen + rhs.GetLen();
132:       String temp(totalLen);
133:       for (int i = 0; i<itsLen; i++)
134:          temp[i] = itsString[i];
135:       for (int j = 0; j<rhs.GetLen(); j++, i++)
136:          temp[i] = rhs[j];
137:       temp[totalLen]='\0';
138:       return temp;
139:    }
140:
141:    // changes current string, returns nothing
142:    void String::operator+=(const String& rhs)
143:    {
144:       unsigned short rhsLen = rhs.GetLen();
```

```
145:        unsigned short totalLen = itsLen + rhsLen;
146:        String  temp(totalLen);
147:        for (int i = 0; i<itsLen; i++)
148:            temp[i] = itsString[i];
149:        for (int j = 0; j<rhs.GetLen(); j++, i++)
150:            temp[i] = rhs[i-itsLen];
151:        temp[totalLen]='\0';
152:        *this = temp;
153:    }
154:
155:    // int String::ConstructorCount = 0;
156:
157:    ostream& operator<<( ostream& theStream,String& theString)
158:    {
159:        theStream << theString.GetString();
160:        return theStream;
161:    }
162:
163:    class pAddress
164:    {
165:    public:
166:        pAddress(SERVICE theService,
167:                    const String& theAddress,
168:                    const String& theDisplay):
169:            itsService(theService),
170:            itsAddressString(theAddress),
171:            itsDisplayString(theDisplay)
172:            {}
173:        // pAddress(String, String);
174:        // pAddress();
175:        // pAddress (const pAddress&);
176:        ~pAddress(){}
177:        friend ostream& operator<<( ostream& theStream, pAddress& theAddress);
178:        String& GetDisplayString() { return itsDisplayString; }
179:    private:
180:        SERVICE itsService;
181:        String itsAddressString;
182:        String itsDisplayString;
183:    };
184:
185:    ostream& operator<<( ostream& theStream, pAddress& theAddress)
186:    {
187:        theStream << theAddress.GetDisplayString();
188:        return theStream;
189:    }
190:
191:    class PostMasterMessage
192:    {
193:    public:
194:        // PostMasterMessage();
195:
196:        PostMasterMessage(const pAddress& Sender,
197:                            const pAddress& Recipient,
198:                            const String& Subject,
199:                            const pDate& creationDate);
```

continues

Listing 18.3. continued

```
200:
201:      // other constructors here
202:      // remember to include copy constructor
203:      // as well as constructor from storage
204:      // and constructor from wire format
205:      // Also include constructors from other formats
206:      ~PostMasterMessage(){}
207:
208:      void Edit(); // invokes editor on this message
209:
210:      const pAddress& GetSender() const { return itsSender; }
211:      const pAddress& GetRecipient() const { return itsRecipient; }
212:      const String& GetSubject() const { return itsSubject; }
213:      //   void SetSender(pAddress& );
214:      // other member accessors
215:
216:      // operator methods here, including operator equals
217:      // and conversion routines to turn PostMaster messages
218:      // into messages of other formats.
219:
220:   private:
221:      pAddress itsSender;
222:      pAddress itsRecipient;
223:      String  itsSubject;
224:      pDate itsCreationDate;
225:      pDate itsLastModDate;
226:      pDate itsReceiptDate;
227:      pDate itsFirstReadDate;
228:      pDate itsLastReadDate;
229:   };
230:
231:   PostMasterMessage::PostMasterMessage(
232:         const pAddress& Sender,
233:         const pAddress& Recipient,
234:         const String& Subject,
235:         const pDate& creationDate):
236:         itsSender(Sender),
237:         itsRecipient(Recipient),
238:         itsSubject(Subject),
239:         itsCreationDate(creationDate),
240:         itsLastModDate(creationDate),
241:         itsFirstReadDate(0),
242:         itsLastReadDate(0)
243:      {
244:        cout << "Post Master Message created. \n";
245:      }
246:
247:      void PostMasterMessage::Edit()
248:      {
249:          cout << "PostMasterMessage edit function called\n";
250:      }
251:
252:
253:   void main()
```

```
254:    {
255:        pAddress Sender(PostMaster, "jliberty@PostMaster", "Jesse Liberty");
256:        pAddress Recipient(PostMaster, "sliberty@PostMaster","Stacey Liberty");
257:        PostMasterMessage PostMasterMessage(Sender, Recipient, "Saying Hello", 0);
258:        cout << "Message review... \n";
259:        cout << "From:\t\t" << PostMasterMessage.GetSender() << endl;
260:        cout << "To:\t\t" << PostMasterMessage.GetRecipient() << endl;
261:        cout << "Subject:\t" << PostMasterMessage.GetSubject() << endl;
262:    }
```

```
Post Master Message created.
Message review...
From:      Jesse Liberty
To:        Stacey Liberty
Subject:   Saying Hello
```

On line 4 pDate is type-defined to be an unsigned long. It is not uncommon for dates to be stored as a long integer; typically as the number of seconds since an arbitrary starting date such as January 1, 1900. In this program, this is a place holder; you would expect to eventually turn pDate into a real class.

On line 5 an enumerated constant, SERVICE, is defined to allow the address objects to keep track of what type of address they are, including PostMaster, CompuServe, and so forth.

Lines 7–161 represents the interface to and implementation of String, along much the same lines as you have seen in previous chapters. The String class is used for a number of member variables in all of the message classes, and various other classes used by messages, and as such it is pivotal in your program. A full and robust String class will be essential to making your message classes complete.

On lines 162–182 the pAddress class is declared. This represents only the fundamental functionality of this class, and you would expect to flesh this out once your program is better understood. These objects represent essential components in every message: both the sender's address and that of the recipient. A fully functional pAddress object will be able to handle forwarding messages, replies, and so forth.

It is the pAddress object's job to keep track of both the display string as well as the internal routing string for its service. One open question for your design is whether there should be one pAddress object, or if this should be subclassed for each service type. For now the service is tracked as an enumerated constant, which is a member variable of each pAddress object.

Lines 191–229 shows the interface to the PostMasterMessage class. In this particular listing this class stands on its own, but very soon you'll want to make this part of its inheritance hierarchy. When you do redesign this to inherit from Message, some of the

18

member variables may move into the base classes, and some of the member functions may become overrides of base class methods.

A variety of other constructors, accessor functions and other member functions will be required to make this class fully functional. Note that what this listing illustrates is that your class does not have to be 100 percent complete before you can write a simple driver program to test some of your assumptions.

On lines 247–250 the `Edit()` function is "stubbed-out" in just enough detail to indicate where the editing functionality will be put once this class is fully operational.

Lines 253–262 represent the driver program. Currently this program does nothing more than exercise a few of the accessor functions and the `operator<<` overload. Nonetheless, this gives you the starting point for experimenting with `PostMasterMessages` and a framework within which you can modify these classes and examine the impact.

Summary

Today you saw a review of how to bring together many of the elements of C++ syntax, and apply them to object-oriented analysis, design, and programming. The development cycle is not a linear progression from clean analysis through design and culmination in programming: rather it is, in fact, cyclical. The first phase is typically analysis of the problem, with the results of that analysis forming the basis for the preliminary design.

Once a preliminary design is complete, programming can begin, but the lessons learned during the programming phase are fed back into the analysis and design. As programming progresses, testing and then debugging begins. The cycle continues, never really ending though discreet points are reached, at which time it is appropriate to ship the product.

When analyzing a large problem from an object-oriented viewpoint, the interacting parts of the problem are often the objects of the preliminary design. The designer keeps an eye out for process, hoping to encapsulate discreet activities into objects whenever possible.

A class hierarchy must be designed, and fundamental relationships among the interacting parts must be established. The preliminary design is not meant to be final, and functionality will migrate among objects as the design solidifies.

It is a principal goal of object-oriented analysis to hide as much of the data and implementation as possible and to build discreet objects, which have a narrow and well-defined interface. The clients of your object should not need to understand the implementation details of how they fulfill their responsibilities.

Q&A

Q **In what way is object-oriented analysis and design fundamentally different from other approaches.**

A Prior to the development of these object-oriented techniques, analysts and programmers tended to think of programs as functions that acted on data. Object-oriented programming focuses on the integrated data and functionality as discreet units that have both knowledge (data) and capabilities (functions). Procedural programs, on the other hand, focus on functions and how they act on data. It has been said that Pascal and C programs are collections of procedures and C++ programs are collections of classes.

Q **Is object-oriented programming finally the silver bullet that will solve all programming problems?**

A No, it was never intended to be. For large, complex problems, however, object-oriented analysis, design and programming can provide the programmer with tools to manage enormous complexity in ways that were previously impossible.

18

Q **Is C++ the perfect object-oriented language?**

A C++ has a number of advantages and disadvantages when compared with alternative object-oriented programming languages, but it has one killer advantage above and beyond all others: it is the single most popular object-oriented programming language on the face of the Earth. Frankly, most programmers don't decide to program in C++ after an exhaustive analysis of the alternative object-oriented programming languages; they go where the action is, and in the 1990s the action is with C++. There are good reasons for that, C++ has a lot to offer, but this book exists, and I'd wager you are reading it because C++ is the development language of choice at so many corporations.

Q **Where can I learn more about object-oriented analysis and design?**

A Day 21 offers some further suggestions, but it is *my* personal opinion that there are a number of terrific object-oriented analysis and design books available. My personal favorites include:

Object-Oriented Analysis and Design with Applications by Grady Booch (2nd Edition). Published by Benjamin/Cummings Publishing Company, Inc., ISBN: 0-8053-5340-2.

Object-Oriented Modeling and Design by Rumbaugh, Blaha, Premerlani, Eddy and Lorenson. Published by Prentice-Hall, ISBN 0-13-629841-9.

There are many other excellent alternatives. Also be sure to join one of the news groups or conferences on the Internet, Interchange or one of the alternative dial-up services.

Workshop

The Workshop provides quiz questions to help you solidify your understanding of the material covered and exercises to provide you with experience in using what you've learned. Try to answer the quiz and exercise questions before checking the answers in Appendix D, and make sure you understand the answers before continuing to the next chapter.

Quiz

1. What is the difference between object-oriented programming and procedural programming?

2. To what does "event-driven" refer?

3. What are the stages in the development cycle?

4. What is a rooted hierarchy?

5. What is a driver program?

6. What is encapsulation?

Exercises

1. Suppose you had to simulate the intersection of Massachusetts Avenue and Vassar Street—two typical two-lane roads, with traffic lights and crosswalks. The purpose of the simulation is to determine if the timing of the traffic signal allows for a smooth flow of traffic.

   What kinds of objects should be modelled in the simulation? What would the classes be for the simulation?

2. Suppose the intersections from Question 1 were in a suburb of Boston, which has arguably the unfriendliest streets in the U.S. At any time there are three kinds of Boston drivers:

Locals, who continue to drive through intersections after the light turns red; tourists, who drive slowly and cautiously (in a rental car, typically); and taxis, which have a wide variation of driving patterns depending on the kinds of passengers in the cabs.

Also, Boston has two kinds of pedestrians: locals, who cross the street whenever they feel like it, and seldom use the crosswalk buttons; and tourists, who always use the crosswalk buttons and only cross when the Walk/Don't Walk light permits. Finally, Boston has bicyclists who never pay attention to stop lights.

How do these considerations change the model?

3. You are asked to design a group scheduler. The software allows you to arrange meetings among individuals or groups, and to reserve a limited number of conference rooms. Identify the principle subsystems.

4. Design and show the interfaces to the classes in the room reservation portion of the program discussed in Question 3.

18

19

Templates

WEEK
3

On Day 17 you saw how to use macros to create various lists using the concatenation operator.

Today you will learn:

- ☐ What templates are and how to use them.
- ☐ Why templates supply a better alternative to macros.
- ☐ How to create class templates.
- ☐ How to create function templates.

What are Templates?

At the end of Week 2 you saw how to build a `PartsList` object and how to use that to create a `PartsCatalog`. If you want to build on the `PartsList` object to make a list of cats, you have a problem: `PartsList` only knows about parts.

To solve this problem, you can create a list base class and derive from it the `PartsList` and `CatsList` classes. You could then cut and paste much of the `PartsList` class into the new `CatsList` declaration. Next week, when you want to make a list of `Car` objects, you would then have to make a new class, and again you'd cut and paste.

Needless to say, this is not a satisfactory solution. Over time the `List` class and its derived classes will have to be extended. Making sure that all the changes are propagated to all the related classes would be a nightmare.

On Day 17 one approach to parameterizing lists was briefly demonstrated—using macros and name concatenation. Although macros do save much of the cutting and pasting, they have one killer disadvantage: like everything else in the preprocessor, they are not type-safe.

Templates offer the preferred method of creating parameterized lists in C++. They are an integrated part of the language, they are type-safe, and they are very flexible.

Parameterized Types

Templates allow you to teach the compiler how to make a list of any type of thing, rather than creating a set of type-specific lists. A `PartsList` is a list of parts, a `CatList` is a list of cats. The only way in which they differ is the type of the thing on the list. With templates, the type of the thing on the list becomes a parameter to the definition of the class.

A common component of virtually all C++ libraries is an array class. As you saw with Lists, it is tedious and inefficient to create one array class for integers, another for doubles, and yet another for an array of Animals. Templates let you declare a parameterized array class, and then specify what type of object each *instance* of the array will hold.

 Instantiation The act of creating a specific type from a template is called instantiation, and the individual classes are called instances of the template.

Parameterized Templates provide you with the ability to create a general class, and pass types as *parameters* to that class, in order to build specific instances.

Template Definition

You declare a parameterized array object (a template for an array) by writing

```
1: template <class T>     // declare the template and the parameter
2: class Array            // the class being parameterized
3: {
4:    public:
5:       Array();
6:    // full class declaration here
7: };
```

The keyword template is used at the beginning of every declaration and definition of a template class. The parameters of the template are after the keyword template. The parameters are the things that will change with each instance. For example, in the array template shown previously, the type of the objects stored in the array will change. One instance might store an array of integers, while another might store an array of Animals.

In this example, the keyword class is used, followed by the identifier T. The keyword class indicates that this parameter is a *type*. The identifier T is used throughout the rest of the template definition to refer to the parameterized type. One instance of this class will substitute int everywhere T appears, and another will substitute Cat.

To declare an int and a Cat instance of the parameterized array class you would write

```
Array<int> anIntArray;
Array<Cat> aCatArray;
```

The object anIntArray is of the type *array of integers*; the object aCatArray is of the type *array of Cats*. You can now use the type Array<int> anywhere you would normally use a type—as the return value from a function, as a parameter to a function, and so forth. Listing 19.1 provides the full declaration of this stripped-down array template.

19

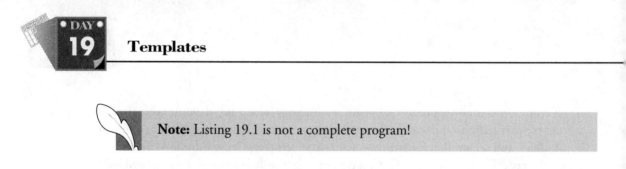
> **Note:** Listing 19.1 is not a complete program!

Listing 19.1. A template of an array class.

```
1: Listing 19.1 A template of an array class
2:     #include <iostream.h>
3:     const int DefaultSize = 10;
4:
5:     template <class T>  // declare the template and the parameter
6:     class Array              // the class being parameterized
7:     {
8:     public:
9:         // constructors
10:        Array(int itsSize = DefaultSize);
11:        Array(const Array &rhs);
12:        ~Array() { delete [] pType; }
13:
14:        // operators
15:        Array& operator=(const Array&);
16:        Type& operator[](int offSet) { return pType[offSet]; }
17:
18:        // accessors
19:        int getSize() { return itsSize; }
20:
21:    private:
22:        Type *pType;
23:        int  itsSize;
24:    };
```

There is no output. This is an incomplete program.

The definition of the template begins on line 5 with the keyword `template` followed by the parameter. In this case the parameter is identified to be a type by the keyword `class`, and the identifier `T` is used to represent the parameterized type.

From line 6 until the end of the template on line 24, the rest of the declaration is like any other class declaration. The only difference is that wherever the type of the object would normally appear, the identifier `T` is used instead. For example, `operator[]` would be expected to return a reference to an object in the array, and in fact it is declared to return a reference to a `T`.

When an instance of an integer array is declared, the operator= that is provided to that array will return a reference to an integer. When an instance of an Animal array is declared, the operator= provided to the Animal array will return a reference to an Animal.

Using the Name

Within the class declaration the word Array may be used without further qualification. Elsewhere in the program this class will be referred to as Array<T>. For example, if you do not write the constructor within the class declaration, you must write

```
template <class T>
Array<T>::Array(int size):
itsSize = size
{
  pType = new T[size];
  for (int i = 0; i<size; i++)
      pType[i] = 0;
}
```

The declaration on the first line of this code fragment is required to identify the type (class T). The template name is Array<T> and the function name is Array(int size).

The remainder of the function is exactly the same as it would be for a non-template function. It is a common and preferred method to get the class and its functions working as a simple declaration before turning it into a template.

Implementing the Template

The full implementation of the template class array requires implementation of the copy constructor, operator=, and so forth. Listing 19.2 provides a simple driver program to exercise this template class.

19

> **Note:** Some older compilers do not support templates. Templates are, however, part of the emerging C++ standard. All major compiler vendors have committed to supporting templates in their next release, if they have not already done so. If you have an older compiler, you won't be able to compile and run the exercises in this chapter. It's still a good idea to read through the entire chapter, however, and return to this material when you upgrade your compiler.

Listing 19.2. The implementation of the template array.

```
1:    #include <iostream.h>
2:
3:    const int DefaultSize = 10;
4:
5:    // declare a simple Animal class so that we can
6:    // create an array of animals
7:
8:    class Animal
9:    {
10:   public:
11:      Animal(int);
12:      Animal();
13:      ~Animal() {}
14:      int GetWeight() const { return itsWeight; }
15:      void Display() const { cout << itsWeight; }
16:   private:
17:      int itsWeight;
18:   };
19:
20:   Animal::Animal(int weight):
21:   itsWeight(weight)
22:   {}
23:
24:   Animal::Animal():
25:   itsWeight(0)
26:   {}
27:
28:
29:   template <class T>  // declare the template and the parameter
30:   class Array           // the class being parameterized
31:   {
32:   public:
33:      // constructors
34:      Array(int itsSize = DefaultSize);
35:      Array(const Array &rhs);
36:      ~Array() { delete [] pType; }
37:
38:      // operators
39:      Array& operator=(const Array&);
40:      T& operator[](int offSet) { return pType[offSet]; }
41:      const T& operator[](int offSet) const { return pType[offSet]; }
42:
43:      // accessors
44:      int GetSize() const { return itsSize; }
45:
46:   private:
47:      T *pType;
48:      int  itsSize;
49:   };
50:
51:   // implementations follow...
52:
53:   // implement the Constructor
54:   template <class T>
```

```
55:     Array<T>::Array(int size = DefaultSize):
56:     itsSize(size)
57:     {
58:        pType = new T[size];
59:        for (int i = 0; i<size; i++)
60:           pType[i] = 0;
61:     }
62:
63:     // copy constructor
64:     template <class T>
65:     Array<T>::Array(const Array &rhs)
66:     {
67:        itsSize = rhs.GetSize();
68:        pType = new T[itsSize];
69:        for (int i = 0; i<itsSize; i++)
70:           pType[i] = rhs[i];
71:     }
72:
73:     // operator=
74:     template <class T>
75:     Array<T>& Array<T>::operator=(const Array &rhs)
76:     {
77:        if (this == &rhs)
78:           return *this;
79:        delete [] pType;
80:        itsSize = rhs.GetSize();
81:        pType = new T[itsSize];
82:        for (int i = 0; i<itsSize; i++)
83:           pType[i] = rhs[i];
84:        return *this;
85:     }
86:
87:     // driver program
88:     void main()
89:     {
90:        Array<int> theArray;        // an array of integers
91:        Array<Animal> theZoo;       // an array of Animals
92:        Animal *pAnimal;
93:
94:        // fill the arrays
95:        for (int i = 0; i < theArray.GetSize(); i++)
96:        {
97:           theArray[i] = i*2;
98:           pAnimal = new Animal(i*3);
99:           theZoo[i] = *pAnimal;
100:       }
101:
102:       // print the contents of the arrays
103:       for (int j = 0; j < theArray.GetSize(); j++)
104:       {
105:          cout << "theArray[" << j << "]:\t" << theArray[j] << "\t\t";
106:          cout << "theZoo[" << j << "]:\t";
107:          theZoo[j].Display();
108:          cout << endl;
109:       }
```

continues

Listing 19.2. continued

```
110:
111:        // return the allocated memory before the arrays are destroyed.
112:        for (int k = 0; k < theArray.GetSize(); k++)
113:            delete &theZoo[j];
114:    }
```

theArray[0]:	0	theZoo[0]:	0
theArray[1]:	2	theZoo[1]:	3
theArray[2]:	4	theZoo[2]:	6
theArray[3]:	6	theZoo[3]:	9
theArray[4]:	8	theZoo[4]:	12
theArray[5]:	10	theZoo[5]:	15
theArray[6]:	12	theZoo[6]:	18
theArray[7]:	14	theZoo[7]:	21
theArray[8]:	16	theZoo[8]:	24
theArray[9]:	18	theZoo[9]:	27

Lines 8 to 26 provide a stripped-down Animal class, created here so that there are objects of a user-defined type to add to the array.

Line 29 declares that what follows is a template, and that the parameter to the template is a *type*, designated as T. The Array class has two constructors as shown, the first of which takes a size and defaults to the constant integer DefaultSize.

The assignment and offset operators are declared, with the latter declaring both a const and a non-const variant. The only accessor provided is GetSize(), which returns the size of the array.

One can certainly imagine a fuller interface, and for any serious Array program what has been supplied here would be inadequate. At a minimum, operators to remove elements, to expand the array, to pack the array, and so forth, would be required.

The private data consists of the size of the array and a pointer to the actual in-memory array of objects.

Template Functions

If you wish to pass an array object to a function, you must pass a particular *instance* of the array, and not a template. Thus, if SomeFunction() takes an integer array as a parameter, you may write

```
void SomeFunction(Array<int>&);    // ok
```

but you may not write

```
void SomeFunction(Array<T>&);    // error!
```

because there is no way to know what a `T&` is. You also may not write

```
void SomeFunction(Array &);    // error!
```

as there is no class `Array`, only the template and the instances.

To accomplish the more general approach, you must declare a function template.

```
template <class T>
void MyTemplateFunction(Array<T>&);    // ok
```

Here the function `MyTemplateFunction()` is declared to be a template function by the declaration on the top line. Note that template functions can have any name, just as other functions can.

Template functions can also take instances of the template, in addition to the parameterized form. The following is an example.

```
template <class T>
void MyOtherFunction(Array<T>&, Array<int>&);    // ok
```

Note that this function takes two arrays: a parameterized `array` and an `array` of integers. The former can be an array of any object, but the latter is always an array of integers.

Templates and Friends

Template classes can declare three types of friends:

1. A non-template friend class or function.

2. A general template friend class or function.

3. A type-specific template friend class or function.

Non-Template Friend Classes and Functions

It is possible to declare any class or function to be a friend to your template class. Each instance of the class will treat the friend properly, as if the declaration of friendship had been made in that particular instance. Listing 19.3 adds a trivial friend function, `Intrude()`, to the template definition of the `Array` class, and the driver program invokes

Templates

Intrude(). Because it is a friend, Intrude() can then accesses the private data of the Array. Because this is *not* a template function, it can only be called on Arrays of int.

> **Note:** To use Listing 19.3, copy lines 1-26 of Listing 19.2 after 1 of this listing, and then copy lines 51-86 of listing 19.2 after line 37 of this listing.

Listing 19.3. Non-template **friend** function.

```
1:   // Listing 19.3 - Type specific friend functions in templates
2:
3:      template <class T>  // declare the template and the parameter
4:      class Array              // the class being parameterized
5:      {
6:      public:
7:          // constructors
8:          Array(int itsSize = DefaultSize);
9:          Array(const Array &rhs);
10:         ~Array() { delete [] pType; }
11:
12:         // operators
13:         Array& operator=(const Array&);
14:         T& operator[](int offSet) { return pType[offSet]; }
15:         const T& operator[](int offSet) const { return pType[offSet]; }
16:
17:         // accessors
18:         int GetSize() const { return itsSize; }
19:
20:       // friend function
21:       friend void Intrude(Array<int>);
22:
23:      private:
24:          T *pType;
25:          int  itsSize;
26:      };
27:
28:         // friend function. Not a template, can only be used
29:         // with int arrays! Intrudes into private data.
30:         void Intrude(Array<int> theArray)
31:         {
32:         cout << "\n*** Intrude ***\n";
33:         for (int i = 0; i < theArray.itsSize; i++)
34:            cout << "i: " <<    theArray.pType[i] << endl;
35:         cout << "\n";
36:         }
37:
38:      // driver program
39:      int main()
40:      {
41:         Array<int> theArray;       // an array of integers
```

```
42:         Array<Animal> theZoo;      // an array of Animals
43:         Animal *pAnimal;
44:
45:         // fill the arrays
46:         for (int i = 0; i < theArray.GetSize(); i++)
47:         {
48:             theArray[i] = i*2;
49:             pAnimal = new Animal(i*3);
50:             theZoo[i] = *pAnimal;
51:         }
52:
53:         // print the contents of the arrays
54:         for (int j = 0; j < theArray.GetSize(); j++)
55:         {
56:             cout << "theZoo[" << j << "]:\t";
57:             theZoo[j].Display();
58:             cout << endl;
59:         }
60:         cout << "Now use the friend function to find the members of Array<int>";
61:         Intrude(theArray);
62:
63:         // return the allocated memory before the arrays are destroyed.
64:         for (int k = 0; k < theArray.GetSize(); k++)
65:             delete &theZoo[j];
66:
67:         cout << "\n\nDone.\n";
68:         return 0;
69:     }
```

```
theZoo[0]:      0
theZoo[1]:      3
theZoo[2]:      6
theZoo[3]:      9
theZoo[4]:      12
theZoo[5]:      15
theZoo[6]:      18
theZoo[7]:      21
theZoo[8]:      24
theZoo[9]:      27
```

Now use the friend function to find the members of Array<int>.

```
i: 0
i: 2
i: 4
i: 6
i: 8
i: 10
i: 12
i: 14
i: 16
i: 18
```

The declaration of the array template has been extended to include the friend function Intrude(). This declares that every instance of an array will consider Intrude() to be a friend function, and thus Intrude() will have access to the private member data and functions of the array instance.

On line 33 Intrude() accesses itsSize directly, and on line 33 it accesses pType directly. This trivial use of these members was unnecessary as the array class provides public accessors for this data, but it serves to demonstrate how friend functions can be declared with templates.

General Template Friend Class or Function

It would be helpful to add a display operator to the array class. One approach would be to declare a display operator for each possible type of array, but this would undermine the whole point of having made array a template.

What is needed is an insertion operator that works for any possible type of array.

```
ostream& operator<< (ostream& Array<T>&);
```

To make this work, we need to declare operator<< to be a template function.

```
template <class T> ostream& operator<< (ostream&, Array<T>&)
```

Now that operator<< is a template function, you only need to provide an implementation. Listing 19.4 shows the array template extended to include this declaration, and provides the implementation for the operator<<.

Note: To compile this listing, copy lines 8-26 of Listing 19.2 and insert them between lines 3 and 4. Also copy lines 51-86 of 19.2 and insert them between lines 37 and 38.

Listing 19.4. Using operator ostream.

```
1:    #include <iostream.h>
2:
3:    const int DefaultSize = 10;
4:
5:    template <class T>   // declare the template and the parameter
6:    class Array          // the class being parameterized
7:    {
```

```
8:     public:
9:         // constructors
10:        Array(int itsSize = DefaultSize);
11:        Array(const Array &rhs);
12:        ~Array() { delete [] pType; }
13:
14:        // operators
15:        Array& operator=(const Array&);
16:        T& operator[](int offSet) { return pType[offSet]; }
17:        const T& operator[](int offSet) const { return pType[offSet]; }
18:
19:        // accessors
20:        int GetSize() const { return itsSize; }
21:
22:      template <class T> friend ostream& operator<< (ostream&, Array<T>&);
23:
24:    private:
25:        T *pType;
26:        int  itsSize;
27:    };
28:
29:    template <class T>
30:    ostream& operator<< (ostream& output, Array<T>& theArray)
31:    {
32:        for (int i = 0; i<theArray.GetSize(); i++)
33:            output << "[" << i << "] " << theArray[i] << endl;
34:    }
35:
36:    enum BOOL { FALSE, TRUE};
37:
38:    void main()
39:    {
40:        BOOL Stop = FALSE;          // flag for looping
41:        int offset, value;
42:        Array<int> theArray;
43:
44:        while (!Stop)
45:        {
46:            cout << "Enter an offset (0-9) and a value. (-1 to stop): " ;
47:            cin >> offset >> value;
48:
49:            if (offset < 0)
50:                break;
51:
52:            if (offset > 9)
53:            {
54:                cout << "***Please use values between 0 and 9.***\n";
55:                continue;
56:            }
57:
58:            theArray[offset] = value;
59:        }
60:
61:        cout << "\nHere's the entire array:\n";
62:        cout << theArray << endl;
63:    }
```

19

```
Enter an offset (0-9) and a value. (-1 to stop): 1 10
Enter an offset (0-9) and a value. (-1 to stop): 2 20
Enter an offset (0-9) and a value. (-1 to stop): 3 30
Enter an offset (0-9) and a value. (-1 to stop): 4 40
Enter an offset (0-9) and a value. (-1 to stop): 5 50
Enter an offset (0-9) and a value. (-1 to stop): 6 60
Enter an offset (0-9) and a value. (-1 to stop): 7 70
Enter an offset (0-9) and a value. (-1 to stop): 8 80
Enter an offset (0-9) and a value. (-1 to stop): 9 90
Enter an offset (0-9) and a value. (-1 to stop): 10 10
***Please use values between 0 and 9. ***
Enter an offset (0-9) and a value. (-1 to stop): -1 -1

Here's the entire array:
[0] 0
[1] 10
[2] 20
[3] 30
[4] 40
[5] 50
[6] 60
[7] 70
[8] 80
[9] 90
```

On line 22 the function template operator<<() is declared to be a friend of the Array class template. Because operator<<() is implemented as a template function, every instance of this parameterized array type will automatically have an operator<<(). The implementation for this operator starts on line 29. Every member of an array is called in turn. This only works if there is an operator<< definded for every type of object stored in the array.

A Type-Specific Template Friend Class or Function

Although the insertion operator shown in Listing 19.4 works, it is still not quite what is needed. Because the declaration of the friend operator on line 22 declares a template, it will work for any instance of Array and any insertion operator taking an array of any type.

The insertion operator template shown in Listing 19.4 makes all instances of the insertion operator<< a friend of any instance of Array, whether the instance of the insertion operator is an integer, an Animal, or a Car. It makes no sense, however, for an Animal insertion operator to be a friend to the insertion operator for an integer Array.

What is wanted is for the insertion operator for an Array of *int* to be a friend to the Array of int class, and for the insertion operator of an Array of Animals to be a friend to the Array of *animals* instance.

To accomplish this, modify the declaration of the insertion operator on line 22 of Listing 19.4, and remove the words `template <class T>`. That is, change line 22 to read

```
friend ostream& operator<< (ostream&, Array<T>&);
```

This will use the type (T) declared in the template of `Array`. Thus, the `operator<<` for an integer will only work with an array of integers, and so forth.

Using Template Items

You can treat template items as you would any other type. You can pass them as parameters, either by reference or by value, and you can return them as the return values of functions, also by value or by reference. Listing 19.5 demonstrates how to pass template objects.

Listing 19.5. Passing template objects to and from functions.

```
1:      #include <iostream.h>
2:
3:      const int DefaultSize = 10;
4:
5:      // A trivial class for adding to arrays
6:      class Animal
7:      {
8:      public:
9:      // constructors
10:         Animal(int);
11:         Animal();
12:         ~Animal();
13:
14:         // accessors
15:         int GetWeight() const { return itsWeight; }
16:         void SetWeight(int theWeight) { itsWeight = theWeight; }
17:
18:          // friend operators
19:         friend ostream& operator<< (ostream&, const Animal&);
20:
21:      private:
22:         int itsWeight;
23:      };
24:
25:      // extraction operator for printing animals
26:      ostream& operator<< (ostream& theStream, const Animal& theAnimal)
27:      {
28:      theStream << theAnimal.GetWeight();
29:      return theStream;
30:      }
31:
```

continues

Listing 19.5. continued

```
32:    Animal::Animal(int weight):
33:    itsWeight(weight)
34:    {
35:        // cout << "Animal(int)\n";
36:    }
37:
38:    Animal::Animal():
39:    itsWeight(0)
40:    {
41:        // cout << "Animal()\n";
42:    }
43:
44:    Animal::~Animal()
45:    {
46:        // cout << "Destroyed an animal...\n";
47:    }
48:
49:    template <class T>   // declare the template and the parameter
50:    class Array             // the class being parameterized
51:    {
52:    public:
53:        Array(int itsSize = DefaultSize);
54:        Array(const Array &rhs);
55:        ~Array() { delete [] pType; }
56:
57:        Array& operator=(const Array&);
58:        T& operator[](int offSet) { return pType[offSet]; }
59:        const T& operator[](int offSet) const { return pType[offSet]; }
60:        int GetSize() const { return itsSize; }
61:
62:        // friend function
63:      friend ostream& operator<< (ostream&, const Array<T>&);
64:
65:    private:
66:        T *pType;
67:        int  itsSize;
68:    };
69:
70:    template <class T>
71:    ostream& operator<< (ostream& output, const Array<T>& theArray)
72:    {
73:        for (int i = 0; i<theArray.GetSize(); i++)
74:            output << "[" << i << "] " << theArray[i] << endl;
75:        return output;
76:    }
77:
78:    void IntFillFunction(Array<int>& theArray);
79:    void AnimalFillFunction(Array<Animal>& theArray);
80:    enum BOOL {FALSE, TRUE};
81:
82:    void main()
83:    {
84:        Array<int> intArray;
```

```
85:        Array<Animal> animalArray;
86:        IntFillFunction(intArray);
87:        AnimalFillFunction(animalArray);
88:        cout << "intArray...\n" << intArray;
89:        cout << "\nanimalArray...\n" << animalArray << endl;
90:    }
91:
92:    void IntFillFunction(Array<int>& theArray)
93:    {
94:        BOOL Stop = FALSE;
95:        int offset, value;
96:        while (!Stop)
97:        {
98:            cout << "Enter an offset (0-9) and a value. (-1 to stop): " ;
99:            cin >> offset >> value;
100:           if (offset < 0)
101:               break;
102:           if (offset > 9)
103:           {
104:               cout << "***Please use values between 0 and 9.***\n";
105:               continue;
106:           }
107:           theArray[offset] = value;
108:       }
109:   }
110:
111:
112:   void AnimalFillFunction(Array<Animal>& theArray)
113:   {
114:       Animal * pAnimal;
115:       for (int i = 0; i<theArray.GetSize(); i++)
116:       {
117:           pAnimal = new Animal;
118:           pAnimal->SetWeight(i*100);
119:           theArray[i] = *pAnimal;
120:           delete pAnimal;   // a copy was put in the array
121:       }
122:   }
```

```
Enter an offset (0-9) and a value. (-1 to stop): 1 10
Enter an offset (0-9) and a value. (-1 to stop): 2 20
Enter an offset (0-9) and a value. (-1 to stop): 3 30
Enter an offset (0-9) and a value. (-1 to stop): 4 40
Enter an offset (0-9) and a value. (-1 to stop): 5 50
Enter an offset (0-9) and a value. (-1 to stop): 6 60
Enter an offset (0-9) and a value. (-1 to stop): 7 70
Enter an offset (0-9) and a value. (-1 to stop): 8 80
Enter an offset (0-9) and a value. (-1 to stop): 9 90
Enter an offset (0-9) and a value. (-1 to stop): 10 10
***Please use values between 0 and 9. ***
Enter an offset (0-9) and a value. (-1 to stop): -1 -1

intArray:...
[0] 0
```

```
[1] 10
[2] 20
[3] 30
[4] 40
[5] 50
[6] 60
[7] 70
[8] 80
[9] 90

animalArray:...
[0] 0
[1] 100
[2] 200
[3] 300
[4] 400
[5] 500
[6] 600
[7] 700
[8] 800
[9] 900
```

Most of the Array class implementation is left out to save space. The Animal class is declared on lines 6-23. Although this is a stripped down and simplified class, it does provide its own insertion operator (<<) to allow the printing of Animals. Printing simply prints the current weight of the Animal.

Note that Animal has a default constructor. This is necessary, because when you add an object to an array the object's default constructor is used to create the object. This creates some difficulties, as you'll see.

On line 78 the function IntFillFunction() is declared. The prototype indicates that this function takes an *integer array*. Note that this is *not* a template function. IntFillFunction() expects only one type of an array—an integer array. Similarly, on line 79 AnimalFillFunction() is declared to take an Array of Animal.

The implementations for these functions are different from one another, because filling an array of integers does not have to be accomplished in the same way as filling an array of Animals.

Specialized Functions

If you uncomment the print statements in Animal's constructors and destructor in Listing 19.5, you'll find that there are unanticipated extra constructions and destructions of Animals.

When an object is added to an array, the object's default constructor is called. The Array constructor, however, goes on to assign 0 to the value of each member of the array, as shown on lines 59 and 60 of Listing 19.2.

When you write someAnimal = (Animal) 0; you call the default operator= for Animal. This causes a temporary Animal object to be created, using the constructor, which takes an integer (zero). That temporary is used as the right-hand side of the operator equals, and then is destroyed.

This is an unfortunate waste of time, because the Animal object was already properly initialized. However, you can't remove this line, because integers are not automatically initialized to value 0. The solution is to teach the template not to use this constructor for Animals, but to use a special Animal constructor.

You can provide an explicit implementation for the Animal class, as indicated in Listing 19.6.

Listing 19.6. Specializing template implementations.

```
1:     #include <iostream.h>
2:
3:     const int DefaultSize = 3;
4:
5:     // A trivial class for adding to arrays
6:       class Animal
7:       {
8:       public:
9:          // constructors
10:         Animal(int);
11:         Animal();
12:         ~Animal();
13:
14:         // accessors
15:         int GetWeight() const { return itsWeight; }
16:         void SetWeight(int theWeight) { itsWeight = theWeight; }
17:
18:         // friend operators
19:         friend ostream& operator<< (ostream&, const Animal&);
20:
21:       private:
22:          int itsWeight;
23:       };
24:
25:       // extraction operator for printing animals
26:       ostream& operator<< (ostream& theStream, const Animal& theAnimal)
27:       {
28:         theStream << theAnimal.GetWeight();
29:         return theStream;
30:       }
31:
32:       Animal::Animal(int weight):
33:       itsWeight(weight)
34:       {
35:          cout << "animal(int) ";
```

continues

603

Listing 19.6. continued

```
36:      }
37:
38:      Animal::Animal():
39:      itsWeight(0)
40:      {
41:          cout << "animal() ";
42:      }
43:
44:      Animal::~Animal()
45:      {
46:        cout << "Destroyed an animal...";
47:      }
48:
49:   template <class T>  // declare the template and the parameter
50:   class Array              // the class being parameterized
51:   {
52:   public:
53:      // constructors
54:      Array(int itsSize = DefaultSize);
55:      Array(const Array &rhs);
56:      ~Array() { delete [] pType; }
57:
58:      // operators
59:      Array& operator=(const Array&);
60:      T& operator[](int offSet) { return pType[offSet]; }
61:      const T& operator[](int offSet) const { return pType[offSet]; }
62:
63:      // accessors
64:      int GetSize() const { return itsSize; }
65:
66:      // friend function
67:     friend ostream& operator<< (ostream&, const Array<T>&);
68:
69:   private:
70:      T *pType;
71:      int  itsSize;
72:   };
73:
74:   template <class T>
75:   Array<T>::Array(int size = DefaultSize):
76:   itsSize(size)
77:   {
78:      pType = new T[size];
79:      for (int i = 0; i<size; i++)
80:        pType[i] = (T)0;
81:   }
82:
83:   template <class T>
84:   Array<T>& Array<T>::operator=(const Array &rhs)
85:   {
86:      if (this == &rhs)
87:         return *this;
88:      delete [] pType;
89:      itsSize = rhs.GetSize();
```

```
90:        pType = new T[itsSize];
91:        for (int i = 0; i<itsSize; i++)
92:            pType[i] = rhs[i];
93:    }
94:
95:    template <class T>
96:    Array<T>::Array(const Array &rhs)
97:    {
98:        itsSize = rhs.GetSize();
99:        pType = new T[itsSize];
100:       for (int i = 0; i<itsSize; i++)
101:           pType[i] = rhs[i];
102:   }
103:
104:
105:   template <class T>
106:   ostream& operator<< (ostream& output, const Array<T>& theArray)
107:   {
108:       for (int i = 0; i<theArray.GetSize(); i++)
109:           output << "[" << i << "] " << theArray[i] << endl;
110:       return output;
111:   }
112:
113:
114:   Array<Animal>::Array(int AnimalArraySize):
115:   itsSize(AnimalArraySize)
116:   {
117:       pType = new T[AnimalArraySize];
118:   }
119:
120:
121:   void IntFillFunction(Array<int>& theArray);
122:   void AnimalFillFunction(Array<Animal>& theArray);
123:   enum BOOL {FALSE, TRUE};
124:
125:   void main()
126:   {
127:       Array<int> intArray;
128:       Array<Animal> animalArray;
129:       IntFillFunction(intArray);
130:       AnimalFillFunction(animalArray);
131:       cout << "intArray...\n" << intArray;
132:       cout << "\nanimalArray...\n" << animalArray << endl;
133:   }
134:
135:   void IntFillFunction(Array<int>& theArray)
136:   {
137:       BOOL Stop = FALSE;
138:       int offset, value;
139:       while (!Stop)
140:       {
141:           cout << "Enter an offset (0-9) and a value. (-1 to stop): " ;
142:           cin >> offset >> value;
143:           if (offset < 0)
144:               break;
```

continues

Listing 19.6. continued

```
145:         if (offset > 9)
146:         {
147:             cout << "***Please use values between 0 and 9.***\n";
148:             continue;
149:         }
150:         theArray[offset] = value;
151:     }
152: }
153:
154:
155: void AnimalFillFunction(Array<Animal>& theArray)
156: {
157:     Animal * pAnimal;
158:     for (int i = 0; i<theArray.GetSize(); i++)
159:     {
160:         pAnimal = new Animal(i*10);
161:         theArray[i] = *pAnimal;
162:         delete pAnimal;
163:     }
164: }
```

Note: Line numbers have been added to the output to make analysis easier. Line numbers will *not* appear in your output.

```
1:  animal() animal() animal()
2:  Enter an offset (0-9) and a value. (-1 to stop): 0 0
3:  Enter an offset (0-9) and a value. (-1 to stop): 1 1
4:  Enter an offset (0-9) and a value. (-1 to stop): 2 2
5:  Enter an offset (0-9) and a value. (-1 to stop): 3 3
6:  animal(int)
7:  Destroyed an animal...
8:  animal(int)
9:  Destroyed an animal...
10: animal(int)
11: Destroyed an animal...
12: initArray...
13: [0] 0
14: [1] 1
15: [2] 2
16:
17: animal array...
18: [0] 0
19: [1] 10
20: [2] 20
21:
22: Destroyed an animal...
23: Destroyed an animal...
```

```
24: Destroyed an animal...
25:
<<< Second run >>>

26: animal() animal() animal()
27: animal(int)  Destroyed an animal...
28: animal(int)  Destroyed an animal...
29: animal(int)  Destroyed an animal...
30: Enter an offset (0-9) and a value. (-1 to stop): 0 0
31: Enter an offset (0-9) and a value. (-1 to stop): 1 1
32: Enter an offset (0-9) and a value. (-1 to stop): 2 2
33: Enter an offset (0-9) and a value. (-1 to stop): 3 3
34: animal(int)
35: Destroyed an animal...
36: animal(int)
37: Destroyed an animal...
38: animal(int)
39: Destroyed an animal...
40: initArray...
41: [0] 0
42: [1] 1
43: [2] 2
44:
45: animal array...
46: [0] 0
47: [1] 10
48: [2] 20
49:
50: Destroyed an animal...
51: Destroyed an animal...
52: Destroyed an animal...
```

Listing 19.6 reproduces both classes in their entirety so that you can see the creation and destruction of temporary Animal objects. The value of DefaultSize has been reduced to 3 to simplify the output.

The Animal constructors and destructors on lines 32-47 each print a statement indicating when they are called.

On lines 74-81 the template behavior of an array constructor is declared. On lines 114-118 the specialized constructor for an Array of Animals is demonstrated. Note that in this special constructor, the default constructor is allowed to set the initial value for each animal, and no explicit assignment is done.

The first time this program is run, the first set of output is shown. Line 1 of the output shows the three default constructors called by creating the array. The user enters four numbers, and these are entered into the integer array.

Execution jumps to AnimalFillFunction(). Here a temporary animal is created on the heap on line 160, and its value is used to modify the Animal object in the array on line 161. On line 162 the temporary Animal is destroyed. This is repeated for each member of the array, and is reflected in the output on lines 6-11.

At the end of the program the arrays are destroyed, and when their destructors are called all their objects are destroyed as well. This is reflected in the output on lines 22-24.

For the second set of output (lines 26-52) the special implementation of the array of character constructor, shown on lines 114-118 of the program, is commented out. When the program is run again the template constructor, shown on lines 74-81 of the program, is run when the Animal array is constructed.

This causes temporary Animal objects to be called for each member of the array on lines 79 and 80 of the program, and is reflected in the output on lines 26 to 29 of the output.

In all other respects the output for the two runs is identical, as you would expect.

Static Members and Templates

A template can declare static data members. Each instantiation of the template then has its own set of static data, one per class *type*. That is, if you add a static member to the Array class (for example, a counter of how many arrays have been created) you will have one such member per type: one for all the arrays of Animals, and another for all the arrays of integers. Listing 19.7 adds a static member and a static function to the Array class.

Listing 19.7. Using static member data and functions with templates.

```
1:     #include <iostream.h>
2:
3:     template <class T>  // declare the template and the parameter
4:     class Array          // the class being parameterized
5:     {
6:     public:
7:         // constructors
8:         Array(int itsSize = DefaultSize);
9:         Array(const Array &rhs);
10:        ~Array() { delete [] pType;   itsNumberArrays—; }
11:
12:        // operators
13:        Array& operator=(const Array&);
14:        T& operator[](int offSet) { return pType[offSet]; }
15:        const T& operator[](int offSet) const { return pType[offSet]; }
16:
17:        // accessors
18:        int GetSize() const { return itsSize; }
19:        static int GetNumberArrays() { return itsNumberArrays; }
20:
21:        // friend function
22:       friend ostream& operator<< (ostream&, const Array<T>&);
23:
24:     private:
25:        T *pType;
26:        int  itsSize;
```

```
27:        static int itsNumberArrays;
28:    };
29:
30:    template <class T>
31:        int Array<T>::itsNumberArrays = 0;
32:
33:    template <class T>
34:    Array<T>::Array(int size = DefaultSize):
35:    itsSize(size)
36:    {
37:        pType = new T[size];
38:        for (int i = 0; i<size; i++)
39:          pType[i] = (T)0;
40:        itsNumberArrays++;
41:    }
42:
43:    template <class T>
44:    Array<T>& Array<T>::operator=(const Array &rhs)
45:    {
46:        if (this == &rhs)
47:            return *this;
48:        delete [] pType;
49:        itsSize = rhs.GetSize();
50:        pType = new T[itsSize];
51:        for (int i = 0; i<itsSize; i++)
52:            pType[i] = rhs[i];
53:    }
54:
55:    template <class T>
56:    Array<T>::Array(const Array &rhs)
57:    {
58:        itsSize = rhs.GetSize();
59:        pType = new T[itsSize];
60:        for (int i = 0; i<itsSize; i++)
61:            pType[i] = rhs[i];
62:        itsNumberArrays++;
63:    }
64:
65:
66:    template <class T>
67:    ostream& operator<< (ostream& output, const Array<T>& theArray)
68:    {
69:        for (int i = 0; i<theArray.GetSize(); i++)
70:            output << "[" << i << "] " << theArray[i] << endl;
71:        return output;
72:    }
73:
74:
75:    Array<Animal>::Array(int AnimalArraySize):
76:    itsSize(AnimalArraySize)
77:    {
78:        pType = new T[AnimalArraySize];
79:        itsNumberArrays++;
80:    }
```

continues

19

Listing 19.7. continued

```
81:
82:    void main()
83:    {
84:
85:        cout << Array<int>::GetNumberArrays() << " integer arrays\n";
86:        cout << Array<Animal>::GetNumberArrays() << " animal arrays\n\n";
87:
88:        Array<int> intArray;
89:        Array<Animal> animalArray;
90:
91:        cout << intArray.GetNumberArrays() << " integer arrays\n";
92:        cout << animalArray.GetNumberArrays() << " animal arrays\n\n";
93:
94:        Array<int> *pIntArray = new Array<int>;
95:
96:        cout << Array<int>::GetNumberArrays() << " integer arrays\n";
97:        cout << Array<Animal>::GetNumberArrays() << " animal arrays\n\n";
98:
99:        delete pIntArray;
100:
101:        cout << Array<int>::GetNumberArrays() << " integer arrays\n";
102:        cout << Array<Animal>::GetNumberArrays() << " animal arrays\n\n";
103:    }
```

Output

```
0 integer array
0 animal arrays

1 integer array
1 animal arrays

2 integer array
1 animal arrays

1 integer array
1 animal arrays
```

Analysis The declaration of the Animal class has been left out to save space. The Array class has added the static variable itsNumberArrays on line 27, and because this data is private, the static public accessor GetNumberArrays() was added on line 19.

Initialization of the static data is accomplished with a full template qualification, as shown on lines 30 and 31. The constructors of Array and the destructor are each modified to keep track of how many arrays exist at any moment.

Accessing the static members is exactly like accessing the static members of any class: you can do so with an existing object, as shown on lines 91 and 92, or by using the full class specification, as shown on lines 85 and 86. Note that you must use a specific *type* of array when accessing the static data. There is one variable for each type.

DO	DON'T

DO use statics with templates as needed.

DO specialize template behavior by overriding template functions by type.

DO use the parameters to template functions to narrow their instances to be type-safe.

Summary

Today you learned how to create and use templates. Templates are a built-in facility of C++ used to create parameterized types: types that change their behavior based on parameters passed in at creation. They are a way to reuse code safely and effectively.

The definition of the template determines the parameterized type. Each instance of the template is an actual object, which can be used like any other object—as a parameter to a function, as a return value, and so forth.

Template classes can declare three types of friend functions: non-template, general templates, and type-specific templates. A template can declare static data members, in which case each instance of the template has its own set of static data.

If you need to specialize behavior for some template functions based on the actual type, you can override a template function with a particular type. This works for member functions as well.

Q&A

Q Why use templates when macros will do?

A Templates are type safe and built into the language.

Q What is the difference between the parameterized type of a template function, and the parameters to a normal function?

A A regular function (non-template) takes parameters on which it may take action. A template function allows you to parameterize the type of a particular parameter to the function. That is, you can pass an Array of Type to a function, and then have the Type determined by the template instance.

Q Why bother with templates when macros will work?

A All the usual reasons apply here: Templates are an integrated part of the language, macros are not. Templates are "type-safe" and macros are not.

Q When do you use templates and when do you use inheritance?

A Use templates when all the behavior or virtually all of the behavior is unchanged, except in regard to the type of the item on which your class acts. If you find yourself copying a class and changing only the type of one or more of its members, it may be time to consider using a template.

Q When do you use general template friend classes?

A When every instance, regardless of type, should be a friend to this class or function.

Q When do you use type-specific template friend classes or functions?

A When you wish to establish a one-to-one relationship between two classes. For example, array<int> should match iterator<int> but not iterator<Animal>.

Workshop

The Workshop provides quiz questions to help you solidify your understanding of the material covered, and exercises to provide you with experience in using what you've learned. Try to answer the quiz and exercise questions before checking the answers in Appendix D, and make sure you understand the answers before continuing to the next chapter.

Quiz

1. What is the difference between a template and a macro?

2. What is the difference between the parameter in a template and the parameter in a function?

3. What is the difference between a type-specific template friend class and a general template friend class?

4. Is it possible to provide special behavior for one instance of a template but not for other instances?

5. How many static variables are created if you put one static member into a template class definition?

Exercises

1. Create a template based on this list class:

```
class List
{
private:

public:
        List():head(0),tail(0),theCount(0) {}
        virtual ~List();

        void insert( int value );
        void append( int value );
        int is_present( int value ) const;
        int is_empty() const { return head == 0; }
        int count() const { return theCount; }
private:
        class ListCell
        {
        public:
                ListCell(int value, ListCell *cell = 0):val(value),next(cell){}
                int val;
                ListCell *next;
        };
        ListCell *head;
        ListCell *tail;
        int theCount;
};
```

2. Write the implementation for the `List` class (non-template) version.

3. Write the template version of the implementations.

4. Declare three list objects: a list of strings, a list of `Cat`s, and a list of ints.

5. **BUG BUSTERS:** What is wrong with the following code? (Assume the `List` template is defined and `Cat` is the class defined earlier in the book.)

```
List<Cat> Cat_List;
Cat Felix;
CatList.append( Felix );
```

```
cout << "Felix is " <<
    ( Cat_List.is_present( Felix ) ) ? "" : "not " << "present\n";
```

HINT (this is tough): What makes `Cat` different from `int`?

6. Declare friend operator == for `List`.

7. Implement friend operator == for `List`.

8. Does `operator==` have the same problem as in Exercise 5?

9. Implement a template function for swap, which exchanges two variables.

20

Exceptions and Error Handling

WEEK
3

Introduction

The code you've seen in this book has been created for illustration purposes. It has not dealt with errors so that you would not be distracted from the central issues being presented. Real-world programs must take error conditions into consideration.

Today you will learn:

- [ ] What exceptions are.

- [ ] How exceptions are used and what issues they raise.

- [ ] How to build exception hierarchies.

- [ ] How exceptions fit into an overall error-handling approach.

- [ ] What a debugger is.

Bugs, Errors, Mistakes, and Code Rot

All programs have bugs. The bigger the program the more bugs, and many of those bugs actually "get out the door" and into final, released software. That this is true does not make it okay, and making robust, bug-free programs is the number one priority of anyone serious about programming.

The single biggest problem in the software industry is buggy, unstable code. The biggest expense in many major programming efforts is testing and fixing. The person who solves the problem of producing good, solid, bulletproof programs at low cost and on time will revolutionize the software industry.

There are a number of discreet kinds of bugs that can trouble a program. The first is poor logic: the program does just what you asked, but you haven't thought through the algorithms properly. The second is syntactic: you used the wrong idiom, function, or structure. These two are the most common, and they are the ones most programmers are on the lookout for.

Research and real-world experience have shown beyond a doubt that the later in the development process you find a problem, the more it costs to fix it. The least expensive problems or bugs to fix are the ones you manage to avoid creating. The next cheapest are those the compiler spots. The C++ standards force compilers to put a lot of energy into making more and more bugs show up at compile time.

Bugs that get compiled in but that are caught at the first test—those that crash *every time*—are less expensive to find and fix than those that are flaky and only crash once in a while.

A bigger problem than logic or syntactic bugs is unnecessary fragility: your program works just fine if the user enters a number when you ask for one, but it crashes if the user enters letters. Other programs crash if they run out of memory, or if the floppy disk is left out of the drive, or if the modem drops the line.

To combat this kind of fragility, programmers strive to make their programs "bulletproof." A bulletproof program is one that can handle anything that comes up at runtime, from bizarre user input to running out of memory.

It is important to distinguish between bugs, which arise because the programmer made a mistake in syntax; logic errors, which arise because the programmer misunderstood the problem or how to solve it; and exceptions, which arise because of unusual but predictable problems such as running out of resources (memory or disk space).

Exceptions

Programmers use powerful compilers and sprinkle their code with asserts, as discussed on Day 17, to catch programming errors. They use design reviews and exhaustive testing to find logic errors.

Exceptions are different, however. You can't eliminate exceptional circumstances; you can only prepare for them. Your users *will* run out of memory from time to time, and the only question is what you will do. Your choices are limited to these:

1. Crash the program.

2. Inform the user and exit gracefully.

3. Inform the user and allow the user to try to recover and continue.

4. Take corrective action and continue without disturbing the user.

While it is not necessary or even desirable for every program you write to automatically and silently recover from all exceptional circumstances, it is clear that you must do better than crashing.

C++ exception handling provides a type-safe, integrated method for coping with the predictable but unusual conditions that arise while running a program.

A Word About Code Rot

Code rot is a well-proven phenomenon. Code rot is when code deteriorates due to being neglected. Perfectly well-written, fully debugged code will develop new and bizarre behavior six months after you release it, and there isn't much you can do to stop it. What you *can* do, of course, is write your programs so that when you go back to fix the spoilage, you can quickly and easily identify where the problems are.

 **Note:** Code rot is somewhat of a programmer's joke used to explain how bug-free code suddenly becomes unreliable. It does, however, teach an important lesson. Programs are enormously complex, and bugs, errors, and mistakes can hide for a long time before turning up. Protect yourself by writing easy-to-maintain code.

This means that your code must be commented even if you don't expect anyone else to ever look at it but you. Six months after you deliver your code, you will read it with the eyes of a total stranger, bewildered by how anyone could ever have written such convoluted and twisty code and expected anything but disaster.

Exceptions

In C++, an exception is an object that is passed from the area of code where a problem occurs to the part of the code that is going to handle the problem. The type of the exception determines which area of code will handle the problem, and the contents of the object thrown, if any, may be used to provide feedback to the user.

The basic idea behind exceptions is fairly straightforward:

- [ ] The actual allocation of resources (for example, the allocation of memory or the locking of a file) is usually done at a very low level in the program.

- [ ] The logic of what to do when an operation fails, memory cannot be allocated, or a file cannot be locked is usually high in the program, with the code for interacting with the user.

- [ ] Exceptions provide an express path from the code that allocates resources to the code that can handle the error condition. If there are intervening layers of

functions, they are given an opportunity to clean up memory allocations, but are not required to include code whose only purpose is to pass along the error condition.

How Exceptions Are Used

try blocks are created to surround areas of code that may have a problem. For example:

```
try
{
    SomeDangerousFunction();
}
```

catch blocks handle the exceptions thrown in the try block. For example:

```
try
{
    SomeDangerousFunction();
}
catch(OutOfMemory)
{
    // take some actions
}
catch(FileNotFound)
{
    // take other action
}
```

The basic steps in using exceptions are:

1. Identify those areas of the program in which you begin an operation that might raise an exception, and put them in try blocks.

2. Create catch blocks to catch the exceptions if they are thrown, and to clean up allocated memory and inform the user as appropriate. Listing 20.1 illustrates the use of both try blocks and catch blocks.

Exceptions are objects used to transmit information about a problem.

A *try block* is a block surrounded by braces in which an exception may be thrown.

A *catch block* is the block immediately following a try block, in which exceptions are handled.

When an exception is *thrown* (or *raised*) control transfers to the catch block immediately following the current try block.

Exceptions and Error Handling

> **Note:** Some older compilers do not support exceptions. Exceptions are, however, part of the emerging C++ standard. All major compiler vendors have committed to supporting exceptions in their next release, if they have not already done so. If you have an older compiler, you won't be able to compile and run the exercises in this chapter. It's still a good idea to read through the entire chapter, however, and return to this material when you upgrade your compiler.

Listing 20.1. Raising an exception.

```
1:    #include <iostream.h>
2:
3:    const int DefaultSize = 10;
4:
5:    class Array
6:    {
7:    public:
8:       // constructors
9:       Array(int itsSize = DefaultSize);
10:      Array(const Array &rhs);
11:      ~Array() { delete [] pType;}
12:
13:      // operators
14:      Array& operator=(const Array&);
15:      int& operator[](int offSet);
16:      const int& operator[](int offSet) const;
17:
18:      // accessors
19:      int GetitsSize() const { return itsSize; }
20:
21:      // friend function
22:     friend ostream& operator<< (ostream&, const Array&);
23:
24:      class xBoundary {};  // define the exception class
25:    private:
26:      int *pType;
27:      int  itsSize;
28:    };
29:
30:
31:    Array::Array(int size):
32:    itsSize(size)
33:    {
34:       pType = new int[size];
35:       for (int i = 0; i<size; i++)
36:          pType[i] = 0;
37:    }
38:
39:
```

```
40:    Array& Array::operator=(const Array &rhs)
41:    {
42:       if (this == &rhs)
43:          return *this;
44:       delete [] pType;
45:       itsSize = rhs.GetitsSize();
46:       pType = new int[itsSize];
47:       for (int i = 0; i<itsSize; i++)
48:          pType[i] = rhs[i];
49:    }
50:
51:    Array::Array(const Array &rhs)
52:    {
53:       itsSize = rhs.GetitsSize();
54:       pType = new int[itsSize];
55:       for (int i = 0; i<itsSize; i++)
56:          pType[i] = rhs[i];
57:    }
58:
59:
60:    int& Array::operator[](int offSet)
61:    {
62:       int size = GetitsSize();
63:       if (offSet >= 0 && offSet < GetitsSize())
64:          return pType[offSet];
65:       throw xBoundary();
66:    }
67:
68:
69:    const int& Array::operator[](int offSet) const
70:    {
71:       int mysize = GetitsSize();
72:       if (offSet >= 0 && offSet < GetitsSize())
73:          return pType[offSet];
74:       throw xBoundary();
75:    }
76:
77:    ostream& operator<< (ostream& output, const Array& theArray)
78:    {
79:       for (int i = 0; i<theArray.GetitsSize(); i++)
80:          output << "[" << i << "] " << theArray[i] << endl;
81:       return output;
82:    }
83:
84:    void main()
85:    {
86:       Array intArray(20);
87:       try
88:       {
89:          for (int j = 0; j< 100; j++)
90:          {
91:             intArray[j] = j;
92:             cout << "intArray[" << j << "] okay..." << endl;
93:          }
94:       }
```

20

continues

621

Listing 20.1. continued

```
95:        catch (Array::xBoundary)
96:        {
97:            cout << "Unable to process your input!\n";
98:        }
99:        cout << "Done.\n";
99:    }
```

```
intArray[0] okay...
intArray[1] okay...
intArray[2] okay...
intArray[3] okay...
intArray[4] okay...
intArray[5] okay...
intArray[6] okay...
intArray[7] okay...
intArray[8] okay...
intArray[9] okay...
intArray[10] okay...
intArray[11] okay...
intArray[12] okay...
intArray[13] okay...
intArray[14] okay...
intArray[15] okay...
intArray[16] okay...
intArray[17] okay...
intArray[18] okay...
intArray[19] okay...
Unable to process your input!
Done.
```

Listing 20.1 presents a somewhat stripped-down Array class, based on the template developed on Day 19. On line 24 a new class is contained within the declaration of the Array: boundary.

This new class is not in any way distinguished as an exception class. It is just a class like any other. This particular class is incredibly simple: it has no data and no methods. Nonetheless, it is a valid class in every way.

In fact, it is incorrect to say it has no methods, because the compiler automatically assigns it a default constructor, destructor, copy constructor, and the copy operator (operator equals); so it actually has four class functions, but no data.

Note that declaring it from within Array serves only to couple the two classes together. As discussed on Day 15, Array has no special access to xBoundary, nor does xBoundary have preferential access to the members of Array.

On lines 60–66 and 69–75, the offset operators are modified to examine the offset requested and, if it is out of range, to "throw" the xBoundary class as an exception. The parentheses are required to distinguish between this call to the xBoundary constructor and the use of an enumerated constant.

On line 87, the keyword try begins a try block that ends on line 94. Within that try block, 100 integers are added to the array that was declared on line 86.

On line 95, the catch block to catch xBoundary exceptions is declared.

In the driver program on lines 84–89 a try block is created in which each member of the array is initialized. When j (line 89) is incremented to 20 the member at offset 20 is accessed. This causes the test on line 63 to fail, and operator[] raises an xBoundary exception on line 65.

Program control switches to the catch block block on line 95 and the exception is caught or handled by the case on the same line, which prints an error message. Program flow drops through to the end of the catch block on line 98.

Syntax

try Blocks

A try block is a set of statements that begin with the word try, are followed by an opening brace, and end with a closing brace.

Example:

```
try
{
    Function();
};
```

Syntax

catch Blocks

A catch block is a series of statements, each of which begins with the word catch, followed by an exception type in parentheses, followed by an opening brace, and ending with a closing brace.

Example:

```
Try
{
    Function();
};
Catch (OutOfMemory)
{
    // take action
}
```

20

Using *try* Blocks and *catch* Blocks

Figuring out where to put your `try` blocks is non-trivial: it is not always obvious which actions might raise an exception. The next question is where to catch the exception. It may be that you'll want to throw all memory exceptions where the memory is allocated, but you'll want to catch the exceptions high in the program, where you deal with the user interface.

When trying to determine `try` block locations, look to where you allocate memory or use resources. Other things to look for are out-of-bounds errors, illegal input, and so forth.

Catching Exceptions

Here's how it works: when an exception is thrown, the call stack is examined. The call stack is the list of function calls created when one part of the program invokes another function.

The call stack tracks the execution path. If `main()` calls the function `Animal::GetFavoriteFood()`, and `GetFavoriteFood()` calls `Animal::LookupPreferences()`, which in turn calls `fstream::operator>>()`, all of these are on the call stack. A recursive function might be on the call stack many times.

The exception is passed up the call stack to each enclosing block. As the stack is "unwound," the destructors for local objects on the stack are invoked, and the objects are destroyed.

After each `try` block there is one or more `catch` statements. If the exception matches one of the `catch` statements, it is considered to be handled by having that statement execute. If it doesn't match any, the unwinding of the stack continues.

If the exception reaches all the way to the beginning of the program (`main()`) and is still not caught, a built-in handler is called that terminates the program.

It is important to note that the exception unwinding of the stack is a one-way street. As it progresses, the stack is unwound and objects on the stack are destroyed. There is no going back: once the exception is handled, the program continues after the `try` block of the `catch` statement that handled the exception.

Thus, in Listing 20.1, execution will continue on line 99, the first line after the `try` block of the `catch` statement that handled the `xBoundary` exception. Remember that when an exception is raised, program flow continues after the `catch` block, *not* after the point where the exception was thrown.

More Than One *catch* Specification

It is possible for more than one condition to cause an exception. In this case, the catch statements can be lined up one after another, much as the conditions in a switch statement. The equivalent to the default statement is the "catch everything" statement indicated by catch(...). Listing 20.2 illustrates multiple exception conditions.

Listing 20.2. Multiple exceptions.

```
1:     #include <iostream.h>
2:
3:     const int DefaultSize = 10;
4:
5:     class Array
6:     {
7:     public:
8:         // constructors
9:         Array(int itsSize = DefaultSize);
10:        Array(const Array &rhs);
11:        ~Array() { delete [] pType;}
12:
13:        // operators
14:        Array& operator=(const Array&);
15:        int& operator[](int offSet);
16:        const int& operator[](int offSet) const;
17:
18:        // accessors
19:        int GetitsSize() const { return itsSize; }
20:
21:        // friend function
22:       friend ostream& operator<< (ostream&, const Array&);
23:
24:      // define the exception classes
25:        class xBoundary {};
26:        class xTooBig {};
27:        class xTooSmall{};
28:        class xZero {};
29:        class xNegative {};
30:    private:
31:        int *pType;
32:        int  itsSize;
33:    };
34:
35:
36:     Array::Array(int size):
37:     itsSize(size)
38:     {
39:         if (size == 0)
40:             throw xZero();
41:         if (size < 10)
42:             throw xTooSmall();
43:         if (size > 30000)
```

continues

Listing 20.2. continued

```
44:           throw xTooBig();
45:      if (size < 1)
46:           throw xNegative();
47:
48:      pType = new int[size];
49:      for (int i = 0; i<size; i++)
50:        pType[i] = 0;
51:   }
52:
53:
54:
55:   void main()
56:   {
57:
58:      try
59:      {
60:         Array intArray(0);
61:         for (int j = 0; j< 100; j++)
62:         {
63:             intArray[j] = j;
64:             cout << "intArray[" << j << "] okay..." << endl;
65:         }
66:      }
67:      catch (Array::xBoundary)
68:      {
69:         cout << "Unable to process your input!\n";
70:      }
71:      catch (Array::xTooBig)
72:      {
73:         cout << "This array is too big..." << endl;
74:      }
75:      catch (Array::xTooSmall)
76:      {
77:         cout << "This array is too small..." << endl;
78:      }
79:      catch (Array::xZero)
80:      {
81:         cout << "You asked for an array of zero objects!" << endl;
82:      }
83:      catch (...)
84:      {
85:         cout << "Something went wrong, but I've no idea what!" << endl;
86:      }
87:      cout << "Done.\n";
88:   }
```

Output

```
You asked for an array of zero objects!
Done.
```

Analysis

The implementation of all of Array's methods, except for its constructor, have been left out because they are unchanged from Listing 20.1.

Four new classes are created in lines 26–29: xTooBig, xTooSmall, xZero, and xNegative. In the constructor, on lines 36–51, the size passed to the constructor is examined. If it's too big, too small, negative, or zero, an exception is thrown.

The try block is changed to include catch statements for each condition other than negative, which is caught by the "catch everything" statement catch(...) shown on line 83.

Try this with a number of values for the size of the array. Then try putting in -5. You might have expected xNegative to be called, but the order of the tests in the constructor prevented this: size < 10 was evaluated before size < 1. To fix this, swap lines 41 and 42 with lines 45 and 46 and recompile.

Exception Hierarchies

Exceptions are classes, and as such they can be derived from. It may be advantageous to create a class xSize, and to derive from it xZero, xTooSmall, xTooBig, and xNegative. Thus, some functions might just catch xSize errors, while other functions might catch the specific type of xSize error. Listing 20.3 illustrates this idea.

Listing 20.3. Class hierarchies and exceptions.

```
1:     #include <iostream.h>
2:
3:     const int DefaultSize = 10;
4:
5:     class Array
6:     {
7:     public:
8:         // constructors
9:         Array(int itsSize = DefaultSize);
10:        Array(const Array &rhs);
11:        ~Array() { delete [] pType;}
12:
13:        // operators
14:        Array& operator=(const Array&);
15:        int& operator[](int offSet);
16:        const int& operator[](int offSet) const;
17:
18:        // accessors
19:        int GetitsSize() const { return itsSize; }
20:
21:        // friend function
22:       friend ostream& operator<< (ostream&, const Array&);
23:
24:     // define the exception classes
25:        class xBoundary {};
```

continues

Listing 20.3. continued

```
26:        class xSize {};
27:        class xTooBig : public xSize {};
28:        class xTooSmall : public xSize {};
29:        class xZero  : public xTooSmall {};
30:        class xNegative  : public xSize {};
31:    private:
32:        int *pType;
33:        int  itsSize;
34:    };
35:
36:
37:    Array::Array(int size):
38:    itsSize(size)
39:    {
40:       if (size == 0)
41:          throw xZero();
42:       if (size > 30000)
43:          throw xTooBig();
44:       if (size <1)
45:          throw xNegative();
46:       if (size < 10)
47:          throw xTooSmall();
48:
49:       pType = new int[size];
50:       for (int i = 0; i<size; i++)
51:         pType[i] = 0;
52:    }
```

This array is too small...
Done.

This listing leaves out the implementation of the array functions because they are unchanged, and it leaves out main() because it is identical to that in Listing 20.2.

The significant change is on lines 26–30, where the class hierarchy is established. Classes xTooBig, xTooSmall, and xNegative are derived from xSize, and xZero is derived from xTooSmall.

The Array is created with size zero, but what's this? The wrong exception appears to be caught! Examine the catch block carefully, however, and you will find that it looks for an exception of type xTooSmall *before* it looks for an exception of type xZero. Since an xZero object is thrown and an xZero object *is an* xTooSmall object, it is caught by the handler for xTooSmall. Once handled, the exception is *not* passed on to the other handlers, so the handler for xZero is never called.

The solution to this problem is to carefully order the handlers so that the most specific handlers come first and the less specific handlers come later. In this particular example, switching the placement of the two handlers xZero and xTooSmall will fix the problem.

Data in Exceptions and Naming Exception Objects

Often you will want to know more than just what type of exception was thrown so you can respond properly to the error. Exception classes are like any other class. You are free to provide data, initialize that data in the constructor, and read that data at any time. Listing 20.4 illustrates how to do this.

Listing 20.4. Getting data out of an exception object.

```
1:     #include <iostream.h>
2:
3:     const int DefaultSize = 10;
4:
5:     class Array
6:     {
7:     public:
8:        // constructors
9:        Array(int itsSize = DefaultSize);
10:       Array(const Array &rhs);
11:       ~Array() { delete [] pType;}
12:
13:       // operators
14:       Array& operator=(const Array&);
15:       int& operator[](int offSet);
16:       const int& operator[](int offSet) const;
17:
18:       // accessors
19:       int GetitsSize() const { return itsSize; }
20:
21:       // friend function
22:      friend ostream& operator<< (ostream&, const Array&);
23:
24:    // define the exception classes
25:       class xBoundary {};
26:       class xSize
27:       {
28:       public:
29:          xSize(int size):itsSize(size) {}
30:          ~xSize(){}
31:          int GetSize() { return itsSize; }
```

continues

Listing 20.4. continued

```
32:        private:
33:            int itsSize;
34:        };
35:
36:        class xTooBig : public xSize
37:        {
38:        public:
39:            xTooBig(int size):xSize(size){}
40:        };
41:
42:        class xTooSmall : public xSize
43:        {
44:        public:
45:            xTooSmall(int size):xSize(size){}
46:        };
47:
48:        class xZero   : public xTooSmall
49:        {
50:        public:
51:            xZero(int size):xTooSmall(size){}
52:        };
53:
54:        class xNegative : public xSize
55:        {
56:        public:
57:            xNegative(int size):xSize(size){}
58:        };
59:
60:    private:
61:        int *pType;
62:        int  itsSize;
63:    };
64:
65:
66:    Array::Array(int size):
67:    itsSize(size)
68:    {
69:       if (size == 0)
70:           throw xZero(size);
71:       if (size > 30000)
72:           throw xTooBig(size);
73:       if (size <1)
74:           throw xNegative(size);
75:       if (size < 10)
76:           throw xTooSmall(size);
77:
78:       pType = new int[size];
79:       for (int i = 0; i<size; i++)
80:         pType[i] = 0;
81:    }
82:
83:
84:    void main()
85:    {
```

```
86:
87:        try
88:        {
89:            Array intArray(9);
90:            for (int j = 0; j< 100; j++)
91:            {
92:                intArray[j] = j;
93:                cout << "intArray[" << j << "] okay..." << endl;
94:            }
95:        }
96:        catch (Array::xBoundary)
97:        {
98:            cout << "Unable to process your input!\n";
99:        }
100:       catch (Array::xZero theException)
101:       {
102:           cout << "You asked for an array of zero objects!" << endl;
103:           cout << "Received " << theException.GetSize() << endl;
104:       }
105:       catch (Array::xTooBig theException)
106:       {
107:           cout << "This array is too big..." << endl;
108:           cout << "Received " << theException.GetSize() << endl;
109:       }
110:       catch (Array::xTooSmall theException)
111:       {
112:           cout << "This array is too small..." << endl;
113:           cout << "Received " << theException.GetSize() << endl;
114:       }
115:       catch (...)
116:       {
117:           cout << "Something went wrong, but I've no idea what!" << endl;
118:       }
119:       cout << "Done.\n";
120:    }
```

```
This array is too small...
Received 9
Done.
```

The declaration of xSize has been modified to include a member variable, itsSize, on line 33 and a member function, GetSize(), on line 31. Additionally, a constructor has been added that takes an integer and initializes the member variable, as shown on line 29.

The derived classes declare a constructor that does nothing but initialize the base class. No other functions were declared, in part to save space in the listing.

The catch statements on lines 100 to 118 are modified to name the exception they catch, theException, and to use this object to access the data stored in itsSize.

> **Note:** Keep in mind that if you are constructing an exception, it is because
> an exception has been raised: something has gone wrong and your exception
> should be careful not to kick off the same problem. Thus, if you are creating
> an OutOfMemory exception, you probably don't want to allocate memory in
> its constructor.

It is tedious and error-prone to have each of these catch statements individually print the
appropriate message. This job belongs to the object, which knows what type of object
it is and what value it received. Listing 20.5 takes a more object-oriented approach to this
problem, using virtual functions so that each exception "does the right thing."

**Listing 20.5. Passing by reference and using virtual functions in
exceptions.**

```
1:    #include <iostream.h>
2:
3:    const int DefaultSize = 10;
4:
5:    class Array
6:    {
7:    public:
8:        // constructors
9:        Array(int itsSize = DefaultSize);
10:       Array(const Array &rhs);
11:       ~Array() { delete [] pType;}
12:
13:       // operators
14:       Array& operator=(const Array&);
15:       int& operator[](int offSet);
16:       const int& operator[](int offSet) const;
17:
18:       // accessors
19:       int GetitsSize() const { return itsSize; }
20:
21:       // friend function
22:      friend ostream& operator<< (ostream&, const Array&);
23:
24:     // define the exception classes
25:      class xBoundary {};
26:      class xSize
27:      {
28:      public:
29:          xSize(int size):itsSize(size) {}
30:          ~xSize(){}
31:          virtual int GetSize() { return itsSize; }
32:          virtual void PrintError() { cout << "Size error. Received: " << itsSize
<< endl; }
33:        protected:
```

```
34:            int itsSize;
35:        };
36:
37:        class xTooBig : public xSize
38:        {
39:        public:
40:            xTooBig(int size):xSize(size){}
41:            virtual void PrintError() { cout << "Too big! Received: " <<
            ➥xSize::itsSize << endl; }
42:        };
43:
44:        class xTooSmall : public xSize
45:        {
46:        public:
47:            xTooSmall(int size):xSize(size){}
48:            virtual void PrintError() { cout << "Too small! Received: " <<
            ➥xSize::itsSize << endl; }
49:        };
50:
51:        class xZero   : public xTooSmall
52:        {
53:        public:
54:            xZero(int size):xTooSmall(size){}
55:            virtual void PrintError() { cout << "Zero!!. Received: " <<
            ➥xSize::itsSize << endl; }
56:        };
57:
58:        class xNegative : public xSize
59:        {
60:        public:
61:            xNegative(int size):xSize(size){}
62:            virtual void PrintError() { cout << "Negative! Received: " <<
            ➥xSize::itsSize << endl; }
63:        };
64:
65:    private:
66:        int *pType;
67:        int  itsSize;
68:    };
69:
70:    Array::Array(int size):
71:    itsSize(size)
72:    {
73:        if (size == 0)
74:            throw xZero(size);
75:        if (size > 30000)
76:            throw xTooBig(size);
77:        if (size <1)
78:            throw xNegative(size);
79:        if (size < 10)
80:            throw xTooSmall(size);
81:
82:        pType = new int[size];
83:        for (int i = 0; i<size; i++)
84:          pType[i] = 0;
```

20

continues

Listing 20.5. continued

```
85:    }
86:
87:    void main()
88:    {
89:
90:       try
91:       {
92:          Array intArray(9);
93:          for (int j = 0; j< 100; j++)
94:          {
95:             intArray[j] = j;
96:             cout << "intArray[" << j << "] okay..." << endl;
97:          }
98:       }
99:       catch (Array::xBoundary)
100:      {
101:         cout << "Unable to process your input!\n";
102:      }
103:      catch (Array::xSize& theException)
104:      {
105:         theException.PrintError();
106:      }
107:      catch (...)
108:      {
109:         cout << "Something went wrong, but I've no idea what!" << endl;
110:      }
111:      cout << "Done.\n";
112:   }
```

```
Too small! Received 9
Done.
```

Listing 20.5 declares a virtual method in the xSize class, PrintError(), which prints an error message and the actual size of the class. This is overridden in each of the derived classes.

On line 103, the exception object is declared to be a reference. When PrintError() is called with a reference to an object, polymorphism causes the correct version of PrintError() to be invoked. The code is cleaner, easier to understand, and easier to maintain.

Exceptions and Templates

When creating exceptions to work with templates, you have a choice: you can create an exception for each instance of the template, or you can use exception classes declared outside of the template declaration. Listing 20.6 illustrates both approaches.

Listing 20.6. Using exceptions with templates.

```
1:     #include <iostream.h>
2:
3:     const int DefaultSize = 10;
4:     class xBoundary {};
5:
6:     template <class T>
7:     class Array
8:     {
9:     public:
10:        // constructors
11:        Array(int itsSize = DefaultSize);
12:        Array(const Array &rhs);
13:        ~Array() { delete [] pType;}
14:
15:        // operators
16:        Array& operator=(const Array<T>&);
17:        T& operator[](int offSet);
18:        const T& operator[](int offSet) const;
19:
20:        // accessors
21:        int GetitsSize() const { return itsSize; }
22:
23:        // friend function
24:         friend ostream& operator<< (ostream&, const Array<T>&);
25:
26:      // define the exception classes
27:
28:         class xSize {};
29:
30:     private:
31:         int *pType;
32:         int  itsSize;
33:     };
34:
35:     template <class T>
36:     Array<T>::Array(int size):
37:     itsSize(size)
38:     {
39:        if (size <10 || size > 30000)
40:           throw xSize();
41:        pType = new T[size];
42:        for (int i = 0; i<size; i++)
43:          pType[i] = 0;
44:     }
45:
46:     template <class T>
47:     Array<T>& Array<T>::operator=(const Array<T> &rhs)
48:     {
49:        if (this == &rhs)
50:           return *this;
51:        delete [] pType;
52:        itsSize = rhs.GetitsSize();
```

continues

Listing 20.6. continued

```
53:         pType = new T[itsSize];
54:         for (int i = 0; i<itsSize; i++)
55:             pType[i] = rhs[i];
56:     }
57:     template <class T>
58:     Array<T>::Array(const Array<T> &rhs)
59:     {
60:         itsSize = rhs.GetitsSize();
61:         pType = new T[itsSize];
62:         for (int i = 0; i<itsSize; i++)
63:             pType[i] = rhs[i];
64:     }
65:
66:     template <class T>
67:     T& Array<T>::operator[](int offSet)
68:     {
69:         int size = GetitsSize();
70:         if (offSet >= 0 && offSet < GetitsSize())
71:             return pType[offSet];
72:         throw xBoundary();
73:     }
74:
75:     template <class T>
76:     const T& Array<T>::operator[](int offSet) const
77:     {
78:         int mysize = GetitsSize();
79:         if (offSet >= 0 && offSet < GetitsSize())
80:             return pType[offSet];
81:         throw xBoundary();
82:     }
83:
84:     template <class T>
85:     ostream& operator<< (ostream& output, const Array<T>& theArray)
86:     {
87:         for (int i = 0; i<theArray.GetitsSize(); i++)
88:             output << "[" << i << "] " << theArray[i] << endl;
89:         return output;
90:     }
91:
92:
93:     void main()
94:     {
95:
96:         try
97:         {
98:             Array<int> intArray(9);
99:             for (int j = 0; j< 100; j++)
100:            {
101:                intArray[j] = j;
102:                cout << "intArray[" << j << "] okay..." << endl;
103:            }
104:        }
105:        catch (xBoundary)
106:        {
```

```
107:          cout << "Unable to process your input!\n";
108:      }
109:      catch (Array<int>::xSize)
110:      {
111:          cout << "Bad Size!\n";
112:      }
113:
114:      cout << "Done.\n";
115:  }
```

```
Bad Size!
Done.
```

The first exception, xBoundary, is declared outside the template definition on line 4. The second exception, xSize, is declared from within the definition of the template.

The exception xBoundary is not tied to the template class, but can be used like any other class. xSize is tied to the template, and must be called based on the instantiated Array. You can see the difference in the syntax for the two catch statements. Line 105 shows catch (xBoundary), but line 109 shows catch (Array<int>::xSize). The latter is tied to the *instantiation* of an integer Array.

Exceptions Without Errors

When C++ programmers get together for a virtual beer in the cyberspace bar after work, talk often turns to whether exceptions should be used for routine conditions. Some maintain that by their nature exceptions should be reserved for those predictable but exceptional circumstances (hence the name!) that a programmer must anticipate, but that are not part of the routine processing of the code.

Others point out that exceptions offer a powerful and clean way to return through many layers of function calls without danger of memory leaks. A frequent example is this: the user requests an action in a GUI environment. The part of the code that catches the request must call a member function on a dialog manager, which in turn calls code that processes the request, which calls code that decides which dialog box to use, which in turn calls code to put up the dialog box, which finally calls code that processes the user's input. If the user presses Cancel, the code must return to the very first calling method, where the original request was handled.

One approach to this problem is to put a try block around the original call and catch CancelDialog as an exception, which can be raised by the handler for the Cancel button. This is safe and effective, but pressing cancel is a routine circumstance, not an exceptional one.

This frequently becomes something of a religious argument, but there is a reasonable way to decide the question: Does use of exceptions in this way make the code easier or harder to understand? Are there fewer risks of errors and memory leaks or more? Will it be harder or easier to maintain this code? These decisions, like so many others, will require an analysis of the trade-offs; there is no single, obvious right answer.

Bugs and Debugging

You saw on Day 17 how to use asserts to trap runtime bugs during the testing phase, and today you saw how to use exceptions to trap runtime problems. There is one more powerful weapon you'll want to add to your arsenal as you attack bugs: the debugger.

Nearly all modern development environments include one or more high-powered debuggers. The essential idea of using a debugger is this: you run the debugger, which loads your source code, and then you run your program from within the debugger. This allows you to see each instruction in your program as it executes, and to examine your variables as they change during the life of your program.

All compilers will let you compile with or without symbols. Compiling with symbols tells the compiler to create the necessary mapping between your source code and the generated program; the debugger uses this to point to the line of source code that corresponds to the next action in the program.

Full-screen symbolic debuggers make this chore a delight. When you load your debugger, it will read through all your source code and show the code in a window. You can step over function calls or direct the debugger to step into the function, line by line.

With most debuggers, you can switch between the source code and the output to see the results of each executed statement. More powerfully, you can examine the current state of each variable, you can look at complex data structures, examine the value of member data within classes, and look at the actual values in memory of various pointers and other memory locations. You can execute several types of control within a debugger that include setting breakpoints, setting watch points, examining memory, and looking at the assembler code.

Breakpoints

Breakpoints are instructions to the debugger that when a particular line of code is ready to be executed, the program should stop. This allows you to run your program unimpeded until the line in question is reached. Breakpoints help you analyze the current condition of variables just before and after a critical line of code.

Watch Points

It is possible to tell the debugger to show you the value of a particular variable, or to break when a particular variable is read or written to. Watch points allow you to set these conditions, and at times to even modify the value of a variable *while the program is running*.

Examining Memory

At times it is important to see the actual values held in memory. Modern debuggers can show values in the form of the actual variable; that is, strings can be shown as characters, longs as numbers rather than as four bytes, and so forth. Sophisticated C++ debuggers can even show complete classes, providing the current value of all the member variables, including the *this* pointer.

Assembler

Although reading through the source can be all that is required to find a bug, when all else fails it is possible to instruct the debugger to show you the actual assembly code generated for each line of your source code. You can examine the memory registers and flags, and generally delve as deep into the inner workings of your program as required.

Learn to use your debugger. It can be the most powerful weapon in your holy war against bugs. Runtime bugs are the hardest to find and squash, and a powerful debugger can make it possible, if not easy, to find nearly all of them.

Summary

20

Today you learned how to create and use exceptions. Exceptions are objects that can be created and thrown at points in the program where the executing code cannot handle the error or other exceptional condition that as arisen. Other parts of the program, higher in the call stack, implement catch blocks that catch the exception and take appropriate action.

Exceptions are normal user-created objects, and as such may be passed by value or by reference. They may contain data and methods, and the catch block may use that data to decide on how to deal with the exception.

It is possible to create multiple catch blocks, but once an exception matches a catch block's signature, it is considered to be handled and is not given to the subsequent catch blocks. It is important to order the catch blocks appropriately, so that more specific catch blocks have first chance and more general catch blocks handle those not otherwise handled.

This chapter also examined some of the fundamentals of symbolic debuggers, including using watch points, breakpoints, and so forth. These tools can help you zero in on the part of your program that is causing the error, and let you see the value of variables as they change during the course of the execution of the program.

Q&A

Q Why bother with raising exceptions? Why not handle the error right where it happens?

A Often the same error can be generated in a number of different parts of the code. Exceptions let you centralize the handling of errors. Additionally, the part of the code that generates the error may not be the best place to determine *how* to handle the error.

Q Why generate an object? Why not just pass an error code?

A Objects are more flexible and powerful than error codes. They can convey more information, and the constructor/destructor mechanisms can be used for the creation and removal of resources that may be required to properly handle the exceptional condition.

Q Why not use exceptions for non-error conditions? Isn't it convenient to be able to express-train back to previous areas of the code, even when non-exceptional conditions exist?

A Yes, some C++ programmers use exceptions for just that purpose. The danger is that exceptions might create memory leaks as the stack is unwound and some objects are inadvertently left in the free store. With careful programming techniques and a good compiler, this can usually be avoided. Otherwise, it is a matter of personal aesthetic; some programmers feel that by their nature exceptions should not be used for routine conditions.

Q Does an exception have to be caught in the same place where the try block created the exception?

A No, it is possible to catch an exception anywhere in the call stack. As the stack is unwound, the exception is passed up the stack until it is handled.

Q **Why use a debugger when you can use cout with conditional (#ifdef debug) compiling?**

A The debugger provides a much more powerful mechanism for stepping through your code and watching values change without having to clutter your code with thousands of debugging statements.

Workshop

The Workshop contains quiz questions to help solidify your understanding of the material covered and exercises to provide you with experience in using what you've learned. Try to answer the quiz and exercise questions before checking the answers in Appendix D, and make sure you understand the answers before going to the next chapter.

Quiz

1. What is an exception?

2. What is a try block?

3. What is a catch statement?

4. What information can an exception contain?

5. When are exception objects created?

6. Should you pass exceptions by value or by reference?

7. Will a catch statement catch a derived exception if it is looking for the base class?

8. If there are two catch statements, one for base and one for derived, which should come first?

9. What does catch(...) mean?

10. What is a breakpoint?

Exercises

1. Create a try block, a catch statement, and a simple exception.

2. Modify the answer from Exercise 1, put data into the exception, along with an accessor function, and use it in the catch block.

3. Modify the class from Exercise 2 to be a hierarchy of exceptions. Modify the catch block to use the derived objects and the base objects.

4. Modify the program from Exercise 3 to have three levels of function calls.

5. **BUG BUSTERS:** What is wrong with the following code?

```
class xOutOfMemory
{
public:
    xOutOfMemory( const String& message ) : itsMsg( message ){}
    ~xOutOfMemory(){}
    virtual const String& Message(){ return itsMsg};
private:
    String itsMsg;          // assume you are using the string class as
    previously defined
}


main()
{
    try {
        char *var = new char;
        if ( var == 0 )
            throw xOutOfMemory();
    }
    catch( xOutOfMemory& theException )
    {
        cout <<  theException.Message() << "\n";
    }
}
```

What's Next

Introduction

Congratulations! You are nearly done with a full three-week intensive introduction to C++. By now you should have a solid understanding of C++, but in modern porgramming there is always more to learn. This chapter will fill in some missing details and then set the course for continued study.

Today you will learn:

☐ What the standard libraries are.

☐ How to manipulate individual bits and use them as flags.

☐ What the next steps are in learning to use C++ effectively.

The Standard Libraries

Every implementation of C++ includes the standard libraries, and most include additional libraries as well. Libraries are sets of functions that can be linked into your code. You've already used a number of standard library functions and classes, most notably from the iostreams library.

To use a library, you typically include a header file in your source code, much as you did by writing #include <iostreams.h> in many of the examples in this book. The angle brackets around the filename are a signal to the compiler to look in the directory where you keep the header files for your compiler's standard libraries.

There are dozens of libraries, covering everything from file manipulation to setting the date and time to math functions. Today we will review just a few of the most popular functions and classes in the standard library that have not yet been covered in this book.

String

The most popular library is almost certainly the string library, with perhaps the function strlen() called most often. Strlen() returns the length of a null-terminated string. Listing 21.1 illustrates its use.

Listing 21.1. strlen().

```
1:      #include <iostream.h>
2:      #include <string.h>
3:
```

```
4:      void main()
5:      {
6:          char buffer[80];
7:          do
8:          {
9:              cout << "Enter a string up to 80 characters: ";
10:             cin.getline(buffer,80);
11:             cout << "Your string is " << strlen(buffer) << " characters long." <<
                   ➥endl;
12:         }   while (strlen(buffer));
13:         cout << "\nDone." << endl;
14:     }
```

```
Enter a string up to 80 characters: This sentence has 28 characters
Your string is 28 characters long.
Enter a string up to 80 characters: This sentence no verb
Your string is 21 characters long.
Enter a string up to 80 characters:
Your string is 0 characters long.

Done.
```

On line 6 a character buffer is created, and on line 9 the user is prompted to enter a string. As long as the user enters a string, the length of the string is reported on line 10.

Note the test in the do...while() statement: while (strlen(buffer)). Since strlen() will return 0 when the buffer is empty, and since 0 evaluates false, this while loop will continue as long as there are any characters in the buffer.

strcpy() and *strncpy()*

The second most popular function in STRING.H probably *was* strcpy(), which copied one string to another. This may now be diminished somewhat as C-style null-terminated strings have become somewhat less important in C++; typically, string manipulation is done from within a vendor-supplied or user-written string class. Nonetheless, your string class must support an assignment operator and a copy constructor, and often these are implemented using strcpy(), as illustrated in Listing 21.2.

Listing 21.2. Using strcpy.

```
1:      #include <iostream.h>
2:      #include <string.h>
3:
4:      void main()
5:      {
```

continues

21

Listing 21.2. continued

```
6:      char stringOne[80];
7:      char stringTwo[80];
8:
9:      stringOne[0]='\0';
10:     stringTwo[0]='\0';
11:
12:     cout << "String One: " << stringOne << endl;
13:     cout << "String Two: " << stringTwo << endl;
14:
15:     cout << "Enter a string: ";
16:     cin.getline(stringOne,80);
17:
18:     cout << "\nString One: " << stringOne << endl;
19:     cout << "String Two: " << stringTwo << endl;
20:
21:     cout << "copying..." << endl;
22:     strcpy(stringTwo,stringOne);
23:
24:     cout << "\nString One: " << stringOne << endl;
25:     cout << "String Two: " << stringTwo << endl;
26:     cout << "\nDone " << endl;
27:   }
```

```
String One:
String Two:
Enter a string: Test of strcpy()

String One:  Test of strcpy()
String Two:
copying...

String One:  Test of strcpy()
String Two:  Test of strcpy()

Done.
```

Two C-style null-terminated strings are declared on lines 6 and 7. They are initialized to empty on lines 9 and 10, and their values are printed on lines 12 and 13. The user is prompted to enter a string, and the result is put in stringOne; the two strings are printed again, and only stringOne has the input. Strcpy() is then called, and stringOne is copied into stringTwo.

Note that the syntax of strcpy() can be read as "copy into the first parameter the string in the second parameter." What happens if the target string (stringTwo) is too small to hold the copied string? This problem and its solution is illustrated in Listing 21.3.

Listing 21.3. Using strncpy().

```
1:     #include <iostream.h>
2:     #include <string.h>
3:
4:     void main()
5:     {
6:        char stringOne[80];
7:        char stringTwo[10];
8:        char stringThree[80];
9:
10:       stringOne[0]='\0';
11:       stringTwo[0]='\0';
12:       stringThree[0]='\0';
13:
14:       cout << "String One: " << stringOne << endl;
15:       cout << "String Two: " << stringTwo << endl;
16:       cout << "String Three: " << stringThree << endl;
17:
18:       cout << "Enter a long string: ";
19:       cin.getline(stringOne,80);
20:       strcpy(stringThree,stringOne);
21:    //    strcpy(stringTwo,stringOne);
22:
23:       cout << "\nString One: " << stringOne << endl;
24:       cout << "String Two: " << stringTwo << endl;
25:       cout << "String Three: " << stringThree << endl;
26:
27:       strncpy(stringTwo,stringOne,9);
28:
29:       cout << "\nString One: " << stringOne << endl;
30:       cout << "String Two: " << stringTwo << endl;
31:       cout << "String Three: " << stringThree << endl;
32:
33:       stringTwo[9]='\0';
34:
35:       cout << "\nString One: " << stringOne << endl;
36:       cout << "String Two: " << stringTwo << endl;
37:       cout << "String Three: " << stringThree << endl;
38:       cout << "\nDone." << endl;
39:    }
```

```
String One:
String Two:
String Three:

Enter a long string: Now is the time for all...

String One:    Now is the time for all...
String Two:
String Three:  Now is the time for all...
```

```
String One:    Now is the time for all...
String Two:    Now is th_+||
String Three:  Now is the time for all...

String One:    Now is the time for all...
String Two:    Now is th
String Three:  Now is the time for all...

Done.
```

 On lines 6, 7, and 8, three string buffers are declared. Note that `stringTwo` is declared to be only 10 characters, while the others are 80. All three are initialized to zero length on lines 10 to 12 and are printed on lines 14 to 16.

The user is prompted to enter a string, and that string is copied to string three on line 20. Line 21 is commented out; copying this long string to `stringTwo` caused a crash on my computer because it wrote into memory that was critical to the program.

The standard function `strcpy()` starts copying at the address pointed to by the first parameter (the array name), and it copies the entire string without ensuring that you've allocated room for it!

The standard library offers a second, safer function, `strncpy()`, which copies only a specified number of characters to the target string. The n in the middle of the function name `strncpy()` stands for *number*. This is a convention used throughout the standard libraries.

On line 27, the first nine characters of `stringOne` are copied to `stringTwo` and the result is printed. Because `strncpy()` does *not* put a null at the end of the copied string, the result is not what was intended. Note that `strcpy()` does null-terminate the copied string, but `strncpy()` does not; just to keep life interesting.

The null is added on line 33, and the strings are then printed a final time.

strcat() and strncat()

Related to `strcpy()` and `strncpy()` are the standard functions `strcat()` and `strncat()`. The former con*cat*enates one string to another; that is, it appends the string it takes as its second parameter to the end of the string it takes as its first parameter. `strncat()`, as you might expect, appends the first n characters of one string to the other. Listing 21.4 illustrates their use.

Listing 21.4. Using `strcat()` and `strncat()`.

```
1:    #include <iostream.h>
2:    #include <string.h>
```

```
3:
4:
5:      void main()
6:      {
7:          char stringOne[255];
8:          char stringTwo[255];
9:
10:         stringOne[0]='\0';
11:         stringTwo[0]='\0';
12:
13:         cout << "Enter a  string: ";
14:         cin.getline(stringOne,80);
15:
16:         cout << "Enter a second string: ";
17:         cin.getline(stringTwo,80);
18:
19:         cout << "String One: " << stringOne << endl;
20:         cout << "String Two: " << stringTwo << endl;
21:
22:         strcat(stringOne," ");
23:         strncat(stringOne,stringTwo,10);
24:
25:         cout << "String One: " << stringOne << endl;
26:         cout << "String Two: " << stringTwo << endl;
27:
28:     }
```

```
Enter a string: Oh beautiful
Enter a second string: for spacious skies for amber waves of grain

String One: Oh beautiful
String Two: for spacious skies for amber waves of grain

String One: Oh beautiful for spacio
String Two: for spacious skies for amber waves of grain
```

On lines 7 and 8 two character arrays are created, and the user is prompted for two strings, which are put into the two arrays.

A space is appended to stringOne on line 22, and then on line 23 the first ten characters of stringTwo are appended to stringOne. The result is printed on lines 25 and 26.

Other String Functions

The string library provides a number of other string functions, including those used to find occurrences of various characters or "tokens" within a string. If you need to find a comma or a particular word as it occurs in a string, look to the string library to see if the function you need already exists.

Time and Date

The time library provides a number of functions for obtaining a close approximation of the current time and date, and for comparing times and dates to one another.

The center of this library is a structure, tm, which consists of nine integer values for the second, minute, hour, day of the month, number of the month (where January=0), the number of years since 1900, the day (where Sunday=0), the day of the year (0-365) and a Boolean value establishing whether Daylight Savings Time is in effect. (This last may not be supported on some systems.)

Most time functions expect a variable of type time_t, or a pointer to a variable of this type. There are conversion routines to turn such a variable into a tm data structure.

The standard library supplies the function time(), which takes a pointer to a time_t variable and fills it with the current time. It also provides ctime(), which takes the time_t variable filled by time() and returns an ASCII string that can be used for printing. If you need more control over the output, however, you can pass the time_t variable to local_time(), which will return a pointer to a tm structure. Listing 21.5 illustrates these various time functions.

Listing 21.5. Using ctime().

```
1:      #include <time.h>
2:      #include <iostream.h>
3:
4:      void main()
5:      {
6:          time_t currentTime;
7:
8:          // get and print the current time
9:          time (&currentTime); // fill now with the current time
10:         cout << "It is now " << ctime(&currentTime) << endl;
11:
12:         struct tm * ptm= localtime(&currentTime);
13:
14:         cout << "Today is " << ((ptm->tm_mon)+1) << "/";
15:         cout << ptm->tm_mday << "/";
16:         cout << ptm->tm_year << endl;
17:
18:         cout << "\nDone.";
19:     }
```

```
It is now Tue Jul 19 11:14:27 1994

Today is 7/19/94

Done.
```

On line 6, CurrentTime is declared to be a variable of type time_t. The address of this variable is passed to the standard time library function time(), and the variable currentTime is set to the current date and time. The address of this variable is then passed to ctime(), which returns an ASCII string that is in turn passed to the cout statement on line 12.

The address of currentTime is then passed to the standard time library function localtime(), and a pointer to a tm structure is returned, which is used to initialize the local variable ptm. The member data of this structure is then accessed to print the current month, day of the month, and year.

stdlib

stdlib is something of a miscellaneous collection of functions that did not fit into the other libraries. It includes simple integer math functions, sorting functions (including qsort(), one of the fastest sorts available), and text conversions for moving from ASCII text to integers, long, float, and so forth.

The functions in stdlib you are likely to use most often include atoi(), itoa(), and the family of related functions. atoi() provides ASCII to integer conversion. atoi() takes a single argument, a pointer to a constant character variable. It returns an integer (as you might expect). Listing 21.6 illustrates its use.

Listing 21.6. Using atoi() and related functions.

```
1:      #include <stdlib.h>
2:      #include <iostreams.h>
3:
4:      void main()
5:      {
6:          char buffer[80];
7:          cout << "Enter a number: ";
8:          cin >> buffer;
9:
10:         int number;
11:         // number = buffer; compile error
12:         number = atoi(buffer);
13:         cout << "here's the number: " << number << endl;
14:
15:         // int sum = buffer + 5;
16:         int sum = atoi(buffer) + 5;
17:         cout << "here's sum: " << sum << endl;
18:
19:     }
```

21

```
Enter a number: 9
Here's the number: 9
Here's sum: 14
```

On line 6 of this simple program an 80-character buffer is allocated, and on line 7 the user is prompted for a number. The input is taken as text and written into the buffer.

On line 10 an `int` variable, `number`, is declared, and on line 11 the program attempts to assign the contents of the buffer to the `int` variable. This generates a compile-time error and is commented out.

On line 12 the problem is solved by invoking the standard library function `atoi()`, passing in the buffer as the parameter. The return value, the integer value of the text string, is assigned to the integer variable `number` and printed on line 13.

On line 15 a new integer variable, `sum`, is declared, and an attempt is made to assign to it the result of adding the integer constant 5 to the buffer. This, too, fails and is solved by calling the standard function `atoi()`.

> **Note:** Some compilers implement standard conversion procedures (such as `atoi()`) using macros. You can usually use these functions without worrying about how they are inplemented. Check your compiler's documentation for details.

qsort()

At times you may want to sort a table or an array; `qsort()` provides a quick and easy way to do so. The hard part of using `qsort()` is setting up the structures to pass in.

`qsort()` takes four arguments. The first is a pointer to the start of the table to be sorted (an array name works just fine), the second is the number of elements in the table, the third is the size of each element, and the fourth is a pointer to a comparison function.

The comparison function must return an `int`, and must take as its parameters two constant void pointers. Void pointers aren't used very often in C++, as they diminish the type checking, but they have the advantage that they can be used to point to items of any type. If you were writing your own `qsort()` function, you might consider using templates instead. Listing 21.7 illustrates how to use the standard `qsort()` function.

Listing 21.7. Using qsort().

```
1:      /* qsort example */
2:
3:      #include <iostream.h>
4:      #include <stdlib.h>
5:
6:      // form of sort_function required by qsort
7:      int sortFunction( const void *intOne, const void *intTwo);
8:
9:      const int TableSize = 10;   // array size
10:
11:     void main(void)
12:     {
13:         int table[TableSize];
14:
15:         // fill the table with values
16:         for (int i = 0; i<TableSize; i++)
17:         {
18:             cout << "Enter a number: ";
19:             cin >> table[i];
20:         }
21:         cout << "\n";
22:
23:         // sort the values
24:         qsort((void *)table, TableSize, sizeof(table[0]), sortFunction);
25:
26:         // print the results
27:         for (i = 0; i < TableSize; i++)
28:             cout << "Table [" << i << "]: " << table[i] << endl;
29:
30:         cout << "Done." << endl;
31:     }
32:
33:     int sortFunction( const void *a, const void *b)
34:     {
35:         int intOne = *((int*)a);
36:         int intTwo = *((int*)b);
37:         if (intOne < intTwo)
38:             return -1;
39:         if (intOne == intTwo)
40:             return 0;
41:         return 1;
42:     }
```

Output

```
Enter a number: 2
Enter a number: 9
Enter a number: 12
Enter a number: 873
Enter a number: 0
Enter a number: 45
Enter a number: 93
Enter a number: 2
Enter a number: 66
Enter a number: 1
```

21

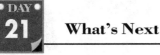

```
Table[0]: 0
Table[1]: 1
Table[2]: 2
Table[3]: 2
Table[4]: 9
Table[5]: 12
Table[6]: 45
Table[7]: 66
Table[8]: 93
Table[9]: 873
Done.
```

 On line 4 the standard library header is included, which is required by the qsort() function. On line 7 the function sortFunction() is declared, which takes the requisite four parameters.

An array is declared on line 13 and filled by user input on lines 16-20. qsort() is called on line 24, casting the address of the array name table to be a void*.

Note that the parameters for sortFunction are not passed to the call to qsort(). The name of the sortFunction, which is itself a pointer to that function, is the parameter to qsort().

Once qsort() is running, it will fill the constant void pointers a and b with each value of the array. If the first value is smaller than the second, the comparison function must return -1. If it is equal, the comparison function must return 0. Finally, if the first value is greater than the second value, the comparison function must return 1. This is reflected in the sortFunction(), as shown on lines 33 to 42.

Other Libraries

Your C++ compiler supplies a number of other libraries, among them the standard input and output libraries and the stream libraries that you've been using throughout this book. It is well worth your time and effort to explore the documentation that came with your compiler to find out what these libraries have to offer.

Bit Twiddling

Often you will want to set flags in your objects to keep track of the state of your object. (Is it in AlarmState? Has this been initialized yet? Are you coming or going?)

You can do this with user-defined Booleans, but when you have many flags, and when storage size is an issue, it is convenient to be able to use the individual bits as flags.

Each byte has eight bits, so in a four-byte `long` you can hold 32 separate flags. A bit is said to be "set" if its value is 1, and clear if its value is 0. When you set a bit, you make its value 1, and when you clear it, you make its value 0. (Set and clear are both nouns and verbs). You can set and clear bits by changing the value of the `long`, but that can be tedious and confusing.

Note: Appendix C provides valuable additional information about binary and hexidecimal manipulation.

C++ provides bitwise operators that act upon the individual bits. These look like, but are different from, the logical operators, so many novice programmers confuse them. The bitwise operators are presented in Table 21.1.

Table 21.1. The bitwise operators.

symbol	operator
&	AND
¦	OR
^	exclusive OR
~	complement

Operator *AND*

The AND operator (&) is a single ampersand, as opposed to the logical AND, which is two ampersands. When you AND two bits, the result is 1 if both bits are 1, but 0 if either bit is 0 or both are. The way to think of this is: the result is 1 if bit 1 is set *and* if bit 2 is set.

Operator *OR*

The second bitwise operator is OR (¦). Again, this is a single vertical bar, as opposed to the logical OR, which is two vertical bars. When you OR two bits, the result is 1 if either bit is set or if both are.

Operator Exclusive *OR*

The third bitwise operator is exclusive OR (^). When you exclusive OR two bits, the result is 1 if the two bits are different.

The Complement Operator

The complement operator (~) clears every bit in a number that is set and sets every bit that is clear. If the current value of the number is 1010 0011, the complement of that number is 0101 1100.

Setting Bits

When you want to set or clear a particular bit, you use masking operations. If you have a 4-byte flag and you want to set bit 8 true, you need to OR the flag with the value 128. Why? 128 is 1000 0000 in binary; thus the value of the eighth bit is 128. Whatever the current value of that bit (set or clear), if you OR it with the value 128 you will set that bit and not change any of the other bits. Let's assume that the current value of the 8 bits is 1010 0110 0010 0110. ORing 128 to it looks like this:

```
          9 8765 4321
   1010 0110 0010 0110     // bit 8 is clear
|  0000 0000 1000 0000     // 128
---------------------
   1010 0110 1010 0110     // bit 8 is set
```

There are a few things to note. First, as usual, bits are counted from right to left. Second, the value 128 is all zeros except for bit 8, the bit you want to set. Third, the starting number 1010 0110 0010 0110 is left unchanged by the OR operation, except that bit 8 was set. Had bit 8 already been set, it would have remained set, which is what you want.

Clearing Bits

If you want to clear bit 8, you can AND the bit with the complement of 128. The complement of 128 is the number you get when you take the bit pattern of 128 (1000 0000), set every bit that is clear, and clear every bit that is set (0111 1111). When you AND these numbers, the original number is unchanged, except for the eighth bit, which is forced to zero.

```
   1010 0110 1010 0110     // bit 8 is set
 & 1111 1111 0111 1111     // ~128
---------------------
   1010 0110 0010 0110     // bit 8 cleared
```

To fully understand this solution, do the math yourself. Each time both bits are 1, write 1 in the answer. If either bit is 0, write 0 in the answer. Compare the answer with the original number. It should be the same except that bit 8 was cleared.

Flipping Bits

Finally, if you want to flip bit 8, no matter what its state, you exclusive OR the number with 128. Thus:

```
  1010 0110 1010 0110   // number
^ 0000 0000 1000 0000   // 128
---------------------
  1010 0110 0010 0110   // bit flipped
^ 0000 0000 1000 0000   // 128
---------------------
  1010 0110 1010 0110   // flipped back
```

DO	DON'T
DO set bits by using masks and the OR operator.	
DO clear bits by using masks and the AND operator.	
DO flip bits using masks and the exclusive OR operator.	

Bit Fields

There are circumstances under which every byte counts, and saving six or eight bytes in a class can make all the difference. If your class or structure has a series of Boolean variables, or variables that can have only a very small number of possible values, you may save some room using bit fields.

Using the standard C++ data types, the smallest type you can use in your class is a type char, which is one byte. More often, you'll end up using an int, which is two or more often four bytes. By using bit fields, you can store eight binary values in a char and 32 such values in a long.

Here's how bit fields work: bit fields are named and accessed like any class member. Their type is always declared to be unsigned int. After the bit field name, write a colon followed by a number. The number is an instruction to the compiler as to how many bits to assign to this variable. If you write 1, the bit will represent either the value 0 or 1. If you write 2, the bit can represent 0, 1, 2, or 3; a total of four values. A three-bit field can represent

21

eight values, and so forth. Appendix C reviews binary numbers. Listing 21.8 illustrates the use of bit fields.

Listing 21.8. Using bit fields.

```
1:    #include <iostream.h>
2:    #include <string.h>
3:
4:    enum STATUS { FullTime, PartTime } ;
5:    enum GRADLEVEL { UnderGrad, Grad } ;
6:    enum HOUSING { Dorm, OffCampus };
7:    enum FOODPLAN { OneMeal, AllMeals, WeekEnds, NoMeals };
8:
9:    class student
10:   {
11:   public:
12:   student():myStatus(FullTime),myGradLevel(UnderGrad)
      ➥,myHousing(Dorm),myFoodPlan(NoMeals){}
13:       ~student(){}
14:       STATUS GetStatus();
15:       void SetStatus(STATUS);
16:       FOODPLAN GetPlan() { return myFoodPlan; }
17:
18:   private:
19:       unsigned myStatus : 1;
20:       unsigned myGradLevel: 1;
21:       unsigned myHousing : 1;
22:       unsigned myFoodPlan : 2;
23:   };
24:
25:   STATUS student::GetStatus()
26:   {
27:       if (myStatus)
28:           return FullTime;
29:       else
30:           return PartTime;
31:   }
32:   void student::SetStatus(STATUS theStatus)
33:   {
34:       myStatus = theStatus;
35:   }
36:
37:
38:   void main()
39:   {
40:       student Jim;
41:
42:       if (Jim.GetStatus()== PartTime)
43:           cout << "Jim is part time" << endl;
44:       else
45:           cout << "Jim is full time" << endl;
46:
47:       Jim.SetStatus(PartTime);
48:
49:       if (Jim.GetStatus())
```

```
50:        cout << "Jim is part time" << endl;
51:    else
52:        cout << "Jim is full time" << endl;
53:
54:    cout << "Jim is on the " ;
55:
56:    char Plan[80];
57:    switch (Jim.GetPlan())
58:    {
59:        case  OneMeal: strcpy(Plan,"One meal"); break;
60:        case  AllMeals: strcpy(Plan,"All meals"); break;
61:        case WeekEnds: strcpy(Plan,"Weekend meals"); break;
62:        case NoMeals: strcpy(Plan,"No Meals");break;
63:        default : cout << "Something bad went wrong!\n"; break;
64:    }
65:    cout << Plan << " food plan." << endl;
66:
67:  }
```

```
Jim is part time
Jim is full time
Jim is on the No Meals food plan.
```

On lines 4 to 7, a number of enumerated types are defined. These serve to define the possible values for the bit fields within the student class.

Student itself is declared in lines 9–23. While this is a trivial class, it is interesting in that all the data is packed into five bits. The first bit represents the student's status, full-time or part-time. The second bit represents whether or not this is an undergraduate. The third bit represents whether or not the student lives in a dorm. The final two bits represent the four possible food plans.

The class methods are written as for any other class, and are in no way affected by the fact that these are bit fields and not integers or enumerated types.

The member function GetStatus() reads the Boolean bit and returns an enumerated type, but this is not necessary. It could just as easily have been written to return the value of the bit field directly. The compiler would have done the translation.

To prove that to yourself, replace the GetStatus() implementation with this code:

```
STATUS student::GetStatus()
{
    return myStatus;
}
```

There should be no change whatsoever to the functioning of the program. It is a matter of clarity when reading the code; the compiler isn't particular.

Note that the code on line 42 *must* check the status and then print the meaningful message. It is tempting to write this:

```
cout << "Jim is " << Jim.GetStatus() << endl;
```

That will simply print this:

```
Jim is 0
```

The compiler has no way to translate the enumerated constant `PartTime` into meaningful text.

On line 57 the program switches on the food plan, and for each possible value it puts a reasonable message into the buffer, which is then printed on line 65. Note again that the switch statement could have been written as follows:

```
case  0: strcpy(Plan,"One meal"); break;
case  1: strcpy(Plan,"All meals"); break;
case  2: strcpy(Plan,"Weekend meals"); break;
case  3: strcpy(Plan,"No Meals");break;
```

The most important thing about using bit fields is that the client of the class need not worry about the data storage implementation. Because the bit fields are private, you can feel free to change them later and the interface will not need to change.

Style

As stated elsewhere in this book, it is important to adopt a consistent coding style, though in many ways it doesn't matter which style you adopt. A consistent style makes it easier to guess what you meant by a particular part of the code, and you avoid having to look up whether you spelled the function with an initial cap or not the last time you invoked it.

The following guidelines are arbitrary; they are based on the guidelines used in projects I've worked on in the past, and they've worked well. You can just as easily make up your own, but these will get you started.

As Emerson said, "Foolish consistency is the hobgoblin of small minds," but having some consistency in your code is a good thing. Make up your own, but then treat it as if it was dispensed by the Programming Gods.

Indenting

Tab size should be four spaces. Make sure your editor converts each tab to four spaces.

Braces

How to align braces can be the most controversial topic between C and C++ programmers. Here are the tips I suggest:

☐ Matching braces should be aligned vertically.

☐ The outermost set of braces in a definition or declaration should be at the left margin. Statements within should be indented. All other sets of braces should be in line with their leading statement.

☐ No code should appear on the same line as a brace. For example:

```
if (condition==true)
{
    j = k;
    SomeFunction();
}
m++;
```

Long Lines

Keep lines to the width displayable on a single screen. Code that is off to the right is easily overlooked, and scrolling horizontally is annoying. When a line is broken, indent the following lines. Try to break the line at a reasonable place, and try to leave the intervening operator at the end of the previous line (as opposed to the beginning of the following line) so that it is clear that the line does not stand alone and that there is more coming.

In C++ functions tend to be far shorter than they were in C, but the old, sound advice still applies. Try to keep your functions short enough to print the entire function on one page.

switch Statements

Indent switches as follows to conserve horizontal space:

```
switch(variable)
{
case ValueOne:
    ActionOne();
    break;
case ValueTwo:
    ActionTwo();
    break;
default:
    assert("bad Action");
    break;
}
```

21

Program Text

There are several tips you can use to create code which is easy to read. Code which is easy to read is easy to maintain.

- ☐ Use whitespace to help readability.

- ☐ Objects and arrays are really referring to one thing. Don't use spaces within object references (., ->, [ ]).

- ☐ Unary operators are associated with their operand, so don't put a space between them. Do put a space on the side away from the operand. Unary operators include !, ~, ++, --, -, * (for pointers), & (casts), sizeof.

- ☐ Binary operators should have spaces on both sides: +, =, *, /, %, >>, <<, <, >, ==, !=, &, ¦, &&, ¦¦, ?:, =, +=, etc.

- ☐ Don't use lack of spaces to indicate precedence (4+ 3*2).

- ☐ Put a space after commas and semicolons, *not* before.

- ☐ Parentheses should not have spaces on either side.

- ☐ Keywords, such as if, should be set off by a space: if (a == b).

- ☐ The body of a comment should be set off from the // with a space.

- ☐ Place the pointer or reference indicator next to the type name, not the variable name:

```
char* foo;
int& theInt;


rather than


char *foo;
int &theInt;
```

- ☐ Do *not* declare more than one variable on the same line.

Identifier Names

Here are some guideline for working with identifiers.

- ☐ Identifier names should be long enough to be descriptive.

- ☐ Avoid cryptic abbreviations.

- Take the time and energy to spell things out.

- Do not use Hungarian notation. C++ is strongly typed and there is no reason to put the type into the variable name. With user-defined types (classes), Hungarian notation quickly breaks down. The exceptions to this may be to use a prefix for pointers (p) and references (r) as well as for class member variables (its).

- Short names (i, p, x, etc.) should only be used where their brevity makes the code more readable *and* where the usage is so obvious that a descriptive name is not needed.

- The length of a variable's name should be proportional to its scope.

- Make sure identifers look and sound different from one another to minimize confusion.

- Function (or method) names are usually verbs or verb-noun phrases: Search(), Reset(), FindParagraph(), ShowCursor(). Variable names are usually abstract nouns, possibly with an additional noun: count, state, windSpeed, windowHeight. Boolean variables should be named appropriately: windowIconized, fileIsOpen.

Spelling and Capitalization of Names

Spelling and capitalization should not be overlooked when creating your own style. Some tips for these areas include the following:

- Use all uppercase and underscore to separate the logical words of names, such as SOURCE_FILE_TEMPLATE. Note, however, that these are rare in C++. Consider using constants and templates in most cases.

- All other identifiers should use mixed case—no underscores. Function names, methods, class, typedef, and struct names should begin with a capitalized letter. Elements like data members or locals should begin with a lowercase letter.

- Enumerated constants should begin with a few lowercase letters as an abbreviation for the enum. For example:

```
enum TextStyle
{
    tsPlain,
    tsBold,
```

```
        tsItalic,
        tsUnderscore,
    };
```

Comments

Comments can make it much easier to understand a program. Oftentimes you will not work on a program for several days or even months. In this time you can forget what certain code does or why it has been included. Problems in understanding code can also occur when someone else reads your code. Comments that are applied in a consistent, well thought out style can be well worth the effort. There are several tips to remember concerning comments:

☐ Wherever possible, use C++ // comments rather than the /* */ style.

☐ Higher-level comments are infinitely more important than process details. Add value; do not merely restate the code.

```
n++;    // n is incremented by one
```

This line isn't worth the time it takes to type it in. Concentrate on the semantics of functions and blocks of code. Say what a function does. Indicate side effects, types of parameters, and return values. Describe all assumptions that are made (or not made), such as "assumes n is non-negative" or "will return -1 if x is invalid". Within complex logic, use comments to indicate the conditions that exist at that point in the code.

☐ Use complete English sentences with appropriate punctuation and capitalization. The extra typing is worth it. Don't be overly cryptic and don't abbreviate. What seems exceedingly clear to you as you write code will be amazingly obtuse in a few months.

☐ Use blank lines freely to help the reader understand what is going on. Separate statements into logical groups.

Access

The way you access portions of your program should also be consistent. Some tips for access include these:

☐ Always use public:, private:, and protected: labels; don't rely on the defaults.

□ List the public members first, then protected, then private. List the data members in a group after the methods.

□ Put the constructor(s) first in the appropriate section, followed by the destructor. List overloaded methods with the same name adjacent to each other. Group accessor functions together when possible.

□ Consider alphabetizing the method names within each group and alphabetizing the member variables. Be sure to alphabetize the filenames in `include` statements.

□ Even though the use of the `virtual` keyword is optional when overriding, use it anyway; it helps to remind you that it is virtual, and also keeps the declaration consistent.

Class Definitions

Try to keep the definitions of methods in the same order as the declarations. It makes things easier to find.

When defining a function, place the return type and all other modifiers on a previous line so that the class name and function name begin on the left margin. This makes it much easier to find functions.

include Files

Try as hard as you can to keep from including files into header files. The ideal minimum is the header file for the class this one derives from. Other mandatory includes will be those for objects that are members of the class being declared. Classes that are merely pointed to or referenced only need forward references of the form.

Don't leave out an `include` file in a header just because you assume that whatever `.cpp` file includes this one will also have the needed `include`.

 Tip: All header files should use inclusion guards.

assert()

Use assert() freely. It helps find errors, but it also greatly helps a reader by making it clear what the assumptions are. It also helps to focus the writer's thoughts around what is valid and what isn't.

const

Use const wherever appropriate: for parameters, variables, and methods. Often there is a need for both a const and a non-const version of a method; don't use this as an excuse to leave one out. Be very careful when explicitly casting from const to non-const and vice versa—there are times when this is the only way to do something—but be certain that it makes sense, and include a comment.

Next Steps

You've spent three long, hard weeks working at C++, and you are now a competent C++ programmer, but you are by no means finished. There is much more to learn, and many more books to read as you move from novice C++ programmer to expert.

The following sections recommend a number of specific books, and these recommendations reflect only my personal experience and opinions. There are dozens of books on each of these topics, however, so be sure to get other opinions before purchasing.

Where to Get Help and Advice

The very first thing you will want to do as a C++ programmer will be to tap into one or another C++ conference on an online service. These groups supply immediate contact with hundreds or thousands of C++ programmers who can answer your questions, offer advice, and provide a sounding board for your ideas.

I participate in the C++ discussions on Interchange (of course), as well as many C++ forums on Ziffnet, CompuServe, and other dial-in services. I'm also active in the C++ Internet news group (comp.lang.c++), and I recommend all of these as good sources of information and support.

Also, you may want to look for local user groups. Many cities have C++ interest groups where you can meet other programmers and exchange ideas.

Required Reading

The very next book I'd run out and buy and read is:

Meyers, Scott. *Effective C++* (ISBN: 0-201-56364-9). Addison-Wesley Publishing, 1993.

This is by far the most useful book I've ever read, and I've read it three times.

Object-Oriented Analysis and Design

If you are serious about object-oriented programming and design, be sure to pick up a good book on the subject. This book only scratches the surface of this complex topic, and either of the following books will be a valuable addition to your library:

Booch, Grady. *Object-Oriented Analysis and Design with Applications*, 2nd Edition (ISBN: 0-8053-5340-2). The Benjamin/Cummings Publishing Company, Inc., 1994.

Rumbaugh, *et al. Object-Oriented Modeling and Design* (ISBN: 0-13-629841-9). Prentice Hall, Inc., 1991.

Writing Solid Code

A number of books have been published lately about writing high-quality code. I highly recommend these three:

McConnel, Steve. *Code Complete* (ISBN: 1-55615-484-4). Microsoft Press, 1993.

Maguire, Steve. *Writing Solid Code* (ISBN: 1-55615-551-4). Microsoft Press, 1993.

Thielen, David. *No Bugs! Delivering Error-Free Code in C and C++* (ISBN: 0-201-60890-1). Addison-Wesley Publishing, 1992.

Data Structures

Any reasonably advanced C++ program will require extensive and expert use of complex data structures. A number of good books have been written on this topic, but few from the perspective of object-oriented programming using C++.

21

Windows and Mac

Now that you've accomplished a good fundamental understanding of C++, you may want to apply it to your operating environment. Now is a good time to tackle Windows or Mac development, or one of the other graphical environments such as X Window. There are scores of good books on this subject, many of them from Sams Publishing.

If you are serious about learning Windows, there is one book you must consider, even though it was written for C programmers and not for C++. The absolute, rock-solid bible on Windows development is:

Petzold, Charles. *Programming Windows 3.1*, Third Edition (ISBN: 1-55615-395-3). Microsoft Press, 1992.

Once you understand Windows, you'll immediately want to look at a C++ perspective, and I recommend these:

Shammas, Namir. *Teach Yourself Visual C++ in 21 Days* (ISBN: 0-672-30372-8). Sams Publishing, 1993.

Kruglinski, David. *Inside Visual C++* (ISBN: 1-55615-511-5). Microsoft Press, 1993.

Magazines

Reading all these books and more is vitally important, and going online will give you day-to-day access to other C++ programmers, but there is one more thing you can do to strengthen your skills: subscribe to a good magazine on C++ programming. The absolute best magazine of this kind in my opinion is *C++ Report* from SIGS Publications. Every issue is packed with useful articles. Save them; what you don't care about today will become critically important tomorrow.

You can reach them at SIGS Publications, P.O. Box 2031, Langhorne, PA 19047-9700. I have no affiliation with the magazine (I work for two other publishers!) but their magazine is the best, bar none.

Staying in Touch

If you have comments, suggestions, or ideas about this book or other books, I'd love to hear them. Please write to me on Interchange, or on the Internet at jliberty@zdi.ziff.com. I look forward to hearing from you.

DO	**DON'T**

DO look at other books. There's plenty to learn and no single book can teach you everything you need to know.

DON'T just read code! The best way to learn C++ is to write C++ programs.

DO subscribe to a good C++ magazine and join a good C++ user group.

Summary

Today you saw how some of the standard libraries, shipped with your C++ compiler, can be used to manage some routine tasks. Strcpy(), strlen(), and related functions can be used to manipulate null-terminated strings. Although these won't work with the string classes you create, you may find that they provide functionality essential to implementing your own classes.

The time and date functions allow you to obtain and manipulate time structures. These can be used to provide access to the system time for your programs, or they can be used to manipulate time and date objects you create.

You also learned how to set and test individual bits, and how to allocate a limited number of bits to class members.

Finally, C++ style issues were addressed, and resources were provided for further study.

Q&A

Q Why are the standard libraries included with C++ compilers, and when would you use them?

A They are included for backwards-compatability with C. They are not type-safe, and they don't work well with user-created classes, so their use is limited. Over time, you might expect all of their functionality to be migrated into C++ specific libraries, at which time the standard C libraries would become obsolete.

Q When would you use bit structures rather than simply using integers?

A When the size of the object is crucial. If you are working with limited memory or with communications software, you may find that the savings offered by these structures is essential to the success of your product.

Q Why do style wars generate so much emotion?

A Programmers become very attached to their habits. If you are used to this indentation,

```
if (SomeCondition){
    // statements
}     // closing brace
```

it is a difficult transition to give it up. New styles look wrong and create confusion. If you get bored, try logging onto a popular online service and asking which indentation style works best, which editor is best for C++, or which product is the best word processor. Then sit back and watch as ten thousand messages are generated, all contradicting one another.

Q What is the very next thing to read?

A Tough question. If you want to review the fundamentals, read one of the other primers. If you want to hone C++, run out and get Scott Meyer's *Effective C++*. If you want to expand your object-oriented skills, read one of the recommended books on object-oriented analysis and design. Finally, if you want to write for Windows or the Mac, it might make sense to pick up a primer on the platform. Sooner or later you should read them all!

Q Is that it?

A Yes! You've learned C++, but...no. Ten years ago it was possible for one person to learn all there was to know about microcomputers, or at least to feel pretty confident that he was close. Today it is out of the question: you can't possibly catch up, and even as you try the industry is changing. Be sure to keep reading, and stay in touch with the resources that will keep you up with the latest changes: magazines and online services.

Quiz

1. What is the difference between `strcpy()` and `strncpy()`?

2. What does `ctime()` do?

3. What is the function to call to turn an ASCII string into a `long`?

4. What does the complement operator do?

5. What is the difference between `OR` and exclusive `OR`?

6. What is the difference between & and &&?

7. What is the difference between | and ||?

Exercises

1. Write a program to safely copy the contents of a 20-byte string to a 10-byte string, truncating whatever won't fit.

2. Write a program that tells the current date in the form 7/28/94.

3. Write a program that creates 26 flags (labeled a-z). Prompt the user to enter a sentence, and then quickly report on which letters were used by setting and then reading the flags.

4. Write a program that adds two numbers without using the addition operator (+). Hint: use the bit operators!

3

The following program brings together many of the advanced techniques you've learned during the past three weeks of hard work. Week 3 in Review provides a template-based linked list with exception handling. Examine it in detail; if you understand it fully, you *are* a C++ programmer.

Listing R3.1. Week 3 in Review listing.

```
 1:     // ****************************************************
 2:     //
 3:     // Title:        Week 3 in review
 4:     //
 5:     // File:         Week3
 6:     //
 7:     // Description:  Provide a template-based linked list
 8:     //                   demonstration program with exception handling
 9:     //
10:     // Classes:      PART - holds part numbers and potentially other
11:     //                     information about parts. This will be the
12:     //                     example class for the list to hold
13:     //                     Note use of operator<< to print the
14:     //                     information about a part based on its
15:     //                     run time type.
16:     //
17:     //               Node - acts as a node in a List
18:     //
19:     //               List - template based list which provides the
20:     //                     mechanisms for a linked list
21:     //
22:     //
23:     // Author:       Jesse Liberty (jl)
24:     //
25:     // Developed:    486/66 32mb RAM  MVC 1.5
26:     //
27:     // Target:       Platform independent
28:     //
29:     // Rev History:  9/94 - First release (jl)
30:     // ****************************************************
31:
32:     #include <iostreams.h>
33:
34:     typedef unsigned long ULONG;
35:     typedef unsigned short USHORT;
36:
37:     // exception classes
38:     class Exception {};
39:     class OutOfMemory : public Exception{};
40:     class NullNode : public Exception{};
41:     class EmptyList : public Exception {};
42:     class BoundsError : public Exception {};
43:
44:
45:     // *************** Part ************
46:     // Abstract base class of parts
47:     class Part
48:     {
49:     public:
50:         Part():itsObjectNumber(1) {}
51:         Part(ULONG ObjectNumber):itsObjectNumber(ObjectNumber){}
52:         virtual ~Part(){};
53:         ULONG GetObjectNumber() const { return itsObjectNumber; }
54:         virtual void Display() const =0;  // must be overridden
```

```
55:
56:     private:
57:         ULONG itsObjectNumber;
58:     };
59:
60:     // implementation of pure virtual function so that
61:     // derived classes can chain up
62:     void Part::Display() const
63:     {
64:         cout << "\nPart Number: " << itsObjectNumber << endl;
65:     }
66:
67:     // this one operator<< will be called for all part objects.
68:     // It need not be a friend as it does not access private data
69:     // It calls Display() which uses the required polymorphism
70:     // We'd like to be able to override this based on the real type
71:     // of thePart, but C++ does not support contravariance
72:     ostream& operator<<( ostream& theStream,Part& thePart)
73:     {
74:         thePart.Display();  // virtual contravariance!
75:         return theStream;
76:     }
77:
78:     // *************** Car Part ************
79:     class CarPart : public Part
80:     {
81:     public:
82:         CarPart():itsModelYear(94){}
83:         CarPart(USHORT year, ULONG partNumber);
84:         USHORT GetModelYear() const { return itsModelYear; }
85:         virtual void Display() const;
86:     private:
87:         USHORT itsModelYear;
88:     };
89:
90:     CarPart::CarPart(USHORT year, ULONG partNumber):
91:         itsModelYear(year),
92:         Part(partNumber)
93:     {}
94:
95:     virtual void CarPart::Display() const;
96:     {
97:         Part::Display();
98:         cout << "Model Year: " << itsModelYear << endl;
99:     }
100:
101:    // *************** AirPlane Part ************
102:    class AirPlanePart : public Part
103:    {
104:    public:
105:        AirPlanePart():itsEngineNumber(1){};
106:        AirPlanePart(USHORT EngineNumber, ULONG PartNumber);
107:        virtual void Display() const;
108:        USHORT GetEngineNumber()const { return itsEngineNumber; }
109:    private:
```

continues

Listing R3.1. continued

```
110:      USHORT itsEngineNumber;
111:   };
112:
113:   AirPlanePart::AirPlanePart(USHORT EngineNumber, ULONG PartNumber):
114:       itsEngineNumber(EngineNumber),
115:       Part(PartNumber)
116:   {}
117:
118:   virtual void AirPlanePart::Display() const
119:   {
120:       Part::Display();
121:       cout << "Engine No.: " << itsEngineNumber << endl;
122:   }
123:
124:   // forward declaration of class List
125:   template <class T>
126:   class List;
127:
128:   // ****************  Node ************
129:   // Generic node, can be added to a list
130:   // ***********************************
131:
132:   template <class T>
133:   class Node
134:   {
135:   public:
136:       friend class List<T>;
137:       Node (T*);
138:       ~Node();
139:       void SetNext(Node * node) { itsNext = node; }
140:       Node * GetNext() const;
141:       T * GetObject() const;
142:   private:
143:       T* itsObject;
144:       Node * itsNext;
145:   };
146:
147:   // Node Implementations...
148:
149:   template <class T>
150:   Node<T>::Node(T* pOjbect):
151:   itsObject(pOjbect),
152:   itsNext(0)
153:   {}
154:
155:   template <class T>
156:   Node<T>::~Node()
157:   {
158:       delete itsObject;
159:       itsObject = 0;
160:       delete itsNext;
161:       itsNext = 0;
162:   }
```

```
163:
164:    // Returns NULL if no next Node
165:    template <class T>
166:    Node<T> * Node<T>::GetNext() const
167:    {
168:         return itsNext;
169:    }
170:
171:    template <class T>
172:    T * Node<T>::GetObject() const
173:    {
174:        if (itsObject)
175:           return itsObject;
176:        else
177:           throw NullNode();
178:    }
179:
180:    // *************** List ***********
181:    // Generic list template
182:    // Works with any numbered object
183:    // *********************************
184:    template <class T>
185:    class List
186:    {
187:    public:
188:       List();
189:       ~List();
190:
191:       void     Iterate(void (T::*f)()const) const;
192:       T*         Find(ULONG & position, ULONG ObjectNumber)  const;
193:       T*       GetFirst() const;
194:       void      Insert(T *);
195:       T*        operator[](ULONG) const;
196:       ULONG    GetCount() const { return itsCount; }
197:    private:
198:       Node<T> * pHead;
199:       ULONG itsCount;
200:    };
201:
202:    // Implementations for Lists...
203:    template <class T>
204:    List<T>::List():
205:       pHead(0),
206:       itsCount(0)
207:       {}
208:
209:    template <class T>
210:    List<T>::~List()
211:    {
212:       delete pHead;
213:    }
214:
215:    template <class T>
216:    T*   List<T>::GetFirst() const
217:    {
```

continues

Listing R3.1. continued

```
218:        if (pHead)
219:            return pHead->itsObject;
220:        else
221:            throw EmptyList();
222:    }
223:
224:    template <class T>
225:    T *  List<T>::operator[](ULONG offSet) const
226:    {
227:        Node<T>* pNode = pHead;
228:
229:        if (!pHead)
230:            throw EmptyList();
231:
232:        if (offSet > itsCount)
233:            throw BoundsError();
234:
235:        for (ULONG i=0;i<offSet; i++)
236:            pNode = pNode->itsNext;
237:
238:        return   pNode->itsObject;
239:    }
240:
241:    // find a given object in list based on its unique number (id)
242:    template <class T>
243:    T*   List<T>::Find(ULONG & position, ULONG ObjectNumber)   const
244:    {
245:        Node<T> * pNode = 0;
246:        for (pNode = pHead, position = 0;
247:             pNode!=NULL;
248:             pNode = pNode->itsNext, position++)
249:        {
250:            if (pNode->itsObject->GetObjectNumber() == ObjectNumber)
251:                break;
252:        }
253:        if (pNode == NULL)
254:            return NULL;
255:        else
256:            return pNode->itsObject;
257:    }
258:
259:    // call function for every object in list
260:    template <class T>
261:    void List<T>::Iterate(void (T::*func)()const) const
262:    {
263:        if (!pHead)
264:            return;
265:        Node<T>* pNode = pHead;
266:        do
267:            (pNode->itsObject->*func)();
268:        while (pNode = pNode->itsNext);
269:    }
270:
271:    // insert if the number of the object is unique
```

```
272:     template <class T>
273:     void List<T>::Insert(T* pObject)
274:     {
275:         Node<T> * pNode = new Node<T>(pObject);
276:         Node<T> * pCurrent = pHead;
277:         Node<T> * pNext = 0;
278:
279:         ULONG New =  pObject->GetObjectNumber();
280:         ULONG Next = 0;
281:         itsCount++;
282:
283:         if (!pHead)
284:         {
285:             pHead = pNode;
286:             return;
287:         }
288:
289:         // if this one is smaller than head
290:         // this one is the new head
291:         if (pHead->itsObject->GetObjectNumber() > New)
292:         {
293:             pNode->itsNext = pHead;
294:             pHead = pNode;
295:             return;
296:         }
297:
298:         for (;;)
299:         {
300:             // if there is no next, append this new one
301:             if (!pCurrent->itsNext)
302:             {
303:                 pCurrent->itsNext = pNode;
304:                 return;
305:             }
306:
307:             // if this goes after this one and before the next
308:             // then insert it here, otherwise get the next
309:             pNext = pCurrent->itsNext;
310:             Next = pNext->itsObject->GetObjectNumber();
311:             if (Next > New)
312:             {
313:                 pCurrent->itsNext = pNode;
314:                 pNode->itsNext = pNext;
315:                 return;
316:             }
317:             pCurrent = pNext;
318:         }
319:     }
320:
321:
322:     int main()
323:     {
324:         List<Part> theList;
325:         int choice;
326:         ULONG ObjectNumber;
```

continues

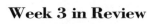

Listing R3.1. continued

```
327:     USHORT value;
328:     Part * pPart;
329:     while (1)
330:     {
331:        cout << "(0)Quit (1)Car (2)Plane: ";
332:        cin >> choice;
333:
334:        if (!choice)
335:           break;
336:
337:        cout << "New ObjectNumber?: ";
338:        cin >>  ObjectNumber;
339:
340:        if (choice == 1)
341:        {
342:           cout << "Model Year?: ";
343:           cin >> value;
344:           try
345:           {
346:              pPart = new CarPart(value,ObjectNumber);
347:           }
348:           catch (OutOfMemory)
349:           {
350:              cout << "Not enough memory; Exiting..." << endl;
351:              return 1;
352:           }
353:        }
354:        else
355:        {
356:           cout << "Engine Number?: ";
357:           cin >> value;
358:           try
359:           {
360:              pPart = new AirPlanePart(value,ObjectNumber);
361:           }
362:           catch (OutOfMemory)
363:           {
364:              cout << "Not enough memory; Exiting..." << endl;
365:              return 1;
366:           }
367:        }
368:        try
369:        {
370:           theList.Insert(pPart);
371:        }
372:        catch (NullNode)
373:        {
374:           cout << "The list is broken, and the node is null!" << endl;
375:           return 1;
376:        }
377:        catch (EmptyList)
378:        {
379:           cout << "The list is empty!" << endl;
```

```
380:            return 1;
381:        }
382:     }
383:     try
384:     {
385:        for (int i = 0; i < theList.GetCount(); i++ )
386:            cout << *(theList[i]);
387:     }
388:        catch (NullNode)
389:        {
390:            cout << "The list is broken, and the node is null!" << endl;
391:            return 1;
392:        }
393:        catch (EmptyList)
394:        {
395:            cout << "The list is empty!" << endl;
396:            return 1;
397:        }
398:        catch (BoundsError)
399:        {
400:            cout << "Tried to read beyond the end of the list!" << endl;
401:            return 1;
402:        }
403:    return 0;
404:    }
```

```
(0)Quit (1)Car (2)Plane: 1
New PartNumber?: 2837
Model Year? 90

(0)Quit (1)Car (2)Plane: 2
New PartNumber?: 378
Engine Number?: 4938

(0)Quit (1)Car (2)Plane: 1
New PartNumber?: 4499
Model Year? 94

(0)Quit (1)Car (2)Plane: 1
New PartNumber?: 3000
Model Year? 93

(0)Quit (1)Car (2)Plane: 0

Part Number: 378
Engine No. 4938

Part Number: 2837
Model Year: 90

Part Number: 3000
Model Year: 93

Part Number 4499
Model Year: 94
```

Analysis The Week 3 in Review modifies the program provided in Week 2 to add templates, ostream processing and exception handling. The output is identical.

On lines 37–42 a number of exception classes are declared. In the somewhat primitive exception handling provided by this program, no data or methods are required of these exceptions; they serve as flags to the catch statements, which print out a very simple warning and then exit. A more robust program might pass these exceptions by reference and then extract context or other data from the exception objects in an attempt to recover from the problem.

On line 45 the abstract base class Part is declared exactly as it was in Week 2. The only interesting change here is in the *non-class member* operator<<() which is declared on lines 72–76. Note that this is neither a member of Part nor a friend of part, it simply takes a Part reference as one of its arguments.

You might want to have operator<< take a CarPart and an AirPlanePart in the hopes that the correct operator<< would be called based on whether a car part or an airplane part is passed. Since the program passes a pointer to a part, however, and not a pointer to a carpart or an airplane part, C++ would have to call the right function based on the real type of one of the arguments to the function. This is called *contravariance* and is not supported in C++.

There are only two ways to achieve polymorphism in C++: function polymorphism and virtual functions. Function polymorphism won't work here because in every case you are matching the same signature: the one taking a reference to a Part.

Virtual functions won't work here because operator<< is not a member function of Part. You can't make operator<< a member function of Part because you want to invoke

```
cout << thePart
```

and that means that the actual call would be to cout.operator<<(Part&) and cout does not have a version of operator<< which takes a part reference!

To get around this limitation, the Week 3 program uses just one operator<<, taking a reference to a Part. This then calls Display(), which *is* a virtual member function and thus the right version is called.

On lines 132–145, Node is defined as a template. It serves the same function as Node did in the Week 2 review program, but this version of Node is *not* tied to a Part object. It can, in fact, be the node for any type of object.

Note that if you try to get the object from the Node and there is no object this is considered an exception, and the exception is thrown on line 177.

On lines 180–200 a generic List class template is defined. This list class can hold nodes of any objects that have unique identification numbers, and it keeps them sorted in ascending order. Each of the list functions checks for exceptional circumstances and throws the appropriate exceptions as required.

On lines 322–404 the driver program creates a list of two types of Part objects, and then prints out the values of the objects in the list by using the standard streams mechanism.

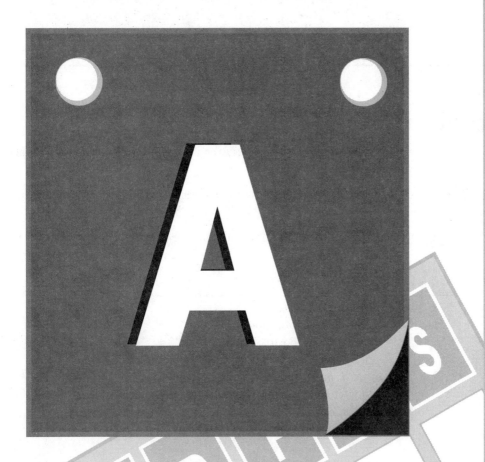

Operator
Precedence

Introduction

It is important to understand that operators *have* a precedence, but it is not essential to memorize the precedence.

NEW TERM *Precedence* is the order in which a program performs the operations in a formula. If one operator has precedence over another operator, it is evaluated first.

Higher precedence operators "bind tighter" than lower precedence operators; they will be evaluated first. The *lower* the rank in the following chart, the *higher* the precedence.

Rank	Name	Operator
1	scope resolution	`::`
2	member selection, subscripting,	`.` `->`
	function calls, postfix increment	`( )`
	and decrement	`++ --`
3	`sizeof`, prefix increment and decrement	`++ --`
	complement and not unary minus and plus	`^ !`
	address of and dereference new and delete	`- +`
	casting `sizeof()` new delete delete[]	`& *`
		`( )`
4	member selection for pointer	`.* ->*`
5	multiply, divide, modulo	`* / %`
6	add, subtract	`+ -`
7	shift	`<< >>`
8	inequality relational	`< <= > >=`
9	equality, inequality	`== !=`
10	bitwise and	`&`
11	bitwise exclusive or	`^`
12	bitwise OR	`¦`
13	logical AND	`&&`
14	logical OR	`¦¦`
15	conditional	`?:`
16	assignment operators	`= *= /= %=`
		`+= -= <<= >>=`
		`&= ¦= ^=`
17	throw operator	`throw`
18	comma	`,`

B

C++ Keywords

Introduction

Keywords are reserved to the compiler for use by the language. You cannot define classes, variables, or functions that have these keywords as their names. The list is a bit arbitrary as some of the keywords are specific to a given compiler. Your milage may vary slightly:

```
auto
break
case
catch
char
class
const
continue
default
delete
do
double
else
enum
extern
float
for
friend
goto
if
int
long
mutable
new
operator
private
protected
public
register
return
short
signed
sizeof
static
struct
switch
template
this
throw
typedef
union
unsigned
virtual
void
volatile
while
```

Binary and
Hexadecimal

Introduction

You learned the fundamentals of arithmetic so long ago, it is hard to imagine what it would be like without that knowledge. When you look at the number 145 you instantly see "one-hundred and forty-five" without much reflection.

Understanding binary and hexadecimal requires that you reexamine the number 145 and see it not as a number, but as a code for a number.

Start small: examine the relationship between the number three and "3." The *numeral* 3 is a squiggle on a piece of paper, the number three is an idea. The numeral is used to represent the number.

The distinction can be made clear by realizing that *three, 3, |||, III,* and *** can all be used to represent the same idea of three.

In base 10 (decimal) math you use the numerals 0, 1, 2, 3, 4, 5, 6, 7, 8, 9 to represent all numbers. How is the number ten represented?

One can imagine that we would have evolved a strategy of using the letter A to represent ten; or we might have used IIIIIIIII to represent that idea. The romans used X. The Arabic system, which we use, makes use of *position* in conjunction with numerals to represent values. The first (right most) column is used for "ones" and the next column is used for tens. Thus the number fifteen is represented as 15 (read that one-five); that is 1 ten and 5 ones.

Certain rules emerge, from which some generalizations can be made:

1. Base 10 uses the digits 0–9

2. The columns are powers of ten: 1s, 10s, 100s, etc.

3. If the third column is 100, the largest number you can make with two columns is 99. More generally, with n columns you can represent 0 to (10^n-1). Thus with 3 columns you can represent 0 to (10^3-1) or 0–999.

Other Bases

It is not a coincidence that we use base 10; we have 10 fingers. One can imagine a different base, however. Using the rules found in base 10, you can describe base 8:

1. The digits used in base 8 are 0–7.

2. The columns are powers of 8: 1s, 8s, 72, etc.

3. With n columns you can represent 0 to 8^n-1.

To distinguish numbers written in each base, write the base as a subscript next to the number. The number fifteen in base 10 would be written as 15_{10} and read as "one-five, base ten."

Thus, to represent the number 15_{10} in base 8 you would write 17_8. This is read "one seven base eight." Note that it can also be read "fifteen" as that is the number it continues to represent.

Why 17? The 1 means 1 eight, and the 7 means 7 ones. One eight plus seven ones equals fifteen. Consider fifteen asterisks:

```
*****     *****
*****
```

The natural tendency is to make two groups, a group of ten asterisks and another of five. This would be represented in decimal as 15 (1 ten and 5 ones). You can also group the asterisks as

```
****          *******
****
```

That is, eight asterisks and seven. That would be represented in base nine as 17_8. That is one eight and seven ones.

Around the Bases

You can represent the number fifteen in base ten as 15, in base nine as 16_9, in base 8 as 17_8, in base 7 as 21_7. Why 21_7? In base 7 there is no numeral 8. In order to represent fifteen, you will need two sevens and one 1.

How do you generalize the process? To convert a base ten number to base 7 think about the columns: in base 7 they are ones, sevens, forty-nines, three-hundred forty-threes, etc. Why these columns? They represent $7^0, 7^1, 7^2, 7^3$ and so forth. Create a table for yourself:

4	3	2	1
7^3	7^2	7^1	7^0
343	49	7	1

The first row represents the column number. The second row represents the power of 7. The third row represents the binary value of each number in that row.

To convert from a decimal value to base 7, here is the procedure: examine the number and decide which column to use first. If the number is 200, for example, you know that column 4 (343) is 0 and you don't have to worry about it.

To find out how many 49s there are, divide 200 by 49. The answer is 4, so put 4 in column 3 and examine the remainder: 4. There are no 7s in 4, so put a zero in the sevens column. There are 4 ones in 4, so put a 4 in the 1s column. The answer is 404_7.

To convert the number 968 to base 6:

5	4	3	2	1
6^4	6^3	6^2	6^1	6^0
1296	216	36	6	1

There are no 1296s in 968, so column 5 has 0. Dividing 968 by 216 yields 4 with a remainder of 104. Column 4 is 4. Dividing 104 by 36 yields 2 with a remainder of 32. Column 3 is 2. Dividing 32 by 6 yields 5 with a remainder of 2. The answer therefore is 4252_6.

5	4	3	2	1
6^4	6^3	6^2	6^1	6^0
1296	216	36	6	1
0	4	2	5	2

There is a shortcut when converting from one base to another base (such as 6) to base 10. You can multiply:

```
4 * 216 = 864
2 * 36  =  72
5 * 6   =  30
2 * 1   =   2
          968
```

Binary

Base 2 is the ultimate extension of this idea. There are only two digits: 0 and 1. The columns are:

Col:	8	7	6	5	4	3	2	1
Power:	2^7	2^6	2^5	2^4	2^3	2^2	2^1	2^0
Value:	128	64	32	16	8	4	2	1

To convert the number 88 to base 2, you follow the same procedure: there are no 128s, so column 8 is 0.

There is one 64 in 88, so column 7 is 1 and 24 is the remainder. There are no 32s in 24 so column 6 is 0.

There is 1 sixteen in 24 so column 5 is 1. The remainder is 8. There is one 8 in 8, and so column 4 is 1. There is no remainder, so the rest of the columns are 0.

| 0 | 1 | 0 | 1 | 1 | 0 | 0 | 0 |

To test this answer, convert it back:

```
1 * 64 =  64
0 * 32 =   0
1 * 16 =  16
1 *  8 =   8
0 *  4 =   0
0 *  2 =   0
0 *  1 =   0
          88
```

Why Base 2?

The power of base 2 is that it corresponds so cleanly to what a computer needs to represent. Computers do not really know anything at all about letters, numerals, instructions or programs. At their core they are just circuitry, and at a given juncture there either is a lot of power or there is very little.

To keep the logic clean engineers do not treat this as a relative scale: "a little power, some power, more power, lots of power, tons of power," but rather as a binary scale: "enough power or not enough power." Rather than saying even enough or not-enough, they simplify it down to "yes or no." Yes or no, or TRUE or FALSE, can be represented as 1 or 0. By convention 1 means TRUE or Yes, but that is just a convention: it could just as easily have meant false or no.

Once you make this great leap of intuition, the power of binary becomes clear: with 1s and 0s you can represent the fundamental truth of every circuit: there is power or there isn't. All a computer ever knows is "Is you is, or is you ain't?" Is you is = 1; is you ain't = 0.

Bits, Bytes, and Nybbles

Once the decision is made to represent truth and falsehood with 1s and 0s, BInary digiTS (or BITS) become very important. Since early computers could send 8 bits at a time, it was natural to start writing code using 8 bit numbers—called bytes.

Note: Half a byte (4 bits) is called a nybble!

With 8 binary digits you can represent up to 256 different values. Why? Examine the columns: if all 8 bits are set (1) the value is 255. If none is set (all the bits are clear or zero) the value is 0. 0-255 is 256 possible states.

What's a K?

It turns out that 2^{10} (1024) is roughly equal to 10^3 (1,000). This coincidence was too good to miss, so computer scientists started referring to 2^{10} bytes as 1K or 1 kilobyte, based on the scientific prefix of kilo for thousand.

Similarly 1024 * 1024 (1,048,576) is close enough to one million to receive the designation 1M or 1 megabyte, and 1024 megabytes is called 1 gigabyte (giga implies thousand-million or billion.)

Binary Numbers

Computers use patterns of 1s and 0s to encode everything they do. Machine instructions are encoded as a series of 1s and 0s and interpreted by the fundamental circuitry. Arbitrary sets of 1s and 0s can be translated back into numbers by computer scientists, but it would be a mistake to think that these numbers have intrinsic meaning.

For example, the Intel 80×6 chip set interprets the bit pattern 1001 0101 as an instruction. You certainly can translate this into decimal (149) but that number per se has no meaning.

Sometimes the numbers are instructions, sometimes they are values, and sometimes they are codes. One important standardized code set is ASCII. In ASCII every letter and punctuation is given a 7-digit binary representation. For example, the lowercase letter, a, is represented by 0110 0001. This is *not* a number, though you can translate it to the number 97 (64 + 32 + 1). It is in this sense that people say that the letter 'a' is represented by 97 in ASCII; but the truth is that the binary representation of 97, 01100001, is the encoding of the letter 'a', and the decimal value 97 is a human convenience.

Hexadecimal

Because binary numbers are difficult to read, a simpler way to represent the same values is sought. Translating from binary to base 10 involves a fair bit of manipulation of numbers; but it turns out that translating from base 2 to base 16 is very simple because there is a very good shortcut.

To understand this, first you must understand base 16, which is known as hexadecimal. In base 16 there are sixteen numerals: 0, 1, 2, 3, 4, 5, 6, 7, 8, 9, A, B, C, D, E, F. The last six are arbitrary; the letters A to F were chosen because they are easy to represent on a keyboard. The columns in hexadecimal are:

4	3	2	1
16^3	16^2	16^1	16^0
4096	256	16	1

To translate from hexadecimal to decimal, you can multiply. Thus the number F8C represents:

```
F * 256 = 15 * 256 = 3840
8 * 16 =              128
C * 1 = 12 * 1 =       12
                     3980
```

Translating the number FC to binary is best done by translating first to base 10, and then to binary:

```
F * 16 = 15 * 16 =  240
C * 1 = 12 * 1 =     12
                    252
```

Converting 252_{10} to binary requires the chart:

```
Col:       9    8    7   6    5   4   3   2   1
Power:    2⁸   2⁷   2⁶  2⁵   2⁴  2³  2²  2¹  2⁰
Value:    256  128  64  32   16  8   4   2   1
```

```
There are no 256's.
            1 128 leaves 124
                 1 64 leaves 60
                      1 32 leaves 28
                           1 16 leaves 12
                                1 8 leaves 4
                                     1 4 leaves 0
                                          0
                                               0
            1    1    1    1    1    1    0    0
```

Thus the answer in binary is 1111 1100

Now, it turns out that if you treat this binary number as two sets of 4 digits, you can do a magical transformation.

The right set is 1100. In decimal that is 12 or in hexadecimal it is C.

The left set is 1111, which in base 10 is 15, or in hex is F.

Thus you have:

```
1111 1100
F    C
```

Putting the two hex numbers together is FC, which is the real value of 1111 1100. This shortcut always works. You can take any binary number of any length, and reduce it to sets of 4, translate each set of four to hex, and put the hex numbers together to get the result in hex. Here's a much larger number:

```
1011 0001 1101 0111
```

The columns are 1, 2, 4, 8, 16, 32, 64, 128, 256, 512, 1024, 2048, 4096, 8192, 16384, and 32768.

```
1 x 1 =           1
1 x 2=            2
1 x 4 =           4
0 x 8 =           0

1 x 16 =         16
0 x 32 =          0
1 x 64 =         64
1 x 128 =       128

1 x 256 =       256
0 x 512 =         0
0 x 1024 =        0
0 x 2048 =        0

1 x 4096 =    4,096
1 x 8192 =    8,192
0 x 16384 =       0
1 x 32768 = 32,768
Total:       45,527
```

Converting this to hexadecimal requires a chart with the hexadecimal values.

```
65535      4096      256      16      1
```

There are no 65,535's in 45,527 so the first column is 4096. There are 11 4096's (45,056), with a remainder of 471. There is 1 256 in 471 with a remainder of 215. There are 13 16s (208) in 215 with a remainder of 7. Thus the hexadecimal number is B1D7.

Checking the math:

```
B (11) * 4096 =    45,056
1 * 256 =             256
D (13) * 16 =         208
7 * 1 =                 7
Total              45,527
```

The shortcut version would be to take the original binary number, 1011000111010111 and break it into groups of 4: 1011 0001 1101 0111. Each of the four is then evaluated as a hexadecimal number:

```
1011 =
1 x 1 =       1
1 x 2 =       2
0 x 4 =       0
1 x 8 =       8
Total        11
Hex:          B

0001 =
1 x 1 =       1
0 x 2 =       0
0 x 4 =       0
0 * 8 =       0
Total         1
Hex:          1

1101 =
1 x 1 =       1
0 x 2 =       0
1 x 4 =       4
1 x 8 =       8
Total        13
Hex =         D

0111 =
0 x 1 =       1
1 x 2 =       2
1 x 4 =       4
0 x 8 =       0
Total         7
Hex:          7

Total Hex:  B1D7
```

D

Answers

Day 1
Quiz

1. What is the difference between interpreters and compilers?

   Interpreters read through source code and translate a program, turning the programmer's "code," or program instructions, directly into actions. Compilers translate source code into an executable program that can be run at a later time.

2. How do you compile the source code with your compiler?

   Every compiler is different. Be sure to check the documentation which came with your compiler.

3. What does the linker do?

   The linker's job is to tie together your compiled code with the libraries supplied by your compiler vendor and other sources. The linker lets you build your program in "pieces" and then link together the pieces into one big program.

4. What are the steps in the development cycle?

   Edit source code, compile, link, test, repeat.

Exercises

1. Initializes two integer variables and then prints out their sum and their product.

2. See your compiler manual.

3. You must put a # symbol before the word `include` on the first line.

4. This program prints the words `Hello World` to the screen, followed by a new line (carriage return).

Day 2
Quiz

1. What is the difference between the compiler and the preprocessor?

   Each time you run your compiler, the pre-processor runs first. It reads through your source code and includes the files you've asked for, and performs other housekeeping chores. The preprocessor is discussed in detail on Day 18.

2. Why is the function `main()` special?

   `Main()` is called automatically, each time your program is executed.

3. What are the two types of comments, and how do they differ?

   C++-style comments are two slashes (`//`) and they comment out any text until the end of the line. C-style comments come in pairs (`/* */`) and everything between the matching pairs is commented out. You must be careful to ensure you have matched pairs.

4. Can comments be nested?

   Yes, C++-style comments can be nested within C-style comments. You can, in fact, nest C-style comments within C++-style comments, as long as you remember that the C++-style comments end at the end of the line.

5. Can comments be longer than one line?

   C-style comments can. If you want to extend C++-style comments to a second line, you must put another set of double slashes (`//`).

Exercises

1. Write a program that writes `I love C++` to the screen.

   ```
   1: #include <iostream.h>
   2:
   3: void main()
   4: {
   5:     cout << "I love C++\n";
   6: }
   ```

2. Write the smallest program that can be compiled, linked and run.

   ```
   void main(){}
   ```

3. **BUG BUSTER:** Enter this program and compile it. Why does it fail? How can you fix it?

   ```
   1: #include <iostream.h>
   2: main()
   3: {
   4:     cout << Is there a bug here?";
   5: }
   ```

   Line 4 is missing an opening quote for the string.

4. Fix the bug in Exercise 3 and recompile, link and run it.

```
1: #include <iostream.h>
2: main()
3: {
4:     cout << "Is there a bug here?";
5: }
```

Day 3
Quiz

1. What is the difference between an integral variable and a floating-point variable?

   Integer variables are whole numbers; floating-point variables are "reals" and have a "floating" decimal point. Floating-point numbers can be represented using a mantissa and exponent.

2. What are the differences between an unsigned short int and a long int?

   The keyword unsigned means that the integer will hold only positive numbers. On most computers, short integers are 2 bytes and long integers are 4.

3. What are the advantages of using a symbolic constant rather than a literal?

   A symbolic constant explains itself; the name of the constant tells what it is for. Also, symbolic constants can be redefined at one location in the source code, rather than the programmer having to edit the code everywhere the literal is used.

4. What are the advantages of using the const keyword rather than #define?

   const variables are "typed," and thus the compiler can check for errors in how they are used. Also, they survive the preprocessor, and thus the name is available in the debugger.

5. What makes for a good or bad variable name?

   A good variable name tells you what the variable is for; a bad variable name has no information. myAge and PeopleOnTheBus are good variable names, but xjk and prndl are probably less useful.

6. Given this enum, what is the value of `Blue`?

```
enum COLOR { WHITE, BLACK = 100, RED, BLUE, GREEN = 300 };
```

```
BLUE = 102
```

7. Which of the following variable names are good, which are bad, and which are invalid?

   a. `Age`

      Good

   b. `!ex`

      Not legal

   c. `R79J`

      Legal, but a bad chioce

   d. `TotalIncome`

      Good

   e. `Invalid`

      Not legal

Exercises

1. What would be the correct variable type in which to store the following information?

   a. Your age.

      Unsigned short integer.

   b. The area of your backyard.

      Unsigned long integer or unsigned float.

   c. The number of stars in the galaxy.

      Unsigned double.

   d. The average rainfall for the month of January.

      Unsigned short integer.

2. Create good variable names for this information.

     a. `myAge`

     b. `backYardArea`

     c. `StarsInGalaxy`

     d. `averageRainFall`

3. Declare a constant for pi as 3.14159.

```
const float PI = 3.14159;
```

4. Declare a float variable and initialize it using your pi constant.

```
float myPi = PI;
```

Day 4

Quiz

1. What is an expression?

Any statement that returns a value.

2. Is `x = 5 + 7` an expression? What is its value?

Yes, `12`.

3. What is the value of `201 / 4`?

`50`.

4. What is the value of `201 % 4`?

`1`.

5. If `myAge`, `a`, and `b` are all int variables, what are their values after:

```
myAge = 39;
a = myAge++;
b = ++myAge;
```

`myAge: 41, a: 39, b: 41`.

6. What is the value of `8+2*3`?

`14`.

7. What is the difference between `if(x = 3)` and `if(x == 3)`?

The first one assigns 3 to x and returns true. The second one tests whether x is equal to 3; it returns true if the value of x is equal to 3 and false if it is not.

Exercises

1. Write a single `if` statement that examines two integer variables and changes the larger to the smaller, using only one `else` clause.

```
if (x > y)
    x = y;
else            // y > x ¦¦ y == x
    y = x;
```

2. Examine the following program. Imagine entering three numbers, and write what output you expect.

```
1:    #include <iostream.h>
2:    void main()
3:    {
4:        int a, b, c;
5:        cout << "Please enter three numbers\n";
6:        cout << "a: ";
7:        cin >> a;
8:        cout << "\nb: ";
9:        cin >> b;
10:       cout << "\nc: ";
11:       cin >> c;
12:
13:       if (c = (a-b))
14:           cout << "a: " << a << " minus b: " << b << "
              ➥equals c: " << c;
15:       else
16:           cout << "a-b does not equal c: ";
17:   }
```

D

3. Enter the program from exercise 2; compile, link, and run it. Enter the numbers 20, 10, and 50. Did you get the output you expected? Why not?

Enter 20, 10, 50.

Get back a: 20 b: 30 c: 10.

Line 13 is assigning, not testing for equality.

4. Examine this program and anticipate the output:

```
1:      #include <iostream.h>
2:      void main()
3:      {
4:          int a = 2, b = 2, c;
5:          if (c = (a-b))
6:              cout << "The value of c is: " << c;
7:      }
```

5. Enter, compile, link, and run the program from Exercise 4. What was the output? Why?

Because line 5 is assigning the value of a-b to c, the value of the assignment is a (1) minus b (1), or 0. Because 0 is evaluated as false, the `if` fails and nothing is printed.

Day 5
Quiz

1. What are the differences between the function prototype and the function definition?

The function prototype declares the function; the definition defines it. The prototype ends with a semicolon; the definition need not. The declaration can include the keyword `inline` and default values for the parameters; the definition cannot. The declaration need not include names for the parameters; the definition must.

2. Do the names of parameters have to agree in the prototype, definition, and call to the function?

No; all parameters are identified by position, not name.

3. If a function doesn't return a value, how do you declare the function?

Declare the function to return `void`.

4. If you don't declare a return value, what type of return value is assumed?

Any function that does not explicitly declare a return type returns `int`.

5. What is a local variable?

A local variable is a variable passed into or declared within a block, typically a function. It is visible only within the block.

6. What is scope?

Scope refers to the visibility and lifetime of local and global variables. Scope is usually established by a set of braces.

7. What is recursion?

Recursion generally refers to the ability of a function to call itself.

8. When should you use global variables?

Global variables are typically used when many functions need access to the same data. Global variables are very rare in C++; once you know how to create static class variables, you will almost never create global variables.

9. What is function overloading?

Function overloading is the ability to write more than one function with the same name, distinguished by the number or type of the parameters.

10. What is polymorphism?

Polymorphism is the ability to treat many objects of differing—but related—types without regard to their differences. In C++, polymorphism is accomplished by using class derivation and virtual functions.

Exercises

1. Write the prototype for a function named `Perimeter`, which returns an unsigned long int and which takes two parameters, both unsigned short `int`s.

   ```
   unsigned long int Perimeter(unsigned short int, unsigned short int);
   ```

2. Write the definition of the function `Perimeter` as described in Exercise 1. The two parameters represent the length and width of a rectangle and have the function return the perimeter (twice the length plus twice the width).

   ```
   unsigned long int Perimeter(unsigned short int length, unsigned short int width)
   {
       return 2*length + 2*width;
   }
   ```

3. **BUG BUSTER:** What is wrong with the function?

```
#include <iostreams.h>
void myFunc(unsigned short int x);
void main()
{
    unsigned short int x, y;
    y = myFunc(int);
    cout << "x: " << x << " y: " << y << "\n";
}


void myFunc(unsigned short int x)
{
    return (4*x);
}
```

The function is declared to return void and it cannot return a value.

4. **BUG BUSTER:** What is wrong with the function?

```
#include <iostreams.h>
int myFunc(unsigned short int x);
void main()
{
    unsigned short int x, y;
    y = myFunc(int);
    cout << "x: " << x << " y: " << y << "\n";
}


int myFunc(unsigned short int x)
{
    return (4*x);
}
```

This function would be fine, but there is a semicolon at the end of the function definition's header.

5. Write a function which takes two unsigned short int arguments and returns the result of dividing the first by the second. Do not do the division if the second number is 0, but do return −1.

```
short int Divider(unsigned short int valOne, unsigned short int valTwo)
{
    if (valTwo == 0)
```

```
            return -1;
        else
            return valOne / valTwo;
}
```

6. Write a program which asks the user for two numbers and calls the function you wrote in Exercise 5. Print the answer, or print an error message if you get −1.

```
#include <iostream.h>
typedef unsigned short int USHORT;
typedef unsigned long int ULONG;
short int divider(
unsigned short int val one,
unsigned short into val two);
void main()
{
    USHORT one, two;
    short int answer;
    cout << "Enter two numbers.\n Number one: ";
    cin >> one;
    cout << "Number two: ";
    cin >> two;
    answer = Divider(one, two);
    if (answer > -1)
        cout << "Answer: " << answer;
    else
        cout << "Error, can't divide by zero!";
}
```

7. Write a program which asks for a number and a power. Write a recursive function which takes the number to the power. Thus, if the number is 2 and the power is 4, the function will return 16.

```
#include <iostream.h>
typedef unsigned long ULONG
ULONG GetPower(USHORT n, USHORT power);
void main()
{
    USHORT number, power;
    ULONG answer;
```

```
        cout << "Enter a number: ";
        cin >> number;
        cout << "To what power? ";
        cin >> power;
        answer = GetPower(number,power);
        cout << number << " to the " << power << "th power is " << answer << endl;
    }


    ULONG GetPower(USHORT n, USHORT power)
    {
        if(power == 1)
          return n;
        else
            return (n * GetPower(n,power-1));
    }
```

Day 6
Quiz

1. What is the dot operator, and what is it used for?

   The dot operator is the period (.). It is used to access the members of the class.

2. Which sets aside memory—declaration or definition?

   Definitions of variables set aside memory. Declarations of classes don't set aside memory.

3. Is the declaration of a class its interface or its implementation?

   The declaration of a class is its interface; it tells clients of the class how to interact with the class. The implementation of the class is the set of member functions stored—usually in a related .CPP file.

4. What is the difference between public and private data members?

   Public data members can be accessed by clients of the class. Private data members can be accessed only by member functions of the class.

5. Can member functions be private?

   Yes. Both member functions and member data can be private.

6. Can member data be public?

Although member data can be public, it is good programming practice to make it private and to provide public accessor functions to the data.

7. If you declare two `Cat` objects, can they have different values in their `itsAge` member data?

Yes. Each object of a class has its own data members.

8. Do class declarations end with a semicolon? Do class method definitions?

Declarations end with a semicolon after the closing brace; function definitions do not.

9. What would the header for a `Cat` function, `Meow`, that takes no parameters and returns `void` look like?

The header for a `Cat` function, `Meow()`, that takes no parameters and returns `void` looks like this:

```
void Cat::Meow()
```

10. What function is called to initialize a class?

The constructor is called to initialize a class.

Exercises

1. Write the code that declares a class called `Employee` with these data members: `age`, `yearsOfService`, and `Salary`.

```
class Employee
{
    int Age;
    int YearsOfService;
    int Salary;
};
```

2. Rewrite the `Employee` class to make the data members private, and provide public accessor methods to get and set each of the data members.

```
class Employee
{
public:
    int GetAge() const;
```

```
        void SetAge(int age);
        int GetYearsOfService()const;
        void SetYearsOfService(int years);
        int GetSalary()const;
        void SetSalary(int salary);

    private:
        int Age;
        int YearsOfService;
        int Salary;
    };
```

3. Write a program with the `Employee` class that makes two `Employees`; sets their age, `YearsOfService`, and `Salary`; and prints their values.

```
    main()
    {
        Employee John;
        Employee Sally;
        John.SetAge(30);
        John.SetYearsOfService(5);
        John.SetSalary(50000);

        Sally.SetAge(32);
        Sally.SetYearsOfService(8);
        Sally.SetSalary(40000);

        cout << "At AcmeSexist company, John and Sally have the same job.\n";
        cout << "John is " << John.GetAge() << " years old and he has been with";
        cout << "the firm for " << John.GetYearsOfService << " years.\n";
        cout << "John earns $" << John.GetSalary << " dollars per year.\n\n";
        cout << "Sally, on the other hand is " << Sally.GetAge() << " years old and
has";
        cout << "been with the company " << Sally.GetYearsOfService;
        cout << " years. Yet Sally only makes $" << Sally.GetSalary();
        cout << " dollars per year!  Something here is unfair.";
```

4. Continuing from Exercise 3, provide a method of `Employee` that reports how many thousands of dollars the employee earns, rounded to the nearest 1,000.

```
float Employee:GetRoundedThousands()const
{
    return Salary % 1000;
}
```

5. Change the `Employee` class so that you can initialize age, `YearsOfService`, and `Salary` when you create the employee.

```
class Employee
{
public:

    Employee(int age, int yearsOfService, int salary);
    int GetAge()const;
    void SetAge(int age);
    int GetYearsOfService()const;
    void SetYearsOfService(int years);
    int GetSalary()const;
    void SetSalary(int salary);

private:
    int Age;
    int YearsOfService;
    int Salary;
};
```

6. **BUG BUSTERS**: What is wrong with the following declaration?

```
class Square
{
public:
    int Side;
}
```

Class declarations must end with a semicolon.

7. **BUG BUSTERS**: Why isn't the following class declaration very useful?

```
class Cat
{
    int GetAge()const;
private:
    int itsAge;
};
```

The accessor `GetAge()` is private. Remember: All class members are private unless you say otherwise.

8. **BUG BUSTERS**: What three bugs in this code will the compiler find?

```
class  TV
{
public:
    void SetStation(int Station);
    int GetStation() const;
private:
    int itsStation;
};

main()
{
    TV myTV;
    myTV.itsStation = 9;
    TV.SetStation(10);
    TV myOtherTv(2);
}
```

You can't access `itsStation` directly. It is private.

You can't call `SetStation()` on the class. You can call `SetStation()` only on objects.

You can't initialize `itsStation` because there is no matching constructor.

Day 7
Quiz

1. How do I initialize more than one variable in a `for` loop?

   Separate the initializations with commas, such as

   `for (x = 0, y = 10; x < 100; x++, y++).`

2. Why is `goto` avoided?

   `Goto` jumps in any direction to any arbitrary line of code. This makes for source code, which is difficult to understand and therefore difficult to maintain.

3. Is it possible to write a `for` loop with a body that is never executed?

   Yes, if the condition is false after the initialization, the body of the `for` loop will never execute. Here's an example:

   ```
   for (int x = 100; x < 100; x++).
   ```

4. Is it possible to nest `while` loops within `for` loops?

   Yes, any loop may be nested within any other loop.

5. Is it possible to create a loop that never ends? Give an example.

   Yes. Following are examples for both a `for` loop and a `while` loop:

   ```
   for(;;)
   {
       // This for loop never ends!
   }
   while(1)
   {
       // This while loop never ends!
   }.
   ```

6. What happens if you create a loop that never ends?

   Your program "hangs" and you usually must reboot the computer.

Exercises

1. What is the value of x when the `for` loop completes?

   ```
   for (int x = 0; x < 100; x++)
   ```

   100

2. Write a nested `for` loop which prints a 10x10 pattern of 0's.

   ```
   for (int i = 0; i< 10; i++)
   {
       for ( int j = 0; j< 10; j++)
          cout << "0";
       cout << "\n";
   }
   ```

3. Write a `for` statement to count from 100 to 200 by 2s.

   ```
   for (int x = 100; x<=200; x+=2)
   ```

4. Write a `while` loop to count from 100 to 200 by 2s.

```
int x = 100;
while (x <= 200)
    x+= 2;
```

5. Write a `do...while` loop to count from 100 to 200 by 2s.

```
int x = 100;
do
{
    x+=2;
} while (x <= 200);
```

6. **BUG BUSTERS:** What is wrong with this code?

```
int counter = 0
while (counter < 10)
{
    cout << "counter: " << counter;
    counter++;
}
```

`counter` is never incremented and the `while` loop will never terminate.

7. **BUG BUSTERS:** What is wrong with this code?

```
for (int counter = 0; counter < 10; counter++);
    cout << counter << "\n";
```

There is a semicolon after the loop and the loop does nothing. The programmer may have intended this, but if `counter` was supposed to print each value, it won't.

8. **BUG BUSTERS:** What is wrong with this code?

```
int counter = 100;
while (counter < 10)
{
    cout << "counter now: " << counter;
    counter--;
}
```

`counter` is initialized to 100, but the test condition is that if it is less than 10, the test will fail and the body will never be executed. If line 1 were changed to

int counter = 5; the loop would not terminate until it had counted down past the smallest possible int. Since int is signed by default, this would not be what was intended.

9. **BUG BUSTERS:** What is wrong with this code?

```
cout << "Enter a number between 0 and 5: ";
cin >> theNumber;
switch (theNumber)
{
    case 0:
          doZero();
    case 1:                 // fall through
    case 2:                 // fall through
    case 3:                 // fall through
    case 4:                 // fall through
    case 5:
          doOneToFive();
          break;
    default:
          doDefault();
          break;
}
```

Case 0 probably needs a break statement. If not, it should be documented with a comment.

Day 8
Quiz

1. What operator is used to determine the address of a variable?

   The address of operator (&) is used to determine the address of any variable.

2. What operator is used to find the value stored at an address held in a pointer?

   The dereference operator (*) is used to access the value at an address in a pointer.

3. What is a pointer?

   A pointer is a variable that holds the address of another variable.

4. What is the difference between the address stored in a pointer and the value at that address?

The address stored in the pointer is the address of another variable. The value stored at that address is any value stored in any variable. The indirection operator (*) returns the value stored at the address, which itself is stored in the pointer.

5. What is the difference between the indirection operator and the `address of` operator?

The indirection operator returns the value at the address stored in a pointer. The `address of` operator (&) returns the memory address of the variable.

6. What is the difference between `const int * ptrOne` and `int * const ptrTwo`?

The `const int * ptrOne` declares that `ptrOne` is a pointer to a constant integer. The integer itself cannot be changed using this pointer.

The `int * const ptrTwo` declares that `ptrTwo` is a constant pointer to integer. Once it is initialized, this pointer cannot be reassigned.

Exercises

1. What do these declarations do?

   a. `int * pOne;`

   b. `int vTwo;`

   c. `int * pThree = &vTwo;`

   a. `int * pOne;` declares a pointer to an integer.

   b. `int vTwo;` declares an integer variable.

   c. `int * pThree = &vTwo;` declares a pointer to an integer and initializes it with the address of another variable.

2. If you have an `unsigned short` variable named `yourAge`, how would you declare a pointer to manipulate `yourAge`?

   `unsigned short pAge = &yourAge;`

3. Assign the value `50` to the variable `yourAge` by using the pointer that you declared in Exercise 2.

   `*pAge = 50;`

4. Write a small program that declares an integer and a pointer to integer. Assign the address of the integer to the pointer. Use the pointer to set a value in the integer variable.

```
int theInteger;
int *pInteger = &theInteger;
*pInteger = 5;
```

5. **BUG BUSTERS**: What is wrong with this code?

```
#include <iostream.h>
void main()
{
    int *pInt;
    *pInt = 9;
    cout << "The value at pInt: " << *pInt;
}
```

pInt should have been initialized. More important, because it was not initialized and was not assigned the address of any memory, it points to a random place in memory. Assigning 9 to that random place is a dangerous bug.

6. **BUG BUSTERS**: What is wrong with this code?

```
void main()
{
    int SomeVariable = 5;
    cout << "SomeVariable: " << SomeVariable << "\n";
    int *pVar = & SomeVariable;
    pVar = 9;
    cout << "SomeVariable: " << *pVar << "\n";
}
```

Presumably, the programmer meant to assign 9 to the value at pVar. Unfortunately, 9 was assigned to be the value of pVar because the indirection operator (*) was left off. This will lead to disaster if pVar is used to assign a value.

Day 9
Quiz

1. What is the difference between a reference and a pointer?

A reference is an alias, and a pointer is a variable that holds an address. References cannot be null and cannot be assigned to.

2. When must you use a pointer rather than a reference?

   When you may need to reassign what is pointed to, or when the pointer may be null.

3. What does *new* return if there is insufficient memory to make your new object?

   A null pointer (0).

4. What is a constant reference?

   This is a shorthand way of saying a reference to a constant object.

5. What is the difference between passing *by* reference and passing *a* reference?

   Passing *by* reference means not making a local copy. It can be accomplished by passing a reference or by passing a pointer.

Exercises

1. Write a program that declares an int, a reference to an int, and a pointer to an int. Use the pointer and the reference to manipulate the value in the int.

```
void main()
{
int varOne;
int& rVar = varOne;
int* pVar = &varOne;
rVar = 5;
*pVar = 7;
}
```

2. Write a program that declares a constant pointer to a constant integer. Initialize the pointer to an integer variable, varOne. Assign 6 to varOne. Use the pointer to assign 7 to varOne. Create a second integer variable, varTwo. Reassign the pointer to varTwo.

```
void main()
{
    int varOne;
    const int * const pVar = &varOne;
    *pVar = 7;
    int varTwo;
    pVar = &varTwo;
}
```

3. Compile the program in Exercise 2. What produces errors? What produces warnings?

You can't assign a value to a constant object, and you can't reassign a constant pointer.

4. Write a program that produces a stray pointer.

```
void main()
{
int * pVar;
*pVar = 9;
}
```

5. Fix the program from Exercise 4.

```
void main()
{
int VarOne;
int * pVar = &varOne;
*pVar = 9;
}
```

6. Write a program that produces a memory leak.

```
int FuncOne();
void main()
{
    int localVar = FunOne();
    cout << "the value of localVar is: " << localVar;
}

int FuncOne()
{
    int * pVar = new int (5);
    return *pVar;
}
```

7. Fix the program from Exercise 6.

```
void FuncOne();
void main()
{
    FunOne();
}
```

```
void FuncOne()
{
   int * pVar = new int (5);
   cout << "the value of *pVar is: " << *pVar ;
}
```

8. **BUG BUSTERS:** What is wrong with this program?

```
1:      #include <iostreams.h>
2:
3:      class CAT
4:      {
5:         public:
6:            CAT(int age) { itsAge = age; }
7:            ~CAT(){}
8:            int GetAge() const { return itsAge;}
9:         private:
10:           int itsAge;
11:     };
12:
13:     CAT & MakeCat(int age);
14:     void main()
15:     {
16:        int age = 7;
17:        CAT Boots = MakeCat(age);
18:        cout << "Boots is " << Boots.GetAge() << " years old\n";
19:     }
20:
21:     CAT & MakeCat(int age)
22:     {
23:        CAT * pCat = new CAT(age);
24:        return *pCat;
25:     }
```

MakeCat returns a reference to the CAT created on the free store. There is no way to free that memory, and this produces a memory leak.

9. Fix the program from Exercise 8.

```
1:      #include <iostreams.h>
2:
```

```
3:    class CAT
4:    {
5:      public:
6:          CAT(int age) { itsAge = age; }
7:          ~CAT(){}
8:          int GetAge() const { return itsAge;}
9:      private:
10:         int itsAge;
11:   };
12:
13:   CAT * MakeCat(int age);
14:   void main()
15:   {
16:     int age = 7;
17:     CAT * Boots = MakeCat(age);
18:     cout << "Boots is " << Boots->GetAge() << " years old\n";
19:     delete Boots;
20:   }
21:
22:   CAT * MakeCat(int age)
23:   {
24:     return new CAT(age);
25:   }
```

Day 10
Quiz

1. When you overload member functions, in what ways must they differ?

   Overloaded member functions are functions in a class that share a name, but that differ in the number or type of their parameters.

2. What is the difference between a declaration and a definition?

   A definition sets aside memory, but a declaration does not. Almost all declarations *are* definitions; the major exceptions are class declarations, function prototypes, and typedef statements.

3. When is the copy constructor called?

Whenever a temporary copy of an object is created. This happens every time an object is passed by value.

4. When is the destructor called?

The destructor is called each time an object is destroyed, either because it goes out of scope or because you call `delete` on a pointer pointing to it.

5. How does the copy constructor differ from the assignment operator (=)?

The assignment operator acts on an existing object; the copy constructor creates a new one.

6. What is the `this` pointer?

The `this` pointer is a hidden parameter in every member function that points to the object itself.

7. How do you differentiate between overloading the prefix and postfix increments?

The prefix operator takes no parameters. The postfix operator takes a single `int` parameter, which is used as a signal to the compiler that this is the postfix variant.

8. Can you overload the operator+ for short integers?

No, you cannot overload any operator for built-in types.

9. Is it legal in C++ to overload operator++ so that it decrements a value in your class?

It is legal, but it is a bad idea. Operators should be overloaded in a way that is likely to be readily understood by anyone reading your code.

10. What return value must conversion operators have in their declaration?

None. Like constructors and destructors, they have no return values.

Exercises

1. Write a `SimpleCircle` class declaration (only) with one member variable: `itsRadius`. Include a default constructor, a destructor, and accessor methods for radius.

```
class SimpleCircle
{
```

```
public:
    SimpleCircle();
    ~SimpleCircle();
    void SetRadius(int);
    int GetRadius();
private:
    int itsRadius;
};
```

2. Using the class you created in Exercise 1, write the implementation of the default constructor, initializing itsRadius with the value 5.

```
SimpleCircle::SimpleCircle():
itsRadius(5)
{}
```

3. Using the same class, add a second constructor that takes a value as its parameter and assigns that value to itsRadius.

```
SimpleCircle::SimpleCircle(int radius):
itsRadius(radius)
{}
```

4. Create a prefix and postfix increment operator for your SimpleCircle class that increments itsRadius.

```
SimpleCircle SimpleCircle::operator++()
{
    itsRadius++;
    return *this;
}


SimpleCircle SimpleCircle::operator++ (int)
{
    itsRadius++;
    return *this;
}
```

5. Change SimpleCircle to store itsRadius on the free store, and fix the existing methods.

```
class SimpleCircle
{
public:
```

```
        SimpleCircle();
        SimpleCircle(int);
        ~SimpleCircle();
        void SetRadius(int);
        int GetRadius();
        SimpleCircle operator++();
        SimpleCircle operator++(int);
private:
        int *itsRadius;
};


SimpleCircle::SimpleCircle()
{itsRadius = new int(5);}

SimpleCircle::SimpleCircle(int radius)
{itsRadius = new int(radius);}

SimpleCircle SimpleCircle::operator++()
{
        (*itsRadius)++;
        return *this;
}

SimpleCircle SimpleCircle::operator++ (int)
{
        (*itsRadius)++;
        return *this;
}
```

6. Provide a copy constructor for SimpleCircle.

```
SimpleCircle::SimpleCircle(const SimpleCircle & rhs)
{
        int val = rhs.GetRadius();
        itsRadius = new int(val);
}
```

7. Provide an operator= for SimpleCircle.

```
SimpleCircle& SimpleCircle::operator=(const SimpleCircle & rhs)
{
```

```
        if (this == &rhs)
            return *this;
        *itsRadius = rhs.GetRadius();
    }
```

8. Write a program that creates two `SimpleCircle` objects. Use the default constructor on one and instantiate the other with the value 9. Call increment on each and then print their values. Finally, assign the second to the first and print its values.

```
#include <iostreams.h>

class SimpleCircle
{
public:
        // constructors
    SimpleCircle();
    SimpleCircle(int);
    SimpleCircle(const SimpleCircle &);
    ~SimpleCircle() {}

// accessor functions
    void SetRadius(int);
    int GetRadius()const;

// operators
    SimpleCircle operator++();
    SimpleCircle operator++(int);
    SimpleCircle& operator=(const SimpleCircle &);

private:
    int *itsRadius;
};


SimpleCircle::SimpleCircle()
{itsRadius = new int(5);}

SimpleCircle::SimpleCircle(int radius)
{itsRadius = new int(radius);}
```

```
SimpleCircle::SimpleCircle(const SimpleCircle & rhs)
{
    int val = rhs.GetRadius();
    itsRadius = new int(val);
}
SimpleCircle& SimpleCircle::operator=(const SimpleCircle & rhs)
{
    if (this == &rhs)
        return *this;
    *itsRadius = rhs.GetRadius();
    return *this;
}


SimpleCircle SimpleCircle::operator++()
{
    (*itsRadius)++;
    return *this;
}


SimpleCircle SimpleCircle::operator++ (int)
{
    (*itsRadius)++;
    return *this;
}
int SimpleCircle::GetRadius() const
{
    return *itsRadius;
}
void main()
{
    SimpleCircle CircleOne, CircleTwo(9);
    CircleOne++;
    ++CircleTwo;
    cout << "CircleOne: " << CircleOne.GetRadius() << endl;
    cout << "CircleTwo: " << CircleTwo.GetRadius() << endl;
    CircleOne = CircleTwo;
    cout << "CircleOne: " << CircleOne.GetRadius() << endl;
    cout << "CircleTwo: " << CircleTwo.GetRadius() << endl;
}
```

9. **BUG BUSTERS:** What is wrong with this implementation of the assignment operator?

```
SQUARE SQUARE ::operator=(const SQUARE & rhs)
{
        itsSide = new int;
        *itsSide = rhs.GetSide();
        return *this;
}
```

You must check to see if rhs equals this, or the call to a = a will crash your program.

10. **BUG BUSTERS:** What is wrong with this implementation of operator+?

```
VeryShort  VeryShort::operator+ (const VeryShort& rhs)
{
    itsVal += rhs.GetItsVal();
    return *this;
}
```

This operator+ is changing the value in one of the operands, rather than creating a new VeryShort object with the sum. The right way to do this is as follows:

```
VeryShort  VeryShort::operator+ (const VeryShort& rhs)
{
    return VeryShort(itsVal + rhs.GetItsVal());
}
```

Day 11

Quiz

1. What are the first and last elements in SomeArray[25]?

   SomeArray[0], SomeArray[24]

2. How do you declare a multidimensional array?

   Write a set of subscripts for each dimension. For example, SomeArray[2][3][2] is a three-dimensional array. The first dimension has two elements; the second has three; and the third has two.

3. Initialize the members of the array in Question 2.

```
SomeArray[2][3][2] = { { {1,2},{3,4},{5,6} } , { {7,8},{9,10},{11,12} } };
```

4. How many elements are in the array `SomeArray[10][5][20]`?

```
10*5*20=1,000
```

5. What is the maximum number of elements that you can add to a linked list?

There is no fixed maximum. It depends on how much memory you have available.

6. Can you use subscript notation on a linked list?

You can use subscript notation on a linked list only by writing your own class to contain the linked list and overloading the subscript operator.

7. What is the last character in the string "Brad is a nice guy?"?

The null character.

Exercises

1. Declare a two-dimensional array that represents a tic-tac-toe game board.

```
int GameBoard[3][3];
```

2. Write the code that initializes all the elements in the array you created in Exercise 1 to the value 0.

```
int GameBoard[3][3] = { {0,0,0},{0,0,0},{0,0,0} }
```

3. Write the declaration for a `Node` class that holds unsigned short integers.

```
class Node
{
public:
    Node ();
    Node (int);
    [126]Node();
    void SetNext(Node * node) { itsNext = node; }
    Node * GetNext() const { return itsNext; }
    int GetVal() const { return itsVal; }
    void Insert(Node *);
    void Display();
private:
```

```
    int itsVal;
    Node * itsNext;
};
```

4. **BUG BUSTERS**: What is wrong with this code fragment?

```
unsigned short SomeArray[5][4];
for (int i = 0; i<4; i++)
    for (int j = 0; j<5; j++)
        SomeArray[i][j] = i+j;
```

The array is 5 elements by 4 elements, but the code initializes 4×5.

5. **BUG BUSTERS**: What is wrong with this code fragment?

```
unsigned short SomeArray[5][4];
for (int i = 0; i<=5; i++)
    for (int j = 0; j<=4; j++)
        SomeArray[i][j] = 0;
```

You wanted to write i<5, but you wrote i<=5 instead. The code will run when i == 5 and j == 4, but there is no such element as SomeArray[5][4].

Day 12
Quiz

1. What is a v-table?

   A v-table, or virtual function table, is a common way for compilers to manage virtual functions in C++. The table keeps a list of the addresses of all the virtual functions, and depending on the run-time type of the object pointed to, invokes the right function.

2. What is a virtual destructor?

   A destructor of any class can be declared to be virtual. When the pointer is deleted, the run-time type of the object will be assessed and the right derived destructor invoked.

3. How do you show the declaration of a virtual constructor?

   There are no virtual constructors.

4. How can you create a virtual copy constructor?

By creating a virtual method in your class, which itself calls the copy constructor.

5. How do you invoke a base member function from a derived class in which you've overridden that function?

```
Base::FunctionName();
```

6. How do you invoke a base member function from a derived class in which you have *not* overridden that function?

```
FunctionName();
```

7. If a base class declares a function to be virtual, and a derived class does not use the term virtual when overriding that class, is it still virtual when inherited by a third-generation class?

Yes, the virtualness is inherited and *cannot* be turned off.

8. What is the `protected` keyword used for?

`protected` members are accessible to the member functions of derived objects.

Exercises

1. Show the declaration of a virtual function taking an integer parameter and returning void.

```
virtual void SomeFunction(int);
```

2. Show the declaration of a class `Square`, which derives from `Rectangle`, which in turn derives from `Shape`.

```
class Square : public Rectangle
{};
```

3. If, in Example 2, `Shape` takes no parameters, `Rectangle` takes two (length and width), but `Square` takes only one (length), show the constructor initialization for `Square`.

```
Square::Square(int length):
    Rectangle(length, length){}
```

4. Write a virtual copy constructor for the class `Square` (above).

```
Square& Square::Clone()
{ return new Square(*this); }
```

5. **BUG BUSTERS:** What is wrong with this code snippet?

```
void SomeFunction (Shape);
Shape * pRect = new Rectangle;
SomeFunction(*pRect);
```

Perhaps nothing. `SomeFunction` expects a `Shape` object. You've passed it a `Rectangle` "sliced" down to a `Shape`. As long as you don't need any of the `Rectangle` parts, this will be fine. If you do need the `Rectangle` parts, you'll need to change `SomeFunction` to take a pointer or a reference to a `Shape`.

6. **BUG BUSTERS:** What is wrong with this code snippet?

```
class Shape()
{
public:
    Shape();
    virtual ~Shape();
    virtual Shape(const Shape&);
};
```

You can't declare a copy constructor to be virtual.

Day 13

Quiz

1. What is a down cast?

   A down cast (also called "casting down") is a declaration that a pointer to a base class is to be treated as a pointer to a derived class.

2. What is the v-ptr?

   The v-ptr, or virtual-function pointer, is an implementation detail of virtual functions. Each object in a class with virtual functions has a v-ptr, which points to the virtual function table for that class.

3. If a round-rectangle has straight edges and rounded corners, and your `RoundRect` class inherits both from `Rectangle` and from `Circle`, and they in turn both inherit from `Shape`, how many `Shapes` are created when you create a `RoundRect`?

If neither class inherits using the keyword virtual, two Shapes are created, one for Rectangle and one for Shape. If the keyword virtual is used for both classes, only one shared Shape is created.

4. If Horse and Bird inherit virtual public from Animal, do their constructors initialize the Animal constructor? If Pegasus inherits from both Horse and Bird, how does it initialize Animal's constructor?

Both Horse and Bird initialize their base class, Animal, in their constructors. Pegasus does as well, and when a Pegasus is created, the Horse and Bird initializations of Animal are ignored.

5. Declare a class, vehicle and make it an Abstract Data Type.

```
class Vehicle
{
    virtual void Move() = 0;
}
```

6. If a base class is an ADT, and it has three pure virtual functions, how many of these *must* be overridden in its derived classes?

None must be overridden unless you want to make the class non-abstract, in which case all three must be overridden.

Exercises

1. Show the declaration for a class JetPlane, which inherits from Rocket and Airplane.

```
class JetPlane : public Rocket, public Airplane
```

2. Show the declaration for 747, which inherits from the JetPlane class described in Exercise 1.

```
class 747 : public JetPlane
```

3. Show the declarations for the classes Car and Bus, which each derive from the class Vehicle. Make Vehicle an ADT with two pure virtual functions. Make Car and Bus not be ADTs.

```
class Vehicle
{
    virtual void Move() = 0;
    virtual void Haul() = 0;
```

```
};

class Car : public Vehicle
{
    virtual void Move();
    virtual void Haul();
};

class Bus : public Vehicle
{
    virtual void Move();
    virtual void Haul();
};
```

4. Modify the program in Exercise 1 so that `Car` is an ADT, and derive `SportsCar` and `Coupe` from `Car`. In the `Car` class, provide an implementation for one of the pure virtual functions in `Vehicle` and make it non-pure.

```
class Vehicle
{
    virtual void Move() = 0;
    virtual void Haul() = 0;
};

class Car : public Vehicle
{
    virtual void Move();
};

class Bus : public Vehicle
{
    virtual void Move();
    virtual void Haul();
};

class SportsCar : public Car
{
    virtual void Haul();
};
```

```
class Coupe : public Car
{
    virtual void Haul();
};
```

Day 14

Quiz

1. Can static member variables be private?

   Yes, they are member variables and their access can be controlled like any other. If they are private, they can be accessed only by using member functions or, more commonly, static member functions.

2. Show the declaration for a static member variable.

   ```
   static int itsStatic;
   ```

3. Show the declaration for a static function pointer.

   ```
   static int SomeFunction();
   ```

4. Show the declaration for a pointer to function returning `long` and taking an integer parameter.

   ```
   long (* function)(int);
   ```

5. Modify the pointer in Exercise 4 to be a pointer to member function of class `Car`.

   ```
   long (* Car::function)(int);
   ```

6. Show the declaration for an array of 10 pointers as defined in Exercise 5.

   ```
   (long (* Car::function)(int) theArray [10];
   ```

Exercises

1. Write a short program declaring a class with one member variable and one static member variable. Have the constructor initialize the member variable and increment the static member variable. Have the destructor decrement the member variable.

   ```
   1:    class myClass
   2:    {
   ```

```
3:      public:
4:          myClass();
5:          ~myClass();
6:      private:
7:          int itsMember;
8:          static int itsStatic;
9:      };
10:
11:     myClass::myClass():
12:      itsMember(1)
13:     {
14:         itsStatic++;
15:     }
16:
17:     myClass::~myClass()
18:     {
19:         itsStatic—;
20:     }
21:
22:     int myClass::itsStatic = 0;
23:
24:     void main()
25:     {}
```

2. Using the program from Exercise 1, write a short driver program that makes three objects and then displays their member variables and the static member variable. Then destroy each object and show the effect on the static member variable.

```
1:      #include <iostream.h>
2:
3:      class myClass
4:      {
5:      public:
6:          myClass();
7:          ~myClass();
8:          void ShowMember();
9:          void ShowStatic();
10:     private:
11:         int itsMember;
```

```
12:        static int itsStatic;
13:    };
14:
15:    myClass::myClass():
16:     itsMember(1)
17:    {
18:       itsStatic++;
19:    }
20:
21:    myClass::~myClass()
22:    {
23:       itsStatic—;
24:       cout << "In destructor. ItsStatic: " << itsStatic << endl;
25:    }
26:
27:    void myClass::ShowMember()
28:    {
29:       cout << "itsMember: " << itsMember << endl;
30:    }
31:
32:    void myClass::ShowStatic()
33:    {
34:       cout << "itsStatic: " << itsStatic << endl;
35:    }
36:    int myClass::itsStatic = 0;
37:
38:    void main()
39:    {
40:       myClass obj1;
41:       obj1.ShowMember();
42:       obj1.ShowStatic();
43:
44:       myClass obj2;
45:       obj2.ShowMember();
46:       obj2.ShowStatic();
47:
48:       myClass obj3;
49:       obj3.ShowMember();
50:       obj3.ShowStatic();
51:    }
```

3. Modify the program from Exercise 2 to use a static member function to access the static member variable. Make the static member variable private.

```
1:     #include <iostream.h>
2:
3:     class myClass
4:     {
5:     public:
6:         myClass();
7:         ~myClass();
8:         void ShowMember();
9:         static int GetStatic();
10:    private:
11:        int itsMember;
12:        static int itsStatic;
13:    };
14:
15:    myClass::myClass():
16:     itsMember(1)
17:    {
18:        itsStatic++;
19:    }
20:
21:    myClass::~myClass()
22:    {
23:        itsStatic--;
24:        cout << "In destructor. ItsStatic: " << itsStatic << endl;
25:    }
26:
27:    void myClass::ShowMember()
28:    {
29:        cout << "itsMember: " << itsMember << endl;
30:    }
31:
32:    int myClass::itsStatic = 0;
33:
34:    void myClass::GetStatic()
35:    {
36:        return itsStatic;
```

```
37:      }
38:
39:   void main()
40:   {
41:      myClass obj1;
42:      obj1.ShowMember();
43:      cout << "Static: " << myClass::GetStatic() << endl;
44:
45:      myClass obj2;
46:      obj2.ShowMember();
47:      cout << "Static: " << myClass::GetStatic() << endl;
48:
49:      myClass obj3;
50:      obj3.ShowMember();
51:      cout << "Static: " << myClass::GetStatic() << endl;
52:   }
```

4. Write a pointer to member function to access the non-static member data in the program in Exercise 3, and use that pointer to print the value of that data.

```
1:    #include <iostream.h>
2:
3:    class myClass
4:    {
5:    public:
6:       myClass();
7:       ~myClass();
8:       void ShowMember();
9:       static int GetStatic();
10:   private:
11:      int itsMember;
12:      static int itsStatic;
13:   };
14:
15:   myClass::myClass():
16:    itsMember(1)
17:   {
18:      itsStatic++;
19:   }
20:
21:   myClass::~myClass()
```

```
22:     {
23:         itsStatic--;
24:         cout << "In destructor. ItsStatic: " << itsStatic << endl;
25:     }
26:
27:     void myClass::ShowMember()
28:     {
29:         cout << "itsMember: " << itsMember << endl;
30:     }
31:
32:     int myClass::itsStatic = 0;
33:
34:     int myClass::GetStatic()
35:     {
36:         return itsStatic;
37:     }
38:
39:     void main()
40:     {
41:         void (myClass::*PMF) ();
42:
43:         PMF=myClass::ShowMember;
44:
45:         myClass obj1;
46:         (obj1.*PMF)();
47:         cout << "Static: " << myClass::GetStatic() << endl;
48:
49:         myClass obj2;
50:         (obj2.*PMF)();
51:         cout << "Static: " << myClass::GetStatic() << endl;
52:
53:         myClass obj3;
54:         (obj3.*PMF)();
55:         cout << "Static: " << myClass::GetStatic() << endl;
56:     }
```

5. Add two more member variables to the class from the previous questions. Add accessor functions that get the value of these data and give all the member functions the same return values and signatures. Use the pointer to member function to access these functions.

```
1:      #include <iostream.h>
2:
3:      class myClass
4:      {
5:      public:
6:          myClass();
7:          ~myClass();
8:          void ShowMember();
9:          void ShowSecond();
10:         void ShowThird();
11:         static int GetStatic();
12:     private:
13:         int itsMember;
14:         int itsSecond;
15:         int itsThird;
16:         static int itsStatic;
17:     };
18:
19:     myClass::myClass():
20:      itsMember(1),
21:      itsSecond(2),
22:      itsThird(3)
23:     {
24:         itsStatic++;
25:     }
26:
27:     myClass::~myClass()
28:     {
29:         itsStatic--;
30:         cout << "In destructor. ItsStatic: " << itsStatic << endl;
31:     }
32:
33:     void myClass::ShowMember()
34:     {
35:         cout << "itsMember: " << itsMember << endl;
36:     }
37:
38:     void myClass::ShowSecond()
39:     {
```

```
40:        cout << "itsSecond: " << itsSecond << endl;
41:    }
42:
43:    void myClass::ShowThird()
44:    {
45:        cout << "itsThird: " << itsThird << endl;
46:    }
47:    int myClass::itsStatic = 0;
48:
49:    int myClass::GetStatic()
50:    {
51:        return itsStatic;
52:    }
53:
54:    void main()
55:    {
56:        void (myClass::*PMF) ();
57:
58:        myClass obj1;
59:        PMF=myClass::ShowMember;
60:        (obj1.*PMF)();
61:        PMF=myClass::ShowSecond;
62:        (obj1.*PMF)();
63:        PMF=myClass::ShowThird;
64:        (obj1.*PMF)();
65:        cout << "Static: " << myClass::GetStatic() << endl;
66:
67:        myClass obj2;
68:        PMF=myClass::ShowMember;
69:        (obj2.*PMF)();
70:        PMF=myClass::ShowSecond;
71:        (obj2.*PMF)();
72:        PMF=myClass::ShowThird;
73:        (obj2.*PMF)();
74:        cout << "Static: " << myClass::GetStatic() << endl;
75:
76:        myClass obj3;
77:        PMF=myClass::ShowMember;
78:        (obj3.*PMF)();
```

```
79:        PMF=myClass::ShowSecond;
80:        (obj3.*PMF)();
81:        PMF=myClass::ShowThird;
82:        (obj3.*PMF)();
83:        cout << "Static: " << myClass::GetStatic() << endl;
84:    }
```

Day 15
Quiz

1. How do you establish an *is-a* relationship?

   With public inheritance.

2. How do you establish a *has-a* relationship?

   With containment; that is, one class has a member that is an object of another type.

3. What is the difference between containment and delegation?

   Containment describes the idea of one class having a data member that is an object of another type. Delegation expresses the idea that one class uses another class to accomplish a task or goal. Delegation is usually accomplished by containment.

4. What is the difference between delegation and implemented-in-terms-of?

   Delegation expresses the idea that one class uses another class to accomplish a task or goal. Implemented-in-terms-of expresses the idea of inheriting implementation from another class.

5. What is a friend function?

   A friend function is a function declared to have access to the protected and private members of your class.

6. What is a friend class?

   A friend class is a class declared so that all of its member functions are friend functions of your class.

7. If Dog is a friend of Boy, is Boy a friend of Dog?

   No, friendship is not commutative.

8. If Dog is a friend of Boy, and Terrier derives from Dog, is Terrier a friend of Boy?

   No, friendship is not inherited.

9. If Dog is a friend of Boy and Boy is a friend of House, is Dog a friend of House?

   No, friendship is not associative.

10. Where must the declaration of a friend function appear?

    Anywhere within the class declaration. It makes no difference whether you put the declaration within the public:, protected:, or private: access areas.

Exercises

1. Show the declaration of a class Animal that contains a data member that is a string object.

```
class Animal:
{
private:
    String itsName;
};
```

2. Show the declaration of a class BoundedArray that *is* an array.

```
class boundedArray : public Array
{
//...
}
```

3. Show the declaration of a class Set that is declared in terms of an array.

```
class Set : private Array
{
// ...
}
```

4. Modify Listing 15.11 to provide the String class with an extraction operator (>>).

```
1:        #include <iostreams.h>
2:        #include <string.h>
3:
4:        class String
```

```
5:        {
6:           public:
7:               // constructors
8:               String();
9:                String(const char *const);
10:               String(const String &);
11:               ~String();
12:
13:               // overloaded operators
14:               char & operator[](int offset);
15:               char operator[](int offset) const;
16:               String operator+(const String&);
17:               void operator+=(const String&);
18:               String & operator= (const String &);
19:               friend ostream& operator<<( ostream&
                  ➥theStream,String& theString);
20:               friend istream& operator>>( istream&
                  ➥theStream,String& theString);
21:               // General accessors
22:               int GetLen()const { return itsLen; }
23:               const char * GetString() const { return itsString; }
24:               // static int ConstructorCount;
25:
26:           private:
27:               String (int);          // private constructor
28:               char * itsString;
29:               unsigned short itsLen;
30:
31:        };
32:
33:        ostream& operator<<( ostream& theStream,String& theString)
34:        {
35:            theStream << theString.GetString();
36:            return theStream;
37:        }
38:
39:        istream& operator>>( istream& theStream,String& theString)
40:        {
41:            theStream >> theString.GetString();
```

```
42:            return theStream;
43:        }
44:
45:        void main()
46:        {
47:            String theString("Hello world.");
48:            cout << theString;
49:        }
```

5. **BUG BUSTER**: What is wrong with this program?

```
1:      #include <iostream.h>
2:
3:      class Animal;
4:
5:      void setValue(Animal& , int);
6:
7:
8:      class Animal
9:      {
10:     public:
11:         int GetWeight()const { return itsWeight; }
12:         int GetAge() const { return itsAge; }
13:     private:
14:         int itsWeight;
15:         int itsAge;
16:     };
17:
18:     void setValue(Animal& theAnimal, int theWeight)
19:     {
20:         friend class Animal;
21:         theAnimal.itsWeight = theWeight;
22:     }
23:
24:     void main()
25:     {
26:         Animal peppy;
27:         setValue(peppy,5);
28:     }
```

D

You can't put the friend declaration into the function. You must declare the
function to be a friend in the class.

6. Fix the listing in Exercise 5 so it compiles.

```
1:      #include <iostream.h>
2:
3:      class Animal;
4:
5:      void setValue(Animal& , int);
6:
7:
8:      class Animal
9:      {
10:     public:
11:         friend void setValue(Animal&, int);
12:         int GetWeight()const { return itsWeight; }
13:         int GetAge() const { return itsAge; }
14:     private:
15:         int itsWeight;
16:         int itsAge;
17:     };
18:
19:     void setValue(Animal& theAnimal, int theWeight)
20:     {
21:         theAnimal.itsWeight = theWeight;
22:     }
23:
24:     void main()
25:     {
26:         Animal peppy;
27:         setValue(peppy,5);
28:     }
```

7. **BUG BUSTERS:** What is wrong with this code?

```
1:      #include <iostream.h>
2:
3:      class Animal;
4:
5:      void setValue(Animal& , int);
6:      void setValue(Animal& ,int,int);
7:
```

```
8:      class Animal
9:      {
10:     friend void setValue(Animal& ,int); // here's the change!
11:     private:
12:        int itsWeight;
13:        int itsAge;
14:     };
15:
16:     void setValue(Animal& theAnimal, int theWeight)
17:     {
18:         theAnimal.itsWeight = theWeight;
19:     }
20:
21:
22:     void setValue(Animal& theAnimal, int theWeight, int theAge)
23:     {
24:        theAnimal.itsWeight = theWeight;
25:        theAnimal.itsAge = theAge;
26:     }
27:
28:     void main()
29:     {
30:        Animal peppy;
31:        setValue(peppy,5);
32:        setValue(peppy,7,9);
33:     }
```

The function setValue(Animal&,int) was declared to be a friend, but the overloaded function setValue(Animal&,int,int) was not declared to be a friend.

8. Fix Exercise 7 so it compiles.

```
1:      #include <iostream.h>
2:
3:      class Animal;
4:
5:      void setValue(Animal& , int);
6:      void setValue(Animal& ,int,int); // here's the change!
7:
8:      class Animal
```

```
9:      {
10:     friend void setValue(Animal& ,int);
11:     friend void setValue(Animal& ,int,int
12:     private:
13:         int itsWeight;
14:         int itsAge;
15:     };
16:
17:     void setValue(Animal& theAnimal, int theWeight)
18:     {
19:         theAnimal.itsWeight = theWeight;
20:     }
21:
22:
23:     void setValue(Animal& theAnimal, int theWeight, int ➥theAge)
24:     {
25:         theAnimal.itsWeight = theWeight;
26:         theAnimal.itsAge = theAge;
27:     }
28:
29:     void main()
30:     {
31:         Animal peppy;
32:         setValue(peppy,5);
33:         setValue(peppy,7,9);
34:     }
```

Day 16

Quiz

1. What is the insertion operator and what does it do?

   The insertion operator (<<) is a member operator of the ostream object and is used for writing to the output device.

2. What is the extraction operator and what does it do?

   The extraction operator (>>) is a member operator of the istream object and is used for writing to your program's variables.

3. What are the three forms of `cin.get()` and what are their differences?

The first form of `get()` is without parameters. This returns the value of the character found, and will return EOF (end of file) if the end of the file is reached.

The second form of `get()` takes a character reference as its parameter; that character is filled with the next character in the input stream. The return value is an `iostream` object.

The third form of `get()` takes an array, a maximum number of characters to get, and a terminating character. This form of `get()` fills the array with up to one fewer characters than the maximum (appending null) unless it reads the terminating character, in which case it immediately writes a null and leaves the terminating character in the buffer.

4. What is the difference between `cin.read()` and `cin.getline()`?

`cin.read()` is used for reading binary data structures.

`getline()` is used to read from the `istream`'s buffer.

5. What is the default width for ouputting a long integer using the insertion operator?

Wide enough to display the entire number.

6. What is the return value of the insertion operator?

A reference to an `istream` object.

7. What parameter does the constructor to an `ofstream` object take?

The filename to be opened.

8. What does the `ios::ate` argument do?

`ios::ate` places you at the end of the file, but you can write data anywhere in the file.

Exercises

1. Write a program that writes to the four standard `iostream` objects: `cin`, `cout`, `cerr`, and `clog`.

```
1:    #include <iostream.h>
2:    void main()
```

D

```
3:     {
4:         int x;
5:         cout << "Enter a number: ";
6:         cin >> x;
7:         cout << "You entered: " << x << endl;
8:         cerr << "Uh oh, this to cerr!" << endl;
9:         clog << "Uh oh, this to clog!" << endl;
10:    }
```

2. Write a program that prompts the user to enter her full name and then displays it on the screen.

```
1:     #include <iostream.h>
2:     void main()
3:     {
4:         char name[80];
5:         cout << "Enter your full name: ";
6:         cin.getline(name,80);
7:         cout << "\nYou entered: " << name << endl;
8:     }
```

3. Rewrite Listing 16.9 to do the same thing, but without using putback() or ignore().

```
1:     // Listing
2:     #include <iostream.h>
3:
4:     void main()
5:     {
6:         char ch;
7:         cout << "enter a phrase: ";
8:         while ( cin.get(ch) )
9:         {
10:             switch (ch)
11:             {
12:             case '!':
13:                 cout << '$';
14:                 break;
15:             case '#':
16:                 break;
17:             default:
18:                 cout << ch;
```

```
19:                    break;
20:            }
21:        }
22:    }
```

4. Write a program that takes a filename as a parameter and opens the file for reading. Read every character of the file and display only the letters and punctuation to the screen. (Ignore all non-printing characters.) Then close the file and exit.

```
1:     #include <fstream.h>
2:     enum BOOL { FALSE, TRUE };
3:
4:     int main(int argc, char**argv)    // returns 1
on error
5:     {
6:
7:         if (argc != 2)
8:         {
9:             cout << "Usage: argv[0] <infile>\n";
10:            return(1);
11:        }
12:
13:    // open the input stream
14:        ifstream fin (argv[1],ios::binary);
15:        if (!fin)
16:        {
17:            cout << "Unable to open " << argv[1] <<
" for reading.\n";
18:            return(1);
19:        }
20:
21:        char ch;
22:        while ( fin.get(ch))
23:            if ((ch > 32 && ch < 127) || ch == '\n'
|| ch == '\t')
24:                cout << ch;
25:        fin.close();
26:    }
```

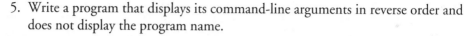

5. Write a program that displays its command-line arguments in reverse order and does not display the program name.

```
1:      #include <fstream.h>
2:
3:      int main(int argc, char**argv)    // returns 1
on error
4:      {
5:          for (int ctr = argc; ctr ; ctr—)
:              cout << argv[ctr] << " ";
7:      }
```

Day 17
Quiz

1. What is an inclusion guard?

   Inclusion guards are used to protect a header file from being included into a program more than once.

2. How do you instruct your compiler to print the contents of the intermediate file showing the effects of the preprocessor?

   This quiz question must be answered by you, depending on the compiler you are using.

3. What is the difference between #define debug 0 and #undef debug?

   #define debug 0 defines the term debug to equal 0 (zero). Everywhere the word debug is found, the character 0 will be substituted. #undef debug removes any definition of debug; when the word debug is found in the file, it will be left unchanged.

4. Name four predefined macros.

   __DATE__ __TIME__ __FILE__ __LINE__

5. Why can't you call invariants() as the first line of your constructor?

   The job of your constructor is to create the object; the class invariants cannot and should not exist before the object is fully created, and so any meaningful use of invariants() will return false until the constructor is finished.

Exercises

1. Write the inclusion guard statements for the header file STRING.H.

```
#ifndef STRING_H
#define STRING_H

...

#endif
```

2. Write an assert() macro which prints an error message and the file and line number if debug level is 2, just a message (without file and line number) if the level is 1, and does nothing if the level is 0.

```
1:      #include <iostream.h>
2:
3:      #ifndef DEBUG
4:      #define ASSERT(x)
5:      #elif DEBUG == 1
6:      #define ASSERT(x) \
7:                  if (! (x)) \
8:                  { \
9:                      cout << "ERROR!! Assert " <<
#x << " failed\n"; \
10:                 }
11:     #elif DEBUG == 2
12:     #define ASSERT(x) \
13:                 if (! (x) ) \
14:                 { \
15:                     cout << "ERROR!! Assert " <<
#x << " failed\n"; \
16:                     cout << " on line " <<
__LINE__ << "\n"; \
17:                     cout << " in file " <<
__FILE__ << "\n";  \
18:                 }
19:     #endif
```

3. Write a macro DPrint which tests if debug is defined, and if it is, prints the value passed in as a parameter.

```
#ifndef DEBUG
#define DPRINT(string)
```

```
#else
#define DPRINT(STRING) cout << #STRING ;
#endif
```

4. Write a function that prints an error message. The function should print the line number and filename where the error occurred. Note that the line number and filename are passed in to this function.

```
1:      #include <iostream.h>
2:
3:       void ErrorFunc(
4:           int LineNumber,
5:           const char * FileName)
6:      {
7:           cout << "An error occurred in file ";
8:            cout << FileName;
9:            cout << " at line "
10:           cout << LineNumber << endl;
11:      }
```

5. How would you call the preceding error function?

```
1:      // driver program to exercise ErrorFunc
2:      void main()
3:      {
4:           cout << "An error occurs on next line!";
5:           ErrorFunc(__LINE__, __FILE__);
6:      }
```

Note that the __LINE__ macro and the __FILE__ macro are used at the point of the error, and not in the error function. If you used them in the error function, they would report the line and file for the error function itself.

6. Write an assert() macro that uses the error function from Exercise 4, and write a driver program which calls that assert() macro.

```
1:      #include <iostream.h>
2:
3:      #define DEBUG // turn error handling on
4:
5:      #ifndef DEBUG
6:      #define ASSERT(x)
```

```
7:      #else
8:      #define ASSERT(X) \
9:         if (! (X)) \
10:       { \
11:            ErrorFunc(__LINE__, __FILE__); \
12:       }
13:     #endif
14:
15:     void ErrorFunc(int LineNumber, const char * FileName)
16:     {
17:          cout << "An error occurred in file ";
18:          cout << FileName;
19:          cout << " at line ";
20:          cout << LineNumber << endl;
21:     }
22:
23:     // driver program to exercise ErrorFunc
24:     void main()
25:     {
26:        int x = 5;
27:        ASSERT(x >= 5);  // no error
28:        x = 3;
29:        ASSERT(x >= 5); // error!
30:     }
```

D

Note that in this case, the __LINE__ and __FILE__ macros can be called in the assert() macro and will still give the correct line (line 29). This is because the assert() macro is expanded in place, where it is called. Thus, this program is evaluated exactly as if main() were written as

```
1:      // driver program to exercise ErrorFunc
2:      void main()
3:      {
4:         int x = 5;
5:         if (! (x >= 5)) {ErrorFunc(__LINE__, __FILE__);}
6:         x = 3;
7:         if (! (x >= 5)) {ErrorFunc(__LINE__, __FILE__);}
8:      }
```

Day 18
Quiz

1. What is the difference between object-oriented programming and procedural programming?

   Procedural programming focuses on functions separate from data. Object-oriented programming ties data and functionality together into objects, and focuses on the interaction among the objects.

2. To what does "event-driven" refer?

   Event-driven programs are distinguished by the fact that action is taken only in response to some form of (usually external) simulation such as a user's keyboard or mouse input.

3. What are the stages in the development cycle?

   Typically, the development cycle includes analysis, design, coding, testing, programming, and an interaction and feedback among these stages.

4. What is a rooted hierarchy?

   A rooted hierarchy is one in which all the classes in the program derive directly or indirectly from a single base class.

5. What is a driver program?

   A driver program is simply a function which is designed to exercise whatever objects and functions you are currently programming.

6. What is encapsulation?

   Encapsulation refers to the (desirable) trait of bringing together in one class all the data and functionality of one discreet entity.

Exercises

1. Suppose you had to simulate the intersection of Massachusetts Avenue and Vassar Street—two typical two-lane roads with traffic lights and crosswalks. The purpose of the simulation is to determine if the timing of the traffic signal allows for a smooth flow of traffic.

   What kinds of objects should be modelled in the simulation? What should be the classes defined for the simulation?

Cars, motorcycles, trucks, bicycles, pedestrians, and emergency vehicles all use the intersection. In addition, there is a traffic signal with Walk/Don't Walk lights.

Should the road surface be included in the simulation? Certainly, road quality can have an affect on the traffic, but for a first design, it may be simpler to leave this consideration aside.

The first object is probably the intersection itself. Perhaps the intersection object maintains lists of cars waiting to pass through the signal in each direction, as well as lists of people waiting to cross at the crosswalks. It will need methods to choose which and how many cars and people go through the intersection.

There will only be one intersection, so you may want to consider how you will ensure that only one object is instantiated (hint: think about static methods and protected access).

People and cars are both clients of the intersection. They share a number of characteristics: they can appear at any time, there can be any number of them, and they both wait at the signal (although in different lines). This suggests that you will want to consider a common base class for pedestrians and cars.

The classes would therefore include:

```
class Entity;                  // a client of the
intersection
class Vehicle : Entity ...;          // the root of
all cars, trucks, bicycles and emergency vehicles.
class Pedestrian : Entity...;     // the root of all
People
class Car : public Vehicle...;
class Truck : public Vehicle...;
class Motorcycle : public Vehicle...;
class Bicycle : public Vehicle...;
class Emergency_Vehicle : public Vehicle...;
class Intersection;            // contains lists of
cars and people waiting to pass
```

2. Suppose the intersections from Exercise 1 were in a suburb of Boston, which has arguably the unfriendliest streets in the U.S. At any time, there are three kinds of Boston drivers:

Locals, who continue to drive through intersections after the light turns red; tourists, who drive slowly and cautiously (in a rental car, typically); and taxis, which have a wide variation of driving patterns, depending on the kinds of passengers in the cabs.

Also, Boston has two kinds of pedestrians: locals, who cross the street whenever they feel like it, and seldom use the crosswalk buttons; and tourists, who always use the crosswalk buttons and only cross when the Walk/Don't Walk light permits. Finally, Boston has bicyclists who never pay attention to stoplights.

How do these considerations change the model?

A reasonable start on this would be to create derived objects which model the refinements suggested by the problem:

```
class Local_Car : public Car...;
        class Tourist_Car : public Car...;
        class Taxi : public Car...;
        class Local_Pedestrian : public
Pedestrian...;
        class Tourist_Pedestrian : public
Pedestrian...;
        class Boston_Bicycle : public Bicycle...;
```

By using virtual methods, each class can modify the generic behavior to meet its own specifications. For example, the Boston driver can react to a red light differently than a tourist does, while still inheriting the generic behaviors which continue to apply.

3. You are asked to design a group scheduler. The software allows you to arrange meetings among individuals or groups, and to reserve a limited number of conference rooms. Identify the principle subsystems.

Two discreet programs need to be written for this project: the client, which the users run; and the server, which would run on a separate machine. In addition, the client machine would have an administrative component to enable a system administrator to add new people and rooms.

If you decide to implement this as a client/server model, the client would accept input from users and generate a request to the server. The server would service the request and send back the results to the client. With this model, many people can schedule meetings at the same time.

On the client's side, there are two major subsystems in addition to the administrative module: the user interface and the communications subsystem. The server's side consists of three main subsystems: communications, scheduling, and a mail interface, which would announce to the user when changes have occurred in the schedule.

4. Design and show the interfaces to the classes in the room reservation portion of the program discussed in Exercise 3.

A meeting is defined as a group of people reserving a room for a certain amount of time. The person making the schedule may wish for a specific room, or a specified time; but the scheduler must always be told how long the meeting will last and who is required.

The objects will probably include the users of the system as well as the conference rooms. Don't forget to include classes for the calendar, and perhaps a class Meeting which encapsulates all that is known about a particular event.

The prototypes for the classes might include:

```
class Calendar_Class;          // forward reference
class Meeting;                 // forward reference
class Configuration
{
public:
    Configuration();
    ~Configuration();
    Meeting Schedule( ListOfPerson&, Delta Time
duration );
    Meeting Schedule( ListOfPerson&, Delta Time
duration, Time );
    Meeting Schedule( ListOfPerson&, Delta Time
duration, Room );
    ListOfPerson&    People();    // public
accessors
    ListOfRoom&      Rooms();     // public accessors
protected:
    ListOfRoom       rooms;
    ListOfPerson     people;
};
typedef long         Room_ID;
class Room
```

```
{
public:
     Room( String name, Room_ID id, int capacity,
String directions = "", String description = "" );
     ~Room();
     Calendar_Class Calendar();

protected:
     Calendar_Class      calendar;
     int            capacity;
     Room_ID        id;
     String         name;
     String         directions;          // where is
this room?
     String         description;
};
typedef long Person_ID;
class Person
{
public:
     Person( String name, Person_ID id );
     ~Person();
     Calendar_Class Calendar();          // the access
point to add meetings
protected:
     Calendar_Class      calendar;
     Person_ID      id;
     String         name;
};
class Calendar_Class
{
public:
     Calendar_Class();
     ~Calendar_Class();

     void Add( const Meeting& );           // add a
meeting to the calendar
     void Delete( const Meeting& );
     Meeting* Lookup( Time );              // see if
```

```
there is a meeting at the
                                        // given time

    Block( Time, Duration, String reason = "" );
// allocate time to yourself...

protected:
    OrderedListOfMeeting meetings;
};
class Meeting
{
public:
    Meeting( ListOfPerson&, Room room,
        Time when, Duration duration, String purpose
= "" );
    ~Meeting();
protected:
    ListOfPerson      people;
    Room          room;
    Time          when;
    Duration      duration;
    String          purpose;
};
```

Day 19
Quiz

1. What is the difference between a template and a macro?

    Templates are built into the C++ language and are type-safe. Macros are implemented by the preprocessor and are not type-safe.

2. What is the difference between the parameter in a template and the parameter in a function?

    The parameter to the template creates an instance of the template for each type. If you create six template instances, six different classes or functions are created. The parameters to the function change the behavior or data of the function, but only one function is created.

3. What is the difference between a type-specific template friend class and a general template friend class?

   The general template friend function creates one function for every type of the parameterized class; the type-specific function creates a type-specific instance for each instance of the parameterized class.

4. Is it possible to provide special behavior for one instance of a template but not for other instances?

   Yes, create a specialized function for the particular instance. In addition to creating `Array<t>::SomeFunction()`, also create `Array<int>::SomeFunction()` to change the behavior for integer arrays.

5. How many static variables are created if you put one static member into a template class definition?

   One for each instance of the class.

Exercises

1. Create a template based on this list class:

```
class List
{
private:

public:
    List():head(0),tail(0),theCount(0) {}
    virtual ~List();

    void insert( int value );
    void append( int value );
    int is_present( int value ) const;
    int is_empty() const { return head == 0; }
    int count() const { return theCount; }
private:
    class ListCell
    {
    public:
        ListCell(int value, ListCell *cell = 0):val(value),next(cell){}
        int val;
```

```
        ListCell *next;
    };
    ListCell *head;
    ListCell *tail;
    int theCount;
};
```

One way to implement this template:

```
template <class Type>
class List
{

public:
    List():head(0),tail(0),theCount(0) { }
    virtual ~List();

    void insert( Type value );
    void append( Type value );
    int is_present( Type value ) const;
    int is_empty() const { return head == 0; }
    int count() const { return theCount; }

private:
    class ListCell
    {
    public:
        ListCell(Type value, ListCell *cell = 0):val(value),next(cell){}
        Type val;
        ListCell *next;
    };

    ListCell *head;
    ListCell *tail;
    int theCount;
};
```

2. Write the implementation for the List class (non template) version.

```
void List::insert(int value)
{
    ListCell *pt = new ListCell( value, head );
```

D

765

```
        assert (pt != 0);

        // this line added to handle tail
        if ( head == 0 ) tail = pt;

        head = pt;
        theCount++;
    }


void List::append( int value )
{
    ListCell *pt = new ListCell( value );
    if ( head == 0 )
        head = pt;
    else
        tail->next = pt;

    tail = pt;
    theCount++;
}


int List::is_present( int value ) const
{
    if ( head == 0 ) return 0;
    if ( head->val == value || tail->val == value )
        return 1;

    ListCell *pt = head->next;
    for (; pt != tail; pt = pt->next)
        if ( pt->val == value )
            return 1;

    return 0;
}
```

3. Write the template version of the implementations.

```
template <class Type>
List<Type>::~List()
{
```

```
        ListCell *pt = head;

        while ( pt )
        {
            ListCell *tmp = pt;
            pt = pt->next;
            delete tmp;
        }
        head = tail = 0;
}


template <class Type>
void List<Type>::insert(Type value)
{
        ListCell *pt = new ListCell( value, head );
        assert (pt != 0);

        // this line added to handle tail
        if ( head == 0 ) tail = pt;

        head = pt;
        theCount++;
}


template <class Type>
void List<Type>::append( Type value )
{
        ListCell *pt = new ListCell( value );
        if ( head == 0 )
            head = pt;
        else
            tail->next = pt;

        tail = pt;
        theCount++;
}


template <class Type>
int List<Type>::is_present( Type value ) const
```

```
    {
        if ( head == 0 ) return 0;
        if ( head->val == value || tail->val == value )
            return 1;


        ListCell *pt = head->next;
        for (; pt != tail; pt = pt->next)
            if ( pt->val == value )
                return 1;


        return 0;
    }
```

4. Declare three list objects: a list of strings, a list of `Cats` and a list of `ints`.

```
    List<String> string_list;
    List<Cat> Cat_List;
    List<int> int_List;
```

5. **BUG BUSTERS:** What is wrong with the following code? (Assume the `List` template is defined and `Cat` is the class defined earlier in the book.)

```
    List<Cat> Cat_List;
    Cat Felix;
    CatList.append( Felix );
    cout << "Felix is " <<
        ( Cat_List.is_present( Felix ) ) ? "" : "not " << "present\n";
```

HINT (this is tough): What makes `Cat` different from `int`?

`Cat` doesn't have operator `==` defined; all operations that compare the values in the `List` cells, such as `is_present`, will result in compiler errors. To reduce the chance of this, put copious comments before the template definition stating what operations must be defined for the instantiation to compile.

6. Declare friend operator `==` for `List`.

```
    friend int operator==( const Type& lhs, const Type& rhs );
```

7. Implement friend operator `==` for `List`.

```
    template <class Type>
    int List<Type>::operator==( const Type& lhs, const Type& rhs )
    {
        // compare lengths first
```

```
        if ( lhs.theCount != rhs.theCount )
            return 0;        // lengths differ

        ListCell *lh = lhs.head;
        ListCell *rh = rhs.head;

        for(; lh != 0; lh = lh.next, rh = rh.next )
            if ( lh.value != rh.value )
                return 0;

        return 1;            // if they don't differ, they must match
    }
```

8. Does operator== have the same problem as in Exercise 4?

   Yes, because comparing the array involves comparing the elements, operator!= must be defined for the elements as well.

9. Implement a template function for swap, which exchanges two variables.

```
// template swap:
// must have assignment and the copy constructor defined for the Type.
template <class Type>
void swap( Type& lhs, Type& rhs)
{
    Type temp( lhs );
    lhs = rhs;
    rhs = temp;
}
```

Day 20
Quiz

1. What is an exception?

   An exception is an object that is created as a result of invoking the keyword throw. It is used to signal an exceptional condition, and is passed up the call stack to the first catch statement that handles its type.

2. What is a try block?

   A try block is a set of statements that might generate an exception.

3. What is a catch statement?

   A catch statement has a signature of the type of exception it handles. It follows a try block and acts as the receiver of exceptions raised within the try block.

4. What information can an exception contain?

   An exception is an object and can contain any information that can be defined within a user-created class.

5. When are exception objects created?

   Exception objects are created when you invoke the keyword throw.

6. Should you pass exceptions by value or by reference?

   In general, exceptions should be passed by reference. If you don't intend to modify the contents of the exception object, you should pass a const reference.

7. Will a catch statement catch a derived exception if it is looking for the base class?

   Yes, if you pass the exception by reference.

8. If there are two catch statements, one for base and one for derived, which should come first?

   catch statements are examined in the order they appear in the source code. The first catch statement whose signature matches the exception is used.

9. What does catch(...) mean?

   Catch(...) will catch any exception of any type.

10. What is a breakpoint?

    A breakpoint is a place in the code where the debugger will stop execution.

Exercises

1. Create a try block, a catch statement, and a simple exception.

```
#include <iostreams.h>
class OutOfMemory {};
void main()
{
```

SAMS
Learning
Center
Sams
SAMS
PUBLISHING

```
    try
    {
        int *myInt = new int;
        if (myInt == 0)
            throw OutOfMemory();
    }
    catch (OutOfMemory)
    {
        cout << "Unable to allocate memory!\n";
    }
}
```

2. Modify the answer from Exercise 1, put data into the exception along with an accessor function, and use it in the catch block.

```
#include <iostreams.h>
#include <stdio.h>
#include <string.h>
class OutOfMemory
{
public:
    OutOfMemory(char *);
    char* GetString() { return itsString; }
private:
    char* itsString;
};


OutOfMemory::OutOfMemory(char * theType)
{
    itsString = new char[80];
    char warning[] = "Out Of Memory! Can't allocate room for: ";
    strncpy(itsString,warning,60);
    strncat(itsString,theType,19);
}


void main()
{

    try
    {
```

D

```
             int *myInt = new int;
             if (myInt == 0)
                  throw OutOfMemory("int");
         }
         catch (OutOfMemory& theException)
         {
             cout << theException.GetString();
         }
     }
```

3. Modify the class from Exercise 2 to be a hierarchy of exceptions. Modify the catch block to use the derived objects and the base objects.

```
1:      #include <iostreams.h>
2:
3:      // Abstract exception data type
4:      class Exception
5:      {
6:      public:
7:          Exception(){}
8:          virtual ~Exception(){}
9:          virtual void PrintError() = 0;
10:     };
11:
12:     // Derived class to handle memory problems.
13:     // Note no allocation of memory in this class!
14:     class OutOfMemory : public Exception
15:     {
16:     public:
17:         OutOfMemory(){}
18:         ~OutOfMemory(){}
19:         virtual void PrintError();
20:     private:
21:     };
22:
23:     void OutOfMemory::PrintError()
24:     {
25:         cout << "Out of Memory!!\n";
26:     }
27:
```

```
28:    // Derived class to handle bad numbers
29:    class RangeError : public Exception
30:    {
31:    public:
32:        RangeError(unsigned long number){badNumber = number;}
33:        ~RangeError(){}
34:        virtual void PrintError();
35:        virtual unsigned long GetNumber() { return badNumber; }
36:        virtual void SetNumber(unsigned long number) {badNumber = number;}
37:    private:
38:        unsigned long badNumber;
39:    };
40:
41:    void RangeError::PrintError()
42:    {
43:        cout << "Number out of range. You used " << GetNumber() << "!!\n";
44:    }
45:
46:    void MyFunction();   // func. prototype
47:
48:    void main()
49:    {
50:        try
51:        {
52:            MyFunction();
53:        }
54:        // Only one catch required, use virtual functions to do the
55:        // right thing.
56:        catch (Exception& theException)
57:        {
58:            theException.PrintError();
59:        }
60:    }
61:
62:    void MyFunction()
63:    {
64:        unsigned int *myInt = new unsigned int;
65:        long testNumber;
66:        if (myInt == 0)
```

```
67:              throw OutOfMemory();
68:
69:          cout << "Enter an int: ";
70:          cin >> testNumber;
71:          // this weird test should be replaced by a series
72:          // of tests to complain about bad user input
73:          if (testNumber > 3768 || testNumber < 0)
74:              throw RangeError(testNumber);
75:
76:          *myInt = testNumber;
77:          cout << "Ok. myInt: " << *myInt;
78:          delete myInt;
79:      }
```

4. Modify the program from Exercise 3 to have three levels of function calls.

```
1:      #include <iostreams.h>
2:
3:      // Abstract exception data type
4:      class Exception
5:      {
6:      public:
7:          Exception(){}
8:          virtual ~Exception(){}
9:          virtual void PrintError() = 0;
10:     };
11:
12:     // Derived class to handle memory problems.
13:     // Note no allocation of memory in this class!
14:     class OutOfMemory : public Exception
15:     {
16:     public:
17:         OutOfMemory(){}
18:         ~OutOfMemory(){}
19:         virtual void PrintError();
20:     private:
21:     };
22:
23:     void OutOfMemory::PrintError()
24:     {
```

```
25:        cout << "Out of Memory!!\n";
26:     }
27:
28:     // Derived class to handle bad numbers
29:     class RangeError : public Exception
30:     {
31:     public:
32:         RangeError(unsigned long number){badNumber = number;}
33:         ~RangeError(){}
34:         virtual void PrintError();
35:         virtual unsigned long GetNumber() { return badNumber; }
36:         virtual void SetNumber(unsigned long number) {badNumber = number;}
37:     private:
38:         unsigned long badNumber;
39:     };
40:
41:     void RangeError::PrintError()
42:     {
43:         cout << "Number out of range. You used " << GetNumber() << "!!\n";
44:     }
45:
46:     // func. prototypes
47:     void MyFunction();
48:     unsigned int * FunctionTwo();
49:     void FunctionThree(unsigned int *);
50:
51:     void main()
52:     {
53:        try
54:        {
55:            MyFunction();
56:        }
57:        // Only one catch required, use virtual functions to do the
58:        // right thing.
59:        catch (Exception& theException)
60:        {
61:            theException.PrintError();
62:        }
63:     }
```

D

```
64:
65:    unsigned int * FunctionTwo()
66:    {
67:       unsigned int *myInt = new unsigned int;
68:       if (myInt == 0)
69:          throw OutOfMemory();
70:       return myInt;
71:    }
72:
73:
74:    void MyFunction()
75:    {
76:          unsigned int *myInt = FunctionTwo();
77:
78:          FunctionThree(myInt);
79:          cout << "Ok. myInt: " << *myInt;
80:          delete myInt;
81:    }
82:
83:    void FunctionThree(unsigned int *ptr)
84:    {
85:          long testNumber;
86:          cout << "Enter an int: ";
87:          cin >> testNumber;
88:          // this weird test should be replaced by a series
89:          // of tests to complain about bad user input
90:          if (testNumber > 3768 || testNumber < 0)
91:             throw RangeError(testNumber);
92:          *ptr = testNumber;
93:    }
```

5. **BUG BUSTERS:** What is wrong with the following code?

```
#include "stringc.h"          // our string class

class xOutOfMemory
{
public:
    xOutOfMemory( const String& where ) : location( where ){}
    ~xOutOfMemory(){}
    virtual String where(){ return location };
```

```
private:
    String location;
}

main()
{
    try {
        char *var = new char;
        if ( var == 0 )
            throw xOutOfMemory();
    }
    catch( xOutOfMemory& theException )
    {
        cout << "Out of memory at " << theException.location() << "\n";
    }
}
```

In the process of handling an "out of memory" condition, a string object is created by the constructor of xOutOfMemory. This exception can only be raised when the program is out of memory, and so this allocation must fail.

It is possible that trying to create this string will raise the same exception, creating an infinite loop until the program crashes. If this string is really required, you can allocate the space in a static buffer before beginning the program, and then use it as needed when the exception is thrown.

Day 21
Quiz

1. What is the difference between strcpy() and strncpy()?

    strcpy(char* destination, char* source) copies source to destination, and puts a null at the end of destination. destination *must* be large enough to accommodate source, or strcpy() will simply write past the end of the array. strncpy(char* destination char* source, int howmany) will write howmany bytes of source to destination, but will not put a terminating null.

2. What does ctime() do?

    ctime() takes a time_t variable and returns an ASCII string with the current time. The time_t variable is typically filled by passing its address to time().

3. What is the function to call to turn an ASCII string into a `long`?

   `atol()`

4. What does the complement operator do?

   It flips every bit in a number.

5. What is the difference between OR and exclusive OR?

   OR returns TRUE if either or both bits is set; exclusive OR returns TRUE only if one, but not both, is set.

6. What is the difference between & and &&?

   & is the bitwise AND operator and && is the logical AND operator.

7. What is the difference between ¦ and ¦¦?

   ¦ is the bitwise OR operator and ¦¦ is the logical OR operator.

Exercises

1. Write a program to safely copy the contents of a 20-byte string into a 10-byte string, truncating whatever won't fit.

```
1:      #include <iostreams.h>
2:      #include <string.h>
3:
4:      void main()
5:      {
6:         char bigString[21] = "12345678901234567890";
7:         char smallString[10];
8:         strncpy(smallString,bigString,9);
9:         smallString[9]='\0';
10:        cout << "BigString: " << bigString << endl;
11:        cout << "smallString: " << smallString << endl;
12:     }
```

2. Write a program that tells the current date in the form 7/28/94.

```
1:      #include <iostreams.h>
2:      #include <time.h>
3:
4:      void main()
5:      {
```

```
6:        time_t currentTime;
7:        struct tm *timeStruct;
8:        time (&currentTime);
9:        timeStruct = localtime(&currentTime);
10:
11:       cout << timeStruct->tm_mon+1 << "/";
12:       cout << timeStruct->tm_mday << "/";
13:       cout << timeStruct->tm_year << " ";
14:   }
```

3. Write the definition of a class that uses bit fields to store, whether the computer is monochrome or color, a PC or Macintosh, a laptop or a desktop, and whether or not it has a CD-ROM.

```
#include <iostream.h>
enum Boolean { FALSE = 0, TRUE = 1 };


class Computer
{
public:  // types
     enum Machine { Mac = 0, PC };


public:  // methods
     Computer( Boolean color, Boolean laptop, Machine kind, Boolean cdrom )
          : Color( color ), Laptop( laptop ), Kind( kind ), CDRom( cdrom ){}
     ~Computer(){}


     friend ostream& operator<<( ostream& os, const Computer& computer );


private:
     Boolean Color : 1;
     Boolean Laptop : 1;
     Machine Kind : 1;
     Boolean CDRom : 1;
};


     ostream&
operator<<( ostream& os, const Computer& computer )
{
     os << "[";
```

```
        ( computer.Color ) ? os << "color" : os << "monochrome";
        os << ", ";
        ( computer.Laptop ) ? os << "laptop" : os << "desktop";
        os << ", ";
        ( computer.Kind ) ? os << "PC" : os << "Mac";
        os << ", ";
        ( computer.CDRom ) ? os << "" : os << "no ";
        os << "CD-Rom";
        os << "]";
        return os;
}

        void
main()
{
        Computer pc( TRUE, TRUE, Computer :: PC, TRUE );

        cout << pc << '\n';
}
```

4. Write a program that creates a 26-bit mask. Prompt the user to enter a word, and then quickly report on which letters were used in setting and reading the bits (one bit per character). The program should treat upper and lowercase letters as the same.

```
#include <ctype.h>
#include <iostream.h>

class Bits
{
public:
    enum { BITS_PER_INT = 16 };
    Bits( int cnt );
    virtual ~Bits();

    void clear();
    void set( int position );
    void reset( int position );
    int is_set( int position );
private:
    unsigned int * bits;
```

```
        int count;
        int Ints_Needed;
};

class AlphaBits : private Bits
{
public:
        AlphaBits() : Bits( 26 ){}
        ~AlphaBits(){}

        void clear() { Bits::clear(); }
        void set( char );
        void reset( char );
        int is_set( char );
};

Bits :: Bits( int cnt ) : count( cnt )
{
        Ints_Needed = count / BITS_PER_INT;

        // if there is a remainder, you need one more member in array
        if ( 0 != count % BITS_PER_INT )
            Ints_Needed++;

        // create an array of ints to hold all the bits
        bits = new unsigned int[ Ints_Needed ];

        clear();
}

Bits :: ~Bits()
{
        delete [] bits;
}

void Bits :: clear()
{
        // clear the bits
        for ( int i = 0; i < Ints_Needed; i++ )
```

```
            bits[ i ] = 0;
}

void Bits :: set( int position )
{
      // find the bit to set
      int Int_Number = position / BITS_PER_INT;
      int Bit_Number = position % BITS_PER_INT;

      // create mask with that one bit set
      unsigned int mask = 1 << Bit_Number;

      // set the bit
      bits[ Int_Number ] |= mask;
}

// clear the bit
void Bits :: reset( int position )
{
      int Int_Number = position / BITS_PER_INT;
      int Bit_Number = position % BITS_PER_INT;

      unsigned int mask = ~( 1 << Bit_Number );

      bits[ Int_Number ] &= mask;
}

int Bits :: is_set( int position )
{
      int Int_Number = position / BITS_PER_INT;
      int Bit_Number = position % BITS_PER_INT;

      unsigned int mask = 1 << Bit_Number;

      return ( 0 != ( bits[ Int_Number ] & mask ) );
}

void AlphaBits :: set( char s )
{
```

```
        // make sure the requested character is an alphabetic character
        // if so, force it to lower case, then subtract the ascii value
        // of 'a' to get its ordinal (where a = 0, b =1) and set that bit
        if ( isalpha( s ) )
            Bits :: set( tolower( s ) - 'a' );
    }

    void AlphaBits :: reset( char s )
    {
        if ( isalpha( s ) )
            Bits :: reset( tolower( s ) - 'a' );
    }

    int AlphaBits :: is_set( char s )
    {
        if ( isalpha( s ) )
            return Bits :: is_set( tolower( s ) - 'a' );
        else
            return 0;
    }

    void main()
    {
        AlphaBits letters;

        char buffer[512];

        for (;;)
        {
            cout << "\nPlease type a word (0 to quit): ";
            cin >> buffer;

            // set the bits
            for ( char *s = buffer; *s; s++ )
                letters.set( *s );

            // print the results
            cout << "The letters used were: ";
```

D

```
            for ( char c = 'a'; c <= 'z'; c++ )
                if ( letters.is_set( c ) )
                    cout << c << ' ';
        cout << '\n';


        // clear the bits
        letters.clear();

    }


}
```

5. Write a program that sorts the command-line parameters. If the user enters SortFunc cat bird fish dog, the program prints bird cat dog fish.

```cpp
#include <string.h>
#include <iostream.h>

void swap ( char* &s, char* &t )
{
    char* temp = s;
    s = t;
    t = temp;
}


void main( int argc, char* argv[] )
{
    // Since argv[0] is the program name, we don't want to sort or print it;
    // we start sorting at element 1 (not 0).

    // a "Bubble Sort" is used because of the small number of items.
    for ( int i = 1; i < argc; i++ )
        for ( int j = i + 1; j < argc; j++ )
            if ( 0 < strcmp( argv[i], argv[j] ) )
                swap( argv[i], argv[j] );

    for ( i = 1; i < argc; i++ )
        cout << argv[i] << ' ';

    cout << '\n';
}
```

6. Write a program that adds two numbers without using the addition operator (+), subtraction operator (-), increment (++), or decrement (--). Hint: Use the bit operators!

If you take a look at the addition of two bits, you'll notice the answer will contain two bits: the result bit and the carry bit. Thus, adding 1 and 1 in binary results in 1 with a carry of 1. If we add 101 to 001, here are the results:

```
101  // 5
001  // 1
110  // 6
```

If you add two "set" bits (each is valued as one), the result is that the result bit is 0 but the carry bit is 1. If you add two clear bits, both the result and the carry are 0. If you add two bits with one set and the other clear, the result bit is 1, but the carry bit is 0. Here is a table that summarizes these rules:

```
lhs   rhs  ¦  carry   result
-----------+------------------
0     0    ¦  0       0
0     1    ¦  0       1
1     0    ¦  0       1
1     1    ¦  1       0
```

Examine the logic of the carry bit. If both bits to be added (lhs and rhs) are 0 or either side is 0, the answer is 0. Only if both bits are 1 is the answer 1. This is exactly the same as the AND operator (&).

In the same way, the result is an XOR (^) operation: if either bit is 1 but not both, the answer is 1; otherwise, 0.

When you get a carry, the carry is added to the next most significant (leftmost) bit. This implies either iterating through each bit or recursion.

```
#include <iostream.h>

unsigned int add( unsigned int lhs, unsigned int rhs )
{
    unsigned int result, carry;

    while ( 1 )
    {
        result = lhs ^ rhs;
        carry = lhs & rhs;
```

```
            if ( carry == 0 )
                break;

            lhs = carry << 1;
            rhs = result;
        };

        return result;
}

void main()
{
    unsigned long a, b;
    for (;;)
    {
        cout << "Enter two numbers. (0 0 to stop): ";
        cin >> a >> b;
        if (!a && !b)
            break;
        cout <<a << " + " << b << " =  " << add(a,b) << endl;
    }
}
```

Alternatively, you can solve this problem with recursion:

```
#include <iostream.h>

unsigned int add( unsigned int lhs, unsigned int rhs )
{
    unsigned int carry = lhs & rhs;
    unsigned int result = lhs ^ rhs;

    if ( carry )
        return add( result, carry << 1 );
    else
        return result;
}

void main()
{
```

```
unsigned long a, b;
for (;;)
{
    cout << "Enter two numbers. (0 0 to stop): ";
    cin >> a >> b;
    if (!a && !b)
        break;
    cout <<a << " + " << b << " =  " << add(a,b) << endl;
}
}
```

Index

Symbols

A

derived classes

Sams
Learning
Center

SAMS
PUBLISHING

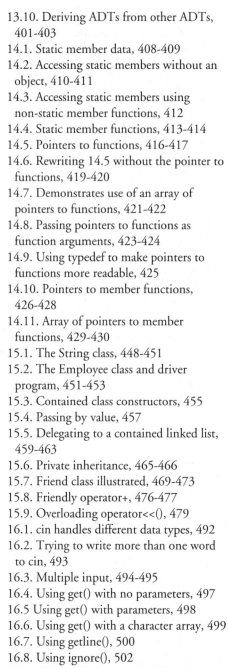

R

S

Disk Offer

The complete listings of the example programs in *Teach Yourself C++ in 21 Days* are available on disk from the author. Use this form, or a photocopy, to place your order.

Please send me __ copies of the *Teach Yourself C++ in 21 Days* program disk.

Mail the disks to:

Name _____

Company (for company name) _____

Street _____

City _____

State/Province _____

ZIP or Postal Code _____

Include your name, mailing address, and ZIP code. Orders delivered by U.S. Postal Service.

United States: $20.00 each
Foreign: $25.00 (U.S.) each

☐ 3-1/2" (default) or ☐ 5-1/4" (All disks are IBM format.)

☐ **RUSH** Federal Express $25.00 additional per copy (total $45.00 each)

Please make check or money order payable to: **The Liberty Group, Inc.** and mail to:

> **The Liberty Group, Inc.**
> P.O. Box 410144
> Cambridge MA 02141

Note: Every effort is made to ensure that the listings match the text in the book and compile and run on a C++ compiler, but there is no warranty of any kind expressed or implied, and no responsibility is accepted for any inaccuracy, loss, or damage. The listings are offered for illustration purposes only. Foreign orders must be paid in U.S. dollars by postal money order or check drawn on a U.S. bank. While disks are sent upon receipt of the order, please allow 3-4 weeks for delivery.

Add to Your Sams Library Today with the Best Books for Programming, Operating Systems, and New Technologies

The easiest way to order is to pick up the phone and call

1-800-428-5331

between 9:00 a.m. and 5:00 p.m. EST.

For faster service, please have your credit card available.

ISBN	Quantity	Description of Item	Unit Cost	Total Cost
0-672-30363-9		Your Borland C++ Consultant (Book/Disk)	$29.95	
0-672-30158-1		Advanced C++ (Book/Disk)	$39.95	
0-672-30370-1		Visual C++ Developer's Guide (Book/Disk)	$49.95	
0-672-48470-6		Assembly Language: For Real Programmers Only!	$44.95	
0-672-30481-3		Teach Yourself NetWare in 14 Days	$29.95	
0-672-30308-6		Tricks of the Graphics Gurus (Book/Disk)	$49.95	
0-672-30507-0		Tricks of the Game-Programming Gurus (Book/CD-ROM)	$45.00	
0-672-30362-0		Navigating the Internet	$24.95	
0-672-30440-6		Database Developer's Guide with Visual Basic 3	$44.95	
0-672-30413-9		Multimedia Madness! Deluxe Edition (Book/2 CD-ROMs)	$55.00	
0-672-30343-4		Even You Can Soup Up and Fix PCs	$16.95	
❏ 3 ½" Disk		Shipping and Handling: See information below.		
❏ 5 ¼" Disk		TOTAL		

Shipping and Handling: $4.00 for the first book, and $1.75 for each additional book. Floppy disk: add $1.75 for shipping and handling. If you need to have it NOW, we can ship product to you in 24 hours for an additional charge of approximately $18.00, and you will receive your item overnight or in two days. Overseas shipping and handling adds $2.00 per book and $8.00 for up to three disks. Prices subject to change. Call for availability and pricing information on latest editions.

201 W. 103rd Street, Indianapolis, Indiana 46290

1-800-428-5331 — Orders   1-800-835-3202 — FAX   1-800-858-7674 — Customer Service